2011
Children's Writer's & Illustrator's Market.

includes a 1-year online subscription to
Children's Writer's & Illustrator's Market on **WritersMarket.com**

Where & How to Sell What You Write

THE ULTIMATE MARKET RESEARCH TOOL FOR WRITERS

To register your *2011 Children's Writer's & Illustrator's Market* book and **start your 1-year online genre only subscription**, scratch off the block below to reveal your activation code, then go to www.WritersMarket.com. Click on "Sign Up Now" and enter your contact information and activation code. It's that easy!

UPDATED MARKET LISTINGS FOR YOUR INTEREST AREA

EASY-TO-USE SEARCHABLE DATABASE

RECORD KEEPING TOOLS

INDUSTRY NEWS

PROFESSIONAL TIPS AND ADVICE

Your purchase of *Children's Writer's & Illustrator's Market* gives you access to updated listings related to this genre of writing (valid through 1/31/12). For just $9.99, you can upgrade your subscription and get access to listings from all of our best-selling Market books. Visit **www.WritersMarket.com** for more information.

WritersMarket.com
Where & How to Sell What You Write

ACTIVATE YOUR WRITERSMARKET.COM SUBSCRIPTION TO GET INSTANT ACCESS TO:

- **UPDATED LISTINGS IN YOUR WRITING GENRE** — Find additional listings that didn't make it into the book, updated contact information and more. WritersMarket.com provides the most comprehensive database of verified markets available anywhere.

- **EASY-TO-USE SEARCHABLE DATABASE** — Looking for a specific magazine or book publisher? Just type in its name. Or widen your prospects with the Advanced Search. You can also search for listings that have been recently updated!

- **PERSONALIZED TOOLS** — Store your best-bet markets, and use our popular record-keeping tools to track your submissions. Plus, get new and updated market listings, query reminders, and more – every time you log in!

- **PROFESSIONAL TIPS & ADVICE** — From pay rate charts to sample query letters, and from how-to articles to Q&A's with literary agents, we have the resources freelance writers need.

- **INDUSTRY UPDATES** — Debbie Ridpath Ohi's Market Watch column keeps you up-to-date on the latest publishing industry news, so you'll always be in-the-know.

YOU'LL GET ALL OF THIS WITH YOUR INCLUDED SUBSCRIPTION TO

WritersMarket.com

11CMI0M

To put the full power of WritersMarket.com to work for you, upgrade your subscription and get access to listings from all of our best-selling Market books. Find out more at **www.WritersMarket.com**

2011
Children's Writer's & Illustrator's Market®

23RD ANNUAL EDITION

ALICE POPE, EDITOR

WRITER'S DIGEST
BOOKS
WritersDigest.com
Cincinnati, Ohio

Publisher & Community Leader, Writing Communities: Phil Sexton
Director, Content & Community Development: Jane Friedman

Children's Writer's & Illustrator's website: www.cwim.com
Writer's Market website: www.writersmarket.com
Writer's Digest website: www.writersdigest.com
Writer's Digest Bookstore: www.writersdigestshop.com

Distributed in Canada by Fraser Direct
100 Armstrong Avenue
Georgetown, ON, Canada L7G 5S4
Tel: (905) 877-4411

Distributed in the U.K. and Europe by David & Charles
Brunel House, Newton Abbot, Devon, TQ12 4PU, England
Tel: (+ 44) 1626 323200, Fax: (+ 44) 1626 323319
E-mail: mail@davidandcharles.co.uk

Distributed in Australia by Capricorn Link
Loder House, 126 George Street
Windsor, NSW 2756 Australia
Tel: (02) 4577-3555

ISSN: 0897-9790
ISBN-13: 978-1-58297-952-6
ISBN-10: 1-58297-952-9

Cover design by Claudean Wheeler
Production coordinated by Greg Nock

Attention Booksellers: This is an annual directory of F + W Media, Inc.
Return deadline for this edition is December 31, 2011.

Contents

Reprinted with permission.

INTERVIEWS

Reprinted with permission.

THE MARKETS

RESOURCES

INDEXES

How to Use This Book

As a writer, illustrator, or photographer first picking up *Children's Writer's & Illustrator's Market*, you may not know quite how to start using the book. Your impulse may be to flip through the book and quickly make a mailing list, then submit to everyone in hopes that someone will take interest in your work. Well, there's more to it. Finding the right market takes time and research. The more you know about a company that interests you, the better chance you have of getting work accepted.

We've made your job a little easier by putting a wealth of information at your fingertips. Besides providing listings, this directory includes a number of tools to help you determine which markets are the best ones for your work. By using these tools, as well as researching on your own, you raise your odds of being published.

USING THE INDEXES

This book lists hundreds of potential buyers of freelance material. To learn which companies want the type of material you're interested in submitting, start with the indexes.

Names Index

This index lists book and magazine editors and art directors as well as agents and art reps, indicating the companies they work for. Use this index to find company and contact information for individual publishing professionals.

Age-Level Index

Age groups are broken down into these categories in the Age-Level Index:

- **Picture books or picture-oriented material** are written and illustrated for preschoolers to 8-year-olds.
- **Young readers** are for 5- to 8-year-olds.
- **Middle readers** are for 9- to 11-year-olds.
- **Young adults** is for ages 12 and up.

Age breakdowns may vary slightly from publisher to publisher, but using them as general guidelines will help you target appropriate markets. For example, if you've written an article about trends in teen fashion, check the Magazines Age-Level Index under the Young Adult subheading. Using this list, you'll quickly find the listings for young adult magazines.

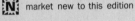

2011 CHILDREN'S WRITER'S & ILLUSTRATOR'S MARKET KEY TO SYMBOLS

 market new to this edition

 Canadian agents

 listing outside U.S. and Canada

 publisher producing educational material

 electronic publisher or producer

📖 book package/producer

Ⓐ publisher accepts agented submissions only

🏆 award-winning publisher

ms, mss manuscript(s)

SCBWI Society of Children's Book Writers and Illustrators

SASE self-addressed, stamped envelope

SAE self-addressed envelope

IRC International Reply Coupon, for use in countries other than your own

b&w black & white (photo)

(For definitions of unfamiliar words and expressions relating to writing, illustration and publishing, see the Glossary.)

Subject Index

But let's narrow the search further. Take your list of young adult magazines, turn to the Subject Index, and find the Fashion subheading. Then highlight the names that appear on both lists (Young Adult and Fashion). Now you have a smaller list of all the magazines that would be interested in your teen fashion article. Read through those listings and decide which ones sound best for your work.

Illustrators and photographers can use the Subject Index as well. If you specialize in painting animals, for instance, consider sending samples to book and magazine publishers listed under Animals and, perhaps, Nature/Environment. Since illustrators can simply send general examples of their style to art directors to keep on file, the indexes may be more helpful to artists sending manuscripts/illustration packages who need to search for a specific subject. Always read the listings for the potential markets to see the type of work art directors prefer and what type of samples they'll keep on file, and obtain art or photo guidelines if they're available through the mail or online.

Photography Index

In this index you'll find lists of book and magazine publishers that buy photos from freelancers. Refer to the list and read the listings for companies' specific photography needs. Obtain photo guidelines if they're offered through the mail or online.

USING THE LISTINGS

Many listings begin with one or more symbols. Refer to the inside covers of the book for quick reference and find a handy pull-out bookmark (shown at left) right inside the front cover.

Many listings indicate whether submission guidelines are available. If a publisher you're interested in offers guidelines, get them and read them. The same is true with catalogs. Sending for and reading catalogs or browsing them online gives you a better idea of whether your work would fit in with the books a publisher produces. (You should also look at a few of the books in the catalog at a library or bookstore to get a feel for the publisher's material.)

Especially for artists & photographers

Along with information for writers, listings provide information for illustrators and photographers. Illustrators will find numerous markets that maintain files of samples for possible future assignments. If you're both a writer and an illustrator, look for markets that accept manuscript/illustration packages and read the information offered under the **Illustration** subhead within the listings.

If you're a photographer, after consulting the Photography Index, read the information under the **Photography** subhead within listings to see what format buyers prefer. For example, some want 35mm color transparencies, others want black and white prints. Note the type of photos a buyer wants to purchase and the procedures for submitting. It's not uncommon for a market to want a resume and promotional literature, as well as tearsheets from previous work. Listings also note whether model releases and/or captions are required.

Especially for young writers

If you're a parent, teacher, or student, you may be interested in Young Writer's & Illustrator's Markets. The listings in this section encourage submissions from young writers and artists. Some may require a written statement from a teacher or parent noting the work is original. Also watch for age limits.

Young people should also check Contests & Awards for contests that accept work by young writers and artists. Some of the contests listed are especially for students; others accept both student and adult work. These listings contain the phrase **open to students** in bold. Some listings in Clubs & Organizations and Conferences & Workshops may also be of interest to students. Organizations and conferences which are open to or are especially for students also include **open to students**.

SPECIFIC CONTACT NAMES

INFO ON WHAT A PUBLISHER HANDLES

E-MAIL ADRESSES AND WEB SITES

DETAILED SUBMISSION GUIDELINES

TIPS DIRECTLY FROM EDITORS

FLUX

Llewellyn Worldwide, Ltd., 2143 Wooddale Drive, Woodbury MN 55125. (651)312-8613. Fax: (651)291-1908. E-mail: submissions@fluxnow.com. Web site: www.fluxnow.com. **Acquisitions Editor:** Brian Farrey. Imprint estab. 2005; Llewellyn estab. 1901. Publishes 21 young abult titles/year. 50% of books by first-time authors. "Flux seeks to publish authors who see YA as a point of view, not a reading level. We look for books that try to capture a slice of teenage experience. We are particularly interested in books that tell the stories of young adults in unexpected or surprising situations around the globe."

* See First Books for an interview with Carrie Jones, author of Flux title *Tips on Having a Gay (ex) Boyfriend.*

Fiction Young Adults: adventure, contemporary, fantasy, history, humor, problem novels, religion, science fiction, sports, suspense. Average word length: 50,000. Recently published *Blue Is for Nightmares*, by Laurie Faria Stolarz; *Dream Spinner*, by Bonnie Dobkin; *How It's Done*, by Christine Kole MacLean.

How to Contact/Writers Query. Responds to queries in 1-2 weeks; mss in 1-3 months. Will consider simultaneous submissions and previously published work.

Terms Pays royalties of 10-15% based on wholesale price. Offers advance. Authors see galleys for review. Book catalog available on Web site. Writer's guidelines available for SASE or available online.

Tips "Read contemporary teen books. Be aware of what else is out there. If you don't read teen books, you probably shouldn't write them. Know your audience. Write incredibly well. Do not condescend."

Quick Tips for Writers & Illustrators

If you're new to the world of children's publishing, buying *Children's Writer's & Illustrator's Market* may have been one of the first steps in your journey to publication. What follows is a list of suggestions and resources that can help make that journey a smooth and swift one:

1. Make the most of *Children's Writer's & Illustrator's Market*. Be sure to read How to Use This Book on page 1 for tips on reading the listings and using the indexes. Also be sure to take advantage of the articles and interviews in the book. The insights of the authors, illustrators, editors, and agents we've interviewed will inform and inspire you.

2. Join the Society of Children's Books Writers and Illustrators. SCBWI, more than 19,000 members strong, is an organization for both beginners and professionals interested in writing and illustrating for children. They offer members a slew of information and support through publications, a website, and a host of Regional Advisors overseeing chapters in almost every state in the U.S. and in a growing number of locations around the globe (including France, Canada, Japan, and Australia). SCBWI puts on a number of conferences, workshops, and events on the regional and national levels (many listed in the Conferences & Workshops section of this book). For more information, contact SCBWI, 8271 Beverly Blvd., Los Angeles CA 90048, (323)782-1010, or visit their website: www.scbwi.org.

3. Read newsletters. Newsletters, such as *Children's Book Insider*, *Children's Writer*, and the *SCBWI Bulletin*, offer updates and new information about publishers on a timely basis and are relatively inexpensive. Many local chapters of SCBWI offer regional newsletters as well. (See Helpful Books & Publications on page 359 for contact information on the newsletters listed above and others. For information on regional SCBWI newsletters, visit www.scbwi.org and click on "Publications."

4. Read trade and review publications. Magazines like *Publishers Weekly* (which offers two special issues each year devoted to children's publishing and is available on newsstands), *The Horn Book*, and *Booklinks* offer news, articles, reviews of newly-published titles, and ads featuring upcoming and current releases. Referring to them will help you get a feel for what's happening in children's publishing.

5. Read guidelines. Most publishers and magazines offer writer's and artist's guidelines that provide detailed information on needs and submission requirements, and some magazines offer theme lists for upcoming issues. Many publishers and magazines state the availability of guidelines within their listings. Send a self-addressed, stamped envelope (SASE) to publishers who offer guidelines. You'll often find submission information on publishers' and magazines' websites.

6. Look at publishers' catalogs. Perusing publishers' catalogs can give you a feel for their line of books and help you decide where your work might fit in. If catalogs are available (often stated within listings), send for them with a SASE. Visit publishers' websites, which often contain their full catalogs. You can also ask librarians to look at catalogs they have on hand. You can even search Amazon.com by publisher and year. (Click on "book search" then "publisher, date" and plug in, for example, "Lee & Low" under "publisher" and "2006" under year. You'll get a list of Lee & Low titles published in 2006, which you can peruse.)

7. Visit bookstores. It's not only informative to spend time in bookstores—it's fun, too! Frequently visit the children's section of your local bookstore (whether a chain or an independent) to see the latest from a variety of publishers and the most current issues of children's magazines. Look for books in the genre you're writing or with illustrations similar in style to yours, and spend some time studying them. It's also wise to get to know your local booksellers; they can tell you what's new in the store and provide insight into what kids and adults are buying.

8. Read, read, read! While you're at that bookstore, pick up a few things, or keep a list of the books that interest you and check them out of your library. Read and study the latest releases, the award winners, and the classics. You'll learn from other writers, get ideas, and get a feel for what's being published. Think about what works and doesn't work in a story. Pay attention to how plots are constructed and how characters are developed or the rhythm and pacing of picture book text. It's certainly enjoyable research!

9. Take advantage of Internet resources. There are innumerable sources of information available on the Internet about writing for children (and anything else you could possibly think of). It's also a great resource for getting (and staying) in touch with other writers and illustrators through listservs, blogs, social networking sites and e-mail, and it can serve as a vehicle for self-promotion. (Visit some authors' and illustrators' sites for ideas. See Useful Online Resources on page 363 for a list of websites.)

10. Consider attending a conference. If time and finances allow, attending a conference is a great way to meet peers and network with professionals in the field of children's publishing. As mentioned above, SCBWI offers conferences in various locations year round. (See www.scbwi.org and click on "Events" for a full conference calendar.) General writers' conferences often offer specialized sessions just for those interested in children's writing. Many conferences offer optional manuscript and portfolio critiques as well, giving you a chance for feedback from seasoned professionals. See the Conferences & Awards section for information on SCBWI and other conferences. The section features a Conferences & Workshops Calendar to help you plan your travel.

11. Network, network, network! Don't work in a vacuum. You can meet other writers and illustrators through a number of the things listed above—SCBWI, conferences, online. Attend local meetings for writers and illustrators whenever you can. Befriend other writers in your area (SCBWI offers members a roster broken down by state)— share guidelines, share subscriptions, be conference buddies and roommates, join a critique group or writing group, exchange information, and offer support. Get online— sign on to listservs, post on message boards and blogs, visit social networking sites and chatrooms. (The Institute of Children's Literature offers regularly scheduled live chats and open forums. Visit www.institutechildrenslit.com and click on Scheduled Events. Also, visit author Verla Kay's website, www.verlakay.com, for information on workshops. See Useful Online Resources on page 363 for more information.) Exchange addresses, phone numbers, and e-mail addresses with writers or illustrators you meet at events. And at conferences, don't be afraid to talk to people, ask strangers to join you for lunch, approach speakers and introduce yourself, or chat in elevators and hallways.

12. Perfect your craft and don't submit until your work is its best. It's often been said that a writer should try to write every day. Great manuscripts don't happen overnight; there's time, research, and revision involved. As you visit bookstores and study what others have written and illustrated, really step back and look at your own work and ask yourself—honestly—*How does my work measure up? Is it ready for editors or art directors to see?* If it's not, keep working. Join a critique group or get a professional manuscript or portfolio critique.

13. Be patient, learn from rejection, and don't give up! Thousands of manuscripts land on editors' desks; thousands of illustration samples line art directors' file drawers. There are so many factors that come into play when evaluating submissions. Keep in mind that you might not hear back from publishers promptly. Persistence and patience are important qualities in writers and illustrators working toward publication. Keep at it—it will come. It can take a while, but when you get that first book contract or first assignment, you'll know it was worth the wait. (For proof, read First Books on page 116.)

Before Your First Sale

If you're just beginning to pursue your career as a children's book writer or illustrator, it's important to learn the proper procedures, formats, and protocol for the publishing industry. This article outlines the basics you need to know before you head to the post office with your submissions.

FINDING THE BEST MARKETS FOR YOUR WORK

Researching publishers thoroughly is a basic element of submitting your work successfully. Editors and art directors hate to receive inappropriate submissions; handling them wastes a lot of their time, not to mention your time and money, and they are the main reason some publishers have chosen not to accept material over the transom. By randomly sending out material without knowing a company's needs, you're sure to meet with rejection.

If you're interested in submitting to a particular magazine, write to request a sample copy or see if it's available in your local library or bookstore. For a book publisher, obtain a book catalog and check a library or bookstore for titles produced by that publisher. Most publishers and magazines have Web sites that include catalogs or sample articles (websites are given within the listings). Studying such materials carefully will better acquaint you with a publisher's or magazine's writing, illustration, and photography styles and formats.

Most of the book publishers and magazines listed in this book offer some sort of writer's, artist's, or photographer's guidelines for a self-addressed, stamped envelope (SASE). Guidelines are also often found on publishers' websites. It's important to read and study guidelines before submitting work. You'll get a better understanding of what a particular publisher wants. You may even decide, after reading the submission guidelines, that your work isn't right for a company you considered.

SUBMITTING YOUR WORK

Throughout the listings, you'll read requests for particular elements to include when contacting markets. Here are explanations of some of these important submission components.

Queries, cover letters, & proposals

A query letter is a no-more-than-one-page, well-written piece meant to arouse an editor's interest in your work. Many query letters start with leads similar to those of actual manuscripts. In the rest of the letter, briefly outline the work you're proposing and include facts, anecdotes, interviews, or other pertinent information that give the editor a feel for the manuscript's premise—entice her to want to know more. End your letter with a straightforward request to write or submit the work, and include information on its approximate length, date it could be completed, and whether accompanying photos or artwork are available.

In a query letter, think about presenting your book as a publisher's catalog would present it. Read through a good catalog and examine how the publishers give enticing summaries of their books in a spare amount of words. It's also important that query letters give editors a taste of your writing style. For good advice and samples of queries, cover letters, and other correspondence, consult *Formatting & Submitting Your Manuscript*, Second Edition, by Cynthia Laufenberg and the editors of *Writer's Market* and *How to Write Attention-Grabbing Query & Cover Letters*, by John Wood (both Writer's Digest Books).

For More Info

- **Query letters for nonfiction.** Queries are usually required when submitting nonfiction material to a publisher. The goal of a nonfiction query is to convince the editor your idea is perfect for her readership and that you're qualified to do the job. Note any previous writing experience and include published samples to prove your credentials, especially samples related to the subject matter you're querying about.
- **Query letters for fiction.** More and more, queries are being requested for fiction manuscripts. For a fiction query, explain the story's plot, main characters, conflict, and resolution. Just as in nonfiction queries, make the editor eager to see more.
- **Cover letters for writers.** Some editors prefer to review complete manuscripts, especially for picture books or fiction. In such cases, the cover letter (which should be no longer than one page) serves as your introduction, establishes your credentials as a writer, and gives the editor an overview of the manuscript. If the editor asked for the manuscript because of a query, note this in your cover letter.
- **Cover letters for illustrators and photographers.** For an illustrator or photographer, the cover letter serves as an introduction to the art director and establishes professional credentials when submitting samples. Explain what services you can provide as well as what type of follow-up contact you plan to make, if any. Be sure to include the URL of your online portfolio if you have one.
- **Resumes.** Often writers, illustrators, and photographers are asked to submit resumes with cover letters and samples. They can be created in a variety of formats, from a single page listing information to color brochures featuring your work. Keep your resume brief, and focus on your achievements, including your clients and the work you've done for them, as well as your educational background and any awards you've received. Do not use the same resume you'd use for a typical job application.
- **Book proposals.** Throughout the listings in the Book Publishers section, publishers refer to submitting a synopsis, outline, and sample chapters. Depending on an editor's preference, some or all of these components, along with a cover letter, make up a book proposal.

A *synopsis* summarizes the book, covering the basic plot (including the ending). It should be easy to read and flow well.

An *outline* covers your book chapter by chapter and provides highlights of each. If you're developing an outline for fiction, include major characters, plots and subplots, and book length.

Sample chapters give a more comprehensive idea of your writing skill. Some editors may request the first two or three chapters to determine if she's interested in seeing the whole book.

Manuscript formats

When submitting a complete manuscript, follow some basic guidelines. In the upper-left corner of your title page, type your legal name (not pseudonym), address, and phone number. In the upper-right corner, type the approximate word count. All material in the upper corners should be single-spaced. Then type the title (centered) almost halfway down that page, the word "by" two spaces under that, and your name or pseudonym two spaces under "by."

The first page should also include the title (centered) one-third of the way down. Two spaces under that type "by" and your name or pseudonym. To begin the body of your manuscript, drop down two double spaces and indent five spaces for each new paragraph. There should be one-inch margins around all sides of a full typewritten page. (Manuscripts with wide margins are more readable and easier to edit.)

Set your computer to double-space for the manuscript body. From page two to the end of the manuscript, include your last name followed by a comma and the title (or key words of the title) in the upper-left corner. The page number should go in the top right corner. Drop down two double spaces to begin the body of each page. If you're submitting a novel, type each chapter title one-third of the way down the page. For more information on manuscript formats, read *Formatting & Submitting Your Manuscript*, by Cynthia Laufenberg and the editors of *Writer's Market* (Writer's Digest Books). SCBWI members and nonmembers can refer to their publication *From Keyboard to Printed Page: Facts You Need to Know*. Visit their website www.scbwi.org and click on "Publications."

For More Info

Picture book formats

The majority of editors prefer to see complete manuscripts for picture books. When typing the text of a picture book, don't indicate page breaks and don't type each page of text on a new sheet of paper. And unless you are an illustrator, don't worry about supplying art. Editors will find their own illustrators for picture books. Most of the time, a writer and an illustrator who work on the same book never meet or interact. The editor acts as a go-between and works with the writer and illustrator throughout the publishing process. *How to Write and Sell Children's Picture Books*, by Jean E. Karl (Writer's Digest Books), offers advice on preparing text and marketing your work.

If you're an illustrator who has written your own book, consider creating a dummy or storyboard containing both art and text, and then submit it along with your complete manuscript and sample pieces of final art (color photocopies or computer printouts—never originals). Publishers interested in picture books specify in their listings what should be submitted. For tips on creating a dummy, refer to *How to Write and Illustrate Children's Books and Get Them Published*, edited by Treld Pelkey Bicknell and Felicity Trotman (North Light Books), or Frieda Gates' book, *How to Write, Illustrate, and Design Children's Books* (Lloyd-Simone Publishing Company).

For More Info

Writers may also want to learn the art of dummy making to help them through their writing process with things like pacing, rhythm, and length. For a great explanation and helpful hints, see *You Can Write Children's Books*, by Tracey E. Dils (Writer's Digest Books).

Getting Started

Mailing submissions

Your main concern when packaging material is to be sure it arrives undamaged. If your manuscript is less than six pages, simply fold it in thirds and send it in a #10 (business-size) envelope. For a SASE, either fold another #10 envelope in thirds or insert a #9 (reply) envelope which fits in a #10 neatly without folding.

Another option is folding your manuscript in half in a 6X9 envelope, with a #9 or #10 SASE enclosed. For larger manuscripts, use a 9X12 envelope both for mailing the submission and as a SASE (which can be folded in half). Book manuscripts require sturdy packaging for mailing. Include a self-addressed mailing label and return postage.

If asked to send artwork and photographs, remember they require a bit more care in packaging to guarantee they arrive in good condition. Sandwich illustrations and photos between heavy cardboard that is slightly larger than the work. The cardboard can be secured by rubber bands or with tape. If you tape the cardboard together, check that the artwork doesn't stick to the tape. Be sure your name and address appear on the back of each piece of art or each photo in case the material becomes separated. For the packaging, use either a manila envelope, a foam-padded envelope, brown paper, or a mailer lined with plastic air bubbles. Bind nonjoined edges with reinforced mailing tape and affix a typed mailing label or clearly write your address.

Mailing material first class ensures quick delivery. Also, first-class mail is forwarded for one year if the addressee has moved, and it can be returned if undeliverable. If you're concerned about your original material safely reaching its destination, consider other mailing options, such as UPS or certified mail. If material needs to reach your editor or art director quickly, use overnight delivery services.

Remember, companies outside your own country can't use your country's postage when returning a manuscript to you. When mailing a submission to another country, include a self-addressed envelope and International Reply Coupons, or IRCs. (You'll see this term in many listings in the Canadian & International Book Publishers section.) Your postmaster can tell you, based on a package's weight, the correct number of IRCs to include to ensure its return.

If it's not necessary for an editor to return your work (such as with photocopies), don't include return postage. You may want to track the status of your submission by enclosing a postage-paid reply postcard with options for the editor to check, such as "Yes, I am interested," "I'll keep the material on file," or "No, the material is not appropriate for my needs at this time."

Some writers elect to include a deadline date. If you don't hear from the editor by the specified date, your manuscript is automatically withdrawn from consideration. Because many publishing houses and companies are overstocked with material, a minimum deadline should be at least three months.

Unless requested, it's never a good idea to use a company's fax number or e-mail address to send manuscript submissions. This can disrupt a company's internal business. Some publishers and magazines, however, may be open to e-mail submissions. Study the listings for specifics and visit publishers' and publications' websites for more information.

Keeping submission records

It's important to keep track of the material you submit. When recording each submission, include the date it was sent, the business and contact name, and any enclosures (such as samples of writing, artwork, or photography). You can create a record-keeping system of your own or look for record-keeping software in your area computer store.

Keep copies of articles or manuscripts you send together with related correspondence to make follow-up easier. When you sell rights to a manuscript, artwork, or photos, you can "close" your file on a particular submission by noting the date the material was accepted, what rights were purchased, the publication date, and payment.

Often writers, illustrators, and photographers fail to follow up on overdue responses. If you don't hear from a publisher within their stated response time, wait another month or so and follow up with a note asking about the status of your submission. Include the title or description, date sent, and a SASE for response. Ask the contact person when she anticipates making a decision. You may refresh the memory of a buyer who temporarily forgot about your submission. At the very least, you'll receive a definite "no" and free yourself to send the material to another publisher.

Simultaneous submissions

If you opt for simultaneous (also called "multiple") submissions—sending the same material to several publishers at the same time—be sure to inform each editor to whom you submit that your work is being considered elsewhere. Many editors are reluctant to receive simultaneous submissions but understand that for hopeful writers and illustrators, waiting several months for a response can be frustrating. In some cases, an editor may actually be more inclined to read your manuscript sooner if she knows it's being considered by another publisher. The Society of Children's Book Writers and Illustrators cautions writers against simultaneous submissions. They recommend simultaneously submitting to publishers who state in their submission guidelines that they accept multiple submissions. In such cases, always specify in your cover letter that you've submitted to more than one editor.

It's especially important to keep track of simultaneous submissions, so if you get an offer on a manuscript sent to more than one publisher, you can instruct other publishers to withdraw your work from consideration.

AGENTS & ART REPS

Most children's writers, illustrators, and photographers, especially those just beginning, are confused about whether to enlist the services of an agent or representative. The decision is strictly one that each writer, illustrator, or photographer must make for herself. Some are confident with their own negotiation skills and believe acquiring an agent or rep is not in their best interest. Others feel uncomfortable in the business arena or are not willing to sacrifice valuable creative time for marketing.

About half of children's publishers accept unagented work, so it's possible to break into children's publishing without an agent. Some agents avoid working with children's books because traditionally low advances and trickling royalty payments over long periods of time make children's books less lucrative. Writers targeting magazine markets don't need the services of an agent. In fact, it's practically impossible to find an agent interested in marketing articles and short stories—there simply isn't enough financial incentive.

One benefit of having an agent, though, is it may speed up the process of getting your work reviewed, especially by publishers who don't accept unagented submissions. If an agent has a good reputation and submits your manuscript to an editor, that manuscript will likely bypass the first-read stage (which is generally done by editorial assistants and junior editors) and end up on the editor's desk sooner.

When agreeing to have a reputable agent represent you, remember that she should be familiar with the needs of the current market and evaluate your manuscript/artwork/

photos accordingly. She should also determine the quality of your piece and whether it is saleable. When your manuscript sells, your agent should negotiate a favorable contract and clear up any questions you have about payments.

Keep in mind that however reputable the agent or rep is, she has limitations. Representation does not guarantee sale of your work. It just means an agent or rep sees potential in your writing, art, or photos. Though an agent or rep may offer criticism or advice on how to improve your work, she cannot make you a better writer, artist, or photographer.

Literary agents typically charge a 15 percent commission from the sale of writing; art and photo representatives usually charge a 25 to 30 percent commission. Such fees are taken from advances and royalty earnings. If your agent sells foreign rights to your work, she will deduct a higher percentage because she will most likely be dealing with an overseas agent with whom she must split the fee.

Be advised that not every agent is open to representing a writer, artist, or photographer who lacks an established track record. Just as when approaching a publisher, the manuscript, artwork, or photos and query or cover letter you submit to a potential agent must be attractive and professional looking. Your first impression must be as an organized, articulate person. For listings of agents and reps, turn to the Agents & Art Reps section.

For additional listings of art reps, consult *Artist's & Graphic Designer's Market*; for photo reps, see *Photographer's Market*; for more information and additional listings of agents see *Guide to Literary Agents* (all Writer's Digest Books).

Running Your Business

The Basics for Writers & Illustrators

A career in children's publishing involves more than just writing skills or artistic talent. Successful authors and illustrators must be able to hold their own in negotiations, keep records, understand contract language, grasp copyright law, pay taxes, and take care of a number of other business concerns. Although agents and reps, accountants and lawyers, and writers' organizations offer help in sorting out such business issues, it's wise to have a basic understanding of them going in. This article offers just that—basic information. For a more in-depth look at the subjects covered here, check your library or bookstore for books and magazines to help you. We also tell you how to get information on issues like taxes and copyright from the federal government.

CONTRACTS & NEGOTIATION

Before you see your work in print or begin working with an editor or art director on a project, there is negotiation. And whether negotiating a book contract, a magazine article assignment, or an illustration or photo assignment, there are a few things to keep in mind. First, if you find any clauses vague or confusing in a contract, get legal advice. The time and money invested in counseling up front could protect you from problems later. If you have an agent or rep, she will review any contract.

Sources for Contract Help

Writers organizations offer a wealth of information to members, including contract advice:

Society of Children's Book Writers and Illustrators members can find information in the SCBWI publication Answers to Some Questions About Contracts. Contact SCBWI at 8271 Beverly Blvd., Los Angeles CA 90048, (323)782-1010, or visit their website: www.scbwi.org.

The Authors Guild also offers contract tips. Visit their website, www.authorsguild.org. (Members of the guild can receive a 75-point contract review from the guild's legal staff.) See the website for membership information and application form, or contact The Authors Guild at 31 E. 28th St., 10th Floor, New York NY 10016, (212)563-5904. Fax: (212)564-5363. E-mail: staff@authorsguild.org. Website: www.authorsguild.org.

A contract is an agreement between two or more parties that specifies the fees to be paid, services rendered, deadlines, rights purchased, and for artists and photographers, whether original work is returned. Most companies have standard contracts for writers, illustrators, and photographers. The specifics (such as royalty rates, advances, delivery dates, etc.) are typed in after negotiations.

Though it's okay to conduct negotiations over the phone, get a written contract once both parties have agreed on terms. Never depend on oral stipulations; written contracts protect both parties from misunderstandings. Watch for clauses that may not be in your best interest, such as "work-for-hire." When you do work-for-hire, you give up all rights to your creations.

When negotiating a book deal, find out whether your contract contains an option clause. This clause requires the author to give the publisher a first look at her next work before offering it to other publishers. Though it's editorial etiquette to give the publisher the first chance at publishing your next work, be wary of statements in the contract that could trap you. Don't allow the publisher to consider the next project for more than 30 days and be specific about what type of work should actually be considered "next work." (For example, if the book under contract is a young adult novel, specify that the publisher will receive an exclusive look at only your next young adult novel.)

For More Info

(For more information about SCBWI, The Authors Guild, and other organizations, turn to the Clubs & Organizations section and read the listings for the organizations that interest you.)

Book publishers' payment methods

Book publishers pay authors and artists in royalties, a percentage of either the wholesale or retail price of each book sold. From large publishing houses, the author usually receives an advance issued against future royalties before the book is published. Half of the advance amount is issued upon signing the book contract; the other half is issued when the book is finished. For illustrations, one-third of the advance should be collected upon signing the contract; one-third upon delivery of sketches; and one-third upon delivery of finished art.

After your book has sold enough copies to earn back your advance, you'll start to get royalty checks. Some publishers hold a reserve against returns, which means a percentage of royalties is held back in case books are returned from bookstores. If you have a reserve clause in your contract, find out the exact percentage of total sales that will be withheld and the time period the publisher will hold this money. You should be reimbursed this amount after a reasonable time period, such as a year. Royalty percentages vary with each publisher, but there are standard ranges.

Book publishers' rates

According to figures from the Society of Children's Book Writers and Illustrators, first-time picture book authors can expect advances of $2,000-3,000; first-time picture book illustrators' advances range from $5,000-7,000; text and illustration packages for first-timers can score $6,000-8,000. Rates go up for subsequent books: $3,500-5,000 for picture book text; $7,000-10,000 for picture book illustration; $8,000-10,000 for text and illustration. Experienced authors can expect higher advances. Royalties for picture books are generally about five percent (split between the author and illustrator) but can go as high as ten percent. Those who both write and illustrate a book, of course, receive the full royalty.

Advances for hardcover novels and nonfiction can fetch author's advances of $4,000-6,000 and 10 percent royalties; paperbacks bring in slightly lower advances of $3,000-

5,000 and royalties of 6-8 percent.

As you might expect, advance and royalty figures vary from house to house and are affected by the time of year, the state of the economy, and other factors. Some smaller houses may not even pay royalties, just flat fees. Educational houses may not offer advances or offer smaller amounts. Religious publishers tend to offer smaller advances than trade publishers. First-time writers and illustrators generally start on the low end of the scale, while established and high-profile writers are paid more. For more information SCBWI members can request or download SCBWI publication "Answer to Some Questions About Contracts." (Visit www.scbwi.org.)

Pay rates for magazines

For writers, fee structures for magazines are based on a per-word rate or range for a specific article length. Artists and photographers have a few more variables to contend with before contracting their services.

Payment for illustrations and photos can be set by such factors as whether the piece(s) will be black and white or four-color, how many are to be purchased, where the work appears (cover or inside), circulation, and the artist's or photographer's prior experience.

Remaindering

When a book goes out of print, a publisher will sell any existing copies to a wholesaler who, in turn, sells the copies to stores at a discount. When the books are "remaindered" to a wholesaler, they are usually sold at a price just above the cost of printing. When negotiating a contract with a publisher, you may want to discuss the possibility of purchasing the remaindered copies before they are sold to a wholesaler, then you can market the copies you purchased and still make a profit.

KNOW YOUR RIGHTS

A copyright is a form of protection provided to creators of original works, published or unpublished. In general, copyright protection ensures the writer, illustrator, or photographer the power to decide how her work is used and allows her to receive payment for each use.

Essentially, copyright also encourages the creation of new works by guaranteeing the creator power to sell rights to the work in the marketplace. The copyright holder can print, reprint, or copy her work; sell or distribute copies of her work; or prepare derivative works such as plays, collages, or recordings. The Copyright Law is designed to protect work (created on or after January 1, 1978) for her lifetime plus 70 years.

If you collaborate with someone else on a written or artistic project, the copyright will last for the lifetime of the last survivor plus 70 years. The creators' heirs may hold a copyright for an additional 70 years. After that, the work becomes public domain. Works created anonymously or under a pseudonym are protected for 120 years, or 95 years after publication. Under work-for-hire agreements, you relinquish your copyright to your "employer."

Copyright notice & registration

Some feel a copyright notice should be included on all work, registered or not. Others feel it is not necessary and a copyright notice will only confuse publishers about whether the material is registered (acquiring rights to previously registered material is a more complicated process).

Although it's not necessary to include a copyright notice on unregistered work, if you don't feel your work is safe without the notice, it is your right to include one. Including a copyright notice—(c) (year of work, your name)—should help safeguard against plagiarism.

Registration is a legal formality intended to make copyright public record, and it can help you win more money in a court case. By registering work within three months of publication or before an infringement occurs, you are eligible to collect statutory damages and attorney's fees. If you register later than three months after publication, you will qualify only for actual damages and profits.

Ideas and concepts are not copyrightable, only expressions of those ideas and concepts. A character type or basic plot outline, for example, is not subject to a copyright infringement lawsuit. Also, titles, names, short phrases or slogans, and lists of contents are not subject to copyright protection, though titles and names may be protected through the Trademark Office.

You can register a group of articles, illustrations, or photos if it meets these criteria:

- the group is assembled in order, such as in a notebook
- the works bear a single title, such as "Works by (your name)"
- it is the work of one writer, artist, or photographer
- the material is the subject of a single claim to copyright

It's a publisher's responsibility to register your book for copyright. If you've previously registered the same material, you must inform your editor and supply the previous copyright information, otherwise, the publisher can't register the book in its published form.

For More Info

For more information about the proper way to register works and to order the correct forms, contact the U.S. Copyright Office, (202)707-3000. The forms available are TX for writing (books, articles, etc.); VA for pictures (photographs, illustrations); and PA for plays and music. For information about how to use the copyright forms, request a copy of Circular I on Copyright Basics. All of the forms and circulars are free. Send the completed registration form along with the stated fee and a copy of the work to the Copyright Office.

For specific answers to questions about copyright (but not legal advice), call the Copyright Public Information Office at (202)707-3000 weekdays between 8:30 a.m. and 5 p.m. EST. Forms can also be downloaded from the Library of Congress website: www.copyright.gov. The site also includes a list of frequently asked questions, tips on filling out forms, general copyright information, and links to other sites related to copyright issues. For members of SCBWI, information about copyrights and the law is available in their publication: Copyright Facts for Writers.

The rights publishers buy

The copyright law specifies that a writer, illustrator, or photographer generally sells one-time rights to her work unless she and the buyer agree otherwise in writing. Many publications will want more exclusive rights to your work than just one-time usage; some will even require you to sell all rights. Be sure you are monetarily compensated for the additional rights you relinquish. If you must give up all rights to a work, carefully consider the price you're being offered to determine whether you'll be compensated for the loss of other potential sales.

Writers who only give up limited rights to their work can then sell reprint rights to other publications, foreign rights to international publications, or even movie rights, should the opportunity arise. Artists and photographers can sell their work to other markets such as paper product companies who may use an image on a calendar, greeting card, or mug. Illustrators and photographers may even sell original work after it has been published. And there are a number of galleries throughout the U.S. that display and sell the original work of children's illustrators.

Rights acquired through the sale of a book manuscript are explained in each publisher's contract. Take time to read relevant clauses to be sure you understand what rights each contract is specifying before signing. Be sure your contract contains a clause allowing all rights to revert back to you in the event the publisher goes out of business. (You may even want to have the contract reviewed by an agent or an attorney specializing in publishing law.)

The following are the rights you'll most often sell to publishers, periodicals, and producers in the marketplace:

First rights. The buyer purchases the rights to use the work for the first time in any medium. All other rights remain with the creator. When material is excerpted from a soon-to-be-published book for use in a newspaper or periodical, first serial rights are also purchased.

One-time rights. The buyer has no guarantee that she is the first to use a piece. One-time permission to run written work, illustrations, or photos is acquired, then the rights revert back to the creator.

First North American serial rights. This is similar to first rights, except that companies who distribute both in the U.S. and Canada will stipulate these rights to ensure that another North American company won't come out with simultaneous usage of the same work.

Second serial (reprint) rights. In this case, newspapers and magazines are granted the right to reproduce a work that has already appeared in another publication. These rights are also purchased by a newspaper or magazine editor who wants to publish part of a book after the book has been published. The proceeds from reprint rights for a book are often split evenly between the author and his publishing company.

Simultaneous rights. More than one publication buys one-time rights to the same work at the same time. Use of such rights occurs among magazines with circulations that don't overlap, such as many religious publications.

All rights. Just as it sounds, the writer, illustrator, or photographer relinquishes all rights to a piece—she no longer has any say in who acquires rights to use it. All rights are purchased by publishers who pay premium usage fees, have an exclusive format, or have other book or magazine interests from which the purchased work can generate more mileage. If a company insists on acquiring all rights to your work, see if you can negotiate for the rights to revert back to you after a reasonable period of time. If they agree to such a proposal, get it in writing. Note: Writers, illustrators, and photographers should be wary of "work-for-hire" arrangements. If you sign an agreement stipulating that your work will be done as work-for-hire, you will not control the copyrights of the completed work—the company that hired you will be the copyright owner.

Foreign serial rights. Be sure before you market to foreign publications that you have sold only North American—not worldwide—serial rights to previous markets. If so, you are free to market to publications that may be interested in material that's appeared in a North American-based periodical.

Syndication rights. This is a division of serial rights. For example, if a syndicate prints portions of a book in installments in its newspapers, it would be syndicating second serial rights. The syndicate would receive a commission and leave the remainder to be split between the author and publisher.

Subsidiary rights. These include serial rights, dramatic rights, book club rights, or translation rights. The contract should specify what percentage of profits from sales of these rights go to the author and publisher.

Dramatic, television, and motion picture rights. During a specified time, the interested party tries to sell a story to a producer or director. Many times options are renewed because the selling process can be lengthy.

Display rights or electronic publishing rights. They're also known as "Data, Storage, and Retrieval." Usually listed under subsidiary rights, the marketing of electronic rights in this era of rapidly expanding capabilities and markets for electronic material can be tricky. Display rights can cover text or images to be used in a CD-ROM or online, or they may cover use of material in formats not even fully developed yet. If a display rights clause is listed in your contract, try to negotiate its elimination. Otherwise, be sure to pin down which electronic rights are being purchased. Demand the clause be restricted to things designed to be read only. By doing this, you maintain your rights to use your work for things such as games and interactive software.

STRICTLY BUSINESS

An essential part of being a freelance writer, illustrator, or photographer is running your freelance business. It's imperative to maintain accurate business records to determine if you're making a profit as a freelancer. Keeping correct, organized records will also make your life easier as you approach tax time.

When setting up your system, begin by keeping a bank account and ledger for your business finances apart from your personal finances. Also, if writing, illustration, or photography is secondary to another freelance career, keep separate business records for each.

You will likely accumulate some business expenses before showing any profit when you start out as a freelancer. To substantiate your income and expenses to the IRS, keep all invoices, cash receipts, sales slips, bank statements, canceled checks, and receipts related to travel expenses and entertaining clients. For entertainment expenditures, record the date, place, and purpose of the business meeting, as well as gas mileage. Keep records for all purchases, big and small. Don't take the small purchases for granted; they can add up to a substantial amount. File all receipts in chronological order. Maintaining a separate file for each month simplifies retrieving records at the end of the year.

Record keeping

When setting up a single-entry bookkeeping system, record income and expenses separately. Use some of the subheads that appear on Schedule C (the form used for recording income from a business) of the 1040 tax form so you can easily transfer information onto the tax form when filing your return. In your ledger include a description of each transaction—the date, source of income (or debts from business purchases), description of what was purchased or sold, the amount of the transaction, and whether payment was by cash, check, or credit card.

Don't wait until January 1 to start keeping records. The moment you first make a business-related purchase or sell an article, book manuscript, illustration, or photo, begin tracking your profits and losses. If you keep records from January 1 to December 31, you're using a calendar-year accounting period. Any other accounting period is called a fiscal year.

There are two types of accounting methods you can choose from—the cash method and the accrual method. The cash method is used more often: You record income when it is received and expenses when they're disbursed.

Using the accrual method, you report income at the time you earn it rather than when it's actually received. Similarly, expenses are recorded at the time they're incurred rather than when you actually pay them. If you choose this method, keep separate records for "accounts receivable" and "accounts payable."

Satisfying the IRS

To successfully—and legally—work as a freelancer, you must know what income you should report and what deductions you can claim. But before you can do that, you must prove to the IRS you're in business to make a profit, that your writing, illustration, or photography is not merely a hobby.

The Tax Reform Act of 1986 says you should show a profit for three years out of a five-year period to attain professional status. The IRS considers these factors as proof of your professionalism:

- accurate financial records
- a business bank account separate from your personal account
- proven time devoted to your profession
- whether it's your main or secondary source of income
- your history of profits and losses
- the amount of training you have invested in your field
- your expertise

If your business is unincorporated, you'll fill out tax information on Schedule C of Form 1040. If you're unsure of what deductions you can take, request the IRS publication containing this information. Under the Tax Reform Act, only 30 percent of business meals, entertainment and related tips, and parking charges are deductible. Other deductible expenses allowed on Schedule C include: car expenses for business-related trips; professional courses and seminars; depreciation of office equipment, such as a computer; dues and publication subscriptions; and miscellaneous expenses, such as postage used for business needs.

If you're working out of a home office, a portion of your mortgage interest (or rent), related utilities, property taxes, repair costs, and depreciation may be deducted as business expenses—under special circumstances. To learn more about the possibility of home office deductions, consult IRS Publication 587, Business Use of Your Home.

The method of paying taxes on income not subject to withholding is called "estimated tax" for individuals. If you expect to owe more than $500 at year's end and if the total amount of income tax that will be withheld during the year will be less than 90 percent of the tax shown on the current year's return, you'll generally make estimated tax payments. Estimated tax payments are made in four equal installments due on April 15, June 15, September 15, and January 15 (assuming you're a calendar-year taxpayer). For more information, request Publication 533, Self-Employment Tax.

The Internal Revenue Service's website (www.irs.gov) offers tips and instant access to IRS forms and publications. **For More Info**

Social Security tax

Depending on your net income as a freelancer, you may be liable for a Social Security tax. This is a tax designed for those who don't have Social Security withheld from their paychecks. You're liable if your net income is $400 or more per year. Net income is the difference between your income and allowable business deductions. Request Schedule SE, Computation of Social Security Self-Employment Tax, if you qualify.

If completing your income tax return proves to be too complex, consider hiring an accountant (the fee is a deductible business expense) or contact the IRS for assistance. (Look in the White Pages under U.S. Government—Internal Revenue Service or check their website, www.irs.gov.) In addition to offering numerous publications to instruct you in various facets of preparing a tax return, the IRS also has walk-in centers in some cities.

Insurance

As a self-employed professional, be aware of what health and business insurance coverage is available to you. Unless you're a Canadian who is covered by national health insurance or a full-time freelancer covered by your spouse's policy, health insurance will no doubt be one of your biggest expenses. Under the terms of a 1985 government act (COBRA), if you leave a job with health benefits, you're entitled to continue that coverage for up to 18 months—you pay 100 percent of the premium and sometimes a small administration fee. Eventually, you must search for your own health plan. You may also choose to purchase disability and life insurance. Disability insurance is offered through many private insurance companies and state governments. This insurance pays a monthly fee that covers living and business expenses during periods of long-term recuperation from a health problem. The amount of money paid is based on the recipient's annual earnings.

Before contacting any insurance representative, talk to other writers, illustrators, or photographers to learn which insurance companies they recommend. If you belong to a writers' or artists' organization, ask the organization if it offers insurance coverage for professionals. (SCBWI has a plan available to members in certain states. Look through the Clubs & Organizations section for other groups that may offer coverage.) Group coverage may be more affordable and provide more comprehensive coverage than an individual policy.

An Agent/Author's Crash Course in Getting Published

by John M. Cusick

My career began with an American Bulldog. I'd climbed five flights to interview at S©ott Treimel NY, a boutique juvenile literary agency in the LaGrange Terrace penthouse at Astor Place. Five months previous I'd graduated college, set to dazzle the world with the profundity of metaphor in Russian literature. I wanted to be a novelist, and was also interested in the book business. Now, 20 interviews later, beat and red-eyed, I clasped my double-espresso like a scabbard and faced 100 pounds of slobbering Cerberus. Its nametag read "Petey."

Speaking of metaphor, Petey was an apt one for what I hoped to become. Agents can seem like fanged gatekeepers, blocking the entry to literary success. I didn't know what lay beyond the big dog, and neither do most writers. Getting past doesn't mean getting published. In fact an agent's inbox is just the beginning of the fraught, uncanny journey to the bookstore. I know this well. Now that I'm an agent, I read dozens of queries a day—vetting, culling, and mostly rejecting. I crumple with prejudice. I delete with a vengeance. But I'm also a writer, and know what it's like to send a query hoping someone will discover my talent. It's a Jeckle & Hyde identity—part fiendish rejecter, part doe-eyed scribbler.

Writer-agents aren't unheard of, though my situation is a bit unique, as *my* agent is also my boss. Not long after starting at STNY, Scott suggested I write something for teens. *Solicited*? Woot! I'd have a book deal by Christmas. Right?

...Right?

Writing young adult after four years studying 19th century novels wasn't easy. I couldn't hide behind complex literary tricks or sweeping description. I had to tell a good story. Period. My characters would have to *do* things, not just sit around *feeling* and *thinking*. Feeling blocked, I flew to L.A. to attend the Book Expo America on behalf of STNY. Landing at LAX, I glanced out the window and saw a city where I knew virtually no one. I thought of the first day of school, when everyone seems to be friends but you. And then *BAM* I had it. My story was about *isolation*, feeling alone in a crowd. I opened

---

JOHN M. CUSICK is from a small town in Massachusetts and a 2007 graduate of Wesleyan University. John is a literary agent of books for children and teens with S©ott Treimel NY. His debut young adult novel, Girl Parts was released by Candlewick Press in August, 2010. He lives in Brooklyn.

John M. Cusick's debut young adult novel *Girl Parts* was released by Candlewick Press in 2010. As an agent, he cautions potential authors, "Your first book probably won't get published."

girl parts

JOHN M. CUSICK

my lap top and started typing furiously— just in time to hear, "Excuse me sir, you'll need to stow that."

Four months later I presented my manuscript, and immediately wished my agent didn't read *literally* 10 feet from my desk. As Scott read, I tried to concentrate on work, jumping out of my seat whenever he went *"Hmm."* This went on for days (an eye-blink compared to most agency turn-around times), Scott scribbling in the margins, me grinding the enamel from my teeth. I knew to expect notes, but wasn't prepared for anything so exhaustive. Scott said he had "some thoughts": My story was set in the future. Scott suggested a contemporary setting. It was told in the present-tense. He wanted simple past. It was in the first person. It should be in third. And that was just the *beginning*.

Getting notes is like being punched in the nose and saying, "Thanks!" Revision is resetting the bone. It *hurts*. But I was lucky. Not only did Scott hold my hand through months of rewrites, everyday I saw our clients—veteran writers—take their notes and go back to work, rethinking, refining, and polishing. Without their example I'd have despaired. More than ever, agents develop manuscripts before submitting—editors can't risk purchasing underdeveloped material—but it still shocked me how many drafts any manuscript undergoes before it's acquired, let alone hits the shelves.

At last my manuscript, *Girl Parts*, was ready to submit. Scott hand-picked a list of editors, and the waiting began. I learned to fear the sound of Scott's email alert and his sigh *"Oh well."* More distracting than rejection was the eventual interest from three major houses. There were a few awkward moments when editors called for Scott and got me instead. It was like an Abbot and Costello routine:

> Editor: *Is John willing to discuss edits?*
> Me: *I am, sure.*
> Editor: *No, John.*
> Me: *I'm John.*
> Editor: *No, no. John the author.*
> Me: *Yes. That's me. I'm the author.*
> Editor: *Oh! I'm sorry, John. I thought I dialed STNY.*
> And so on.

When at last we accepted an offer from Candlewick, I helped negotiate my own contract, a privilege few authors are afforded. I'd aided Scott on dozens of contracts, but the fine print looked much different when it was *my* name on the signatory line. Then came my editor's notes, and jacket design, and marketing...but that's all the fun stuff.

With the emphasis on creative development in MFA and undergrad programs and critique groups, writers aren't always aware of what to expect from the agenting process. As an agent and author I've had a crash course in the business of getting published, and so here are six things I wish someone had told me.

1. Your first book probably won't get published.

One of STNY's authors has for jacket copy: "This is not Mr. Scrimger's first novel; but it is the first one anyone apart from his wife has liked." It's sad but true. Writing something saleable (and by this I mean not just artistically coherent but marketable) takes practice, and most authors have a few unsold first-tries lurking in a drawer somewhere. The good news for first-timers: the pressure is off. Experiment. Type (or scribble) with impunity! Consider your first novel a warm-up, part classroom, part playground. Down the line you may even return and cull great things from it—or better yet, revise and publish! But don't get discouraged if first time isn't the charm. In the words of Beckett: "Try again. Fail again. Fail better."

2. Writing "The End" is far from the end.

I wrote my first novel in college on a Smith Corona Electric (just for fun), and typing "The End" at the bottom of page 300, I felt I'd just climbed Everest. There it was—my book, all seven pounds of it. A work of flawless genius. *Finito.* Months later an agent friend sent me a three-page letter of editorial suggestions, and I nearly stroked. "But the book is *done*," I whined. "You want me to *change it*?" I didn't understand that the first draft is step one on a long journey of revision that can take months or even years. I had the gist on paper, now it was time to dig deeper, enrich my characters, their motivation and psychology, the reality of the story's world, everything. Agents *assume* writers are willing (and eager) to revise. Even best selling authors with awards coming out their ears go through draft after draft. Some writers freak after receiving their first critique from an agent or editor, when they should be popping champagne. STNY rarely sends notes to writers without (in our opinion) potential. Criticism means *interest*, or at least a measure of respect in your talent. Moreover, notes are a grad school creative writing course for the price of an SASE. Value them!

3. Let the work speak for itself.

An author once sent chocolate chip cookies with her query. That author instantly became my best friend forever. But, as far as I know, she remains unpublished.

I look for three things in a query, in this order: First, did the author follow our guidelines? It may seem picayune, but it's a litmus test of professionalism. Second, I look for a strong, coherent story concept. If it's too familiar, or too generic (i.e. "loner kid comes of age and struggles with bullies and first love"), I know we'll have trouble selling it.

Finally, I look for superlative writing—exquisitely fresh observation, ingenious details and a startling voice. Professionalism, strong story, strong writing. That's what I (and I think all agents) look for.

It's true that agents read thousands of queries a year, and it's important to stand out: but stand by being a desirable author with a great story and strong writing. Believe me, that's enough! Avoid colorful fonts, gimmicky ideas, and presents. Also, professional websites, business cards and fancy letterhead may look cool, but they won't save a boring story.

4. A good idea is better than good writing, but you need both.

I hear it everywhere. Editors, agents, librarians and booksellers are all looking for "high-concept" books. What makes a book "high-concept?" If the central idea of the story is clear, precise, and unique, it's probably "high-concept." Lauren McLaughlin's *Cycler* is an excellent example: Every time a girl has her period, she transforms into a boy. Bam! That is *different*, easy to grasp (conceptually if not scientifically), and gets our imagination spinning before we read the first page. Note too that *Cycler*'s concept can be described in a brief sentence. Learning to distill your story into its basic element this way is an important skill.

Is concept more important than strong writing? No, but it will get your foot in the door, as most agents read query letters *before* sample pages. And strong writing rarely sells a book. This fact is oft lamented in our office: sometimes a truly talented writer can't get published because his or her stories are just, well, boring.

5. Follow your muse, not the trends.

Boy, I wish I'd written a vampire book back in 2006. Instead I was writing about dinosaurs. Oh well. Trends are difficult to anticipate, even for industry professionals. Trying to follow them rarely succeeds. By the time your book is finished, chances are editors' lists are already saturated with zombie-pirate-mysteries, or whatever the next hot thing is. Your best bet is to follow your muse. Write what inspires you, what moves you, what you can write truthfully and with personal understanding.

That said, you probably have more than one good idea, and it doesn't hurt to pick the most market-friendly. Look for what's out there, and what isn't. The other day Scott said to me, "You should write a novel set in the Roaring Twenties. No one's done that lately." Next day, *Going Bovine* author Libba Bray signed a seven-figure deal for just such a series. Whoops, we were too late. But she certainly wasn't, and I'm willing to wager Ms. Bray had a dozen worthy ideas and chose one that was market-friendly. (See the inerview with Libba Bray on page 81.)

6. It's not impossible!

My grandmother once told me, "John, surviving a hand grenade going off in your hat is a miracle. Getting published happens everyday." She was right. Work hard, keep at it, be smart, be ready to give yourself entirely to your work, and chances are you will either (A) realize you have better things to do, or (B) get published. It's not impossible. It happens every day. And remember, there's an entire industry of professional bookmakers out there who truly want you to be the next J.K. Rowling.

Ignore those who say it's hard. You know that already. Ignore those who say there's no money in it. They're right, and it doesn't matter. You're a writer. You'd write stories if you lived alone on a desert island, using the bark of coconut trees for paper. Forget the naysayers, listen and appreciate criticism, and keep at it every day. Stranger things have happened. So go for it!

Agents Tell All

*Literary agents answer some common
(and not-so-common) questions*

by Chuck Sambuchino & Ricki Schultz

Whether during their travels to conferences or on their personal blogs, literary agents get a lot of questions from writers, some over and over. Below is a roundup of such questions answered by some of the top children's agents in the business.

ON STARTING STRONG

When you're reviewing a partial fiction manuscript, what do you hate to see in Chapter 1?

I hate to see a whiny character who's in the middle of a fight with one of their parents, slamming doors, rolling eyes, and displaying all sorts of other stereotypical behavior. I hate seeing character "stats" ("Hi, I'm Brian, I'm 10 years and 35 days old with brown hair and green eyes"). I also tend to have a hard time bonding with characters who talk to the reader ("Let me tell you about the summer when I...").

—**Kelly Sonnack** *is a literary agent with the Andrea Brown Literary Agency*

In YA and teen, what are some page 1 clichés you come across?

The most common problem I see is a story that's been told a million times before, without any new twists to make it unique enough to stand out. Same plot, same situations, same set up = the same ol' story. For example: abusive parents/kid's a rebel; family member(s) killed tragically/kid's a loner; divorced parents/kid acts out. Another problem I often see is when the protagonist/main characters don't have an age-appropriate voice. For example: if your main character is 14, let him talk like a 14-year-old. And lastly, being unable to "connect" with the main character(s). For example: characters are too whiny or bratty, or a character shows no emotion/angst.

—**Christine Witthohn** *is the founder of Book Cents Literary*

What are some Chapter 1 clichés you often come across when reading a partial manuscript?

One of my biggest pet peeves is when writers try to stuff too much exposition into dialogue

---

CHUCK SAMBUCHINO is the editor of Guide to Literary Agents (guidetoliteraryagents.com/blog) and the author of the reference book Formatting & Submitting Your Manuscript, 3rd Ed., and the humor book How to Survive a Garden Gnome Attack. **RICKI SCHULTZ** (rickischultz.com) is a Virginia-based freelancer.

rather than trusting their abilities as storytellers to get information across. I'm talking stuff like the mom saying, "Listen, Jimmy, I know you've missed your father ever since he died in that mysterious boating accident last year, but I'm telling you, you'll love this summer camp!" So often writers feel like they have to hook the reader right away. In some ways that's true, but in others you can hook a reader with things other than explosions and big secrets being revealed. Good, strong writing and voice can do it, too.

—**Chris Richman** *is a literary agent with Upstart Crow Literary*

What are some reasons you stop reading a YA manuscript?

Once I've determined that the writing is strong enough, it's usually a question of plot (we receive many works that are derivative or otherwise unoriginal) or voice. As we know from the young adults in our lives, anything that sounds even vaguely parental will not be well received. And there's nothing worse than narration that reads like a text message from a grandmother. In the past month, I've received 29 YA partials. Looking back on my notes, I see that I rejected eight for writing, seven for voice, six for derivative or unoriginal plots, four because they were inappropriate for the age group, and two that simply weren't a good fit for the agency but may find a home elsewhere. Then there were two I liked and passed them on to others in my office. Also, I think a lot of writers, seeing the success of *Twilight*, have tried to force their manuscripts into this genre. I know you've heard it before, but it's so true: write what you are meant to write—don't write what you think will sell.

—**Jessica Sinsheimer** *is a literary agent with the Sarah Jane Freymann Literary Agency*

ON VOICE, CONCEPT AND SUBJECT MATTER

I've heard that nothing is taboo anymore in young adult books, and you can write about topics such as sex and drugs. Is this true?

I would say this: Nothing is taboo if it's done well. Each scene needs to matter in a novel. I've read a number of "edgy" young adult books where writers seem to add in scenes just for shock value and it doesn't work with the flow of the rest of the novel. "Taboo" subjects need to have a purpose in the progression of the novel—and of course, need to be well written! If it does, then yes, I would say nothing is taboo. Taboo topics do, however, affect whether the school and library market will pick up the book—and this can have an effect on whether a publisher feels they can sell enough copies.

—**Jessica Regel** *is a literary agent with the Jean V. Naggar Literary Agency*

What are some subjects or styles of writing that you rarely receive in a submission and wonder why more writers don't tackle such a subject/style?

In terms of style and execution, I'd love to see more MG and YA submissions use innovative narrative strategies deliberately and well. For example: alternating voices/points of view, or a structure that plays with narrative time. Kids are sophisticated readers. Books that engage them on the level of storytelling, as well as story, could break out. In terms of subject matter, I don't see as many stories as you'd think about multicultural families and friendships. I'd also love to see more YA submissions depict awkward, funny and real—rather than flat and glossy—teen romance.

—**Michelle Andelman** *is a literary agent with Lynn C. Franklin Associates*

Articles

Regarding submissions, what do you see too much of? What do you see too little of?

I'm definitely looking for projects with something timeless at their core, whether it's the emotional connection a reader feels to the characters, or the universal humor, or issues that are relevant now and will still be relevant years from now. Can readers truly understand what it's like to be the prince of Denmark? Probably not, but they can identify with feeling disconnected from a dead loved one and the anger at watching him be replaced by a conniving uncle. I want stories that, no matter what the setting, feel true in some way to the reader. I definitely see too many people trying to be something else. I used to make the mistake of listing Roald Dahl as one of my favorite writers from my childhood, but I've found that just inspires a bunch of Dahl knockoffs. And trust me, it's tough to imitate the greats. I get far too much emulation of Dahl, Snicket, Rowling, and whatever else has worked in the past. It's one thing to aspire to greatness; it's another to imitate it. I want people who can appeal to me in the same way as successful writers of yore, with a style that's their own. I see too few writers willing to take chances. I just finished Markus Zusak's wonderful novel *The Book Thief*. It breaks so many so-called rules for kids' books—there are tons of adult characters and points of view, it's a historical at heart, and it's narrated by Death for crying out loud. It's one of the best young adult novels I've read recently.

—**Chris Richman** *is a literary agent at Upstart Crow Literary*

Are there any subjects you feel are untapped and would, therefore, be a refreshing change from the typical multicultural story?

When I was a [bookstore buyer], I was tired of certain subject matters only because those subjects have been explored so well, so often, that you really needed to bring something special to the page to make anyone take notice. Send me a story about some modern immigrant stories, some multi-generational stuff, like the forthcoming (in the U.S.) YA novels of Carlos Ruiz Zafon. There are deeply rich stories about being an outsider, and yet how assimilation means a compromise and loss. I'd also love to see more issues of race discussed in modern terms, where there is the melting pot happening across the U.S., yet the tensions are still there, like the fear of the other. I think these stories, when done well, are universal stories, as we all feel that way at some point. Look at Junot Diaz's *The Brief Wondrous Life of Oscar Wao* as exhibit A.

—**Joe Monti** *is a literary agent with Barry Goldblatt Literary*

ON PICTURE BOOKS & ILLUSTRATIONS

Do you often get queries from authors who have also illustrated their children's book? Are the illustrations usually of enough quality to include them with the submission to publishers?

I do receive many queries from author/illustrators, or from authors who aren't necessarily illustrators but fail to understand that they don't have to worry about submitting illustrations. But most often I find that most illustrators are not the best at coming up with compelling story lines or can't execute the words like a well-seasoned writer (or vice versa: The better writers usually are not the best illustrators).

—**Regina Brooks** *is the founder of Serendipity Literary*

With picture books, I suspect you get a lot of submissions and most of them get rejected. Where are writers going wrong?

Rhyming! So many writers think picture books need to rhyme. There are some editors who won't even look at books in rhyme, and a lot more who are extremely wary of them, so it limits an agent on where it can go and the likelihood of it selling. It's also particularly hard to execute perfectly. Aside from rhyming, I see way too many picture books about a family pet or bedtime.

—**Kelly Sonnack** *is a literary agent with Andrea Brown Literary Agency*

Many people tend to try their hand at children's writing and picture books, but it's often said that writing such books is much more difficult than writers first consider. Why is this so?

I suspect the common thinking goes that if a writer "knows" children, she can write for them. But a successful children's author doesn't simply "know" children—what makes them tick, what their internal and emotional lives are like—she also knows children's literature. She's an avid reader, so she's familiar with what's age-appropriate and authentic to her category of the market. If she's writing a picture book, she's a skilled visual storyteller and can offer up a plot, character, relationship, or emotional arc in miniature—but still, and this is the difficult part, in full.

—**Michelle Andelman** *is a literary agent with Lynn C. Franklin Associates*

What can writers do to enhance their chances of getting a picture book published?

I know it sounds simplistic, but write the very best picture books you can. I think the market contraction has been a good thing, for the most part. I'm only selling the very best picture books my clients write—but I'm definitely selling them. Picture books are generally skewing young, and have been for some time, so focus on strong read-alouds and truly kid-friendly styles. I'm having a lot of luck with projects that have the feel of being created by an author-illustrator even if the author is not an artist, in that they're fairly simple, have all kinds of room for fun and interpretation in the illustrations, and have a lot of personality. I see a lot of picture book manuscripts that depend too heavily on dialogue, which tends to give them the feel of a chapter book or middle-grade novel. The style isn't a picture book style.

—**Erin Murphy** *is the founder of the Erin Murphy Literary Agency*

ON CHILDREN'S NONFICTION
Can you give us some 101 tips on writing nonfiction for kids?

You can write about almost anything when it comes to children's nonfiction, even if it's been done before. But you need to come at the subject from a different angle. If there is already a book on tomatoes and how they grow, then try writing about tomatoes from a cultural angle. There are a ton of books on slavery, but not many on slaves in Haiti during the Haitian Revolution (is there even one? There's an idea—someone take it and query me!). Another thing to always consider is your audience. Kids already have textbooks at school, so you shouldn't write your book like one. Come at the subject in a way that kids can relate to and find interesting. Humor is always a useful tool in nonfiction for kids. Adding to a series is a great way to get started as a writer of nonfiction. But it can't hurt to research the market and try to come up with an idea of your own.

—**Joanna Stampfel Volpe** *is an agent with Nancy Coffey Literary*

You're looking for nonfiction for young adults, such as picture book biographies. Can you give a few good examples of this for people to read and learn from?

The most important thing to me is that the nonfiction reads like fiction—that there is a "story behind the story." For example, Pamela S. Turner's *George Schaller: Life in the Wild*, forthcoming from FSG/Kroupa, is a biography of the great field biologist George Schaller. The book explores Dr. Schaller's career both as a scientist and as an advocate for vanishing wildlife. Appealing to children who are interested in animals, science, adventure and the outdoors, each chapter of the book will also be a "mini-biography" of the species being studied. Several of Pamela's other books study certain environments or animals and make science fun and interesting for kids.

—**Caryn Wiseman** *is a literary agent with the Andrea Brown Literary Agency*

ON CHILDREN'S WRITING CATEGORIES

If someone asked about the line between middle grade and young adult, how would you explain the difference?

Is there a line? It seems to me there is scale more than a line. An editor said to me recently that if the main character is 14, it automatically gets shelved in YA in the chain stores. There's a line. But I work with authors whose light and wholesome novels, with teen main characters, are read mostly by tweens; and others whose novels are populated by middle graders going through such intense experiences that the readership skews to the high end of MG/low end of YA. I try to focus on helping my clients make their stories the best stories they can be rather than fitting them into boxes. The line sometimes feels like a moving target, and the writer has little control over it; better to focus on what you can control, which is how good it is. That said, characters should feel as though they are truly the age they are supposed to be—and that age *today*. Kids are savvier than they used to be even five or ten years ago. They are exposed to more and more at a younger age. Writers should respect their readership accordingly.

—**Erin Murphy** *is the founder of the Erin Murphy Literary Agency*

Can you explain exactly how chapter books differ from middle grade?

There is a lot of overlap between categories, so the difference between older chapter books and younger middle grade is often just a matter of marketing. Younger chapter books are for kids who have graduated from easy readers and are starting to read more fluently. They usually have 8-10 short chapters, each with a cliffhanger ending. They are often a series, like Captain Underpants or Magic Tree House, and can be lightly or heavily illustrated. Middle grade is for readers in the 8-12 age group. They can have a complex plot and subplot, and while often humorous, they can certainly be more serious. The vocabulary is more sophisticated than chapter books, and the emphasis is on character. *The Qwikpick Adventure Society* by Sam Riddleburger (Dial) is an example of a middle grade book in which the targeted reader is at the younger end of the spectrum. At the older end of the middle grade spectrum is "tween." It's realistic, often contemporary, often edgier than traditional middle-grade, and deals with identity issues, school-based situations, family vs. friends, and just how hard it is to be 12.

—**Caryn Wiseman** *is a literary agent with the Andrea Brown Literary Agency*

Does "tween" exist as a category?

Tween does exist, and various publishers even have specific tween imprints in place. As for queries, the same standard holds true for me in terms of tween as it does with YA or MG: If the voice is authentic, then I'm probably interested. However, I do look more at plot with tween novels: right now, it's not enough just to have a great tween voice—the storyline also needs to be unique enough to stand out in the marketplace.

, —**Meredith Kaffel** *is a literary agent at The Charlotte Sheedy Literary Agency*

ON ADVICE TO WRITERS
What's your best piece of advice for new writers who wish to submit children's work to agents?

My best one word of advice: professionalize. A new writer who has done her homework on the children's market ahead of time, and submits to agents in a way that suggests a professional approach to a writing career, is going to stand out. Professionalizing may mean doing a few different things that make all the difference: joining a critique group that can help you polish your manuscript before you query, researching and approaching agents according to submission guidelines, crafting a query that aims to pique interest in—rather than fully explain—your project, and joining the Society of Children's Book Writers & Illustrators (SCBWI).

—**Michelle Andelman** *is a literary agent with Lynn C. Franklin Associates*

Best piece of advice we haven't talked about yet?

Don't hold back from your passion. Too many folks get caught up in what the marketplace is supposedly looking for, and they lose sight of what they're trying to write. That and read your drafts (Note the plural usage!) aloud for imperfections of language and cadence. It's an old horse, but not done enough because it may take you days to finish—but the results are astounding.

—**Joe Monti** *is a literary agent with Barry Goldblatt Literary*

Telling Your Secrets

by Holly Cupala

Five years ago, my writing career was just beginning to take flight—I had articles in *Cricket* and *Spider* and saw my first story published in a *Chicken Soup* anthology. I'd begun a middle grade novel, and everyone kept telling me how much they loved the voice.

But I knew I would never write another word.

In April, after months of hoping and planning, the unthinkable had happened. My husband and I lost our first daughter at birth.

Along with the grief, a sudden clarity enveloped me that what I was writing, what I had been writing, was a sham. It felt hollow and meaningless, devoid of emotional truths. I'd been writing to please other people, and I didn't have the heart for it anymore. To write about Ezri? That would be nothing short of exploitation. My only option to quell the cry of my spirit was to quit writing altogether.

During that time, friends and especially the writing and illustrating community smothered us with love, support, and a lot of fresh meals. Even more, they encouraged me in ways I didn't fully grasp until later—namely, they shared their insights on searching these deep and difficult personal experiences to put truth on the page.

That summer, I attended the SCBWI conference in Los Angeles on scholarship and surrounded by friends. One friend, Justina Chen, had just published her first novel, *Nothing But the Truth (and a few white lies)*. She invited me out to lunch and asked, very kindly, "Are you thinking of writing about Ezri?"

Her question turned a key, opened a door, gave me permission to walk through.

Moments later, we headed into a session with Libba Bray, who had just come out with *A Great and Terrible Beauty*. Libba was sharing with incredible candor about "How to Shut Off Your Brain and Get to the Heart of Your Writing," when...

WHOMP.

An entire novel dropped into my lap: concept, characters, and story arc. I started

---

HOLLY CUPALA wrote teen romance novels before she ever actually experienced teen romance. When she did, it became all about tragic poetry and slightly less tragic novels. When she isn't writing and contributing readergirlz.com, she spends time with her husband and daughter in Seattle, Washington. These days, her writing is less about tragedy and more about hope. Tell Me a Secret is her first novel. Visit her online at www.hollycupala.com.

writing notes as fast as I could as I listened to Libba for clues on how to write it from the heart.

Then, months later, when my character, a pregnant teen, was passed out in a pool of blood and I couldn't bring myself to write the next scene, my friend Janet Lee Carey, author of such stunning fantasies as *Dragon's Keep*, gently suggested, "Maybe it doesn't have to be that way."

And *Tell Me a Secret* was born.

Giving your story permission

If Justina hadn't asked me that question, if she hadn't opened that door, I'm not sure if *Tell Me a Secret* would have ever been written. For years, I'd penned clever fairy tales and rhymed allegories, all of them aimed at staying a safe distance from what really mattered to me. We, as humans, are wired to avoid pain. We seek approval. When we face difficult events in our lives, sometimes those things fall away. Sometimes we come away with the courage to dig deeper.

Justina Chen's award-winning novels are a study in transforming pain into truthful narratives. *Nothing but the Truth (and a few white lies)* confronts the subtleties of racism and identity. *Girl Overboard* addresses a teen struggling with feelings of inadequacy. In *North of Beautiful*, she delivers a girl challenging her beliefs about herself and what true beauty means.

"Every single one of my novels comes from a deep emotional reservoir of personal experiences," says Justina. "I know what it's like to be discriminated against based on my race—and I know how it feels to have someone spit upon my face. I know what it feels like to be used by people who want something from me—and I know what betrayal feels like. I know how it feels to look different from everybody else…and to feel ugly because of it. So for me, "Write what you know" is all about writing what I *feel*."

But mining deep emotions and personal experiences can incite opposition from many corners—not the least of which is facing the experiences themselves. "The hard part," says Justina, "is that you must stare unflinchingly at what you dredge up: the gunk of bad memories. But if you listen carefully to those bad memories, you can hear the soft heartbeat of your story." For me, during the writing of *Tell Me a Secret*, that meant making trails through sadness and loss. It meant reliving the emotions of painful relationships—but unexpectedly, it meant transforming them into hope.

At first, Justina tried her hand at picture books—funny, rhyming, counting, serious. She sold her first picture book, *The Patch*, on the last day of the writing class where we met! But something kept her from writing novels, especially novels touching on her own experiences. "The voice in my head," she says, "sounded surprisingly like a certain creative writing professor at Stanford who told me I had no talent with words and I'd never publish. So I put away my writing for years and years."

Then someone turned a key.

"I went to a conference, and an editor read one of my manuscripts out loud and very thoughtfully, very deliberately announced before hundreds of people, 'This author should be a novelist.'" That editor opened a door for Justina much in the same way she opened a door for me.

The next step we had to take on our own: walking through the door, and giving *ourselves* permission. Justina describes that vivid turning point: "I remember quite

Articles

With a few gentle nudges from writing friends, Holly Cupala wrote her debut novel *Tell Me a Secret*, inspired by the loss of her first daughter at childirth.

Reprinted with permission.

distinctly looking at my kids and thinking to myself, How can I expect my children to go for their dreams if I don't?"

For me, that step meant a battle between a story I knew I needed to tell and the certain belief that I would not be capable of telling it.

Getting out of your own way

Writers face doubts—on ideas, on our instincts, on words that come one painful drop at a time. Learning to navigate the minefield of challenges is much more than just deciding to write from the heart one day and pouring out a novel the next. It's a process.

For months after *Tell Me a Secret* landed in my lap, I confined myself to writing notes, not trusting my mind to translate what was in my heart. I might have continued writing notes forever if two things hadn't happened: first, Justina called me to say, "You *have* to write this." Then another friend, unrelated to my writing life, called to say he'd had a dream: I was supposed to be working on something, and I'd better get to it.

What followed was a year of wrestling myself to get words, emotions onto the page. In essence, I learned to take Libba Bray's advice and make it my own.

"You have to plunge yourself down into the depths of what you want to write and why you want to write the book in the first place," says Libba Bray, author of The Gemma Doyle Trilogy and recipient of the 2010 Michael L. Printz Award for *Going*

Bovine. (See page 81 for an in-depth interview with Libba.) "There's this great quote from Jennifer Jacobsen: when she sits down to write, she asks herself, *is it true yet?* You can feel it. There's that moment where you're kind of hollowed out by it. There are no shortcuts."

If anyone has triumphed in the battle of getting truth onto the page, it is Libba. The summer after high school, she was in a wreck that demolished her face. What followed was a long, drawn-out, frustrating process that left her isolated and devastated. "It was like having the house land in the *Wizard of Oz*. I didn't have any way to talk about what was going on inside of me. Who could understand what I was going through?"

Libba had been writing before, but now it provided deliverance. "One of my graduation gifts was this little yellow journal. That's where I had a voice. It was a really self-destructive year, and the journal was my lifeline. It kept me from killing myself, basically."

Outside of her journal, Libba turned to humor to mask the deeper things. She wrote plays, but looking back, she felt like she was circling. "There were times when I would touch on something that felt sort of real, but there was this sense of being tuned to the outside, to what you think something should be. I had this friend in college, Christopher Rao, who said, 'If you would take this writing thing seriously, you could really be something.' He told me I was hiding."

At first, she didn't get it, though she had moments of breaking through. "I wrote this monologue in my twenties all about a girl who was not beautiful, and she was trying to reconcile with that fact. It was very honest, and I'm not sure how I got out of my own way on that."

After that, she continued circling until her son was born. "It's ripping yourself open in more ways than one—making you very, very aware of all kinds of thoughts and feelings. I started realizing, I've got to write." Libba signed up for a writing workshop. "In the beginning, I felt very stilted—we read our work aloud, and people would only comment on what was strong. It was too embryonic for criticism. I learned to take risks, get comfortable with my own voice.

"One night, I was in a bad mood, angry, just really raw, and I thought, *I will write whatever comes into my head.* Then I read it aloud, and it was the piece that everyone responded to. A friend said, 'One of the things I love about your writing, Libba, is that it's angry. It's got this edge to it.' At first I was horrified, and then I realized, yeah, I do have an edge. Those were the things I was always trying to hide before—it was really liberating."

Writing is never an easy process, but something clicked for Libba as she wrote *Going Bovine*. "Structure is my *bête noir*—I am more interested in character and atmosphere and scene. *Going Bovine* was episodic, so I was free to make up episodes on the way like *Don Quixote*. I do feel like revision is where it happens for me—it's where I can tunnel deeper."

In writing the first draft of *Tell Me a Secret*, I resisted tunneling deeper. Just getting words onto the page, addressing those emotions, felt like battle enough. It wasn't until the middle of the night, a month after our second daughter was born, that I responded to the call of my character's voice: *It's tough, living in the shadow of a dead girl.* Shortly afterward, I applied for an SCBWI Work-In-Progress Grant—receiving one served as a signpost.

I continued writing until I could go no further.

Letting your story have a life of its own

My character was passed out in a pool of blood. I knew the ending would bring loss and devastation, a family shattered by grief brought together again by forgiveness. But I couldn't bring myself to write a word of it.

"Maybe it doesn't have to be that way. Maybe the baby doesn't have to die." Janet Lee Carey, award-winning author of *Dragon's Keep* and *Stealing Death*, said this after weeks of watching me try to break through to that pivotal scene, when my character's reality would meet mine. Instead, I had been writing earlier, happy scenes. A funny Christmas flashback, a steamy kiss. When she asked me, I cried.

Janet recognized my dilemma because she knew it intimately. Every one of her books comes from a deep well of memories, questions that must be answered. *Dragon's Keep* tells the story of a princess with a dragon's claw, a kind of beauty and beast combined. In *Stealing Death*, Kipp tries to stop Death from taking the girl he loves and asks, what if the thing we fear most is not what we imagined?

"The emotional core of *Dragon's Keep* came from my own experience as an overweight teen," says Janet. "I felt imperfect, awkward, beautiful inside and ugly outside. Princess Rosalind's feelings of inadequacy and longing to be loved propel her through the story. Her 'flaw' was different than mine, but the feelings were the same." Readers have told Janet they could relate to the flawed princess with the ugly secret.

Although the idea for *Stealing Death* had come twelve years before, Janet didn't begin writing it until the year her mother was dying. She sang the song Kipp sings in the book

Writing Advice from the Trenches

From Justina Chen: Close your eyes and type. I mean it. Close your eyes and let the words flow in one passionate rush...or one painful trickle, however the scene comes. Then, without looking at your pages, save and close the document. Reward yourself for the rest of the day. The hard part is over. What comes next—revision—will be much, much easier to face.

From Libba Bray: I am utterly terrified every time I sit down to write something. I always feel like I can avoid the fire—I'll go around, there will be a detour, a nice scenic drive. But I can't. It's bloody, brutal, a fight—but you are going to get through the fire. You are going to come out through the other side. Otherwise, what's the point?

From Janet Lee Carey: If you are having difficulty bringing personal experiences to the page, try flipping things around. Changing some of the basic facts surrounding the emotional memory frees you to write passionately. You might set the incident in another world, another time, or with completely different people. The key is to be real when it comes to the emotional center.

My own advice: Make a choice to be transparent, a choice to tell the truth. Every character must be some aspect of yourself, showing something that, in your heart of hearts, you know to be true. My loss stripped away all of the worries I had about what people would think, about not revealing too much about myself, about not digging deeper. But truth is in the deep parts. Writers, keep digging.

to her mother as she was slipping away. "I finished it just a week before my stepfather died," says Janet. "Kipp's story helped me through both losses. My stepfather's longing to be reunited with my mother after she died paralleled Sor Joay's longing to be with his wife. I was telling myself this as I wrote but didn't realize it until much later. Sometimes art shines a light on life in miraculous ways."

Each of her novels unwrap deeper issues about life, beauty, and the nature of our beliefs about ourselves, and the challenge is to write them with honesty and integrity. If the character is holding something back, Janet says, "then I have to sit very still and really listen. I have to get out of the way, let them move, breathe, and speak. The art wants to burst through. The story wants out."

Sometimes that means letting the story have a life of its own on the page. "I have learned I can trust art to transform the original experience. When I bring a strong emotional experience into my novel, I know it's not about 'sticking to the facts.' It's about listening to the truth I want to tell myself."

Janet wasn't offering an open door for me—instead, she gently closed the one I wasn't supposed to walk through again. This book would be about healing. The more I thought about it, the more I could see the possibilities.

Writing what is meaningful to you

The rest of the story is written. After I finished and revised and searched for an agent with whom the novel would resonate, I found him—he sold *Tell Me a Secret* to our top choice in the space of a few weeks. I have had to adjust to the idea of my secrets making their way into the world and meeting an unknown fate. Our daughter now urgently whispers to friends, "I'm writing a *book*. It's called *Tell Me a Secret...*" And I have begun the process all over again.

Giving your story permission is an act of faith—that the story of your heart has a heartbeat of its own. Getting out of the way means letting the page be messy and honest so that you can scratch the surface and find truth. The hardest part may be letting the story go, trusting that it will find its way amidst a universe of possibilities.

How do you do it?

Surround yourself with fellow travelers. Prioritize time to soak in inspiration, time to create. Learn to recognize the voices (many of them in your own heart, or voices from the past or present) that would stop you. Listen to the One True Voice, the one that knows your story with absolute certainty.

There is a touch of destiny about writing what you are meant to write. You will feel it, and your readers will, too.

Trust yourself to write it.

Articles

Creating a Strong Sense of Place

by Jill Alexander

I know at least three truths about Prosper County that don't appear in *Sweetheart* or *Paradise and His Smokin' Squeezebox*: When the blacktop roads spidering through the piney woods soak up the August sun, the tar turns to modeling clay beneath the bare feet of children whose hearts are equally impressionable. I know too that in town, the big town with the mall and the downtown square, there's a shiny-shoed preacher standing high on a Bible and with a trumpeting, confident voice leads a whole congregation of believers down a narrow rabbit hole. And I know that for the kids whose toes shape the tar and whose minds find before they follow, dreams don't stop at the city limit sign.

Indeed by the time a novel is complete, I have a much larger sense of the story's setting than what I reveal to the reader. Those intimate, unspoken and unwritten details of time and place enhance my ability to shape a story, build a world. I certainly did not know all the details of setting on the front end of writing my stories. However, as with character development, setting a story begins with a broad stroke of understanding. As I began in the first chapter of *The Sweetheart of Prosper County* to paint the downtown square through the narrator Austin's eyes, the basic foundations of her community became clear. And in *Paradise and His Smokin' Squeezebox*, the setting extends naturally into the rural countryside.

Prosper County—the place, the people, the atmosphere—exists only between the pages of my books. Although realistic, Prosper County is a work of fiction in the same way that Hogwarts and Middle-earth are. A strong sense of place transcends genre and tethers the reader to the story, gives them terra firma on which to stand and experience right along side the characters.

JILL ALEXANDER grew up in rural East Texas with no public library and few books at home. The love of reading fiction she developed in high school combined with her passion for storytelling led her to study literature and creative writing. She's taught AP English and Spanish. Her debut novel *The Sweetheart of Prosper County* was discovered through the SCBWI Annual Winter Conference critique process and has received a starred review from *School Library Journal* as well as being awarded to the 2010 Texas Lonestar Reading List. Her second novel *Paradise and His Smokin' Squeezebox* is set for release in Spring 2011. Visit her at www.jillsalexander.com or follow her twang on twitter http://twitter.com/jillsalexander.

YA Novels Strong on Setting

- *The Underneath*, by Kathi Appelt
- *The Compound*, by S.A. Bodeen
- *Hunger Games*, by Suzanne Collins
- *Lock and Key*, by Sarah Dessen
- *The Graveyard Book*, by Neil Gaiman
- *Out of The Dust*, by Karen Hesse
- *Love is the Higher Law*, by David Levithan
- *Soul Enchilada*, by David Macinnis Gill
- *Jellicoe Road*, by Melina Marchetta
- *Hatchet*, by Gary Paulsen
- *The Adoration of Jenna Fox*, by Mary E. Pearson
- *In the Path of Falling Objects*, by Andrew Smith
- *Espressologist*, by Kristina Springer
- *How to Say Goodbye in Robot*, by Natalie Standiford
- *Shiver*, by Maggie Stiefvater

Articles

The basics of setting

At a superficial minimum, setting is simply physical background. The first task of any storyteller is to know the basic setting just like he or she knows the narrator, the characters and their fears and desires. Whether writing fantasy or realistic fiction—any genre—consider and convey these beginning elements:

- **Landscape.** More than town, landscape is topography. The characters may find hills to climb or quicksand to avoid.
- **Time and Season.** Plot occurs within a time block, so a setting should be textured with details and images evocative of the period. In Prosper County, springtime brings bluebonnets. In Dickens' 19th Century in England, debtor's prisons and poverty weigh heavily.
- **Community.** The inhabitants (not necessarily the characters) of a place have jobs and pastimes, social norms and manners. Perhaps a population in a sci-fi novel moves about with absolutely no eye contact, unlike a genteel Southern family where the door of welcome is flung wide.
- **Atmosphere.** The setting can illustrate the emotional and spiritual climate, as in using a barren landscape to suggest a greater sense of loneliness or isolation.

One of my favorite American authors, Eudora Welty, had this to say about setting: "Every story would be another story, and unrecognizable if it took up its characters and plot and happened somewhere else . . . Fiction depends for its life on place. Place is the crossroads of circumstance, the proving ground of What happened? Who's here? Who's coming?"

Now, as they'd say in Prosper County, sit on that notion and spin a while. Think about it. Can you imagine *Twilight* taking place somewhere other than Forks? How would the story have changed had the setting been different? What about a classic like *The Great Gatsby* and West Egg/East Egg/ Wilson's garage as the "crossroads of circumstance?" Even consider the work of Jack London.

Building a world, creating a setting, requires a sensory journey on the part of the writer. An archeological dig. A futuristic trip. A visit back home. Followed then by a fearless effort to show the world the place the characters will call home.

The building of setting

Developing a strong sense of place—a place that is the "proving ground"—requires attention to the little things. Not only do I need to know and convey the basics of my setting, I must also provide the sensory detail necessary for a reader to experience that world.

- **Sight.** This goes beyond a straightforward scene description and becomes an opportunity to color hope across a broad, blue sky and contour stubbornness into a weathered old barn.
- **Sound.** Every community and place has familiar sounds—from chiming church bells to clanging death knells—that once revealed anchor a reader to the scene.
- **Smell.** To be real and tangible, every setting needs a scent. Perhaps it is the salt air of the sea or maybe the sour stench from a chicken processing plant.
- **Taste.** Settings should be savored like the sweet, palatable aroma floating from an orchard full and ripe with peaches.

Setting for me, however, is more than just detail and background; it is backbone. More than time and place. More than an opportunity to tickle a reader's senses. When I'm writing, I'm very conscious of how setting both affects and interacts with plot and characters. One of the best examples in classic literature of the fullness of setting— where sensory details interact with plot to become "the crossroads of circumstance"—is in Harper Lee's Pulitzer prize-winning novel *To Kill a Mockingbird*. Lee uses contrasting cabin settings to introduce the character Robert Ewell and to illustrate racial prejudice. She leaves no detail unearthed:

> Maycomb's Ewells lived behind the town garbage dump in what was once a Negro cabin. The cabin's plank walls were supplemented with sheets of corrugated iron, its roof shingled with tin cans hammered flat, so only its general shape suggested its original design: square, with four tiny rooms opening onto a shotgun hall, the cabin rested uneasily upon four irregular lumps of limestone. Its windows were merely open spaces in the walls, which in the summertime were covered with greasy strips of cheesecloth to keep out the varmints that feasted on Maycomb's refuse. The varmints had a lean time of it, for the Ewells gave the dump a thorough gleaning everyday, and the fruits of their industry (those that were not eaten) made the plot of ground around the cabin look like the playhouse of an insane child.

Austin is tired of standing at the curb and watching the parade pass her by. Literally.

the sweetheart of prosper county

by jill s. alexander

Reprinted with permission.

Jill Alexander's debut noel *The Sweetheart of Prosper County* was discovered through the SCBWI Annual Winter Conference critique process.

In contrast:

> A dirt road ran from the highway past the dump, down to a small Negro settlement some five hundred yards beyond the Ewells . . . In the frosty December dusk, their cabins looked neat and snug with pale blue smoke rising from the chimneys and doorways glowing amber from the fires inside. There were delicious smells about: chicken, bacon frying crisp as the twilight air. Jem and I detected squirrel cooking, but it took an old country man like Atticus to identify possum and rabbit, aromas that vanished when we rode back past the Ewell residence.

Lee then reveals her theme and the absurdity of racial prejudice by immediately following with the narrator Scout's observation of Robert Ewell:

> "All the little man on the witness stand had that made him any better than his nearest neighbors was, that if scrubbed with lye soap in very hot water, his skin was white."

The breadth of setting

In the above passages, Harper Lee sets the scene with sensory language—using the setting to create an atmosphere, develop character, further the voice of the story, and point to theme. Setting permeates all facets of the storytelling.

- **Character.** Setting shapes a character from his or her roots but also can function as character. Alive. Fully drawn and detailed. An environment, not only *in which*, but *to which* characters react.
- **Voice.** Writers often hear that their work must have a strong, clear voice. Yet voice is an intangible that is as hard to identify as it is to achieve. I've heard voice defined as "I know it when I see it." Going with that definition, consider that setting can strengthen voice, maybe even make it more outstanding to a reader. In my Prosper County, the hardworking, blue collar community influenced the sassy, southern narrative voice in both my novels. My first person narrators are as hearty and stubborn as their surroundings. The setting lifts the voice of the story because the two share the similar characteristics.
- **Mood.** Setting helps to create a mood and reflects the emotional condition of the narrator and characters. In *Sweetheart*, Austin looks at the abandoned downtown on Christmas Eve and her own loneliness from the loss of her father surfaces. In contrast, a lively celebration around the downtown square depicted much later in the novel supports her excitement as she hangs out with her new friends.
- **Theme.** The setting is the "crossroads of circumstance," the place where the character makes his or her stand. If theme is the universal truth in a story, then that truth rises naturally from the conflicts. As much as setting influences a story's conflict, setting should be considered in the resolution. In so many words, what happens in Vegas stays in Vegas. Carry the setting through to the end. Leave the readers knowing where they've been.

What setting isn't

Setting is not description in isolation from the plot or the narrator or character's emotional state. Again, I know many things about my setting that I don't reveal to the reader. However, the only physical scene descriptions that matter are those that directly involve the character and are filtered by the narrator. The power in setting comes in its connection to the novel as a whole.

Setting is also not decorative imagery—a pretty picture or information dump. A strong sense of time and place should be evocative and even provocative.

In her novel *Their Eyes Were Watching God*, Zora Neale Hurston achieves both the evocative and provocative power of setting. Through an intense description, Hurston conveys young Janie's sexual awakening. Interestingly, the imagery and emotion in this setting is so powerful that the passage has been cited in attempts to ban the book:

> It was a spring afternoon in West Florida. Janie had spent most of the day under a blossoming pear tree in the back-yard . . . She was stretched on her back beneath the pear tree soaking in the alto chant of the visiting bees, the gold of the sun and the panting breath of the breeze when the inaudible voice of it all came to her. She saw a dust-bearing bee sink into the sanctum of a bloom; the thousand sister-calyxes arch to meet the love embrace and the ecstatic shiver of the tree from root to tiniest branch creaming in every blossom and frothing with delight . . . Then Janie felt a pain remorseless and sweet that left her limp and languid.

The surprise in the setting

Setting is not merely established early then left behind. Woven throughout the story, setting—much like character and plot—adds a layer of depth and can take surprising twists and turns. Although I start with the basic elements, I enjoy those writing moments when organically, as if by magic, a new facet to the setting appears that enriches the entire work. Staying open to the possibilities and in touch with the story's environment gives me the good stuff, the details to create a strong sense of place—a place both familiar and new to which a reader can run, escape or even hide.

Articles

Don't Parent Your Characters

by Sue Bradford Edwards

Ask writers about problems in their work and you'll get a variety of responses:
"The adults keep taking my story over."
"I don't want my characters to suffer."
"I have problems creating enough tension in my plot."
"I don't want to write edgy even thought that's what sells."

If you have one or more of these problems, then I'm issuing you a challenge: Stop parenting your characters. There are a lot of ways that writers parent their characters but no matter how you do it the end result is the same—a story that just doesn't work and ultimately won't sell.

Fortunately, it is a habit you *can* break.

Getting in the way of a good story

The number one parenting problem that characters face is adults, usually parents, who stop the fun and solve all of the problems instead of letting the characters get into trouble and then get back out again. The solution is somewhat obvious. Get Mom and Dad out of the way.

"I recall my horror when first starting out to hear Betsy Byars recommend killing off my characters' parents," says author and writing coach Esther Hershenhorn. "But she was right. A young character *acting*, moving forward on his plotline, against all odds, is what ultimately empowers the character and thus the reader." From The Boxcar Children to Harry Potter, there is a long tradition of killing off Mom and Dad to get the story underway. Even Hershenhorn opted for this solution. "I have indeed orphaned a few characters, namely Pippin Biddle and his sisters in my picture book *Fancy That.*"

If burying Mom and Dad doesn't work for your story, don't worry. There are other ways to get them out of the way. Adults, both real and imagined, are wonderfully self-absorbed and don't always notice what is going on under their own noses. "In my novel, *Grace Happens*, I kept the parents out of the main character's way by making the

SUE BRADFORD EDWARDS writes from her office in St. Louis, Missouri. You can find her work in Children's Writer newsletter and on the web site Prayables.com. She has also been offering a series of free writing workshops in the St. Louis area. Find out more about her and her work on her website (www.suebradfordedwards.com) and her blogs (suebe.wordpress.com and suebe2.wordpress.com).

mother so self involved in her career as a movie star that she left her daughter's care to a nanny and a tutor who do their jobs and are caring but not overly so," says Jan Czech.

You can also stop parenting your characters by putting someone more permissive in charge. "For my YA mystery, *Suspect,* I sent the father off to a week-long conference. Other adults surrounded my main character, but they were inclined to give her more autonomy," says Kristin Wolden Nitz. This approach worked in the Boxcar Children and it still works today.

You can also keep Mom and Dad busy with what so often keeps real parents busy—work. "In my book *The Lucky Star,* set during the Great Depression, I sent Dad off to a work camp with the CCC, and Mom found part-time work," says author Judy Young. "This left the main character, Ruth, alone to figure out how to help her younger sister learn to read when their school shut down."

Can't work a full-time job into the story? "In *Rules,* the character's mother was an accountant, so Cynthia Lord set the story during tax season!" says Hershenhorn. Seasonal jobs, job related travel and a handy deadline can all work to keep pesky adults out of the main story line.

Worried such solutions won't be believable? "So many kids understand what it feels like to fly beneath the radar in a hectic household," says Sydney Salter. It may not be the norm in your household, but it happens in most households at one time or another.

Not part of the solution

If you simply cannot get the parents out of your story, then make good use of them. "I think children solve their own problems no matter what the adults around them are

Articles

Sometimes You Just Gotta

No matter how often a rule applies, sometimes you simply have to break the rule to make a story work. This is true even in terms of not letting adults interfere in the young character's story.

"In my picture book *Chicken Soup by Heart* (Simon & Schuster) my very young character Rudie Dinkins cooks chicken soup to make his beloved flu-ridden after-school babysitter Mrs. Gittel instantly better in time to watch him the next day," says Esther Hershenhorn.

"My savvy editor Stephanie Owens Lurie reminded me that (a) little children need to be supervised when chopping vegetables and cooking soup on a stove, (b) Mothers often object when their children idolize another, say a babysitter, and (c) Mothers happen to purchase a lot of children's books.

"Thus, when Rudie chose to act by deciding to cook and deliver chicken soup, based on *his* needs, *his* ideas, and *his* solutions, he cooked that chicken soup with his Mama beside him. Of course, Rudie delivered the soup and instructions sans-Mama; otherwise the story wouldn't be his."

Mama may have been necessary, both in terms of reality and marketability, but Hershenhorn still didn't let her steal the show.

doing," says A.S. King. "For example, take an overprotective parent who is trying to solve every problem a kid has. Underneath it all, the child is actually dealing with the problem of having an overprotective parent, whether by acting out or retracting into a shell where they have some level of control over their life."

Salter also uses adults to complicate the lives of young characters. "I do sometimes have older characters give misguided advice to younger characters," says Salter. "That way rather than solving problems, the adults complicate them. Polly's grandmother in *Swoon at Your Risk* is an advice columnist, but she isn't helping Polly solve her boy problems at all—she's only making things worse!"

King agrees and adds that problem adults are a very real problem. "For the most part, adults are a very real and very constant obstacle to my characters. I don't keep them out of the way at all. During teen years, it's often adults—teachers, parents, coaches—who cause problems. Why get rid of them when they are an authentic and usable resource?"

If this is a technique you plan to use, be warned. There is a balancing act between making your adults part of the problem and inhumanly dense. "They may not know how to help, or they may be misguided, but most of the time, adults are simply trying to do the best they can at parenting, teaching, coaching, etc. Maybe it's not good enough," says Salter. "But have sympathy for your adult characters, even if your younger characters don't. In other words, give each of your characters a mixture of many good and bad traits. That's what makes them human." Even if your adult characters are werewolves or zombies, they need to be believable and somewhat sympathetic.

It's my problem!

There is one final way to keep from writing a story where Mom and Dad solve the problem—make that reality an absolute impossibility. "In my novel *The Dark Divine* my main character Grace comes from a close-knit family that is very involved in each other's lives. She has a father who is interested in helping her solve the problem she faces in the book, but even though he provides her with some of the information she needs, ultimately the problem is something that only Grace can solve," says Bree Despain. "No matter how much her father wants to help her, he can't. He has to step aside in order to let Grace figure out how to solve the problem on her own. However, I did put him on an airplane at the climax of the book just to ensure that he didn't get in the way."

Nitz used this technique equally well in her middle grade novel. "In *Defending Irene*, the parents were aware of the problem, but knew that they couldn't really do anything about it. My parents were wise enough to know that nothing good comes of parents going to coaches to complain unless there is a physically unsafe situation," says Nitz. "They had to release my main character to the game and support her without intervening."

Think you can't use this technique in your picture book? Think again. "In my picture book *The Garden Angel*, the main character, grieving the loss of her beloved grandfather, plants a garden, something they used to do together—all by herself and dresses the scarecrow in her grandfather's gardening clothes," says Czech. "She's not aware of course that she is consciously working through her grief—she's simply doing something that gives her some control of the situation."

Carefully select the problem that your character has and, no matter how much the adults want to help, it simply will not be an option. But you also need to remember that this isn't the only problem we create when we parent our characters.

Even good kids need room to grow

Another way we parent our characters is by making them too good to be true. A bit of "bad" behavior may be necessary both to make your character believable and to move the story forward.

"Allowing my characters to do a little bit of rebellious sneaking around helps me keep parents out of the way. In *My Big Nose and Other Natural Disasters,* Jory doesn't tell her parents that she's saving money for a nose job because she knows they disapprove of plastic surgery for teens," says Salter. "Readers relate to keeping a few secrets from parents so it makes the plot, as well as my characters, believable."

Nitz seconds this approach. "In *Saving the Griffin*, my young characters kept everything secret from the parents. The mother saw signs that things were going on, but misinterpreted them completely."

Not only is this type of behavior more realistic, it also leads to a better story. "Let your character learn from small mistakes early in the story so that they will be able to make bigger leaps in problem solving by the end," says Salter. "Otherwise, the resolution will appear forced or unrealistic. Characters need to show incremental changes all through the story so they have the strength to overcome the biggest conflicts by the end." Getting Mom and Dad out of the way is pointless if your character isn't willing to make mistakes that make things happen, lead to later solutions and character growth.

Give 'em hell

In addition to wanting your characters to behave better than any real kid we've ever met, another parenting problem comes when we aren't willing to make our characters suffer for the sake of a good story. "You should run your main character up a tree and then start throwing rocks at her metaphorically speaking," Despain says. "I'm not afraid to be too hard on my characters." Still can't bring yourself to make your character suffer? Not even for a top-notch story? Then maybe you aren't parenting your character, but your reader. "I think if an author is overly worried about putting their character in 'too much' danger, then he is probably trying too hard to 'parent' the reader, and not just the character," says Despain. "It is easy to get caught up in the idea of writing a character who is too perfect. They don't want to let their characters make unwise decisions, disobey the adult characters in the book, etc. because they want their main character to be a good example for the reader. However, no reader, or publisher, out there is going to identify with a character who doesn't ever make mistakes. If you want your characters to feel real, then you have to allow them to act like real people."

King agrees. "I think a lot of people feel that every story for teens needs a wholesome moral. And while I agree to some extent, I feel there are many ways to get to that moral, and many ways to express it. For example, we don't always learn from people who make great choices or who reap oversimplified consequences. I reckon I've learned more in my life from people who have made the wrong choices. We often hear censors lashing out at YA authors for their characters using drugs or having sex, as if all readers will run out and do the same things. Fact is, teenagers are really smart and we rarely give them credit for that."

In addition to respecting your reader, as an author you must recognize that your readers have a different set of experiences than you do. "Children don't have as much of a sense of mortality and don't see as much inherent danger lurking in every shadow as adults do, so may more readily accept that the child character can survive in situations which an adult would say, 'no, you should never do that.' But child readers will also know when the character has reached the 'no way' limit which will make the story unbelievable," says Young. "It is a fine line to draw between wanting the excitement to build up and letting it get way out of hand, but a writer needs to think about whether it's perceived danger or real danger. Is it really an impossible situation, or can your character get out of it in a reasonably believable manner? And, also, don't forget the age of the intended reader."

That doesn't mean that a character will never do something they know is dangerous. "I think that one of the keys is that children shouldn't be putting themselves stupidly into harm's way. They should evaluate the options and figure that everything will be fine if they carry out their plans. The one exception to this is when a person who the main character loves is in serious danger," says Nitz. "Survivor's guilt is a real thing. People will go to the rescue even when they're not confident that they can make it out intact."

Handle dangerous situations in an age-appropriate way. "One of my favorite books for kids is *Henry's Freedom Box*. Henry is in such danger due to the historical setting of the novel. Without going into too much detail, the author showed us that danger by putting the boy in a box and sending him north. But the author did not show the physical consequences of not putting Henry in that box, because the age group would not have been ready for the brutal realities of what happened to child slaves at the time," says King. "That said, the book included the savage separation of Henry's family, and the selling of people, which children of that age group can grasp and learn from. In short, I feel the truth is never dangerous, as long as it's age-appropriate."

Respect both your young characters and your young readers. As much as we adults want to keep our characters and our readers safe, we simply can't if we want to create literature that is believable and exciting, enlightening and empowering.

Step back and take a look at some of your rejected manuscripts. If your plot is ho hum, you may need to put your character in a bad place or at least mess up his day. Give your young character the tools and the drive to solve his own problems. It isn't bad for grade schoolers, tweens or teens to want to solve their own problems so much as it is natural. Keep things age-appropriate and this is what will drive your story forward.

Give your readers and your characters the chance to surprise you with what they can handle. You just might grow as a writer in the process.

Testing the Waters

Still not sure it is your young character who holds center stage instead of an interfering adult? Then its time to test your manuscript.

"This allows me to keep my camera lens, like the reader's eye, focused on the young character who claims my story. Once I write a complete draft, I bracket and study each scene to determine who is acting and re-acting, who is emoting, who is speaking and how those words serve the story," says Hershenhorn. "The Ah-Hah! Moment on which the climax and resolution depend must *always* belong to my story's main character, whether he's the stuff of a picture book or a middle grade novel."

Narrow your focus and see who is acting. If it is an adult when your main character should be driving the story forward, you still have some work to do.

Creating Quirky Characters

by Donna Gephart

I spent a year researching and writing a 400-page novel told from the viewpoints of four separate characters. When finished, I sent it to my agent. After reading it, my agent politely told me to scrap the project and start something new. "Your characters," she said, "are stereotypes."

What?!

Had she read the same manuscript I'd sent? I had a deaf character, a character with OCD, a character who played the cello and...oh, I can't even remember. My agent—as usual—was right. I hadn't developed fully realized characters; I'd created caricatures.

Young readers won't lose themselves in books populated with caricatures and stereotypes. They'll lose interest.

How does a writer populate stories and novels with fully realized, well-developed, quirky characters?

Three places from which to create characters

1. Memory. What were you like as a child? What mattered to you? What was your favorite way to spend a Saturday morning? Where would you go on your bicycle? Who were your best friends? Enemies? What was your most traumatic experience? Which year in school do you remember most clearly?

It's all fodder for your character.

The main character of my novel, *As If Being 12¾ Isn't Bad Enough, My Mother Is Running for President!*, Vanessa Rothrock has big feet, a flat chest and loves the color purple—like, ahem, yours truly at that age. (OK, I still have big feet and love the color purple.) Vanessa is also klutzy, sports wild hair and has a penchant for spelling impossibly difficult words. Not me.

Our characters shouldn't be clones of us; we are not writing memoirs. But they can share some of our attributes, thoughts, feelings and desires.

DONNA GEPHART's newest novel, *How to Survive Middle School*, garnered excellent reviews, including a starred review from *Kirkus*. Her first novel, *As if Being 12 3/4 Isn't Bad Enough, My Mother Is Running for President!* won the prestigious Sid Fleischman Humor Award. To learn more about Donna and to watch the most amazing singing hamster video, check out www.donnagephart.com.

Donna Gephart's newest novel, *How to Survive Middle School*, garnered excdellent reviews, including a starred review from Kirkus.

2. Observation/Fact. I wear a T-shirt that reads: "Careful, or you'll end up in my novel." It's true. Friends, family, strangers at the mall—none are safe from an observant writer. Borrow physical traits, speech patterns, hobbies and quirks for your characters.

When I created Vanessa, I had a friend's daughter in mind. She was the jumping off point, but I did not borrow her completely. It's not good form to use an actual person for your character. Borrow a sprinkling of traits or just one, but not enough that the person would recognize him or herself.

Have you read an article about a kid who donated all his birthday money to buy food for the hungry? Did you learn about a man who lost a finger wrestling alligators? Have you seen a sit-com about a guy who fears clowns—coulrophobia? It's all material for the creation of unique characters…or characters' parents.

3. Imagination. Sometimes your mind combines elements of memory and observation/fact in unexpected ways to create interesting character quirks. For example, in my novel, *How to Survive Middle School*, the main character's mother lives on an organic beet farm in Maine. I don't know anyone who lives on an organic beet farm, but I had eaten organic beets when I was working on that part of the book. And I don't live near Maine, but visited once. Honestly, I have no idea from where the idea actually sprang; it was a bit of mind magic. But it gave my character's mother just the right quirk for the story.

Creating characters with whom young readers can connect

Young readers must find ways to connect to your character, ways in which your character is "like me."

Many young readers tell me Vanessa, the main character in my first book, is exactly like them. But these readers each picked different traits and quirks that they had in common with Vanessa. Some focused on her physical appearance. Others focused on her quirks and faults. And still others focused on her family structure. I'd given my main character many traits—both external and internal—that young readers could relate to.

One of the ways we achieve this "like me" factor is making sure our characters are imperfect.

Faults, foibles & flubs

Characters, like people, have things wrong with them, things they need to improve, things that get in the way of achieving dreams and desires, things that annoy others. Even Superman has his little Kryptonite issue.

What will your character's Kryptonite be?

Perhaps your character has a particular fear or worry that plagues her. Perhaps he's not good at a particular skill. Or maybe she's stuck in a family with problems.

Whatever the case, be sure your character has at least one fault. It will make him/her more human and will help kids connect.

Strengths, strong suits & superpowers

At what does your character excel? Solving mysteries? Fixing cars? Caring for siblings? Drawing? Growing organic beets, or in the case of *Squashed* by Joan Bauer, giant pumpkins?

Your character's strength may inform his or her overwhelming desire that drives the story (plot).

In *A Crooked Kind of Perfect* by Linda Urban, Zoe Elias liked playing the piano and wanted to become a famous concert pianist. Life had other plans...when, instead of buying her a piano, her father purchased a wood-grained, vinyl-seated, wheeze-bag organ, The Perfectone D-60.

Your character doesn't live on an island of one

(Unless he's Chuck Noland, Tom Hank's character in *Cast Away*, but even *he* had a volleyball for company.)

Give your character a rich internal and external life.

Your character's internal life will encompass memorable moments in her past, fears and worries, joy and passions and sensory stimulation that triggers memories and feelings. That internal life will inform how your character reacts to his or her environment.

Your character's external life will encompass home (parents, siblings, pets, extended family), school (teachers, classmates), and neighborhood (library, supermarket, park, friends' homes).

It's the interaction between your character and his or her internal and external world that creates a fully realized character who lives beyond the confines of the page.

Interview Method

Pull out your reporter's notebook and ask your character a few questions. Here are some to get you started:

1. What is your most treasured possession?

2. What is your greatest regret?

3. Which talent would you most like to have?

4. Which trait in yourself do you most like/dislike?

5. Whom do you most admire?

6. What is the one thing you hope no one ever finds out about you?

Or have your character fill in the blanks from this psychological survey:

1. The happiest time _____.

2. At home _____.

3. I can't _____.

4. I'm best when _____.

5. I wish _____.

6. At school _____.

7. I secretly _____.

8. My greatest worry is _____.

Put the quirk in your character

With 175,000 books published each year, your character must stand out. How do you make your character similar to your readers yet unique?

While your character has universal feelings and emotions, she has quirks that make her unusual, like these beloved characters:

- *Stargirl* by Jerry Spinelli. Stargirl dresses differently and plays "Happy Birthday" on the ukulele to her classmates, but her feelings of needing to be loved are universal.
- *Millicent Min, Girl Genius* by Lisa Yee. Millicent has an I.Q. that eclipses her peers, but she wants to be liked and included.
- *Marcelo in the Real World* by Francisco X. Stork. Marcelo sees the world through Asperger's Syndrome and, like most kids, desires to be appreciated for who he is.

What quirks will your character have? An unusual hobby? An unusual ability? Or a typical trait taken to an extreme, like high intelligence or exceptional musical ability? An unusual way of looking at the world? An atypical fear? An unusual friend or family member?

The best way to uncover quirks for your characters are to refer to the three methods for character creation: memory, observation/fact and imagination.

Do you remember an unusual child when you went to school? What was that person's quirk? Did you have a particular way in which you stood out? A particular incident that happened to you that you could attribute to your character? Have you observed fascinating people in your community, in the newspaper or on TV? Have you come across someone with a unique job—perhaps the person who wakes at 3 a.m. to make donuts? Remember, unique jobs can be attributed to your character's parents.

What is the function of character?

Your character is the heart of your story; he or she is the vehicle that will drive your reader through each page.

Your character wants something desperately, or wants to avoid something desperately. This desire will stem from your character's basic personality, likes, dislikes, etc. This desire will drive the story forward. Your character's deepest desire might not be the one that first appears; it might be something deeper that you discover as your write. And this desire is the seed from which your plot grows.

You, as god of your fictional universe, will plunk roadblocks along your character's path to attaining her greatest desire. Like when Zoe Elias wanted to become a famous pianist and a wheeze-bag organ was plunked in her path. What was she to do?

The answer to that question is what keeps readers turning pages.

Dunk your character into hot water. Provide increasingly difficult obstacles. Be mean! Give her something she does not want, but has to face. Then watch how she reacts. The tougher the dilemma, the harder the decision, the more deeply we'll get to know the character from her reaction.

That's how a story moves forward. That's how readers get to know a character. And ultimately, that's how the character grows and changes. We get to know the character's world and meet him or her just before that world is about to change. Then we follow the character through a series of difficult experiences and decisions until we emerge at a place where the character can't go back to the world he or she knew, but lands somewhere else and is changed from the experience.

Methods of creating characters

While there isn't a blueprint for creating characters, there are various means by which to get to know your character. Characters aren't described, by the way. They are revealed through action, thought and dialogue. Their true nature is revealed slowly, like peeling layers of an onion, the same way we get to know new friends. First we see them, then we hear them, then we learn about their values, likes and dislikes and then we see how they react in challenging situations.

Write your way into your character

Sometimes, I'll write 50 pages until I know my character, until I can hear her unique voice. Sometimes it takes that much writing to reveal the quirk that makes my character unique.

You don't have to jump into writing your story to get to know your character. You can begin by writing a diary entry from your character. You can write a letter from your character. You can have your character write a series of IMs to a friend...or an enemy. My first novel began as a series of diary entries from my character, until I got to know her, then I could begin telling her story.

Articles

Character Profile

(Adapted from Paula Danziger's workshop)

Name, age, grade

Parents, relationship with parents, parents' jobs, siblings, pets

Socioeconomic level

Public, private or home school

What does your character's closet look like?

Organized? Messy?

Favorite expression to say, music, books

Lot of friends, few friends

Favorite food, if Dad's cooking, if Mom's cooking, if no one is looking on a Saturday morning

Idiosyncrasies, parents' idiosyncrasies If she has a happy family, she has to have a problem outside the home

Interview your character

Coming from a journalism background, I can appreciate the need to interview people to get to know what's different and interesting about them. You can interview your characters. You can ask about their families and how they feel about those families. You can inquire about what they're afraid of, what makes them zing with happiness, what they're looking forward to and dreading. You can even find out their favorite color.

Character inventory

You might want to use the character inventory method from the outset or once you've created a character and want to know him better. In this method, you list all the pertinent things about your character's internal and external life.

I was fortunate to attend a character workshop given by the late, great Paula Danziger. She asked us what secret is hidden in our character's closet. Answering this question led me to deeper character discoveries in two of my novels. David Greenberg from *How to Survive Middle School* has a shoe box full of letters written by his mother, who no longer lives with the family. Those letters became significant to my character's motivation.

What secret lies in the back of *your* character's closet?

At the end of Paula Danziger's workshop, she said, "Did you notice one thing I didn't ask?" She never asked us to tell what our character looked like.

I love when readers "see" my characters physically when I haven't described her. This means you've done your job and your reader has done hers as well.

Character webbing

In the center of your page, put your character's name. Draw lines from the name. On each line, list a character trait or family detail. From each of those, draw lines and list further details.

This organized brainstorming technique might turn up surprises about your character's internal and external life.

Don't censor yourself while webbing. And push yourself to keep going with more and more lines. While all the details about your character probably won't end up in your story, they will help your character seem more fully alive. They will keep your characters from becoming stereotypes or caricatures.

Human beings are complicated, surprising, creatures of habit, afraid, joyous, remarkable, etc. And with hard work on your part, your characters will be all these things, too. Then, when a young reader recalls her favorite character, she might be describing one you created.

Naming Your Quirky Characters

Choose names that give a feel for your character. For example, I needed the mother who is running for president in my novel to have a strong name so I picked Rothrock as her last name. A humorous character will have a funny sounding name, like Ramona Quimby, Frankie Farkle McBride and Mrs. Piggle-Wiggle.

Writer Linda Salem Marlow reads the obituary pages from West Virginia, and has discovered such gems for her characters as Pie and Froggy Landon. If your character lives in a certain area, check the obituary listings for that area or the birth or wedding announcements from their online newspapers.

Check out listings of pet names for inspiration:

- www.infoplease.com/spot/petnamespot.html
- www.babynames.com/Names/Pets

Look in playbills, baby naming books and mastheads in magazines. Pay attention when introduced to people. If you hear an interesting name, jot it in a character notebook.

Hook Readers with Strong Beginnings & Endings

by Sue Bradford Edwards

Writing well means honing your words to fast, furious precision, writing and rewriting. Rewriting often focuses on the beginning and the ending of the manuscript. This isn't surprising given their importance.

The beginning has to hook your reader—fast. Bore the reader and off they go to the next article, a different book, or a computer game.

The ending must tie things up in a satisfying package. Fail and the reader feels cheated out of both time and effort.

Fortunately, you can learn to excel at both.

A HOOK IS . . .

First and foremost, the very first line of a manuscript has to introduce the reader to the manuscript in such a way that they simply have to read more. This is the same whether you are writing a novel or a picture book.

"The beginning of a picture book is a promise and an invitation to the reader: stick with me, readers, and you will be richly rewarded," says author Leda Schubert. "So it should ideally provide a character the reader cares about and enough action and tension to propel that page turn. If brilliant, it can contain so much: point of view, trajectory, setting, rhythm, and it can even carry theme. Not an easy task, by any means."

A novel works much the same way. "An opening has to introduce the main character, establish the setting, and capture the author's/character's voice," says author Chris Eboch. "Ideally, it will clarify the genre and give the reader an idea of what to expect from the rest of the book. That's a lot to get into a page or two."

Author Fiona Bayrock does this within a nonfiction framework. "I design my beginnings with two main goals in mind: to get kids interested in the subject so they want to read more, and to get them asking questions so they keep reading to find the answers," she says. "Kids won't stick around to see if the pace picks up or things get

SUE BRADFORD EDWARDS writes from her office in St. Louis, Missouri. You can find her work in Children's Writer newsletter and on the web site Prayables.com. She has also been offering a series of free writing workshops in the St. Louis area. Find out more about her and her work on her website (www.suebradfordedwards.com) and her blogs (suebe.wordpress.com and suebe2.wordpress.com).

Fine Tune Your Work

Think you have the best possible hook and ending? Get ready to fine tune.

Start with your beginning. "What if you delete the first sentence, the first paragraph, the first page? Does the story still make sense? Does it get off to a faster start? What if you cut the whole first chapter, or several chapters?" asks author Chris Eboch. Does the story still work? If so, you need to cut. "If you can't cut, can you condense?" she asks.

"Try the same trick with the ending. How quickly can you end, after the climax? If you ramble on for pages, wrapping things up, see how much you can condense or eliminate. If you have subplots to wrap up, try to do that before you wrap up the main plot. You probably need some dénouement after the climax, where the main character reflects on what he or she has learned, and we get a glimpse of the future. But keep it brief."

The more effort you put into it, the more likely you are to hook an editor and leave them satisfied in the end.

better later. I know that whatever the topic, I have three or four sentences max to win over young readers."

The hook must excite the reader and get them invested in finding out more. Just how this is done varies from manuscript to manuscript. "I get a lot of people who start with dialogue," says Charlesbridge Editor Randi Rivers. "Right away you get an idea who the character is and you get an idea of the situation."

When asked about her favorite hook, Rivers shared one in which the narrator speaks directly to the reader. "The one I have up on my door is from M. T. Anderson's *Feed*. 'We went to the moon to have fun, but the moon turned out to completely suck.'" She then explains why it works so well. "You're getting this switcheroo—shouldn't going to the moon be cool? Why does it suck? It makes you want to find out why." You also meet the irreverent teen narrator and find out *Feed* is science fiction—people are traveling to the moon. As a novelist, Anderson could have taken a page or more to do this but in just 16 words, he gives us voice, genre and a tantalizing hook.

In nonfiction, a high interest topic often supplies its own hook. "The immediacy and 'weird' quality of my topics act as pretty strong hooks from the onset, so I don't have a problem with setting the tone," says Kelly Milner Halls who has written about dinosaur mummies as well as cryptids.

Another way to hook the reader in nonfiction is with a fact that makes the reader react. "I spend a lot of time deciding how to approach a topic. I write mostly science, so that usually means finding the 'Ew!,' 'Cool!,' or 'Phew!' in my subject. I want an angle that is fresh and unusual and something kids will easily relate to," says Bayrock. "For example, Klingons fictitiously blew up the Pioneer 10 space probe as part of target practice during one of the Star Trek movies, so when I wrote about the real Pioneer 10 for *YES Mag*, I started the article with Klingon target practice."

IT AIN'T EASY

Finding just the right voice or an intriguing fact doesn't come easily and many writers simply don't put enough effort into this task. "I see people who don't take time with it," Rivers says. "As a result, I'm not intrigued by the character or the situation. The hook should immediately spark my interest."

There's no easy way to hook a reader, but many writers try to take shortcuts. One way that some nonfiction writers try to do this by asking the reader a question in the very first line. "Have you ever looked at your neighborhood as if it was a maze?" Nope, and an easy "no" isn't the response you want. "Questions make me think of text books or rote nonfiction—not interesting nonfiction," says Rivers. "There's no effort put into it."

If you want to start with a question, give the reader something to contemplate. "Sometimes I get readers to put themselves in strange situations and feel certain emotions as they hear sounds or experience sights, tastes, and textures I've described," says Bayrock. "For a *YES Mag* article on how wood mice use waymarkers like Hansel & Gretel crumbs to find their way through the maze of vegetation in the fields where they live, I started with: 'Imagine your neighborhood is one giant maze. When you stop in the middle, you see twisty pathways going off in every direction. And they all look alike. How would you know the way to school? To your friend's house? Back home again?'" Bayrock doesn't use the question as a short cut. Instead, she weaves a rich scene and then uses her question to engage the reader.

Sometimes Bayrock implies a question. "While researching an article for *Odyssey* about hearing loss—a subject that has great potential to be dry and boring—I learned that two tiny ear muscles work to keep the eardrum from vibrating too much to prevent ear damage from dangerously loud noises. That something designed to *hear* sound also deliberately works to *prevent* sound being heard is surprising and an odd little fact that most people probably don't know," she says. "To make it relevant to my tween audience, I used rock music as the specific example. 'Your ears work hard to keep loud rock music out of your head.' Reader reaction is a double-take followed by disbelief and a 'How can that be?' Bingo. The question has hooked readers into reading more because they want to find out, even if they wouldn't otherwise be interested in an article on hearing loss."

If you think editors are tough, think again. They want to find manuscripts to publish. Young readers, with multiple demands on their time, are the real tough sell. Your hook must work *fast*. "I love expository pastoral moments with fluffy clouds and beautiful mountains. I hear the welling music, 'The hills are alive with the sound of music...,'" says author Molly Blaisdell. "The first lines of a book are a bad place for such a moment. That's visual storytelling. It's called a movie. Not hooky at all in fiction. And Problem #2: Why, oh, why, must a character get out of bed first thing in a new book. Big mistake. Delete getting out bed. Just do it."

Eboch discovered a similar problem in her own work. "In *The Well of Sacrifice*, I started too slow, with too many details of setting and culture before we got to a problem," she says. "You want to start in a moment of action, where something is changing, and cut the background. But don't rush things—take a little time to set up the situation, so it makes sense and we care about the characters, and what's happening to them."

Last of all, many writers fail to make their hook honest. "Sometimes writers worry too much about flashy writing, and come up with openings that are confusing or misleading," says Eboch. "Suzanne Morgan Williams, author of *Bull Rider*, talks about the promise of the first chapter. The first chapter tells you what to expect from the rest of the book, whether it's humor, action, tragedy or whatever. So you don't just need a good hook—you need the best hook for this novel, a hook that will attract those readers who will most enjoy the book. A clever, funny hook is great—but only if the rest of the book is also clever and funny."

Find the hook that works for *that* manuscript and it will give you the opportunity to pen your way to the end with your reader in tow.

THE LEARNING PROCESS

Be prepared to rewrite your beginning several times.

"In every case but one, I've written that first line over and over and over and over. When I started work on *Ballet of the Elephants,* I had an idea that it would begin something like this: 'George Balanchine loved to tell others how to dance. Even elephants.' That didn't last long—it wasn't really true, and as the pieces of the story became more and more complex, I realized I couldn't begin with Balanchine at all," says Schubert. "It was a story about an event, not a specific person, so it finally began with the event."

Nonfiction is equally complicated. "Because beginnings are so important, crafting them can take me ten or more times longer than writing any other part of an article or book," says Bayrock. "I just keep thinking about it, and working it and working it until I get something I'm happy with."

If you find beginnings particularly difficult, listen to as many as possible. "Go to first pages panels at conferences," says Rivers. "I've seen some really great lines and some that really fall flat. It's the first paragraph that has to catch you." Listen to what other writers have done. Watch the audience react. What works? What doesn't?

But don't let a bad beginning bring you to a halt. "Don't worry about the beginning during the first draft. Chances are it will change completely anyway. Wait until you have a solid plot before you start fine-tuning your opening and ending," says Eboch. "Many authors write a novel, then throw away the first chapter and write a new first chapter— the one that belongs there. It seems like it's almost impossible to write a strong opening until you've finished the rest of the book." This isn't surprising given the connection between the beginning and the end of a manuscript.

THE END

A strong hook demands a lot of effort on the part of the writer, but the ending is just as critical. An ending is more than a place where the words stop. "In your first chapter, you make a promise. That last chapter is going to fulfill your promise," says Blaisdell.

This means that the beginning and ending are tied closely together. "A good ending follows from a strong beginning. It is both inevitable and unexpected. It delights, it completes, and it sends us back to the beginning to see what was promised or just for the joy of rereading and understanding," says Schubert. "The greatest picture book ending of all time is, of course, 'And it was still hot.'" *Where the Wild Things Are* brings the reader back to Max's room, a place where he is loved, monster or no.

"An ending should feel complete. The main character, and thus the reader, may not know exactly what will happen in the future, but readers still want a sense of closure," says Eboch. "In my Mayan historical novel, *The Well of Sacrifice*, the main character overcomes her enemy and tells people they must abandon their city. The book ends with Eveningstar and her family preparing to travel and start a new life. They may have more adventures, but this adventure is complete. Teachers often have their students write the story of what happens next."

Serious About Series Endings

When writing a series, authors are often tempted to have a series' wide story arc without tying things up in each book. "Even in series books, most readers prefer that each book wraps up the main plot in that book. You can have an ongoing overall story arc, and unfinished subplots, but readers want to feel that the characters are, for the moment, safe and reasonably happy," says Chris Eboch.

This means a satisfying ending is needed for each and every title in the series. "In my Haunted series, each book features the ghost hunter TV show researching a new ghost in a new location, such as on a riverboat (*The Riverboat Phantom*) or at an art museum (*The Knight in the Shadows*). Each book ends with the children helping the current ghost, and then they hear about the show's next project. Hopefully this satisfies readers, while encouraging them to seek out the next book."

One book leads to the next, but not without tying up the current adventure.

The nonfiction ending functions a bit differently. Says Rivers, "Nonfiction needs to give a summation of what we've learned in the text. The conclusion needs to tie up why it was important to learn about Abraham Lincoln or the Rovers on Mars."

Bayrock agrees. "The ending is me wrapping things up by referring to the hook I used at the beginning—a kind of 'See? I gave you what I promised I would. We're done now.' The reader leaves satisfied that we accomplished what we set out to do," says Bayrock. "For example, *Bubble Homes and Fish Farts* (Charlesbridge) begins with kids blowing bubbles, and after going through many animals and how they use bubbles, it ends with humans again, this time using bubbles to save animals." The beginning and ending don't duplicate each other, but they do make strong connections.

FIXING POTENTIAL PROBLEMS

If you can't tie up your ending neatly, it may indicate a problem with something other than that last chapter, page or paragraph, especially in nonfiction. "That usually means I need to start over—find a more energetic focus or hook," says Halls. "With my work, you have to walk a fine line, presenting the facts without sensationalizing. That was especially true with *Albino Animals* and *Mysteries of the Mummy Kids*. If I hadn't been cautious, the books could have been disrespectful and might have offended people with albinism or the cultures who honor the mummies as their ancestors. By keeping those people in mind, I was able to write endings that left the readers and the potential critics satisfied and certain my intentions were good."

Another problem comes when the nonfiction author forgets to wrap things up. "A lot of people forget the conclusion. They just stop," says Rivers. "They feel like this is where it ended and that's enough, but for the picture book age group especially, you need that summary to tie things together."

Creating a satisfactory fiction ending is more complicated. "The beginning and ending should also form a kind of circle. Issues raised at the beginning are resolved in the ending. Questions are answered. The main character has changed, and can look back at her earlier self with a new understanding," says Eboch. "The ending is an echo of the beginning, but with everything now in its proper place, as if a kaleidoscope turned and formed a new image with the same colors." The same elements must be present, but if the ending too closely mirrors the beginning, it is likely your character didn't grow. Ask yourself how your character changed? What is different in the end than in the beginning? You may have a bit more work to do.

If you find yourself having trouble writing a solid ending, study what is in print. If that doesn't help, Rivers has one more word of advice. "Endings are really hard. You have to put the story away and see if it still satisfies you. Read it to others and see if it satisfies them," she says. "An outline will tell you if your story arc is there or if it falls flat. Outlining is a lost art. When you do an outline for nonfiction, make sure you've hit all the points you need to tie it together. It's about organization, almost like a check list."

It seems like a lot of work, and it is. But every manuscript you submit needs a worthy ending and a powerful beginning. Whether you are working in fiction of nonfiction, picture book or novel-length, every manuscript is a journey. The beginning hooks the reader with an interesting voice and the promise of adventure ahead. The ending ties things up in a hopeful package.

Just what is in that package depends on you, the writer.

Picture Book Pace

Verbal & Visual Tools for Writers

by Jodell Sadler

When a writer is looking to share the emotional intensity of her story and fill it with heart, she only needs to investigate a powerful, one-syllable word: Pace. Pacing presents the kind of magic every manuscript needs. When it comes to picture books, the art and words must gel, and pacing is a fabulous tool.

Pacing moves the story in a picture book. It's the rate the writer reveals the story to the reader. With careful pacing, writers can pull back or zoom in close, slow down or speed up as necessary to reveal the relevant details of a story. Often, writers stop the action of a story to allow the art to carry the story. One thing is sure, great pacing may catapult a writer's manuscript to a whole new level of Wow!

Good pacing makes or breaks a story. A slow or monotonous pace kills a story. And a well-paced picture book invites the reader in—even reluctant ones—again and again. Writers who hone pace enough may even invite readers in by creating an interactive or guessing game.

When considering pace, the writer chooses words purposefully. When one word may elate us, or break our heart, the selection and placement of each word becomes crucial. Words, rhythm, repetition, details, white space, page turns and art of a story matter and must work together to support a story's theme. Every thing should contribute to pace.

EXAMINE VERBAL PACING TOOLS
Words

In *Looking for a Moose*, Phyllis Root paces through her infectious language fun. As four children's and a dog journey through the woods, swamps, bushes and hilltops in search of a moose, they discover Root's love of adventure, the great outdoors, and language.

Root's adventure begins with a question. "Have you ever seen a moose—a long-leggy moose—a branchy-antler, dinner-diving, bulgy-nose moose?" This line, its sound and word fun galore, makes the reader want to hear it again.

JODELL SADLER is a writer, freelance designer, and marketing professional. She's an adjunct by day and writer/illustrator by night who recently completed her MFA in Writing for Children and Young Adults at Hamline University in St. Paul, MN, where she received mentoring from great writers like Ron Koertge, Marsha Wilson Chall, Lisa Jahn-Clough, and Jacqueline Briggs Martin. She currently enjoys speaking engagements, teaching online Children's Writing workshops, and looks forward to working on children's projects of all kinds. Her illustration portfolio may be seen online at www.jodellsadler.com.

B Reading List

Study the books mention in this article for lessons on picture book pacing:

* *Looking for a Moose*, by Phyllis Root, illustrated by Randy Cecil (Candlewick)

* *Banjo Granny*, by Sarah Martin Busse and Jacqueline Briggs Martin, illustrated by Barry Root (Hougton)

* *Leonardo the Terrible Monster*, written and illustrated by Mo Willems (Hyperion)

* *I Ain't Gonna Paint No More!*, by Karen Beaumont, illustrated by David Cartrow (Harcourt)

* *Where the Wild Things*, written and illustrated by Maurice Sendak (HarperCollins)

She uses the words "never," "ever," and "really" to pick up the pace. "No! We've never, ever, ever, ever, ever seen a moose. And we really, really, really, really want to see a moose." She draws attention to how difficult—near impossible—it will be to see a moose.

Then, "OR-ROOG!" halts the action for the reader to consider the question, "What's that?" as they discover a surprise twist in the end. "LOOK THERE!" ...a moose...and a moose...and a moose." And the opening flips on its head, in the same frolicking sound. "I've never, ever, ever seen so many moose!" Words, every word, even words within a sentence need to be paced. Each word makes a big difference.

Rhythm, repetition, questions

In *Looking for a Moose*, pace is all about language and sound. Root uses questions, repetition and rhythmic descriptions to pace, and the sound of language matters.

Just as in poetry, the sound and flow of the language—variety and structure—impacts the reader. Root shares an ear for good rhythm. She pays attention to meaning and sound. Meaning merges with rhythm. Repetition races, and her descriptions become infectious. Her joy comes through as she creates her fabulous string of words that tickles her reader's fancy, too.

With picture books, a unique style and voice is essential. Like the lyrics of a song, if pace and rhythm are well crafted, the reader will recite the words again and again.

Even questions can pace. Root asks the question, "What now?" and it pulls readers through the story. She invites them to "TROMP STOMP! TROMP STOMP! treesy-breezy, tilty-stilty, wobbly-knobbly woods." Not just any woods. Root's very original, built-out-of-words woods, with its rich rhythm and passionate energies that entice the reader to join in and explore.

Root uses onomatopoeia, alliteration, assonance, and consonance to increase the pace, so where the descriptions would normally slow, the aural energy of Root's words speed the reader along. Her writing exudes tone, energy, sound, action, and language that's so infectious it frolics. This is the power of pace.

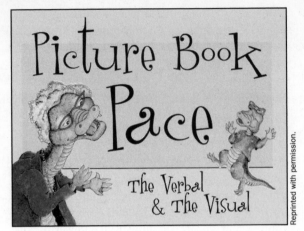

Picture books are paced by more than just the words and more than just the illustrations. It's a combined effect that makes a successful book.

Setting, details, objects

In *Banjo Granny*, Sarah Martin Busse and Jacqueline Briggs Martin use details, objects, and the back and forth motion between two vivid settings to pace a story.

Time waltzes between Granny's and Owen's worlds in a way that imitates walking itself. The reader moves from Granny to Owen and Granny to Owen until Granny's "thousand mile shoes" firmly land on Owen's doorstep.

Granny faces three obstacles. "She must cross one river, one mountain and a desert." While this list slows the pace, the reader discovers a Granny who is determined to do anything to reach the baby who goes "wiggly, jiggly, all-around giggly, and tip over tumble for bluegrass music."

When Granny moves, the story moves and objects set the pace.

Granny comes to a river and pulls out an oar to paddle across. She walks on. Granny comes to the mountain and pulls out a big red balloon to fly high above. She walks on. Granny comes to the desert and pulls out a long nightgown to sail across the sands. Each obstacle looks impossible, but the authors write "...she thought of Owen and her heart was set to see him," and the reader sails out of harms way. An oar, a red balloon, a long nightgown, and these authors' genius are at their aid.

Granny's desire moves the story along at a pace filled with delightful detail. "The river was fast. The river was deep ... The mountain was high. The mountain was steep ... The desert was hot. The desert was wide and worrisome." Here, when the pattern brakes, the words "wide and worrisome" alert the reader to the importance of what is to come.

Meanwhile, the words sing. Sound, rhythm, and meaning unite in a fabulous word strings. "Baby goes wiggly, jiggly, all-around giggly, and tip over tumble for bluegrass music," introduced early on, the line rolls right off the tongue. The reader learns more about a Granny, who holds her instrument in "her banjo case with the taped-up handle." This phrase not only paces, the words exude aural energy and reveal Granny's character.

The reader learns Granny is someone who loves something so much—even though worn and far from perfect—that she might possibly represent love itself. Granny treasures something despite its flaws. She's keeps her banjo a long time. She cherishes it.

Granny's banjo case serves the pace as well. It's an endowed object and metaphor that carries the reader forward. Granny pulls from inside its casing the objects she needs to overcome obstacles that stand in her way. Just as children pull from themselves to overcome problems, so does Granny. This revelation is as powerful and we see how details, objects, and setting pace and support a story's theme.

EXPLORE VISUAL PACING TOOLS
White space

In *Leonardo the Terrible Monster*, Mo Willems uses white space to pace. White space forces the reader to entertain expressions, feelings, and changes in the character's emotional journey. It intensifies the emotional bent. It's powerful.

When nothing appears on a page besides Leonardo, the focus shifts to the character's expression and body language. That's all there is. The story stops. Pace halts, and the character's plight reveals itself like a freeze frame as "Leonardo is a terrible monster" begs the question: is he terrible good or terrible bad?

Willems shows us how lists can assist pace. A list can be a list, or launch into a lengthy interplay between the art and words of a story. A list slows the pace, and Willems list casts out over eight pages allows readers opportunity to explore Leonardo's character:

> "He (Leonardo) couldn't scare anyone.
> He didn't have 1,642* teeth, like Tony. * Note: Not all teeth shown.
> He wasn't big, like Eleanor.
> And he wasn't just plain weird, like Hector."

This list builds tension through page turns and art. New questions pop up: What lies ahead for poor Leonardo? Will he be a scary? And, if he is not like Tony or Eleanor or Hector, just who is he?

Leonardo is then defined as a monster that sees a good fright is in his future. He searches for the perfect candidate, "the most scaredy-cat kid in the whole world," to scare. He wants to terrify "the tuna fish" out of him. Will he?

The reader turns the page to find Sam in the opposite corner from where Leonardo appeared a few spreads earlier. This identifies him as the opponent. Willems suspends the moment. He adds white space and an additional page turn before Leonardo sneaks up on Sam. Tension surrounds the question: What is Leonardo capable of?

Immediately, Willems speeds the pacing with back and forth banter between his characters. Short sentences speed the pace.

Leonardo scares Sam. "… the monster gave it all he had. Until the little boy cried."
Leonardo revels in scaring Sam and clamors, "Yes."
Sam snaps. "No you didn't!"
"Oh, yeah?" Leonardo asks, "Then why are you crying?"
The pace quickens—Snap, snap, snap. The page turns, and the pace slows.

Graphics immediately demand the reader's attention. Sam rants up a whole breathless page. White space disappears. Sam loses it. Pace halts, and the art shouts, "Pay attention!" Sam's words appear in large creamy pastel letters and cover and clip off the pages behind Sam and Leonardo. The art matches the intensity of the scene. What's next?

When white space returns, two short, small words float in a one-inch bubble above Sam's head. "That's why." Leonardo observes this from across the page and BAM!

Willems pumps up pace by breaking his rhythm to interject vitality into his story. A close up of Leonardo's face appears large and screams, Hey, reader, this is pivotal! The text reads: "Then Leonardo made a very big decision." The art matches the moment: big decision, big change, big bold face.

Another page turn reveals Leonardo and Sam hugging and this satisfies. Both characters are small. A mass of white space surrounds them, and Willem writes, "Instead of being a terrible monster, he would become a wonderful friend." The page turns and shows Leonardo and Sam walking across the page, hand-in-hand, on a wordless spread. Knowing precisely when to pull back or zoom in close, Willems lets the art carry the story at times.

There are key moments of action and deep emotion, when the writer allows the art to carry the reader forward with more than words might express. It's a bold move when a writer steps aside to allow the heart of the story to shine through but an important one.

White space and art pace, and may even inspire an interactive game.

Art games

What's great about *Looking for a Moose* is that artist, Randy Cecil, creates a game of hide-and-seek and picks up the pace where Root leaves off.

Root asks, "Have you ever seen a moose—a long-leggy moose—a branchy-antler, dinner-diving, bulgy-nose moose?" Then she breaks down these descriptive phrases to use as steppingstones that serve pace. She writes, "We don't see any long-leggy moose." Then, "We don't see any long-leggy, dinner-diving moose" and so on. Meanwhile, Cecil hides long-leggy legs among trees; dinner-divers in the swamp; branchy-antlers in the bushes; and bulgy-noses alongside the hilltops... so once the reader catches on, her picture book offers page-after-page surprise.

When writers start to see picture books as a performance with words, they begin to see new ways to interact and participate in their story through pace.

Page turns

In *I Ain't Gonna Paint No More!* Karen Beaumont uses repetition, rhymes, and objects to pace. Artsy body parts pace. The rhythm and repetition of "I ain't gonna paint no more, no more" paces. Page turns pace and invites interaction that actively engages the reader with the text, which is a key element in many successful picture books.

Set to the musical tune of "It Ain't Gonna Rain No More," this picture book tells a story about a creative child who floods his world with color—and scribbles silliness into the fine art of self-expression.

Mama enters the story on page one and eyes up the disaster. Beaumont slows the pace with a list of damage done to the house. Unlike Willems' list that cast over eight pages, this list is simply a list. Catrow's art shows what appears in the text to be true and accurate. This slows the reader to reveal details and add tension and drama to an already colorful scene:

> "One day my mama caught me
> paintin' pictures on the floor

and the ceiling
and the walls
and the curtains
and the door,
and I heard my mama holler like I never did before…"

On the next page, the reader views large print. "YA AINT GONNA PAINT NO MORE!" Our art enthusiast sits in a tub, and we discover a beagle—not mentioned in the text— that becomes a pacing marker through his behaviors. Beagle hides behind Mama, hops into the bath, buries snout in stairs, and adds a new dynamic to the unfolding story. Beagle slows the pace and entertains.

While the writer's job is to whittle a story experience down its essence, the illustrator's job is to expand story by art. While Beaumont whittles down story, Catrow expands as page turns create a guessing game.

The body parts add rhythm and beg for the reader's interaction. "So I take some red and I paint my—" interrupts for a page turn, leaving the reader guessing "HEAD!" This continues. "Aw, what the heck! Gonna paint my—" and a page turn shares the word "NECK!" The last body part breaks this pattern. "But I'm such a nut, gonna paint my—." The reader, knowing what word comes next, is surprised to read "WHAT?"

It's a hoot! Beaumont's story becomes infectious, and Catrow hits exclamation marks as his art and page turns create a guessing game. When it comes to good pace, it's magic.

Art amplified

Art in the picture book must marry with the text. Not holy matrimony, but holy moly! Writers who do what Maurice Sendak had the fortitude to do many years ago in *Where the Wild Things Are* will see the payoff. He used art—and its relative size—to pace. Created in 1963, this story gave Sendak the daring to start his art small and have it grow in size along with the story's intensity. The art expands in proportion to the forest that grows in Max's room. Sendak then breaks free from the text all together and shares Max's wild side over the course of three two-page spreads. No words. Just the emotion of the scene raises a ruckus until Max himself shouts, "Halt!" and the pace shifts again…

What becomes clear? When it comes to picture books, the art and words must gel, and pacing is a fabulous tool. Pacing presents the kind of magic every manuscript needs.

When a writer is looking to share the emotional intensity of her story and fill it with heart, she only needs to investigate a powerful, one-syllable word: Pace.

Articles

Don't Just Blog—Glog!

The Pleasures (& Perils) of Group Blogging

by Carmela A. Martino

For years, I'd heard the buzz about the value of blogging as a promotional tool for writers and illustrators. Yet I procrastinated about entering the blogosphere. My main concern: How could I blog regularly without taking significant chunks of time away from my own writing?

I found the answer on the *Writer's Digest* website, in an article called "Two Simple Blogging Exercises." (See Online Resources sidebar.) In the article, best-selling author M.J. Rose recommends forming or joining a group blog, or what she calls a "glog." As Rose explains, glogs "can be a great alternative to individual blogs because you have four to seven writers all blogging and taking turns . . . . Each writer feels less pressure and the readers don't get tired of the same voice or same type of post." A glog sounded like the perfect answer—it would not only allow me to share the blogging burden with others, but it would also distinguish my blog from those by individual authors. (Note: the term "glog" sometimes refers to a "graphics blog," but in this article, it means "group blog.")

Before founding my glog, I studied some by other children's authors and illustrators. (See Sample Glogs sidebar.) I noticed that the ones I admired most all had a specific niche or focus. For example, **I.N.K.: Interesting Nonfiction for Kids** features 15-25 authors discussing the craft behind creating fascinating nonfiction for children. Another Kidlit glog, **Three Silly Chicks,** is all about making readers laugh. The "Chicks" describe themselves as: "Readers, Writers, and Reviewers of Funny Books for Kids." Interestingly, the number of members in both examples is outside the range of four to seven M.J. Rose recommends, proof that there are no real rules when it comes to group blogs.

I wanted my glog to have a focus, too. But what would it be? I considered my personal interests and my qualifications: in addition to my publishing credits, I am a writing teacher, with an MFA in Writing for Children and Young Adults. After much thought, an idea finally came to me—I could blog about my role as an author who teaches other

CARMELA MARTINO founded www.TeachingAuthors.com, a group blog of writing and teaching tips by six children's authors who are also writing teachers. Carmela first children's novel, *Rosa, Sola,* (Candlewick Press) was named to Booklist magazine's "Top Ten First Novels for Youth: 2006." Her most recent publication is a humorous short story in the middle-grade anthology *I Fooled You: Ten Stories of Tricks, Jokes, and Switcheroos,* edited by Johanna Hurwitz (Candlewick Press). Carmela teaches writing workshops for both children and adults. To learn more, visit www.carmelamartino.com.

Six Children's Authors
Who Also Teach Writing

TeachingAuthors.com is a group blog of writing and teaching
tips by six children's authors who are also writing teachers.

authors. I invited several friends who are also writing teachers to join me. During a brainstorming session, we decided to call ourselves the "teaching authors." I searched the blogosphere and was relieved not to find any similar glogs. We launched **Teaching Authors: Six Children's Book Authors Who Also Teach Writing** in April 2009.

Establishing and running a group blog turned out to be more challenging than I expected. However, the rewards have been greater than I expected, too. I recently surveyed a number of group bloggers to find out how the pleasures and perils they experienced compared with mine. Following are the most common issues they shared.

THE PERILS

1. Member Conflicts

One of the greatest challenges for group blogs is assembling a team that works well together. Team members don't have to always agree, but when they disagree, they need to do so amicably. As Michelle Ehrich of **Slushbusters** explains, "It's important to have a cohesive group dynamic before starting a blog." The **Slushbusters** created their dynamic as a critique group long before they considered launching a glog.

An established relationship is not necessarily a requirement for a successful group blog, however. The **Enchanted Inkpot** began when author Malinda Lo posted a call for young adult fantasy authors on an online discussion board. Many of the group's 55 members have never met in person. Yet, according to author Marissa Doyle, one of the **Enchanted Inkpot's** founders, the group is "running smoothly." The key to their success? They spent almost four months "planning and working things out via a Yahoo group (which has a handy polling feature) so that we were able to come to a consensus on pretty much everything."

Rather than put out a call for members, Linda Salzman, founder of **I.N.K.: Interesting Nonfiction for Kids**, personally invited nonfiction authors whose work she admired to join her blog. Her leadership has helped minimize problems. She says, "We haven't had a lot of conflict because I'm pretty much in charge of all of the decisions. This seems to work well mostly because I also do all of the work. I do all of the updates, scheduling, add to the sidebars, etc." Salzman adds that some decisions are still put to the whole group: "For example, when we were choosing our logo we had a vote between two. People voiced their opinions and then voted. Everyone participated and yet was willing to go along with the majority."

Even when a team gets along well, though, an individual member's opinions about controversial issues may create difficulties for other members. To avoid such problems, some group blogs post a disclaimer on their website. As Newbery-honor-winning author-illustrator Grace Lin of the **Blue Rose Girls** explains, "We definitely did not want to censor anyone, so instead we put up this statement on the sidebar: The opinions expressed on this blog are not affiliated with our respective publishers or employers, nor should they be seen as a representation of the companies we work for or with. The individual opinions expressed on this blog also do not necessarily reflect the opinions of the other contributors to this blog." We have a similar disclaimer on our **Teaching Authors** site.

Most people join a group blog with honest intentions. However, one of the greatest perils arises when a member has ulterior motives. A writer who asked not to be identified shared what happened when she accepted someone she knew "only through an online presence" into her group blog. She says, "After a few months of blogging with us, this person threatened me with a frivolous six-figure lawsuit for copyright infringement of materials posted on the blog. The lawsuit was unfounded and ultimately settled in my favor. But I was still forced to hire an attorney and file for declaratory judgment in federal court to clear my name." She now encourages others to "ask for references before entering into any relationship with someone you don't know."

2. Intense Competition

According to M.J. Rose, "there are thousands of writers blogging about writing." Therefore, new bloggers would do well to research the competition. Author Tami Lewis Brown of **Through The Tollbooth** advises, "Read established group blogs and consider their strengths and weaknesses. Just as if you were writing a book, you'll be more successful if your blog has a unique focus and you're uniquely qualified to blog about your topic." A good place to start your research is at Kidlitosphere Central, the Web site of the Society of Bloggers in Children's and Young Adult Literature. (See Online Resources sidebar.) The site provides links to members' blogs, as well as information regarding resources for bloggers.

Before launching **Teaching Authors**, my co-bloggers and I spent several months discussing how to make our blog stand out. We asked ourselves: What specific topics could we address uniquely as authors who teach? Who would our audience be? What could we offer that would keep them coming back? We eventually decided to target our posts to both writers and those who teach writing. And we developed special features unique to our site, such as our "Writing Workouts," which can be used by both writers and teachers.

For the **Pen Tales,** their uniqueness came from being an online critique group with members scattered across the United States. According to founding member Elise Murphy, they were often asked about the logistics of how an online critique group works. "We looked around the blogosphere and didn't really find any other group blogs focused on online critique groups. It's a different type of relationship . . . and we felt we had a lot of insight into how to make it work."

With so many blogs about writing, authors may want to consider shifting the focus a bit. Grace Lin of the **Blue Rose Girls** says, "Many blogs deal with writing techniques and publishing issues—our blog is not about getting a book published, it's about what it's like to have a career in the industry." She adds, "Because we are authors and illustrators of different genres, as well as an editor and a former librarian, our viewpoints span all areas of children's literature."

Guys Lit Wire is another group blog with members from multiple fields. The glog began after a discussion among bloggers about the lack of books for teenage boys. According to founder Colleen Mondor, "The site brings literary news and reviews to the attention of teenage boys and the people who care about them. The group of contributors includes many of the bloggers involved in the original discussion, as well as teen librarians, writers, and non-bloggers who answered the call to discuss great books for boys."

Another way to make a blog unique is by *vlogging*—posting video instead of text. The group vlog **YARebels** launched in January 2010. Their YouTube profile describes the **YARebels** as "Seven young adult writers and authors, in different stages of the publishing world, vlogging about what it's really like behind the scenes." Their initial response was impressive—within the first month of launch, the site had over 9000 views.

3. Inconsistent Posting

Group blogs face this peril when members don't fulfill their posting obligations. Vicki Cobb, a founding member of I.N.K.: Interesting Nonfiction for Kids, says, "bloggers have to make a commitment to doing the blog in a professional manner. Deadlines must be met. . . . The success of a blog comes from producing over time. It takes time to build a following and it takes producing excellence again and again."

Most successful group blogs have explicit schedules, with members assigned to post on specific days of the week or month. In some cases, the schedule is set far in advance. For example, at **Through The Tollbooth**, each member posts for an entire week approximately every 10 weeks. Their current 10-week schedule is published in the "about us" section of their Web site for all their followers to see.

The Spectacle, however, has a more relaxed approach; members sign up each month for their posting dates. Founder Parker Peevyhouse admits that this has led to problems: "We have a casual, friendly set-up, so it can be hard to enforce our requirement of two posts per month from each member. Since we are such a small group, it feels awkward to tell a member, 'You haven't met your quota this month.'" Peevyhouse adds, "our biggest challenge so far was when a member went incommunicado for a few months and we were forced to oust him from the group."

PLEASURES

1. Sharing the workload

One of the most obvious benefits of a group blog is the shared workload. As Marissa Doyle of the **Enchanted Inkpot** explains, "Blogging with others means the workload is spread around—you're not having to generate a post every other day—and you keep each other honest: it's a lot harder to think, 'Eh, I don't feel like blogging right now; I'll post later' when you've got partners relying on you to hold up your end of the deal." Doyle adds, "And having many of us means we have lots of connections to draw on,

Online Resources for Bloggers

- The Society of Bloggers in Children's and Young Adult Literature
- www.kidlitosphere.org
- M.J. Rose's article: "Two Simple Blogging Exercises"
- www.writersdigest.com/article/2-simple-blogging-exercises-february
- From editorial director Jane Friedman's blog: "Should You Blog? And If So, What Are Best Practices?"
- blog.writersdigest.com/norules/2009/09/14/ShouldYouBlogAndIfSoWhatAreBest Practices.aspx
- Maria Schneider's "20 Tips for Good Blogging"
- blog.writersdigest.com/writersperspective/20+Tips+For+Good+Blogging.aspx
- "8 Blogging Tips for Beginning Bloggers"
- www.problogger.net/archives/2009/12/31/blogging-tips-for-beginners-best-of-problogger/
- "The Power of Uniqueness (19 Starting Points for Being a Unique Blogger)"
- www.problogger.net/archives/2010/01/23/the-power-of-uniqueness-19-starting-points-for-being-a-unique-blogger

Below is a sampling of group blogs and their taglines.

Author2Author, http://author2author.blogspot.com
"5 YA Authors, 5 Journeys" (5 members)

Blue Rose Girls, http://bluerosegirls.blogspot.com
"In the tradition of the Red Rose Girls, seven children's book professionals discuss their lives in books" (7 members)

Class of 2K10, http://community.livejournal.com/classof2k10/876.html
"A group of 2010 debut young adult and middle grade authors" (23 members)

Enchanted Inkpot, http://community.livejournal.com/enchantedinkpot
"A community for writers and readers of high, historical, traditional and cross-genre fantasy intended for middle-grade and young adult readers" (55 members)

Guys Lit Wire, http://guyslitwire.blogspot.com
"Helping you find the reading material YOU want" (23 members)

I.N.K.: Interesting Nonfiction for Kids, www.inkrethink.blogspot.com (15-25 members

The Longstockings, http://thelongstockings.com
"We who write, blog and ♥ children's books" (6 members)

Pen Tales, http://pentales.blogspot.com
"Writers on the Path to Publication and Beyond (4 members)

Readergirlz, http://readergirlz.blogspot.com
"Read, Reflect, and Reach Out" (6 members)

Slushbusters, http://www.slushbusters.blogspot.com
"The adventures of 7 children's writers as they critique, support, and cheer each other on while fighting their way to the top of the slush pile." (7 members)

The Spectacle, http://thespectacleblog.wordpress.com
"Authors talk about writing speculative fiction for teens and pre-teens." (6 members)

Teaching Authors, http://www.TeachingAuthors.com
"Six Children's Book Authors Who Also Teach Writing" (6 members)

Three Silly Chicks, http://threesillychicks.com
"Readers, Writers, and Reviewers of Funny Books for Kids" (3 members)

Through The Tollbooth, www.ThroughTheTollbooth.com
"What do nine writing women have in common? An MFA in writing for children and young adults from Vermont College ... And a blog." (9 members)

YA Rebels, http://www.youtube.com/yarebels
"Seven young adult writers and authors, in different stages of the publishing world, vlogging about what it's really like behind the scenes." (7 members)

Articles

which makes doing fun things like interviews easier."

Tami Lewis Brown says, "At **Through The Tollbooth** we post every day, Monday through Friday. We don't even take holiday or vacation breaks. It would be nearly impossible for any one person to create that much substantive content and get other writing done."

A group blog needn't have many members to benefit from sharing the workload. As Emily Marshall of **Author2Author** says, "Each of us five writers brings unique strengths, ideas, and connections. The impact we can have by working together is much greater than by ourselves."

Parker Peevyhouse of **The Spectacle** also points out that with a group blog, "each post is guaranteed to get comments, and a few comments from blog members can open the gates for more comments from readers."

2. Increased exposure

Most writers and illustrators, both published and unpublished, blog as a promotional tool. As Elise Murphy of **Pen Tales** says, "it allows us to establish an online presence, which is helpful now while some of our members are seeking agents, and will be helpful in the future when we all sell books!"

According to Gretchen McNeil, a member of **YARebels,** group blogging definitely yields results. After the launch of **YARebels,** she noticed an increase in the number of followers of her personal blog. "I feel like I've gotten my name 'out there,'" she says. "Self-promotion can be very valuable in this business."

Deena Lipomi, one of the yet-to-be-published members of **Author2Author**, has also seen tangible results. She says, "We had an editor from Scholastic e-mail us to ask for manuscripts." While the request didn't lead to a sale, it was an important connection. And, as Lipomi says, "it was nice to be asked!"

Even established authors like Karen Romano Young of **I.N.K.: Interesting Nonfiction for Kids** appreciate the increased exposure group blogging provides, especially when teammates publish a new book or receive an award. She says, "We ride each other's waves. Every book that is published raises all boats. When your own book comes out, the attention it gets assists the others." The success of **I.N.K.** has also led to other joint ventures, including the INK Think Tank, an online database of member books with curriculum tie-ins, and the formation of a new company offering videoconferencing and webinars.

3. Sense of Community

By far the greatest pleasure cited by those I surveyed comes from the sense of community group blogging creates. First-time author Leah Cypess of **Enchanted Inkpot** says, "being part of a group blog has been fantastic for me—it allows me to have a web presence. More important to me, though, is the 'non-blog' aspect of the **Enchanted Inkpot**, the listserv on which we discuss both blog-related and non-blog-related topics. It's allowed me to be part of a community of talented and thoughtful writers, and I've benefited enormously from that."

Her co-blogger, Ellen Oh, was especially touched by the support she received from fellow members during a family crisis: "All the Inkies rallied around me to offer warmth and support and to tell me not to worry about a thing. They were my online family whose kindnesses during this period deeply moved me."

One of the longest running glogs I surveyed was **The Longstockings,** which launched in August 2006. Its members first met while pursuing MFAs in Writing for Children. According to author Caroline Hickey, "The blog has been a great way for the six of us to stay close as a group, and to remind ourselves that you can't write in isolation. You have to have some contact with the outside world!"

Entering the blogosphere has definitely expanded my world. Not only has it deepened my relationship with my co-bloggers, it's also allowed me to connect with people I would never have met any other way, including authors, illustrators, editors, teachers, librarians, reviewers, and, best of all, young writers. And that has been *my* greatest pleasure.

Authors Unite Online

Support, Sharing & Celebration During the Debut Year

by Sara Bennett Wealer

Writing may be a solitary profession but, as I learned when I sold my first book (*Rival*, HarperTeen), the journey toward launching a debut novel should not be taken alone. You need the companionship of others who are traveling the same path.

Friends and family know you've realized a dream, but better yet are people who appreciate how it feels to break through after years of scrapped drafts, agent searches, revisions and rejections. And when the dream becomes a bumpy reality (Your editorial letter is 14 pages, single spaced! You hate your cover! Your book gets skipped by a major retailer!), you'll want those same people to hold your hand through the twists and turns.

No one appreciates the sweetness of reaching a longed-for destination better than someone who's in the same boat. That's why I formed the Elevensies along with fellow debut author Sheela Chari (*Vanished*, Disney-Hyperion).

The Elevensies is an online group of young adult and middle grade authors whose first novels come out in 2011. We meet at our home base, a Live Journal blog, to share information, offer support and celebrate as we prepare to see our books on the shelves for the very first time.

"My agent, Steven Malk, said to me, 'You can only debut once,'" says Sheela. "I think this is so true. No matter what your life might have been like before your book deal, it will certainly change afterwards. The Elevensies community is a great place to find writing friends, share experiences, and promote our books."

Carrying on the tradition

The Elevensies actually represent the third generation of a tradition that started when Jackson Pearce (*Sisters Red*; Little, Brown) founded the 2009 Debutantes, also known as

SARA BENNETT WEALER grew up in Manhattan, Kansas (the "Little Apple"), where she sang with the show choir and wrote for her high school newspaper. She majored in voice performance at the University of Kansas before ditching her operatic dreams and transferring to journalism school instead. Since then, Sara has been fortunate to make her living as a writer. She lives in Cincinnati with her husband and two daughters, and still sings when her schedule allows—most recently with the May Festival Chorus, the official choir of the Cincinnati Symphony Orchestra. Her first book Rival, will be published by HarperTeen in early 2011.

The Debs or "The Feast of Awesome." Jackson had just sold her first book, *As You Wish* (HarperTeen), and was looking for a casual setting to connect with others like her.

"I was lonely," she says. "Well, not just me—so were the other debut authors I knew. I wanted to provide a social arena where we could get to know one another outside the context of marketing and business networking."

The Debs took off quickly, attracting more than 50 authors and establishing itself in YA and MG circles as *the* place to be for friendship, fun and a safe haven in which to freak out about copyedits, first reviews and other stresses related to launching a debut novel.

Next came the 2010 Tenners, founded by Heidi R. Kling (*Sea*, Putnam) and Lindsey Leavitt (*Princess for Hire*, Disney-Hyperion). Heidi started as a Deb before her launch date was moved and couldn't imagine not having a similar group for debut authors in 2010.

"I'm a very social person," she says. "I like having like-minded folks to bounce things off of. I like being part of a supportive group of friends, and I like being surrounded by incredibly talented minds. It's like a virtual writer's retreat every day."

Sheela and I felt the same way. We both began as Tenners, and when our launch dates were changed it seemed only natural to form a group for 2011 debuts. We wanted others to experience the vibrancy, good will and pooling of multiple talents that we'd enjoyed with our 2010 friends.

Other authors were eager to join. Before the blog was up and running I had inquiries. And as the months progressed I found that a debut YA or MG sale listed on Publisher's Marketplace would soon be followed by a new member request in my inbox.

For me, that's part of the fun: seeing our membership grow and getting acquainted with so many great titles. I'm excited to be able to walk into a bookstore and know the authors of virtually every new novel on the shelves, along with the stories that went behind those books. It's a privilege that makes my own debut experience even more special.

Informal & invaluable

The concept behind the Elevensies, Debs and Tenners isn't that revolutionary. Authors have been connecting via list servs for years, while groups such as the highly successful 2K classes (of which several Debs, Tenners and Elevensies are members) offer the chance for YA and MG authors to pool marketing resources and build buzz as a team.

What makes our groups unique is that they exist, first and foremost, as places for debut authors to support each other. And unlike, say, a Yahoo Group, we often open ourselves to the public, allowing fans and fellow writers to comment and join in on our ongoing discussions about writing, books and the path to publication.

"Certainly there's a writers community at large online, but most of it is for adult fiction," says Saundra Mitchell (*Shadowed Summer*, Delacorte), a member of the 2009 Debs. "That's why these groups are so special. We're all going through the same thing in the same genre with the same publishers and it's a relief to talk about your issues without first having to explain *why* they're issues."

The Elevensies are dues-free, and members can participate as much or as little as they'd like. While we might do a marketing activity every now and then, we're more likely to spend our time cheering each other through revisions, squeeing about blurbs from our favorite authors, or offering virtual hugs when someone's editor leaves.

Reprinted with permission.

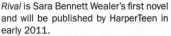

Rival is Sara Bennett Wealer's first novel and will be published by HarperTeen in early 2011.

It's that informal vibe that has contributed to the popularity of the Debs, Tenners and Elevensies. The Tenners closed their membership with more than 90 members, and at the time of this printing the Elevensies were already up to 45.

There are, of course, a few ground rules for those wishing to join. Authors must have contracts with houses listed in *Children's Writer's & Illustrator's Market*. And they must be publishing their debut novel, though we have made some exceptions for those with previous work-for-hire titles.

Within the group there also are some understandings. One is that we respect each other's feelings. Some authors get bigger advances, better buzz, and more marketing support—that's a fact of life. But the Elevensies operate as equals whether we are being sent on multi-city book tours or footing the bill for our own book trailers. And it goes without saying that we all try to keep in mind the difference between sharing and bragging.

"I'm learning from everyone," says Shawn Goodman, whose book, *Something Like Hope*, won the Delacorte Prize for a first YA novel. "In isolation there's a tendency toward self-doubt; however, being a member of a group like the Elevensies is reaffirming in so many ways. We're all at roughly the same point in our careers, yet the array of personalities, voices and writing styles is amazing."

No-pressure marketing

While the Debs, Tenners and Elevensies are not focused on marketing, each group has done its share of outreach projects. For example:

- The Debs sponsored a giveaway contest for libraries, with each author contributing a book to the winner's package. Seventy librarians entered by submitting photos of their libraries' pets or mascots.
- Both the Debs and Tenners hosted regular contests gifting readers with packages of swag items relating to various members' books. The Elevensies are planning a similar activity.
- The Tenners hosted interviews at their blog with Deb authors as their books came out, and the Elevensies have continued that tradition with our "Tennerviews" series.
- The Tenners featured regular "Ask a Tenner" forums, which were wildly popular with online followers. The Elevensies, meanwhile, will host a "Second Breakfast" feature where authors will take turns "hosting" a virtual brunch to answer questions from visitors.
- The Tenners teamed up for a group book trailer, and members of all groups band together whenever possible for multiple-author signings.

These activities have been successful, in part, because people are drawn to groups of authors who are having fun together. Bookstores and librarians also appreciate being able to feature several authors at once.

No-Stress, No-Strings Group Marketing

While groups like the Elevensies are more about support than marketing, we have been successful at building buzz for our books—often without trying very hard. Here are a few of our secrets.

We're just having fun. Most of the time we aren't trying to sell ourselves or our books. We're just sharing the journey to publication. People are attracted to that, and it makes them curious to find out more.

We keep it casual. Most of our projects come about because someone had an idea and ran with it. While we might put certain things up for a vote, members are free to organize their own initiatives, and everything is opt-in. People can participate in the projects they're passionate about.

We're part of the bigger conversation. Most of us were already active in social networking before joining the Elevensies, and those who weren't got active by virtue of spending time with the group. We like chatting with fans, librarians and other writers. That gives us credibility. So when we do switch into marketing mode, people are willing to listen and excited to participate.

We like hanging out together. Often when members travel, they put out feelers to see who else is in the area. If we can, we set up joint book signings, school visits and other events. We get to hang out with other Elevensies and stores, libraries and schools get several authors at once. It's a win-win!

No project is ever mandatory. "Most of our 'networking,' like blog tours and book signings, are the result of someone saying, 'Hey, I'll be in New York this March! Who's with me?'" says Lindsey Leavitt. "The promotion activities are there if you want them, but if you want a place to hang out in a safe, private setting, we're there for that as well."

Jackson Pearce credits the groups' success, in part, to the freedom that members have to be as active as they like.

"The community has developed beautifully in part because of our 'just do it' policy," she says. "If you want to organize a giveaway, a meet-up, a blog tour, whatever, you just post and get a few people to help you, then go for it. There are no committees, no one has to run anything past the moderator or get something approved, and everything is opt-in."

And membership does have its benefits. The fact that we're grouped under a catchy name makes it easy for people to create lists of our books on Goodreads or Amazon. Another benefit: book bloggers are fond of following debut groups on Twitter, Facebook, and other online meeting spots. In fact, *Shelf Awareness* cited Becca Fitzpatrick's affiliation with the Tenners and their close relationship to bloggers as a factor in helping her debut novel, *Hush Hush* (Simon & Schuster), reach the New York Times bestseller list.

"I've been in awe of the support given to me by the Tenners," says Fitzpatrick. "Members have posted reviews of the book on their blogs, gifted the book to friends and family, helped spread word by announcing contests I've held to build buzz for the book, and given me feedback on the book's sequel, *Crescendo*. Each member of the group brings their own talents and strengths to the community, and it makes for an incredible bunch of authors!"

Connections that count

From year to year and group to group, we've been able to learn from each other and build upon what worked in the past. But we also benefit from being in the now.

"Technologies change, the industry changes, trends come and go in a heartbeat," says Sheela. "Two years ago, book trailers were barely getting off the ground and no one really knew about Twitter. That's hardly the case now. Having a community in place each year helps authors meet these changes as a group and find the best ways to reach readers that makes sense for them."

And the fun doesn't end once the debut year is over. Both the Debs and Tenners continue to update their blogs, celebrating awards and highlighting appearances by their authors. They've also continued their outreach activities, for example when the Debs donated copies of their books to a fundraiser sponsored by the Leaky Caldron fansite for victims of the January 2010 earthquake in Haiti.

To me, that's what's most inspiring about belonging to the Elevensies. We get to share this once-in-a-lifetime experience, but we're also forging friendships that will last far beyond what we're going through now. In an industry that sometimes feels isolating and cut-throat, we know we can count on each other for support, advice and a heartfelt congratulations no matter where our careers take us.

"Publishing could be a vicious, competitive cycle, but we've avoided most of that," says Saundra Mitchell. "I feel like we've gotten the most amazing experience of publishing by being together. The Debs will always be the Debs. Tenners will always be Tenners.

Elevensies will always be Elevensies. And I hope the chain continues on because the whole point of writing is to make connections. And these are the connections I'm happiest I made."

Where to Find Us

The Elevensies, and those who've gone before us, can be found on Twitter, Facebook and other online gathering places. But our home bases are at Live Journal. Here's where we hang out!

- The Elevensies: community.livejournal.com/2011debuts
- The Tenners: community.livejournal.com/10_ers
- The Debs: community.livejournal.com/debut2009

Libba Bray

'You just give yourself permission to fail,'
says Prinz winner

by Jolie Stekly

Growing up, Libba Bray wanted to be the Queen of England, a champion figure skater, and David Bowie. Luckily for readers, those three options didn't work out so well.

Readers first fell in love with her *Gemma Doyle* trilogy. Then Bray left behind the fantasy-based historical fiction for a comic, contemporary road trip called *Going Bovine*.

It's possibly the trippiest road trip story ever, telling the story of how a 16-year-old with mad cow disease set out to save himself and the world with the help of a dwarf, a garden gnome, and a punk-rock guardian angel.

Now, Bray is fresh off winning the 2010 Michael L. Printz award for the funny and thought-provoking novel.

Now that there's been a little time to settle into your Printz win, how has it changed life, if at all?

Right now I am typing from my rose-strewn throne while resting my feet upon the back of David Levithan, who has graciously agreed to act as my foot stool until my new one arrives. (It will have the "Ask Me about My Printz Award!" upholstery. The nailhead trim takes a while, I'm told.) Every day, when I come down to write, woodland creatures sing me songs about the fact that my hair smells like brilliance. And my bum is a thing of firm beauty. It's good to be me. So good.*

* Resemblance between this and author's actual daily life of missed deadlines, ferrying child to and from school and activities, doing laundry, and occasionally showering is iffy. Mostly, author's life has been affected by a feeling of deep gratitude to the fabulous Printz committee and by overuse of the word, "Wow!" to describe how good it felt to be honored by the receipt of said prize.

You spent many years with the character Gemma Doyle. Does your mind ever drift back to her story and what might come next?

JOLIE STEKLY is a writer, fitness instructor, former SCBWI Regional Advisor, and the 2009 Society of Children's Book Writers & Illustrators Member of the Year. She's a member of SCBWI TEAM BLOG which offers live blogging at the organization's annual summer and winter conferences, and maintains her own blog at cuppajolie. blogspot.com.

Sometimes, though lately there hasn't been time for much drift. Last year, I went through a temporary psychosis wherein I contemplated a fourth Gemma book. My family staged an intervention. But yes, I have thought occasionally about what fun it might be to continue their adventures. I had always wanted to take Gemma back to India at some point to investigate the connection between The Order and the Rakshana there. I definitely felt we weren't finished with Sarita. And seeing Ann have a life on the stage and Felicity reign in Paris would be delicious fun, I'm sure. I had entertained the idea of setting a novel in 1901, just as Queen Victoria dies, but that made them all about 21/22, and then I wasn't sure it was YA anymore.

Going Bovine is a considerably different book than your Gemma Doyle trilogy. What sparked the idea to write Cameron's funny yet very personal story?

I'd had the idea knocking around in my head for some time. I'd always been interested in riffing on Don Quixote. I love road trips and quests. And I have a soft spot for sardonic outsiders. I also really, really wanted to write a comedy.

I never really know what stars align to form each book, but certainly this one started many years ago with the tale of a man from my hometown who contracted Creutzfeldt-Jakob's disease. He had powerful hallucinations including fire imagery. His mind and reality were being eroded, which played at one of my most primal fears, and also made me question the nature of reality. I also realized after the fact that the many experiences I'd had relating to my car accident at eighteen came into play—not just the hospital stays and the endless doctors' office rounds but the depression and isolation, the reconstruction of an identity. And many of the central questions of the book—Who are we? Why are we here? What gives life its meaning? Is there a God? What is reality, anyway?—are questions I've wrestled with my whole life, starting in childhood, and I wanted room to explore them.

As for the rest, well, as Dulcie says in the book: "Mystery!" I'm comfortable with that.

Did you find the process of writing a male point-of-view different than a female's? Or writing the contemporary vs. historical voice?

Well, I think there is a lot more wiggle room between male and female than our cultural gender ideas seem to allow for. I don't know that Cameron and Gonzo's feelings, their doubts, insecurities, anger or frustrations are so different from mine or any number of girls'. I think we do allow our boys more room for directness and less apology in their anger and aggression, and frankly, I found that a relief to write. My hope is that we will allow more room for that in our girls. The novel I'm working on now, *Beauty Queens*, is girl-centric, and I'm really trying to explore the boundaries of gender.

Writing contemporary is much easier than writing historical in some obvious ways—not as much painstaking research into whether or not you can use the word "audition," for instance, or not having to come up with believable ways for your Victorian female characters to be somewhere unchaperoned, which, at times, resembled a game of Mouse Trap. But in the end, it's still about the characters and their journey, and that's tough no matter the time period in which you're placing that puppy.

Reprinted with permission.

Going Bovine won Libba Bray the 2010 Michael L. Printz award.

There were so many threads and themes running through *Going Bovine*. How did you keep it all straight?

I'm not sure I did. To quote Monty Python, "My brain hurts!" It's called a writing process for a reason—there's a lot to process. Things would just occur to me as I'd go along. I'd make the connection: "Oh! It should be Bifrost Road, like the road the dead travel in Norse mythology!" But honestly, that's so much of the fun. I'm absolutely useless at math and music theory but that's the closest I come to being able to move in that world and understand the beauty of how things work, how the long algebra problem on the chalkboard gets solved or the musical score gets fleshed out with a descant and a descending bass line and a lyric that is a play on another lyric. That "Aha!" moment when you make the connections and it all comes together. It's great. But for every one of those, there's a lot of "Huh, I wonder how this sounds?" (Plays dissonant chord) "Oh, it sounds like Hell is coming for your soul, that's what."

Really, it's a matter of working and reworking, revising, paying attention, asking, "Is there a connection there?" I'd also have to give credit to my mother, a former high school English teacher. In a sense, she "trained" me to be looking for those associations and allusions, those connections by constantly asking questions. So thanks, Mom. (And by the way, the reason my bedroom screen was off the window that time in eighth grade was because Jeannie and I snuck out in the middle of the night. Sorry.) And of course, it never hurts to have the expert help of a good editor and other writers to say, "Hey, missed a spot." Thank God for them.

Which part of the writing process do find is your biggest challenge? And, how do you go about conquering it?

The fear. It's so easy to doubt myself and criticize every choice even before it's on the page. I don't know of any foolproof way of avoiding that. In fact, I think the fear might be necessary—at least for me. I think it's probably not too far removed from being in any social situation where you feel awkward and afraid of saying the wrong thing and certain that it was a mistake to wear your Converse, and why can't you just be like all those *normal* people here? And at some point you just go, "Fuck it. This is who I am. I have to go with that or it's not going to work in the long run." I guess you just give yourself permission to fail. I mean, if you're gonna go down in flames, go down as who you really are, you know? (I can only hear the *Zombieland* Woody Harrelson in my head saying, "Time to nut up or shut up." But yeah. That.)

The other big challenge is time. Despite my research into parallel worlds and time travel, I have not come up with a way to be both at my computer writing and at the gym running. Nor do I know how to freeze the editorial timeline so that my books are not actually late. If anyone knows how to do this, please contact me.

Not only have you written many novels, but short stories as well. Is your approach to writing your short stories any different than your novels?

I try not to make the short stories 500 + pages.

I get slightly less freaked out about short stories only in that I know they can't be 500 + pages and so that makes it seem a tad more manageable. Of course, I say this, but I've had short stories that took me months to write, so maybe *I do* get freaked out about it.

I really love reading short stories, and I so admire writers who manage to plunk you down right at a pivotal moment without floundering around, and so I try to remember that when I'm writing a short story, that it is as if we have joined the program already in progress, and my job should be to make the reader say, "Oooh, what's going on here? This seems odd/intriguing/mysterious."

Possibly my favorite short story collection is George Saunders' *Pastoralia*. I distinctly remember reading the title story. I was in the waiting room of my doctor's office, feeling icky, and when I read that first page, I laughed out loud. Then I had to read it again to make sure I wasn't hallucinating. Talk about odd and what's going on here? But he just creates his own ecosystems in those stories. It's George Saunders World, and we've just gotten a day pass, and I love that. I also love Raymond Carver and Lorrie Moore and David Levithan and Junot Diaz and Kelly Link and Holly Black and so many more. So, I guess I have answered your question about how I approach writing short stories by talking about the short story writers I love. Reading the good ones. Not a bad place to start.

Little, Brown will be publishing a young adult series The Diviners scheduled for fall of 2012. Can you give us a little taste of what readers will get from this series?

Yes, but only if you promise not to double dip.

I'm really excited about diving in. I started doing the research and jotting down ideas, playing around with this world about two, two-and-a-half years ago, and I've continued playing with it in between working on other books and stories. So it's nice to move it from the back burner to the front. The main character is a flapper party girl with a sort of Zelda Fitzgerald/Dorothy Parker bent. It's set in New York City, which was such a vibrant place in the 1920's. I can tell you that it involves supernatural elements and powers and a deep, dark secret from the past which has placed the world in jeopardy. There are a lot of political overtones as well. There is romance and horror. I don't want to say too much beyond that. But I hope it will be a hell of a ride.

There are countless writers who admire you and your work, writers who want to "grow up" to be like Libba Bray. Who was your Libba Bray when you were moving toward publication?

There were so many people whose work I admired on the road to publication…

But if I'm going to single out one writer, I guess I'd have to say John Irving has always held a special place in my heart. His stuff is so weird and gorgeous and it never fails to gut me. It's also just thoroughly John Irving-ish. It speaks to me.

By the way, you really don't want to grow up to be me. I'm pretty short and I can never remember anything.

Music seems to be of great importance to you. What role does it play in your personal and writing life?

Oh wow. I'm just a huge music freak. It does something for me that I can't always put into words. It is like a sense memory exercise. Music helped define me as a teen and was my salvation in many ways, and I find that it still functions as muse, balm, restorative, energizer, thought provoker. There's something about music that opens me up to the possible. I make an iPod playlist for everything I write, and picking the songs that feel "right" for that mix is a fun part of the writing process. I also play in an all-YA author rock band, Tiger Beat, with Natalie Standiford, Daniel Ehrenhaft, and Barnabas Miller. Coming soon to a bookstore near you. Possibly. If we don't get sucked into a parallel world first.

Marketing and the use of social networking, youtube, etc. has changed so much since the release of *A Great And Terrible Beauty*. For *Going Bovine* you created a wonderfully funny book trailer and did a Skype tour. Have you noticed a difference in how you are able to reach readers? And how readers react and reach out?

For the most part, the various social networking aspects are great. I don't do a lot of travel because I find it disruptive to the family and writing life. (Please see above.) So things like Twitter and Live Journal and Facebook (although I hate FB—it feels like going into Macy's on a packed Sunday afternoon) and YouTube make it possible to communicate and bring the world a bit closer. It's cool that there is accessibility. I know people from their Twitter and Live Journal names, and when they come out, there's that great feeling of, "Oh! You're LadyHawke96! So nice to meet you in person." I did a Skype tour, and I enjoyed the intimacy of being able to talk to people from my home office, to say, "Look, there are my cats being all cat-like, which is to say, lazy!" But I have the sense that Skype works better in, say, a classroom setting where you have a captive audience and it beats taking a geology exam than, say, showing up to a bookstore where seeing someone live and in person and perhaps having a book signed is the objective. It will be interesting to see where Skype might go from here. Anyway, I'm terrible with technology, but I do love all the options. I hope to make better use of them in the future. (That sounds like I'm answering a pageant question. Sorry. I'm writing about beauty queens right now. Occupational hazard.)

Truth in storytelling is important to you. How do you ensure that you get to the heart of truth in each of your stories? Do you have some sort of BS censor? And if so, what sets it off?

I can't claim to "ensure" that I get there. But I spend an awful lot of time trying. Honestly, it's just the daily grind. It's the work. You keep writing until you hit something that feels like a vein and you keep going. Or you go for a walk and let it sink in. You do something else, come back to it. But you keep coming back. You keep sitting with it, asking yourself if it's true or if you've got another layer to go. For me, I can't always see that the first time. It's the second or third or tenth time. It's reading over it the next day and seeing the joke or the obfuscating language that hides the more truthful approach. Sometimes, I've written funny passages that I've cut because they didn't serve the story. And I think each story has its own voice, so it's about finding what's true for that particular story. Anyway, it's just sitting there slogging through. No secret BS devices. No decoder rings. Sorry.

In such an isolated and lonely profession, what role do writer friends play in your life?

I am so grateful for them. It's great to have a community, people you can turn to when things aren't going so well and you're struggling, and those people understand! They will listen and nod sympathetically or distract you by suddenly blurting out, "Would you rather be forced to relive your 7th grade prom or wear a satin jumpsuit and roller skate in public?" Sometimes they even buy you a cookie and tell you to put the whole thing in your mouth and not think or write until it's gone. And this is sound advice. Community. It's important, people. [*Author wipes away a solitary tear*]

Do you remember when you made the decision to *be a writer*?

Which time? Sometimes I think I should have stuck with my original game plan, which was to be Queen of England. After all, I like Corgis. And diamonds.

Jacqueline Woodson

'I write because I have questions, not answers'

by Lee Wind

Jacqueline Woodson is an amazingly talented writer. Her picture books (seven of them so far, three more coming soon) sweep you in and up every time you read them with a child. Her middle grade titles (six of them) are almost deceptively light, fast reads—and yet have amazing depth to the characters' emotions and stories. And her 10 young adult novels are masterful—the characters, their lives, their stories stay with you long after you've finished reading them.

She has won major awards in every genre she's written (see sidebar), including the Margaret A. Edwards award for Lifetime Achievement from the Young Adult Library Service Association of the ALA for her body of work "helping adolescents become aware of themselves and addressing questions about their role and importance in relationships, society, and the world."

Here, Woodson talks about the difference in writing picture books and books for teens, the "why" behind the choices she makes in her books, and shares some wonderful advice on how to tackle the big "issues" in your writing.

So I have this theory where we writers tend to set our main characters at ages that were really pivotal in our own development. As if we all have this age of arrested development, this time in our own childhoods where we keyed into the world and our lives more intensely—and in the alchemy of writing fiction that memory lets us go back and write through the eyes of that age. As you write both picture books and books for teens, I'm wondering if you feel you have two (or more) ages of arrested development?

I think your theory of arrested development is true. As writers, we do want to go back to the place that, in a lot of ways, we never left. Mostly, to change the world it was when we were in it—a world where too often, we didn't know our own power. We didn't know how to create change or if we actually had the ability to do so. So as an adult, going "home" to that past is an amazing feeling. That said, I think it's bigger somehow at the

---

LEE WIND is the author of the how-to e-book guide, *The Zen OfBlogging: 7 Steps On The Virtual Path To Real Success*. His award- winning blog, "I'm Here. I'm Queer. What the Hell do I Read?" covers GLBTQ Teen Books, Culture and Politics. He is currently working on both a YA and a MG novel. You can find out more about Lee, his e-book, and his blog at www.zenofblogging.com and www.leewind.org.

Feathers earned a Newberry Honor Medal for Jacqueline Woodson.

same time. As a writer, I often say that it's important to walk through the world with your eyes wide open. A lot of people are afraid to do this because of what they might see. It's hard being hyper-aware of the many injustices in the world and sometimes, it can make a person feel *very* young, *very* powerless—hence, it can take you back to that world of childhood where adults seemed to be making all the decisions. Replace the word 'adult' with whatever force/person is in the moment causing the disruption and you have the *now* world that you're walking through. So I feel like, as a writer, I exist in both those worlds—the past and the present. In my books, the two worlds meet but the young people are stronger than I was as a child, more articulate and vocal, more in the world—more who I am now.

In terms of writing both picture books and books for teens, all this is true. It's a continuum—I don't see a divide between the worlds of being 7 and 14. The people in the stories are all on the same journey—just at different points on the road.

You are remarkably prolific. When you get an idea for a new story, at what point do you figure out how you're going to approach it (if it's going to be a picture book, or a novel)? Do you generally start with a character, or with a story element?

I usually have a character in my head and start writing whatever that character is bringing

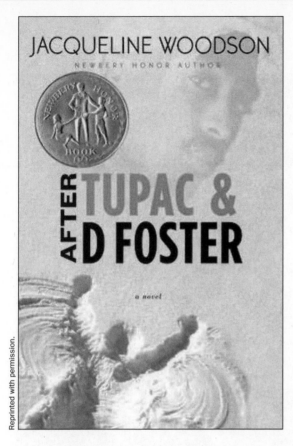

Reprinted with permission.

After Tupac & D Foster won Jacqueline Woodson another Newberry Honor Medal.

with him/her. Usually, the way the story comes to the page determines what it's going to be. If the narrative is immediate with lines breaking it, with clear imagery—I know it's a picture book. If it feels more contemplative and questioning on a broader, more vague level—then I know it's going to be for middle graders and/or young adults.

Sometimes writers try to tackle a huge topic—like racism, or homophobia—and the result is a story that's overburdened with "morals" and "lessons" and feels, well, preachy. Your picture book *The Other Side* is one of the most beautiful stories about overcoming racism, and yet it feels so real, so natural, so *not* didactic. How do you pull that off?

Talking about stuff like racism, homophobia, activism, gender issues, etc. can't be a *new* dialogue. It has to be part of the everyday conversation. I never feel like I'm *introducing* a new idea to my readers. We're more like close friends talking about the same things we've always talked about.

I think what's most important is that what your writing matters to you on some deep and familiar level. Like I said, your ideas, your "morals," your thoughts about the world should be part of a bigger conversation that you're not having for the first time but that you've always had and plan to continue having.

Show Way earned Woodson one of many Newberry Honor Medals.

In *Visiting Day* you tell the story of a young girl going to visit her father who is in prison. In OUR GRACIE AUNT a brother and sister are abandoned by their mother and taken into foster care with their aunt. These are scary, hard situations, and yet you managed to make them picture books that tug at the hearts of readers, adults and children alike. When you take on stories like these, are you concerned with feeding into negative stereotypes about black people in our culture?

I am one black person telling one black story. If people want to take that story and make it about something big and deep and dysfunctional, then that need in them has nothing to do with me or what I'm trying to do in fiction. If people need to look at one book and say "these are all 'those people,'" then all I can feel is sad for them (which is what I feel whenever I hear someone say "those people") because in my community, we call that racism. I can't imagine a backlash for putting the stories of strong black people on the page. If people need to look through those stories, to not see them, to only see what's "wrong" in the story, again, it saddens me. People go to jail. People can't raise their children. This happens across all lines of race and class.

One of many beautiful moments in *After Tupac & D Foster* is where the main character considers why she reads so much: "I read all those books and watched those educational shows and peeped the newspapers and people's biographies and autobiographies because I was trying to see some tiny bit of myself up in those books. And even though I didn't ever find it, I kept on

Woodson's Awards by Genre

- *Show Way*, Newbery Honor Medal

- *Coming On Home Soon*, Caldecott Honor, ALA Notable

- *The Other Side*, ALA Notable and 14 additional honors

- *Feathers*, Newbery Honor Medal

- *Locomotion*, National Book Award Finalist, Coretta Scott King Honor, Boston Globe-Horn Book Award

- *After Tupac & D Foster*, Newbery Honor Medal

- *Hush*, National Book Award Nominee

- *Miracle's Boys*, Coretta Scott King Award, Los Angeles Times Book Prize, ALA Best Book for Young Adults

- *If You Come Softly*, ALA Best Book for Young Adults

For more information about Woodson, her books and her awards, check out her website, www.jacquelinewoodson.com.

looking." Is that moment you? Is that what made you a writer—to help kids finally see some tiny bit of themselves in *your* books?

All the moments in all of my books are me. I wasn't a big reader as a young person and it wasn't until I was grown that I realized the absence of people like me in the pages of the literature I grew up reading. I actually am not sure I'm writing to "help kids." I think that's the gravy. I'm writing to grow, to learn, to make discoveries about who I am in the world and about the world itself. Writing helps me do this. It allows me to step outside of my everyday life and really examine so much around me.

As I've said before, I write because I have questions, not answers. In terms of my narrator in *After Tupac*, she's still trying to find herself. Fortunately, I have a *very* clear sense of who I am. Goodness, to get this age and not know would be heartbreaking. But even having a clear sense of myself doesn't mean I can't continue to grow and learn and explore.

Do you feel a writer needs to have a personal connection to tackle a "minority" character, or can you get by with just research? Did you have a personal connection with Sean, the main character's deaf brother in *Feathers*?

I don't like the word "minority" so let's not use it anymore. Minority to whom? To what? Also, in terms of thinking "bigger" (because this is what writing is about), let's stop and ponder—how many times are white writers asked "Do you feel a writer needs a personal connection to tackle a "white" character? Making a character white is as much of a choice as making a character a person of color yet this doesn't get discussed.

I have a personal connection to each character that walks across the page. I write across all lines of race and class. Mainly, because I exist in a world and in a community where all kinds of people are present. I've made very conscious choices about everything from where my child goes to school to where I live to who gets represented in the pages of my literature.

Why? Because all people are people—not "minorities," not "other," not the many things so many people feel they need to call people in order to feel power over them. I love Sean because he knows who he is and what he wants. Yes, he's deaf. Yes, there are deaf people in the world. Yes, the deafness adds to who he is and how he walks through the world. And this too, I love about him.

***Feathers* had this fascinating duality, where on the one hand the book was soft, and on the other it dealt with major internal conflict, including dealing with hard stuff like death. How did your novel dealing with the subject of death and loss and moving on evolve?**

Feathers was originally called *Still Winter* from the line in Oscar Wilde's *The Selfish Giant*. All over the world it was spring but in the giant's garden, it was still winter. *The Selfish Giant* was the biggest inspiration for *Feathers* and there is a lot of the essence of that story moving through the novel.

I think it is *very* scary for people to imagine worlds they've never been a part of. As I wrote and re-wrote *Feathers*, I knew, eventually, that the book was way bigger than the story of the Jesus Boy. Bigger than *The Selfish Giant*. That it was becoming the story of kids figuring out their way in a world where adult-laden hopes and ideas have always been central to their lives. I think death is hard but only if you believe that death is the absolute end of things.

Three months ago, my mom died suddenly at the age of 67. I live in the world these days still surprised by it and at peace with her presence a constant in my life. I think when you're open to truly being a part of the world, you can't help but exist in many worlds—as writers, we live in the worlds of our characters' lives, our personal worlds, our public worlds, and on and on. Having all those doors open is a gift and a means in which to explore some of the harder stuff life brings our way. So I close no doors and write what I know.

Did dealing with something so difficult shift the tone of the rest of the book as you wrote it? Did you feel you had to make other parts lighter or funnier to "even it out"?

I'm not conscious of how the story shifts and stuff. I just write. I knew what I wanted to do (The Selfish Giant thing) but the book had a different plan. Having kids has definitely given me more of a sense of humor and my friends and I joke and laugh a lot. My two closest friends, Toshi (my daughter's godmom) and Jana (my son's godmom) and I go out once a month to eat good food, drink good wine and generally get the world off our shoulders. They're two of the funniest people I know. I grew up with my grandmother and mom and my grandmother *loved* good jokes so I would constantly look for good ones to tell her and she'd just crack up. Growing up with a gaggle of siblings in a religious household where we weren't allowed to curse, watch much television or stay out past dark, we found ways to entertain each other and, mostly, I told jokes or acted the clown. So laughter has always been a part of my life and in fiction you need both—the darkness and the light, you need the hope that goes along with the loss, you need the spring that comes after winter.

Perhaps it's because you write so much in the first person, but sometimes we readers don't even learn your main character's name! (Like in *Visiting Day* and *After Tupac & D Foster*.) And yet, it works because the voice of that main character is so strong.

If *You Come Softly* is written in first person (Ellie) and third person (Miah) for the obvious reason—the reader finds out—that Miah doesn't live to tell his story. *After Tupac.* has an unnamed narrator because the book is about that intimacy and false sense of intimacy—here is a girl who has told us her life and we *really* think we know her—but do we? Do the girls *really* know Tupac? Does it matter?

I love how you echoed this with the main character realizing toward the end of *After Tupac & D Foster* that she hadn't known D's real name—and wondering how much did she really knows about this close friend of hers? And all the while we the readers feel so close to the narrator and we don't know her name. So elegantly done. How do you go about finding the voice for each story?

Mainly, however the character first shows up in my head is how they end up telling their story. Parts of *Behind You* are written in second person because Miah is talking to us—the readers. So I don't find the voices—they find themselves. I have to figure out what the story is trying to say but usually the characters come to me pretty much with their voices intact. Thank goodness!

Some of your picture books are rollicking while some feel almost reverent. *We Had a Picnic This Sunday Past* **is hysterical—I laugh each time I read it with my daughter.** *Show Way* **gives me goose bumps every single time. Do you have any special techniques or tricks that keep you "on tone" when you're writing?**

I read everything I write out loud—again and again. If it doesn't sound right, it gets edited. I can't sing at all so whenever I hear someone talk about my pitch and tone as a writer, I'm beside myself because *no one* has ever said that about my singing!

You've done so many books, so many different styles—Is there another genre/type of story you're itching to try?

I'm trying it now. But can't talk about it because it's too new.

Do you work on multiple projects at a time? What are you working on now?

Yup. I'll talk about the ones that are finished: *Pecan Pie Baby*—a picture book illustrated by Sophie Blackall about a girl who doesn't want a new baby. (Our children are six years apart. Somewhat autobiographical.) *The Rope*—a picture book illustrated by James Ransome about a rope that travels with a family through generations ending up in Brooklyn, NY. *Each Kindness*—a picture book illustrated by Shadra Strickland. I'm psyched about this one. I think Shadra will rock it.

What's the best piece of writing advice you've ever received, and that you would like to share with aspiring writers?

From Dorothy Allison—Tell Your Story. Everybody has a story and a right to tell it.

Two Writers on the Duet of Co-Authorship

by Fiona Bayrock

As a general rule, writing isn't a group activity. Most of the time, the act of stringing words together is, as the saying goes, a solitary occupation. But every once in a while we find writers who combine their talents to write books together. What is such a writing partnership like? How do co-authors successfully mesh their writing habits, styles, goals, schedules, and personalities to become a team? What does it take to share a process over which each writer is used to having sole autonomy? We sat down with award-winning Vancouver authors Shar Levine and Leslie Johnstone to find out. After 16 years of writing over 50 children's books together, they have co-authoring down to a fine art.

Levine and Johnstone were experienced writers when they met; Levine had a few books under her belt, and Johnstone was editing and writing for a science teachers' magazine. Since the two began writing together, they've published children's hands-on science books with Sterling, Scholastic, becker&mayer!, John Wiley and Sons, Mud Puddle, and Silver Dolphin. Their titles include: *Shocking Science, Sports Science, Bathtub Science, Magnet Power,* and *The Icky Sticky and Gross Fascinating Fact Book,* as well as several SMARTLAB, Extreme 3-D, and Build Your Own books, to name a few. Levine and Johnstone share a knack for digging up cool, quirky science facts and activities, and then writing about them in a way that appeals to kids, parents, and teachers. The partnership is a professional success whichever way you cut it. Over a million of their books are in print in more than seven languages, and have received nods from the National Science Teachers Association, Parents' Choice Awards, and others, including two books shortlisted for the AAAS Subaru SB&F Prize for Excellence in Science Books (*Backyard Science*, 2005) and *The Ultimate Guide to Your Microscope*, 2008). The

FIONA BAYROCK is the author of *Bubble Homes and Fish Farts* (Charlesbridge, 2009; a Junior Library Guild selection and finalist for the BC Book Prizes), 14 other quirky science books for the school and education market, and 60+ articles, stories, and poems in children's magazines such as Highlights for *Children, KNOW,* and *Odyssey.* Over the years, Fiona has delighted in chasing questions through most of the "ologies," talking to scientists around the world about all kinds of neat stuff, from palindromes to solar wind. She currently lives with her zany family on the side of a mountain in rural British Columbia, Canada, where she is constantly in search of the "Aha!", clever puns, and her coffee. She enjoys visiting schools and speaking at conferences. Visit her at www.fionabayrock.com.

partnership is a personal success, too. After so many years and books together, they love what they do and love doing it together.

By day, Leslie Johnstone heads the science department at a large Vancouver high school, while Shar Levine takes on the public face of the duo as "The Science Lady" (www.sciencelady.com). Here they talked candidly about their writing relationship and methods, spilling a few secrets of their success in the process.

How did you become writing partners?

Shar Levine: A mutual friend introduced us at a New Year's party. We sat up all night and talked about science. It was like finding a soul mate. When I had an opportunity to write a new book, I phoned Leslie and said, "Can we do this together?"

Leslie Johnstone: We just kind of clicked...you know, the old L.M. Montgomery kindred spirit thing from *Anne of Green Gables*. Even so, we were friends for two years before we started writing together. I don't think we could have stepped in and started writing the very first day, but when Shar called, it turned out the timing was right. Doing that first pair of books was kind of scary because we didn't know how it was all going to turn out.

Levine: We ended up doing several books together within about two years—*Silly Science* (1995), *Everyday Science* (1995), and *Science Around the World* (1996) with John Wiley and Sons, and *The Microscope Book* (Sterling, 1996). They all did well, and we had a great time writing together.

Johnstone: And we've been writing together ever since.

So, what's it like writing with a partner? Give us a peek.

Levine: Imagine traveling with your best friend, working with your best friend, giggling—it's such a joy. When I talk to kids I ask, "Who likes to do an assignment with their best friend?" and everybody puts their hand up. It's fun to work together. And we just get each other, so it's very easy. For example, one time I was in the middle of a pitch to a publisher, free-forming some ideas, and this idea for a backpack alarm popped out of my mouth (it ended up as *Build Your Own Backpack Alarm*, Scholastic, 2006). Leslie went, "Oh!" and you see this little light there—an "Oh, I get that!"—so when the publisher said, "Tell me more about it.", Leslie and I sort of looked at each other and proceeded to tap dance our way through it together. We do that a lot.

Johnstone: *(nodding)* If one of us starts a sentence, the other one can always figure out the finish the other person intended. It's really quite remarkable.

Levine: Having a writing partner is also a great bring-forward thing for the odd facts we collect. (We find out all sorts of really weird things, which makes us very interesting at cocktails parties!) The extra brain is like having another hard drive. Leslie will remember something I've forgotten and vice versa.

Johnstone: Invariably, if Shar loses something on her hard drive, it's on mine. Shar once sent me this thing about blue lobsters (I didn't know they came in blue!), and she said, "I'm sure we can use this somewhere." Years later, I was buying lobsters in Halifax and they had one in a tank, so I took a picture of it. Eventually, the blue lobsters—and why they're blue—made it into one of our books. For another project, we needed something on horseshoe crabs and I knew that we'd written something about them in a previous book but couldn't remember which one. Shar did, and we managed to look back at what we'd written before so we didn't repeat ourselves.

Shar Levine and Leslie Johnstone have collaborated on several children's books now, including *Sports Science*.

Do you have different strengths you bring to the partnership?

Johnstone: It's one of the main reasons we work so well together. Shar's very good at making connections to things in kids' everyday lives. Sometimes I'll come at something from a very teacher/academic kind of direction and she'll go, "No, no, no, it'll have to be more fun than that," and she'll write something about skateboarding, or chewing bubblegum, or something, that would never have occurred to me.

Levine: Leslie is better at the hard science. (She hates the way I pronounce things in Latin!) Having different strengths and different weaknesses is beneficial. If you have two people who do the same things equally well, I think they'd butt heads more than we do.

How do you divide the work?

Levine: It depends on the book. Sometimes Leslie is busier and I can do more of

Co-author Checklist

- know each other well?

- like and respect each other a lot?

- enjoy each other's company?

- trust each other?

- communicate easily and well together?

- have different strengths and weaknesses and complementary skills and abilities so that the product of your collaboration will be better than either of you could produce on your own?

- have compatible personalities and work habits?

- work well together?

- have similar writing styles? (If not, how will you mesh them?)

- have the same expectations of the time and effort involved and volume of work you'll create together?

- how you'll divide the work.

- whether you'll work together or apart.

- how you'll make creative and business decisions.

- how you'll resolve disagreements. Will one of you have the final say over anything?

- how you'll split the royalties. Include the percentage split in your contracts, and have publishers send individual royalty statements and checks to each of you.

- a time schedule (at least to start).

- deadlines.

- leave your ego at the door. Be willing to put the project before yourself.

- don't sweat the small stuff.

- don't try to take ownership.

- it's a collaboration...that means give and take.

a book, so I'll take first stab and work out a rough outline for her input. And if I'm busier, she'll do more of a book. Sometimes we literally draw a line down the middle. Or we might say, "Oh, I'd like to write this." "I'd like to write that." We don't have an accounting of words or chapters or anything, though. We don't count up the number of pages and say, "All right, I wrote 30 pages and you wrote 20, and now next time you have to write 30 and I write 20."

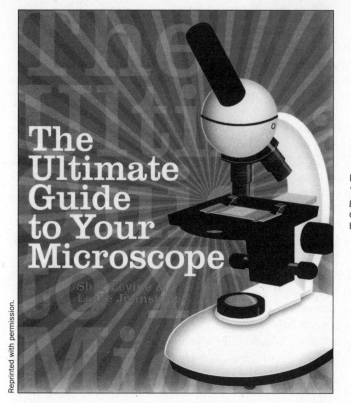

Reprinted with permission.

Levine says of collaborating, "Having two perspectives is good," while Johnstone says co-authoring really helps keep both authors sane.

Johnstone: I remember we had two books at one point where Shar started one and I started the other. We each got as far as we wanted to go, traded books, and finished up each other's book.

Levine: We know what the other is thinking. It's like we share the same brain.

Walk us through some of the nitty gritty of how you work together.

Johnstone: Because we've been doing it for so long we have our own little shorthand ways of doing things and can get through it pretty quickly.

Levine: I do lots of the pre-research. Often I'll prep the stuff and get what we need together, and then when we sit down everything is roughly in component pieces. This goes with this experiment. This goes with this activity. This is the information we need for what we're doing here.

Johnstone: But nowadays we don't even have to be together to write together because we can do it over the phone and internet. Sometimes Shar's at her place in Hawaii and I'm here in Vancouver, and we're writing a book together. We can literally email each other the document back and forth five or six times in an hour. So, [grin] I don't have to go to Shar's and be subjected to her horrible dogs and she doesn't have to come to my house and deal with my chaos. (I actually do like her dogs, but I'm allergic) Although we don't necessarily have to spend a huge amount of time together to do the writing, it's fun when we do, and it's certainly faster if we're working on a project with a really tight deadline to both be there and on two computers and able to…

Levine: ...literally stand up, change places, finish our sentences, and go back.

How do you divide the business end of things?

Johnstone: Shar is more contactable than I am, and I don't talk to people on the phone if I can avoid it, so she's usually the contact person for contracts and that kind of thing. Basically, Shar acts as my agent, I buy her a bottle of champagne when we sign contracts, and it seems to work out pretty well.

Levine: Leslie digs me out when I yell at publishers. As for royalties, we split everything 50-50. It's in the contracts that way, so we each get a check and royalty statement from each publisher. It's great being able to compare royalty statements: "What? You got a thousand dollars more than I did on that book? That makes no sense. We wrote the book together!" Thanks to that second statement, we know when to chase down a larger check.

Does having a partner help you through the negative aspects of the business, as well?

Johnstone: We've had publishers go bankrupt and not pay us. We've had publishers be bought by other companies and change their mind mid-project in a way that made it impossible to continue. One editor added up to 14 exclamation marks per paragraph. Yes, it`s nice to have someone to drink with.

Levine: Having two perspectives is good. Like when we get an edit back, and we're not happy with the cuts or rewrites, or it feels overwhelming. It's really helpful to have that other person.

Johnstone: Sometimes what Shar looks at and thinks is a terrible edit and way too much work to deal with and total chaos, I'll look at and go, "No, it's just this and it's this and it's this. It's fine." And she'll do the same for me. When one of us is having a bad day, it's nice to be able to say, "Can you look at this because I can't make any sense of it. It's making me crazy."

What's your biggest challenge?

Johnstone: Time. I have a full-time job and three children.

Levine: Yes, time. We tend to write on weekends, in summers, and over Christmas vacation and spring break. We go skiing together. We take work with us in the oddest places and do whatever it is we're supposed to do during the day, and in the evening we find time to write a book.

Johnstone: Sometimes. Sometimes we just go and have fun.

Levine: Very true.

What are the essential components of your writing partnership that make it so successful?

Levine: Friendship and respect. A sense of humor. Trust is also very important. We had one publisher who was mad at me and asked Leslie to write the book without me. Uh-uh...we won't go behind each other's back. It's a partnership. Whenever I get offered something, Leslie's the first person I turn to. I would never, ever accept something without presenting it to her, and vice versa.

Johnstone: *(nodding)* We really respect each other's abilities. We know the product we get when we write together is better than what we could do separately.

Levine: We have a style. We both think science should be interesting and fun and alive. Our books have a sort of, I don't know...a cadence, a rhythm, an energy.

Johnstone: There are some sections of some books that we look at and Shar will say, "I wrote this." and I'll say, "No, I wrote it." and we go back and forth. You really can't tell most of the time.

Johnstone: You also have to be able to tell the other person things they don't want to hear.

Levine: ...and be receptive to hearing those things. We put ego aside when we write. It's not like I'm right and you're wrong, or the other way around. We've got a very close friendship. We can tell each other anything. But working with a friend can destroy the friendship. When you're writing with a partner you have to decide what's more important—the book or your friendship. If I never wrote another book, it would be fine by me, but if I didn't have Leslie as my friend, it would be something I would always regret.

What happens when you disagree about something?

Johnstone: If it's about the business, we usually discuss it back and forth and Shar's usually right. If it's about the science, Shar always defers to me. I can't think of a circumstance where one of us really felt strongly about something and the other person felt strongly about it, too. We've always managed to come to a consensus.

Levine: Yeah, just minor quibbling. And if there's been a mistake, it's like, well, we're just not going to do that again.

What if one of you doesn't like something the other person has written?

Johnstone: We separate the business from the personal. If she doesn't like something I've written, I don't take it personally. Usually I don't like it either. If Shar tells me something's lame, I usually agree with her. Sometimes when I'm going through something she's written, I'll say to myself, What's Shar thinking here? What's she doing there? It's not a personal thing, though. Of course, [grin] if something's brilliant, we both recognize that it's brilliant, so it's no issue.

Levine: *(laughing)* Yeah, and that I wrote it. Seriously, though, the truth is that aside from getting the science right, none of our sentences are ever that important that we have to fight over the wording of it. Nothing is ever that critical.

Johnstone: We're only part of the process. Editors want to put their slant on things, too. So, rather than worrying about where the semicolon goes, or what three words we're putting at the end of that sentence, or whether it's this word or that word, in the grand scheme of things, it's better to just get it done, move on to the next thing, and not worry about it too much because often what you get back from the editors doesn't bear a whole lot of resemblance to what you wrote in the first place. We may argue with a publisher—remember the exclamation marks?—but there's never an argument between the two of us.

Have you ever had a time when one of you had writer's block?

Levine: Sure. Often it's end-of-sentence block.

Johnstone: That's where collaboration is very helpful. When you reach the point where you honestly don't know where to go next, you just send it to the other person and say "Finish this, please." I'll be reading something Shar wrote and it'll say, "Leslie, add something in here about such-and-such." Or I'll write a paragraph and tell Shar, "This is a bad paragraph. Please make it pretty."

Have you ever had a situation where neither of you wanted to "make it pretty", or there was something neither of you wanted to do?

Levine: When that happens we suck it up and we do it. For example, we know that on Saturday when I show up at Leslie's house at 10 a.m. with coffees for her entire family (and lunch!), that we're going to work through X number of hours on a project, even though we'd really prefer to be somewhere else, like on the ski hill or with our families.

Johnstone: Sometimes we'll skip bits and move on to something else that's not as irritating. It is work, though. I mean it's mostly play, and it's mostly fun, and it beats the heck out of your day job most of the time, but it is work. And sometimes when there's work to be done, you just have to do the work.

Any final thoughts?

Johnstone: *(grinning)* Writing with a partner has added benefits. Both of our families think we work a lot more than we do. If we want to go shopping for an afternoon... "Oh, we're working on a book. I'm going to Shar's to write."

Levine: *(grinning)* Sometimes we do a lot of "work" when relatives are in town.

Jack Martin

NYC Public Library Assistant Director on Reaching the YA Audience

by Lee Wind

H. "Jack" Martin is a young adult librarian out to dismantle the "traditional stereotype of a librarian who scowls and 'shushes' kids in the library." Currently the Assistant Director for Public Programs and Lifelong Learning at the New York Public Library, he is the mastermind behind video game tournaments throughout the NYPL system and even on giant screens just past those famous lions.

He was a contributor to *The Librarian's Guide to Gaming: An Online Toolkit for Building Gaming @ Your Library*, http://librarygamingtoolkit.org/nypl.html. He's on the review team for *Stuff for the Teen Age*, The NYPL's annual list of the best books, music, movies and video games for teens. And the STA website, with awesome categories like "The Undead," "LOL," and "For Real," (www.nypl.org/books/sta2009) is packed with videos of teens sharing their own reviews.

Martin was also the 2008 committee chair of the Quick Picks for Reluctant Young Adult Readers, an annual best-of list put out by the YALSA, the Young Adult Library Services Association of the ALA, the American Library Association.

Not only does he pull off an annual "Anti-Prom" at the library, he gets Tim Gunn from TV's "Project Runway" to mentor six teens on video. And the teens drew on the library's collection of books on fashion and photography as inspiration for their Anti-Prom outfits. Martin wrote of the free-to-attend Anti-Prom, "Offer teens a prom where they can wear what they like, dress how they like, choose the music they like, and bring whomever they like? That's real empowerment."

He co-wrote with his husband James R. Murdock *Serving lesbian, gay, bisexual, transgender and questioning teens: a how-to-do-it manual for librarians*. It is a remarkable—and practical—guide for librarians to understand how they can be there for the LGBTQ members of the Young Adult community they serve.

Martin is the quintessential "out-of-the-box" thinker, and here he speaks about what teens want, how to navigate cursing and sex in YA novels, and the opportunities for writers in the mix of collaboration, technology and untold teen stories.

LEE WIND is the author of the how-to e-book guide, *The Zen Of Blogging: 7 Steps On The Virtual Path To Real Success*. His award-winning blog, "I'm Here. I'm Queer. What the Hell do I Read?" covers GLBTQ Teen Books, Culture and Politics. He is currently working on both a YA and a MG novel. You can find out more about Lee, his e-book, and his blog at www.zenofblogging.com and www.leewind.org.

You've written that "Being a young adult librarian means more than just recommending good books; rather it means listening to teens, treating them with respect, thinking about the impact that the library can have on their lives, and helping teens contribute to their world." That's an amazing way to approach being a librarian, and I think that if we substitute "author" for librarian, it's rather profound. Are authors and librarians out to do the same thing?

I think they're on parallel missions. We're there to help them become healthy, happy, world-wise, self-sufficient adults.

When I talk with YA authors, they always talk about reaching teens. Helping them succeed and survive by finding stories about themselves is always central to their mission, no matter what they write, whether it's realistic fiction, horror, nonfiction... anything.

Librarians are more like the lamplighters who help show the way. We help teens find the stories they need in those books (and other resources). We build relationships with teens in our libraries so they trust us to know that we're giving them something that is right and good for them. But we're also about more than books.

You don't seem to see or be limited by boundaries: TV, videogames, music, movies, books, even prom—they all feed into the lives of teens and you've made the library a hub for all of it. Is there a lesson for authors in that?

I think the key is finding teens where they are, and then working back from there. That's not saying that authors should think about writing books about video games, but rather think about the context and the format of a game... How can that carry over into the book world? How can you make it interactive? Competitive, even?

In terms of listening to teens, what are they telling you they want from a YA novel?

They want it to be about themselves, or about their friends (in terms of age, sex, ethnicity). That is they want to see themselves in the eyes of the characters. They want the book to be full of action, romance and mystery. They want to read about things that affect them in their everyday lives, but they also want to escape. They're always looking for the ring of truth in novels, and are always asking if fictional stories are real.

They're looking for a book they can read quickly, or they're looking for a deliciously long work that seems to end all too quickly.

What are the ways authors can treat teens with respect?

They can tell the truth in the books they write and talk honestly and openly about the issues that teens are facing. Talking down to teens in a book is always a bad move, so they should try to avoid that.

I think they can also seek out stories that teens are looking for, especially those whose stories don't often get told.

They can also respect the way teens speak and behave. Too often in their work writers try too hard to mimic trendy language that may be outside their realm of understanding. In other words, if an author doesn't know what street means, they're probably not going to be able to write about it.

Some YA librarians told me that even one use of the f-word made it very difficult for them to buy a book for their collection. What would you tell authors about balancing being "real" about teens' lives with trying to get their books into teens' hands?

I don't necessarily think authors have to drop the f-bomb to come across as real. There are lots of great YA books out there that avoid it really well. I think understanding the language of teenspeak and grasping its nuances and flow is much more important in the long run. Then, if you can drop a well-timed f-bomb in there, you'll get a lot more respect from the teen readers. That said, f-bombs don't have to be blatant, and they can be interpreted in a thematic sense rather than in the literal sense.

The comedian Jackie Mason has a schtick about how every movie has a sex scene, and the excuse Hollywood uses is that everyone has sex. He argues that everyone eats soup, too, so where are all the soup-eating scenes in Hollywood blockbusters? What's your advice for authors on including sex in stories for teens?

That's tricky. It depends on the audience, the author's voice, and the situation in the book itself. I don't want to misquote too much, but I once heard Cecily von Ziegesar (the author of the Gossip Girl books) say something along the lines of giving teens enough to think about, but not enough to gross them out.

I think authors have to think about how would this/that character describe what's happening to him/her, and take it from there. Some will probably recount stuff a lot more intensely than others, and that's where authors and editors will have to come together to make the right decisions.

David Levithan, in his introduction to your how-to-do-it manual, wrote that "the right book at the right time can make such a difference. Books do not create identities, but they can affirm identities." He was speaking about LGBTQ teens reading books with LGBTQ characters and content, but do you see that across the board? Are big teens drawn to K.L. Going's *Fat Kid Rules the World* as much as gay teens are to Levithan's *Boy Meets Boy*? Are teens always going to pick up the book with someone who looks like them on the cover?

Teens are definitely drawn in by book covers...that's a fact across the board.

And LGBTQ teens are definitely drawn towards books about themselves.

Books about big kids? Probably so. I've met lots of girls who talk very deeply about the main character in Carolyn Mackler's *The Earth, My Butt and Other Big Round Things*. Ditto for lots of other books with big kids in them.

Funny, not so much about *Fat Kid Rules the World*, though. That book tends to draw more music fans than anything.

How do we encourage teens to read beyond the reflection of their own identities?

Reflecting their identities is only a starting point. Once librarians can prove to teens that they understand who they are and where they're coming from (by showing them the books that reflect who they are at that given time), then teens will eventually be much more open to exploring the world beyond their comfort zone. That said, many teens are at many different stages of this equation. Some are already comfortable outside of their world. Others need more guidance.

In your book you present 18 Successful LGBTQ Programs for Librarians to put on in their libraries. One of the most surprising ideas to me was the "Living Library" program—where visitors to the library get to check out an actual LGBTQ person for a 45 minute conversation. On paper it seems to be saying two things: 1) that everybody has a story to tell, and 2) we need to get past our fear of "other" people—and the way to do that is to hear their stories. How does this program play out in reality?

This idea was inspired from a story about a library in Sweden who had actually tried this, and it worked! Obviously the LGBTQ person being "checked out" would need to be a good moderator with excellent communication skills and a very thick skin. I see this as an extension of a discussion/life skills-based workshop where teens are engaged by a presenter and are invited into a conversation. The "check-out" session does raise the level of anonymity for the audience, and participants might be more comfortable to ask the questions they need to ask instead of when they're in a group.

You've created some amazing programs with video games, encouraging teens to come into the library and kick some serious virtual butt. The New York Times reported in an October 2008 article that in six months the New York Public Library "hosted more than 500 events, drawing nearly 8,300 teenagers." Do you see a progression with actual teens, or is it just a theory, that they'll go from playing video games, to reading graphic novels, to reading novels? And is that the goal?

There are several forces at play when it comes to gaming at the library:

1. Gaming brings new audiences into the library. It brings kids who are gamers and kids who might never have thought to set foot in a library before by reinvigorating the perception of the library inside the youths' minds.
2. We have documented that gaming in the library does introduce new audiences to the other materials in the library. Teens have told us that they now prioritize their homework and research first so they'll have plenty of time to game with their friends in the library. Also, we've heard from teens that when they're waiting for the gaming event to begin, that they do pick up a book, or magazine or another library material.
3. There's the whole notion that gaming itself is literacy. Games are puzzle and strategy-based. They often require the player to learn a new language or the history behind a character. Many are story-driven. Many are education... It's all about the blending of formal and informal learning processes. We're actually in the midst of developing Serious Video Game design workshops, where teens work collaboratively to create a game based on real issues that are affecting the world such as media consolidation, drug trafficking, genocide, global warming, and more. We piloted this project last spring and are aiming for a second iteration starting in February 2010.

"Everybody" says that boys don't read as they become teenagers. It's a belief that has skewed book marketing and cover design, and often has

authors feeling they can't write the "boy" book they really have inside them. Is "everybody" wrong on this?

Interesting. I think that boys do read; I just think they probably don't read the majority of what's being published and promoted these days, such as chick lit, girly vampire novels, etc. Whenever I go to a publisher presentation, usually more than half of the titles are geared towards 14- to 15-year-old white girls. I remember thumbing through a publisher's catalogue thinking to myself, "another book about a white girl," over and over again.

I think this is definitely a marketing issue, and we as librarians work hard to help boy readers move past their initial impressions of books and reading. One way we do this is through book-talking titles that we think have crossover appeal to both boys and girls. I've hand-sold many titles with girls on the cover and girl main characters to boys. It's often not easy, but I've seen it work.

Maybe publishers could push harder to find more titles not just for boys, but for other non-white girl readers as well. For NYC, we are always looking for titles that will appeal to the kids in our neighborhoods, and it's not always easy.

Madeline L'Engel had this great quote: "You have to write the book that wants to be written. And if the book will be too difficult for grown-ups, then you write it for children." Do you see that in books for teens today?

With titles like *The Book Thief; Living Dead Girl*; and *Under the Wolf, Under the Dog*, it's hard to say. These are tough, hard-hitting books published for teens that feel like adult books, so I'm not sure if the same equation applies. Instead, books like these blur the lines between teen and adult (you also find many more adults reading from the teen market too). I think publishers are picking up on this by giving new teen book covers a more adult look to reach both audiences.

With the future of publishing changing dramatically, with fewer editors at fewer major publishing houses, with e-books, and print on demand, and on-line offerings of entire works for free where do you see writing stories and books for teens going?

I definitely see lots of potential for authors to publish online, like Cory Doctorow. I also see explosions of fan-fiction happening on the blogs of upcoming teen writers who want to recreate their favorite stories. I also am intrigued by the 22nd Century notion of collaboration and the collaborate novel. There have been lots of them popping up in the past few years, and I expect to see more.

That said, I think the printed book still has lots of cred for teens. Many of them still see "reading" as something they do with paper rather than something online. And, most of those teens still prefer to read stories on paper. Maybe this is because they like to keep their different worlds separated, or maybe it's because they can't afford Kindles.

Is there an opportunity for new writers to "break in" by experimenting with the new technology, or do you have to be an established author like National Book Award Finalist Kathleen Duey (Skin Hunger) to get away with writing a novel on Twitter, like her remarkable *Russett*? (http://russet-one-wing. blogspot.com/)?

I wonder if there's a way for authors to experiment by engaging their teen readers in the

Interviews

writing process? This could definitely be done online with something social like Twitter or Facebook. Collaboration is huge with today's teens, and I think engaging them is a great way to get the word out.

I think there's lots of ground to break as well—in the more traditional sense—of finding stories that haven't yet been told, or told well. In my office we dream of a Girl Meets Girl lesbian love story for teens. And that's probably just the tip of the iceberg.

Laurent Linn

'Sharing the Responsibility of Storytelling'
in Your Art

by Lee Wind

L aurent Linn has designed costumes and sets for theater companies. He won an Emmy Award for his puppets and design work on Sesame Street. He is an illustrator, a book designer, and is currently Art Director for Simon and Schuster Books for Young Readers. He has designed books across genres, including picture books, poetry books, chapter books, and even young adult novels.

Check out his stylish and very cool website at www.laurentlinn.com

The Title of your workshop at a recent SCBWI conference was "The Real Deal About Visual Story Telling." It made me think about Alfred Hitchcock, who was famous for saying "Dialog should simply be a sound among other sounds, just something that comes out of the mouths of people whose eyes tell the story in visual terms." Do you think a kid, before they can read, should be able to "get" the story of a picture book without the words? Is that a kind of "test" that you put illustrations through?

We know that creating a picture book starts with the story and text, but it is the illustrations that bring the kids into the book. Meaning that, just as you say, children at this age aren't reading yet, so the art must truly tell the story. As anyone who has read a picture book aloud to a child knows, kids soak up the words told to them and remember them. But they will really pour over the art and interact with the characters and scenes visually—it's a unique experience that is their own. As an adult, when we read aloud the text, we put our own inflections and interpretations into the telling, so in essence we interpret the words for the child. But, in looking at the illustrations, kids are allowed to interpret the story they see unfiltered—getting to have their own "first read," arriving at their own conclusions.

Of course, we always try to NOT say in the art what is said in the text, and vice versa (why waste those few, precious words in the text to tell about something that is easily shown in the art?) But the art and words must always go together, sharing the responsibilities of storytelling.

LEE WIND is the author of the how-to e-book guide, *The Zen OfBlogging: 7 Steps On The Virtual Path To Real Success*. His award-winning blog, "I'm Here. I'm Queer. What the Hell do I Read?" covers GLBTQ Teen Books, Culture and Politics. He is currently working on both a YA and a MG novel. You can find out more about Lee, his e-book, and his blog at www.zenofblogging.com and www.leewind.org.

Laurent Linn says, "the art and words must always go together, sharing the responsibilities of storytelling."

The National Book Award Winner, "The Absolutely True Diary of a Part-Time Indian," by Sherman Alexie, is a book I first listened to on audio. When I mentioned to a friend that I loved hearing the author read it himself, she insisted I get a hard copy so I could see the illustrations. And she was right, they were amazing, and really did add a whole other dimension to the story and the character.

When you're looking at a Chapter Book, MG or YA manuscript, how do you make the decision about interior illustrations? Where they should be? How many? What goes into that process?

I'd say that the age of the intended reader determines how many illustrations in a novel, and what art style. As well as the story and type of book, of course. For chapter books, since the readers are just coming from knowing picture books and perhaps easy readers and are learning to read longer books, many illustrations are included, often one on each page. Then, as the readership gets older, you'd want fewer illustrations, like having one or two pages of art per chapter for older middle-grade. Teens are also reading books written for adults, so we design them to have the look and feel of adult books, but often with a design sensibility that reflects that age, and rarely with art in the interior pages.

Then the type of book determines a lot as well. Fantasy novels will often get a bit more art than contemporary, real-life novels (like chapter-opener art, for example.)

Often in picture books an illustrator will add a whole new story layer. I know you worked on *Chaucer's First Winter*, by Stephen Krensky, illustrated by Henry Cole, where there was a whole new visual storyline where the little bear cub Chaucer's parents, who he thinks are hibernating in the cave, appear in the background here and there to reassure the readers that Chaucer is being looked after.

How can an illustrator's portfolio give you the sense that they can do that—add that extra dimension, or that counterpoint, to the story?

One thing that is essential in art sample pieces is creating a moment in a story that pulls you in. While portraits and landscapes may help to show an artist's talents and skills, they're not the type of art we're looking for. We want to see real storytelling, with a clear emotion of the moment. What is the character feeling? And we want to wonder what will happen next.

As for how to show added layers of storytelling, often illustrating a scene from a well-known folktale or story can do that. It could show how an artist would interpret a text everyone knows, and offer an opportunity to add nuances that are not in the classic tale.

It seems that another side of an illustrator being a super-creative half of the picture book team is this fear that some writers have that their picture book manuscript, if purchased, will be taken by the illustrator and flung into a

different time frame than they envisioned. Or that their main characters, who they had thought of as human kids, will suddenly become hedgehogs who ride bicycles. Should writers really be afraid of that?

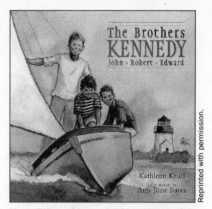

For the most part, it's usually very clear when a story takes place, or who the characters are. But, when a story is up to interpretation, those instances can occur. What writers should keep in mind is that a picture book truly is 50% the author's vision, and 50% the illustrator's. We get the best and most creative illustrators for each book, and we really do want their vision and imagination. And, overall, editors and art directors want a book to be the best it can be, and if characters are to become hedgehogs (for

Linn: "What writers should understand is that a picture book truly is 50% the author's vision, and 50% the illustrator's."

example), it would be discussed and determined that doing that would be the absolute best thing for the book.

Of course, authors feel ownership of the story (they did come up with the idea and write it, after all), and may have spent a lot of time visualizing it in the writing process. But picture books are truly a collaboration, and the illustrator's vision is equally as important. In most all instances, an illustrator will spend months and months of their life with a book, so they have ownership as well. And we on the publishing end spend many months collaborating on the book, too, so it's a group creation.

Laurent, you have a great sense of humor. Do you find that you're drawn to (pun intended) illustrators who show humor in their work? Can you explain how you think humor can come through via illustrations?

I'm glad you bring up humor, which is often such a huge part of picture books. As we know, kids are hysterical, and when they laugh, they *really* laugh! For those books that are appropriate for humor, it's essential that it's in the art. Often the humor will be in another "layer," like we were talking about. For example, in a book I recently worked on called *Christian, the Hugging Lion* (by Justin Richardson & Peter Parnell, illustrated by Amy June Bates), a lion cub is living with a family in an apartment. He grows so big they have to find another place for him to live, and the text says so in a very matter-of-fact way. But in the art, the illustrator added so many wonderful details (of a shredded couch, pawed pillows, scratched wall paper, terrified birds outside the window, bewildered humans . . . and a lion who's very satisfied with his handiwork!), that there's a great deal of humor to go back to again and again.

So, I'd say that for illustration art samples, if the subject has potential humor, crank it up! Adding the humor on varying levels will only add to the depth of a piece, as well as show that you can create art that will be worth going back to over and over.

How important is a website and/or blog for an illustrator's chances of getting hired?

Since websites have really replaced portfolios, I'd say having a website is essential if an illustrator is serious about getting work. It certainly doesn't have to be fancy, just

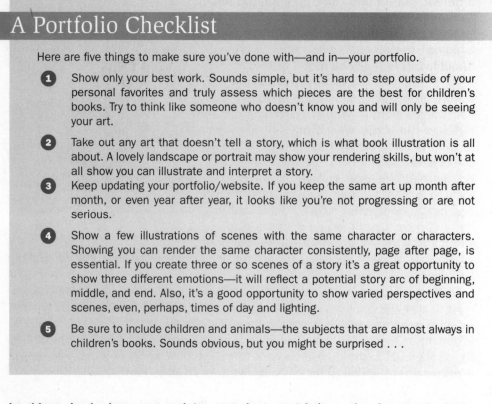

A Portfolio Checklist

Here are five things to make sure you've done with—and in—your portfolio.

1 Show only your best work. Sounds simple, but it's hard to step outside of your personal favorites and truly assess which pieces are the best for children's books. Try to think like someone who doesn't know you and will only be seeing your art.

2 Take out any art that doesn't tell a story, which is what book illustration is all about. A lovely landscape or portrait may show your rendering skills, but won't at all show you can illustrate and interpret a story.

3 Keep updating your portfolio/website. If you keep the same art up month after month, or even year after year, it looks like you're not progressing or are not serious.

4 Show a few illustrations of scenes with the same character or characters. Showing you can render the same character consistently, page after page, is essential. If you create three or so scenes of a story it's a great opportunity to show three different emotions—it will reflect a potential story arc of beginning, middle, and end. Also, it's a good opportunity to show varied perspectives and scenes, even, perhaps, times of day and lighting.

5 Be sure to include children and animals—the subjects that are almost always in children's books. Sounds obvious, but you might be surprised . . .

be able to clearly show your work in a way that's straightforward and easy to navigate. Since most illustrators have websites now (or have their work on a group website), an artist not having their work online is at a disadvantage.

As for blogging, since the art really should speak for itself, blogs aren't as important for illustrators in getting hired. Of course, that doesn't mean one shouldn't do it! It can be an essential tool to reach fellow illustrators, one's book readers, teachers, etc. It's just that when I'm specifically looking at illustration, I rarely read someone's blog. But, if it's an artist whose illustrations I like, I will scroll down and look at what art they have on their blog that may not be on their website.

Do you like seeing (and would you advise artists to share online) the evolution of a work of art (i.e., showing thumbnails and rough sketches) or do you think artists should only show their finished, most polished pieces?

For the most part, seeing finished pieces is most important. But I (and I believe other art directors) like to see how an illustrator thinks. So showing the sketch process for a particularly interesting piece can be good to do. Also, a few character development sketches can be good to show the creative process as well. But just a few. Or, if an artist wants to show a lot of sketches, she could simply have a separate gallery section for sketches, which is great.

What about the balance in a portfolio between consistency (so you know they could do an entire book in the same style) and variety (showing you that

they have more than one "look" they can achieve?)

No matter in what style, showing that you can illustrate characters consistently is very important. Then, if an artist does have more than one style, it's fine to show that as well. I'd just group all the art in one style together, then group the pieces of a second style together, etc. If it's made clear that the illustrator is intentionally showing art in varied styles, it won't look jumbled and will look more professional.

Scott M. Fischer

Laurent Linn advises illustrators, "Don't work in a vacuum."

On that idea of more than one look, can illustrators genre-hop? Or is a picture book illustrator always a picture book illustrator, and not really considered for a MG or YA book?

If an illustrator is good at creating art for various readers/ages, then by all means, create art! Many picture book illustrators not only have older middle-grade and teen styles, but also do art for adult editorial work, like magazines and newspapers, etc. If an artist is good at more than picture book illustration styles, then absolutely show it. Just be sure to group and name the separate galleries on a website so the styles don't mix. That includes black and white illustration as well, which is used frequently in middle-grade novels.

We hear all the time that picture book writers should let the editor and art director choose the illustrator for their project (unless they're a writer/ illustrator.) But I've also heard that graphic novel writers can team up independently with graphic novel illustrators and then approach publishers as a team. Are graphic novels still the Wild West, where the only rule that applies is that it works?

I think graphic novels are not as much the Wild West as they are just a different species. The text and art are so intertwined, so it really is a unique type of book. Most publishers that do graphic novels have a separate imprint that puts out only graphic novels, so that the editors and art directors in those imprints work exclusively on this book format. So sometimes there are different rules, and different publishers have different guidelines. Unfortunately, it seems there's not one rule that applies to all!

As an artist, what's the best piece of advice you've ever gotten?

You know, surprisingly, no one has ever asked me this. You're making me think! Which is great. I feel I'm always learning with every new experience, which is so essential for all of us, isn't it? But, to your question . . . I had a phenomenal college art professor, Dr. Larry Bakke, who really helped me understand new ways to see the world as an artist. One thing he taught me in particular, which I'd say is the best piece of advice I've had as an artist, is to truly be specific in your art—to truly *see* the world, even if it's a world of your own imagining.

Interviews

How an Illustrator's Portfolio is Judged

Here are a few things art directors, editors, and judges consider when reviewing a portfolio:

1 **Consistency of quality.** One or two stellar pieces are wonderful, but if the entire portfolio doesn't stand up to the best pieces then it reflects on the portfolio as a whole.

2 **Order of art.** Start with a bang and go from there—think of the flow of your portfolio as you would the flow of a book, with one piece logically leading to the next. Also, if you have more than one style or technique, group them together in sections so the varied styles don't look jumbled.

3 **Si mplify, simplify, simplify.** Don't put in too many pieces—you don't want each illustration getting lost. There's no magic number, but roughly between 10-20 illustrations is a good balance. During a judging session, time is limited, and you don't want a judge to lose interest because there are simply too many pages to turn in the time allotted.

4 **No bells and whistles.** While mounting each piece on separate boards may look lovely, for example, it's not practical for quickly looking at the art. A standard portfolio with clear-sleeved pages that are easy to flip through is best. Your art should stand out, not the fashion you've presented it in.

5 **Each piece should be appropriate.** Avoid including any art that isn't right for children's or teen books. Even one piece that is too adult, or graphic, or unrelated to children's literature, etc., could throw off how the entire portfolio is viewed.

One day, he gave us a pop quiz: to draw a tree. Well, we laughed and everyone drew a tree. Without even looking at our sketches, he gave us all an F. It took a while for my mind to wrap around this idea, but basically he explained that there's no such thing as "a tree." There's that tall maple tree that was outside your childhood bedroom that used to scare you when it scraped on your window, or that bare poplar tree you pass on your way to work that looks so old and serene, or that little pine tree that bends away from the road near the highway like it's longing for a forest, etc. In other words, everything you draw, whether real or imagined, should be a specific thing. If not, you're not illustrating the truth . . . your truth.

This applies to children's illustration in every way. So often I see art samples where an illustrator has drawn children in "clothes," like generic jeans and a t-shirt. That doesn't show us much about this character, does it? Just like the specifics of a tree show not only what kind of tree it is, but let us know so much more, like where we are, the emotional setting and tone, as well as how that particular artist interprets the world. As an illustrator, you're set designer and costume designer, so use those roles to let us know specifically who your character is before we even turn to the second page. It will enrich the story, the art, and the reader's experience—as well as help make you stand apart as an artist.

I think that applies to writers as well—there really shouldn't be any generic trees! Now, as an art director, what advice would you like to share with aspiring illustrators?

First, don't work in a vacuum. Meaning, take art classes if you like, and/or find fellow illustrators and share your work and join or create a critique group (I'm currently in two myself, and have been for years.) This can be in person or online. Publishing is very collaborative, and you need to be open to other opinions and, in fact, welcome them if they can help you improve and see your art in a new way.

Second, draw draw draw! The only way to improve is to keep drawing and learning. One idea is to create one new promotional piece a month (or every two months, or whatever time frame works for you.) Not only could it help you learn a lot and improve, but it would enable you to constantly update your website (or portfolio), frequently showing new work, which is important.

First Books

Novels—Past, Present & Future

by Alice Pope

There's something particularly amazing about debut novels that I often feel is not repeated in subsequent works. Not that those later books aren't wonderful in their own right, but, like a first album, first books have a certain indescribable special quality, a freshness of sorts (even if the author had several unsuccessful draft in the proverbial drawer).

The three first books featured here have that quality, although they are, of course, different from one another. Angie Frazier's *Everlasting* is set in the past. Blythe Woolston's *The Freak Observer* is contemporary. Joelle Anthony's *Restoring Harmony* takes place in a not-so-distant future. Each has a teenage girl main character making her way through the world and somehow finding herself. They all reflect the diversity that is YA. And I couldn't put any of them down once I started reading. Here are their stories.

Blythe Woolston
The Freak Observer (Carolrhoda Lab)
blythewoolston.blogspot.com

Before she found her main character Loa, before *The Freak Observer* had a name, says Blythe Woolston, "I had a working title: *Not Bestiality*.

"I can't remember if it was Amalia Elison or Alexandra Penfold who said it, but it was at SCBWI Big Sky in 2007. Someone asked, 'What is YA?' and one of them, or both of them—they were riffing on each other like jazz musicians—said, 'It's not bestiality.' That just clicked with me. I had my limits; I could play with the variables, all of the variables, within those limits. What can I say? It worked for me."

This one phrase that changed Woolston's writing life, drove home for her the fact that "good YA isn't 'edgy' for the sake of being titillating or peeing in somebody's cornflakes. It's edgy because is about real people, real young adults, who are testing the boundaries and making choices. When I see discussions about whether a scene can be set in a bathroom or if a subject is 'inappropriate,' I think of that."

ALICE POPE is the editor of *Children's Writer's & Illustrator's Market.*

Having this clearer sense of what young adult literature is was helpful to Woolston as she forged ahead on more than one work in progress—including *The Freak Observer*—after hearing from more than one reader—including an agent—that her work wasn't YA. "I think YA has an ancestor, *Bildungsroman*, which I choose to define as the story of self-cultivation," she says. "YA is the story of building ourselves from the inside out, about finding an individual identity. YA can appear in different modes—dystopian sci-fi, realistic, high fantasy—but it is that essential struggle to know the self that makes YA. The process can sometimes be brutal. It is always a venture into uncharted territory. It is the defining experience that we carry within us forever after."

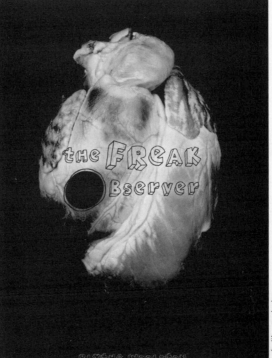

Blythe Woolston's debut novel *The Freak Observer* was inspired by something overheard at SCBWI Big Sky.

These standards hold true in Woolston's debut novel *The Freak Observer* as her main character Loa gives readers a first-person perspective as she copes with tragedies, endures regular hallucinations, and discovers herself.

"An early reader thought there were too many problems loaded on Loa. I felt that, if anything, I had already streamlined the complications," says Woolston. "Problems don't queue up in an orderly line and wait their turn. Problems spawn problems, they mutate, and they grow. Denying that pretty much denies reality—at least as I know it."

Woolston says she had confidence in Loa's resilience, ingenuity, and gumption. "But I still cried while I wrote. That wasn't much of a comfort to her...but, if I'd interceded like a fairy godmother and un-kinked her life, I don't think I would have been doing her or her story justice."

The story in the *The Freak Observer* is interspersed with theoretical physics. Unusual in YA, yes—but Woolston simply finds physics fascinating. "Physics is the rules of operation for the real world. Physics is also a field where original thinking—imagination and creativity—is essential. And have you seen the Hubble pictures? Physics is beautiful, absolutely beautiful.

"Freak observers—also known as Boltzmann's brains—are hypothetical conscious beings," explains Woolston. "Ludwig Boltzmann, the freak observers' namesake, was a physicist who wondered (as everyone probably does) why time seems to move only in one direction. He also wondered why the universe seems to naturally become more chaotic. As part of that thinking, he suggested that there might be pockets of order in

Interviews

the chaos—and that sometimes fragmentary beings, like a naked brain floating in space, might emerge.

"I need to emphasize that physicists don't actually believe that this is how things work," she says. "The concept is a tool to help them think about the universe and infinite possibilities. In my book, Loa uses the idea of the freak observer in a similar way to help her think about and deal with the apparent chaos of her life."

Woolston fell in love with physics (and a lot of other subjects) in high school, thanks to "brilliant, excited, passionate teachers," she says. "For me, for Loa, for a lot of people I think, high school is not just a flat backdrop for social dramas or an irritating interlude before real life gets started. It's an incredibly rich environment where ideas matter and experiences happen."

To help make her writing life happen, Woolston participated in SCBWI events. "I live in Montana. On one hand there is a literary tradition here that is pure genius. On the other hand there is the simple fact that living here is not like being in New York or San Francisco or Bologna," she says. "If you say you want to write, people give you a sort of alrighty-then-pull-up-your-socks-and-get-on-with-it-but-don't-forget-to-milk-the-cow look."

Woolston doesn't belong to a critique group. Instead, she says, the SCBWI Big Sky is her critique group. "There are writers in my community, my husband is a science and travel writer, but I am not a member of a regular YA crit group. You need to have critical mass for that. It's an annual rendezvous and Maker Faire," she says. "I heard Linda Sue Park talk about writing at SCWBI Big Sky. I learned about how editorial meetings happen while I was soaking in a hot spring under shooting stars. I have to give credit to Michele Corriel, another 2010 debut author, for being able to put those experiences together for me."

When Woolston began working on getting published, she started by querying five agents. Querying, she says, is a learning process. "I'm the sort of person who likes to have information so those stats and tips and other resources helped me form realistic expectations and think about how to proceed. Some authors cast a wide net, but I decided on a trout fishing model. One of my problems was that my book is a little weird; I had to try to figure out where to cast. Googling 'YA agent seeking physics,' is less productive than Googling 'chiffon wombat.' I did watch for clues like 'quirky' or other words that might mean the agent was open to the peculiar. I had a couple of nibbles… that was encouraging."

According to Woolston, each rejection she received had its value. "A couple came back within minutes, snappy fast. OK. No reason for sorrow, just get on with new submissions equally fast. Each one helped me rethink what I was offering, so when I saw the call for small books 'filled with such raw emotion that going beyond 35,000 words would be considered hazardous to the reader's health' I thought, 'My little book is like that.' I sent it off. Then I got on with my work as an indexer and spent time with my interesting companions in an interesting world," she says. "Months later, Andrew Karre called me and asked if my book was still available, and then my life got interesting in a whole new direction."

Woolston says she waited about a month between the first indication of interest and the call where she learned that her book had survived acquisitions. "It's a good thing I have interesting work and live with interesting people; without those distractions my brain would have just crawled out my ears and hid under the bed. Andrew had been encouraging, and I knew he was the perfect champion for my book, but I also knew that this was huge event. The acquisition meeting is when people say, 'This book is worth it.' Imagine that. When I heard, I was reduced to a blithering idiot. Andrew will confirm that. He is very patient with blithering idiots."

So Woolston signed with Andrew Karre, and *The Freak Observer* is one of the first three books from Carolrhoda Lab, Carolrhoda's new imprint just for YA. "I still don't have an agent. I do think of it sometimes, but I haven't been pursuing it. Clearly there can be advantages to having an agent; an agent opens up different opportunities and can be a real ally. Right now, my focus is on getting *The Freak Observer* launched and writing my next book. (I'm writing another YA. It's a halieutic novel—a book about fishing. I'm not certain if there are already YA novels about trout, but it's the book that's fun to make right now. Maybe trout are the new vampires—or the new zombie chickens.)"

As far as her unagented relationship with Carolrhoda and Andrew Karre, Woolston says, "I put my trust there and it was rewarded. I wanted to know that my work would be made into a well-bound, beautiful book that could wait on library shelves until someone needed to read it. I wanted to know that it might also become a digital book, easy to get and easy to read. Everything that has happened so far has been evidence that my desires are respected."

As a freelancer, Woolston had worked with editors before, "and they had always made the work better," she says. "As result, I tend to be optimistic about the results of collaboration. What happened working with Andrew blew me out of the water.

"First of all, there is a difference between technical or purely professional writing to convey information, and a novel. Part of that difference is emotional, but another part is the realm of possibilities. The editorial guidance I received was remarkable. It was like a gesture that called my attention to something hovering just below the surface—all I had to do was lift it up. It was a revelation.

"I work as an academic indexer so I spend my time reading complicated texts—seeing through them to the bones, the essential structure. I needed to learn how to do that with my own fiction. Then I needed revise, to mend the broken bones and reroute the nerves to make my book stronger and smarter. Andrew showed me how to do that."

What's it like being in the freshman class of a brand new imprint? "I didn't really understand the magnitude of this until I found out about the other books and their authors: Ilsa Bick's *Draw the Dark*, Steve Brezenoff's | -1 |, and Gudrun Pausewang's *Traitor*. There is a synergy in the collection that Andrew put together," she says. "He made my little book part of a constellation. I feel a great responsibility to hold up my corner of the sky."

When is comes to promoting her debut novel, Woolston says, "I'm lucky I have Carolrhoda on my side, because I had no idea how to build an online presence and they take that very seriously. They are wonderfully supportive. I have autonomy and creative control, but they nudge me in the direction of new opportunities. I learned a lot by watching what other authors were doing—and by reading Andrew's blog. In the past six months, I've built a website, created a book trailer, and have even had comments on some of my blog posts. It is actually a pleasure, and that is a surprise to me."

She says she's thinking about ways to make her book a richer experience for her readers. "That's the whole reason for the online presence. So I'm creating links to Loa's world. I want the readers to be able to find the books she found in the library. I want them to see the images she witnessed. And since postcards are such an important part of Loa's world, I also hope to create or share a Mail Art experience with the readers. For me, it's a new dimension of the narrative. I hope it will become that for the readers as well."

For others writing YA, Woolston says, "Writing is the best part. Really, it is. If you can love writing for the experience, then the book will be worth it. I can easily imagine another me out there in the multiverse, one who didn't see the call for 'small books' and never sent *The Freak Observer* in response. I can't imagine that I would have stopped writing books, though, because I love it. I love it as much as I love reading. So just write that book. (It's good advice. I intend to follow it myself.)"

Angie Frazier
Everlasting (Scholastic)
www.angiefrazier.com

"I'm definitely a 'slow and steady wins the race' type of writer," says Angie Frazier. "From elementary school through college I dreamed about being an author. After graduating with a degree in journalism, I decided just to dream about it wasn't good enough. I needed to make it a reality. So I started writing at night and on weekends while I worked full time as an editorial assistant at a regional New England magazine. Since this was during the pre-motherhood years, I managed to pull all-nighters writing. It was in that first year out of college that I wrote the first version of what is now *Everlasting*."

It took Frazier about four months to complete her first manuscript, and after a quick revision, she sent it out to dozens of agents. "When the only agent who asked for a partial bluntly replied, 'I don't like your style of writing *at all*,' I decided to shelve the manuscript and work on other things. I didn't know what craft was at that point, but I knew I needed to improve—drastically. I wrote a handful of other manuscripts, but I kept coming back to *Everlasting* and revising it. I couldn't give up on it, or the possibility of what it could be."

Fast forwarding six years, Frazier was freelancing and staying home with children as she continued to write and query. "The rejections streamed in, but I was blind to them. I told myself I was either an optimist or delusional to keep trying for so long! But at last I had a revelation about the shelved draft of *Everlasting*, totally rewrote it, and sent that new version out to agents. Fulls or partials were being requested by nearly every agent I queried and I knew I had finally found the right story for my cast of characters."

One of the agents who requested her full manuscript was Ted Malawer of Upstart Crow Literary (upstartcrowliterary.com), who was a junior agent at the time and building his client list. "He wrote back saying how much he loved my manuscript, and that he wanted to do a revision," says Frazier. "If we worked well together, he wanted to represent me. The revision lasted all summer, but in the fall of 2007 he did sign me as a client, and then in early 2008, eight years after I wrote that first draft, *Everlasting* went to auction."

Frazier says finding an agent, someone who believed in her and in her writing, was the best moment of her writing career so far. "Ted 'got' my story, he loved my characters as much I did, and he worked tirelessly with me to make the book everything it could be."

What Malawer no doubt appreciated in Frazier's writing is a plucky main character Camille (likable from the first page) and her love interest/ partner in adventure Oscar (who's brave and complicated and pretty darn dreamy) along with some terrific secondary characters, a romp of a plot set in 19th century San Francisco, Australia, and a merchant ship, with just a touch of magic in the mix.

"Camille was the toughest character for me to write," says Frazier. "I knew her perfectly in my mind, but getting her out onto paper was a challenge. All I can say is that developing my characters took a long time. I have a process that might sound a bit odd, but it worked for me. What I did was take Oscar and Camille and imagine them in entirely different situations from the one in *Everlasting*. I wouldn't write these 'stories' down, but just kept them running in my head, thinking them out chapter by chapter until the final scene. At the end of each of these imagined stories I would feel like I knew Camille and Oscar a little bit better. These episodic stories helped me write their characters. And for me, Camille and Oscar live on outside the real book. *Everlasting* is just one of their stories."

The original draft of Angie Frazier's debut novel *Everlasting* was written in four months, but it took six years of rejections before she had a breakthrough in her revisions that led to publication.

Despite being so close to her main character, Frazier made Camille endure some harrowing situations, constantly raising the stakes for her. "As much as I adore Camille, it wasn't difficult for me to be hard on her. Tough love was really the only way for me to be certain that she was growing as the story progressed," she says. "Forcing her to deal with heartache, with hatred, and with failure shaped her character as much as allowing her the comforts and victories she experiences in the novel. I absolutely wanted her to have a happy ending, but it wouldn't feel genuine if it came without a price. I hope by being tough on Camille I've revealed her as strong and capable, yet also vulnerable and real."

And just as Camille often dealt with the unexpected, Frazier encountered some surprises throughout her publishing process—but they were positive surprises. "The biggest surprise has been finding out just how slow the process is," she says. "I assumed my revision letter would zing into my mailbox within a few weeks after signing the contract. In the end it took a full year! I wouldn't say it was a bad surprise though. As frustrating as it was to be put on hold for so long, it gave me plenty of time to get the second *Everlasting* book (releasing in June 2011) finished and revised. I also had enough time to get used to the idea of being published, to let the excitement mellow, and to read up on other authors and how they worked with their editors."

Another surprise, she says, was how much fun the revising and copyediting stages were. "I've been told by a few other authors that I'm clearly insane to have loved revisions and copyedits! But revision has always been my favorite part of the writing process, and I had such a blast working with my editor, Jennifer Rees. I was in constant awe of her insight and ideas, and I couldn't wait to work everything she suggested into the story."

Frazier's book, set in the 1850s, is rife with historical detail—clothing, ships, towns small and large. Historical research, she says, was one of the foundations of her novel and she spent years conducting it. "Every detail needed to be verified, from what kind of clock would have been in the foyer of Camille's San Francisco home, to the route her father's merchant ship would have taken across the Pacific, to what kind of trees and animals Camille might have encountered on her trek through the Victoria wilderness," Frazier says. "I also needed to figure out how Camille would have seen the world as a 17-year-old girl of her class in 1855 California. How would she have been raised? What would she value? What would her mannerisms most likely be? How would she interact with strangers, or even with people she cared for, like Oscar? All of those details are small, and yet make a huge difference in whether or not the story and the characters ring true."

Frazier says she tended to research as she wrote, both online and through books. "When I came upon a scene or a sentence that required research, I would stop and do it. I read nonfiction and fiction alike, gleaning what I could, double-checking facts, making notes on Post-its, and jotting things down in notebooks. Keeping a research notebook was one of the more organized things I did! I would also bookmark sites I visited online so I could go back to them time and again."

Everlasting is an action-packed adventure, but at its heart is romance. "I had a brief romance novel reading phase during high school," confesses Frazier, "but quickly abandoned it when every book started to blend together and feel the same. It was all so formulaic and I knew I didn't want to do that with my own writing."

So, she says, actually writing the romance between Oscar and Camille was extremely difficult. "I couldn't seem to get their love, respect, and attraction for one another out of my head and onto the page. I think I was afraid of turning my book into one of those formulaic romance novels. I wanted more for my book, and for the characters in it. My agent and I went back and forth for many rounds of revisions while we worked on drawing out the romance between Oscar and Camille. It was exhausting, and I had many moments when I wondered if I was at all capable of writing romance. But with each round of revision, Ted and I saw progress being made. And then, with my editor, I worked on building Oscar's character more, which in turn helped the romance between him and Camille. I'm really pleased with how things turned out, and now when I read a book that has a romantic storyline that I love, I pick it apart to try and learn from it."

When is comes to promoting her book, Frazier admits that the idea "strikes a little bit of fear into my heart, but Scholastic has a great history of introducing new authors and their books so I'm confident that I'm in the best of hands." As for her own promotional efforts, she has a website and blog, for which she's planning some Australia-themed posts, and will be holding giveaways for signed copies of *Everlasting*, bookmarks, and other swag. "I'm looking forward to visiting lots of YA book review blogs to talk about my book, too."

And she's got lots on her plate for the future. "Next up is my first middle grade novel, *Suzanna Snow and the Mystery of the Midnight Tunnel*, releasing Spring 2011. Suzanna's debut story (a second Suzanna Snow book is forthcoming in 2012) is a coming-of-age mystery set against the disappearance of a young girl at a grand hotel in 1905 New Brunswick, Canada. Then in the summer of 2011, the sequel to *Everlasting* will be published, which I'm already so excited for! Meanwhile, I'll be working on a handful of other YA and MG projects that are all vying for my attention."

For first-time novel writers Frazier advises, "Please don't do what I did in the beginning, which was write a first draft, spell check and revise lightly, and then send out a mass mailing of untargeted queries. Have someone you trust and respect as a writer read and critique your work. Join an online or in-person writing group, take a workshop, and attend conferences. Concentrate on the craft first, and that includes reading scores of books in the genre you're writing. This all takes time and patience. And when your manuscript is finally ready to submit, research which editors or agents to query. Targeted queries bring better results. Lastly, don't give up, even when the rejections seem endless. It sounds cliché but it really does only take that one 'yes.' And trust me, it is well worth the patience and persistence!"

Joelle Anthony
Restoring Harmony (Putnam)
http://joelleanthony.com

"May I use all the clichés?" asks Joelle Anthony when asked about her path to publication. "It was a rough road, a long haul, a tough row to hoe... I started pursuing writing when I was 22. My first published novel will be released a couple of weeks after I turn 42. There are reasons it took me so long," she says. "One is that I tend to do things on my own. Essentially, I taught myself to write (as opposed to taking classes or reading many books on craft). This can really slow a person down, and I don't necessarily recommend it! On the plus side, it allows me to absorb

It took Joelle Anthony 20 years to publish her debut novel *Restoring Harmony*.

Reprinted with permission.

things and process them too. Another reason is because I always had to have a day job, and it wasn't until my husband made it financially possible for me to commit to being a writer and stay home that I made real progress. Some people are good at catching snatches of writing time, but I need hours in big chunks. That happened six years ago and I really mark that as the beginning of taking it seriously."

Anthony's debut *Restoring Harmony* was not the first novel she submitted. "I'd had some interest from an editor on a young adult novel (now hidden in the proverbial drawer) and she suggested I look for an agent, so that's what got me started querying," she says. "My agent search was so crazy it's hard to contain it to a few sentences. Let me put it this way: I sent out more than 40 queries over a year and a half, had around 10 requests for partials and fulls, wrote two more novels (one of which was *Restoring Harmony*), started querying for both of the new manuscripts, got multiple offers, and found out Michael could tell the future."

The "Michael" she refers to is her agent Michael Bourret of Dystel & Goderich Literary Management. "At the time of my multiple agent offers, Michael passed, but he said to me, 'If you're ever looking for an agent again, feel free to contact me.' To be honest, I

RESTORING HARMONY

JOËLLE ANTHONY

Reprinted with permission.

Restoring Harmony is a journey story set in a dystopian not-so-distant future.

thought he was crazy because I was planning to sign with my choice for life! But seven months later I'd left my agent (just not a good match—she has clients very happy with her), revised *Restoring Harmony,* and queried him again, reminding him of his prophecy," she says. "This time, after reading the revision, he offered to rep me. He recently told me that he finds it odd he made the offer to me to get in touch again because he never tells people that, although he remembers doing it. We were obviously meant to be!"

Anthony originally found Bourret on his agency's website (www.dystel.com). "He looked so cheerful and happy in his picture," she says, "but the real reason I queried him was because I did a little research and discovered he'd sold books to a house where I thought I would fit in well. I noted that in my query."

Restoring Harmony is a journey story set in a dystopian not-so-distant future, centering on Molly, her fiddle, and her difficult quest to help her family. Anthony thinks it's more interesting "to have people who remember what life is like now and struggle with the changes to contrast with someone who has practically grown up with that way of life, like Molly. That's why I set it only 30 years in the future, instead of say, a hundred."

Anthony says the setting for her book was sparked by that fact that "many people are predicting the end of oil and a collapse of life as we know it. While I'm not saying that I'm onboard for all of these predictions, I do find them both intriguing and possible. This 'after-oil' time period drew me in as a perfectly scary and exciting setting for a book, and I couldn't resist. However, the more I thought about the actual story, the clearer it became to me that this world would have to be the *setting*. That's why the book takes place ten years after the fictional Collapse instead of during it, or because of it. I didn't want the actual Collapse to get muddled up with Molly's story."

Anthony enjoyed the editorial phase for her *Restoring Harmony.* "I love edits. I love to revise. It's my favorite part of writing," she says. "Getting the words down the first time is so hard, but editing is just a great joy. Like Michael, my editor Stacey Barney tends to take the approach of asking questions as opposed to making suggestions. Sometimes they're very thoughtful questions, but often times they're simple ones like, 'Why?' or 'What does she think here?' I love questions and my imagination just takes off when she asks them."

She admits she didn't really know what to expect when it came to the editorial process. "I think the biggest surprise was the amount of work we had to do on *Restoring Harmony*. I was naïve in thinking that because a great agent had loved it, and a fabulous editor had bought it, it must mean it was pretty much ready to go!" she says. "The thing I didn't know at the time, but can see very clearly now, is that Stacey made a great leap of faith with a new writer. I had no idea how to shape or pace a novel and Stacey essentially walked me through it. I had a severe problem with repetition and ended up cutting over 150 of the 375 pages. I also wrote about 50 new ones to take their place.

"I was pretty clueless and I think in part it's because what happens after you get an agent is just not on the web that much. I know that part of it is a privacy thing, but I think it's a disservice to other writers to just sort of close up providing info after the agent is secured."

Luckily, she says, she knew a few experienced writers who she'd met online and they were there to answer her questions. "I could ask things like, 'How long does an agent generally take before reading a revision?' so I would know when it was OK to ask Michael and not be a pest. Or 'What do I do when they send me the copyedits?' It is surprising how things just arrive in your inbox or your mailbox without directions on how to do them. I guess editors are really busy and they forget that as new writers, we're usually winging it."

Anthony is in a critique group with two writers—one has an agent and one has not even started querying yet. "I share a lot of info with them about what happens along the way. I've told them things I wouldn't share with just anyone, like how much my publisher offered, and what I ended up with, how long it takes to get a contract, when you get paid, what happens after you sign, etc. I can't put that info on the web, but it would've been so great if I'd known what normal procedure was."

She says of her agent: "I can ask him anything, but I know a lot of people who have agents they love and respect, but don't talk to very often and would feel uncomfortable e-mailing every little question to. I've been trying to think how to make this info available to aspiring writers without disclosing private info and I can't see how to do it other than anonymously and with a bunch of other authors involved too. I don't really have time for that though."

Anthony has a background as and actor, something she feels absolutely affects her writing. "Voice has been my strength all along, and I'm certain that comes from my training as an actor and improviser," she says. "In my new book, my main character dreams of being an actress and so the theatre is an important part in the story. In Molly's book, she plays her fiddle fearlessly, and that comes from me being an actor. It never occurred to me to have her be inhibited about performing for a crowd because everyone I know is used to performing."

She says that there are similarities between acting and writing. "It goes beyond creating characters, although that is one element that comes to mind right away. You learn to play the love in scenes when you act, and that's an important element in writing novels too. Conflict comes from love, but it's easy to get carried away when writing and forget that and just write the conflict," she says. "If you just write the conflict, your story is flat and uninteresting. The other thing is, in every play or scene I've ever improvised, the character has to want something and needs to change by the end. Those are essential in writing as well. And then there are all the structural elements too, which I studied in college in regards to plays."

During the course of working on the manuscript for *Restoring Harmony*, Anthony met a teenage fiddle player names Sarah who is strikingly similar in looks and age to her character Molly, and who, she says, changed her life. Not only did Sarah serve as Anthony's technical advisor on fiddle playing, "she and her parents have started coming up to stay with us regularly, and are possibly even looking to move to our island. She and my husband have both recorded and performed together, and Sarah and are in touch several times a week," Anthony says.

"Professionally, getting *Restoring Harmony* published is the most exciting thing to happen to me so far, but personally, meeting Sarah and her family is the most important thing that has come out of this experience."

Anthony's second book *The Right & the Real* also offers readers a teen character who is thrust into a new world, learns to navigate it, and finds her inner hero. She's drawn to write about such journeys, she says, partly because "if I'm going to spend years with a character and story, then I want it to be exciting and interesting, and yes, even a bit scary at times. Also, I think we all have the ability to rise up and meet adversity, and a story like this may lend a bit of courage to a reader going through tough times. And if it doesn't do that, then perhaps it will offer distraction."

Anthony advises writers to read, read, read, but says "I'm of two minds about whether you should read your genre of interest or not. About five years ago, I found my writing had plateaued at good, but not good enough. I looked into masters programs, but realized not only did I not want to go to school, but I couldn't afford it anyway. While researching them though, someone told me that they read 150 books in their genre each year while doing the program at Vermont College. I decided I could do that on my own, and I set out to do it. It made all the difference in the world for my writing. Not only did I learn more about how a novel is put together, but I began to see what I liked, what I didn't, and why."

To those already querying agents or editors, she says, "Query widely and keep writing something new. I believe that comes from Miss Snark, although you'll find it all over the web. I've helped several writers, answered questions and read their queries and things while they try to find agents and the one thing I really seem to have trouble getting them to do is to keep querying once someone expresses interest. I know from experience that the interest can drag on for months and then just not pan out. You really have to keep querying or you'll be at it for years. You might be anyway," she says. "And you must keep writing and it needs to be something new. If I'd just waited around, or continued to polish the first book, I never would've written *Restoring Harmony*."

First Books

Picture Book Authors

by Alice Pope

The picture book is the most special of formats as the synergy of words and art create an experience that's generally shared by a child and a grown-up. Picture books are true collaborations between writers, illustrators, editors, art directors and designers, each handling their pieces, each adding their special touch.

But it all starts with the text. There are few words in a picture book, and each and every one is oh so important. And writing a good one is no easy task. The three debut authors featured here, Jean Reidy, Nancy Gow and Candace Ryan, were drawn to the task and pulled it offer wonderfully, the first two in rhyme and Ryan with wordplay. Here's a look at their paths to publication, their process, and their picture books.

Jean Reidy
Too Purpley! (Bloomsbury)
www.jeanreidy.com

Writers are often struck by inspiration at random times. For Jean Reidy, it happened on a road trip with her kids while listening to the book on tape of Sharon Creech's *Bloomability*. "I was completely enchanted with the voice of the novel, and that voice inspired me to write fiction," says Reidy. "So there on Interstate 80, I began to develop an idea for a middle grade novel. With scenes, dialog and narrative bubbling from my brain, I had my daughter jot down my dictated thoughts in the margins of a map."

Soon after, Reidy began to explore children's writing in earnest, enrolling in classes and attending conferences. And it was at a conference that the world of picture book writing opened up to her. "But I knew it wouldn't be easy," she says. "I was actually a bit intimidated by the thought of packing so much into so few words, and humbled by the many great picture books I love."

During that conference she took a workshop that required participants to write the opening pages of a picture book, an exercise she found "challenging yet really fun. I was hooked and took off on a whole new journey into picture book writing."

ALICE POPE is the editor of *Children's Writer's & Illustrator's Market*.

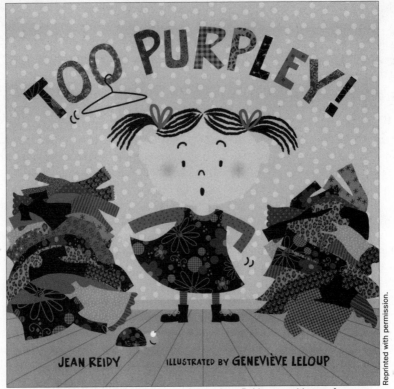

The world of picture book writing opened up to Jean Reidy at a writing conference.

Next she won a picture book manuscript contest at a writer's conference, and, Reidy says, she "made the mistake of thinking that very first picture book would be snapped up in a flash by an editor or agent. Silly me. That manuscript still sits in a file waiting to be reworked."

Putting the focus back on finishing her middle grade novel, Reidy then just "dabbled in picture books whenever an idea struck me" and she sent queries, pursuing editors and agents in tandem. "I knew that for picture books especially, finding an agent would be more difficult. So I submitted my middle grade novel to agents instead [and my picture book manuscripts to editors].

"Around the time that I wrote *Too Purpley!* I read in the Society of Children's Book Writers & Illustrators *Bulletin* that a veteran editor was moving to Bloomsbury and that her specialty was books for very young children. Bloomsbury was open to unagented submissions, so I sent her the manuscript, which her intern pulled from the slush pile. That intern is now an editorial assistant at another major house."

The Bloomsbury editor asked for companion manuscripts to go with *Too Purpley!* because the text was so slight, so Reidy wrote three additional books, one of which was *Too Pickley!* (a July 2010 release).

In *Too Purpley!*, a young main character is having wardrobe issues. Everything she tries on is just not right: "too purpley, too tickly, too puckery, too prickly." The idea for Reidy's book was apparently percolating in her subconscious writer's mind for years. "When my niece Sarah was a little girl (Sarah now has children of her own) she complained that every article of clothing in her closet was either too itchy or too prickly or too taggy," Reidy says. "Not being a mom at the time, I thought that was hilarious. Then I had my own kids, and they were tortured by too-tight turtlenecks and creepy jeans. Children of friends registered similar complaints, and it struck me how universal the theme was. Maybe the search for comfy clothes was as common as getting dressed."

As Reidy's debut picture book manuscript was on its way to acquisitions, agent Erin Murphy was in the process of reading her middle grade novel. "She was my dream agent and I knew she'd be a perfect fit for both picture books and novels," Reidy says. "Having significant editor interest in my books certainly enhanced the agent interest. So in May, I signed on with Erin and in June we signed the contract for *Too Purpley!* and *Too Pickley!* Erin has negotiated and sold all four of my books.

"As for a timeline, *Too Purpley!* was first submitted to Bloomsbury in September 2006 and I got the intern's e-mail in October. In May of 2007 I received sample illustrations."

Reidy's debut books, "*Too Purpley!* and *Too Pickley!* feature rhyming text and her third book, *My Own Little Piece of the Universe*, is a cumulative verse also in rhyme. "I feel that when rhyme is done well, it can facilitate a child's own ability to read and enjoy a book," she says.

"Before I use rhyme, I ask, 'Why does this story need to rhyme?,'" says Reidy. "I often read manuscripts that have fantastic premises but are restricted by the rhyme. Or they grow to be hundreds of words too long for the sake of the rhyme. I think rhyming writers need to honestly assess if the story is better because of the rhyme."

If you do decide to write in rhyme, Reidy advises lining up "loads of fresh readers for your story. And I'd have them read the text out loud, noting where the rhythm or rhyme trips them up. So often, rhythm perfects itself via repetitive reading. And as writers we can trick our own ears quite easily. But with fresh readers, you only get one chance.

"Your story needs to rhyme perfectly on the first read," says Reidly. Natural accents and beats must roll off the reader's tongue. Editor, Allyn Johnston calls the perfect picture book "a dance between text and illustrations." Your rhyme must essentially disappear in that dance and not call attention to itself. It's a bit like background music in that regard.

Bad rhyme, she says, jolts readers out of the story, "which more or less ties in to my best advice for picture book writers: Remember, research shows that the picture book experience is the magical interaction of the reader, the book and the child. Make sure your writing doesn't stand in the way of the magic."

Bloomsbury wisely paired Reidy's fun, rhyming text with the art of Geneviève Lebloup, who is also a textile designer, making for a picture book full of delicious colors and textures.

"The first illustration I saw for *Too Purpley!* was of my little main character in her underwear with her pet turtle. I loved them both," says Reidy. "There is a certain amount of trust that goes into being a picture book writer—allowing your editor and illustrator the freedom to follow their creative vision. I think the finished product shows that my trust was well-placed.

"I was simply amazed at the level of professionalism, thought and care that goes into each stage of publishing a picture book—from editors analyzing every word and punctuation mark in the text, to design directors studying minute details of an illustration, to marketing departments exploring appropriate pricing, promotion and placement," says Reidy. "The people working in this genre of the industry care intensely about children's literature."

Throughout her writing and submitting process, Reidy surrounded herself with writers who care intensely about creating children's books in the form of two critique groups and SCBWI.

"My two critique groups—one online and one face-to-face—are completely indispensable. They not only offer support and mentoring but they keep me laughing," she says. "I was invited to join my face-to-face group after a member read an essay of mine, and those writers have been by my side from freelancing through kid lit. I love the variety of work brought to the table and the camaraderie I've found in that group throughout this journey."

Reidy found her online group through Verla Kay's Blue Boards (at www.verlakay. com). "They focus on middle grade and young adult literature, but I'll send them my picture books every once in a while too. The members of both groups are exceptionally talented and each member brings unique input to their critiques."

As for SCBWI? "Oh my goodness, I could go on and on. Our local Rocky Mountain Chapter hosts the most fabulous conferences with top notch speakers. That's how I found Erin Murphy," Reidy say. "And I found my first picture book editor in the SCBWI *Bulletin*. I read the *Bulletin* cover to cover and have gathered a wealth of timely advice on everything from submissions to school visits. I also love to keep up with the successes of my fellow writers via the announcement pages."

Nancy Gow
Tens Big Toes and a Prince's Nose (Sterling)
www.nancygow.com

"It never occurred to me to look for an agent," says debut author Nancy Gow. *"Children's Writer's & Illustrator's Market* had all the publisher information I needed—addresses, editors, the types of books they were looking for—so sending out my own manuscripts seemed like the natural thing to do. It was a lot of work, mind you, and being the perfectionist that I am, I researched appropriate publishing houses, sent out carefully composed letters, neatly typed up my manuscripts, and enclosed an SASE when necessary. I really tried to do things the right way so that I could stand a chance of having someone seriously consider my story.

"Nowadays," says Gow, "I think that having an agent would be great. It would be far less work for me, and the idea of having someone 'in the know' representing my manuscripts would be a dream come true."

Gow's first book, *Ten Big Toes and a Prince's Nose*, is told in rhyme. It begins: "There once was a princess so lovely and fair / with ruby red lips and a mane of brown hair. / Her voice was like honey, her smile soft and sweet.../ ...but the beautiful princess had gigantic feet." Gow never hesitated to write in rhyme despite tales from the trenches about the difficulties of getting rhyming manuscripts past the slush pile. "Some of the best children's books I've ever read—both past and present—are written in rhyme.

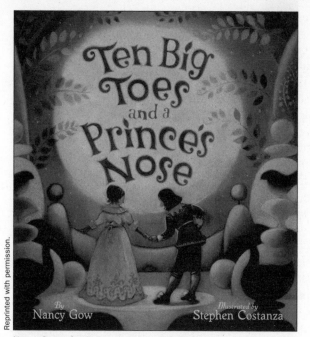

Nancy Gow used *Children's Writer's & Illustrator's Market* to place her debut picture book *Ten Big Toes and a Prince's Nose*.

How could I believe it wasn't possible when there are so many funny, imaginative rhyming picture books constantly being published?" she says. "I did realize very quickly, though, that editors aren't interested in 'bad' rhyme.

There's something in all of us that loves the rhythm of bouncy, well-metered rhyme, while we cringe at rhythms that don't flow or words that don't fit," she says. "I can't say enough about the pleasures of good rhyme. I'll always be a kid in that respect, letting myself be carried along by joyous wordplay and spontaneous rhythms."

Why this love of verse? "Two words: Dr. Seuss," says Gow. "When I was a teenager, I used to read Dr. Seuss books to my younger sister. Man, did I ever get into those books! I mean, it was so much fun to recite those preposterous little stories that I think I enjoyed it more than she did! Seuss created a world of intelligent fun and creativity that showed me how much joy there could be in well-written rhyme."

As she delved into her writing, Gow studied current rhyming books to find out what was out there, and, she says, "I was bowled over. Books like *Finklehopper Frog* (by Irene Livingston, illustrated by Brian Lies) and *I Saw an Ant on the Railroad Track* (by Joshua Prince, illustrated by Macky Pamintuan) just blew me away. It was as if someone had thrown down the gauntlet and said, 'Look what's being written now. Do you think you can match it? ...And I took up the challenge!

"The act of writing is a mystery to me," she says "for I never know what's going to come out of my pen or keyboard. I haven't had much instruction in writing, but I have read many children's books and I know what captures my attention. I study those books to understand the structure, but what I'm really interested in is the person behind the book—their sense of humor, their love of, and ability to play with words, and their willingness to take a chance and write something new."

Ten Big Toes, Gow says, came to her during about bought of sleepy inspiration—she continued to lie down and get back up as text popped into her head. "As far as I'm concerned, the best way to come up with new ideas is to place your body in a horizontal position!" she says. "I'll be laboring on a rhyme—trying this, trying that—and then when I simply can't come up with any more ideas, I'll take a break. I'll lie on my bed and just drift, without any expectations—and that's when something fresh will often arise. Working on the text seems to be a necessary first step, but when that's done, inspiration can take over."

When her manuscript was ready she sent it to an editor who had been mentoring her. "She was always prompt in her replies, but this time I heard nothing," Gow says. "I waited for about four months then status-queried her, only to receive a vague apology from 'the editors,' stating that it could take up to six months to receive an answer on my submission."

This caused Gow feelings of discouragement and doubt, but she kept something in mind: "If you love something, do it. I've always lived my life that way; I've been a rock singer, a yoga teacher and now a children's writer. I'm happy that I did the things I felt passionate about. It's much better than looking back and saying "If only....'

"Doing what you love can involve dedication, hard work and learning," she says, "but as long as the enjoyment is there, those things will never be a burden. If writing stops being enjoyable, however, I could see that as being a reason to quit. But that wasn't the case for me. Even when I felt discouraged and doubtful, I still wanted to write. I still wanted to see if I could find that illusive word or the perfect rhyme. And I kept hoping that I would eventually find an editor who would enjoy reading my stories as much as I enjoyed writing them."

Then she came across "a wonderful picture book which was published by Sterling," *I Saw an Ant on the Railroad Track*. "I was so inspired that I sent my manuscript off to Sterling the next week and received an e-mail reply a week and a half later! I couldn't believe it when I saw the email address in my inbox. I thought surely it must have been a mistake, or that I was being rejected electronically! Who knew that one little email message could change my whole world."

There were some surprised throughout her editorial process, Gow says. "When I submitted my story I knew every syllable by heart. I knew every beat and every nuance, and I figured the final product would be an exact rendering of my labor of love. In other words, I thought the book would be all about me! But my editor saw the story totally fresh and she had her own ideas of how to make it better. So little by little I had to let go of my attachments, and it ended up being a better story for our collaboration. Then the art director had her unique view, and I began to realize that a book—and particularly a picture book that is filled with illustrations—is the product of not just my vision, but the vision of other creative people as well. I had no idea of this at the beginning, but now I see it as a natural process. Even though I wrote the text, the book ends up being as much of a surprise to me as to the person who eventually buys it—and I thinks that's cool!"

As she moved through the editorial process, Gow was very curious about how the illustrations for *Ten Big Toes* would turn out. "I mean, how do you illustrate a big-footed princess gliding down the slopes of the Alps without skis, and a big-nosed prince who's charming and full of fun but can never get a date? And I must say Stephen Costanza was up to the challenge. His drawings are very funny, yet sweet and compassionate."

Do help promote her book Gow plans to do a lot of advertising online, "sending my books to be reviewed by bloggers I really like, and participating on message boards. And I love reading and acting out stories for kids, too. I've done a fair amount of acting, and although it still makes me nervous to speak in public, there's nothing like telling a story to an eager group of children. They become so involved, and I just love to take them on a little journey into their own imagination."

For writers on the journey, Gow feels it's terribly important to read a lot of children's books. "Let yourself be inspired, and dare to follow your inspiration," she says. "I also happen to have a lot of respect for publishing houses, as well as compassion for the editorial assistant who has to slog her way through the slush pile. So I would advise beginning writers to make sure your submission is as professional as can be: write a good introductory letter; format your manuscript correctly; follow the guidelines set down by individual publishers; and seek out those houses that publish stories similar to your own."

But the most important thing, she says is to come up with a good story—and then write it well. "Practice makes perfect, so practice, practice, practice. If you love to write, you'll want to work at your craft to make your story the best it can be; it's your love of writing that will get you in the door. That love of the written word will shine through in your rhyme or your novel or your collection of poems. It's what makes people connect with your work—the joy they see in it, even if it's a sad story."

Candace Ryan
Animal House (Walker)
www.bookbookerbookest.blogspot.com

"Like most writers, my path to publication wasn't a straight line," says author Candace Ryan. "While still teaching middle school, I started writing picture books. When I felt like I wasn't making enough progress, I shifted gears and started writing for the adult market. I met with some early success and had a few personal essays published in *The Christian Science Monitor*. This gave me enough momentum to continue exploring my voice. Ironically, I discovered that my voice was better suited to the children's market. I couldn't shake my need to play with words, the way young children do. I'm an eight year-old at heart."

Fortunately for Ryan, she landed an agent not long after she returned to writing for children. "I cold queried Kelly Sonnack with a rudimentary draft of *Animal House* when she was with the Sandra Dijkstra Literary Agency (Since then, I have followed Kelly to the Andrea Brown Literary Agency). We did several rounds of revisions, and then Kelly sold it to Stacy Cantor at Walker. Stacy was so enthusiastic about *Animal House*. She made me feel like the book had found a home in the truest sense."

In *Animal House* Jeremy's teacher Mrs. Nuddles comes to visit his home after he claims his "vulchair" ate his homework, and pretty much as soon as she steps on the "welcome bat" and makes her way to his "kangaroom," she realizes something is amiss. Ryan says that her debut picture book is a reflection of how her brain works. "I'm a language-lover and pattern-seeker. The premise for *Animal House* was the culmination of a typical thought process for me."

She got the idea for this clever premise while reading a list of dinosaur names on a box of magnets. "I discovered a pattern with the dinosaur names, which led me to wonder whether or not I could find a similar pattern with animal names. It wasn't long before I found one. Then, the title *Animal House* popped into my head, and I knew I was onto something."

Beyond the premise, Ryan's book is unique in that it's written in first-person, present-tense—unusual for a picture book. "Neither my agent nor my editor raised any concerns over it," she says. "I had been writing many personal essays at the time, and it was just extension of what felt like a very natural and comfortable voice for me."

Ryan cautions that such rule-breaking isn't for all writers—and that's OK. "But if it's

Reprinted with permission.

Candace Ryan initially found success writing for adults, but kept coming back to writing for children until she found an agent for her debut picture book *Animal House*.

part of who you are, and you can't help but play at the margins, then by all means, play away," she say. "Children desperately need to know that they are smart to play, experiment, and explore, despite negative feedback adults often give them. Many of us probably remember messages from our own childhoods of, 'That's not how you do it... That's wrong...Why can't you do it like the rest of us?' This is why we don't have a cure for cancer. So many kids are taught to value conformity over creativity, but it is only through creativity that breakthroughs are made. Children's book creators can help break that cycle by offering up the blueprints for thinking outside of the box."

Although unusual for a first-time author, Walker allowed Ryan to choose her own illustrator for *Animal House* due to the challenging nature of her book. "At the time, I had recently read Nathan Hale's *Yellowbelly and Plum Go to School* and was impressed with Nathan's style and sensibility. Maybe most importantly, he had a great sense of humor," says Ryan. "Nathan was everything I wanted in an illustrator for *Animal House*, plus he had an existing relationship with my publisher. It seemed meant to be. And after viewing Nathan's final artwork for the book, I couldn't imagine it any other way. "When it came time for Nathan to begin the artwork, I wasn't in direct contact with him. My editor, Stacy Cantor, acted as a liaison. I responded to Nathan's questions and gave feedback via Stacy, which is the traditional way an author and illustrator work together. I respected this model and the need to give Nathan as much space as possible to bring his vision to the book."

Having that level of consultation, says Ryan, was a pleasant surprise. "The main expectation I had about the whole process was having to do more revisions, which certainly held true. I stayed open and flexible to the notion of re-imagining the story, which I think led me to having a relatively smooth experience overall." Ryan learned that the collaborative book-making process is full of pleasant surprises. "It was so much fun to watch Stacy, Nathan, and the book designer, Danielle Delaney, creatively problem-solve their way through different challenges."

As Hale worked on the art for the book, "he wanted to fill the house with as many animals as possible," Ryan says. "In other words, he wanted to create animals that weren't in the text. I supported Nathan's vision with the caveat that each animal's name had to fit into the overall wordplay pattern. Between Nathan's creativity and strong word sense, and a little bit of research and problem-solving skills on my end, we were able to pull it off. For example, when Nathan drew a rabbit-staircase, I was able to come up with the word, "harecase." The harecase ultimately made it into the text during one of the revisions. There are a lot of behind-the-scenes anecdotes like this one. It was a really fun book to make."

Long before her first books hit the shelves, Ryan had created her blog . "I've had my blog since 6/7/08. If you notice the date, you'll see that my love for patterns extends to numbers. I started blogging so that I could be part of a larger conversation about kidlit," she says. "I'm not a clockwork blogger, but hopefully my content is still entertaining and/or useful enough that the blogosphere can forgive my erratic posting schedule. I welcome readers to my blog, 'where picture books are the superlative.' The blog reveals my thoughts on and about picture books. Therefore, it is quite quirky. I also have a feature called 'Librarypalooza,' in which I review super cool L.A. area libraries. If I weren't an author, being a librarian would be the next-best-thing!"

In addition to blogging, Ryan's promotional efforts so far have involved reaching out to local independent booksellers and librarians. "It's a grass-roots approach that oddly feels like being on a campaign trail sometimes, but I've been having a blast! People are starting to recognize me from the bookmarks I've been distributing. It's great to see such immediate results from my efforts.

"After *Animal House* is released, my blog will be a hub of information on signings and appearances. Twitter continues to be an under-explored territory for me, so I'm mulling over how best to use it. I'm also in the planning stages for a fun book launch and blog tour."

Ryan says for now, pre-book release, she's connecting with other writers in-person more than online. "In the next week alone, I have five separate events I'm planning to attend, where I will get excellent face-to-face time with folks in the kidlit community," she says. "I'm not in a critique group or taking any classes right now, but if you live in the L.A. area, you'll likely see me at conferences, signings, book festivals, lectures, and readings."

Her motto, she says, is "Picture books or bust! I'm always working on them. My agent sold my second picture book to Walker in the fall of 2009. I've been able to see some early sketches and nearly got a cavity looking at them, they were so sweet. *Ribbit Rabbit* (illustrated by Mike Lowery) is due out in the spring of 2011. It's for a younger crowd than *Animal House*, and it features a different kind of wordplay, but it is very much from my literary loins."

For other writing working on publishing picture books, Ryan recommends classes in-person or online. "If I can reveal a personal bias based on experience, I recommend courses taught through UCLA Extension (which offers both types of courses). Such classes can form the foundation for a career in writing picture books." Her reasons: "Courses are taught by professionals in the industry who share valuable insider information and who can become powerful networking allies. You develop and strengthen your craft and learn the needs of the marketplace. You develop collegial relations with fellow writers. Some of you may band together to form a critique group that lasts beyond the duration of the class. You share and receive valuable information about which publications to read, organizations to join, or events to attend. The potential camaraderie of everyone "in it together" can help buoy you during times of rejection and self-doubt, helping inspire and encourage you to plow ahead. What more could you ask for?"

Book Publishers

There's no magic formula for getting published. It's a matter of getting the right manuscript on the right editor's desk at the right time. Before you submit it's important to learn publishers' needs, see what kind of books they're producing and decide which publishers your work is best suited for. *Children's Writer's & Illustrator's Market* is but one tool in this process. (Those just starting out, turn to Quick Tips for Writers & Illustrators on page 4.)

To help you narrow down the list of possible publishers for your work, we've included several indexes at the back of this book. The **Subject Index** lists book and magazine publishers according to their fiction and nonfiction needs or interests. The **Age-Level Index** indicates which age groups publishers cater to. The **Photography Index** indicates which markets buy photography for children's publications. The **Poetry Index** lists publishers accepting poetry.

If you write contemporary fiction for young adults, for example, and you're trying to place a book manuscript, go first to the Subject Index. Locate the fiction categories under Book Publishers and copy the list under Contemporary. Then go to the Age-Level Index and highlight the publishers on the Contemporary list that are included under the Young Adults heading. Read the listings for the highlighted publishers to see if your work matches their needs.

Remember, *Children's Writer's & Illustrator's Market* should not be your only source for researching publishers. Here are a few other sources of information:

- The Society of Children's Book Writers and Illustrators (SCBWI) offers members an annual market survey of children's book publishers for the cost of postage or free online at www.scbwi.org (SCBWI membership information can also be found at www. scbwi.org)
- The Children's Book Council website (www.cbcbooks.org) gives information on member publishers.
- If a publisher interests you, send a SASE for submission guidelines or check publishers' websites for guidelines *before* submitting. To quickly find guidelines online, visit The Colossal Directory of Children's Publishers at www.signaleader.com.
- Check publishers' websites. Many include their complete catalogs that you can browse. Web addresses are included in many publishers' listings.
- Spend time at your local bookstore to see who's publishing what. While you're there, browse through *Publishers Weekly* and *The Horn Book*.

SUBSIDY & SELF-PUBLISHING

Some determined writers who receive rejections from royalty publishers may look to subsidy and co-op publishers as an option for getting their work into print. These publishers ask writers to pay all or part of the costs of producing a book. We strongly advise writers and illustrators to work only with publishers who pay them. For this reason, we've adopted a policy not to include any subsidy or co-op publishers in *Children's Writer's & Illustrator's Market* (or any other Writer's Digest Books market books).

If you're interested in publishing your book just to share it with friends and relatives, self-publishing is a viable option, but it involves time, energy, and money. You oversee all book production details. Check with a local printer for advice and information on cost or check online for print-on-demand publishing options (which are often more affordable).

Whatever path you choose, keep in mind that the market is flooded with submissions, so it's important for you to hone your craft and submit the best work possible. Competition from thousands of other writers and illustrators makes it more important than ever to research publishers before submitting—read their guidelines, look at their catalogs, check out a few of their titles and visit their websites.

ABBEVILLE FAMILY

Abbeville Press 137 Varick St. New York NY 10013. Estab. 1977. (212)366-5585. Fax: (212)366-6966. E-mail: cvance@abbeville.com. Website: www.abbeville.com. Specializes in trade books. **Manuscript/ Art Acquisitions:** Cynthia Vance, Director of Abbeville Family. Publishes 8 picture books/year. 10% of books by firs-time authors and 20% for subsidy published.

Fiction Picture Books: Animal, anthology, concept, contemporary, fantasy, folktales, health, hi-lo, history, humor, multicultural, nature/environment, poetry, science fiction, special needs, sports, suspense. Average word length 300-1,000 words. Recently published *Everett, the Incredibly Helpful Helper,* by Sue Anne Morrow with illustrations by CG Williams (ages 1-4, picture/nonfiction book); *Red, Yellow, Blue, and You,* by Cynthia Vance with illustrations by Candace Whitman (ages 2-5 picture/board book) with padded cover and rhyming text; *The Journey: Plateosarus (Dinosaurs illustrated comics series),* by Matteo Bacchin and Marco Signore, with foreword by Mark Norell (ages 9 and up). Educational comic series, 64 pages with hardcover.

How to Contact Fiction: Please refer to website for submission policy. Not accepting unsolicited manuscripts. If you wish to have your manuscript or materials returned, an SASE with proper postage must be included.

Illustration Works with approx 2-4 illustrators/year. Uses color artwork only.

Photography Buys stock and assigns work.

ABRAMS BOOKS FOR YOUNG READERS

115 W. 18th St., New York NY 10011.

- Abrams title *365 Penguins,* by Jean-Luc Fromental, illustrated by Joelle Jolivel, won a Boston Globe-Horn Book Picture Book Honor Award in 2007. *Abrams also publishes Laurent De Brunhoff, Graeme Base, and Laura Numeroff, among others.*

Fiction Picture books ages 0-12, fiction and non-fiction.

How to Contact Does not accept unsolicited manuscripts or queries.

Illustration Illustrations only: Do not submit original material; copies only. Contact: Chad Beckerman, art director.

☐ ABSEY & CO.

23011 Northcrest Dr. Spring TX 77389. (281)257-2340. Fax: (281)251-4676. E-mail: abseyandco@aol.com. Website: www.absey.com. New York address: 45 W. 21st Street, Suite 5, New York NY 10010. (212)277-8028. (Send mss to Spring, TX address only.) **Publisher:** Edward Wilson. "We are looking for education books, especially those with teaching strategies based upon research, for children's picture books and Young Adult fiction. We haven't done much with nonfiction." Publishes hardcover, trade paperback and mass market paperback originals. Publishes 5-10 titles/year. 50% of books from first-time authors; 50% from unagented writers.

Fiction "Since we are a small, new press, we are looking for good manuscripts with a firm intended audience." Recently published *Stealing a Million Kisses* (board book); *Adrift* (YA fiction).

How to Contact Fiction: Query with SASE. Does not consider simultaneous submissions. Responds to queries in 3 months. No e-mail submissions. "We do not download from unknown sources."

Illustration Reviews ms/illustration packages. Send photocopies, transparencies, etc.

Photography Reviews ms/photo packages. Send photocopies, transparencies, etc.

Terms Pays 8-15% royalty on wholesale price. Publishes book 1 year after acceptance of ms. Manuscript guidelines for #10 SASE.

Tips "Absey publishes a few titles every year. We like the author and the illustrator working together to create something magical. Authors and illustrators have input into every phase of production."

ALADDIN/PULSE

1230 Avenue of the Americas, 4th Floor, New York NY 10020. (212)698-2707. Fax: (212)698-7337. Website: www.simonsays.com. Hardcover/paperback imprints of Simon & Schuster Children's Publishing Children's Division. Publishes 175 titles/year. **Vice President/Publisher, Aladdin/Pulse**: Bethany Buck **Vice President/Associate Publisher, Aladdin**: Ellen Krieger; Liesa Abrams, executive editor (Aladdin); Emily Lawrence, associate editor (Aladdin); Kate Angelella, assistant editor (Aladdin) Jennifer Klonsky, Editorial Director (Pulse); Anica Rissi, editor (Pulse); Michael del Rosario, associate editor (Pulse). **Manuscript Acquisitions:** Attn: Submissions Editor. **Art Acquisitions**: Karin Paprocki, Aladdin; Russell Gordon, Simon Pulse.

Fiction Aladdin publishes picture books, beginning readers, chapter books, middle grade and tween fiction and nonfiction, and graphic novels and nonfiction in hardcover and paperback, with an emphasis on commercial, kid-friendly titles. Simon Pulse publishes original teen series, single title fiction, and select nonfiction, in hardcover and paperback. Recently published Nancy Drew and the Clue Crew chapter book series (Emily Lawrence, editor); Pendragon middle grade series (Liesa Abrams, editor); Edgar & Ellen middle grade series (Ellen Krieger, editor); Uglies series (Bethany Buck, editor); *Wake, bloom, Uninvited, Disenchanted Princess, The Straight Road to Kylie* (Jennifer Klonsky, editor); *Chill; Model* (Anica Rissi, editor); *I Heart You, You Haunt Me; Unleashed; My Summer on Earth*; Drama series (Michael del Rosario, editor).

How to Contact Fiction: Accepts query letters with proposals (Aladdin); accepts query letters (Simon Pulse).

ALASKA NORTHWEST BOOKS

Imprint of Graphic Arts Center Publishing Co. P.O. Box 10306, Portland OR 97296-0306. (503)226-2402. Fax: (503)223-1410. E-mail: editorial@gacpc.com. Website: www.gacpc.com. **Executive Editor:** Tim Frew. Imprints: Alaska Northwest Books. Publishes 3 picture books/year; 1 young reader/year. 20% of books by first-time authors. "We publish books that teach and entertain as well as inform the reader about Alaska or the western U.S. We're interested in wildlife, adventure, unusual sports, inspirational nature stories, traditions, but we also like plain old silly stories that make kids giggle. We are particular about protecting Native American story-telling traditions, and ask that writers ensure that it's clear whether they are writing from within the culture or about the culture. We encourage Native American writers to share their stories."

Fiction Picture books, young readers: adventure, animal, contemporary, fantasy, history, humor, multicultural, nature/environment, poetry. Middle readers, young adult/teens: adventure, animal, anthology, contemporary, history, humor, multicultural, nature/environment, suspense/mystery. Average word length: picture books—500-1,000; young readers—500-1,500; middle readers—1,500-2,000; young adults—35,000. Recently published *Seldovia Sam and the Wildfire Rescue*, by Susan Woodward Springer, illustrated by Amy Meissner (ages 6-10, early chapter book); *Ten Rowdy Ravens*, by Susan Ewing, illustrated by Evon Zerbetz (age 5 and up, humor); *Berry Magic*, by Teri Sloat and Betty Huffmon, illustrated by Teri Sloat (age 6 and up, legend).

Nonfiction Picture books: animal. Young readers: animal, multicultural, sports. Middle readers, young adults/teens: animal, history, multicultural, nature/environment, sports, Alaska- or Western-themed adventure. Average word length: picture books—500-1,000; young readers—500-1,500; middle readers—1,500-2,000; young adults—35,000. Recently published *Big-Enough Anna: The Little Sled Dog Who Braved the Arctic*, by Pam Flowers and Ann Dixon, illustrated by Bill Farnsworth (5 and up); *Recess at 20 Below*, by Cindy Lou Aillaud (ages 6-10).

How to Contact Fiction: Submit complete ms for picture books or submit outline/synopsis and 2 sample chapters for YA novels. Nonfiction: Submit complete ms for picture books or submit 2 sample chapters for YA nonfiction chapter books. Responds to queries/mss in 3-5 months. Publishes book 2 years after acceptance. Will consider simultaneous submissions.

Illustration Works with 4-5 illustrators/year. Uses color artwork only. Reviews ms/illustration packages from artists. Submit ms with dummy or scans of final art on CD. Contact: Tricia Brown. Illustrations only: Query with résumé, scans on CD. Responds only if interested. Samples not returned; samples filed.

Photography Buys stock and assigns work. "We rarely illustrate with photos—only if the book is more educational in content." Photo captions required. Uses color and 35mm or 4 × 5 transparencies. Submit cover letter, résumé, slides, portfolio on CD, color promo piece.

Terms Pays authors royalty of 5-7% based on net revenues. Offers advances (average amount: $2,000). Pays illustrators royalty of 5-7% based on net revenues. Pays photographers royalty of 5-7% based on net revenues. Sends galleys to authors; dummies to illustrators. Originals returned to artist at job's completion. Book catalog available for 9 × 12 SASE and $3.85 postage; ms, art, and photo guidelines available for SASE. All imprints included in a single catalog. Catalog available on website.

Tips "As a regional publisher, we seek books about Alaska and the West. We rarely publish YA novels, but are more interested in the pre-school to early reader segment. A proposal that shows that the author has researched the market, in addition to submitting a unique story, will get our attention."

☐ ALL ABOUT KIDS PUBLISHING

P.O. Box 159, Gilroy CA 95021. (408)846-1833. E-mail: lguevara@aakp.com. Website: www.aakp.com. **Acquisitions:** Linda Guevara. Publishes 3-5 picture books/year; 3-5 chapter books/year. 80% of books by first-time authors.

Fiction Picture books, young readers: adventure, animal, concept, fantasy, folktales, history, humor, nature, poetry, suspense/mystery. Average word length: picture books—450 words. Recently published *The Big Blue Lake*, by Robert Armstrong (picture book); *The Titanic Game*, by Mike Warner (chapter book).

Nonfiction Picture books, young readers: activity books, animal, biography, concept, history, nature. Average word length: picture books—450 words. Recently published *Shadowbox Hunt: A Search & Find Odyssey*, by Laura L. Seeley (picture book).

How to Contact Fiction: Submit complete ms. Nonfiction: Submit complete ms for picture books; outline synopsis and complete ms for young readers. Responds to mss in 3 months. Publishes a book 2-3 years after acceptance. Manuscript returned with SASE only.

Illustration Works with 5-10 illustrators/year. Reviews ms/illustration packages from artists. Submit ms with dummy or ms with 2-3 pieces of final art. Contact: Linda Guevara, editor. Illustrations only: Arrange personal portfolio review or send résumé, portfolio and client list. Responds in 3 months. Samples returned with SASE; or samples filed.

Photography Works on assignment only. Contact: Linda Guevara, editor. Model/property releases required. Submit portfolio, résumé, client list.

Terms Pays author royalty. Offers advances (average amount: $1,000). Pays illustrators by the project (range: $3,000 minimum) and/or royalty of 3-5% based on discounted. Pays photographers by the project (range: $500 minimum) or royalty of 5% based on discounted price. Sends galleys to authors; dummies to illustrators. All imprints included in a single catalog. Writer's, artist's and photographer's guidelines available for SASE and on website.

Tips "Not accepting submissions until July 2009. Please check our website in June and December for updates and submission guidelines."

ALPHA WORLD PRESS

530 Oaklawn Avenue, Green Bay WI 54304. (866)855-3720. E-mail: office@alphaworldpress.com. **Contact:** Tracey Vandeveer, owner. "Our press is dedicated to publishing high-quality work by, for

and about lesbians from all walks of life. We publish fiction, non-fiction, and poetry. We welcome all manuscripts from lesbians. We want the voices and perspectives of lesbians from all across the world to be heard through the books that we publish. We work very closely with our authors in all aspects of publishing - from editing, graphic design, to actual production, promotion & marketing." Publishes trade paperback originals, and mass market paperback originals 120 queries received/year. 12 mss received/year.

Fiction We publish only lesbian-themed books for the lesbian market. Submit proposal package, 3 sample chapters, clips. Send it via e-mail in pdf.

Nonfiction Only submit nonfiction if it is written by or relates to lesbians. Submit proposal package, outline.

Tips Our audience is lesbians only.

AMERICAN GIRL PUBLISHING

8400 Fairway Place, Middleton WI 53562-2554. (608)836-4848. Fax: (608)836-1999. Website: www.americangirl.com. **Manuscript Acquisitions:** Submissions Editor. Publishes 30 middle readers/year. 10% of books by first-time authors. Publishes fiction and nonfiction for girls 8-12.

Fiction American Girls publishes 2-3 titles per year for its Girl of the Year character and 3 mystery titles per year for its historical characters. American Girl does not accept ideas or manuscripts.

Nonfiction Middle readers: activity books, arts/crafts, cooking, history, hobbies, how-to self help, sports. Recently published *A Smart Girl's Guide to Friendship Troubles*, by Patti Kelley Crisswell, (ages 8 and up; self-help); *Paper Punch Art*, by Laura Torres (ages 8 and up; craft); *Quiz Book 2*, by Sarah Jane Brian, illustrated by Debbie Tilley (ages 8 and up; activity). Also publishes *American Girl* magazine. See the listing for *American Girl* in the Magazines section.

How to Contact Nonfiction: Submit well-focused concepts for activity, craft or advice books. "Proposals should include a detailed description of your concept, sample chapters or spreads and lists of previous publications. Complete manuscripts also accepted." Responds in 3 months. Will consider simultaneous submissions.

Illustration Works with 10 illustrators/year. Reviews ms/illustration packages from artists. Illustrations only: Query with samples. Contact: Art Director. Responds only if interested. Samples not returned.

Photography Buys stock and assigns work. Submit cover letter, published samples, promo piece.

Terms Pays authors royalty or work purchased outright. Pays illustrators by the project. Pays photographers by the project. Sends galleys to authors; dummies to illustrators. Originals returned to artist at job's completion. Book catalog available for 8½ × 11 SAE and 4 first-class stamps. All imprints included in a single catalog.

AMERICAN PRESS

60 State St., Suite 700, Boston MA 02109. (617)247-0022. E-mail: americanpress@flash.net. *Integrating Technology Into Physical Education and Health*, by Ken Felker and D.J. Bradley. **Contact:** Jana Kirk, editor. Publishes college textbooks 350 queries received/year. 100 mss received/year.

Nonfiction "We prefer that our authors actually teach courses for which the manuscripts are designed." Query, or submit outline with tentative TOC. *No complete mss.*

N AMULET BOOKS

Abrams Books for Young Readers, 115 W. 18th St., New York NY 10001. **Manuscript Acquisitions:** Susan Van Metre, associate publisher. **Art Acquisitions:** Chad Beckerman, art director. Produces 10 middle readers/year, 10 young adult titles/year. 10% of books by first-time authors.

Fiction Middle readers: adventure, contemporary, fantasy, history, science fiction, sports. Young adults/teens: adventure, contemporary, fantasy, history, science fiction, sports, suspense. Recently published *Diary of a Wimpy Kid*, by Jeff Kinney; *The Sisters Grimm*, by Michael Buckley (mid-grade series); *ttyl*, by Lauren Miracle (YA novel).

How to Contact Fiction: Does not accept unsolicited manuscripts or queries.

Illustration Works with 10-12 illustrators/year. Uses both color and b&w. Query with samples. Contact: Chad Beckerman, art director. Samples filed.

Photography Buys stock images and assigns work.

Terms Offers advance against royalties. Illustrators paid by the project. Author sees galleys for review. Illustrators see dummies for review. Originals returned to artist at job's completion.

ANNICK PRESS LTD.

15 Patricia Ave., Toronto ON M2M 1H9, Canada. **Creative Director:** Sheryl Shapiro. Publishes 5 picture books/year; 6 young readers/year; 8 middle readers/year; 9 young adult titles/year. 25% of books by first-time authors. "Annick Press maintains a commitment to high-quality books that entertain and challenge. Our publications share fantasy and stimulate judgment and abilities."

• Annick Press does not accept unsolicited manuscripts.

Fiction Recently published *The Apprentice's Masterpiece: A Story of Medieval Spain*, by Melanie Little, ages 12 and up; *Chicken, Pig, Cow series*, written and illustrated by Ruth Ohi, ages 2-5; *Single Voices series*, Melanie Little, Editor, ages 14 and up; *Crusades*, by Laura Scandiffio, illustrated by John Mantha, ages 9-11.

Nonfiction Recently published *Pharaohs and Foot Soldiers: One Hundred Ancient Egyptian Jobs you Might Have Desired or Dreaded*, by Kristin Butcher, illustrations by Martha Newbigging, ages 9-12; *The Bite of the Mango*, by Mariatu Kamara with Susan McClelland, ages 14 and up; *Adventures on the Ancient Silk Road*, by Priscilla Galloway with Dawn Hunter, ages 10 and up; *The Chinese Thought of it: Amazing Inventions and Innovations*, by Ting-xing Ye, ages 9-11.

Illustration Works with 20 illustrators/year. Illustrations only: Query with samples. Contact: Creative Director. Samples cannot be returned. Response sent only if SASE included and submission being kept on file.

Terms Pays authors royalty of 5-12% based on retail price. Offers advances (average amount: $3,000). Pays illustrators royalty of 5% minimum. Originals returned to artist at job's completion. Book catalog available on website.

ARCHEBOOKS PUBLISHING

ArcheBooks Publishing Inc., 6081 Silver King Blvd., Cape Coral FL 33914. (239)542-7595. Fax: (239)542-0080. E-mail: publisher@archebooks.com. **Contact:** Robert E. Gelinas, publisher & editor-in-chief. Publishes hardcover originals, electronic originals and trade paperback originals 100+ queries received/year. 100+ mss received/year.

Fiction "Writers should be prepared to participate in very aggressive and orchestrated marketing and promotion campaigns, using all the promotional tools and training that we provide, at no charge. We're expanding in all areas." Submit proposal package. See website for complete proposal guidelines.

Nonfiction Submit proposal package. See website for complete proposal guidelines.

Tips " Learn to write a good proposal. An article on this topic can be found for free on our website in the Author's Corner section of Writer's Resources."

⬛ ATHENEUM BOOKS FOR YOUNG READERS

Imprint of Simon & Schuster Children's Publishing Division, 1230 Avenue of the Americas, New York NY 10020. (212)698-2715. Website: www.simonsayskids.com. Estab. 1960. **Publisher:** Vice President: Emma D. Dryden. Editorial Director: Caitlyn Dlouhy, Executive Editor: Namrata Tripathi. "Atheneum publishes original hardcover and paperback trade books for children from pre-school age through young adult. Our list includes picture books, chapter books, mysteries, biography, science fiction, fantasy, graphic novels, middle grade and young adult fiction and nonfiction. The style and subject matter of the books we publish is almost unlimited. We do not, however, publish textbooks, coloring or activity books, greeting cards, magazines or pamphlets or religious publications." *"Simon & Schuster does not accept unsolicited manuscripts.* We suggest that prospective authors submit their manuscripts through a professional literary agent. We cannot recommend specific agents for your work. There are websites, however, that offer resources for authors, such as *Writer's Digest."* Also, Writer's Market has *The Guide to Literary Agents,* which includes a free online subscription.

- Atheneum title *The Underneath,* by Kathi Appelt; illustrated by David Small won a 2009 Newbery Honor. Recently published: *Someday,* by Alison McGhee, illustrated by Peter Reynolds (picture book); *That Book Woman,* by Heather Henson; illustrated by David Small (picture book); *Olivia Helps With Christmas*, by Ian Falconer (picture book); *Dark Dude,* by Oscar Hijuelos (teen novel); *Shift,* by Jennifer Bradbury (debut novel); *Tweak,* by Nic Sheff (teen memoir); *The Higher Power Of Lucky,* by Susan Patron (Newbery Medal).

Terms Pays royalty on hardcover and paperback retail price: 10% fiction; 5% illustrator (picture book). Publishes MSS up to 3 years after acceptance. Pays illustrators advance and royalty or by the project. Pays photographers by the project. Original artwork returned at job's completion.

Tips "Atheneum has a 40 + year tradition of publishing distinguished books for children. Study our titles."

AVALON BOOKS

160 Madison Ave., 5th Floor, New York NY 10016. (212)598-0222. Fax: (212)979-1862. E-Mail: editorial@avalonbooks.com. Website: www.avalonbooks.com. **Acquisitions**: Faith Black, editor. Chelsea Gilmore, assistant editor. Established: 1950. Publishes hardcover originals. **Publishes 60 titles/year**. Publishes manuscript 10-12 months after acceptance. Responds in 6 No Answer to manuscripts. **Pays 15% royalty. Offers advance**.

Fiction "We publish wholesome contemporary romances, mysteries, historical romances and westerns. Our books are read by adults as well as teenagers, and the characters are all adults. All mysteries are contemporary. We publish contemporary romances (4 every 2 months), historical romances (2 every 2 months), mysteries (2 every 2 months) and traditional westerns (2 every 2 months). Submit first 3 sample chapters, a 2-3 page synopsis and SASE. The manuscripts should be 40,000-70,000 words. Manuscripts that are too long will not be considered. The books shall be wholesome fiction, without graphic sex, violence or strong language. We are actively looking for romantic comedy, chick lit."

Needs Mystery, Romance, Western. **Submission method:** Query with SASE

Recent Titles Miss Delacourt Speaks Her Mind, by Heidi Ashworth (historical romance); Everything But A Wedding, by Holly Jacobs (contemporary romance); Murder Express, by Robert Scott (mystery); Judgment at Gold Butte, by Terrell L. Bowers (western).

⬛ AVON BOOKS/BOOKS FOR YOUNG READERS

1350 Avenue of the Americas, New York NY 10019. (212)261-6500. Fax: (212)261-6668. Website: www.harperchildrens.com.

• Avon is not accepting unagented submissions. See listing for HarperCollins Children's Books.

[N] AZRO PRESS

PMB 342, 1704 Llano St. B, Santa Fe NM 87505. (505)989-3272. Fax: (505)989-3832. E-mail: books@azropress.com. Website: www.azropress.com. Estab. 1997. Specializes in illustrated children's books. **Writers contact:** Gae Eisenhardt. Produces 3-4 picture books/year; 1 young reader/year. 75% of books by first-time authors. "We like to publish illustrated children's books by Southwestern authors and illustrators. We are always looking for books with a Southwestern look or theme."

Fiction Picture books: animal, history, humor, nature/environment. Young readers: adventure, animal, hi-lo, history, humor. Average word length: picture books—1,200; young readers—2,000-2,500. Recently published *The Magical Mrs. Iptweet & Me*, by Barbara Mayfield; *T is for Tortilla*, by Jody Alpers, illustration by Celeste Johnson; *Cactus Critter Bash*, by Sid Hausman; *Loco Dog and the Dustdevil in the Railyard*, by Marcy Heller, illustration by Nancy Poes; *Pancho Finds a Home*, by Karen Gogan, illustration by Blanche Davidson.

Nonfiction Picture books: animal, geography, history. Young readers: geography, history.

How to Contact Accepts international submissions. Fiction/nonfiction: Query or submit complete ms. Responds to queries/mss in 3-4 months. Publishes book 1-2 years after acceptance. Considers simultaneous submissions.

Illustration Accepts material from international illustrators. Works with 3 illustrators/year. Uses color and b&w artwork. Reviews ms/illustration packages. Reviews work for future assignments. Query with samples. Submit samples to illustrations editor. Responds in 3-4 months. Samples not returned. Samples are filed.

Terms Pays authors royalty of 5% to 10% based on wholesale price. Pays illustrators by the project ($2,000) or royalty of 5%. Author sees galleys for review. Illustrators see dummies for review. Originals returned to artist at job's completion. Catalog available for #10 SASE and 3 first-class stamps. Catalog on line. See website for artist's, photographer's guidelines.

Tips "We are not currently accepting new manuscripts. Please see our website for acceptance date."

BALZER & BRAY

HarperCollins Children's Books. 1350 Avenue of the America's, New York NY 10019. Estab. 2008. (212)307-3628. Fax: (212)261-6538. Specializes in fiction. Imprints: Balzer & Bray, Alessandra Balzer, Co-Publisher; Donna Bray, Co-Publisher; Jill Santopolo, Senior Editor; Kristin Daly, Editor; Ruta Rimas, Editorial Assistant; Corey Mallonee, Editorial Assistant. Publishes 10 picture books/year; 8 middle reader/year; 7 young adult/year.

Fiction Picture Books, Young Readers: adventure, animal, anthology, concept, contemporary, fantasy, history, humor, multicultural, nature/environment, poetry, science fiction, special needs, sports, suspense. Middle Readers, Young Adults/Teens: adventure, animal, anthology, contemporary, fantasy, history, humor, multicultural, nature/environment, poetry, science fiction, special needs, sports, suspense.

Nonfiction All levels: animal, biography, concept, cooking, history, multicultural, music/dance, nature/environment, other, science, self help, social issues, special needs, sports. "We will publish very few non-fiction titles, maybe 1-2 per year."

How to Contact Interested in agented material. Publishes a book 18 months after acceptance.

Illustration Works with 10 illustrators/year. Uses both color and b&w. Illustrations only: send tearsheets to be kept on file. **Contact:** Ruta Rimas or Corey Mallonee Editorial Assistant. Responds only if interested. Samples are not returned.

Photography Works on assignment only.

Terms Offers advances. Pays illustrators by the project. Sends galleries to authors. Originals returned to artist at job's completion. Catalog is available on our web site.

BAREFOOT BOOKS

2067 Massachusetts Ave., 5th Floor, Cambridge MA 02140. Website: wwwbarefootbookscom.

Fiction Picture books, young readers: animal, anthology, concept, folktales, multicultural, nature/environment, poetry, spirituality. Middle readers, young adults: anthology, folktales. Average word length: picture books—500-1,000; young readers—2,000-3,000; anthologies—10,000-20,000. Recently published *The Prince's Bedtime*, by Joanne Oppenheim; *The Hare and the Tortoise*, by Ranjit Bolt; *Elusive Moose*, by Clare Beaton.

How to Contact Fiction: Submit complete ms for picture books; outline/synopsis and 1 sample story for collections. Responds in 4 months if SASE is included. Will consider simultaneous submissions and previously published work.

Illustration Works with 20 illustrators/year. Uses color artwork only. Reviews ms/illustration packages from artists. Send query and art samples or dummy for picture books. Illustrations only: Query with samples or send promo sheet and tearsheets. Responds only if interested. Samples returned with SASE.

Terms Pays authors royalty of 5% based on retail price. Offers advances. Sends galleys to authors. Originals returned to artist at job's completion. Book catalog available for SAE and 5 first-class stamps; ms guidelines available for SASE.

Tips "We are looking for books that inspire and are filled with a sense of magic and wonder. We also look for strong stories from all different cultures, reflecting the ways of the individual culture while also touching deeper human truths that suggest we are all one. We welcome playful submissions for the very youngest children and also anthologies of stories for older readers, all focused around a universal theme. We encourage writers and artists to visit our website and read some of our books to get a sense of our editorial philosophy and what we publish before they submit to us. Always, we encourage them to stay true to their inner voice and artistic vision that reaches out for timeless stories, beyond the momentary trends that may exist in the market today."

☐ BARRONS EDUCATIONAL SERIES

250 Wireless Blvd. Hauppauge NY 11788. Fax: (631)434-3723. E-mail: waynebarr@barronseduc.com. Website: www.barronseduc.com. **Manuscript Acquisitions:** Wayne R. Barr, acquisitions manager. **Art Acquisitions:** Bill Kuchler. Publishes 20 picture books/year; 20 young readers/year; 20 middle readers/year; 10 young adult titles/year. Most are from packagers.

Fiction Picture books: animal, concept, multicultural, nature/environment. Young readers: adventure, multicultural, nature/environment, fantasy, suspense/mystery. Middle readers: adventure, fantasy, multicultural, nature/environment, problem novels, suspense/mystery. Young adults: problem novels. Examples — *Night at the Smithsonian*, by Leslie Goldman; *Renoir and the Boy in the Long Hair*, by Wendy Wax. Stories with an educational element are appealing.

Nonfiction Picture books: concept, reference. Young readers: biography, how-to, reference, self help, social issues. Middle readers: hi-lo, how-to, reference, self help, social issues. Young adults: reference, self help, social issues, sports.

How to Contact Fiction: Query via e-mail with no attached files. No snail mail. Nonfiction: Submit outline/synopsis and sample chapters. "Nonfiction Submissions must be accompanied by SASE for response." Responds to queries in 2 months; mss in 4 months. Publishes a book 1 year after acceptance. Will consider simultaneous submissions.

Illustration Works with 20 illustrators/year. Reviews ms/illustration packages from artists. Query first; 3 chapters of ms with 1 piece of final art, remainder roughs. Illustrations only: Submit tearsheets or slides plus résumé. Responds in 2 months.

Terms Pays authors royalty of 10-13% based on net price or buys ms outright for $2,000 minimum. Pays illustrators by the project based on retail price. Sends galleys to authors; dummies to illustrators. Book catalog, ms/artist's guidelines for 9 × 12 SAE.

Tips Writers: "We publish preschool storybooks, concept books and middle grade and YA chapter books. No romance novels. Those with an educational element." Illustrators: "We are happy to receive a sample illustration to keep on file for future consideration. Periodic notes reminding us of your work are acceptable." Children's book themes "are becoming much more contemporary and relevant to a child's day-to-day activities, fewer talking animals. We are interested in fiction (ages 7-11 and ages 12-16) dealing with modern problems."

BENCHMARK BOOKS

99 White Plains Rd., Tarrytown NY 10591. Phone/Fax: (914)332-8888. E-mail: mbisson@ marshallcavendish.com. Publishes about 300 young reader, middle reader and young adult books/ year. "We look for interesting treatments of only nonfiction subjects related to elementary, middle school and high school curriculum." **Contact:** Manuscript Acquisitions: Michelle Bisson.

Nonfiction Most nonfiction topics should be curriculum related. Average word length: 4,000-20,000. All books published as part of a series. Recently published *Barbarians, Amazing Machines, Perspectives On*.

How to Contact Nonfiction: "Please read our catalog or view our website before submitting proposals. We only publish series. We do not publish individual titles." Submit outline/synopsis and 1 or more sample chapters. Responds to queries/mss in 3 months. Publishes a book 2 years after acceptance. Will consider simultaneous submissions.

Photography Buys stock and assigns work.

Terms Buys work outright. Sends galleys to authors. Book catalog available online. All imprints included in a single catalog.

BICK PUBLISHING HOUSE

307 Neck Rd., Madison CT 06443. (203)245-0073. Fax: (203)245-5990. "We publish psychological, philosophical, scientific information on health and recovery, wildlife rehabilitation, living with disabilities, teen psychology and science for adults and young adults."

Nonfiction Young adults: nature/environment, religion, science, self help, social issues, special needs. Average word length: young adults-60,000. Recently published *In and Out of Your Mind* (teen science); *Who Said What?* (philosophy quotes for teens); *What are You Doing with Your Life?*, by J. Krishnamurti (philosophy for teens); *The Teen Brain Book*, by Dale Carlson.

How to Contact Fiction: Submit outline/synopsis and 3 sample chapters. Nonfiction: Submit outline/synopsis or outline/synopsis and 3 sample chapters. Responds to queries/mss in 2 weeks. Publishes book 1 year after acceptance. Will consider simultaneous submissions and previously published work.

Illustration Works with 1 illustrator/year. Uses b&w artwork only. Reviews ms/illustration packages from artists. Submit sketches of teens or science drawings. Contact: Dale Carlson, president. Illustrations only: Query with photocopies, résumé, SASE. Responds in 2 weeks. Samples returned with SASE.

Terms Pays authors royalty of 5-10%. Pays illustrators by the project (range: up to $1,000). Sends galleys to authors; dummies to illustrators. Book catalog available for SASE with 1 first-class stamp; writer's guidelines available for SAE. Catalog available on Website.

Tips "Read our books!"

BIRDSONG BOOKS

1322 Bayview Rd. Middletown DE 19709. (302)378-7274. E-mail: Birdsong@BirdsongBooks.com. Website: www.BirdsongBooks.com. **Manuscript & Art Acquisitions:** Nancy Carol Willis, president. Publishes 1 picture book/year. "Birdsong Books seeks to spark the delight of discovering our wild neighbors and natural habitats. We believe knowledge and understanding of nature fosters caring and a desire to protect the Earth and all living things. Our emphasis is on North American animals and habitats, rather than people."

Nonfiction Picture books, young readers: activity books, animal, nature/environment. Average word length: picture books—800-1,000 plus content for 2-4 pages of back matter. Recently published *The Animals' Winter Sleep*, by Lynda-Graham Barber (age 3-6, nonfiction picture book); *Red Knot: A Shorebird's Incredible Journey*, by Nancy Carol Willis (age 6-9, nonfiction picture book); *Raccoon Moon*, by Nancy Carol Willis (ages 5-8, natural science picture book); *The Robins In Your Backyard*, by Nancy Carol Willis (ages 4-7, nonfiction picture book).

How to Contact Nonfiction: Submit complete manuscript package with SASE. Responds to mss in 3 months. Publishes book 2-3 years after acceptance. Will consider simultaneous submissions (if stated).

Illustration Accepts material from residents of U.S. Works with 1 illustrator/year. Reviews ms/illustration packages from artists. Send ms with dummy (plus samples/tearsheets for style). Illustrations only: Query with brochure, résumé, samples, SASE, or tearsheets. Responds only if interested. Samples returned with SASE.

Photography Uses North American animals and habitats (currently wading birds - herons, egrets, and the like). Submit cover letter, résumé, promo piece, stock photo list.

Tips "We are a small independent press actively seeking manuscripts that fit our narrowly defined niche. We are only interested in nonfiction, natural science picture books or educational activity books about North American animals and habitats. We are not interested in fiction stories based on actual events. Our books include several pages of back matter suitable for early elementary classrooms. Mailed submissions with SASE only. No e-mail submissions or phone calls, please. Cover letters should sell author/illustrator and book idea."

BLOOMING TREE PRESS

P.O. Box 140934, Austin TX 78714. Estab. 2000. (512)921-8846. Fax: (512)873-7710. E-mail: email@bloomingtreepress.com. Website: www.bloomingtreepress.com. **Imprints:** Blooming Tree Press (Children's), CBAY Books (Edgier Fiction), Tire Swing Books (Paperback), Ready Blade (Graphic Novels). **Publisher:** Miriam Hees; Madeline Smoot, publisher, CBAY Books; Anna Herrington, editorial director, blooming tree children's and tire swing books, Bradford Hees, publisher, ready blade graphic novels/comics. **Art Acquisitions:** Theresa Tabi, art director. " Blooming Tree Press is dedicated to producing high quality book for the young and the young at heart. It is our hope that you will find your dreams between the pages of our books."

Fiction Picture books: adventure, animal, contemporary, fantasy, folktales, history, humor, multicultural, religion, science fiction, special needs, sports. Young readers: adventure, animal, contemporary, fantasy, folktales, history, humor, multicultural, religion, science fiction, special needs, sports, suspense. Middle readers: adventure, animal, anthology, contemporary, fantasy, folktales, history, humor, multicultural, poetry, religion, science fiction, suspense. Young adults/teens: adventure, animal, anthology, contemporary, fantasy, folktales, history, humor, religion, science fiction, suspense. Average word length: picture books: 300-1,000; young readers: 800-9,000; middle readers: 25,000-40,000; young adult/teens: 40,000-70,000. Recently published *The Kulak's Daughter*, written by Gabrielle Goldstone (mid-grade historical fiction set during the reign of Stalin); *Haven*, by Beverly Patt (mid-grade about interracial friendship); *The Amulet of Amun*

Ra, by Leslie Carmichael (a mid-grade Egyptian time travel book); *The Book of Knowledge*, by David Michael Slater (a middle grade fantasy- 2nd book in the Sacred Book Series).

Nonfiction "We are not accepting nonfiction at this time."

How to Contact Fiction: "Accepting agented, conference attendee and personally requested submissions only. No unsolicited submissions. Check website for dates of entries for the annual "The Bloom Award". Unsolicited submissions mailings received during non-submission dates weill be recycled."

Illustration Works with 6-20 illustrators/year. Send postcard size samples Attention Art Department. Samples not returned; sample filed for six months for future projects.

Terms Pays authors royalty of 10% depending on the project. Pays illustrators by the project or royalty depending on project. Authors see galleys for review; illustrators see dummies. Writer's guidelines on website.

Tips "During submission times follow the guidelines listed on our Website. Send a crisp and clean one-page query letter stating your project, why it is right for the market, and a little about yourself. Write what you know, not what's 'in.' Remember, every great writer/illustrator started somewhere. Keep submitting.. don't ever give up."

BLOOMSBURY CHILDREN'S BOOKS

Imprint of Bloomsbury PLC, 175 Fifth Avenue, 8th Floor, New York NY 10010. Website: www. bloomsburykids.com Specializes in fiction, picture books. Publishes 15 picture books/year; 10 young readers/year; 20 middle readers/year; 25 young adult titles/year. 25% of books by first-time authors.

Fiction Picture books: adventure, animal, contemporary, fantasy, folktales, history, humor, multicultural, poetry, suspense/mystery. Young readers: adventure, animal, anthology, concept, contemporary, fantasy, folktales, history, humor, multicultural, suspense/mystery. Middle readers: adventure, animal, contemporary, fantasy, folktales, history, humor, multicultural, poetry, problem novels. Young adults: adventure, animal, anthology, contemporary, fantasy, folktales, history, humor, multicultural, problem novels, science fiction, sports, suspense/mystery. Recently published *Too Purpley*, by Jean Reidy (picture books); *A Whole Nother Story*, by Dr. Cuthbert Soup (middle reader); *The Captivate*, by Carrie Jones (young adult).

Terms Pays authors royalty or work purchased outright for jackets. Offers advances. Pays illustrators by the project or royalty. Pays photographers by the project or per photo. Sends galleys to authors; dummies to illustrators. Originals returned to artist at job's completion. Writer's and art guidelines available on their website.

Tips "All Bloomsbury Children's Books submissions are considered on an individual basis. Bloomsbury Children's Books will no longer respond to unsolicited manuscripts or art submissions. Please include a telephone AND e-mail address where we may contact you if we are interested in your work. Do NOT send a self-addressed stamped envelope. We regret the inconvenience, but unfortunately, we are too understaffed to maintain a correspondence with authors. We will continue to accept unsolicited manuscripts but we can contact you ONLY if we are interested in acquiring your work. There is no need to send art with a picture book manuscript. Artists should submit art with a picture book manuscript. We do not return art samples. Please do not send us original art! Please note that we do accept simultaneous submissions but please be courteous and inform us if another house has made an offer on your work. Do not send originals or your only copy of anything. We are not liable for artwork or manuscript submissions. Do not send a SASE, as we are no longer responding to submissions. Please address all submissions to the attention of "Manuscript Submissions". Please make sure that everything is stapled, paper-clipped, or rubber-banded together. We do not accept e-mail or CD/DVD submissions. Be sure your work is appropriate for us. Familiarize yourself with our list by going to bookstores or libraries."

ⓝ BOLD STROKES BOOKS, INC.

P.O. Box 249, Valley Falls NY 12185. (518)753-6642. Fax: (518)753-6648. E-mail: publisher@ boldstrokesbooks.com. **Contact:** Len Barot, acq. director (general/genre gay/lesbian fiction). Trade paperback originals and reprints; electronic originals and reprints 300 queries/year; 300 mss/ year.

Fiction "Submissions should have a gay, lesbian, transgendered, or bisexual focus and should be positive and life-affirming." Submit completed ms with bio, cover letter, and synopsis—electronically only.

Nonfiction Submit completed ms with bio, cover letter, and synopsis electronically only.

Tips "We are particularly interested in authors who are interested in craft enhancement, technical development, and exploring and expanding traditional genre definitions and boundaries and are looking for a long-term publishing relationship ."

BOYDS MILLS PRESS

815 Church St., Honesdale PA 18431. Website: www.boydsmillspress.com. Estab. 1990. Imprints: Calkins Creek Books, Front Street, Wordsong. 5% of books from agented writers. "We publish a wide range of quality children's books of literary merit, from preschool to young adult."

Fiction Ages 0-10: adventure, contemporary, humor, multicultural, rhyming. Picture books: all kinds. Multicultural themes include any story showing a child as an integral part of a culture and which provides children with insight into a culture they otherwise might be unfamiliar with.

Nonfiction All levels: nature/environment, history, science. Picture books, young readers, middle readers: animal, multicultural. Does not want to see reference/curricular text.

How to Contact Fiction/nonfiction: Submit complete ms or submit through agent. Label package "Manuscript Submission" and include SASE. Responds in 3 months.

Illustration Works with 25 illustrators/year. Reviews ms/illustration packages from artists. Submit complete ms with 1 or 2 pieces of art. Illustrations only: Query with samples best suited to the art (postcard, 8½ × 11, etc.). Label package "Art Sample Submission." Responds only if interested. Samples returned with SASE.

Photography Assigns work.

Terms Authors paid royalty or work purchased outright. Offers advances. Illustrators paid by the project or royalties; varies. Photographers paid by the project, per photo, or royalties; varies. Manuscripts/artist's guidelines available on Website.

Tips "Picture books with fresh approaches, not worn themes, are our strongest need at this time. Check to see what's already on the market and on our Website before submitting your story. Prose fiction for middle-grade through young adult should be submitted to Boyds Mills' imprint Front Street-see Front Street listing for submission information. Poetry for all ages should be submitted to Boyds Mills' Wordsong imprint-see Wordsong listing for submission information. Historical fiction and nonfiction about the United States for all ages should be submitted to Calkins Creek Books-see Calkins Creek listing for submission information."

ⓓ BRIGHT RING PUBLISHING, INC.

P.O. Box 31338, Bellingham WA 98228. (360)592-9201. Fax: (360)592-4503. E-mail: maryann@ brightring.com. Website: www.brightring.com. **Editor:** MaryAnn Kohl.

- Bright Ring is no longer accepting manuscript submissions.

Ⓝ CALKINS CREEK

815 Church St. Honesdale PA 18431. Website: www.calkinscreekbook.com. Estab. 2004. "We aim to publish books that are a well-written blend of creative writing and extensive research which emphasize important events, people, and places in U.S. history."

Fiction All levels: history. Recently published *Healing Water,* by Joyce Moyer Hostetter (ages 10 and up, historical fiction); *The Shakeress,* by Kimberly Heuston (ages 12 and up, historical fiction).

Nonfiction All levels: history. Recently published *Farmer George Plants a Nation,* by Peggy Thomas (ages 8 and up, nonfiction picture book); *Robert H. Jackson,* by Gail Jarrow (ages 10 and up, historical fiction);

How to Contact Accepts international submissions. Fiction: Submit outline/synopsis and 3 sample chapters. Nonfiction: Submit outline/synopsis and 3 sample chapters. Considers simultaneous submissions. Label package "Manuscript Submissions" and include SASE.

Illustration Accepts material from international illustrators. Works with 25 (for all Boyds Mills Press imprints) illustrators/year. Uses both color and b&w. Reviews ms/illustration packages. For ms/illustration packages: Submit ms with 2 pieces of final art. Submit ms/illustration packages to address above, label package " Manuscript Submission". Reviews work for future assignments. If interested in illustrating future titles, query with samples. Submit samples to address above, label package "Art Sample Submission".

Photography Buys stock images and assigns work. Submit photos to: address above, label package "Art Sample Submission". Uses color or b&w 8 × 10 prints. For first contact, send promo piece (color or b&w).

Terms Authors paid royalty or work purchased outright. Offers advances. Illustrators paid by the project or royalties; varies. Photographers paid by the project, per photo, or royalties; varies. Manuscripts/artist's guidelines available on Website.

Tips "Read through our recently-published titles and review our catalog. When selecting titles to publish, our emphasis will be on important events, people, and places in U.S. history. Writers are encouraged to submit a detailed bibliography, including secondary and primary sources, and expert reviews with their submissions."

CANDLEWICK PRESS

99 Dover S., Somerville MA 02144. (617)661-3330. Fax: (617)661-0565. E-mail: bigbear@candlewick.com. Publishes 160 picture books/year; 15 middle readers/year; 15 young adult titles/year. 5% of books by first-time authors. "Our books are truly for children, and we strive for the very highest standards in the writing, illustrating, designing and production of all of our books. And we are not averse to risk." **Contact:** Karen Lotz, publisher; Liz Bicknell, editorial director and associate publisher; Joan Powers, editorial director; Mary Lee Donovan, executive editor; Sarah Ketchersid, senior editor; Deborah Wayshak, executive editor; Andrea Tompa, associate editor; Katie Cunningham, associate editor; Kaylan Adair, associate editor; Kate Fletcher, associate editor; Jennifer Yoon, associate editor. Art Acquisitions: Anne Moore.

- Candlewick Press is not accepting queries and unsolicited mss at this time. Candlewick title *Good Masters! Sweet Ladies! Voices from a Medieval Village,* by Amy Schlitz won the John Newbery Medal in 2008. Their title *Twelve Rounds to Glory: The Strong of Muhammad Ali,* by Charles R. Smith Jr., illustrated by Bryan Collier, won a Coretta Scott King Author Honor Award in 2008. Their title *The Astonishing Life of Octavian Nothing,* by M.T. Anderson won the Boston Globe-Hornbook Award for Fiction and Poetry in 2007.

Fiction Picture books: animal, concept, contemporary, fantasy, history, humor, multicultural, nature/environment, poetry. Middle readers, young adults: contemporary, fantasy, history, humor, multicultural, poetry, science fiction, sports, suspense/mystery. Recently published *The Astonishing life of Octavian Nothing, Traitor to the Nation: Volume One: The Pox Party* by M.T. Anderson (young adult fiction); *Surrender*, by Sonya Hartnett (young adult fiction); *Good Masters! Sweet Ladies! by* Laura Amy Schlitz, illustrated by Robert Byrd (middle grade poetry collection), *Dragonology,* by Ernest Drake; Encyclopedia Prehistorica*: Dinosaurs,* by Robert Sabuda and Matthew Reinhart.

Nonfiction Picture books: concept, biography, geography, nature/environment. Young readers: biography, geography, nature/environment. Recently published *Twelve Rounds to Glory: The Story of Muhammad Ali*, by Charles R. Smith Jr., illustrated by Bryan Collier.

Illustration Works with approx. 40 illustrators/year. "We prefer to see a range of styles from artists along with samples showing strong characters (human or animals) in various settings with various emotions." *Does not accept unsolicited illustration packages/dummies.*

Terms Pays authors royalty of 2½-10% based on retail price. Offers advances. Pays illustrators 2½-10% royalty based on retail price. Sends galleys to authors; dummies to illustrators. Pays photographers 2½-10% royalty. Original artwork returned at job's completion.

CAROLRHODA BOOKS, INC.

A division of Lerner Publishing Group, 241 First Ave. N. Minneapolis MN 55401. Website: www. lernerbooks.com. Estab. 1969. Publishes hardcover originals. Averages 8-10 picture books each year for ages 3-8, 6 fiction titles for ages 7-18, and 2-3 nonfiction titles for various ages.

- Starting in 2007, Lerner Publishing Group no longer accepts submissions to any of their imprints except for Kar-Ben Publishing.

How to Contact "We will continue to seek targeted solicitations at specific reading levels and in specific subject areas. The company will list these targeted solicitations on our Website and in national newsletters, such as the SCBWI Bulletin."

CARTWHEEL BOOKS

Imprint of Scholastic Inc. 557 Broadway, New York NY 10012. Website: www.scholastic.com. Estab. 1991. Book publisher. Editorial Director: Cecily Kaiser. **Manuscript Acquisitions:** Rotem Moscovich, editor; Jeffrey Salane, editor. **Art Acquisitions:** Daniel Moreton, Creative Director. Publishes 15-25 picture books/year; 10-15 easy readers/year; 40-50 novelty/concept/board books/year.

Fiction Picture books, young readers: humor, seasonal/holiday, humor, family/love. Average word length: picture books—100-500; easy readers-100-1,500.

Nonfiction Picture books, young readers: seasonal/curricular topics involving animals (polar animals, ocean animals, hibernation), nature (fall leaves, life cycles, weather, solar system), history (first Thanksgiving, MLK Jr.George Washington, Columbus). "Most of our nonfiction is either written on assignment or is within a series. We do not want to see any arts/crafts or cooking." Average word length: picture books-100-1,500; young readers-100-2,000.

How to Contact Cartwheel Books is no longer accepting unsolicited mss. All unsolicited materials will be returned unread. Fiction/nonfiction: For previously published or agented authors, submit complete ms. Responds to mss in 6 months. Publishes a book within 2 years after acceptance. SASE required with all submissions.

Illustration Works with 30 illustrators/year. Reviews illustration packages from artists. Illustrations only: Query with samples; arrange personal portfolio review; send promo sheet, tearsheets to be kept on file. Contact: Creative Director. Responds in 6 months. Samples returned with SASE; samples filed. Please do not send original artwork.

Photography Buys stock and assigns work. Uses photos of kids, families, vehicles, toys, animals. Submit published samples, color promo piece.

Terms Pays advance against royalty or flat fee. Sends galley to authors; dummy to illustrators. Originals returned to artist at job's completion.

Tips "With each Cartwheel list, we seek a pleasing balance of board books and novelty books, hardcover picture books and gift books, nonfiction, paperback storybooks and easy readers. Cartwheel seeks to acquire projects that speak to young children and their world: new and exciting novelty formats, fresh seasonal and holiday stories, curriculum/concept-based titles, and books for beginning readers. Our books are inviting and appealing, clearly marketable, and have inherent educational and social value. We strive to provide the earliest readers with relevant and exciting books that will ultimately lead to a lifetime of reading, learning, and wondering. Know what types of books we do. Check out bookstores or catalogs first to see where your work would fit best, and why."

MARSHALL CAVENDISH CHILDREN'S BOOKS

Imprint of Marshall Cavendish, 99 White Plains Rd. Tarrytown NY 10591-9001. (914)332-8888. **Publisher:** Margery Cuyler. **Art Acquisitions:** Anahid Hamparian, art director. Publishes 60-70 books/year.

Fiction Publishes fiction for all ages/picture books.

How to Contact Query nonfiction. Submit 3 chapters (or more) for fiction or for synopsis. For picture books, submit the complete manuscript. Only replies if interested. Authors may submit to other publishers simultaneously.

Illustration Contact: Art Director.

Terms Pays authors/illustrators advance and royalties.

☐ CHARLESBRIDGE

85 Main St. Watertown MA 02472. (617)926-0329. Fax: (617)926-5720. E-mail: tradeeditorial@ charlesbridge.com. Website: www.charlesbridge.com. Estab. 1980. Book publisher. **Contact:** Trade Editorial Department. Publishes 60% nonfiction, 40% fiction picture books and early chapter books. Publishes nature, science, multicultural, social studies, and fiction picture books and transitional "bridge books" (books ranging from early readers to middle-grade chapter books).

Fiction Picture books and chapter books: "Strong, realistic stories with enduring themes." Considers the following categories: adventure, concept, contemporary, health, history, humor, multicultural, nature/environment, special needs, sports, suspense/mystery. Recently published *The Searcher and Old Tree*, by David McPhail; *Good Dog, Aggie,* by Lori Ries; *The Perfect Sword,* by Scott Goto; *Not So Tall for Six*, by Dianna Hutts Aston; *Wiggle and Waggle,* by Caroline Arnold; *Rickshaw Girl,* by Mitali Perkins.

Nonfiction Picture books and chapter books: animal, biography, careers, concept, geography, health, history, multicultural, music/dance, nature/environment, religion, science, social issues, special needs, hobbies, sports. Average word length: picture books-1,000. Recently published *After Gandhi,* by Anne Sibley O'Brien and Perry Edmond O'Brien; *The Mysteries of Beethoven's Hair*, by Russell Martin and Lydia Nibley; *Sea Queens*, by Jane Yolen; *Trout are Made of Trees,* by April Pulley Sayre; *Life on Earth-and Beyond: An Astrobiologist's Quest,* by Pamela S. Turner. Charlesbridge title *Hello, Bumblebee Bat*, written by Darrin Lunde, illustrated by Patricia J. Wynne, won a Theodor Seuss Geisel Award in 2008.

How to Contact Send mss as exclusive submission for three months. Responds only to mss of interest. Full mss only; no queries. Please do not include a self-addressed stamped envelope.

Illustration Works with 5-10 illustrators/year. Uses color artwork only. Illustrations only: Query with samples; provide resume, tearsheets to be kept on file. "Send no original artwork, please." Responds only if interested. Samples returned with SASE; samples filed. Originals returned at job's completion. Pays authors and illustrators in royalties or work purchased outright. Manuscript/art guidelines available for SASE. Exclusive submissions only.

Tips "Charlesbridge publishes picture books and transitional 'bridge books'. We look for fresh and engaging voices and directions in both fiction and nonfiction."

⊞ CHELSEA HOUSE, AN IMPRINT OF INFOBASE PUBLISHING

Facts on File, 132 West 31st Street, 17th Floor, New York, New York 10001. (800)322-8755. Fax: (917)339-0326. E-mail: jciovacco@factsonfile.com. Website: www.chelseahouse.com. Specializes in nonfiction chapter books. **Manuscript Acquisitions:** Laurie Likoff, editorial director; Justine Ciovacco, managing editor. Imprints: Chelsea Clubhouse; Chelsea House. Produces 150 middle readers/year, 150 young adult books/year. No 10% of books by first-time authors.

How to Contact "All books are parts of series. Most series topics are developed by in-house editors, but suggestions are welcome. Authors my query with résumé and list of publications."

⊡ CHRISTIAN ED. PUBLISHERS

P.O. Box 26639, San Diego CA 92196. (858)578-4700. Website: www.ChristianEdWarehouse.com. Book publisher. **Acquisitions:** Janet Ackelson, assistant editor; Carol Rogers, managing editor; Michelle Anson, production coordinator. Publishes 80 Bible curriculum titles/year. "We publish curriculum for children and youth, including program and student books and take-home papers— all handled by our assigned freelance writers only. Do not send unsolicited manuscripts. Ask for a writer's application."

Fiction Young readers: contemporary. Middle readers: adventure, contemporary, suspense/mystery. "We publish fiction for Bible club take-home papers. All fiction is on assignment only. Do not send unsolicited manuscripts. Ask for a writer's application"

Nonfiction Publishes Bible curriculum and take-home papers for all ages. Recently published *All-Stars for Jesus*, by Lucinda Rollings and Laura Gray, illustrated by Aline Heiser (Bible club curriculum for grades 4-6); *Honeybees Classroom Activity Sheets*, by Janet Miller and Wanda Pelfrey, illustrated by Ron Widman (Bible club curriculum for ages 2-3).

How to Contact Fiction/nonfiction: Query. Responds to queries in 5 weeks. Publishes assignments1 year after acceptance. Send SASE for guidelines or contact Christian Editor at crogers@cehouse.com. Ask for a writer's application. Do not send manuscripts.

Illustration Works with 6-7 illustrators/year. Query by e-mail. Contact: Michelle Anson, production coordinator (manson@cehouse.com). Responds in 1 month. Samples returned with SASE.

Terms Work purchased outright from authors for 3¢/word. Pays illustrators $15-18/page. Book catalog available for 9 × 12 SAE and 4 first-class stamps; ms and art guidelines available for SASE or via e-mail.

Tips "Read our guidelines carefully before sending us a manuscript or illustrations. Do not send unsolicited manuscripts. All writing and illustrating is done on assignment only and must be age-appropriate (preschool-6th grade). Ask for a writer's application. Do not send manuscripts."

CHRONICLE BOOKS

680 Second St., San Francisco CA 94107. Publishes 90 (both fiction and nonfiction) books/year; 5-10% middle readers/year; young adult nonfiction titles/year. 10-25% of books by first-time authors; 20-40% of books from agented writers. **Contact:** Acquisitions: Victoria Rock, founding publisher &editor-at-large; Andrea Menotti, senior editor; Julie Romeis, editor; Melissa Manlove, editor, Naomi Kirsten,assistant editor, Mary Colgan, assistant editor].

Fiction Picture books, young readers, middle readers, young adults: "We are open to a very wide range of topics." Recently published *Wave* by Suzy Lee (all ages, picture book); *Ivy and Bean* (series), by Annie Barrows, illustrated by Sophie Blackall (ages 6-10, chapter book).

Nonfiction Picture books, young readers, middle readers, young adults: "We are open to a very wide range of topics." Recently published *Delicious: The Life & Art of Wayne Thiebaud,* by Susan Rubin (Ages 9-14, middle grade).

How to Contact Writers Fiction/nonfiction: Submit complete ms (picture books); submit outline/synopsis and 3 sample chapters (for older readers). Responds to queries in 1 month; will not respond to submissions unless interested. Publishes a book 1-3 years after acceptance. Will consider simultaneous submissions, as long as they are marked "multiple submissions." Will not consider submissions by fax, e-mail or disk. Do not include SASE; do not send original materials. No submissions will be returned; to confirm receipt, include a SASP. **Illustration** Works with 40-50 illustrators/year. Wants "unusual art, graphically strong, something that will stand out on the shelves. Fine art, not mass market." Reviews ms/illustration packages from artists. "Indicate if project *must* be considered jointly, or if editor may consider text and art separately." Illustrations only: Submit samples of artist's work (not necessarily from book, but in the envisioned style). Slides, tearsheets and color photocopies OK. (No original art.) Dummies helpful. Résumé helpful. Samples suited to our needs are filed for future reference. Samples not suited to our needs will be recycled. Queries and project proposals responded to in same time frame as author query/proposals."

Photography Purchases photos from freelancers. Works on assignment only.

Terms Generally pays authors in royalties based on retail price, "though we do occasionally work on a flat fee basis." Advance varies. Illustrators paid royalty based on retail price or flat fee. Sends proofs to authors and illustrators. Book catalog for 9 x 12 SAE and 8 first-class stamps; ms guidelines for #10 SASE.

Tips "Chronicle Books publishes an eclectic mixture of traditional and innovative children's books. We are interested in taking on projects that have a unique bent to them-be it subject matter, writing style, or illustrative technique. As a small list, we are looking for books that will lend us a distinctive flavor. We are also interested in growing our fiction program for older readers, including chapter books, middle grade, and young adult projects."

CLARION BOOKS

215 Park Ave. S. New York NY 10003. (212)420-5889. Website: www.clarionbooks.com. **Manuscript Acquisitions:** Dinah Stevenson, publisher; Virginia Buckley, contributing editor; Jennifer Wingertzahn, editor; Marcia Leonard, editor. **Art Acquisitions:** Christine Kettner, art director.

- Clarion title *The Wednesday Wars,* by Gary D. Schmidt won a Newbery Honor Medal in 2008. Picture book recently published: *The Wonderful Thing about Hiccups,* by Cece Meng, illustrated by Janet Pedersen (ages 4-7, picture book)

Fiction Recently published *The Wonderful Thing About Hiccups,* by Cece Meng, illustrated by Janet Pedersen (ages 4-7, picture book); *The Wednesday Wars,* by Gary D. Schmidt (ages 10-148, historical fiction).

Nonfiction Recently published *Who Was First? Discovering the Americas*, by Russell Freedman (ages 9-12, history).

How to Contact Picture books: Send complete mss. Fiction: Please send first three chapters and a synopsis. Nonfiction: Send query with up to 3 sample chapters. Will only respond to those manuscripts they are interested in. Will accept simultaneous submissions if informed.

Illustration Send samples (no originals).

Terms Pays illustrators royalty; flat fee for jacket illustration. Pays royalties and advance to writers; both vary. Guidelines available on Website.

CLEAR LIGHT PUBLISHERS

823 Don Diego, Santa Fe NM 87505. **Acquisitions:** Harmon Houghton, publisher. Publishes 4 middle readers/year; 4 young adult titles/year.

Nonfiction Middle readers and young adults: multicultural, American Indian and Hispanic only.

How to Contact Fiction/nonfiction: Submit complete ms with SASE. "No e-mail submissions. Authors supply art. Manuscripts not considered without art or artist's renderings." Will consider simultaneous submissions. Responds in 3 months. Only send *copies*.

Illustration Reviews ms/illustration packages from artists. "No originals please." Submit ms with dummy and SASE.

Terms Pays authors royalty of 10% based on wholesale price. Offers advances (average amount: up to 50% of expected net sales within the first year). Sends galleys to authors.

Tips "We're looking for authentic American Indian art and folklore."

CONCORDIA PUBLISHING HOUSE

3558 S. Jefferson Ave. St. Louis MO 63118. (314)268-1187. Fax: (314)268-1329. Website: www.cph. org. **Contact:** Peggy Kuethe. **Art Director:** Norm Simon. "Concordia Publishing House produces quality resources that communicate and nurture the Christian faith and ministry of people of all ages, lay and professional. These resources include curriculum, worship aids, books, and religious supplies. We publish approximately 30 quality children's books each year. We boldly provide Gospel resources that are Christ-centered, Bible-based and faithful to our Lutheran heritage."

Nonfiction Picture books, young readers, young adults: Bible stories, activity books, arts/crafts, concept, contemporary, religion. "All books must contain explicit Christian content." Recently published *Three Wise Women of Christmas*, by Dandi Daley Mackall (picture book for ages 6-10); *The Town That Forgot About Christmas*, by Susan K. Leigh (ages over 5-9, picture book); *Little Ones Talk With God* (prayer book compilation, aged 5 and up).

How to Contact Submit complete ms (picture books); submit outline/synopsis and samples for longer mss. May also query. Responds to queries in 1 month; mss in 3 months. Publishes a book 2 years after acceptance. Will consider simultaneous submissions. "Absolutely no phone queries."

Illustration Works with 20 illustrators/year. Illustrations only: Query with samples. Contact: Norm Simon, art director. Responds only if interested. Samples filed.

Terms Pays authors royalties based on retail price or work purchased outright ($750-2,000). Manuscript guidelines for 1 first-class stamp and a #10 envelope. Pays illustrators by the project.

Tips "Do not send finished artwork with the manuscript. If sketches will help in the presentation of the manuscript, they may be sent. If stories are taken from the Bible, they should follow the Biblical account closely. Liberties should not be taken in fantasizing Biblical stories."

⬛ COTEAU BOOKS LTD.

2517 Victoria Ave.Regina SK S4P 0T2 Canada. (306)777-0170. E-mail: coteau@coteaubooks.com. Website: www.coteaubooks.com. **Acquisitions:** Acquistion editor. Publishes 6 juvenile and/or young adult books/year; 14-16 books/year; 25% of books by first-time authors. "Coteau Books publishes the finest Canadian fiction, poetry, drama and children's literature, with an emphasis on western writers."

- Coteau Books publishes Canadian writers and illustrators only; mss from the U.S. are returned unopened.

Fiction Teen, young readers, middle readers, young adults: adventure, contemporary, fantasy, history, humor, multicultural, nature/environment, science fiction, suspense/mystery. "No didactic, message pieces, nothing religious, no horror. No picture books. Recently published *New: Run Like*

Jäger, by Karen Bass (ages 15 and up); *Longhorns & Outlaws*, by Linda Aksomitis (ages 9 and up); *Graveyard of the Sea*, by Penny Draper (ages 9 and up).

Nonfiction Young readers, middle readers, young adult/teen: biography, history, multicultural, nature/environment, social issues.

How to Contact Accepts unsolicited mss— fiction accepted from Jan. 1 to April 30; Children's/Teen novels from May 1 to August 31, poetry from September 1 to December 31, Nonfiction accepted any time. Submit complete manuscript, or 3-4 sample chapters, author bio. Responds in 2-3 months to queries; 6 months to mss. No simultaneous submissions. Sometimes comments on rejected mss. No e-mail submissions or queries. Include SASE. Responds to queries/mss in 4 months. Publishes a book 1-2 years after acceptance.

Illustration Works with 1-4 illustrators/year. Illustrations only: Submit nonreturnable samples. Responds only if interested. Samples returned with SASE; samples filed.

Photography "Very occasionally buys photos from freelancers." Buys stock and assigns work.

Terms Pays authors royalty based on retail price. Pays illustrators and photographers by the project. Sends galleys to authors; dummies to illustrators. Original artwork returned at job's completion. Book catalog free on request with 9 × 12 SASE.

⬜ ⬜ COTTONWOOD PRESS, INC.

109-B Cameron Drive, Fort Collins CO 80525. Estab. 1986. (970)204-0715. Fax: (970)204-0761. E-mail: cottonwood@cottonwoodpress.com. Website: www.cottonwoodpress.com. Specializes in educational material for the English/language arts classroom. **President:** Cheryl Thurston. Cottonwood Press strives "to publish materials that are effective in the classroom and help kids learn without putting them to sleep, specializing in materials for grades 5-12." No picture books. Publishes 4 middle reader and young adult books/year. 60% of books by first-time authors.

Nonfiction Middle readers: textbooks. Young Adults/Teens: textbooks. Recently published: *UnJournaling: daily writing exercises that are NOT personal, NOT introspective, NOT boring,* by Dawn DiPrince, illustrated by Cheryl Miller Thurston; *Singuini: noodling around with silly songs,* by Heather Stenner and Cheryl Miller Thurston; *Phunny Stuph: Proofreading exercises with a sense of humor,* by M.S. Samston.

How to Contact Nonfiction: Submit complete manuscript. Responds to queries in 2 weeks; mss in 2 months. Publishes a book 6 months-1 year after acceptance. Will consider simultaneous submissions if notified.

Terms Pay royalty of 10-15% based on net sales.

Tips "It is essential that writers familiarize themselves with our website to see what we do. The most successful of our authors have used our books in the classroom and know how different they are from ordinary textbooks."

CREATIVE COMPANY

Imprint of The Creative Company, P.O. Box 227, Mankato MN 56002. (800)445-6209. Fax: (507)388-2746. **Manuscript Acquisitions:** Aaron Frisch. Publishes 5 picture books/year; 40 young readers/year; 70 young adult titles/year. 5% of books by first-time authors. The company name is The Creative Company. It has two imprints: Creative Editons (picture books), and Creative Education (nonfiction series). Either The Creative Company should appear as the header for this entry, or else all picture book references should be removed if Creative Education is given as the header. Currently, we are not accepting submissions for picture books, so it is only of importance to us that the nonfiction series are described here.

Nonfiction Picture books, young readers, young adults: animal, arts/crafts, biography, careers, geography, health, history, hobbies, multicultural, music/dance, nature/environment, religion, science, social issues, special needs, sports. Average word length: young readers—500; young adults-6,000. Recently published *Empire State Building*, by Kate Riggs (age 7, young reader); *The Assassination of Archduke Ferdinand*, by Valerie Bodden (age 14, young adult/teen).

How to Contact We are not accepting fiction submissions. Nonfiction: Submit outline/synopsis and 2 sample chapters, along with division of titles within the series. Responds to queries in 3 months; mss in 3 months. Publishes book 2 years after acceptance. Do not accept illustration packages.

Photography Buys stock. Contact: Tricia Kleist, photo editor. Model/property releases not required; captions required. Uses b&w prints. Submit cover letter, promo piece. Ms. and photographer guidelines available for SAE.

Tips "We are accepting nonfiction, series submissions only. Fiction submissions will not be reviewed or returned. Nonfiction submissions should be presented in series (4,6, or 8) rather than single."

CRICKET BOOKS

Carus Publishing Company, 70 East Lake St., Suite 300, Chicago IL 60601. Website: www.cricketmag. com. Art Acquisitions: John Sandford.

- Cricket Books has a moratorium on manuscripts. Queries from agents and authors who have worked with Cricket Books are still welcome. Direct queries to Jenny Gillespie. Watch Website for updates.

Illustration Works with 4 illustrators/year. Use color and b&w. Illustration only: Please send artwork submissions via e-mail to:mail@cicadamag.com. Make sure "portfolio samples—cricket books" is the subject line of the e-mail. The file should be 72dpi RGB jpg format.Contact: John Sandford. Responds only if interested.

Tips "You may consider submitting your manuscript to one of our magazines, as we sometimes serialize longer selections and always welcome age-appropriate stories, poems, and nonfiction articles."

CROSSWAY BOOKS

Division of Good News Publishers, 1300 Crescent St., Wheaton IL 60187-5800. (630)682-4300. Fax: (630)682-4785. Website: www.crossway.com. **Contact:** Jill Carter. Estab. 1938. "'Making a difference in people's lives for Christ' as its maxim, Crossway Books lists titles written from an evangelical Christian perspective." Midsize evangelical Christian publisher. Publishes hardcover and trade paperback originals. Averages 85 total titles, 1 fiction titles/year. Member ECPA. Distributes titles through Christian bookstores and catalogs. Promotes titles through magazine ads, catalogs.

How to Contact Does not accept unsolicited mss. Agented fiction 5%.

Terms Pays negotiable royalty. Average advance: negotiable. Publishes ms 18 months after acceptance. Ms guidelines online.

DARBY CREEK PUBLISHING

7858 Industrial Pkwy., Plain City OH 43064. (614)873-7955. Fax: (614)873-7135. E-mail: info@ darbycreekpublishing.com. **Manuscript/Art Acquisitions:** Tanya Dean, editorial director. Publishes 10-15 children's books/year.

- Darby Creek does not publish picture books.

Fiction Middle readers, young adult. Recently published *The Warriors*, by Joseph Bruchac (ages 10 and up); *Dog Days*, by David Lubar (ages 10 and up); *Four Things My Geeky-Jock-of-a-Best-Friend Must Do in Europe*, by Jane Harrington.

Nonfiction Middle readers: biography, history, science, sports. Recently published *Albinio Animals*, by Kelly Milner Halls, illustrated by Rick Spears; *Miracle: The True Story of the Wreck of the Sea Venture*, by Gail Karwoski.

How to Contact Accepts international material only with U.S. postage on SASE for return; no IRCs. Fiction/nonfiction: Submit publishing history and/or résumé and complete ms for short works or outline/synopsis and 2-3 sample chapters for longer works, such as novels. Responds in 6 weeks. Does not consider previously published work.

Illustration Illustrations only: Send photocopies and résumé with publishing history. "Indicate which samples we may keep on file and include SASE and appropriate packing materials for any samples you wish to have returned."

Terms Offers advance-against-royalty contracts.

Tips "We are currently not accepting any submissions. If that changes, we will provide all children's writing publications with our new info."

📖 MAY DAVENPORT, PUBLISHERS

26313 Purissima Rd., Los Altos Hills CA 94022-4539. (650)947-1275. Fax: (650)947-1373. E-mail: mdbooks@earthlink.net. Publishes 1-2 picture books/year; 2-3 young adult titles/year. 99% of books by first-time authors. Seeks books with literary merit. "We like to think that we are selecting talented writers who have something humorous to write about today's unglued generation in 30,000-50,000 words for teens and young adults in junior/senior high school before they become tomorrow's 'functional illiterates.' We are interested in publishing literature that teachers in middle and high schools can use in their Language Arts, English and Creative Writing courses. There's more to literary fare than the chit-chat Internet dialog and fantasy trips on television with cartoons or humanoids." This publisher is overstocked with juvenile books, but interested in including poetic verse or prose by teens for teachers' read-aloud lesson plans in multicultural student classrooms K-12. **Contact:** May Davenport, editor/publisher.

Fiction Young readers, young adults: contemporary, humorous fictional literature for use in English courses in junior-senior high schools in U.S. Average word length: 40,000-60,000. Recently published *Charlie and Champ*, by Alysson Wagoner (ages 5-7); *Surviving Sarah, the Sequel: Brown Bug & China Doll*, by Dinah Leigh (ages 15-18);*The Lesson Plan*, by Irvin Gay (ages 15-18); *A Life on the Line*, by Michael Horton (ages 15-18); *Making My Escape*, by David Lee Finkle (ages 12-18); *Summer of Suspense,* by Frances D. Waines; *A Young Girl visits Grandparents Who Rented Rooms to Students with Meals Included; Girl Learns about Freezing Food, Canning, Sleuthing, Too. Modern Equipment of the Grandparents and Sheriff were Gems (ages 14-18)*.

Nonfiction Teens: shocking pathway choices. Recently published *The Runaway Game*, by Kevin Casey (a literary board game of street life in Hollywood, ages 15-18).

How to Contact Fiction: Query. Responds to queries/mss in 3 weeks. Mss returned with SASE. Publishes a book 6-12 months after acceptance.

Illustration Works with 1-2 illustrators/year. "Have enough on file for future reference." Responds only if interested. Samples returned with SASE; samples filed. Originals returned at job's completion.

Terms Pays authors royalty of 15% based on retail price; negotiable. Pays "by mutual agreement, no advances." Pays illustrators by the project (range: $75-350). Guidelines free on request with SASE.

DAWN PUBLICATIONS

12402 Bitney Springs Rd., Nevada City CA 95959. (530)274-7775. Website: www.dawnpub.com. Book publisher. Co-Publishers: Muffy Weaver and Glenn J. Hovemann. **Acquisitions:** Glenn J. Hovemann. Publishes works with holistic themes dealing with nature. "Dawn Publications is dedicated to inspiring in children a deeper appreciation and understanding of nature."

Fiction Picture books exploring relationships with nature. No fantasy or legend.

Nonfiction Picture books: animal, nature/environment. Prefers "creative nonfiction."

How to Contact Query or submit complete ms by mail (enclose self-addressed stamped envelope for reply) or by e-mail (go to the website for e-mail address and instructions). Responds to queries/mss in 3 months.

Illustration Works with 5 illustrators/year. Will review ms/illustration packages from artists. Query; send ms with dummy. Illustrations only: Query with samples, résumé.

Terms Pays authors royalty based on net sales. Offers advance. Book catalog and ms guidelines available online.

Tips Looking for "picture books expressing nature awareness with inspirational quality leading to enhanced self-awareness. Does not publish anthropomorphic works; no animal dialogue."

DELACORTE PRESS

Delacorte Press is an imprint of Random House Children's Books, a division of Random House, Inc., 1745 Broadway, Mail Drop 9-2, New York, NY 10019. (212)782-9000. Websites: www.randomhouse.com/kids, www.randomhouse.com/teens. Publishes middle-grade and young adult fiction in hard cover and trade paperback formats.

- Publishes middle-grade and young adult fiction in hard cover, trade paperback, mass market and digest formats.

How to Contact Unsolicited manuscripts are only accepted as submissions to the Delacorte Dell Yearling Contest for a First Middle Grade Novel Delacorte Press Contest for a First Young Adult Novel. See www.randomhouse.com/kids/writingcontests for rules and guidelines or send a written request addressed to Delacorte Press Contest, Random House, Inc. 1745 Broadway, New York, NY 10019 and include a SASE. All other query letters or manuscript submissions must be submitted through an agent or at the request of an editor. No e-mail queries.

DIAL BOOKS FOR YOUNG READERS

Penguin Young Readers Group, 345 Hudson St., New York NY 10014. Website: www.penguin.com. President and Publisher: Lauri Hornik. **Acquisitions:** Kathy Dawson, Associate Publisher; Kate Harrison, senior editor; Liz Waniewski, editor; Alisha Niehaus, editor; Jessica Garrison, editor. **Art Director:** Lily Malcom. Publishes 20 picture books/year; 3 young readers/year; 12 middle readers/year; 15 young adult titles/year.

Fiction Recently published *Savvy*, by Ingrid Law (ages10-14); *Incarceron* by Catherine Fisher (ages 12 and up); *The Sky Is Everywhere* by Jandy Nelson (ages 14 and up); *Dragonbreath*, by Ursula Vernon (ages 9-11); *Ladybug Girl*, by Jacky Davis and David Soman (ages 3-7).

Nonfiction Will consider query letters for submissions of outstanding literary merit. Recently published *Listen to the Wind* by Greg Mortenson and Susan L. Roth (ages 5-8) and *Omnivore's Dilemma* by Michael Pollan (ages 10-14).

How to Contact "Due to the overwhelming number of unsolicited manuscripts we receive, we at Dial Books for Young Readers have had to change our submissions policy: As of August 1, 2005, Dial will no longer respond to your unsolicited submission unless interested in publishing it. Please do not include SASE with your submission. You will not hear from dial regarding the status of your submission unless we are interested, in which case you can expect a reply from us within four months. We accept entire picture book manuscripts and a maximum of 10 pages for longer works (novels, easy-to-reads). When submitting a portion of a longer work, please provide an accompanying cover letter that briefly describes your manuscript's plot, genre (i.e. easy-to-read, middle grade or YA novel), the intended age group, and your publishing credits, if any."

Illustration "Art samples should be sent to attn: Dial Design and will not be returned without SASE. Never send original art. Please do not phone, fax, or email to inquire after your art submission."

Terms Pays authors and illustrators in royalties based on retail price. Average advance payment varies

DISKUS PUBLISHING

Contact: Joyce McLaughlin, inspirational and children's editor; Holly Janey, submissions editor. Publishes e-books.

Fiction Submit publishing history, bio, Estimated Word Count and Genre. Submit complete ms.

Ⓐ Ⓨ DISNEY HYPERION BOOKS FOR CHILDREN

114 Fifth Ave.New York NY 10011-5690. 914-288-4100. Fax: (212)633-4833. Website: www. hyperionbooksforchildren.com. **Manuscript Acquisitions:** Editorial Director. 10% of books by first-time authors. Publishes various categories. All submissions must come via an agent. b>

- Hyperion title *Are You Ready to Play Outside*, by Mo Willems, won the Theodor Seuss Geisel Award in 2009. Their title *We Are the Ship,* by Kadir Nelson won a Coretta Scott King Author Award. Their title *The Disreputable History of Frankie Landou-Banks*, by E. Lockhart was a National Book Award Finalist and won a Michael L. Printz Honor.

Fiction Picture books, early readers, middle readers, young adults: adventure, animal, anthology (short stories), contemporary, fantasy, history, humor, multicultural, poetry, science fiction, sports, suspense/mystery. Middle readers, young adults: commercial fiction.

Nonfiction Narrative nonfiction for elementary schooler's.

How to Contact Only interested in agented material.

Illustration Works with 100 illustrators/year. "Picture books are fully illustrated throughout. All others depend on individual project." Illustrations only: Submit résumé, business card, promotional literature or tearsheets to be kept on file. Responds only if interested. Original artwork returned at job's completion.

Photography Works on assignment only. Provide résumé, business card, promotional literature or tearsheets to be kept on file.

Terms Pays authors royalty based on retail price. Offers advances. Pays illustrators and photographers royalty based on retail price or a flat fee. Sends galleys to authors; dummies to illustrators.

DIVERSION PRESS

E-mail: diversionpress@yahoo.com. **Contact:** Attn: Acquisition Editor. Publishes hardcover, trade and mass market paperback originals

Fiction "We will happily consider any children's or young adult books if they are illustrated. If your story has potential to become a series, please address that in your proposal. Fiction short stories and poetry will be considered for our anthology series. See website for details on how to submit your ms."

Nonfiction "The editors have doctoral degrees and are interested in a broad range of academic works. We are also interested in how-to, slice of life, and other nonfiction areas." We will not review works that are sexually explicit, religious, or put children in a bad light. Send query/proposal first. Mss accepted by request only.

Tips Check out Ellabug, our first children's book, on Diversion Press Blog.

Ⓐ DK PUBLISHING

375 Hudson St.New York NY 10014. Website: www.dk.com. **Acquisitions:** submissions editor. "DK publishes photographically illustrated nonfiction for children of all ages."

- DK Publishing does not accept unagented manuscripts or proposals.

Ⓐ DOG-EARED PUBLICATIONS

P.O. Box 620863, Middletown WI 53562-0863. (608)831-1410. Fax: (608)831-1410. E-mail: field@dog-eared.com. Website: www.og-eared.com. **Art Acquisitions:** Nancy Field, publisher. Publishes 2-3 middle readers/year. 1% of books by first-time authors. "Dog-Eared Publications creates action-packed nature books for children. We aim to turn young readers into environmentally aware citizens and to foster a love for science and nature in the new generation.

Nonfiction Middle readers: activity books, animal, nature/environment, science. Average word length: varies. Recently published *Discovering Black Bear*, by Margaret Anderson, Nancy Field and Karen Stephenson, illustrated by Michael Maydak (middle readers, activity book); *Leapfrogging Through Wetlands*, by Margaret Anderson, Nancy Field and Karen Stephenson, illustrated by Michael Maydak (middle readers, activity book); *Ancient Forests*, by Margaret Anderson, Nancy Field and Karen Stephenson, illustrated by Sharon Torvik (middle readers, activity book).

How to Contact Nonfiction: **Currently not accepting unsolicited mss**.

Illustration Works with 2-3 illustrators/year. Reviews ms/illustration packages from artists. Submit query and a few art samples. Illustrations only: Query with samples. Responds only if interested. Samples not returned; samples filed. "Interested in realistic, nature art!"

Terms Pays authors royalty based on wholesale price. Offers advances (amount varies). Pays illustrators royalty based on wholesale price. Sends galleys to authors. Originals returned to artist at job's completion. Brochure available for SASE and 1 first-class stamp or on Website.

Ⓜ DUTTON CHILDREN'S BOOKS

Imprint of Penguin Group (USA), Inc. 345 Hudson St., New York NY 10014. (212)4143700. Fax: (212)414-3397. Website: www.penquin.com/youngreaders. **Contact**: Lauri Hornik, president and publisher; Julie Strauss-Gabel, associate publisher (literary contemporary young adult fiction); Lucia Monfried, senior editor (picture books and middle grade fiction); Sara Reynolds, art director. Estab.1852. Dutton Children's Books publishes fiction and nonfiction for readers ranging from preschoolers to young adults on a variety of subjects. Publishes hardcover originals as well as novelty formats. Averages 50 titles/year. **Needs:** Dutton Children's Books has a diverse, general-interest list that includes picture books, and fiction for all ages and occasional retail-appropriate nonfiction. Recently published *Skippyjon Jones Lost in Spice*, by Judy Schachner (picture book); *Thirteen*, by Lauren Myracle (middle grade novel); *Paper Towns*, by John Green (young adult novel); and *If I Stay*, by Gayle Forman (young adult novel).

How to Contact Query letter only; include SASE

Terms Pays royalty on retail price. Offers advance.

Ⓒ EDCON PUBLISHING GROUP

30 Montauk Blvd., Oakdale NY 11769. (631)567-7227. Fax: (631)567-8745. Website: www.edconpublishing.com. **Manuscript Acquisitions:** Editor. Publishes 6 young readers/year, 6 middle readers/year, 6 young adult titles/year. 30% of books by first-time. Looking for educational games and nonfiction work in the areas of math, science, reading and social studies.

Fiction Recently adapted/published *A Christmas Carol*; *Frankenstein*; *Around the World in 80 Days*; *The Picture of Dorian Grey*.

Nonfiction Grades 1-12 though primarily 6-12 remedial.

How to Contact Submit outline/synopsis and 1 sample chapter. Publishes book 6 months after acceptance. Will consider simultaneous submissions. Submission kept on file unless return is requested. Include SASE for return.

Illustration Buys b&w and color illustrations and currently seeking computerized graphic art. Send postcards, samples, links to edcon@EDCONPublishing.com. Mailed Submissions kept on file, not returned.

Terms Work purchased outright from authors for up to $1,000. Pays illustrators by the project (range: $100-$500). Catalog available at Website Catalog available at: https://www.edconpublishing.com/Edcon-Catalog.pdf.

⬚ EDUPRESS, INC.

401 S. Wright Rd., Janesville WI 53546. (800)558-9332. Fax: (800)835-7978. E-mail: edupress@highsmith.com. Website: www.edupressinc.com. **Manuscript Acquisitions:** Elizabeth Bowie, product development manager. "Our mission is to create products that make kids want to go to school!"

How to Contact Nonfiction: Submit complete ms. Responds to queries/mss in 3 months. Publishes book 1-2 years after acceptance.

Illustration Query with samples. Contact: Cathy Baker, product development manager. Responds only if interested. Samples returned with SASE.

Photography Buys stock.

Terms Work purchased outright from authors. Pays illustrators by the project. Book catalog available at no cost. Catalog available on Website.

Tips "We are looking for unique, research-based, quality supplemental materials for Pre-K through eighth grade. We publish all subject areas in many different formats, including games. Our materials are intended for classroom and home schooling use."

EERDMANS BOOKS FOR YOUNG READERS

An imprint of Wm. B. Eerdmans Publishing Co., 2140 Oak Industrial Dr. NE, Grand Rapids, MI 49505 (616) 459-4591. Fax: (616) 776-7683. E-mail: youngreaders@eerdmans.com. Website: www.eerdmans.com/youngreaders. **Writers contact:** Acquisitions Editor. **Illustrators contact:** Gayle Brown, Art director. Produces 10-12 picture books/year; 2 middle readers/year; 2 young adult books/year. 10% of books by first-time authors. " We seek to engage young minds with words and pictures that inform and delight inspire and entertain. From board books for babies to picture books, nonfiction, and novels for children and young adults, our goal is to produce quality literature for a new generation of readers. We believe in books!"

Fiction Picture books: animal, concept, contemporary, folktales, history, humor, multicultural, nature/environment, poetry, religion, special needs, social issues, sports, suspense. Young readers: animal, concept, contemporary, fantasy, folktales, history, humor, multicultural, poetry, religion, special needs, social issues, sports, suspense. Middle readers: adventure, contemporary, history, humor, multicultural, nature/environment, problem novels, religion, social issues, sports, suspense. Young adults/teens: adventure, contemporary, fantasy, folktales, history, humor, multicultural, nature/environment, problem novels, religion, sports, suspense. Average word length: picture books-1,000; middle readers-15,000; young adult-45,000. Recently published *My Name is Sangoel,* by Karen Lynn Williams and Khadra Mohammed, illustrated by Catharine Stock (picture book, ages 7-10); *A River of Words,* written by Jen Bryant, illustrated by Melissa Sweet (picture book, ages 7 & up); *Garmann's Summer,* written and illustrated by Stian Hole (picture book, ages 5-8). *Ethan, Suspended,* by Pamela Ehrenberg (middle reader fiction, ages 11-14)

Nonfiction Middle readers: biography, history, multicultural, nature/environment, religion, social issues. Young adults/teens: biography, history, multicultural, nature/environment, religion, social issues. Average word length: middle readers-35,000; young adult books-35,000. Recently published *Eva's Story,* by Eva Schloss.

How to Contact We only consider submissions sent EXCLUSIVELY to Eerdmans. YA and Middle Reader fiction: Please send query, synopsis, and 3 sample chapters. Responds to exclusive queries/ mss in 3-5 months. "We no longer acknowledge or respond to unsolicited manuscripts. Exceptions will be made only for exclusive submissions marked as such on outside envelope."

Illustration Accepts material from international illustrators. Works with 10-12 illustrators/year. Uses color artwork primarily. Reviews work for future assignments. If interested in illustrating future titles, send promo sheet. Submit samples to Gayle Brown, art director. Samples not returned. Samples filed.

Terms Offers advance against royalties. Author sees galleys for review. Illustrators see proofs for review. Originals returned to artist at job's completion. Catalog available for 8 × 10 SASE and 4 first-class stamps. Offers writer's guidelines for SASE. See Website for writer's guidelines. (www. eerdmans.com/youngreaders/submit.htm)

Tips "Find out who Eerdmans is before submitting a manuscript. Look at our website, request a catalog, and check out our books."

EGMONT USA

443 Park Ave South, New York NY 10016. Estab. 2008. The Egmont Group was founded in 1878. (212)685-0102. Website: egmont-us.com. Specializes in trade books. Imprints: Egmont USA. **Acquisitions:** Elizabeth Law (VP & Publisher), Regina Griffin (Executive Editor). Publishes 5 picture books/year; 5 young readers/year; 20 middle readers/year; 20 young adult/year. 25% of books by first-time authors. "Egmont USA publishes quality commercial fiction. We are committed to editorial excellence and to providing first rate care for our authors. Our motto is that we turn writers in authors and children into passionate readers."

Fiction Picture Books: animal, concept, contemporary, humor, multicultural. Young Readers: adventure, animal, contemporary, humor, multicultural. Middle Readers: adventure, animal, contemporary, fantasy, humor, multicultural, problem novels, science fiction, special needs. Young Adults/Teens: adventure, animal, contemporary, humor, multicultural, problem novels, science fiction, special needs. *Leaving the Belleweathers,* by Kristen Venuti (Fall 09); *Back,* by Julia Keller (Fall 09); *The Cinderella Society,* (Spring 2010).

How to Contact Only interested in agented material. Fiction: Submit complete query. Responds to queries in 4 weeks; mss in 6 weeks. Publishes a book 18 months after acceptance. Will consider e-mail submissions.

Illustration Only interested in agented in material. Works with 5 illustrators/year. Uses both color and b&w. Illustrations only: Query with samples. **Contact:** Alison Weiss (Editorial Assistant). Responds only if interested. Samples are not returned.

Terms Pays authors royalties based on retail price. Pays illustrators royalties.

ENSLOW PUBLISHERS INC.

Box 398, 40 Industrial Rd., Berkeley Heights NJ 07922-0398. Fax: (908)771-0925. E-mail: info@ enslow.com. Website: www.enslow.com or www.myreportlinks.com. **Acquisitions:** Brian D. Enslow, vice president. Imprint: MyReportLinks.com Books. Publishes 30 young readers/year; 70 middle readers/year; 100 young adult titles/year. 30% of books by first-time authors.

- Enslow Imprint MyReportLinks.com Books produces books on animals, states, presidents, continents, countries, and a variety of other topics for middle readers and young adults, and offers links to online sources of information on topics covered in books.

Nonfiction Young readers, middle readers, young adults: animal, arts/crafts, biography, careers, geography, health, history, multicultural, nature/environment, science, social issues, sports. Middle readers, young adults: hi-lo. "Enslow is moving into the elementary (grades 3-4) level and is looking for authors who can write biography and suggest other nonfiction themes at this level."

Average word length: young readers-2,000; middle readers-5,000; young adult-18,000. Published *It's About Time! Science Projects*, by Robert Gardner (grades 3-6, science); *Georgia O'Keeffe: Legendary American Painter*, by Jodie A. Shull (grades 6-12, biography); *California: A MyReportLinks.com Book*, by Jeff Savaga (grades 5-8, social studies/history).

How to Contact Nonfiction: Send for guidelines. Query. Responds to queries/mss in 2 weeks. Publishes a book 18 months after acceptance. Will not consider simultaneous submissions.

Illustration Submit résumé, business card or tearsheets to be kept on file. Responds only if interested. Samples returned with SASE only.

Terms Pays authors royalties or work purchased outright. Pays illustrators by the project. Pays photographers by the project or per photo. Sends galleys to authors. Book catalog/ms guidelines available for $3, along with an 8½ × 11 SASE and $2 postage or via Website.

FACTS ON FILE

132 W. 31st St., New York NY 10001. (212)967-8800. Fax: (212)967-9196. E-mail: editorial@ factsonfile.com. Website: www.factsonfile.com. Estab. 1941. Book publisher. Editorial Director: Laurie Likoff. **Acquisitions:** Frank Darmstadt, science and technology/nature; Andrew Gyory, American history and cultural studies; Jeff Soloway, language and literature; Owen Lancer, world studies; Jim Chambers, arts, health and entertainment. "We produce high-quality reference materials for the school library market and the general nonfiction trade." Publishes 25-30 young adult titles/year. 5% of books by first-time authors; 25% of books from agented writers; additional titles through book packagers, co-publishers and unagented writers.

Nonfiction Middle readers, young adults: animal, biography, careers, geography, health, history, multicultural, nature/environment, reference, religion, science, social issues and sports.

How to Contact Nonfiction: Submit outline/synopsis and sample chapters. Responds to queries in 10 weeks. Publishes a book 10-12 months after acceptance. Will consider simultaneous submissions. Sends galleys to authors. Book catalog free on request. Send SASE for submission guidelines.

Terms Submission guidelines available via website or with SASE.

Tips "Most projects have high reference value and fit into a series format."

🔲 FARRAR, STRAUS & GIROUX INC.

18 West 18th St., New York, NY 10010. (212)741-6900. Website: www.fsgkidsbooks.com. Estab. 1946. Book publisher. Imprints: Frances Foster Books. Children's Books Editorial Director: Margaret Ferguson. **Manuscript Acquisitions:** Margaret Ferguson, editorial director; Frances Foster, Frances Foster Books; Wesley Adams, executive editor; Janine O'Malley, Senior editor. **Art Director:** Robbin Gourley, art director, Books for Young Readers. Publishes 40 picture books/year; 30 middle grade books/year; 10 young adult titles/year. 5% of books by first-time authors; 20% of books from agented writers.

- Farrar title *How I Learned Geography*, by Uri Shulevitz, won a Caldecott Honor in 2009. Farrar/Frances Foster title *The Wall: Growing Up Behind the Iron Curtain*, by Peter Siís, won a Caldecott Honor Medal in 2008. Farrar/Melanie Kroupa title *Rex Zero and the End of the World,* by Tim Wynne-Jones, won a Boston Globe-Horn Book Fiction and Poetry Honor Award in 2007. Farrar/Frances Foster title *Dreamquake: Book Two of the Dreamhunter Duet*, by Elizabeth Knox, won a Michael L. Printz Honor Award in 2008. See First Books on page 133 for interviews with Deborah Diesen and Dan Hanna, author and illustrator of Farrar, Straus & Giroux title *The Pout-Pout Fisho*.

Fiction All levels: all categories. "Original and well-written material for all ages." Recently published *The Cabinet of Wonders*, by Marie Rutkoski; *Last Night*, by Hyewon Yum.

Nonfiction All levels: all categories. "We publish only literary nonfiction."

How to Contact Fiction/nonfiction: for novels, query with outline/synopsis and 3 sample chapters; for picture books send complete ms. Do not fax or e-mail submissions or queries. Responds to queries/mss in 3 months. Publishes a book 18 months after acceptance. Will consider simultaneous submissions.

Illustration Works with 30-60 illustrators/year. Reviews ms/illustration packages from artists. Submit ms with 1 example of final art, remainder roughs. Do not send originals. Illustrations only: Query with tearsheets. Responds if interested in 3 months. Samples returned with SASE; samples sometimes filed.

Terms "We offer an advance against royalties for both authors and illustrators." Sends galleys to authors; dummies to illustrators. Original artwork returned at job's completion. Book catalog available for 9 × 12 SASE with $1.95 postage; ms guidelines for SASE 1 first-class stamp, or can be viewed at www.fsgkidsbooks.com.

Tips "Study our catalog before submitting. We will see illustrator's portfolios by appointment. Don't ask for criticism and/or advice-due to the volume of submissions we receive, it's just not possible. Never send originals. Always enclose SASE."

⊠ FENN PUBLISHING CO.

34 Nixon Rd., Bolton ON L7E 1W2 Canada. (905)951-6600. Fax: (905)951-6601. E-mail: fennpubs@ hbfenn.com. Website: www.hbfenn.com. Manuscript/Art Acquisitions: C. Jordan Fenn, publisher. Publishes 35 books/year. Publishes children's and young adult fiction.

Fiction Picture books: adventure, animal, sports. adult sports.

How to Contact Query or submit complete ms. Responds to queries/mss in 2 months.

Illustration Reviews ms/illustration packages from artists. Responds only if interested. Samples not returned or filed.

⊠ FITZHENRY & WHITESIDE LTD.

195 Allstate Pkwy. Markham ON L3R 4T8 Canada. (905)477-9700. Fax: (905)477-9179. E-mail: charkin@fitzhenry.ca. Website: www.fitzhenry.ca. Book publisher. **President:** Sharon Fitzhenry; Children's Publisher: Cathy Sandusky. Publishes 3 picture books/year; 4 middle novels/year; 3 young adult titles/year; 3 juvenile nonfiction titles/year. 10% of books by first-time authors. Publishes fiction and nonfiction-social studies, visual arts, biography, environment. Emphasis on Canadian authors and illustrators, subject or perspective.

How to Contact Submissions Editor: Christie Harkin. Fiction/nonfiction. Publishes a book 12-24 months after acceptance. See full submission guidelines on website www.fitzhenry.com.

Illustration Works with approximately 10 illustrators/year. Reviews ms/illustration packages from artists. Submit outline and sample illustration (copy). Illustrations only: Query with samples and promo sheet. Samples not returned unless requested.

Photography Buys photos from freelancers. Buys stock and assigns work. Captions required. Uses b&w 8 × 10 prints; 35mm and 4 × 5 transparencies, 300 + dpi digital images. Submit stock photo list and promo piece.

Terms Pays authors 8-10% royalty with escalations. Offers "respectable" advances for picture books, 50/50 split between author and illustrator. Pays illustrators by the project and royalty. Pays photographers per photo. Sends galleys to authors; dummies to illustrators.

Tips "We respond to quality."

⬚ ▭ FIVE STAR PUBLICATIONS, INC.

P.O. Box 6698, Chandler AZ 85246-6698. (480)940-8182. Fax: (480)940-8787. E-mail: info@ fivestarpublications.com. Web sites: www.FiveStarPublications.com, www.LittleFivestar.

com, www.FiveStarLegends,com, www.FiveStarSleuths.com, www.SixPointsPress.com. **Art Acquisitions:** Sue DeFabis. Publishes 7 middle readers/year.

Nonfiction Recently published *Tic Talk Book: Living with Tourette Syndrome*, by Dylan Peters, illustrated by Zachary Wendland (www.TicTalkBook.com); *Alfie's Bark Mitzvah*, by Shari Cohen, songs by Cantor Marcello Gindlin, illustrated by Nadia Komorova (www.AlfiesBarkMitvah.com).

How to Contact Nonfiction: Query.

Illustration Works with 3 illustrators/year. Reviews ms/illustration packages from artists. Query. Illustrations only: Query with samples. Responds only if interested. Samples filed.

Photography Buys stock and assigns work. Works on assignment only. Submit letter.

Terms Pays illustrators by the project. Pays photographers by the project. Sends galleys to authors; dummies to illustrators.

FLUX

Llewellyn Worldwide, Ltd., 2143 Wooddale Drive, Woodbury MN 55125. (651)312-8613. Fax: (651)291-1908. Imprint estab. 2005; Lllewellyn estab. 1901. Publishes 21 young adult titles/year. 50% of books by first-time authors. "Flux seeks to publish authors who see YA as a point of view, not a reading level. We look for books that try to capture a slice of teenage experience, whether in real or imagined worlds." **Contact:** Brian Farrey, acquisitions editor.

Fiction Young Adults: adventure, contemporary, fantasy, history, humor, problem novels, religion, science fiction, sports, suspense. Average word length: 50,000. Recently published *Ballad*, by Maggie Stiefvater; *The Dust of 100 Dogs*, by A.S. King; *Return to Paradise*, by Simone Elkeles; *Gigged*, by Heath Gibson

How to Contact Query. Responds to mss in 3-4 months. Will consider simultaneous submissions and previously published work.

Terms Pays royalties of 10-15% based on wholesale price. Offers advance. Authors see galleys for review. Book catalog available on Website. Writer's guidelines available for SASE or on Website.

Tips "Read contemporary teen books. Be aware of what else is out there. If you don't read teen books, you probably shouldn't write them. Know your audience. Write incredibly well. Do not condescend."

FREE SPIRIT PUBLISHING

217 Fifth Ave. N.Suite 200, Minneapolis MN 55401-1299. (612)338-2068. Fax: (612)337-5050. E-mail: acquisitions@freespirit.com. Website: www.freespirit.com. Publishes 25-30 titles/year for pre-K through 12, educators and parents. "Free Spirit is the leading publisher of learning tools that support young people's social and emotional health, helping children and teens to think for themselves, succeed in life, and make a difference in the world."

• Free Spirit does not accept fiction, poetry or storybook submissions.

How to Contact Accepts nonfiction submissions from prospective authors or through agents. "Please review catalog and author guidelines (both available online) before submitting proposal." Responds to queries in 4-6 months. "If you'd like material returned, enclose an SASE with sufficient postage." Accepts queries only—not submissions—by e-mail.

Illustration Works with 5 illustrators/year. Submit samples to creative director for consideration. If appropriate, samples will be kept on file and artist will be contacted if a suitable project comes up. Enclose SASE if you'd like materials returned.

Photography Uses stock photos. Does not accept photography submissions.

Terms Pays authors royalty based on net receipts. Offers advance. Pays illustrators by the project.

Tips "We do not publish fiction, poetry or picture storybooks, books with animals or mythical characters, books with religious content, or single biographies, autobiographies or memiors. Free Spirit prefers books written in a practical, psychologically sound, and positive style."

FREESTONE/PEACHTREE, JR.

Peachtree Publishers, 1700 Chattahoochee Ave., Atlanta GA 30318-2112. (404)876-8761. Fax: (404)875-2578. E-mail: hello@peachtree-online.com. Website: www.peachtree-online.com. **Acquisitions:** Helen Harriss. Publishes 4-8 young adult titles/year.

- Freestone and Peachtree, Jr. are imprints of Peachtree Publishers. See the listing for Peachtree for submission information. No e-mail or fax queries or submissions, please.

Fiction Picture books: animals, folktales, health, history, humor, multicultural, nature/environment, special needs, sports. Young readers: history, humor, health, multicultural, sports. Middle readers: adventure, contemporary, history, humor, multicultural, problem novels, sports, suspense/mystery. Young adults/teens: adventure, contemporary, history, humor, multicultural, problem novels, sports, suspense/mystery. Recently published *Martina the Beautiful Cockroach,* by Carmen Agra Deedy, illustrated by Michael Austin (ages 4-8, picture book); *Young Charles Darwin and the Voyage of the Beagle*, written by Ruth Ashby (ages 7-10; early reader); *The Sorta Sisters,* , by Adrian Fogelin (ages 8-12, middle reader); *Giving Up the Ghost*, By Sheri Sinykin (ages 12-16, young adult).

Nonfiction Picture books, young readers, middle readers, young adults: history, sports. Picture books: animal, health, multicultural, nature/environment, science, social issues, special needs.

How to Contact Responds to queries/mss in 6 months.

Illustration Works with 10-20 illustrators/year. Responds only if interested. Samples not returned; samples filed. Originals returned at job's completion.

Terms Pays authors royalty. Pays illustrators by the project or royalty. Pays photographers by the project or per photo.

FRONT STREET

Imprint of Boyds Mills Press, 815 Church Street, Honesdale, PA 18431. Website: www.frontstreetbooks. com. Publishes 20-25 titles/year. "We look for fresh voices for children and young adults. Titles on our list entertain, challenge, or enlighten, always employing novel characters whose considered voices resonate." High-end picture books.

- Front Street title *Keturah and Lord Death*, by Martine Leavitt, was a 2007 National Book Award Finalist. Front Street title *One Whole and Perfect Day*, by Judith Clarke won a Michael L. Printz Honor Book Award in 2008.

Fiction Recently published *I'm Being Stalked by a Moonshadow*, by Doug MacLeod; *Runaround*, by Helen Hemphill; *Baby*, by Joseph Monninger.

How to Contact Fiction: Submit cover letter and complete ms if under 30 pages; submit cover letter, 1 or 2 sample chapters and plot summary if over 30 pages. Label package "Manuscript Submission." Include SASE with submissions if you want them returned. "We try to respond within three months."

Illustration "Send sample illustrations. Label package 'Art Sample Submission.'"

Terms Pays royalties.

⬚ FULCRUM PUBLISHING

4690 Table Mountain Drive, Suite 100 Golden CO 80403. (303)277-1623. Fax: (303)279-7111. Website: www.fulcrum-books.com. **Manuscript Acquisitions:** T. Baker, acquisitions editor.

Nonfiction Middle and early readers: Western history, Nature/ Environment, Native American.

How to Contact Submit complete ms or submit outline/synopsis and 2 sample chapters. "Publisher does not send response letters unless we are interested in publishing." Do not send SASE.

Photography Works on assignment only.

Terms Pays authors royalty based on wholesale price. Offers advances. Book catalog available for 9 × 12 SAE and 77¢ postage; Ms submission guidelines available on website under "Authors" tab.

Tips "Research our line first. We look for books that appeal to the school market and trade. "

Ⓐ DAVID R. GODINE, PUBLISHER

9 Hamilton Place, Boston MA 02108. (617)451-9600. Fax: (617)350-0250. Website: www.godine. com. Estab. 1970. Book publisher. Publishes 1 picture book/year; 1 young reader/year; 1 middle reader/year. 10% of books by first-time authors; 90% of books from agented writers. "We publish books that matter for people who care."

- This publisher is no longer considering unsolicited manuscripts of any type.

Fiction Picture books: adventure, animal, contemporary, folktales, nature/environment. Young readers: adventure, animal, contemporary, folk or fairy tales, history, nature/environment, poetry. Middle readers: adventure, animal, contemporary, folk or fairy tales, history, mystery, nature/ environment, poetry. Young adults/teens: adventure, animal, contemporary, history, mystery, nature/environment, poetry. Recently published *Little Red Riding Hood*, by Andrea Wisnewski (picture book); *The Merchant of Noises*, by Anna Rozen, illustrated by François Avril.

Nonfiction Picture books: alphabet, animal, nature/environment. Young readers: activity books, animal, history, music/dance, nature/environment. Middle readers: activity books, animal, biography, history, music/dance, nature/environment. Young adults: biography, history, music/ dance, nature/environment.

How to Contact Only interested in agented material. Query. Include SASE for return of material.

Illustration Only interested in agented material. Works with 1-3 illustrators/year. "Please do not send original artwork unless solicited. Almost all of the children's books we accept for publication come to us with the author and illustrator already paired up. Therefore, we rarely use freelance illustrators." Samples returned with SASE.

Tips "E-mail submissions are not accepted. Always enclose a SASE. Keep in mind that we do not accept unsolicited manuscripts and that we rarely use freelance illustrators."

Ⓐ GOLDEN BOOKS

1745 Broadway, New York NY 10019. (212)782-9000. **Editorial Directors:** Courtney Silk, color and activity; Chris Angelilli, storybooks; Dennis Shealy, novelty. **Art Acquisitions:** Tracey Tyler, executive art director.

- See listing for Random House-Golden Books for Young Readers Group.

Fiction Publishes board books, novelty books, picture books, workbooks, series (mass market and trade).

How to Contact Does not accept unsolicited submissions.

GRAPHIA

Harcourt Houghton Mifflin, 222 Berkeley St., Boston MA 02116. (617)351-5000. Website: www. graphiabooks.com. **Manuscript Acquisitions:** Julia Richardson. "Graphia publishes quality paperbacks for today's teen readers, ages 14 and up. From fiction to nonfiction, poetry to graphic novels, Graphia runs the gamut, all unified by the quality of writing that is the hallmark of this imprint."

Fiction Young adults: adventure, contemporary, fantasy, history, humor, multicultural, poetry. Recently published: *The Off Season,* by Catherine Murdock; *Come in from the Cold,* by Marsha Qualey; *Breaking Up is Hard to Do,* with stories by Niki Burnham, Terri Clark, Ellen Hopkins, and Lynda Sandoval; *Zahrah the Windseeker,* by Nnedi Okorafot-Mbachu.

Nonfiction Young adults: biography, history, multicultural, nature/environment, science, social issues.

How to Contact Query. Responds to queries/mss in 3 months. Will consider simultaneous submissions and previously published work.

Illustration Do not send original artwork or slides. Send color photocopies, tearsheets or photos to Art Dept. Include SASE if you would like your samples mailed back to you.

Terms Pays author royalties. Offers advances. Sends galleys to authors. Catalog available on Website (www.houghtonmifflin.com).

GREENE BARK PRESS

P.O. Box 1108, Bridgeport CT 06601-1108. (610)434-2802. Fax: (610)434-2803. E-mail: greenebark@ aol.com; service@greenebarkpress.com.

Fiction Picture books, young readers: adventure, fantasy, humor. Average word length: picture books—650; young readers-1,400. Recently published *Edith Ellen Eddy*, by Julee Ann Granger; *Would You Invite a Skunk To Your Wedding?*, by Ginger Pate.

How to Contact Responds to queries in 3 months; mss in 6 months; must include SASE. No response without SASE. Publishes a book 18 months after acceptance. Will consider simultaneous submissions. Prefer to review complete mss with illustrations.

Illustration Works with 1-2 illustrators/year. Uses color artwork only. Reviews ms/illustration packages from artists. Submit ms with 3 pieces of final art (copies only). Illustrations only: Query with samples. Responds in 2 months only if interested. Samples returned with SASE; samples filed. Originals returned at job's completion.

Terms Pays authors royalty of 10-12% based on wholesale price. Pays illustrators by the project (range: $1,500-3,000) or 5-7% royalty based on wholesale price. No advances. Sends galleys to authors; dummies to illustrators. Manuscript guidelines available for SASE or per e-mail request.

Tips "As a guide for future publications look to our latest publications, do not look to our older backlist. Please, no telephone, e-mail or fax queries."

GREENHAVEN PRESS

Imprint of the Cengage Gale, 27500 Drake Road, Farmington Hills MI 48331. E-mail: Kristine. burns@cengage.com. Website: www.gale.com/greenhaven. **Acquisitions:** Kristine Burns. Publishes 220 young adult academic reference titles/year. 50% of books by first-time authors. Greenhaven continues to print quality nonfiction anthologies for libraries and classrooms. Our well known Opposing Viewpoints series is highly respected by students and librarians in need of material on controversial social issues. Greenhaven accepts no unsolicited manuscripts. All writing is done on a work-for-hire basis. Also see listing for Lucent Book.

Nonfiction Young adults (high school): controversial issues, social issues, history, literature, science, environment, health. Recently published (series): Issues That Concern You; Writing the Critical Essay: An Opening Viewpoint Guide; Introducing Issue with Opposing Viewpoints; Social Issues in Literature; and Perspectives on Diseases and Disorders.

How to Contact Send query, resume, and list of published works by e-mail.

Terms Work purchased outright from authors; write-for-hire, flat fee.

GREENWILLOW BOOKS

1350 Avenue of the Americas, New York NY 10019. (212)261-6500. Website: www. harpercollinschildrens.com. Book publisher. Imprint of HarperCollins. Vice President/Publisher: Virginia Duncan. **Art Acquisitions:** Paul Zakris, Art Director. Publishes 30 picture books/year; 5 middle readers/year; 5 young adult books/year. "Greenwillow Books publishes picture books, fiction for young readers of all ages, and nonfiction primarily for children under seven years of age."

• Greenwillow Books is currently accepting neither unsolicited manuscripts nor queries. Unsolicited mail will not be opened and will not be returned. Call (212)261-6627 for an update. Greenwillow title *Escape!: The Story of the Great Houdini*, by Sid Fleischman, won a Boston Globe-Horne Book Nonfiction Honor Award in 2007.

Illustration Art samples (postcards only) should be sent in duplicate to Paul Zakris and Virginia Duncan.

Terms Pays authors royalty. Offers advances. Pays illustrators royalty or by the project. Sends galleys to authors.

Ⓐ GROSSET & DUNLAP PUBLISHERS

Penguin Group (USA), Inc 345 Hudson St.New York NY 10014. Website: http://us.penguingroup.com/youngreaders. Estab. 1898. **Acquisitions:** Francesco Sedita, Vice-President/Publisher. Publishes approximately 140 titles/year. "Grosset & Dunlap publishes high interest, affordable books for children ages 0-10 years. We focus on original series, licensed properties, readers and novelty books."

Fiction Recently published series: Frankly Frannie; George Brown, Class Clown; Bedeviled; Hank Zipzer; Camp Confidential; Katie Kazoo; Magic Kitten; Magic Puppy; The Hardy Boys; Nancy Drew; The Little Engine That Could. *Upcoming series*: Splurch Academy for Disruptive Boys; Gladiator Boy; Dinkin Dings; Hello, Gorgeous!; **Licensed series:** Angelina Ballerina; Disney Club Penguin; Charlie & Lola; Star Wars: The Clone Wars; WWE; Disney's Classic Pooh; Max & Ruby; The Penguins of Madagascar; Batman: The Brave and the Bold; Strawberry Shortcake

Nonfiction *Young readers:* nature/environment, science. Recently published series: *All Aboard Reading*; *Who Was..?* series.

How to Contact "We do not accept e-mail submissions. Unsolicited manuscripts usually receive a response in 6-8 weeks."

▨ GROUNDWOOD BOOKS

110 Spadina.Suite 801, Toronto ON M5V 2K4 Canada. (416)363-4343. Fax: (416)363-1017. Website: www.groundwoodbooks.com. **Manuscript Acquisitions:** Acquisitions Editor. **Art Acquisitions:** Art Director. Publishes 10 picture books/year; 3 young readers/year; 5 middle readers/year; 5 young adult titles/year, approximately 2 nonfiction titles/year. 10% of books by first-time authors; Nonfiction: Recently published *Hip Hop* (A Ground Group), by Dalton Higgins; Picture Books: Recently published *When Stella Was Very, Very Small*, by Marie-Louise Gay (ages 2-5); *Bella's Tree*, by Janet Russell, illustrated by Jirina Marton; *Alego*, by Ningeokuluk Teevee; *A Coyote Solstice Tale*, by Thomas King, illustrated by Gary Clement. Fiction: Recently published *Against The Odds*, by Marjolijn Hof; *Rex Zero, The Great Pretender*, by Tim Wynne-Jones; *Poster Boy*, by Dede Crane.

Fiction Recently published *The Shepherd's Granddaughter*, by Anne Laurel Carter (y/a); *The Saver*, by Edeet Ravel (y/a).

How to Contact Fiction: Submit synopsis and sample chapters. Responds to mss in 6-8 months. Will consider simultaneous submissions.

Illustration Works with 20 illustrators/year. Reviews ms/illustration packages from artists. Illustrations only: Send resume, promo sheet, slides, color or b&w copies, and tearsheets. Responds only if interested. Samples not returned.

Terms Offers advances. Pays illustrators by the project for cover art; otherwise royalty. Sends galleys to authors; dummies to illustrators. Originals returned to artist at job's completion. Backlist available on website.

Tips "Try to familiarize yourself with our list before submitting to judge whether or not your work is appropriate for Groundwood. Visit our website for guidelines."

⬚ GRYPHON HOUSE

P.O. Box 207, Beltsville MD 20704-0207. (301)595-9500. Fax: (301)595-0051. E-mail: kathyc@ghbooks.com. Website: www.gryphonhouse.com. **Acquisitions:** Kathy Charner, editor-in-chief.

Nonfiction Parent and teacher resource books, textbooks. Recently published *Reading Games*, by Jackie Silberg; *Primary Art*, by MaryAnn F. Kohl; *Teaching Young Children's with Autism Spectrum Disorder*, by Clarissa Willis; *The Complete Resource Book for Infants*, by Pam Schiller. "At Gryphon House, our goal is to publish books that help teachers and parents enrich the lives of children from birth through age eight. We strive to make our books useful for teachers at all levels of experience, as well as for parents, caregivers, and anyone interested in working with children."

How to Contact Query. Submit outline/synopsis and 2 sample chapters. Responds to queries/mss in 6 months. Publishes a book 18 months after acceptance. Will consider simultaneous submissions, e-mail submissions.

Illustration Works with 4-5 illustrators/year. Uses b&w realistic artwork only. Illustrations only: Query with samples, promo sheet. Responds in 2 months. Samples returned with SASE; samples filed.

Photography Buys photos from freelancers. Buys stock and assigns work. Submit cover letter, published samples, stock photo list.

Terms Pays authors royalty based on wholesale price. Offers advances. Pays illustrators by the project. Pays photographers by the project or per photo. Sends edited ms copy to authors. Original artwork returned at job's completion. Book catalog and ms guidelines available via website or with SASE.

Tips "Send a SASE for our catalog and manuscript guidelines. Look at our books, then submit proposals that complement the books we already publish or supplement our existing books. We are looking for books of creative, participatory learning experiences that have a common conceptual theme to tie them together. The books should be on subjects that parents or teachers want to do on a daily basis."

H & W PUBLISHING INC

531 Conrad Dr., Cincinnati OH 45231. Estab. 2007. (513)675-2968. Fax: (513)761-4221. E-mail: info@handwpublishing.com. Website: www.handwpublishing.com. Specializes in African American children's literature. Publishes 2 books/year. 90% of books by first-time authors. "Our company empowers, inspires, and uplifts."

Fiction Picture Books: concept, contemporary, humor, poetry, religion. Young Readers: adventure, contemporary, nature/environment, poetry. Middle Readers: contemporary, problem novels. Average word length: picture books-1,200; young readers-850; middle readers-2,500. Recently published *Coralee's Best Run Yet*, by Karen N. Harkness, Alpha Frierson, (ages 6-8 picture book); *Obama Our Hero*, by Karen N. Harkness, Elbert Lewis Jr. (ages 5-12, biography).

Nonfiction Young Readers: biography, social issues. Average word length: picture books-700; young readers-1,200.

How to Contact Submit complete manuscript or submit outline/synopsis. Responds to queries in 1 month. Responds to mss in 2 months. Publishes a book 18 months after acceptance.

Illustration Works with 3 illustrators/year. Uses both color and b&w. Submit work history and 3 samples or URL that displays a minimum of 3 original illustrations. Contact: Karen Harkness, submissions department.

Terms Pays authors royalty 5% and work purchased outright for $2,500-4,000. Pays illustrators by the project-range ($1,800-3,500) and royalty of 3-5% based on retail price. Originals returned to artist at job's completion. Writers and artists guidelines available at www.handwpublishing.com.

Tips "We specialize in literature for African American children. Illustrations should be detailed and reflect positive images. Story lines should either be humorist, contemporary, or teach without being preachy. No books on slavery please."

HACHAI PUBLISHING

527 Empire Blvd., Brooklyn NY 11225. (718)633-0100. Fax: (718)633-0103. E-mail: info@hachai. com; hachai1@aol.com. Publishes 4 picture books/year; 1 young reader/year; 1 middle reader/ year. 75% of books published by first-time authors. "All books have spiritual/religious themes, specifically traditional Jewish content. We're seeking books about morals and values; the Jewish experience in current and Biblical times; and Jewish observance, Sabbath and holidays." **Contact:** Devorah Leah Rosenfeld, submissions editor.

Fiction Picture books and young readers: contemporary, historical fiction, religion. Middle readers: adventure, contemporary, problem novels, religion. Does not want to see fantasy, animal stories, romance, problem novels depicting drug use or violence. Recently published *Let's Go To The Farm*, written and illustrated by Rikki Benenfeld (ages 2-5, picture book); *Dear Tree*, written by Doba Rivka Weber, and illustrated by Phyllis Saroff (ages 2-5, picture book); *The Waiting Wall*, by Leah Levy, illustrated by Avi Katz (ages 3-6 picture book); *Gifts to Treasure*, by Tehilla Greenberger (ages 7-10, short chapter book).

Nonfiction Recently published *The Invisible Book*, by Bracha Goetz, illustrated by Patti Agroff; *My Jewish ABC's*, by Draizy Zelcer, illustrated by Patti Nemeroff (ages 3-6, picture book); *Shadow Play*, by Leah Pearl Shollar, illustrated by Pesach Gerber (ages 3-6, picture book); *Much Much Better*, by Chaim Kosofsky, illustrated by Jessica Schiffman (ages 5-8).

How to Contact Fiction/nonfiction: Submit complete ms. Responds to queries/mss in 6 weeks.

Illustration Works with 4 illustrators/year. Uses primary color artwork, some b&w illustration. Reviews ms/illustration packages from authors. Submit ms with 1 piece of final art. Illustrations only: Query with samples; arrange personal portfolio review. Responds in 6 weeks. Samples returned with SASE; samples filed.

Terms Work purchased outright from authors for $800-1,000. Pays illustrators by the project (range: $2,000-4,000). Book catalog, ms/artist's guidelines available for SASE.

Tips "Write a story that incorporates a moral, not a preachy morality tale. Originality is the key. We feel Hachai publications will appeal to a wider readership as parents become more interested in positive values for their children."

Ⓐ Ⓥ HARCOURT CHILDREN'S BOOKS

Imprint of Houghton Mifflin Harcourt Children's Book Group, 215 Park Ave South, New York, NY 10003. Website: www.harcourtbooks.com. **Senior Vice President and Publisher:** Betsy Groban. **Vice President and Editorial Director:** Jeannette Larson. 20% of books by first-time authors; 50% of books from agented writers. "Harcourt Children's Books publishes hardcover picture books and fiction only." Harcourt Children's Books no longer accepts unsolicited manuscripts, queries or illustrations. Recent Harcourt titles *Ten Little Fingers and Ten Little Toes*, by Mem Fox, illustrated by Helen Oxenbury; *Help Me, Mr. Mut!*, by Janet Stevens and Susan Stevens Crummel; *How I Became a Pirate and Pirates Don't Change Diapers*, by Melinda Long, illustrated by David Shannon; and Frankenstein Makes a Sandwich, by Adam Rex, are all New York Times bestsellers. *My Abuelita*, by Tony Johnston, illustrated by Yuyi Morales was named an Ala Notable Children's book for 2010.

How to Contact Only interested in agented material.

Illustration Only interested in agented material.

Photography Works on assignment only.

Terms Pays authors and illustrators royalty based on retail price. Pays photographers by the project. Sends galleys to authors; dummies to illustrators. Original artwork returned at job's completion.

Ⓐ Ⓨ HARPERCOLLINS CHILDREN'S BOOKS

10 East 53rd St., New York NY 10022. (212)261-6500. Website: www.harpercollinschildrens. com. Book publisher. President and Publisher: Susan Katz. Associate Publisher/Editor-in-Chief: Kate Morgan Jackson. Associate Publisher, Fiction: Elise Howard. Editorial Directors: Margaret Anastas, Barbara Lalicki, Maria Modugno, Phoebe Yeh. **Art Acquisitions:** Martha Rago or Barbara Fitzsimmons, director. Imprints: HarperTrophy, HarperTeen, EOS, HarperFestival, Greenwillow Books, Joanna Cotler Books, Laura Geringer Books, Katherine Tegen Books, Balzer and Bray. *HarperCollins Children's Books is not accepting unsolicited and/or unagented manuscripts or queries.* "Unfortunately, the volume of these submissions is so large that we cannot give them the attention they deserve. Such submissions will not be reviewed or returned." Agent submissions may be sent to Kate Morgan Jackson. Responses only if interested. Materials returned with SASE.

- HarperCollins Children's Books title *The Graveyard Book*, by Neil Gaiman won 2009 Newbury Medal, HarperTeen title *Jellicoe Road*, by Melina Marchetta won the 2009 Micael L. Printz Award, HarperCollins Children's Books title *Nation*, by Terry Pratchett won the 2009 Michael L. Printz Honor.

Fiction Publishes picture, chapter, novelty, board and TV/movie books.

Illustration Art samples may be sent to Martha Rago or Stephanie Bart-Horvath. **Please do not send original art.** Works with over 100 illustrators/year. Responds only if interested. Samples returned with SASE; samples filed only if interested.

Ⓐ HARPERTEEN

10 East 53rd Street, New York, NY 10022. (212)207-7000. Fax: (212)702-2583. Websites: www. harpercollins.com, www.harperteen.com. Book publisher. HarperTeen is an imprint of HarperCollins Children's Books. Publishes 65-70 teen titles/year.

- HarperTeen publishes hardcovers, paperback reprints and paperback originals.

How to Contact HarperCollins Children's Books is not accepting unsolicited and/or un-agented manuscripts or queries."Unfortunately the volume of these submissions is so large that we cannot give them the attention they deserve. Such submissions will not be reviewed or returned." Manuscripts and queries: Agent submissions may be sent to Elise Howard.Responses only if interested. Materials returned with SASE.

Ⓒ HAYES SCHOOL PUBLISHING CO. INC.

321 Pennwood Ave.Wilkinsburg PA 15221-3398. (412)371-2373. Fax: (800)543-8771. E-mail: chayes@hayespub.com. Website: www.hayespub.com. Estab. 1940. **Acquisitions:** Mr. Clair N. Hayes. Produces folders, workbooks, stickers, certificates. Wants to see supplementary teaching aids for grades K-12. Interested in all subject areas. Will consider simultaneous and electronic submissions.

How to Contact Query with description or complete ms. Responds in 6 weeks. SASE for return of submissions.

Illustration Works with 3-4 illustrators/year. Responds in 6 weeks. Samples returned with SASE; samples filed. Originals not returned at job's completion.

Terms Work purchased outright. Purchases all rights.

HEALTH PRESS NA INC

P.O. Box 37470, Albuquerque NM 87176-7479. (505)888-1394 or (877)411-0707. Fax: (505)888-1521. E-mail: goodbooks@healthpress.com. Website: www.healthpress.com. **Acquisitions:** Editor. Publishes 4 young readers/year. 50% of books by first-time authors.

Fiction Picture books, young readers: health, special needs. Average word length: young readers—1,000-1,500; middle readers—1,000-3,000. Recently published *The Girl With No Hair*, by Elizabeth Murphy-Melas, illustrated by Alex Hernandez (ages 8-12, picture book); Bug Bites and Campfires: A Story for Kids about Homesickness, by Frank J. Sileo, Ph.D., illustrated by Eric Scott Fisher (ages 6-12).

Nonfiction Picture books, young readers: health, special needs, social issues, self help.

How to Contact Submit complete ms. Responds in 3 month. Publishes a book 1 year after acceptance. Will consider simultaneous submissions.

Terms Pays authors royalty. Sends galleys to authors. Book catalog available.

HENDRICK-LONG PUBLISHING COMPANY

10635 Tower Oaks, Suite D, Houston TX 77070. (832)912-READ. Fax: (832)912-7353. E-mail: hendrick-long@worldnet.att.net. **Acquisitions:** Vilma Long, vice president. Publishes 4 young readers/year; 4 middle readers/year. 20% of books by first-time authors. Publishes fiction/nonfiction about Texas of interest to young readers through young adults/teens.

Fiction Young readers, middle readers: history books on Texas and the Southwest. No fantasy or poetry.

Nonfiction Young readers, middle readers: history books on Texas and the Southwest, biography, multicultural. "Would like to see more workbook-type manuscripts."

How to Contact Fiction/nonfiction: Query with outline/synopsis and sample chapter. Responds to queries in 5 months. Publishes a book 18 months after acceptance. No simultaneous submissions. Include SASE.

HOLIDAY HOUSE INC.

425 Madison Ave., New York NY 10017. (212)688-0085. Fax: (212)421-6134. Publishes 35 picture books/year; 3 young readers/year; 15 middle readers/year; 8 young adult titles/year. 20% of books by first-time authors; 10% from agented writers. Mission Statement: "To publish high-quality books for children."

Fiction *Here We Go Round the Mulberry Bush*, by Jane Cabrera; *Time Zones*, by David A. Adler; *The Day of the Dead/El Dia de los Muertos*, by Bob Barner; *Thank You, Miss Doover*, by Robin Pulver; *Nightshade City*, by Hilary Wagner; *Storm Mountain*, by Tom Birdseye; *Lafayette and the American Revolution*, by Russell Freedman

Nonfiction All levels, but more picture books and fewer middle-grade nonfiction titles: animal, biography, concept, contemporary, geography, historical, math, multicultural, music/dance, nature/environment, religion, science, social issues.

How to Contact Send complete manuscripts to the Acquisitions Editor. "We respond only to manuscripts that meet our current needs."

Illustration Works with 35 illustrators/year. Reviews ms illustration packages from artists. Send ms with dummy. Do not submit original artwork or slides. Color photocopies or printed samples are preferred. Responds only if interested. Samples filed.

Terms Pays authors and illustrators an advance against royalties. Originals returned at job's completion. Book catalog, ms/artist's guidelines available for a SASE.

Tips "We need books with strong stories, writing and art. We do not publish board books or novelties. No easy readers."

HENRY HOLT & COMPANY

175 Fifth Ave, New York NY 10010. Website: www.HenryHoltKids.com. Submissions Website: www.HenryHoltKids.com/submissions.htm. **Manuscript Acquisitions:** Addressed to submissions/Henry Holt books for young readers. **Art Acquisitions:** Patrick Collins, creative director. Publishes

30-35 picture books/year; 6-8 chapter books/year; 10-15 middle readers/year; 8-10 young adult titles/year. 15% of books by first-time authors; 40% of books from agented writers.

- "Henry Holt and Company Books for Young Readers is known for publishing quality books that feature imaginative authors and illustrators. We tend to publish many new authors and illustrators each year in our effort to develop and foster new talent."

Fiction Picture books: animal, anthology, concept, folktales, history, humor, multicultural, nature/environment, poetry, special needs, sports. Middle readers and young adults: adventure, contemporary, fantasy, history, humor, multicultural, special needs, sports, suspense/mystery.

Nonfiction Picture books: animal, arts/crafts, biography, concept, geography, history, hobbies, multicultural, the arts, nature/environment, sports. Middle readers and young readers, young adult: biography, history, multicultural, sports.

How to Contact Fiction/nonfiction: submit complete ms, Attn: submissions; " no SASE please." Responds in 4-6 months only if interested, otherwise mss are not returned or responded to. Will not consider simultaneous or multiple submissions. "We no longer accept unsolicited submissions."

Illustration Works with 50-60 illustrators/year. Reviews ms/illustration packages from artists. Random samples ok. Illustrations only: submit tearsheets, slides. Do not send originals. Responds to art samples only if interested. Samples filed but not returned. If accepted, original artwork returned at job's completion. Portfolios are reviewed every Monday.

Terms Pays authors/illustrators royalty based on retail price. Sends galleys to authors; proofs to illustrators.

⚑ HOUGHTON MIFFLIN HARCOURT

Children's Trade Books, 222 Berkeley St. Boston MA 02116-3764. (617)351-5000. Fax: (617)351-1111. E-mail: Children'sBooks@hmhpub.com. Website: www.houghtonmifflinbooks.com. **Manuscript Acquisitions:** Submissions Coordinator; Betsy Groban, publisher; Margaret Raymo, editorial director; Ann Rider, executive editor; Mary Wilcox, franchise director, Julia Richardson, paperback director; Kate O'Sullivan, senior editor, Monica Perez, franchise senior editor; Erica Zappy, associate editor. **Art Acquisitions:** Sheila Smallwood, creative director. Imprints include Houghton Mifflin, Harcourt, Clarion, Sandpiper and Graphia. Averages 60 titles/year. Publishes hardcover originals and trade paperback reprints and originals. "Houghton Mifflin gives shape to ideas that educate, inform, and above all, delight."

- Houghton title *The House in the Night*, by Susan Marie Swanson, illustrated by Beth Krommes won the 2008 Caldecott award.

Fiction All levels: all categories except religion. "We do not rule out any theme, though we do not publish specifically religious material." Recently published *Red Sings from Treetops: a year in colors*, by Joyce Sidman, illustrated by Pamela Zagarenski (ages 5-8, picture book/poetry); *The Entomological Tales of Augustus T. Percival: Petronella Saves Nearly Everyone* (ages 5 and up, middle-grade); *Cashay* (ages 12 and up, YA novel).

Nonfiction All levels: all categories except religion. Recently published *Down, Down, Down; A Journey to the Bottom of the Sea*, by Steven Jenkins (ages 5-8, picture); *The Frog Scientist*, by Pamela S. Turner photographs by Andy Comins (ages 10 and up);

How to Contact Submit entire ms typed (letter quality), double-spaced manuscript on unfolded plain white paper in a 9 × 12 envelope. "We do not accept manuscripts that are handwritten or submitted on computer disk. You do not have to furnish illustrations, but if you wish, copies of a few comprehensive sketches or duplicate copies of original art will suffice. "Nonfiction: Submit outline/synopsis and sample chapters. Responds within 4 months ONLY if interested —DO NOT SEND SELF-ADDRESSED STAMPED ENVELOPE. All declined material will be recycled.

Illustration Works with 60 illustrators/year. Reviews ms/illustration packages or illustrations only from artists: Query with samples (colored photocopies are fine); provide tearsheets. Responds in 4 months if interested. Samples returned with SASE; samples filed if interested. Address art submissions to: Art Department, Children's Trade Books.

HUNTER HOUSE PUBLISHERS

P.O. Box 2914, Alameda CA 94501-0914. (510)865-5282. Fax: (510)865-4295. E-mail: acquisitions@ hunterhouse.com. Website: www.hunterhouse.com. **Manuscript Acquisitions:** Acquisitions editor. Publishes 1-3 nonfiction titles for children/teens per year. 50% of books by first-time authors. Website: www. hunterhouse.com

Nonfiction Books are fitness/diet/exercise and activity games/social skills/classroom management-oriented. Does *not* want to see books for young children, fiction, illustrated picture books, memoir or autobiography. Published SmartFun activity book series (currently about 20 books): each has 101 games that encourage imagination, social interaction, and self-expression in children (generally between ages 3-15). Widely used in homes, schools, day-care centers, clubs, and camps. Each activity includes set-up, age range, difficulty level, materials list and a time suggestion.

How to Contact Query: visit website for submission guidelines submit overview and chapter-by-chapter synopsis, sample chapters and statistics on your subject area, support organizations or networks, personal bio and marketing ideas. "Testimonials from professionals or well-known authors are helpful, especially for health books." Responds to queries in 1-3 months; mss in 3-6 months. Publishes a book 12-18 months after acceptance. Will consider simultaneous submissions.

Terms Payment varies. Sends galleys to authors. Book catalog available. But most updated information is on website; ms guidelines for standard SAE and 1 first-class stamp.

Tips Looking for children's activity books focused on education, teamwork, skill-building, ETC. The Children's Books we publish are for a select, therapeutic audience. No fiction! Please, no fiction."

IDEALS CHILDREN'S BOOKS AND CANDYCANE PRESS

Imprints of Ideals Publications, 2636 Elm Hill Pike, Suite 120, Nashville TN 37214. Website: www. idealsbooks.com. **Manuscript Acquisitions:** Submissions. **Art Acquisitions:** Art Director. Publishes 4-6 new picture books/year; 4-6 new board books/year. 50% of books by first-time authors.

Fiction Picture books: animal, concept, history, religion. Board books: animal, history, nature/environment, religion. Average word length: picture books—1,500; board books—200.

ILLUMINATION ARTS

P.O. Box 1865, Bellevue WA 98009. (425)644-7185. Fax: (425)644-9274. E-mail: liteinfo@illumin. com. Website: www.illumin.com. **Acquisitions:** Ruth Thompson, editorial director.

Fiction Word length: Prefers under 1,000, but will consider up to 1,500 words. Recently published *God's Promise*, by Maureen Moss, illustrated by Gerald Purnell; *Roonie B. Moonie: Lost and Alone*, by Emma Perry Roberts, illustrated by Robert Rogalski.

How to Contact Fiction: Submit complete ms. Responds to queries in 3 months with SASE only. No electronic or CD submissions for text or art. Publishes a book 1-2 years after acceptance. Will consider simultaneous submissions.

Illustration Works with 3-5 illustrators/year. Uses color artwork only. Reviews ms/illustration packages from artists. Query or send ms with dummy. Illustrations only: Query with color samples, résumé and promotional material to be kept on file or returned with SASE only. Responds in 3 months with SASE only. Samples returned with SASE or filed.

Terms Pays authors and illustrators royalty based on wholesale price. Book fliers available for SASE.

Tips "Read our books and follow our guidelines. Be patient. The market is competitive. We receive 2,000 submissions annually and publish 2-3 books a year. Sorry, we are unable to track unsolicited submissions."

IMPACT PUBLISHERS, INC.

P.O. Box 6016, Atascadero CA 93423-6016. (805)466-5917. E-mail: submissions@impactpublishers. com. Website: www.impactpublishers.com. **Manuscript Acquisitions:** Freeman Porter, submissions editor. **Art Acquisitions:** J. Trumbull, production. Imprints: Little Imp Books, Rebuilding Books, The Practical Therapist Series. Publishes 1 young reader/year; 1 middle reader/year; 1 young adult title/year. 20% of books by first-time authors. "Our purpose is to make the best human services expertise available to the widest possible audience. We publish only popular psychology and self-help materials written in everyday language by professionals with advanced degrees and significant experience in the human services."

Nonfiction Young readers, middle readers, young adults: self-help. Recently published *Jigsaw Puzzle Family: The Stepkids' Guide to Fitting It Together*, by Cynthia MacGregor (ages 8-12, children's/ divorce/emotions).

How to Contact Nonfiction: Query or submit complete ms, cover letter, résumé. Responds to queries in 12 weeks; mss in 3 months. Will consider simultaneous submissions or previously published work.

Illustration Works with 1 illustrator/year. Uses b&w artwork only. Reviews ms/illustration packages from artists. Query. Contact: Children's Editor. Illustrations only: Query with samples. Contact: Jean Trumbull, production manager. Responds only if interested. Samples returned with SASE; samples filed. Originals returned to artist at job's completion.

Terms Pays authors royalty of 10-12%. Offers advances. Pays illustrators by the project. Book catalog available for #10 SAE with 2 first-class stamps; ms guidelines available for SASE. All imprints included in a single catalog.

Tips "Please do not submit fiction, poetry or narratives."

JEWISH LIGHTS PUBLISHING

P.O. Box 237, Rt. 4, Sunset Farm Offices, Woodstock VT 05091. (802)457-4000. Fax: (802)457-4004. E-mail: editorial@jewishlights.com. Website: www.jewishlights.com. **Manuscript Acquisitions:** Submissions Editor. **Art Acquisitions:** Tim Holtz. Publishes 2 picture books/year; 1 young reader/year. 50% of books by first-time authors; 25% of books from agented authors. All books have spiritual/religious themes. "Jewish Lights publishes books for people of all faiths and all backgrounds who yearn for books that attract, engage, educate and spiritually inspire. Our authors are at the forefront of spiritual thought and deal with the quest for the self and for meaning in life by drawing on the Jewish wisdom tradition. Our books cover topics including history, spirituality, life cycle, children, self-help, recovery, theology and philosophy. We do not publish autobiography, biography, fiction, haggadot, poetry or cookbooks. At this point we plan to do only two books for children annually, and one will be for younger children (ages 4-10)."

Fiction Picture books, young readers, middle readers: spirituality. "We are not interested in anything other than spirituality." Recently published *God's Paintbrush*, by Sandy Eisenberg Sasso, illustrated by Annette Compton (ages 4-9).

Nonfiction Picture book, young readers, middle readers: activity books, spirituality. Recently published *When a Grandparent Dies: A Kid's Own Remembering Workbook for Dealing with Shiva and the Year Beyond*, by Nechama Liss-Levinson, Ph.D. (ages 7-11); *Tough Questions Jews Ask: A Young Adult's Guide to Building a Jewish Life*, by Rabbi Edward Feinstein (ages 12 and up).

How to Contact Fiction/nonfiction: Query with outline/synopsis and 2 sample chapters; submit complete ms for picture books. Include SASE. Responds to queries/mss in 4 months. Publishes a book 1 year after acceptance. Will consider simultaneous submissions and previously published work.

Illustration Works with 2 illustrators/year. Reviews ms/illustration packages from artists. Query. Illustrations only: Query with samples; provide résumé. Samples returned with SASE; samples filed.

Terms Pays authors royalty of 10% of revenue received; 15% royalty for subsequent printings. Offers advances. Pays illustrators by the project or royalty. Pays photographers by the project or royalty. Sends galleys to authors; dummies to illustrators. Book catalog available for 612 × 912 SAE and 59¢ postage; ms guidelines available on website.

Tips "Explain in your cover letter why you're submitting your project to *us* in particular. Make sure you know what we publish."

JOURNEYFORTH BOB JONES UNIVERSITY PRESS

1700 Wade Hampton Blvd., Greenville SC 29614. (803)242-5100, ext. 4350. Fax: (864)298-0268. E-mail: jb@bjupress.com. Specializes in trade books. **Acquisitions Editor:** Nancy Lohr. Publishes 1 picture book/year; 2 young readers/year; 4 middle readers/year; 4 young adult titles/year. 10% of books by first-time authors. "We aim to produce well-written books for readers of varying abilities and interests and fully consistent with biblical worldview."

Fiction Young readers, middle readers, young adults: adventure, animal, contemporary, fantasy, folktales, history, humor, multicultural, nature/environment, problem novels, suspense/mystery. Average word length: young readers—10,000-12,000; middle readers—10,000-40,000; young adult/teens—40,000-60,000. Recently published *Tommy's Race,* by Sharon Hambrick, illustrated by Maurie Manning (ages 6-7, contemporary fiction); *Regina Silsby's Secret War*, by Thomas J. Brodeur (young adult historical fiction); *Two Sides to Everything*, by Deb Brammer (ages 9-12, contemporary fiction).

Nonfiction Young readers, middle readers, young adult: biography. Average word length: young readers—10,000-12,000; middle readers—10,000-40,000; young adult/teens—40,000-60,000. Recently published *Children of the Storm*, by Natasha Vius (young adult autobiography); *Fanny Crosby*, by Rebecca Davis (Christian biography).

How to Contact Fiction: Query or submit outline/synopsis and 5 sample chapters. "Do not send stories with magical elements. We are not currently accepting picture books. We do not publish: romance, science fiction, poetry and drama." Nonfiction: Query or submit outline/synopsis and 5 sample chapters. Responds to queries in 4 weeks; mss in 3 months. Publishes book 12-15 months after acceptance. Will consider previously published work.

Illustration Works with 2- 4 illustrators/year. Query with samples. Send promo sheet; will review website portfolio if applicable. Responds only if interested. Samples returned with SASE; samples filed.

Terms Pays authors royalty based on wholesale price. Pays illustrators by the project. Originals returned to artist at job's completion. Book catalog and writers guidelines are at www.bjupress.com/books/freelance.html.

JOURNEY STONE CREATIONS

3533 Danbury Rd., Fairfield OH 45014. Fax: (513)860-0176. E-mail: pat@jscbookscomsubmissions. E-mail: danelle@jscbookscom. Website: wwwjscbookscom. "We specialize in children's book publishing. Over the last five years, we have published 57 books and are now focusing on special markets and private label products. We are also creating customized books for numerous national and regional organizations. Anyone who has a message and wants that message delivered to children, are our potential clients. We will write, illustrate and publish a book with your message to kids. Our new clients include grocery chains, hospitals, banks, safety organizations, ecology and animal rights organizations and the entertainment business."

Fiction Picture books: adventure, animal, contemporary, history, humor, multicultural, nature/environment, poetry, religion, sports. Early readers: adventure, animal, contemporary, health, history, humor, multicultural, nature/environment, poetry, religion, sports, suspense. "We are not accepting middle readers at this time. "Word length: picture books—1200 or less; Early readers—5,000 or less. Recently published *Stranger Danger*, by Patricia Stirnkorb, illustrated by Claudia Wolf (ages 7-12, childhood safety); *Caterpillars Dream*, by Sally Harris.

How to Contact Query only after reviewing needs on website. Reports on queries in 4-6 weeks. Publishes a book up to 2 years after acceptance. Accepts simultaneous and electronic submissions. "At this time we are only accepting picture books and early reader books with less than 5,000 words. We are reviewing books for publication 12-18 months away."However, we are seeking only specific topics and themes. **Do not submit without first checking our website**."

Illustration Work with 25 illustrators/year. Uses color artwork only. Will review ms/illustrations packages from illustrators. Query; submit ms with 2-3 pieces of final art. Contact: Danelle Pickett, creative director. Illustrations only: Query with samples. Send tearsheets or link to online portfolio. Contact: Danelle Pickett, creative director. Samples not returned, samples filed.

Terms Pays authors negotiable based on project price or prefers to purchase work outright. Pays illustrators by the project. Book catalog available on website. Writer's/artist's guidelines available on website.

Tips "Make sure you submit only your best work. For writers, if it is not letter perfect, we don't want to see it. Review our guidelines. We cannot stress the importance of submitting only after you have read our needs. Don't waste your time and money submitting things we do not need. We are only publishing children's fiction/non-fiction, no adult or teen fiction at this time."

☐ KAEDEN BOOKS

P.O. Box 16190, Rocky River, OH 44116-6190. E-mail: lstenger@kaeden.com. Website: www.kaeden.com. **Contact:** Lisa Stenger, Editor. Kaeden Books produces high-quality children's books for the educational market.

Fiction Stories with humor, surprise endings and interesting characters suitable for the education market. "Must have well-developed plots with clear beginnings, middles and endings. No adult or religious themes." Word count range: 25-2,000.

Nonfiction Unique, interesting topics, supported with details and accurate facts. Word count range: 25-2000.

How to Contact Submit complete ms; include SASE. Do not send originals. Respond within 1 year. For complete guidelines see www.kaeden.com. No phone calls please.

Illustration Work with 8-10 illustrators per year. Looking for samples that are appropriate for children's literature. Submit color samples no larger than 8 1/2 × 11. Samples kept on file. Responds only if interested. "No originals, disks or slides please." Samples not returned.

Terms Work purchased outright from authors. Pays royalties to previous authors. Illustrators paid by project (range: $50-150/page).

Tips "We are particularly interested in humorous stories with surprise endings and beginning chapter books."

☐ KAMEHAMEHA PUBLISHING

567 South King St., Suite 118, Honolulu, HI 96813. 808-523-6200, Fax: 808-541-5305. E-mail: kspress@ksbe.edu. Website: www.KamehamehaPublishing.org. **Manuscript Acquisitions:**

Acquisitions Editor. "Kamehameha Schools Press publishes in the areas of Hawaiian history, Hawaiian culture, Hawaiian language and Hawaiian studies."

Fiction Young reader, middle readers, young adults: biography, history, multicultural, Hawaiian folklore.

Nonfiction Young reader, middle readers, young adults: biography, history, multicultural, Hawaiian folklore.

Illustration Uses color and b&w artwork. Illustrations only: Query with samples. Responds only if interested. Samples not returned.

Terms Work purchased outright from authors or by royalty agreement. Pays illustrators by the project. Sends galleys to authors. Book catalog available (call or write for copy). All imprints included in a single catalog. Catalog available on website.

Tips "Writers and illustrators must be knowledgeable in Hawaiian history/culture and be able to show credentials to validate their proficiency. Greatly prefer to work with writers/illustrators available in the Honolulu area."

KANE/MILLER BOOK PUBLISHERS, INC.

4901 Morena Blvd., Suite 213, San Diego, CA 92117. (858)456-0540. Fax: (858)456-9641. E-mail: info@kanemiller.com. Website: www.kanemiller.com. Estab. 1985. Specializes in trade books, fiction, multicultural material. **Manuscript Acquisitions/Art Acquisitions:** Kira Lynn, Editorial Dept. Publishes 20 picture books/year; 4 young readers/year; 8 middle readers/year. 50% of books by first-time authors.

Fiction Picture Books: concept, contemporary, health, humor, multicultural. Young Readers: contemporary, multicultural, suspense. Middle Readers: contemporary, humor, multicultural, suspense.

How to Contact Only interested in agented material. Fiction/nonfiction: submit outline/synopsis and 2 sample chapters. Responds to queries in 3 weeks; mss in 6 weeks. Publishes a book 1 year after acceptance. Will consider simultaneous submissions.

Illustration Only interested in agented material. Uses both color and b&w. Reviews ms/illustration packages from artists. Query. Responds in 3 weeks. Samples returned with SASE.

Terms Book catalog available online; All imprints included in a single catalog; Writer's and artist's guidelines are available. **www.kanemiller.com.**

KAR-BEN PUBLISHING, INC.

A division of Lerner Publishing Group, Inc., 241 First Ave. N., Minneapolis, MN 55401. (612)332-3344. Fax: (612)-332-7615. E-mail: editorial@karben.com\\. Website: www.karben.com. **Manuscript Acquisitions:** Joni Sussman, publisher. Publishes 10-15 books/year (mostly picture books); 20% of books by first-time authors. All of Kar-Ben's books are on Jewish themes for young children and families.

Fiction Picture books: adventure, concept, folktales, history, humor, multicultural, religion, special needs; must be on a Jewish theme. Average word length: picture books-1,000. Recently published *Engineer Ari and the Rosh Hashanah Ride,* by Deborah Bodin Cohen, illustrated by Shahar Kober; and *The Wedding That Saved a Town,* by Yale Strom, illustrated by Jenya Prosmitsky.

Nonfiction Picture books, young readers: activity books, arts/crafts, biography, careers, concept, cooking, history, how-to, multicultural, religion, social issues, special needs; must be of Jewish interest.

How to Contact Submit complete ms. Responds to queries/mss in 6 weeks. Publishes a book 24-36 months after acceptance. Will consider simultaneous submissions.

Illustration Works with 10-12 illustrators/year. Prefers four-color art in any medium that is scannable. Reviews illustration packages from artists. Submit sample of art or online portfolio (no originals).

Terms Pays authors royalties of 3-5% of net against advance of $500-1,000; or purchased outright. Original artwork returned at job's completion. Book catalog free on request. Manuscript guidelines on website.

Tips Looks for books for young children with Jewish interest and content, modern, nonsexist, not didactic. Fiction or nonfiction with a Jewish theme can be serious or humorous, life cycle, Bible story, or holiday-related. Looking in particular for stories that reflect the ethnic and cultural diversity of today's Jewish family."

KEY PORTER BOOKS

6 Adelaide St. E, Toronto ON M5C 1H6 Canada. (416)862-7777. Fax: (416)862-2304. E-mail: info@ keyporter.com. Website: www.keyporter.com. Book publisher. Key Porter Books is the largest independent, 100% Canadian-owned trade publisher.

Fiction Picture books: biographies, memoirs. Middle readers, young adult: adventure, anthology, sports.

Nonfiction Picture books: animal, arts/crafts, cooking, geography, nature/environment, reference, science, photography. Middle readers: history and business. Recently published *Crusade*, by John Wilson; *Gordon Ramsay's Weekend Brunch*, by Gordon Ramsay; *Contact Charlie*, by Chris Wattie; *Stampede: The Rise of the West and Canada's New Power Elite*, by Gordon Pitts; *Hockey Night in Canada: By the Numbers*, by Scott Morrison; *Ted Reader's Napoleon's Everyday Gourmet Grilling*, by Ted Reader; *Global Warring*, by Cleo Paskal; *The Meaning of Puck*, by Bruce Dowbiggin; *The China Wall*, by Johnny Bower; *Canada*, by Mike Grandmaison.

How to Contact Only interested in agented material; no unsolicited mss. "Although Key Porter Books does not review unsolicited manuscript submissions, we do try and review queries and proposals." Responds to queries/proposals in 6 months.

Photography Buys photos from freelancers. Buys stock and assigns work. Captions required. Uses 35mm transparencies. Submit cover letter, résumé, duplicate slides, stock photo list.

Tips "Please note that all proposals and accompanying materials will be discarded unless sufficient postage has been provided for their return. Please do not send any original artwork or other irreplaceable materials. We do not accept responsibility for any materials you submit."

KIDS CAN PRESS

29 Birch Ave., Toronto ON M4V 1E2, Canada.

- •Kids Can Press is currently accepting unsolicited manuscripts from Canadian adult authors only.

Fiction Picture books, young readers: concepts. We do not accept young adult fiction or fantasy novels for any age. Adventure, animal, contemporary, folktales, history, humor, multicultural, nature/environment, special needs, sports, suspense/mystery. Average word length: picture books 1,000-2,000; young readers 750-1,500; middle readers 10,000-15,000; young adults over 15,000. Recently published *Rosie & Buttercup*, by Chieri Ugaki, illustrated by Shephane Jorisch (picture book); *The Landing*, by John Ibbitson (novel); *Scaredy Squirrel*, by Melanie Watt, illustrated by Melanie Watt, (picture book).

Nonfiction Picture books: activity books, animal, arts/crafts, biography, careers, concept, health, history, hobbies, how-to, multicultural, nature/environment, science, social issues, special needs, sports. Young readers: activity books, animal, arts/crafts, biography, careers, concept, history, hobbies, how-to, multicultural. Middle readers: cooking, music/dance. Average word length: picture books 500-1,250; young readers 750-2,000; middle readers 5,000-15,000. Recently published *The Kids Book of Canadian Geography*, by Jane Drake and Ann Love, illustrated by Heather Collins, written and illustrated by Briony Penn (informational activity); *Science, Nature, Environment*; *Moving Day*, by Pamela Hickman, illustrated by Geraldo Valerio (animal/nature); *Everywear*, by Ellen Warwick, illustrated by Bernice Lum (craft book).

How to Contact Fiction/nonfiction: Submit outline/synopsis and 2-3 sample chapters. For picture books submit complete ms. Responds within 6 months only if interested. Publishes a book 18-24 months after acceptance.

Illustration Works with 40 illustrators/year. Reviews ms/illustration packages from artists. Send color copies of illustration portfolio, cover letter outlining other experience. Contact: Art Director. Illustrations only: Send tearsheets, color photocopies. Responds only if interested.

Ⓐ KNOPF, DELACORTE, DELL BOOKS FOR YOUNG READERS

Imprint of Random House Children's Book, Division of Random House, Inc.1745 Broadway, New York NY 10019. (212)782-9000. Website: www.randomhouse.com/kids. Book publisher.

- See listings for Random House/Golden Books for Young Readers Group, Delacorte and Doubleday Books for Young Readers, Alfred A. Knopf and Crown Books for Young Readers, and Wendy Lamb Books.

How to Contact Not seeking manuscripts at this time. **No e-mail samples accepted. No phone calls accepted. Only mailings to the address listed below.**

Illustration Contact: Isabel Warren-Lynch, executive director, art & design. Responds only if interested. Samples returned with SASE; samples filed.

Terms Pays illustrators and photographers by the project or royalties. Original artwork returned at job's completion.

KOENISHA PUBLICATIONS

3196 53rd St., Hamilton MI 49419-9626. Phone/Fax: (269)751-4100. E-mail: koenisha@macatawa. org. **Contact:** Sharolett Koenig, publisher; Earl Leon, acquisition editor. Publishes trade paperback originals. 500 queries received/year. 500 mss received/year.

Fiction "We do not accept manuscripts that contain unnecessary foul language, explicit sex or gratuitous violence." Query with SASE. Submit proposal package, clips, 3 sample chapters.

Nonfiction *Not accepting submissions from new authors at this time.*

Tips "We're not interested in books written to suit a particular line or house or because it's trendy. Instead write a book from your heart—the inspiration or idea that kept you going through the writing process."

KRBY CREATIONS, LLC

P.O. Box 327, Bay Head NJ 08742. Fax: (815)846-0636. E-mail: info@krbycreationscom. Website: wwwkrbycreationscom.

Fiction Recently published *The Snowman in the Moon*, by Stephen Heigh (picture book); *Mulch the Lawnmower*, by Scott Nelson (picture book); *My Imagination*, by Katrina Estes-Hill (picture book).

How to Contact Fiction/nonfiction: Writers *must* request guidelines by e-mail prior to submitting mss. See website. Submissions without annotation found in guidelines will not be considered. Responds to e-mail queries in 1 week; mss in 1-3 months. Publishes book 1 year after acceptance. Considers simultaneous submissions.

Illustration Detailed contact guidelines available on website. Illustrator terms negotiable. Pays advance plus royalties for experienced Illustrators. Avoids work-for-hire contracts. 40-60% of illustrators are first-time children's picture book published. **Terms** Pays authors royalty of 6-15% based on wholesale price. Catalog on website. Offers writer's guidelines by e-mail.

Tips "Submit as professionally as possible; make your vision clear to us about what you are trying to capture. Know your market/audience and identify it in your proposal. Tell us what is new/ unique with your idea. All writers submitting must first request guidelines by e-mail."

▼ WENDY LAMB BOOKS

Imprint of Random House, 1745 Broadway, New York, NY 10019. Website: www.randomhouse. com. **Manuscript Acquisitions:** Wendy Lamb. Receives 1,500-2,000 submissions/year. Publishes 12-15 novels/year for middle grade and young adult readers. WLB does not publish picture books at present. 15% of books by first-time authors and 10% unagented writers.

Fiction Recently published *When You Reach Me*, by Rebecca Stead; *Love, Aubrey*, by Suzanne LaFleur; *Eyes of the Emporer*, by Graham Salisbury; *A Brief Chapter in My Impossible Life*, by Dana Reinhardt; *What They Found: Love on 145th Street*, by Walter Dean Myers; *Eleven*, by Patricia Reilly Giff. Other WLB authors include Christopher Paul Curtis, Gary Paulsen, Donna Jo Napoli, Peter Dickinson, Marthe Jocelyn, Graham McNamee.

How to Contact Query letter with SASE for reply. A query letter should briefly describe the book you have written, the intended age group, and your brief biography and publishing credits, if any. Please send the first 10 pages (or to the end of the chapter) of your manuscript. Our turn-around time is approximately 4 - 8 weeks.

LEE & LOW BOOKS INC.

95 Madison Ave., New York NY 10016-7801. (212)779-4400. Fax: (212)683-1894. E-mail: info@ leeandlow.com; lmay@leeandlow.com. Publishes 12-14 children's books/year. 25% of books by first-time authors. Lee & Low Books publishes books with diverse themes. "One of our goals is to discover new talent and produce books that reflect the diverse society in which we live." **Contact:** Louise May, vice president/editorial director; Emily Hazel, assistant editor.

- Lee & Low Books is dedicated to publishing culturally authentic literature. The company makes a special effort to work with writers and artists of color and encourages new voices.

Fiction Picture books, young readers: anthology, contemporary, history, multicultural, poetry. "We are not considering folktales or animal stories." Picture book, middle reader: contemporary, history, multicultural, nature/environment, poetry, sports. Average word length: picture books-1,000-1,500 words. Recently published *Gracias ~ Thanks*, by Pat Mora; *Balarama*, by Ted and Betsy Lewin; *Yasmin's Hammer*, by Ann Malaspina; *Only One Year*, by Andrea Cheng (chapter book).

Nonfiction Picture books: concept. Picture books, middle readers: biography, history, multicultural, science and sports. Average word length: picture books-1,500-3,000. Recently published *Seeds of Change*, by Jen Cullerton Johnson; *Sharing Our Homeland*, by Trish Marx.

How to Contact Fiction/nonfiction: Submit complete ms. No e-mail submissions. Responds within 6 months, only if interested. Publishes a book 2-3 years after acceptance. Will consider simultaneous submissions. Guidelines on website.

Illustration Works with 12-14 illustrators/year. Uses color artwork only. Reviews ms/illustration packages from artists. Contact: Louise May. Illustrations only: Query with samples, résumé, promo sheet and tearsheets. Responds only if interested. Samples returned with SASE; samples filed. Original artwork returned at job's completion.

Photography Buys photos from freelancers. Works on assignment only. Model/property releases required. Submit cover letter, résumé, promo piece and book dummy.

Terms Pays authors advances against royalty. Pays illustrators advance against royalty. Photographers paid advance against royalty. Book catalog available for 9 × 12 SAE and $1.68 postage; catalog and ms and art guidelines available via website or with SASE.

Tips "We strongly urge writers to visit our website and familiarize themselves with our list before submitting. Materials will only be returned with SASE."

LEGACY PRESS

P.O. Box 261129, San Diego CA 92196. (858) 277-1167. Publishes 3 young readers/year; 3 middle readers/year; 3 young adult titles/year. Publishes nonfiction, Bible-teaching books. "We publish books that build a legacy in kids' faith, targeting kids ages 2-12. Nonfiction, devotional, journals, guide books, young readers, middle readers, young adults. Recently published *The Christian Girl's Guide to Style* and *Bill the Warthog: Bogus Mind Machine*." Nonfiction Young readers, middle readers, young adults: reference, religion. **Contact:** Editorial Department.

How to Contact Nonfiction: Submit outline/synopsis and 3-5 sample chapters. Will consider simultaneous submissions and previously published work.

Illustration Works with 5 illustrators/year. Reviews ms/illustration packages from artists. Submit ms with 5-10 pieces of final art. Illustrations only: Query with samples to be kept on file.

Terms Pays authors royalty or work purchased outright. Offers advances.

Tips "Become familiar with our products and get to know the Christian bookstore market. We are looking for innovative ways to teach and encourage children about the Christian life."

LERNER PUBLISHING GROUP

241 First Ave. N.Minneapolis MN 55401. (612)332-3344. Fax: (612)332-7615. E-mail: info@ lernerbooks.com. Website: www.lernerbooks.com. **Manuscript Acquisitions:** Jennifer Zimian, nonfiction submissions editor; Zelda Wagner, fiction submissions editor. Primarily publishes books for children ages 7-18. List includes titles in geography, natural and physical science, current events, ancient and modern history, high interest, sports, world cultures, and numerous biography series.

- Starting in 2007, Lerner Publishing Group no longer accepts submission in any of their imprints except for Kar-Ben Publishing.

How to Contact "We will continue to seek targeted solicitations at specific reading levels and in specific subject areas. The company will list these targeted solicitations on our website and in national newsletters, such as the SCBWI *Bulletin*."

ARTHUR A. LEVINE BOOKS

Imprint of Scholastic, Inc.557 Broadway, New York NY 10012. (212)343-4436. Fax: (212)343-4890. Website: www.arthuralevinebooks.com. **Acquisitions:** Arthur A. Levine, editorial director; Cheryl Klein, senior editor. Publishes approximately 8 picture books/year; 8 full-length works for middle grade and young adult readers/year. Approximately 25% of books by first-time authors.

Fiction Recently published *Bobby vs. Girls (accidentally)*, by Lisa Yee (chapter book); *The Perfect Gift*, by Mary Newell Depalma, (picture book); *Moribito: Guardian of the Darkness*, by Nahoko Uehashi, trans. by Cathy Hirano (novel); *The Memory Bank*, by Carolyn Coman (chapter book); and *Plain Kate*, by Erin Bow (novel).

Nonfiction Recently published *Peaceful Heroes*, by Johah Winter, illustrated by Sean Addy (picture book); *The Fabulous Feud of Gilbert and Sullivan*, by Jonah Winter, illustrated by Richard Egielski (picture book).

How to Contact Fiction/nonfiction: Accepts queries only. Responds to queries in 1 month; mss in 5 months. Publishes a book 112 years after acceptance.

Illustration Works with 8 illustrators/year. Will review ms/illustration packages from artists. Query first. Illustrations only: Send postcard sample with tearsheets. Samples not returned.

N LILY RUTH PUBLISHING

P.O. Box 6622, Paris TX 75461.Estab. 2008. (903)715-0740. Fax: (903)737-9748. E-mail: lilyruthpublishing@yahoo.com. Website: www.lilyruthpublishing.com. Estab. 2008. Specializes in fiction. **Manuscript Acquisitions/Art Acquisitions:** Jennifer L. Stone. Publishes 2 middle readers/year. 75% of books by first-time authors. "Here at Lily Ruth Publishing we believe that literature for children should be above all, fun. Strong stories from authors with unique voices are what make reading entertaining and exciting, inspiring a love of reading that will last a life time." **Contact:** Acquisitions: Jennifer L. Stone. "We believe that literature for children should be above all, fun. Strong stories from authors with unique voices are what make reading entertaining and exciting, inspiring a love of reading that will last a life time."

Fiction Early & Middle Readers: adventure, fantasy, history, humor. Young Adults/Teens: adventure, fantasy, humor. Average word length: middle readers—25,000; young adults— 50,000. Recently published *My Weird Family Series: My Vampire Cousin*, by J.K. Hawkins (middle reader, adventure, humor); *My Weird Family Series: My Werewolf Brothers,* by J.K. Hawkins (middle reader, adventures, humor). Query with outline/synopsis and 3 sample chapters.

How to Contact Fiction: query or submit outline/synopsis and 3 sample chapters. Responds 3 months; mss in 3 months. Publishes a book 6 mons - 1 year. Will consider simultaneous submissions.

Illustration Works with 1 illustrators/year. Uses primarily black and white artwork. Illustrations only: Query with samples. Contact: Jennifer L. Stone, Editor. Samples returned with SASE.

Photography Work on assignment only.

Terms Pays authors 10%-15% based on retail price. Sends galleys to authors. Originals returned to artist at job's completion. Catalog available on website.

A LITTLE, BROWN AND COMPANY BOOKS FOR YOUNG READERS

Hachette Book Group USA, 237 Park Ave, New York NY 10017. (212)364-1100. Fax: (212)364-0925. Web sites: www.lb-kids.com; www.lb-teens.com. **Senior Vice President, Publisher:** Megan Tingley. Editorial Director, Little, Brown Books for Young Readers (core hardcover and paperback list): Editor-at-Large: Susan Rich (e: Editor-in-Chief: Liza Baker. Senior Executive Editor: Andrea Spooner. Executive Editorial Director, Poppy (young women's commercial fiction imprint): Cynthia Eagan; Editorial Director: Jennifer Hunt. **Creative Director:** Gail Doobinin. Publishes picture books, board books, chapter books, novelty books, and general nonfiction and novels for middle and young adult readers.

• Little, Brown does not accept unsolicited mss or unagented material.

Fiction Picture books: humor, adventure, animal, contemporary, history, multicultural, folktales. Young adults: contemporary, humor, multicultural, suspense/mystery, chick lit. Multicultural needs include "any material by, for and about minorities." Average word length: picture books—1,000; young readers—6,000; middle readers—15,000- 50,000; young adults—50,000 and up. Recently published *South*, by Patrick McDonnell; *The I Love You Book*, by Todd Parr; *Wabi Sabi*, by Mark Reibstein, illustrated by Ed Young; *The Absolutely True Diary of a Part-time Indian,*by Sherman Alexie; *The Mysterious Benedict Society*, by Trenton Lee Stewart; *The Name Of This Book Is Secret,* by Pseudonymous Bosch; *Ghostgirl*, by Tonya Hurley; *North of Beautiful*, by Justina Chen Headley; *Sweethearts*, by Sara Zarr; *Maximum Ride,* by James Patterson; *The Gossip Girl* series, by Cecily Von Ziegesar; *The Clique* series, by Lisi Harrison; *The Twilight Saga*, by Stephenie Meyer.

Nonfiction Middle readers, young adults: arts/crafts, history, multicultural, nature, self help, social issues, sports, science. Average word length: middle readers—15,000-25,000; young adults—20,000-40,000. Recently published *American Dreaming*, by Laban Carrick Hill; *Exploratopia*, by the Exploratorium; *Yeah! Yeah! Yeah!: The Beatles, Beatlemania, and the Music that Changed the World*, by Bob Spitz.

How to Contact Only interested in solicited agented material. Fiction: Submit complete ms. Nonfiction: Submit cover letter, previous publications, a proposal, outline and 3 sample chapters. Do not send originals. Responds to queries in 2 weeks. Responds to mss in 2 months.

Illustration Works with 40 illustrators/year. Illustrations only: Query art director with b&w and color samples; provide résumé, promo sheet or tearsheets to be kept on file. Does not respond to art samples. Do not send originals; copies only.

Photography Works on assignment only. Model/property releases required; captions required. Publishes photo essays and photo concept books. Uses 35mm transparencies. Photographers should provide résumé, promo sheets or tearsheets to be kept on file.

Terms Pays authors royalties based on retail price. Pays illustrators and photographers by the project or royalty based on retail price. Sends galleys to authors; dummies to illustrators.

Tips "In order to break into the field, authors and illustrators should research their competition and try to come up with something outstandingly different."

LOBSTER PRESS

1620 Sherbrooke St. W., Suites C&D, Montreal QC H3H 1C9 Canada. (514)904-1100. Fax: (514)904-1101. E-mail: editoria@lobsterpress.com. Website: www.lobsterpress.com. **Editorial Director**: Meghan Nolan. Publishes picture books, young readers and YA fiction and nonfiction. "Driven by a desire to produce quality books that bring families together." 75 Lobster Press is currently accepting manuscripts and queries for everything except picture books. **Fiction** Young readers, middle readers, young adults: adventure, animal, contemporary, health, history, literary, multicultural, nature/environment, special needs, sports, suspense/mystery, science fiction, historical fiction, teen issues. Average word length: picture books-200-1,000. Average word length: middle, YA readers-40,000-70,000. Recently published *When I Visited the Farm*, written and illustrated by Crystal Beshara (picture book, 3-5); *Grim Hill; The Forgotten Secret* (ages 9 +); *If You Live Like Me*, by Lori Weber (novel, 13 +).

Nonfiction Young readers, middle readers and adults/teens: animal, biography, Canadian history/culture, careers, geography, hobbies, how-to, multicultural, nature/environment, references, science, self-help, social issues, sports, travel. Recently published *Our Powerful Planet: The Curious Kid's guide to Tornadoes, Earthquakes, and other Phenomena*, by Tim O'Shei (ages 8 +); *Pier 21: Stories from Near & Far*, by Anne Renaud (ages 8 +).

How to Contact "Please address all submissions to Editorial, Lobster Press and specify the genre of your work on the envelope; e-mailed or faxed submissions will not be considered. No editorial comment will be forthcoming unless Lobster Press feels that a manuscript is publishable."

Illustration Works with approx. 3 illustrators/year. Uses line drawings as well as digital and color artwork. Reviews ms/illustration packages from artists. Query with samples. Illustrations only: query with samples. Samples not returned; samples kept on file.

Terms Pays authors 5-10% royalty based on retail price. Original artwork returned to artist at job's completion. Writer's and artist's guidelines available on website.

LOLLIPOP POWER BOOKS

Imprint of Carolina Wren Press, 120 Morris Street, Durham NC 27701. (919)560-2738. Fax: (919)560-2759. E-mail: carolinawrenpress@earthlink.net. Website: www.carolinawrenpress.org. **Manuscript Acquisitions:** Children's Book Editor. **Art Acquisitions**: Art Director. "In the past, Carolina Wren Press and Lollipop Power specialize in children's books that counter stereotypes or debunk myths about race, gender, sexual orientation, etc. We are also interested in books that deal with health or mental health issues—our two biggest sellers are *Puzzles* (about a young girl coping with Sickle Cell Disease) and *I Like It When You Joke With Me, I Don't Like It When You Touch Me* (about inappropriate touching) and we are currently promoting *Peace Comes to Ajani*, about anger management. Many of our children's titles are bilingual (English/Spanish)."Please note, however, that as of 2009, we are no longer holding open submission periods for children's literature."

Fiction Average word length: picture books—500.

How to Contact No open submissions at this time. "Please check our website to see if we have re-opened submissions."

Illustration Send one example and link to website with further examples. We will respond only if interested. Samples not returned.

Terms Pays authors royalty of 10% minimum based on retail price or work purchased outright from authors (range: $500-$2,000). Pays illustrators by the project (range: $500-$2,000). Sends galleys to authors; dummies to illustrators. Originals returned to artist at job's completion. Catalog available on website.

LUCENT BOOKS

Imprint of Gale, 27550 Drake Road, Farmington Hills, MI 49331. E-mail: Kristine.burns@cengage.com. Website: www.gale.com/lucent. **Acquisitions:** Kristine Burns. Series publisher of educational nonfiction for junior high school and library markets.

  • See also listing for Greenhaven Press.

Nonfiction Young adult circulating reference: current issues, diseases, drugs, biographies, geopolitics, history. Recently launched Crime Scene Investigations, and Hot Topics (both series). Recently published *Energy Alternatives*; *Hate Crimes*; *Human Papillomavirus*; *Malnutrition*; *Criminal Profiling*; *DNA Evidence*; *Tupac Shakur*; and *Zac Efron*.

How to Contact E-mail query with résumé or list of publications.

Terms Work purchased outright from authors; write-for-hire, flat fee.

Tips No unsolicited manuscripts.

MAGICAL CHILD

Shades of White, 301 Tenth Ave., Crystal City MO 63019. (314)740-0361. E-mail: acquisition@magicalchildbooks.com. Website: www.magicalchildbooks.com. Estab. 2007. Specializes in trade books, fiction. **Manuscript Acquisitions:** Acquisition Editor. **Art Acquisitions:** Art Director. Publishes 1-3 picture books/year; 1-3 young readers/year; 1-3 middle readers/year. 80% of books by first-time authors. "The Neo-Pagan Earth Religions Community is the fastest growing demographic in the spiritual landscape, and Pagan parents are crying out for books appropriate for the Pagan kids. It is our plan to fill this small, but growing a need."

Fiction Picture Books: adventure, contemporary, nature/environment, submit only stories appropriate for Earth Religions NOT Native American. Young Readers: adventure, contemporary, nature/environment. Middle Readers: adventure, contemporary, nature/environment, submit only stories appropriate for Earth Religions NOT Native American. Average word length; picture books-500-8001; young readers-500-4,500; middle readers-11,200-28,000. Recently published *Aiden's First Full Moon Circle*, by W. Lyon Martin (ages 5-8, picture book); *An Ordinary Girl, A Magical Child*, by W. Lyon Martin (ages 5-8, chapter book); Smoky and the Feast of Mabon, by Catherynne M. Valente (ages 4-8, picture book).

Nonfiction Middle Readers: biography, history (earth religions only for both). Average word length: middle readers-11,200-28,000.

How to Contact Fiction: Query or submit outline/synopsis for picture books only or submit outline/synopsis and 3 sample chapters. Nonfiction: Query or submit outline/synopsis and 3 sample chapters. Responds to queries 3 weeks; mss in 3-6 months. Publishes a book 18+ months after acceptance. Will consider simultaneous submissions.

Illustration Works with 1-2 illustrators/year. Uses color artwork only. Reviews ms/illustrations packages from artists. Send manuscript with dummy. Contact: Art Director. Illustrations only: send résumé, client list, tearsheets. Contact: Art Director. Samples returned with SASE; samples filed if interested.

Terms Pays authors royalty based on retail price. Offers advances. Pays illustrators royalty based on wholesale price. Sends galleys to authors; dummies to illustrators. Originals returned to artist at job's completion. Book catalog available for SASE (envelope size #10 and 1 first-class stamps) All imprints included in single catalog.

Tips "Visit our submissions guidelines on the website. Follow the information provided there. We expect our authors to take an active role in promoting their books. If you can't do that, please don't submit your manuscript. NO CALLS, Please. Our list is VERY specific Please do not send us manuscripts outside of our requested needs. "

MAGINATION PRESS

750 First Street, NE, Washington DC 20002-2984. (202)336-5618. Fax: (202)336-5624. Website: www.maginationpress.com. **Acquisitions:** Kristine Enderle, managing editor. Publishes 12 books/year (picture books/year, middle readers/year, teen nonficition). 75% of books by first-time authors. "We publish books dealing with the psycho/therapeutic resolution of children's problems and psychological issues with a strong self-help component."

• Magination Press is an imprint of the American Psychological Association.

Fiction All levels: psychological and social issues, self-help, health, parenting concerns and, special needs. Picture books, middle school readers. Recently published *Nobody's Perfect: A Story for Children about Perfection,* by Ellen Flanagan Burns, illustrated by, Erica Peltron Villnave (ages 8-12); *Murphey's Three Homes; A Story for Children in Foster Care,* by Jan Levinson Gilman, illustrated by Kathy O'Malley (ages 4-8).

Nonfiction All levels: psychological and social issues, self-help, health, multicultural, special needs. Recently published *Putting on the Brakes: Understanding and controlling your ADD or ADHD* (ages 8-13), by Patricia Quinn and Judith M. Stern, illustrated by Joe Lee.

How to Contact Fiction/nonfiction: Submit complete ms. Responds to queries in 1-2 months; mss in 2-6 months. Will consider simultaneous submissions. Materials returned only with a SASE. Publishes a book 18-24 months after acceptance.

Illustration Works with 10-15 illustrators/year. Reviews ms/illustration packages. Will review artwork for future assignments. Responds only if interested, or immediately if SASE or response card is included. We keep samples on file.

⬛ MASTER BOOKS

Imprint of New Leaf Publishing Group, Inc, P.O. Box 726, Green Forest, AR 72638. (870)438-5288. Fax: (870)438-5120. E-mail: nlp@newleafpress.net. Website: www.nlpg.com. **Manuscript Acquisitions:** Craig Froman, acquisitions editor. 3 young readers/year; 3 middle readers/year; 2 young adult titles/year. 10% of books by first-time authors.

Nonfiction Picture books: activity books, animal, nature/environment, creation. Young readers, middle readers, young adults: activity books, animal, biography Christian, nature/environment, science, creation. Recently published *Dragons: Legends & Lore of Dinosaurs* (middle readers); *Our Created Moon*, by Dr. Don Deyoung and Dr. John Whitcomb (science book); *The New Answers Book 3 Compiled*, by Ken Ham (adult series).

How to Contact Nonfiction: Submission guidelines at our website. Responds to queries/mss in 4 months. Publishes book 1 year after acceptance. Will consider simultaneous submissions. Must download submissions form from website.

Illustration We are not looking for illustrations.

Terms Pays authors royalty of 3-15% based on wholesale price. Sends galleys to authors. Book catalog available per request; ms guidelines available website. Catalog available on website.

Tips "All of our children's books are creation-based, including topics from the Book of Genesis. We look also for home school educational material that would be supplementary to a home school curriculum."

⚜ MARGARET K. MCELDERRY BOOKS

Imprint of Simon & Schuster Children's Publishing Division, 1230 Avenue of the Americas, New York NY 10020. (212)698-7000. Website: www.simonsayskids.com. **Publisher**: Vice President, Publisher Emma D. Dryden. Acquisitions: Karen Wojtyla, editorial director; Lisa Cheng, associate editor; Emily Fabre, Editorial Assistant. Art Acquisitions: Ann Bobco, Executive Art Director. Imprint of Simon & Schuster Children's Publishing Division. Publishes 12 picture books/year; 5-8 middle readers/year; 8-10 young adult titles/year. "Margaret K. McElderry Books publishes hardcover and paperback trade books for children from pre-school age through young adult. This list includes picture books, middle grade and teen fiction, poetry, and fantasy. The style and subject matter of the books we publish is almost unlimited. We do not publish textbooks, coloring and activity books, greeting cards, magazines, pamphlets, or religious publications."

Fiction All levels. "Always interested in publishing young read-aloud picture books, humorous middle grade fiction, and original teen fiction or fantasy." Average word length: picture books-500; young readers-2,000; middle readers-10,000-20,000; young adults-45,000-50,000. Recently Published: *Monster Mess*, by Margery Cuyler; illustrated by S. D. Schindler (picture book); *The Joy of Spooking: Fiendish Deeds* by P. J. Bracegirdle (MGF); *Identical*, by Ellen Hopkins (teen); *Where is Home, Little Pip?*, by Karma Wilson; illustrated by Jane Chapman (picture book); *Dr. Ted*, by Andrea Beaty; illustrated by Pascal LeMaitre (picture book); *To Be Mona* by Kelly Easton (teen).

How to Contact Simon & Schuster children's publishing division does not accept unsolicited queries, manuscripts, or art samples unless submitted by an agent.

Terms Pays authors royalty based on retail price. Pays illustrator royalty of by the project. Pays photographers by the project. Original artwork returned at job's completion.

Tips "We're looking for strong, original fiction, especially mysteries and middle grade humor. We are always interested in picture books for the youngest age reader. Study our titles."

MEADOWBROOK PRESS

5451 Smetana Dr., Minnetonka MN 55343-9012. (952)930-1100. Fax: (952)930-1940. Website: www.meadowbrookpress.com. **Manuscript Acquisitions:** Submissions Editor. **Art Acquisitions:** Art Director. 20% of books by first-time authors; 10% of books from agented writers. Publishes children's poetry books, activity books, arts-and-crafts books and how-to books.

- Meadowbrook does not accept unsolicited children's picture books, short stories or novels. They are primarily a nonfiction press. The publisher offers specific guidelines for children's poetry. Be sure to specify the type of project you have in mind when requesting guideline, or visit their website.

Nonfiction Publishes activity books, arts/crafts, how-to, poetry. Average word length: varies. Recently published *The Siblings' Busy Book*, by Heather Kempskie & Lisa Hanson (activity book); *I Hope I Don't Strike Out*, by Bruce Lansky (poetry).

How to Contact Nonfiction: See guidelines on website before submitting. Responds only if interested. Publishes a book 1-2 years after acceptance. Will consider simultaneous submissions.

Illustration Works with 4 illustrators/year. Submit ms with 2-3 pieces of nonreturnable samples. Responds only if interested. Samples filed.

Photography Buys photos from freelancers. Buys stock. Model/property releases required.

Terms Pays authors royalty of 5-7% based on retail price. Offers average advance payment of $1,000-3,000. Pays illustrators per project. Pays photographers by the project. Book catalog available for 5 × 11 SASE and 2 first-class stamps; ms guidelines and artists guidelines available for SASE.

Tips "Writers should visit our website before submitting their work to us. Illustrators should take a look at the books we publish to determine whether their style is consistent with ours. Writers should also note the style and content patterns of our books. No phone calls, please-e-mail us. We work with the printed word and will respond more effectively to your questions if we have something in front of us."

MERIWETHER PUBLISHING LTD.

885 Elkton Dr., Colorado Springs CO 80907-3557. (719)594-9916. Fax: (719)594-9916. E-mail: editor@meriwether.com. Website: www.meriwetherpublishing.com. **Manuscript Acquisitions:** Ted Zapel, comedy plays and educational drama; Rhonda Wray, religious drama. "We do most of our artwork in-house; we do not publish for the children's elementary market." 75% of books by first-time authors; 5% of books from agented writers. "Our niche is drama. Our books cover a wide variety of theatre subjects from play anthologies to theatrecraft. We publish books of monologs, duologs, short one-act plays, scenes for students, acting textbooks, how-to speech and theatre textbooks, improvisation and theatre games. Our Christian books cover worship on such topics as clown ministry, storytelling, banner-making, drama ministry, children's worship and more. We also publish anthologies of Christian sketches. We do not publish works of fiction or devotionals."

Fiction Middle readers, young adults: anthology, contemporary, humor, religion. "We publish plays, not prose-fiction." Our emphasis is comedy plays instead of educational themes.

Nonfiction Middle readers: activity books, how-to, religion, textbooks. Young adults: activity books, drama/theater arts, how-to church activities, religion. Average length: 250 pages. Recently published *Acting for Life*, by Jack Frakes; *Scenes Keep Happening*, by Mary Krell-Oishi; *Service with a Smile*, by Daniel Wray.

How to Contact Nonfiction: Query or submit outline/synopsis and sample chapters. Responds to queries in 3 weeks; mss in 2 months or less. Publishes a book 6-12 months after acceptance. Will consider simultaneous submissions.

Illustration We do our Illustration in house.

Terms Pays authors royalty of 10% based on retail or wholesale price. Book catalog for SAE and $2 postage; ms guidelines for SAE and 1 first-class stamp.

Tips "We are currently interested in finding unique treatments for theater arts subjects: scene books, how-to books, musical comedy scripts, monologs and short comedy plays for teens."

MILKWEED EDITIONS

(612)332-3192. E-mail: editor@milkweed.org. Publishes hardcover, trade paperback, and electronic originals; trade paperback and electronic reprints

Fiction Novels for adults and for readers 8-13. High literary quality. For adult readers: literary fiction, nonfiction, poetry, essays. For children (ages 8-13): literary novels. Translations welcome for both audiences. No romance, mysteries, science fiction. Query with SASE, submit completed ms.

Nonfiction Please consider our previous publications when considering submissions to Milkweed Editions. Submit complete ms with SASE. Milkweed strongly encourages digital submissions through our website.

Tips "We are looking for excellent writing with the intent of making a humane impact on society. Please read submission guidelines before submitting and acquaint yourself with our books in terms of style and quality before submitting. Many factors influence our selection process, so don't get discouraged. Nonfiction is focused on literary writing about the natural world, including living well in urban environments."

MILKWEED EDITIONS

1011 Washington Ave. S.Suite 300, Minneapolis MN 55415-1246. (612)332-3192. Fax: (612)215-2550. E-mail: editor@milkweed.org. Website: www.milkweed.org. **Manuscript Acquisitions:** Daniel Slager, publisher. Publishes 3-4 middle readers/year. 25% of books by first-time authors. "Milkweed Editions publishes with the intention of making a humane impact on society, in the belief that literature is a transformative art uniquely able to convey the essential experiences of the human heart and spirit. To that end, Milkweed Editions publishes distinctive voices of literary merit in handsomely designed, visually dynamic books, exploring the ethical, cultural, and esthetic issues that free societies need continually to address."

Fiction Middle readers: adventure, contemporary, fantasy, multicultural, nature/environment, suspense/mystery. Does not want to see folktales, health, hi-lo, picture books, poetry, religion, romance, sports. Average length: middle readers-90-200 pages. Recently published *Perfect*, by Natasha Friend (contemporary); *The Linden Tree*, by Ellie Mathews(contemporary); *The Cat*, by Jutta Richter (contemporary/translation).

How to Contact Fiction: Use Submissions manager online at www.milkweed.org. Publishes a book 1 year after acceptance. Will consider simultaneous submissions.

Terms Pays authors variable royalty based on retail price. Offers advance against royalties. Sends galleys to authors. Book catalog available for $1.50 to cover postage; ms guidelines available for SASE or at website. Must include SASE with ms submission for its return.

☐ THE MILLBROOK PRESS

A division of Lerner Publishing Group, Inc. 241 First Avenue North Minneapolis, MN 5540. (800)328-4929. Fax: (800)332-1132. Website: www.lernerbooks.com.

- Starting in 2007, Lerner Publishing Group no longer accepts submission in any of their imprints except for Kar-Ben Publishing.

How to Contact "We will continue to seek targeted solicitations at specific reading levels and in specific subject areas. The company will list these targeted solicitations on our website and in national newsletters, such as the SCBWI Bulletin."

MIRRORSTONE

P.O. Box 707, Renton WA 98057. (425)254-2287. **Manuscript and Art Acquisitions:** Nina Hess. Publishes 6 middle readers/year; 4 young adult titles/year. 5% of books by first-time authors. "We publish fantasy novels for young readers based on the lore of the Dungeons & Dragons role-playing game."

Fiction Young readers, middle readers, young adults: fantasy only. Average word length: middle readers-30,000-40,000; young adults-60,000-75,000. Recently published *A Practical Guide to Dragon-Riding*, by Lisa Trumbaur (ages 6 and up); *The Stowaway*, by R.A. Salvatore and Geno Salvatore (10 and up), *Red Dragon Codex*, by R. Henham (ages 8-12)

How to Contact Fiction: Query with samples, writing credits. "No manuscripts, please." Responds to queries if interested. Publishes book 9-24 months after acceptance.

Illustration Works with 4 illustrators/year. Query. Illustrations only: Query with samples, résumé.

Terms Pays authors royalty of 4-6% based on retail price. Offers advances (average amount: $4,000). Pays illustrators by the project. Ms guidelines available on our website. All imprints included in a single catalog. Catalog available on website.

Tips Editorial staff attended or plans to attend ALA conference.

MITCHELL LANE PUBLISHERS, INC.

P.O. Box 196, Hockessin DE 19707. (302)234-9426. Fax: (302)234-4742. E-mail: mitchelllane@mitchelllane.com. Website: www.mitchelllane.com. **Acquisitons:** Barbara Mitchell, president. Publishes 80 young adult titles/year. "We publish nonfiction for children and young adults."

Nonfiction Young readers, middle readers, young adults: biography, multicultural. Average word length: 4,000-50,000 words. Recently published Stephenie Meyer and Drew Brees (both Blue Banner Biographies); Justin Bieber (A Robbie Reader); Earth Science Projects for Kids series; Your Land and My Land: Latin America series; and World Crafts and Recipes series.

How to Contact Most assignments are work-for-hire.

Illustration Works with 2-3 illustrators/year. Reviews ms/illustration packages from artists. Query. Illustration only: Query with samples; send résumé, portfolio, slides, tearsheets. Responds only if interested. Samples not returned; samples filed.

Photography Buys stock images. Needs photos of famous and prominent minority figures. Captions required. Uses color prints or digital images. Submit cover letter, résumé, published samples, stock photo list.

Terms Work purchased outright from authors (range: $350-2,000). Pays illustrators by the project (range: $40-400). Sends galleys to authors.

Tips "Most of our assignments are work-for-hire. Submit résumé and samples of work to be considered for future assignments."

⊠ MOOSE ENTERPRISE BOOK & THEATRE PLAY PUBLISHING

Imprint of Moose Hide Books, 684 Walls Rd., Sault Ste. Marie ON P6A 5K6 Canada. E-mail: mooseenterprises@on.aibn.com. Website: www.moosehidebooks.com. **Manuscript Acquisitions:** Edmond Alcid. Publishes 2 middle readers/year; 2 young adult titles/year. 75% of books by first-time authors. Editorial philosophy: "To assist the new writers of moral standards."

- This publisher does not offer payment for stories published in its anthologies and/or book collections. Be sure to send a SASE for guidelines.

Fiction Middle readers, young adults: adventure, fantasy, humor, suspense/mystery, story poetry. Recently published *Realm of the Golden Feather*, by C.R. Ginter (ages 12 and up, fantasy); *Tell Me a Story*, short story collection by various authors (ages 9-11, humor/adventure); *Spirits of Lost Lake*, by James Walters (ages 12 and up, adventure); *Rusty Butt-Treasure of the Ocean Mist*, by R.E. Forester.

Nonfiction Middle readers, young adults: biography, history, multicultural.

How to Contact Fiction/nonfiction: Query. Responds to queries in 1 month; mss in 3 months. Publishes book 1 year after acceptance. Will consider simultaneous submissions.

Illustration Uses primarily b&w artwork for interiors, cover artwork in color. Illustrations only: Query with samples. Responds in 1 month, if interested. Samples returned with SASE; samples filed.

Terms Pays royalties. Originals returned to artist at job's completion. Manuscript and art guidelines available for SASE.

Tips "Do not copy trends, be yourself, give me something new, something different."

NEW CANAAN PUBLISHING COMPANY LLC.

2384 N. Hwy 341, Rossville, GA 30741. (423)228-2409. Fax: (203)548-9072. E-mail: djm@newcanaanpublishing.com. Website: www.newcanaanpublishing.com. Book publisher. Publishes 1 picture book/year; 1 young reader/year; 1 middle reader/year; 1 young adult title/year. 50% of books by first-time authors. "We seek books with strong educational or traditional moral content and books with Christian themes."

- To curb the number of unsolicited submissions, New Canaan Publishing only accepts: 1—books for children of military families; and 2—middle readers and young adult books addressing Christian themes (e.g.devotionals, books addressing teen or pre-teen issues with a Christian focus, whether in a fictional context or otherwise).

Fiction All levels: adventure, history, religion (Christianity), suspense/mystery. Picture books: Christian themes. Average word length: picture books—1,000-3,000; young readers—8,000-30,000; middle readers—8,000-40,000; young adult s—15,000-50,000.

Nonfiction All levels: religion (Christian only), textbooks. Average word length: picture books—1,000-3,000; young readers—8,000-30,000; middle readers—8,000-40,000; young adults—15,000-50,000.

How to Contact Submit outline/synopsis with biographical information and writing credentials. Does not guarantee a response unless offer to publish is forthcoming. Responds where appropriate in 4-6 months. Publishes a book 12-18 months after acceptance.

Illustration Works with 1-2 illustrators/year. Reviews ms/illustration packages from artists. Query or send ms with dummy. Illustrations only: Query with samples. Responds in 1-2 months if need exists.

Terms Pays authors royalty of 7-12% based on wholesale price. Royalty may be shared with illustrator where relevant. Pays illustrators royalty of 4-6% as share of total royalties. Submission guidelines available on website.

Tips "We are small, so please be patient."

NEW DAY PUBLISHING, INC

New Day Publishing, Inc. 26 Bluff Ridge Court, Greensboro NC 27455.Estab. 2006. (336)545-1545. Fax: (336)545-1640. E-mail: ateich@newdaypublishing. Website: www.newdaypublishing.com.

Fiction Picture Books: religion. Recently published *Who Made the Morning?,* by Jan Godfrey and Honor Ayers (ages 4-7 hardback), *Come to the Party with Jesus*, by Leena Lane and Chris Sanderson (paper back), *Stand up and Walk with Jesus,* by Leena Lane and Chris Sanderson (paper back).

Nonfiction Picture Books: Christian teaching activities-early children. Recently published *Make a Joyful Voice: Music, Movement and Creative Play to Teach Bible Stories; Old Testaments Readers Theater-Read Aloud Scripts for Young Christians; New Testaments Readers Theater-Read Aloud Scripts for Young Christians.*

How to Contact Fiction/nonfiction: submit outline/synopsis. Responds to queries in 2-3 weeks/mss. Publishes 9-12 months after acceptance. Will consider simultaneous submissions.

Illustration Interested in agent material and accepts material from illustrators outside the country. Works with 3-4 illustrators a year. Uses both color and b&w. Submit manuscript to **Contact:** Kathryn Wolf, VP Editorial. Illustrations only: Query with samples. Responds in 2-3 weeks. Samples are returned with SASE.

Photography Buys stock. **Contact:** Kathryn Wolf, VP Editorial.

Terms Pays royalty of 5-10% based on net sales. Pays illustrators by the project based on net sales. Originals returned to artist at job's completion with SASE. Catalog available on website will post writers guidelines soon.

Tips "Have background in early childhood. Must be appropriate for children ages 4-7."

▓N▓ NOMAD PRESS

2456 Christain St., White River Junction VT 05001. (802)649-1995. Fax: (802)649-2667. E-mail: rachel@nomadpress.net. Website: www.nomadpress.net. Estab. 2001. Specializes in nonfiction, educational material. **Contact:** Alex Kahan, publisher. Produces 8-12 young readers/year. 10% of books by first-time authors. "We produce nonfiction children's activity books that bring a particular science or cultural topic into sharp focus."

- Nomad Press does not accept picture books or fiction.

Nonfiction Middle readers: activity books, history, science. Average word length: middle readers—30,000. Recently published *Explore Transportation,* by Marylou Moran Kjelle (ages 6-9); *Discover the Oceans,* by Lauri Berkenkamp (ages 8-12); *Amazing Biomes,* by Donna Latham (ages 9-12); *Explore Colonial America,* by Verna Fisher (ages 6-9); *Discover the Desert,* by Kathy Ceceri (ages 8-12).

How to Contact Accepts international submissions. Nonfiction: "Nomad Press does not accept unsolicited manuscripts. If authors are interested in contributing to our children's series, please send a writing resume that includes relevant experience/expertise and publishing credits." Responds to queries in 1-2 months. Publishes book 1 year after acceptance.

Terms Pays authors royalty based on retail price or work purchased outright. Offers advance against royalties. Catalog on website. All imprints included in single catalog. See website for writer's guidelines.

Tips "We publish a very specific kind of nonfiction children's activity book. Please keep this in mind when querying or submitting."

▢ ONSTAGE PUBLISHING

190 Lime Quarry Road, Suite 106J, Madison AL 35601 35758-8962. (256)461-0661. E-mail: onstage123@knology.net. Website: www.onstagepublishing.com. **Manuscript Acquisitions:** Dianne Hamilton. Publishes 1-2 middle readers/year; 1-2 young adult titles/year. 80% of books by first-time authors.

Fiction Middle readers: adventure, contemporary, fantasy, history, nature/environment, science fiction, suspense/mystery. Young adults: adventure, contemporary, fantasy, history, humor, science fiction, suspense/mystery. Average word length: chapter books—4,000-6,000 words; middle readers—5,000 words and up; young adults—25,000 and up. Recently published *China Clipper,* by Jamie Dodson (an adventure for boys ages 12+); *Merlin's Curse,* by Darren J. Butler (a chapter book for grades 3 to 5). "We do not produce picture books."

Nonfiction Query first; currently not producing nonfiction.

How to Contact Fiction: Send complete ms if under 20,000 words, otherwise send synopsis and first 3 chapters. Responds to queries/mss in 6-8 months. Publishes a book 1-2 years after acceptance. Will consider simultaneous submissions.

Illustration Reviews ms/illustration packages from artists. Submit with 3 pieces of final art. Contact: Dianne Hamilton, senior editor. Illustrations only. Samples not returned.

Terms Pays authors/illustrators/photographers advance plus royalties. Sends galleys to authors; dummies to illustrators. Catalog available on website.

Tips "Study our titles and get a sense of the kind of books we publish, so that you know whether your project is likely to be right for us."

OOLIGAN PRESS

P.O. Box 751, Portland OR 97213. (503)725-9410. E-mail: acquisitions@ooligans.pdx.edu. Website: www.ooliganpress.pdx.edu. Estab. 2001. **Contact:** Acquisitions Committee. "Ooligan Press is a general trade press at Portland State University. As a teaching press, Ooligan makes as little distinction as possible between the press and the classroom. Under the direction of professional faculty and staff, the work of the press is done by students enrolled in the Book Publishing graduate program at PSU. We are especially interested in works with social, literary, or educational value. Though we place special value on local authors, we are open to all submissions, including translated works and writings by children and young adults. We do not currently publish picture books, board books, easy readers, or pop-up books or middle grade readers. 90% of books by first-time authors."

Fiction Young adult with an emphasis on historical fiction or works related to the Pacific Northwest Region. "At this time we cannot accept science fiction or fantasy submissions." Recently published *Ricochet River*, by Robin Cody (YA novel); *A Heart for Any Fate* (YA novel).

Nonfiction Young adult: open to all categories.

How to Contact Query with SASE or submit proposal package including 4 sample chapters, projected page count, intended audience, and marketing ideas. Prefers traditional mail, but will read unattached queries. Do not send proposal package by e-mail. Response to queries in 4-6 weeks. Publishes a book 18 months after acceptance. Will consider simultaneous submissions and previously published work.

Terms Pays negotiable royalty based on retail price. Authors see galleys for review. Book catalog and writer's guidelines available on website.

ORCA BOOK PUBLISHERS

1030 N. Park St., Victoria BC V8T 1C6, Canada. 1016 Balmoral St., Victoria BC V8T 1A8 Canada. (250)380-1229. Fax: (250)380-1892. Website: www.orcabook.com. **Acquisitions:** Christi Howes, children's book editor (young readers); Andrew Wooldridge, editor (Orca Soundings); Bob Tyrrell, editor (teen fiction); Sarah Harvey, editor (juvenile fiction); Melanie Jeffs, editor (Orca Currents). Publishes 7 picture books/year; 16 middle readers/year; 10 young adult titles/year. 25% of books by first-time authors.

• Orca only considers authors who are Canadian or who live in Canada.

Fiction Picture books: animals, contemporary, history, nature/environment. Middle readers: contemporary, history, fantasy, nature/environment, problem novels, graphic novels. Young adults: adventure, contemporary, hi-lo (Orca Soundings), history, multicultural, nature/environment, problem novels, suspense/mystery, graphic novels. Average word length: picture books—500-1,500; middle readers—20,000-35,000; young adult—25,000-45,000; Orca Soundings—13,000-15,000; Orca Currents—13,000-15,000. Published *Tall in the Saddle*, by Anne Carter, illustrated by David McPhail (ages 4-8, picture book); *Me and Mr. Mah*, by Andrea Spalding, illustrated by Janet Wilson (ages 5 and up, picture book); *Alone at Ninety Foot*, by Katherine Holubitsky (young adult).

How to Contact Fiction: Submit complete ms if picture book; submit outline/synopsis and 3 sample chapters. "All queries or unsolicited submissions should be accompanied by a SASE." Responds to queries in 2 months; mss in 3 months. Publishes a book 18-36 months after acceptance. Submission guidelines available online.

Illustration Works with 8-10 illustrators/year. Reviews ms/illustration packages from artists. Submit ms with 3-4 pieces of final art. "Reproductions only, no original art please." Illustrations only: Query with samples; provide résumé, slides. Responds in 2 months. Samples returned with SASE; samples filed.

Terms Pays authors royalty of 5% for picture books, 10% for novels, based on retail price. Offers advances (average amount: $2,000). Pays illustrators royalty of 5% minimum based on retail price and advance on royalty. Sends galleys to authors. Original artwork returned at job's completion if picture books. Book catalog available for SASE with $2 first-class postage. Manuscript guidelines available for SASE. Art guidelines not available.

Tips "We are not seeking seasonal stories, board books, or 'I Can Read' Books. Orca Sounding/Currents lines offer high interest teen novels aimed at reluctant readers. The story should reflect the universal struggles young people face, but need not be limited to 'gritty' urban tales. Can include adventure, mystery/suspense, fantasy, etc. There's a definite need for humorous stories that appeal to boys and girls. Protagonists are between 14 and 17 years old."

ORCHARD BOOKS

Imprint of Scholastic, Inc.557 Broadway, New York NY 10012. (212)343-6782. Fax: (212)343-4890. Website: www.scholastic.com. Book publisher. Editorial Director: Ken Geist. **Manuscript Acquisitions:** Ken Geist, V.P.editorial director. **Art Acquisitions:** Elizabeth B. Parisi, executive art director. "Orchard publishes 30 books yearly including board books, early chapter books, fiction, poetry, picture books, novelty and young adult novels." 10% of books by first-time authors.
• Orchard is not accepting unsolicited manuscripts; query letters only.
Fiction All levels: animal, contemporary, history, humor, multicultural, poetry. Recently published *Maybe a Bear Ate It!*, by Robie Harris, illustrations by Michael Emberley; *Funny Farm,* by Mark Teague; *One Brown Bunny*, by Marion Dane Bauer, illustrations by Ivan Bates; *Charlie Bone and the Shadow,* by Jenny Nimmo; *Lyonesse: The Well Between the Worlds*, by Sam Llewellyn; *Ten Things I Hate About Me,* by Randa Abdel-Fattah. Upcoming publications:*Cat Dreams, by* Ursula Le Guin, illustrations by S. Schindler; *Max Spaniel* series, by David Catrow; *There Was An Old Monster,* by Rebecca and Ed Emberley; *Dogs Don't Brush Their Teeth,* by Diane de Groat, *and Shelley Rotner and the Dragons of Wayward Crescent* series, by Chris d'Lacey.
Nonfiction "We publish nonfiction very selectively." series
How to Contact Query only with SASE. Responds in 3-6 months.
Illustration Works with 15 illustrators/year. Art director reviews ms/illustration portfolios. Submit "tearsheets or photocopies or Photostats of the work." Responds to art samples in 1 month. Samples returned with SASE. No disks or slides, please.
Terms Most commonly offers an advance against list royalties. Sends galleys to authors; dummies to illustrators. Original artwork returned at job's completion.
Tips "Read some of our books to determine first whether your manuscript is suited to our list."

OUR CHILD PRESS

P.O. Box 4379, Philadelphia PA 19118. Phone/fax: (610)308-8088. E-mail: ourchildpress@aol.com. Website: www.ourchildpress.com. **Acquisitions:** Carol Perrott, president. 90% of books by first-time authors.
Fiction All levels: adoption, multicultural, special needs. Published *Like Me*, written by Dawn Martelli, illustrated by Jennifer Hedy Wharton; *Is That Your Sister?*, by Catherine and Sherry Burin; *Oliver: A Story About Adoption*, by Lois Wichstrom.
How to Contact Query or submit complete ms. Responds to queries/mss in 6 months. Publishes a book 6-12 months after acceptance.
Illustration Works with 1-5 illustrators/year. Reviews ms/illustration packages from artists. Manuscript/illustration packages and illustration only: Query first. Submit résumé, tearsheets and photocopies. Responds to art samples in 2 months. Samples returned with SASE; samples kept on file.
Terms Pays authors royalty of 5-10% based on wholesale price. Pays illustrators royalty of 5-10% based on wholesale price. Original artwork returned at job's completion. Book catalog for business-size SAE and 67¢ postage.

⊡ OUR SUNDAY VISITOR, INC.

200 Noll Plaza, Huntington IN 46750. **Acquisitions:** Jacquelyn Lindsey, David Dziena and Bert Ghezzi. **Art Director:** Tyler Ottinger. Publishes religious, educational, parenting, reference and biographies. OSV is dedicated to providing books, periodicals and other products that serve the Catholic Church.

- "Our Sunday Visitor, Inc. is publishing only those children's books that tie in to sacramental preparation and Catholic identity. Contact the acquisitions editor for manuscript guidelines."

Nonfiction Picture books, middle readers, young readers, young adults. Recently published Beatitudes for Children, by Rosemarie Gortler and Donna Piscitelli, illustrated by Mimi Sternhagen.

How to Contact Query, submit complete ms, or submit outline/synopsis and 2-3 sample chapters. Responds to queries/mss in 2 months. Publishes a book 18-24 months after acceptance. Will consider simultaneous submissions, electronic submissions via disk or modem, previously published work.

Illustration Reviews ms/illustration packages from artists. Illustration only: Query with samples. Contact: Art Director. Responds only if interested. Samples returned with SASE; samples filed.

Photography Buys photos from freelancers. Contact: Art Director.

Terms Pays authors royalty of 10-12% net. Pays illustrators by the project (range: $25-1,500). Sends page proofs to authors. Book catalog available for SASE; ms guidelines available for SASE and online at www.osv.com.

Tips "Stay in accordance with our guidelines."

RICHARD C. OWEN PUBLISHERS, INC.

P.O. Box 585, Katonah NY 10536. (800)336-5588. Fax: (914)232-3977. Website: www.rcowen. com. **Acquisitions:** Janice Boland, children's books editor/art director. 90% of books by first-time authors. We publish "child-focused books, with inherent instructional value, about characters and situations with which five-, six-, and seven-year-old children can identify—books that can be read for meaning, entertainment, enjoyment and information. We include multicultural stories that present minorities in a positive and natural way. Our stories show the diversity in America." Is not interested in lesson plans, or books of activities for literature studies or other content areas.

- Due to a high volume of submissions, Richard C. Owen Publishers are currently only accepting nonfiction pieces.

Nonfiction Picture books, young readers: animals, careers, hi-lo, history, how-to, music/dance, geography, multicultural, nature/environment, science, sports. Multicultural needs include: "Good stories respectful of all heritages, races, cultural-African-American, Hispanic, American Indian." Wants lively stories. No "encyclopedic" type of information stories. Average word length: under 500 words. Recently published The Coral Reef.

How to Contact Fiction/nonfiction: Submit complete ms and cover letter. Responds to mss in 1 year. Publishes a book 2-3 years after acceptance. See website for guidelines.

Illustration Works with 20 illustrators/year. Uses color artwork only. Illustration only: Send color copies/reproductions or photos of art or provide tearsheets; do not send slides or originals. Include SASE and cover letter. Responds only if interested; samples filed.

Terms Pays authors royalty of 5% based on net price or outright purchase (range: $25-500). Offers no advances. Pays illustrators by the project (range: $100-2,500). Pays photographers by the project (range: $100-2,000) or per photo ($100-150). Original artwork returned 12-18 months after job's completion. Book brochure, ms/artists guidelines available for SASE.

Tips Seeking "authentic nonfiction that has charm, magic, impact and appeal; that children living in today's society will want to read and reread; books with strong storylines, child-appealing characters, events, language, action. Write for the ears and eyes and hearts of your readers—use an economy of words. Visit the children's room at the public library and immerse yourself in the best children's literature."

PACIFIC PRESS

P.O. Box 5353, Nampa ID 83653-5353. (208)465-2500. Fax: (208)465-2531. E-mail: booksubmissions@ pacificpress.com. Website: www.pacificpress.com/writers/books.htm. **Manuscript Acquisitions:** Scott Cady. **Art Acquisitions:** Gerald Monks, creative director. Publishes 1 picture book/year; 2 young readers/year; 2 middle readers/year. 5% of books by first-time authors. Pacific Press brings the Bible and Christian lifestyle to children.

Fiction Picture books, young readers, middle readers, young adults: religious subjects only. No fantasy. Average word length: picture books-100; young readers—1,000; middle readers—15,000; young adults-40,000. Recently published *A Child's Steps to Jesus* (3 vols) , by Linda Carlyle; *Octopus Encounter*, by Sally Streib; *Sheperd Warrior*, by Bradley Booth.

Nonfiction Picture books, young readers, middle readers, young adults: religion. Average word length: picture books-100; young readers—1,000; middle readers—15,000; young adults-40,000. Recently published *Escape*, by Sandy Zaugg; *What We Believe*, by Seth Pierce.

How to Contact Fiction/nonfiction: Query or submit outline/synopsis and 3 sample chapters. Responds to queries in 3 months; mss in 1 year. Publishes a book 6-12 months after acceptance. Will consider e-mail submissions.

Illustration Works with 2-6 illustrators/year. Uses color artwork only. Query. Responds only if interested. Samples returned with SASE.

Photography Buys stock and assigns work. Model/property releases required.

Terms Pays author royalty of 6-15% based on wholesale price. Offers advances (average amount: $1,500). Pays illustrators royalty of 6-15% based on wholesale price. Pays photographers royalty of 6-15% based on wholesale price. Sends galleys to authors. Originals returned to artist at job's completion. Manuscript guidelines for SASE. Catalog available on website (www. adventistbookcenter.com).

Tips Pacific Press is owned by the Seventh-day Adventist Church. The Press rejects all material that is not Bible-based.

PACIFIC VIEW PRESS

P.O. Box 2897, Berkeley CA 94702. (510)849-4213. Fax: (510)843-5835. E-mail: pvpress@sprynet. com. Website: www.pacificviewpress.com. **Acquisitions:** Pam Zumwalt, president. Publishes 1-2 picture books/year. 50% of books by first-time authors. "We publish unique, high-quality introductions to Asian cultures and history for children 8-12, for schools, libraries and families. Our children's books focus on hardcover illustrated nonfiction. We look for titles on aspects of the history and culture of the countries and peoples of the Pacific Rim, especially China, presented in an engaging, informative and respectful manner. We are interested in books that all children will enjoy reading and using, and that parents and teachers will want to buy."

Nonfiction Young readers, middle readers: Asia-related multicultural only. Recently published *Cloud Weavers: Ancient Chinese Legends*, by Rena Krasno and Yeng-Fong Chiang (all ages); *Exploring Chinatown: A Children's Guide to Chinese Culture*, by Carol Stepanchuk (ages 8-12).

How to Contact Query with outline and sample chapter. Responds in 3 months.

Illustration Works with 2 illustrators/year. Responds only if interested. Samples returned with SASE.

Terms Pays authors royalty of 8-12% based on wholesale price. Pays illustrators by the project (range: $2,000-5,000).

Tips "We welcome proposals from persons with expertise, either academic or personal, in their area of interest. While we do accept proposals from previously unpublished authors, we would expect submitters to have considerable experience presenting their interests to children in classroom or other public settings and to have skill in writing for children."

PAULINE BOOKS & MEDIA

50 Saint. Pauls Ave.Boston MA 02130-3491. (617)522-8911. E-mail: editorial@paulinemedia.com. Website: www.pauline.org. **Children's Editors:** Christina M. Wegendt, FSP; Diane Lynch. **Art Acquisitions:** Mary Joseph Peterson, FSP. Publishes 8 picture books/year; 2 board books/year; 5 young readers/year; 5 middle readers/year. "One to two books per year by first-time authors. Through our children's literature we aim to provide wholesome and entertaining reading that can help children develop strong Christian values."

Nonfiction Picture books, young readers, middle readers: religion. Average word length: picture books-500-1,000; young readers-8,000-10,000; middle readers-15,000-25,000. Recently published *God Made Wonderful Me!*, by Genny Monchamp; *O Holy Night*, by Maite Roche; *Starring Francie O'Leary*, by Maryann; *Adventures of Saint Paul*, by Oldrich Selucky; *Anna Mei, Cartoon Girl*, by Carol A. Grund; *Goodness Graces! Ten Short Stories about the Sacraments*, by Diana R. Jenkins.

How to Contact For board books and picture books, the entire manuscript should be submitted. For easy-to-read, young readers, and middle-reader books, please send a cover letter accompanied by a synopsis and two sample chapters. "Electronic submissions are encouraged. We make every effort to respond to unsolicited submissions within two months."

Illustration Works with 10-15 illustrators/year. Uses color and black-and-white- artwork. Illustrations only: Send résumé and 4-5 color samples. Samples résumé will be kept on file unless return is requested and SASE provided.

Terms Varies by project, but generally are royalties with advance. Flat fees sometimes considered for smaller works. Manuscript and art guidelines available by SASE or on website. Catalog available on website.

Tips "Manuscripts may or may not be explicitly catechetical, but we seek those that reflect a positive worldview, good moral values, awareness and appreciation of diversity, and respect for all people. All material must be relevant to the lives of young readers and must conform to Catholic teaching and practice."

PAULIST PRESS

97 Macarthur Blvd., Mahwah NJ 07430. Website: www.paulistpress.com. Acquisitions: Jennifer Conlan, Children's Book Editor. Publishes 10-12 titles/year. 10% of books by first-time authors. " Our mission is to Foster in Children the Knowledge that they are precious to help the Lord while encouraging a friendship with him that will last for a lifetime."

Fiction and Poetry "We publish fiction for the young adult market. We do not publish poetry."

Nonfiction We publish biographies for the young adult market, books on prayers and sacraments, spiritual books for children, and activity books. Activity book submissions must be writer/illustrator only. We also publish board books and picture books. All of our books must fulfill our mission. Examples of other kinds of books are *Child's Guide to the Stations of the Cross*, by Sue Stanton, illustrated by Anne Catharine Blake; *Yes, Jesus Loves You*, by Heather Tietz, illustrated by Nancy Miller; *Finn's Marching Band*, written and illustrated by Rachelle Evensen; and *I Can Speak Bully*, by Kevin Morrison and illustrated by Mai Kemble.

How to Contact Send complete mss for short books; query, outline, and sample for longer books. No e-mail submissions. No pitching ideas over the phone. Include SASE. Responds in 4-6 months. Simultaneous submissions are OK.

Illustration Send non-returnable samples of your children's art, or a link to your webpage showing the same. Receipt of art samples cannot be acknowledged.

Terms Pays authors royalty of 4-8% based on net sales, depending on whether or not they are split between author and illustrator. Advance payment is $500, payable on publication. Illustrators sometimes receive a flat fee when all we need are spot illustrations.

PEACHTREE PUBLISHERS, LTD.

1700 Chattahoochee Ave., Atlanta GA 30318-2112. (404)876-8761. Fax: (404)875-2578. E-mail: hello@peachtree-online.com. Website: www.peachtree-online.com. **Acquisitions:** Helen Harriss. **Art Director:** Loraine Joyner. Production Manager: Melanie McMahon Ives. Publishes 30-35 titles/year.

Fiction Picture books, young readers: adventure, animal, concept, history, nature/environment. Middle readers: adventure, animal, history, nature/environment, sports. Young adults: fiction, mystery, adventure. Does not want to see science fiction, romance.

Nonfiction Picture books: animal, history, nature/environment. Young readers, middle readers, young adults: animal, biography, nature/environment. Does not want to see religion.

How to Contact Fiction/nonfiction: Submit complete ms (picture books) or 3 sample chapters (chapter books) by postal mail only. Responds to queries/mss in 6-7 months. Publishes a book 1-2 years after acceptance. Will consider simultaneous submissions.

Illustration Works with 8-10 illustrators/year. Illustrations only: Query production manager or art director with samples, résumé, slides, color copies to keep on file. Responds only if interested. Samples returned with SASE; samples filed.

Terms "Manuscript guidelines for SASE, visit website or call for a recorded message. No fax or e-mail submittals or queries please."

⬛ PELICAN PUBLISHING CO. INC.

1000 Burmaster St., Gretna LA 70053-2246. (504)368-1175. Website: www.pelicanpub.com. **Manuscript Acquisitions:** Nina Kooij, editor-in-chief. **Art Acquisitions:** Terry Callaway, production manager. Publishes 20 young readers/year; 3 middle readers/year. **4% of books from agented writers**. " Pelican publishes hardcover and trade paperback originals and reprints. Our children's books (illustrated and otherwise) include history, biography, holiday, and regional. Pelican's mission is " To publish books of quality and permanence that enrich the lives of those who read them."

Fiction Young readers: history, holiday, science, multicultural and regional. Middle readers: Louisiana History. Multicultural needs include stories about African-Americans, Irish-Americans, Jews, Asian-Americans, and Hispanics. Does not want animal stories, general Christmas stories, "day at school" or "accept yourself" stories. Maximum word length: young readers-1,100; middle readers-40,000. Recently published *The Oklahoma Land Run*, by Una Belle Townsend (ages 5-8, historical/regional).

Nonfiction Young readers: biography, history, holiday, multicultural. Middle readers: Louisiana history, holiday, regional. Recently published *Batty about Texas*, by J. Jaye Smith (ages 5-8, science/regional).

How to Contact Fiction/nonfiction: Query. Responds to queries in 1 month; mss in 3 months. Publishes a book 9-18 months after acceptance.

Illustration Works with 20 illustrators/year. Reviews ms/illustration packages from artists. Query first. Illustrations only: Query with samples (no originals). Responds only if interested. Samples returned with SASE; samples kept on file.

Terms Pays authors in royalties; buys ms outright "rarely." Sends galleys to authors. Illustrators paid by "various arrangements." Book catalog and ms guidelines available on website.

Tips "No anthropomorphic stories, pet stories (fiction or nonfiction), fantasy, poetry, science fiction or romance. Writers: be as original as possible. Develop characters that lend themselves to series and always be thinking of new and interesting situations for those series. Give your story a strong hook-something that will appeal to a well-defined audience. There is a lot of competition out there for general themes. We look for stories with specific 'hooks' and audiences, and writers who actively promote their work."

PHILOMEL BOOKS

Penguin Young Readers Group (USA), 345 Hudson St., New York NY 10014. (212)414-3610. Website: www.penguin.com. **Manuscript Acquisitions:** submissions editor. **Art Acquisitions:** Annie Ericsson, junior designer. Publishes 8-10 picture books/year; 15-18 middle-grades/year; 5 young readers/year. 5% of books by first-time authors; 80% of books from agented writers. "We look for beautifully written, engaging manuscripts for children and young adults."

Fiction All levels: adventure, animal, boys, contemporary, fantasy, folktales, historical fiction, humor, sports, multicultural. Middle readers, young adults: problem novels, science fiction, suspense/ mystery. No concept picture books, mass-market "character" books, or series. Average word length: picture books—1,000; young readers—1,500; middle readers—14,000; young adult—20,000.

Nonfiction Picture books.

How to Contact "Philomel will no longer respond to your unsolicited submission unless interested in publishing it. Rejected submissions will be recycled. Please *do not* include a self-addressed stamped envelope with your submission. You will not hear from Philomel regarding the status of your submission unless we are interested in publishing it, in which case you can expect a reply from us within approximately four months. We regret that we cannot respond personally to each submission, but rest assured that we do make every effort to consider each and every one we receive."

Illustration Works with 8-10 illustrators/year. Reviews ms/illustration packages from artists. Query with art sample first. Illustrations only: Query with samples. Send résumé and tearsheets. Responds to art samples in 1 month. Original artwork returned at job's completion. Samples returned with SASE or kept on file.

Terms Pays authors in royalties. Average advance payment "varies." Illustrators paid by advance and in royalties. Sends galleys to authors; dummies to illustrators. Book catalog, ms guidelines free on request with SASE (9 × 12 envelope for catalog).

Tips Wants "unique fiction or nonfiction with a strong voice and lasting quality. Discover your own voice and own story and persevere." Looks for "something unusual, original, well-written. Fine art or illustrative art that feels unique. The genre (fantasy, contemporary, or historical fiction) is not so important as the story itself and the spirited life the story allows its main character."

◘ PIANO PRESS

P.O. Box 85, Del Mar CA 92014-0085. (619)884-1401. Fax: (858)755-1104. E-mail: pianopress@ pianopress.com. Website: www.pianopress.com. **Manuscript Acquisitions:** Elizabeth C. Axford, M.A, editor. "We publish music-related books, either fiction or nonfiction, coloring books, songbooks and poetry."

Fiction Picture books, young readers, middle readers, young adults: folktales, multicultural, poetry, music. Average word length: picture books-1,500-2,000. Recently published *Strum a Song of Angels*, by Linda Oatman High and Elizabeth C. Axford; *Music and Me*, by Kimberly White and Elizabeth C. Axford.

Nonfiction Picture books, young readers, middle readers, young adults: multicultural, music/ dance. Average word length: picture books-1,500-2,000. Recently published *The Musical ABC*, by Dr. Phyllis J. Perry and Elizabeth C. Axford; *Merry Christmas Happy Hanukkah—A Multilingual Songbook & CD*, by Elizabeth C. Axford.

How to Contact Fiction/ nonfiction: Query. Responds to queries in 3 months; mss in 6 months. Publishes a book 1 year after acceptance. Will consider simultaneous submissions, electronic submissions via disk or modem.

Illustration Works with 1 or 2 illustrators/year. Reviews ms/illustration packages from artists. Query. Illustrations only: Query with samples. Responds in 3 months. Samples returned with SASE; samples filed.

Photography Buys stock and assigns work. Looking for music-related, multicultural. Model/ property releases required. Uses glossy or flat, color or b&w prints. Submit cover letter, résumé, client list, published samples, stock photo list.

Terms Pays authors, illustrators, and photographers royalty of 5-10% based on retail price. Sends galleys to authors; dummies to illustrators. Originals returned to artist at job's completion. Book catalog available for #10 SASE and 2 first-class stamps. All imprints included in a single catalog. Catalog available on website.

Tips "We are looking for music-related material only for any juvenile market. Please do not send non-music-related materials. Query first before submitting anything."

PINATA BOOKS

Imprint of Arte Publico Press, University of Houston, 452 Cullen Performance Hall, Houston TX 77204-2004. (713)743-2843. Fax: (713)743-3080. Website: www.artepublicopress.com. **Manuscript Acquisitions:** Dr. Nicholas Kanellos; Gabriela Baeza Ventura, executive editor. **Art Acquisitions:** Adelaida Mendoza, production manager. Publishes 6 picture books/year; 2 young readers/year; 5 middle readers/year; 5 young adult titles/year. 80% of books are by first-time authors. "Arte Publico's mission is the publication, promotion and dissemination of Latino literature for a variety of national and regional audiences, from early childhood to adult, through the complete gamut of delivery systems, including personal performance as well as print and electronic media."

Fiction Recently published *We Are Cousins/ Somos primos* by Diane Gonzales Betrand; *Butterflies on Carmen Street/ Mariposas en la calle Carmen* by Monica Brown; and *Windows into My World: Latino Youth Write Their Lives.*

Nonfiction Recently published *Cesar Chavez: The Struggle for Justice/Cesar Chavez: La Lucha Por La Justicia*, by Richard Griswold del Castillo, illustrated by Anthony Accardo (ages 3-7).

How to Contact Accepts material from U.S./Hispanic authors only (living abroad OK). Manuscripts, queries, synopses, etc. are accepted in either English or Spanish. Fiction: Submit complete ms. Nonfiction: Query. Responds to queries in 2-4 months; mss in 3-6 months. Publishes a book 2 years after acceptance. Will sometimes consider previously published work.

Illustration Works with 6 illustrators/year. Uses color artwork only. Reviews ms/illustration packages from artists. Query or send portfolio (slides, color copies). Illustrations only: Query with samples or send résumé, promo sheet, portfolio, slides, client list and tearsheets. Responds only if interested. Samples not returned; samples filed.

Terms Pays authors royalty of 10% minimum based on wholesale price. Offers advances (average amount $2,000). Pays illustrators advance and royalties of 10% based on wholesale price. Sends galleys to authors. Catalog available on website; ms guidelines available for SASE.

PINEAPPLE PRESS, INC.

P.O. Box 3889, Sarasota FL 34239. (941)739-2219. Fax: (941)739-2296. E-mail: info@pineapplepress. com. Website: www.pineapplepress.com. **Manuscript Acquisitions:** June Cussen. Publishes 1 picture book/year; 1 young reader/year; 1 middle reader/year; 1 young adult title/year. 50% of books by first-time authors. "Our mission is to publish good books about Florida."

Fiction Picture books, young readers, middle readers, young adults: animal, folktales, history, nature/environment. Recently published *The Treasure of Amelia Island*, by M.C. Finotti (ages 8-12).

Nonfiction Picture books: animal, history, nature/environmental, science. Young readers, middle readers, young adults: animal, biography, geography, history, nature/environment, science. Recently published *Those Magical Manatees*, by Jan Lee Wicker and *Those Beautiful Butterflies*, by Sarah Cussen.

How to Contact Fiction: Query or submit outline/synopsis and 3 sample chapters. Nonfiction: Query or submit outline/synopsis and intro and 3 sample chapters. Responds to queries/samples/ mss in 2 months. Will consider simultaneous submissions.

Illustration Works with 2 illustrators/year. Reviews ms/illustration packages from artists. Query with nonreturnable samples. Contact: June Cussen, executive editor. Illustrations only: Query with brochure, nonreturnable samples, photocopies, résumé. Responds only if interested. Samples returned with SASE, but prefers nonreturnable; samples filed.

Terms Pays authors royalty of 10-15%. Pays illustrators royalties. Sends galleys to authors; dummies to illustrators. Originals returned to artist at job's completion. Book catalog available for 9 × 12 SAE with $1.06 postage; all imprints included in a single catalog. Catalog available on website at www. pineapplepress.com.

Tips "Learn about publishing and book marketing in general. Be familiar with the kinds of books published by the publishers to whom you are submitting."

Ⓝ PITSPOPANY PRESS

Simcha Media, P.O. Box 5329, Englewood NJ 07631. (212)444-1657. Fax: (866)205-3966. E-mail: pitspop@netvision.net.il. Website: www.pitspopany.com. Estab. 1992. Specializes in trade books, Judaica, nonfiction, fiction, multicultural material. **Manuscript Acquisitions:** Yaacov Peterseil, publisher. **Art Acquisitions:** Yaacov Peterseil, publisher. Produces 6 picture books/year; 4 young readers/year; 4 middle readers/year; 4 young adult books/year. 10% of books by first-time authors. "Pitspopany Press is dedicated to bringing quality children's books of Jewish interest into the marketplace. Our goal is to create titles that will appeal to the esthetic senses of our readers and, at the same time, offer quality Jewish content to the discerning parent, teacher, and librarian. While the people working for Pitspopany Press embody a wide spectrum of Jewish belief and opinion, we insist that our titles be respectful of the mainstream Jewish viewpoints and beliefs. We are especially interested in chapter books for kids. Most of all, we are committed to creating books that all Jewish children can read, learn from, and enjoy."

Fiction Picture books: animal, anthology, fantasy, folktales, history, humor, multicultural, nature/ environment, poetry. Young readers: adventure, animal, anthology, concept, contemporary, fantasy, folktales, health, history, humor, multicultural, nature/environment, poetry, religion, science fiction, special needs, sports, suspense. Middle readers: animal, anthology, fantasy, folktales, health, hi-lo, history, humor, multicultural, nature/environment, poetry, religion, science fiction, special needs, sports, suspense. Young adults/teens: animal, anthology, contemporary, fantasy, folktales, health, hi-lo, history, humor, multicultural, nature/environment, poetry, religion, science fiction, special needs, sports, suspense. Recently published *Hayyim's Ghost*, by Eric Kimmel, illustrated by Ari Binus (ages 6-9); *The Littlest Pair*, by Syliva Rouss, illustrated by Hally Hannan (ages 3-6); *The Converso Legacy*, by Sheldon Gardner (ages 10-14, historial fiction).

Nonfiction All levels: activity books, animal, arts/crafts, biography, careers, concept, cooking, geography, health, history, hobbies, how-to, multicultural, music/dance, nature/environment, reference, religion, science, self help, social issues, special needs, sports.

How to Contact Accepts international submissions. Fiction/nonfiction: Submit outline/synopsis. Responds to queries/mss in 6 weeks. Publishes book 9 months after acceptance. Considers simultaneous submissions, electronic submissions.

Illustration Accepts material from international illustrators. Works with 6 illustrators/year. Uses color artwork only. Reviews ms/illustration packages. For ms/illustration packages: Submit ms with 4 pieces of final art. Submit ms/illustration packages to Yaacov Peterseil, publisher. Reviews work for future assignments. If interested in illustrating future titles, send promo sheet. Submit samples to Yaacov Peterseil, publisher. Samples returned with SASE. Samples not filed.

Photography Works on assignment only. Submit photos to Yaacov Peterseil, publisher.

Terms Pays authors royalty or work purchased outright. Offers advance against royalties. Author sees galleys for review. Originals returned to artist at job's completion. Catalog on website. All imprints included in single catalog. Offers writer's guidelines for SASE.

PLAYERS PRESS, INC.

P.O. Box 1132, Studio City CA 91614-0132. (818)789-4980. **Manuscript Acquisitions:** Robert W. Gordon, vice president/editorial director. **Art Acquisitions:** Attention: Art Director. Publishes 7-25 young readers, dramatic plays and musicals/year; 2-10 middle readers, dramatic plays and musicals/year; 4-20 young adults, dramatic plays and musicals/year. 35% of books by first-time authors; 1% of books from agented writers. Players Press philosophy: "To create is to live life's purpose."

Fiction All levels: plays. Recently published *Play From African Folktales*, by Carol Korty (collection of short plays); *Punch and Judy*, a play by William-Alan Landes; *Silly Soup!*, by Carol Korty (a collection of short plays with music and dance).

Nonfiction Picture books, middle readers, young readers, young adults. "Any children's nonfiction pertaining to the entertainment industry, performing arts and how-to for the theatrical arts only." Needs include activity books related to theatre: arts/crafts, careers, history, how-to, music/dance, reference and textbook. Recently published *Scenery*, by J. Stell (how to build stage scenery); *Monologues for Teens*, by Vernon Howard (ideal for teen performers); *Humorous Monologues*, by Vernon Howard (ideal for young performers); *Actor's Resumes*, by Richard Devin (how to prepare an acting résumé).

How to Contact Fiction/nonfiction: Submit plays or outline/synopsis and sample chapters of entertainment books. Responds to queries in 2 weeks; mss in 6 months-1 year. Publishes a book 10 months after acceptance. No simultaneous submissions.

Illustration Works with 2-6 new illustrators/year. Use primarily b&w artwork. Illustrations only: Submit résumé, tearsheets. Responds to art samples in 1 week only if interested. Samples returned with SASE; samples filed.

Terms Pays authors royalty based on wholesale price. Pays illustrators by the project (range: $5-1,000). Pays photographers by the project (up to $100); royalty varies. Sends galleys to authors; dummies to illustrators. Book catalog and ms guidelines available for 9 × 12 SASE.

Tips Looks for "plays/musicals and books pertaining to the performing arts only. Illustrators: send samples that can be kept for our files."

N PLUM BLOSSOM BOOKS

Parallax Press, P.O. Box 7355, Berkeley CA 94707. (510)525-0101. Fax: (510)525-7129. E-mail: rachel@parallax.org. Website: www.parallax.org. Estab. 1985. Specializes in nonfiction, fiction. **Writers contact:** Rachel Neuman, senior editor. Produces 2 picture books/year. 30% of books by first-time authors. "Plum Blossom Books publishes stories for children of all ages that focus on mindfulness in daily life, Buddhism, and social justice."

Fiction Picture books: adventure, contemporary, folktales, multicultural, nature/environment, religion. Young readers: adventure, contemporary, folktales, multicultural, nature/environment, religion. Middle readers: multicultural, nature/environment, religion. Young adults/teens: nature/environment, religion. Recently published *The Hermit and the Well*, by Thich Nhat Hanh, illustrated by Dinh Mai (ages 4-8, hardcover); *Each Breath a Smile*, by Sister Thuc Nghiem and Thich Nhat Hanh, illustrated by T. Hop (ages 2-5, paperback picture book); *Meow Said the Mouse*, by Beatrice Barbey, illustrated by Philippe Ames (ages 5-8, picture and activity book).

Nonfiction All levels: nature/environment, religion (Buddhist), Buddhist counting books.

How to Contact Accepts international submissions. Fiction/nonfiction: Query or submit complete ms. Responds to queries in 1-2 weeks. Responds to mss in 4 weeks. Publishes book 9-12 months after acceptance. Considers electronic submissions.

Illustration Accepts material from international illustrators. Works with 3 illustrators/year. Uses both color and b&w. Reviews ms/illustration packages. For ms/illustration packages: Query. Send manuscript with dummy. Reviews work for future assignments. If interested in illustrating future titles, query with samples. Responds in 4 weeks. Samples returned with SASE. Samples filed.

Photography Buys stock images and assigns work. Submit photos to Rachel Neuman, senior editor. Uses b&w prints. For first contact, send cover letter, published samples.

Terms Pays authors royalty of 20% based on wholesale price. Pays illustrators by the project. Author sees galleys for review. Illustrators see dummies for review. Originals returned to artist at job's completion. Catalog available for SASE. Offers writer's, artist's guidelines for SASE. See website for writer's, artist's, photographer's guidelines.

Tips "Read our books before approaching us. We are very specifically looking for mindfulness and Buddhist messages in high-quality stories where the Buddhist message is implied rather than stated outright."

PRICE STERN SLOAN, INC.

Penguin Group (USA), 345 Hudson St., New York NY 10014. (212)414-3590. Fax: (212)414-3396. Estab. 1963. Website: http://us.penguingroup.com/youngreaders. **Acquisitions:** Debra Dorfman, president/publisher. "Price Stern Sloan publishes quirky mass market novelty series for children's as well as licensed movie tie-in books.

• Price Stern Sloan does not accept e-mail submissions.

Fiction Publishes picture books and novelty/board books including Mad Libs Movie and Television Tie-ins, and unauthorized biographies. "We publish unique novelty formats and fun, colorful paperbacks and activity books. We also publish the Book with Audio Series *Wee Sing* and *Baby Loves Jazz*." Recently published: *Baby Loves Jazz* board book with CD Series; new formats in the classic *Mr. Men/Little Miss* series; Movie/TV tie-in titles: *Speed Racers, Journey 3D*. Unauthorized biographies: *Mad for Miley* and *Jammin' with Jonas Brother*.

How to Contact Query. Responds to queries in 6-8 weeks.

Terms Work purchased outright. Offers advance. Book catalog available for 9 × 12 SASE and 5 first-class stamps; address to Book Catalog. Manuscript guidelines available for SASE; address to Manuscript Guidelines.

Tips "Price Stern Sloan publishes unique, fun titles."

📖 PUFFIN BOOKS

Penguin Group (USA), Inc., 345 Hudson St., New York NY 10014-3657. (212)414-3600. Website: www.penguin.com/youngreaders. **Acquisitions:** Sharyn November, senior editor and editorial director of Firebird. Imprints: Speak, Firebird, Sleuth. Publishes trade paperback originals and reprints. Publishes 175-200 titles/year. Receives 600 queries and mss/year. 1% of books by first-time authors; 5% from unagented writers. "Puffin Books publishes high-end trade paperbacks and paperback originals and reprints for preschool children, beginning and middle readers, and young adults."

Fiction Picture books, young adult novels, middle grade and easy-to-read grades 1-3: fantasy and science fiction, graphic novels, classics. Recently Published *Three Cups of Tea* young readers edition, by Greg Mortenson and David Oliver Relin; adapted for young readers by Sarah Thomson; *The Big Field*, by Mike Lupica; *Geek Charming*, by Robin Palmer.

Nonfiction Biography, illustrated books, young children's concept books (counting, shapes, colors). Subjects include education (for teaching concepts and colors, not academic), women in history. "Women in history books interest us."

How to Contact Fiction: Submit 3 sample chapters with SASE. Nonfiction: Submit 5 pages of ms with SASE. "It could take up to 5 months to get response." Publishes book 1 year after acceptance. Will consider simultaneous submissions, if so noted. Does not accept unsolicited picture book mss.

Illustration Reviews artwork. Send color copies.

Photography Reviews photos. Send color copies.

Terms Pays royalty. Offers advance (varies). Book catalog for 9 × 12 SASE with 7 first-class stamps; send request to Marketing Department.

N A PUSH

Scholastic, 557 Broadway, New York NY 10012-3999. Website: www.thisispush.com. Estab. 2002. Specializes in fiction. Produces 6-9 young adult books/year. 50% of books by first-time authors. PUSH publishes new voices in teen literature.

- PUSH does not accept unsolicited manuscripts or queries, only agented or referred fiction/memoir.

Fiction Young adults: contemporary, multicultural, poetry. Recently published *Splintering*, by Eireann Corrigan; *Never Mind the Goldbergs*, by Matthue Roth; *Perfect World*, by Brian James.

Nonfiction Young adults: memoir. Recently published *Talking in the Dark*, by Billy Merrell; *You Remind Me of You*, by Eireann Corrigan.

How to Contact Only interested in agented material. Accepts international submissions. Fiction/nonfiction: Submit complete ms. Responds to queries in 2 months; mss in 4 months. No simultaneous, electronic, or previously published submissions.

Tips "We only publish first-time writers (and then their subsequent books), so authors who have published previously should not consider PUSH. Also, for young writers in grades 7-12, we run the PUSH novel Contest with the Scholastic Art & Writing Awards. Every year it begins in October and ends in March. Rules can be found on our website."

☥ G.P. PUTNAM'S SONS

Penguin Putnam Books For Young Readers, 345 Hudson St.New York NY 10014. (212)414-3610. Website: www.penguinputnam.com. **Manuscript Acquisitions:** Susan Kochan, associate editorial director; John Rudolph, executive editor; Timothy Travaglini, senior editor; Stacey Barney, editor. **Art Acquisitions:** Cecilia Yung, art director, Putnam and Philomel. Publishes 25 picture books/year; 15 middle readers/year; 5 young adult titles/year. 5% of books by first-time authors; 50% of books from agented authors.

- G.P. Putnam's Sons title *After Tupac and D Foster*, by Jacqueline Woodson, won a Newbery Honor Medal in 2009.

Fiction Picture books: animal, concept, contemporary, humor, multicultural. Young readers: adventure, contemporary, history, humor, multicultural, special needs, suspense/mystery. Middle readers: adventure, contemporary, history, humor, fantasy, multicultural, problem novels, sports, suspense/mystery. Young adults: contemporary, history, fantasy, problem novels, special needs. Does not want to see series. Average word length: picture books—200-1,000; middle readers—10,000-30,000; young adults—40,000-50,000. Recently published *Runaway Mummy: A Parody*, by Michael Rex (ages 4-8); *Adventure According to Humphrey*, by Betty G. Birney (ages 7-11).

Nonfiction Picture books: animal, biography, concept, history, nature/environment, science. Subjects must have broad appeal but inventive approach. Average word length: picture books—200-1,500. Recently published River of Dreams, by Hudson Talbot (ages 5 and up, 32 pages).

How to Contact Accepts unsolicited mss. No SASE required, as will only respond if interested. Picture books: send full mss. Fiction: Query with outline/synopsis and 10 manuscript pages. Nonfiction: Query with outline/synopsis, 10 manuscript pages, and a table of contents. Do not send art unless requested. Responds to mss within 4 months if interested. Will consider simultaneous submissions.

Illustration Write for illustrator guidelines. Works with 40 illustrators/year. Reviews ms/illustration packages from artists. Manuscript/illustration packages and illustration only: Query. Responds only if interested. Samples filed.

Terms Pays authors royalty based on retail price. Pays illustrators by the project or royalty based on retail price. Sends galleys to authors. Original artwork returned at job's completion.

Tips "Study our catalogs and get a sense of the kind of books we publish, so that you know whether your project is likely to be right for us."

RAINBOW PUBLISHERS

P.O. Box 261129, San Diego CA 92196. 858)277-1167. E-mail: editor@rainbowpublishers.com. Publishes 4 young readers/year; 4 middle readers/year; 4 young adult titles/year. 50% of books by first-time authors. "Our mission is to publish Bible-based, teacher resource materials that contribute to and inspire spiritual growth and development in kids ages 2-12." **Contact:** Editorial Department.

Nonfiction Young readers, middle readers, young adult/teens: activity books, arts/crafts, how-to, reference, religion.

How to Contact Nonfiction: Submit outline/synopsis and 3-5 sample chapters. Responds to queries in 6 weeks; mss in 3 months. Publishes a book 36 months after acceptance. Will consider simultaneous submissions, submissions via disk and previously published work.

Illustration Works with 2-5 illustrators/year. Reviews ms/illustration packages from artists. Submit ms with 2-5 pieces of final art. Illustrations only: Query with samples. Responds in 6 weeks. Samples returned with SASE; samples filed.

Terms For authors work purchased outright (range: $500 and up). Pays illustrators by the project (range: $300 and up). Sends galleys to authors.

◘ Ⓐ RANDOM HOUSE-GOLDEN BOOKS FOR YOUNG READERS GROUP

Random House, Inc.1745 Broadway, New York NY 10019. (212)782-9000. Estab. 1925. Book publisher. "Random House Books aims to create books that nurture the hearts and minds of children, providing and promoting quality books and a rich variety of media that entertain and educate readers from 6 months to 12 years." Publisher/Vice President: Kate Klimo. VP & Associate Publisher/Art Director: Cathy Goldsmith. **Acquisitions:** Easy-to-Read Books (step-into-reading and picture books), board and novelty books, fiction and nonfiction for young and mid-grade readers: Heidi Kilgras, Editorial Director. Stepping Stones: Jennifer Arena, Executive Editor. Middle grade and young adult fiction: Jim Thomas, Editorial Director. 100% of books published through agents; 2% of books by first-time authors.

- Random House-Golden Books does not accept unsolicited manuscripts, only agented material. They reserve the right not to return unsolicited material.

How to Contact Only interested in agented material. Reviews ms/illustration packages from artists through agent only. Does not open or respond to unsolicited submissions.

Terms Pays authors in royalties; sometimes buys mss outright. Sends galleys to authors. Book catalog free on request.

☑ RAVEN TREE PRESS

1400 Miller Parkway, McHenry IL 60050. (800)323-8270; (815)363-3582. Fax: (800)909-9901. E-mail: raven@raventreepress.com. Website: www.raventreepress.com. Publishes 8-10 picture books/year. 50% of books by first-time authors. "We publish entertaining and educational picture books in a variety of formats. Bilingual (English/Spanish), English-Only, Spanish-Only and Wordless editions."

Fiction Picture books: K-3 focus. No word play or rhyme. Work will be translated into Spanish by publisher. Check website prior to any submissions for current needs. Average word length: 500.

How to Contact Check website for current needs, submission guidelines and deadlines.

Illustration Check website for current needs, submission guidelines and deadlines.

Terms Pays authors and illustrators royalty. Offers advances against royalties. Pays illustrators by the project or royalty. Originals returned to artist at job's completion. Catalog available on website.

Tips "Submit only based on guidelines. No e-mail OR snail mail queries please. Word count is a definite issue, since we are bilingual." Staff attended or plans to attend the following conferences: BEA, NABE, IRA, ALA and SCBWI.

RAZORBILL

Penguin Group, 345 Hudson Street, New York NY 10014. Imprint estab. 2003. (212)414-3448. Fax: (212)414-3343. E-mail: razorbill@us.penguingroup.com. Website: www.razorbillbooks.com. Specializes in fiction. **Acquisitions:** Gillian Levinson; Editorial Assistant: Jessica Rothenberg, Brianne Mulligan, editors. Publishes about 30 middle grade and YA titles/year. "This division of Penguin Young Readers is looking for the best and the most original of commercial contemporary fiction titles for middle grade and YA readers. A select quantity of nonfiction titles will also be considered."

Fiction Middle Readers: adventure, contemporary, graphic novels, fantasy, humor, problem novels. Young adults/teens: adventure, contemporary, fantasy, graphic novels, humor, multicultural, suspense, paranormal, science fiction, dystopian, literary, romance. Average word length: middle readers—40,000; young adult—60,000. Recently published *Thirteen Reason Why*, by Jay Asher (ages 14 and up, a NY Times Bestseller); *Vampire Academy* series, by Richelle Mead (ages 12 and up; NY Times Bestselling series); *The Teen Vogue Handbook* (ages 12 and up; a NY Times Bestseller); and I *Am a Genius of Unspeakable Evil and I Want to Be Your Class President*, by Josh Lieb (ages 12 and up; a NY Times Bestseller).

Nonfiction Middle readers and Young adults/teens: concept.

How to Contact Submit outline/synopsis and 3 sample chapters along with query and SASE. Responds to queries/mss in 1-3 months. Publishes a book 1-2 years after acceptance. Will consider e-mail submissions and simultaneous submissions.

Terms Offers advance against royalties. Authors see galleys for review. Catalog available online at www.razorbillbooks.com.

Tips "New writers will have the best chance of acceptance and publication with original, contemporary material that boasts a distinctive voice and well-articulated world. Check out www.razorbillbooks.com to get a better idea of what we're looking for."

⚏ RED DEER PRESS

195 Allstate Parkway, Markham ON L9P 1R4 Canada. (800)-387-9776/(905)477-9700. Fax: (800)260-9777/(905)477-2834. E-mail: rdp@reddeerpress.com. Website: www.reddeerpress.com. **Manuscript/Art Acquisitions:** Peter Carver, children's editor. Publishes 3 to 5 picture books/year; 4 young adult titles/year per season. Red Deer Press is known for their "high-quality international children's program that tackles risky and/or serious issues for kids."

• Red Deer only publishes books written and illustrated by Canadians.

Fiction Picture books, young readers: adventure, contemporary, fantasy, folktales, history, humor, multicultural, nature/environment, poetry. Middle readers, young adult/teens: adventure, contemporary, fantasy, folktales, hi-lo, history, humor, multicultural, nature/environment, problem novels, suspense/mystery. Recently published *Egghead*, by Caroline Pignat; *Dooley Takes the Fall*, by Norah McClintock; *The End of The World As We Know It,* by Lesley Choyce.

How to Contact Fiction/nonfiction: Query or submit outline/synopsis. Responds to queries in 2 months; mss in 8 months. Publishes a book 18 months after acceptance.

Illustration Works with 4-6 illustrators/year. Illustrations only: Query with samples. Responds only if interested. Samples not returned; samples filed for six months. Canadian illustrators only.

Photography Buys stock and assigns work. Model/property releases required. Submit cover letter, résumé and color promo piece.

Terms Pays authors royalty (negotiated). Advances (negotiated). Pays illustrators and photographers by the project or royalty (depends on the project). Sends galleys to authors. Originals returned to artist at job's completion. Guidelines not available on website.

Tips "Writers, illustrators, and photographers should familiarize themselves with Red Deer Press's children's publishing program, including the kinds of books we do and do not publish."

⚏ ⚏ RENAISSANCE HOUSE

Imprint of Laredo Publishing, Englewood, NJ 07631. (800)547-5113. Fax: (201)408-5011. E-mail: laredo@renaissancehouse.net. Website: www.renaissancehouse.net. **Manuscript Acquisitions:** Raquel Benatar. **Art Acquisitions:** Sam Laredo. Publishes 5 picture books/year; 10 young readers/year; 10 middle readers/year; 5 young adult titles/year. 10% of books by first-time authors.

Fiction Picture books: animal, folktales, multicultural. Young readers: animal, anthology, folktales, multicultural. Middle readers, young adult/teens: anthology, folktales, multicultural, nature/environment. Recently published *Go Milka, Go* (English-Spanish, age 8-10, biography); *Stories of the Americas*, a series of legends by several authors (ages 9-12, legend).

How to Contact Submit outline/synopsis. Responds to queries/mss in 3 weeks. Publishes a book 1 year after acceptance. Will consider simultaneous submissions, e-mail submissions.

Illustration Works with 25 illustrators/year. Uses color artwork only. Reviews ms/illustration packages from artists. Send ms with dummy. Contact: Sam Laredo. Illustrations only: Send tearsheets. Contact: Raquel Benatar. Responds in 3 weeks. Samples not returned; samples filed.

Terms Pays authors royalty of 5-10% based on retail price. Pays illustrators by the project. Sends galleys to authors; dummies to illustrators. Originals returned to artist at job's completion. Book catalog available for 9 × 12 SASE and $3 postage. All imprints included in a single catalog. Catalog available on website.

⚏ ROARING BROOK PRESS

175 Fifth Ave., New Milford CT 10025. (646)438-5226. E-mail: david.langva@roaringbrookpress. com. **Contact:** David Langva.

• Roaring Brook Press is an imprint of MacMillan, a group of companies that includes Henry Holt and Farrar, Straus & Giroux. Roaring Brook is not accepting unsolicited manuscripts.

Roaring Brook title *First the Egg*, by Laura Vaacaro Seeger, won a Caldecott Honor Medal and a Theodor Seuss Geisel Honor in 2008. Their title *Dog and Bear: Two Friends, Three Stories*, also by Laura Vaccaro Seeger, won the Boston Globe-Horn Book Picture Book Award in 2007.

Fiction Picture books, young readers, middle readers, young adults: adventure, animal, contemporary, fantasy, history, humor, multicultural, nature/environment, poetry, religion, science fiction, sports, suspense/mystery. Recently published *Happy Birthday Bad Kitty*, by Nick Bruel; *Cookie*, by Jacqueline Wilson.

Nonfiction Picture books, young readers, middle readers, young adults: adventure, animal, contemporary, fantasy, history, humor, multicultural, nature/environment, poetry, religion, science fiction, sports, suspense/mystery.

How to Contact Primarily interested in agented material. Not accepting unsolicited mss or queries. Will consider simultaneous agented submissions.

Illustration Primarily interested in agented material. Works with 25 illustrators/year. Illustrations only: Query with samples. Do not send original art; copies only through the mail. Samples returned with SASE.

Photography Works on assignment only.

Terms Pays authors royalty based on retail price. Pays illustrators royalty or flat fee depending on project. Sends galleys to authors; dummies to illustrators, if requested.

Tips "You should find a reputable agent and have him/her submit your work."

▓ RONSDALE PRESS

3350 W. 21st Ave., Vancouver BC V6S 1G7, Canada. (604)738-4688. Fax: (604)731-4548. E-mail: ronsdale@shaw.ca. Website: ronsdalepress.com. Estab. 1988. Book publisher. **Manuscript/Art Acquisitions:** Veronica Hatch, children's editor. Publishes 3 children's books/year. 40% of titles by first-time authors. "Ronsdale Press is a Canadian literary publishing house that publishes 12 books each year, three of which are children's titles. Of particular interest are books involving children exploring and discovering new aspects of Canadian history."

Fiction Young adults: Canadian novels. Average word length: middle readers and young adults-50,000. Recently published *Red Goodwin*, by John Wilson (ages 10-14); *Tragic Links*, by Cathy Beveridge (ages 10-14); *Dark Times*, edited by Ann Walsh (anthology of short stories, ages 10 and up); *Submarine Outlaw*, by Phillip Roy; *The Way Lies North*, by Jean Rae Baxter (ages 10-14).

Nonfiction Middle readers, young adults: animal, biography, history, multicultural, social issues. Average word length: young readers-90; middle readers-90.

How to Contact Accepts material from residents of Canada only. Fiction/nonfiction: Submit complete ms. Responds to queries in 2 weeks; mss in 2 months. Publishes a book 1 year after acceptance. Will consider simultaneous submissions.

Illustration Works with 2 illustrators/year. Reviews ms/illustration packages from artists. Requires only cover art. Responds in 2 weeks. Samples returned with SASE. Originals returned to artist at job's completion.

Terms Pays authors royalty of 10% based on retail price. Pays illustrators by the project $400-800. Sends galleys to authors. Book catalog available for 8½ × 11 stet and $1 postage; ms and art guidelines available for SASE.

▢ RUNNING PRESS KIDS

Imprints of Running Press Book Publishers, 2300 Chestnut St., Philadelphia, PA 19103. (215)567-5080. Fax: (215)568-2919. Website: www.runningpress.com. Manuscript Acquisitions: Not accepting unsolicited manuscripts. Art Acquisitions: Design Director.

Fiction Picture books and YA novels: adventure, animal, anthology, concept, contemporary, fantasy, folktales, health, history, humor, multicultural, nature/environment, poetry, suspense/mystery. Recently published Running Press Kids: *Party Animals,* by Kathie Lee Gifford; *One Weighs a Ton, and I Feel Happy,* by Salina Yoon; *Robox,* by Mark Rogalski; *The Seeing Stick*, by Jane Yolen; *Doodle Bugs*, by Nikalas Catlaw; *Doodle Dolls*, by Jessie Eckel; *Get Real*, by Mara Rockliff; *A Feast of Freedom*, by Walter Staib; *Steampotville,* by Steve Ouch.

Nonfiction Picture books: activity books, animal, biography, concept, history. Young readers, middle readers: activity books, animal, biography, concept, cooking, geography, history. Recently published Running Press Teens: *Nanovor series: Hacked, Welcome to the Nanosphere, and Prank Week,* by Jordan Weisman; *Lost Souls: Burning Sky,* by Jordan Weisman; *Tombstone Tea*, by Joanne Dahme; *The Eternal Kiss edited,* by Trisha Telep; *Star Crossed series: Aires Rising, and Taurus Eyes*, by Bonnie Hearn Hill; *Rebel in a Dress series: Adventurers, and Cowgirls*, by Sylvia Branzei.

How to Contact Fiction: Submit complete ms. Nonfiction: Query. Responds to queries in 2 month; mss in 3 months. Publishes book 2 years after acceptance. Will consider simultaneous submissions and previously published work.

Illustration Send postcard sample. Responds only if interested. Samples not returned; samples filed.

Terms Pays authors royalty or work purchased outright from authors. Offers advances. Pays illustrators by the project or royalties. Sends galleys to authors; dummies to illustrators. Originals returned to artist at job's completion. All imprints included in a single catalog. Catalog available on website.

N SASQUATCH BOOKS

119 South Main St.Seattle WA 98104. (800)775-0817. Fax: (206)467-4301. Website: www.sasquatchbooks.com. Estab. 1986. Specializes in trade books, nonfiction,children's fiction. **Writers contact:** The Editors. **Illustrators contact:** Lisa-Brire Dahmen, production manager. Produces 5 picture books/year. 20% of books by first-time authors. "We are seeking quality nonfiction works about the Pacific Northwest and West Coast regions (including Alaska and California). The literature of place includes how-to and where-to as well as history and narrative nonfiction."

Fiction Young readers: adventure, animal, concept, contemporary, humor, nature/environment. Recently published *Amazing Alaska*, by Deb Vanasse, illustrated by Karen Lewis; *Sourdough Man*, by Cherie Stihler, illustrated by Barbara Lavallee

Nonfiction Picture books: activity books, animal, concept, nature/environment. Recently published *Larry Gets Lost in New York*, written and illustrated by John Skewes (picture book); *Searching for Sasqatch,* by Nathaniel Lachenmeyer, illustrated by Vicki Bradley (picture book).

How to Contact Accepts international submissions. Fiction: Query, submit complete ms, or submit outline/synopsis. Nonfiction: Query. Responds to queries in 3 months. Publishes book 6-9 months after acceptance. Considers simultaneous submissions.

Illustration Accepts material from international illustrators. Works with 5 illustrators/year. Uses both color and b&w. Reviews ms/illustration packages. For ms/illustration packages: Query. Submit ms/illustration packages to The Editors. Reviews work for future assignments. If interested in illustrating future titles, query with samples. Samples returned with SASE. Samples filed.

Photography Buys stock images and assigns work. Submit photos to: Lisa-Brire Dahmen, production manager.

Terms Pays authors royalty based on retail price. Offers advance against royalties. Offers a wide range of advances. Author sees galleys for review. Originals not returned. Catalog on website. See website for writer's guidelines.

◼ SCHOLASTIC CANADA LTD.

604 King St. West, ON M5V 1E1 Canada. (416)915-3500. Fax: (416)849-7912. Website: www.scholastic.ca; for ms/artist guidelines: www.scholastic.ca/aboutscholastic/manuscripts.htm. **Acquisitions:** Editor, children's books. Publishes hardcover and trade paperback originals. Imprints: Scholastic Canada; North Winds Press; Les Editions Scholastic. Publishes 70 titles/year; imprint publishes 4 titles/year. 3% of books from first-time authors; 50% from unagented writers. Canadian authors, theme or setting required.

- At press time Scholastic Canada was not accepting unsolicited manuscripts. For up-to-date information on their current submission policy, call their publishing status line at (905)887-7323, ext. 4308 or view their submission guidelines on their website.

Fiction Picture books, young readers, young adult. Average word length: picture books-under 1,000; young readers-7,000-10,000; middle readers-15,000-30,000; young adult-25,000-40,000.

Nonfiction Animals, biography, history, hobbies, nature, recreation, science, sports. Reviews artwork/photos as part of ms package. Send photocopies.

How to Contact Query with synopsis, 3 sample chapters and SASE. Nonfiction: Query with outline, 1-2 sample chapters and SASE (IRC or Canadian stamps only). Responds in 3 months. Publishes book 1 year after acceptance.

Illustration Illustrations only: Query with samples; send résumé. Never send originals. Contact: Ms. Yuksel Hassan.

Terms Pays authors royalty of 5-10% based on retail price. Offers advances. Book catalog for 8½ × 11 SAE with $2.55 postage stamps (IRC or Canadian stamps only).

◼ SCHOLASTIC INC.

557 Broadway, New York NY 10012. (212)343-6100. Website: www.scholastic.com. Arthur A. Levine Books, Cartwheel Books, Chicken House, Graphix, Little Scholastic, Little Shepherd, Michael di Capua Books, Orchard Books, PUSH, Scholastic en español, Scholastic Licensed Publishing, Scholastic Nonfiction, Scholastic Paperbacks, Scholastic Press, Scholastic Reference, Tangerine Press, and The Blue Sky Press are imprints of Scholastic Trade Books Division. In addition, Scholastic Trade Books included Klutz, a highly innovative publisher and creator of "books plus" for children.

- Scholastic Press title *The Invention of Hugo Cabret*, by Brian Selznick won the Caldecott Medal in 2008.

SCHOLASTIC PRESS

557 Broadway, New York NY 10012. (212)343-6100. Website: www.scholastic.com. **Manuscript Acquisitions:** David Saylor, editorial director, Scholastic Press, Creative director and Associate Publisher for all Scholastic hardcover imprints. David Levithan, Executive Editorial Director, Scholastic Press fiction, multimedia publishing, and Push Lisa Sandell, Acquiring Editor; Dianne Hess, Executive Editor (picture book fiction/nonfiction, 2nd-3rd grade chapter books, some middle grade fantasy that is based on reality); Tracy Mack, Executive Editor (picture book, middle grade, YA); Rachel Griffiths, Editor: Jennifer Rees, Associate Editor (picture book fiction/nonfiction, middle grade, YA). **Art Acquisitions:** Elizabeth Parisi, Art Director, Scholastic Press; Marijka Kostiw, Art Director; David Saylor, creative Director and associate publisher for all Scholastic hardcover imprints. Publishes 60 titles/year. 1% of books by first-time authors.

- Scholastic Press title What I Saw and How I Lied won the 2008 National Book Award; Best-selling Hunger Games, by Suzanne Collins; Best-selling 39 Clues Series; Zen Ties, by Jon J. Muth was 42 weeks on the New York Times Best seller list; Elijah of Buxton, by Christopher Paul Curtis won a Newbery Honor Medal and the Coretta Scott King Author Award in 2008.

Their title Henry's Freedom Box: A True Story from the Underground Railroad, by Ellen Levine, illustrated by Kadir Nelson, won a Caldecott Honor Medal in 2008; Hugo Cabaret won the 2008 Caldecott Medal.

Fiction Looking for strong picture books, young chapter books, appealing middle grade novels (ages 8-11) and interesting and well written young adult novels.

Nonfiction Interested in "unusual, interesting, and very appealing approaches to biography, math, history and science."

How to Contact Fiction/nonfiction: "Send query with 1 sample chapter and synopsis. Don't call! Don't e-mail!" Picture books: submission accepted from agents or previously published authors only.

Illustration Works with 30 illustrators/year. Uses both b&w and color artwork. Illustrations only: Query with samples; send tearsheets. Responds only if interested. Samples returned with SASE. Original artwork returned at job's completion.

Terms Pays advance against royalty.

Tips "Read *currently* published children's books. Revise, rewrite, rework and find your own voice, style and subject. We are looking for authors with a strong and unique voice who can tell a great story and have the ability to evoke genuine emotion. Children's publishers are becoming more selective, looking for irresistible talent and fairly broad appeal, yet still very willing to take risks, just to keep the game interesting."

SECOND STORY PRESS

20 Maud St.Suite 401, Toronto ON M5V 2M5 Canada. (416)537-7850. Fax: (416)537-0588. E-mail: info@secondstorypress.ca. Website: www.secondstorypress.ca.

Fiction Considers non-sexist, non-racist, and non-violent stories, as well as historical fiction, chapter books, picture books. Recently published *Lilly and the Paper Man*, by Rebecca Upjohn; *Mom and Mum Are Getting Married!*, by Ken Setterington.

Nonfiction Picture books: biography. Recently published *Hiding Edith: A True Story*, by Kathy Kacer (a new addition to our Holocaust remembrance series for young readers).

How to Contact Accepts appropriate material from residents of Canada only. Fiction and nonfiction: Submit complete ms or submit outline and sample chapters by postal mail only. No electronic submissions or queries.

SEEDLING CONTINENTAL PRESS

520 E. Bainbridge St., Elizabethtown PA 17022. Website: www.continentalpress.com. **Acquisitions:** Megan Bergonzi. 20% of books by first-time authors. Publishes books for classroom use only for the beginning reader in English. "Natural language and predictable text are requisite. Patterned text is acceptable, but must have a unique story line. Poetry, books in rhyme and full-length picture books are not being accepted. Illustrations are not necessary."

Fiction Young readers: adventure, animal, folktales, humor, multicultural, nature/environment. Does not accept texts longer than 12 pages or over 300 words. Average word length: young readers-100.

Nonfiction Young readers: animal, arts/crafts, biography, careers, concept, multicultural, nature/environment, science. Does not accept texts longer than 12 pages or over 300 words. Average word length: young readers-100.

How to Contact Fiction/nonfiction: Submit complete ms with SASE. Responds in 6 months. Publishes a book 1-2 years after acceptance. Will consider simultaneous submissions. Prefers e-mail submissions from authors or illustrators outside the U.S.

Illustration Works with 8-10 illustrators/year. Uses color artwork only. Reviews ms/illustration packages from artists. Submit ms with dummy. Illustrations only: Color copies or line art. Responds only if interested. Samples returned with SASE only; samples filed if interested.

Photography Buys photos from freelancers. Works on assignment only. Model/property releases required. Uses color prints and 35mm transparencies. Submit cover letter and color promo piece.

Terms Work purchased outright from authors. Pays illustrators and photographers by the project. Original artwork is not returned at job's completion. Catalog available on website.

Tips "See our website. Follow writers' guidelines carefully and test your story with children and educators."

ⓝ SHEN'S BOOKS

1547 Palos Verdes Mall, #291, Walnut Creek CA 94597. (925)262-8108. Fax: (888)269-9092. E-mail: info@shens.com. Website: www.shens.com. Estab. 1986. Specializes in multicultural material.

Acquisitions: Renee Ting, president. Produces 2 picture books/year. 50% of books by first-time authors.

Fiction Picture books, young readers: folktales, multicultural with Asian Focus. Middle readers: multicultural. Recently published *Cora Cooks Pacit*, By Dorina Lazo Gilmore, illustrated by Kristi Valiant; *Grandfather's Story Cloth*, by Linda Gerdner, illustrated by Stuart Loughridge (ages 4-8); *The Wakame Gatherers*, by Holly Thompson, illustrated by Kazumi (ages 4-8); *Romina's Rangoli*, by Malathi Michelle Iyengar, illustrated by Jennifer Wanardi (ages 4-8); *The Day the Dragon Danced*, by Kay Haugaard, illustrated by Carolyn Reed Barritt (ages 4-8).

Nonfiction Picture books, young readers: multicultural. Recently published *Chinese History Stories*, edited by Renee Ting; *Selvakumar Knew Better*, by Virginia Kroll, illustrated by Xiaojun Li (ages 4-8).

How to Contact Accepts international submissions. Fiction/nonfiction: Submit complete ms. Responds to queries in 1-2 weeks; mss in 6-12 months. Publishes book 1-2 years after acceptance. Considers simultaneous submissions.

Illustration Accepts material from international illustrators. Works with 2 illustrators/year. Uses color artwork only. Reviews ms/illustration packages. For ms/illustration packages: Send ms with dummy. Submit ms/illustration packages to Renee Ting, president. Reviews work for future assignments. If interested in illustrating future titles, query with samples. Submit samples to Renee Ting, president. Samples not returned. Samples filed.

Photography Works on assignment only. Submit photos to Renee Ting, president.

Terms Authors pay negotiated by the project. Pays illustrators by the project. Pays photographers by the project. Illustrators see dummies for review. Catalog on website.

Tips "Be familiar with our catalog before submitting."

ⓒ SILVER MOON PRESS

381 Park Avenue South, Suite 1121, New York NY 10016. (212)802-2890. Fax: (212)802-2893. E-mail: mail@silvermoonpress.com. Website: www.silvermoonpress.com. **Publisher:** David Katz. **Marketing Coordinator:** Karin Lillebo. Book publisher. Publishes 1-2 books for grades 4-6/year. 25% of books by first-time authors; 10% books from agented authors. Publishes mainly American historical fiction and books of educational value. Develops books which fit neatly into curriculum for grades 4-6. "History comes alive when children can read about other children who lived when history was being made!"

Fiction Middle readers: historical, multicultural and mystery. Average word length: 14,000. Recently published *Liberty on 23rd Street*, by Jacqueline Glasthal; *A Silent Witness in Harlem*, by Eve Creary;

In the Hands of the Enemy, by Robert Sheely; *Ambush in the Wilderness*, by Kris Hemphill; *Race to Kitty Hawk*, by Edwina Raffa and Annelle Rigsby; *Brothers of the Falls*, by Joanna Emery.

How to Contact We are not accepting manuscript submissions at this time.

Illustration Works with 1-2 illustrators/year. Reviews ms/illustration packages from artists. Query. Illustrations only: Query with samples, résumé, client list. Responds only if interested. Samples returned with SASE; samples filed. Original artwork returned at job's completion.

Photography Buys photos from freelancers. Buys stock and assigns work. Uses archival, historical, sports photos. Captions required. Uses color, b&w prints; 35mm, 2¼ × 2¼, 4 × 5, 8 × 10 transparencies. Submit cover letter, résumé, published samples, client list, promo piece.

Terms Pays authors royalty or work purchased outright. Pays illustrators by the project, no royalty. Pays photographers by the project, per photo, no royalty. Sends galleys to authors; dummies to illustrators. Book catalog available for 8½ × 11 SASE and $1.11 postage.

Tips "We do not accept biographies, poetry, or romance. We do not accept fantasy, science fiction, or historical fiction with elements of either. No picture books. Submissions that fit into New York State curriculum topics such as the Revolutionary War, Colonial times, and New York state history in general stand a greater chance of acceptance than those that do not."

SIMON & SCHUSTER BOOKS FOR YOUNG READERS

1230 Avenue of the Americas, New York NY 10020. (212)698-7000. Fax: (212)698-2796. Website: www.kids.simonandschuster.com. **Manuscript Acquisitions:** Justin Chanda, VP and publisher; David Gale, vice president, editorial director; Kevin Lewis, executive director; Emily Meehan, executive editor; Alexandra Cooper, senior editor; Paula Wiseman, VP, publisher, books. **Art Acquisitions:** Dan Potash, vice president, creative director; Lizzy Bromley, executive art director; Laurent Linn, art director. Publishes 95 books/year. "We publish high-quality fiction and nonfiction for a variety of age groups and a variety of markets. Above all we strive to publish books that will offer kids a fresh perspective on their world." 75 Simon & Schuster Books for Young Readers does not accept unsolicited manuscripts or queries.

Fiction Picture books: animal, minimal text/very young readers. Middle readers, young adult: fantasy, adventure, suspense/mystery. All levels: contemporary, history, humor. Recently published *My Father Knows the Names of Things*, written by Jane Yolen, illustrated by Stephane Jorisch (picture book, ages 4-8); *Frankie Pickle and The Pine Run 3000*, by Eric Wight (middle grade fiction illustrated, ages 7-10); *Hush, Hush*, by Becca Fitzpatrick (teen fiction, ages 14 Up).

Nonfiction Picture books: concept. All levels: narrative, current events, biography, history. "We're looking for picture book or middle grade nonfiction that have a retail potential. No photo essays." Recently published Insiders Series (picture book nonfiction, all ages). Paula Deen's cookbook for the lunch-box set 9 cookbook (nonfiction, ages 7 up).

How to Contact Do not accept unsolicited or unagented manuscripts.

Illustration Works with 70 illustrators/year. Do not submit original artwork. Do not accept unsolicited or unagented illustration submissions.

Terms Pays authors royalty (varies) based on retail price. Pays illustrators or photographers by the project or royalty (varies) based on retail price. Original artwork returned at job's completion. Manuscript/artist's guidelines available via website or free on request. Call (212)698-2707.

Tips "We're looking for picture books centered on a strong, fully-developed protagonist who grows or changes during the course of the story; YA novels that are challenging and psychologically complex; also imaginative and humorous middle-grade fiction. And we want nonfiction that is as engaging as fiction. Our imprint's slogan is 'Reading You'll Remember.' We aim to publish books that are fresh, accessible and family-oriented; we want them to have an impact on the reader."

SKINNER HOUSE BOOKS

Unitarian Universalist Association. 25 Beacon St., Boston MA 02108. Estab. 1976. (617)742-2100. Fax: (617)742-7025. E-mail: skinnerhouse@uua.org. Website: www.uua.org/publications/skinnerhouse/. Estab. 1976. Specializes in nonfiction, educational material, multicultural material. **Manuscript Acquisitions:** Betsy Martin, Editorial Assistant. **Art Acquisitions:** Suzanne Morgan, Design Director. Publishes 1 picture books/ year; 1 young readers/year; 1 middle readers/year. 50% of books by first-time authors. "We publish books for Unitarian Universalists. Most of our children's' titles are intended for religious education or worship use. They reflect Unitarian Universalist values."

Fiction All levels: anthology, multicultural, nature/environment, religion. Recently published *A Child's Book of Blessings and Prayers*, by Eliza Blanchard (ages 4-8, picture book); *Meet Jesus: The Life and Lessons of a Beloved Teacher*, by Lynn Gunney (age's 5-8, picture book); *Magic Wanda's Travel Emporium*, by Joshua Searle-White (ages 9 and up, stories).

Nonfiction All levels: activity books, multicultural, music/dance, nature/environment, religion. *Unitarian Universalism Is a Really long Name*, by Jennifer Dant (picture book, resource that answers children's' questions about Unit. Univ. ages 5-9)

How to Contact Fiction/nonfiction: query or submit outline/synopsis and 2 sample chapters. Responds to queries in 3 weeks; Publishes a book 1 year after acceptance. Will consider but prefer e-mail submissions, simultaneous submissions, and sometimes previously published work.

Illustration Works with 2 illustrators/year. Uses both color and b&w. Reviews ms/illustration packages from artists. Query. Contact: Suzanne Morgan, Design Director. Illustrations only: query with samples. Contact: Suzanne Morgan, Design Director. Responds only if interested. Samples returned with SASE.

Photography Buys stock images and assign work. Contact: Suzanne Morgan, Design Director. Uses inspirational types of photo's. Model/property releases required; captions required. Uses color b&w. Submit cover letter, resume.

Terms Pays authors royalty 8% based on retail price. Pays illustrators/photographers by the project. Sends galleys to authors; dummies to illustrators. Book catalog available for SASE.

Tips "Consult our website."

Ⓐ SLEEPING BEAR PRESS

Imprint of Gale Group, 315 East Eisenhower Parkway, Suite 200 Ann Arbor, MI 48108. Website: www.sleepingbearpress.com. Not accepting manuscripts at this time. Publishes 30 picture books/ year. 10% of books by first-time authors.

Fiction Picture books: adventure, animal, concept, folktales, history, multicultural, nature/environment, religion, sports. Young readers: adventure, animal, concept, folktales, history, humor, multicultural, nature/environment, religion, sports. Average word length: picture books—1,800. Recently published *Brewster the Rooster*, by Devin Scillian; *The Orange Shoes*, by Trinka Hakes Noble; *Yatandou*, by Gloria Whelan.

Nonfiction Average word length: picture books-1,800. Recently published *D is for Drinking Gourd: An African American Alphabet*, by E.B. Lewis.

How to Contact Fiction/nonfiction: Submit complete ms or proposal. "We do not return materials, so please only submit copies. SBP will contact you if interested." Publishes book 2 years after acceptance. Will consider simultaneous submissions.

Illustration Works with 30 illustrators/year. Uses color artwork only. Reviews ms/illustration packages from artists. Send ms with dummy. Illustrations only: "Send samples for our files. We will contact you if interested."

Terms Pays authors royalty. Offers advances. Pays illustrators royalty. Sends galleys to authors. Originals returned to artist at job's completion. Book catalog available. All imprints included in a single catalog. Catalog available on website.

Tips "Please review our book on line before sending material or calling." Editorial staff attended or plans to attend the following conferences: BEA, IRA, Regional shows, UMBE, NEBA, AASL, ALA, and numerous local conferences.

SMALLFELLOW PRESS

Imprint of Tallfellow Press, 9454 Wilshire BLVD.Suite 550, Beverly Hills, CA 90212. E-mail: tallfellow@pacbell.net. Website: www.smallfellow.com. **Manuscript/Art Acquisitions:** Claudia Sloan.

• Smallfellow no longer accepts manuscript/art submissions.

ℕ ▢ SOUNDPRINTS/STUDIO MOUSE

Trudy Corporations, 353 Main St., Norwalk CT 06851. (800)228-7839. Fax: (203)864-1776. E-mail: info@soundprints.com;. Publishes mass market books, educational material, multicultural material. **Manuscript Acquisitions**: Anthony Parisi, editorial assistant. **Art Acquisitions:** Katie Sears, designer. 10% of books by first-time authors.

Fiction Picture books, young readers: adventure, animal, fantasy, history, multicultural, nature/environment, sports. Recently published *Smithsonian Alphabet of Earth*, by Barbie Heit Schwaeber, and illustrated by Sally Vitsky (ages preschool-2, hardcover and paperback available with audio CD); *Little Black Ant on Park Street*, by Janet Halfmann and illustrated by Kathleen Rietz (ages preschool-grade 3, hardcover, paperback, micro book available with plush toy and cd); *Oh Where, Oh Where Has My Little Dog Gone?*, edited by Laura Gates Galvin and illustrated by Erica Pelton Villnave (ages 3 and up, die-cut handle paperback book with cd).

How to Contact Query of submit complete manuscript. Responds to queries/mss in 6 months. Publishes a book 1-2 years after acceptance. Illustration: Works with 3-7 illustrators/year. Uses color artwork only. Send tearsheets with contact information, "especially web address if applicable." Samples not returned; samples filed.

Photography Buys stock and assign work. Model/property release and captions required. Send color promo sheet.

Terms Original artwork returned at jobs completion. Catalog available on website. Offers writer's/artist's/photographer's guidelines with SASE.

SPINNER BOOKS

Imprint of University Games, 2030 Harrison St., San Francisco CA 94107. (415)503-1600. Fax: (415)503-0085. E-mail: info@ugames.com. Website: www.ugames.com. Estab. 1985. Specializes in nonfiction. **Contact:** Editorial Department. Publishes 6 young readers/ year; 6 middle readers/ year. " Spinners Books publishes books of puzzles, games and trivia."

Nonfiction Picture books: games & puzzles. Recently published *20 Questions*, by Bob Moog (adult); *20 Questions for Kids*, by Bob Moog (young adult).

How to Contact Only interested in agented material. Nonfiction: Query. Responds to queries in 3 months; mss in 2 months. Publishes a book 6 months after acceptance. Will consider e-mail submissions.

Illustration Only interested in agented material. Uses both color and b&w. Illustrations only: Query with samples. Responds in 3 months only if interested. Samples not returned.

Terms Sends galleys to authors; dummies to illustrators. Originals returned to artist at job's completion. Book catalog available on website: www.ugames.com

STANDARD PUBLISHING

8805 Governor's Hill Drive, Suite 400, Cincinnati, OH 45249. (513)931-4050. E-mail: ministrytochildren@standardpub.com. Web site: www.standardpub.com. Editorial Director: Family Resources; Ruth Frederick, Children 's Product. Estab. 1866. Publishes children's ministry resources and children's books for the religious market.

STARSEED PRESS

Imprint of HJ Kramer in joint venture with New World Library, P.O. Box 1082, Tiburon CA 94920. (415)435-5367. Fax: (415)435-5364. Website: www.newworldlibrary.com. **Manuscript Acquisitions:** Jan Phillips. **Art Acquisitions:** Linda Kramer, vice president. Publishes 2 picture books/year. 50% of books by first-time authors. "We publish 4-color, 32-page children's picture books dealing with self-esteem and positive values, with a non-denominational, spiritual emphasis."

Fiction Picture books: self-esteem, multicultural, nature/environment. Average word length: picture books—500-1,500. Recently published *Lucky Goose Goes to Texas*, by Holly Bea, illustrated by Joe Boddy (ages 3-10, picture book).

Nonfiction Picture books: multicultural, nature/environment.

How to Contact Fiction/nonfiction: Submit outline/synopsis. Responds to queries/mss in 10 weeks. Publishes a book 18 months after acceptance. Will consider simultaneous submissions, previously published work.

Illustration Works with 2 illustrators/year. Uses color artwork only. Illustrations only: Query with samples. Responds only if interested. Samples returned with SASE; samples filed.

Terms Negotiates based on publisher's net receipts. Split between author and artist. Originals returned to artist at job's completion. Book catalog available for 9 × 11 SAE with $1.98 postage; ms and art guidelines available for SASE. All imprints included in a single catalog.

STERLING PUBLISHING CO.INC.

387 Park Ave. S.10th Floor, New York NY 10016-8810. (212)532-7160. Fax: (212)981-0508. Publishes 10 picture books/year; 50 young readers/year; 50 middle readers/year; 10 young adult titles/year. 15% of books by first-time authors. **Contact:** Children's Book Editor; Children's Art Director: Merideth Harte.

Fiction Picture books.

Nonfiction Young readers: activity books, arts/crafts, cooking, hobbies, how-to, science. Middle readers, young adults: activity books, arts/crafts, hobbies, how-to, science, mazes, optical illusions, games, magic, math, puzzles.

How to Contact Nonfiction: Submit outline/synopsis, 1 sample chapter and SASE. Responds to queries/mss in 6 weeks. Publishes book 1 year after acceptance. Will consider simultaneous submissions, previously published work.

Illustration Works with 50 illustrators/year. Reviews ms/illustration packages from artists. Illustrations only: Send promo sheet. Contact: Karen Nelson, creative director. Responds in 6 weeks. Samples returned with SASE; samples filed.

Photography Buys stock and assigns work. Contact: Karen Nelson.

Terms Pays authors royalty or work purchased outright from authors. Offers advances (average amount: $2,000). Pays illustrators by the project. Pays photographers by the project or per photo. Sends galleys to authors; dummies to illustrators. Originals returned to artist at job's completion. Offers writer's guidelines for SASE. Catalog available on website.

ⓝ STONE ARCH BOOKS

7825 Telegraph Rd., Minneapolis MN 55438. (952)224-0514. Fax: (952)933-2410. Website: www. stonearchbooks.com. **Acquisitions Editor:** Michael Dahl. **Art Director:** Heather Kindseth. Specializes in " safe graphic novels and high-interest fiction for striving readers, especially boys."

Fiction Young readers, middle readers, young adults: adventure, contemporary, fantasy, humor, light humor, mystery, science fiction, sports, suspense. Average word length: young readers-1,000-3,000; middle readers and early young adults: 5,000-10,000.

How to Contact Submit outline/synopsis and 3 sample chapters. Electronic submissions are preferred and should be sent to www.author.sub@stonearchbooks.com. Accepts simultaneous submissions. Only submissions with an e-mail addresses will receive a reply.

Illustration Works with 35 illustrators/year. Used both color and b&w.

Terms Work purchased outright from authors. Illustrators paid by the project. Title list and catalog available on website.

Tips "A high-interest topic or activity is one that a young person would spend their free time on without adult direction or suggestion."

SYLVAN DELL PUBLISHING

976 Houston Northcutt Blvd., Suite 3, Mount Pleasant SC 29464 .Estab. 2004. E-mail: donnagerman@ sylvandellpublishing.com. Website: www.sylvandellpublishing.com. **Contact**: Donna German."The books that we publish are usually, but not always, fictional stories that relate to animals, nature, the environment, and science. All books should subtly convey an educational theme through a warm story that is fun to read and that will grab a children's attention. Each book has a 3-5 page "For Creative Minds" section in the back to reinforce the educational component of the book itself. This section will have a craft and/or game as well as "fun facts" to be shared by the parent, teacher, or other adult. Authors do not need to supply this information but may be actively involved in its development if they would like. Please read about our submission guidelines on our website."

• Sylvan Dell only accepts electronic submissions.

Fiction Picture Books: animal, folktales, nature/environment, math-related. Word length—picture books: no more than 1500. Recently published *Whistling Wings,* by first-time author Laura Goering, illustrated by Laura Jacques; *Sort it Out!,* by Barbara Mariconda, illustrated by Sherry Rogers; *River Beds: Sleeping in the World's Rivers,* by Gail Langer Karwoski, illustrated by Connie McLennan; *Saturn for my Birthday,* by first-time author John McGranaghan, illustrated by Wendy Edelson.

How to Contact Submit complete ms. Prefers to work with authors from the US and Canada because of marketing. Responds to mss in 3-4 months. Publishes a book about 2 years after acceptance. Accepts simultaneous submissions. Accepts electronic submissions only. Snail mail submissions are discarded without being opened.

Illustration Works with 10 illustrators/year. Prefers to work with illustrators from the US and Canada. Uses color artwork only. Submit Web link or 2-3 electronic images. Contact: Donna German. "I generally keep submissions on file until I match the manuscripts to illustration needs."

Terms Pays authors and illustrators step-up, advance royalty. "Authors and illustrators see PDFs of book as it goes to the printer. Any concerns or changes are dealt with then. We keep cover art and return all other art to illustrators." Catalog available on website. Writer's and artist's guidelines available on website.

Tips "Please make sure that you have looked at our website to read our complete submission guidelines and to see if we are looking for a particular subject. Manuscripts must meet all four of our stated criteria. We look for fairly realistic, bright and colorful art-no cartoons."

SYNERGEBOOKS

205 S. Dixie Dr., P.O. Box 185, Haines City, FL 33844]., P.O. Box 185, Haines City FL 33844. (863)956-3010. E-mail: synergebooks@aol.com. **Contact:** Debra Staples, publisher/acquisitions editor. Publishes trade paperback and electronic originals 250 queries received/year. 250 mss received/year.

Fiction SynergEbooks published at least 40 new titles a year, and only 1-5 of those are put into print in any given year. "SynergEbooks is first and foremost a digital publisher, so most of our marketing budget goes to those formats. Authors are required to direct-sell a minimum of 100 digital copies of a title before it's accepted for print." Submit proposal package, including synopsis, 1-3 sample chapters, and marketing plans.

Nonfiction Submit proposal package, 1-3 sample chapters.

Tips "At SynergEbooks, we work with the author to promote their work."

N TANGLEWOOD BOOKS

P.O. Box 3009, Terre Haute IN 47803. **Acquisitions Editor:** Erica Bennet. **Illustrators contact:** Peggy Tierney, publisher. Produces 2-3 picture books/year, 1-2 middle readers/year, 1-2 young adult titles/year. 20% of books by first-time authors. "Tanglewood Press strives to publish entertaining, kid-centric books."

Fiction Picture books: adventure, animal, concept, contemporary, fantasy, humor. Average word length: picture books-800. Recently published *68 Knots*, by Micheal Robert Evans (young adult); *The Mice of Bistrot des Sept Freres*, written and illustrated by Marie Letourneau; Chester Raccoon and the Acorn Full of Memories, by Audrey Penn and Barbara Gibson.

How to Contact Accepts international submissions. Fiction: Query with 3-5 sample chapters. Responds to mss in up to 18 months. Publishes book 2 years after acceptance. Considers simultaneous submissions.

Illustration Accepts material from international illustrators. Works with 3-4 illustrators/year. Uses both color and b&w. Reviews ms/illustration packages. For ms/illustration packages: Send ms with sample illustrations. Submit ms/illustration packages to Peggy Tierney, publisher. If interested in illustrating future titles, query with samples. Submit samples to Peggy Tierney, publisher. Samples returned with SASE. Samples filed.

Terms Illustrators paid by the project for covers and small illustrations; royalty of 3-5% for picture books. Author sees galleys for review. Illustrators see dummies for review. Originals returned to artist at job's completion.

Tips "Please see lengthy 'Submissions' page on our website."

THIRD WORLD PRESS

P.O. Box 19730, Chicago IL 60619. (773)651-0700. Fax: (773)651-7286. E-mail: twpress3@aol.com. **Contact:** Bennett J. Johnson. Publishes hardcover and trade paperback originals and reprints 200-300 queries received/year. 200 mss received/year.

Fiction "We primarily publish nonfiction, but will consider fiction by and about Blacks." Query with SASE. Submit outline, clips, 5 sample chapters.

Nonfiction Query with SASE. Submit outline, 5 sample chapters.

THISTLEDOWN PRESS LTD.

633 Main St., Saskatoon SK S7H 0J8 Canada. (306)244-1722. Fax: (306)244-1762. E-mail: tdpress@ thistledown.sk.com. Website: www.thistledown.com. **Acquisitions:** Allan Forrie, publisher. Publishes numerous middle reader and young adult titles/year. "Thistledown originates books by

Canadian authors only, although we have co-published titles by authors outside Canada. We do not publish children's picture books."

 • Thistledown publishes books by Canadian authors only.

Fiction Middle readers, young adults: adventure, anthology, contemporary, fantasy, humor, poetry, romance, science fiction, suspense/mystery, short stories. Average word length: young adults-40,000. Recently published *Up All Night*, edited by R.P. MacIntyre (young adult, anthology); *Offside*, by Cathy Beveridge (young adult, novel); *Cheeseburger Subversive*, by Richard Scarsbrook; *The Alchemist's Daughter*, by Eileen Kernaghan.

How to Contact Submit outline/synopsis and sample chapters. **"We don not accept unsolicited full-length manuscripts. These will be returned."** Responds to queries in 4 months. Publishes a book about 1 year after acceptance. No simultaneous submissions. No e-mailed submissions.

Illustration Prefers agented illustrators but "not mandatory." Works with few illustrators. Illustrations only: Query with samples, promo sheet, slides, tearsheets. Responds only if interested. Samples returned with SASE; samples filed.

Terms Pays authors royalty of 10-12% based on net dollar sales. Pays illustrators and photographers by the project (range: $250-750). Sends galleys to authors. Original artwork returned at job's completion. Book catalog free on request. Manuscript guidelines for #10 envelope and IRC.

Tips "Send cover letter including publishing history and SASE."

N ◪ TIGHTROPE BOOKS

602 Markham St., Toronto ON M6G 2L8, Canada. (647) 348-4460. **Contact:** Shirarose Wilensky, editor (fiction, poetry, nonfiction). Publishes hardcover and trade paperback originals.

Fiction Query with SASE. Submit proposal package, including: synopsis, 1 sample chapter and completed ms.

Nonfiction Query with SASE. Submit proposal package, including outline, 1 sample chapter and complete ms.

Tips "Audience is young, urban, literary, educated, unconventional."

TILBURY HOUSE, PUBLISHERS

103 Brunswick Ave., Gardiner ME 04345. (207)582-1899. Fax: (207)582-8227. E-mail: karen@tilburyhouse.com. Website: www.tilburyhouse.com. **Publisher:** Jennifer Bunting. **Children's Book Editor:** Audrey Maynard. **Children's Book Editor:** Karen Fisk. Publishes 2-4 picture book/year.

Fiction Picture books, young readers, middle readers: multicultural, nature/environment. Special needs include books that teach children about tolerance and honoring diversity. Recently published *Remember Me: Tomah Joseph's Gift to Franklin Roosevelt*, by Donald Soctomah and Jean Flahive; *Bear-ly There*, by Rebekah Raye; *Remember Me*, Jean Reagan.

Nonfiction Picture books, young readers, middle readers: multicultural, nature/environment. Recently published *Just for Elephants,* by Carol Buckley; *Life Under Ice*, by Mary Cerullo, with photography by Bill Curtsinger.

How to Contact Fiction/nonfiction: Submit complete ms or outline/synopsis. Responds to queries/mss in 1 month. Publishes a book 1-2 years after acceptance. Will consider simultaneous submissions "with notification."

Illustration Works with 2-3 illustrators/year. Illustrations only: Query with samples. Responds in 1 month. Samples returned with SASE. Original artwork returned at job's completion.

Photography Buys photos from freelancers. Works on assignment only.

Terms Pays authors royalty based on wholesale price. Pays illustrators/photographers by the project; royalty based on wholesale price. Sends galleys to authors. Book catalog available for SAE and postage.

Tips "We are always interested in stories that will encourage children to understand the natural world and the environment, as well as stories with social justice themes. We really like stories that engage children to become problem solvers as well as those that promote respect, tolerance and compassion." We do not publish books with personified animal characters; historical fiction; chapter books; fantasy."

TORAH AURA PRODUCTIONS

4423 Fruitland Ave., Los Angeles CA 90058. (800)238-6724. Fax: (323)585-0327. E-mail: misrad@ torahaura.com. **Contact:** Jane Golub. Torah Aura publishes educational materials for Jewish classrooms only. Publishes hardcover and trade paperback originals 5 queries received/year. 10 mss received/year.

Fiction All fiction must have Jewish interest. No picture books. Query with SASE. Reviews artwork/ photos as part

Nonfiction No picture books. Query with SASE.

🅽 TOR BOOKS

175 Fifth Ave., New York NY 10010-7703. **Contact:** Juliet Pederson, Publishing Coordinator.

Fiction Average word length: middle readers-30,000; young adults-60,000-100,000. We do not accept queries.

Nonfiction Middle readers and young adult: geography, history, how-to, multicultural, nature/ environment, science, social issues. Does not want to see religion, cooking. Average word length: middle readers-25,000-35,000; young adults-70,000. Published *Strange Unsolved Mysteries*, by Phyllis Rabin Emert; *Stargazer's Guide (to the Galaxy)*, by Q.L. Pearce (ages 8-12, guide to constellations, illustrated).

Tips "Know the house you are submitting to, familiarize yourself with the types of books they are publishing. Get an agent. Allow him/her to direct you to publishers who are most appropriate. It saves time and effort."

🔳 TRADEWIND BOOKS

202-1807 Maritime Mews, Vancouver BC V6H 3W7, Canada. **Manuscript Acquisitions**: Michael Katz, publisher. **Art Acquisitions:** Carol Frank, art director. Senior Editor: R. David Stephens. Publishes 2-3 picture books; 3 young adult titles/year; 1 book of poetry; 1 chapter book. 15% of books by first-time authors.

Fiction Picture books: adventure, multicultural, folktales. Average word length: 900 words. Recently published City Kids, by X.J. Kennedy and illustrated by Phillpe Beha; *Roxy,* by PJ Reece; *Viva Zapata!,* by Emilie Smith and illustrated by Stefan Czernecki.

How to Contact Picture books: submit complete ms. YA novels by Canadian authors only. Chapter books by US authors considered. Will consider simultaneous submissions. Do not send query letter. Responds to mss in 12 weeks. Unsolicited submissions accepted only if authors have read a selection of books published by Tradewind Books. Submissions must include a reference to these books.

Illustration Works with 3-4 illustrators/year. Reviews ms/illustration packages from artists. Send illustrated ms as dummy. Illustrations only: Query with samples. Responds only if interested. Samples returned with SASE; samples filed.

Terms Royalties negotiable. Offers advances against royalties. Originals returned to artist at job's completion. Catalog available on website.

TRICYCLE PRESS

P.O. Box 7123, Berkeley CA 94707. **Acquisitions:** Nicole Geiger, publisher. Publishes 14-18 picture books/year; 2-4 middle readers/year; 3 board books/year. 25% of books by first-time authors. Press looks for something outside the mainstream; books that encourage children to look at the world from a different angle. "We publish high-quality trade books."

Fiction Board books, picture books, young readers: concept. Middle grade: literary fiction, high-quality contemporary, fantasy, history, multicultural, nature, poetry, suspense/mystery; no mass market fiction. Average word length: picture books: 500-1,000. Recently published *Ned's New Home*, written and illustrated, by Kevin Tseng (ages 2-4, picture book); *Yankee at the Seder*, by Elka Weber, illustrated by Adam Gustavson (ages 7-10, picture book); *I am Jack*, by Susanne Gervay, illustrated by Cathy Wilcox (ages 8-11, novel); *The Tilting House*, by Tom Llewellyn (ages 8-11, novel).

Nonfiction Picture books, middle readers: animal, arts/crafts, biography, careers, concept, cooking, history, how-to, multicultural, music/dance, nature/environment, science. Recently published *Where Else in the Wild*, by David M. Schwartz and Yael Schy, Photographs by Dwight Kuhn (ages 4-8, photographic picture book); *Sky High, The True Story of Maggie Gee*, by Marrissa Moss, illustrated by Carl Angel (ages 6-8, picture book); *The Firehouse Light*, by Janet Nolan, illustrated by Marie Lafrance (ages 5-9, picture book).

How to Contact All submissions must come wit an SASE. No Queries will be responded to. Submit complete ms for picture books. Submit outline/synopsis and 2-3 sample chapters for middle grade, young adult and longer nonfiction. Responds to mss in 4-6 months. Publishes a book 1-2 years after acceptance. Welcomes simultaneous submissions. Do not send original artwork; copies only, please. No electronic or faxed submissions.

Illustration Works with 30 illustrators/year. Uses primarily color. Reviews ms/illustration dummies from artists. Submit ms with dummy and/or 2-3 copies of final art. Illustrations only: Query with samples, promo sheet, tearsheets, low res e-mail. Responds only if interested. Samples returned with SASE. Original artwork returned at job's completion unless work for hire.

Photography Works on assignment only. Uses high resolution electronic files. Submit samples.

Terms Pays authors royalty of 7.5% based on net receipts. Offers advances. Pays illustrators and photographers royalty of 7.5% based on net receipts. Sends galleys of novels to authors. Book catalog for 9 × 12 SASE (3 first-class stamps). Manuscript guidelines for SASE (5 first-class stamp). Manuscripts guidelines available at website.

Tips "We are looking for something a bit outside the mainstream and with lasting appeal (no one-shot-wonders)."

TWO LIVES PUBLISHING

191 Water St.Ambler PA 19002. (609)502-8147. Fax: (610)717-1460. E-mail: bcombs@twolives.com. Website: www.twolives.com. **Manuscript Acquisitions:** Bobbie Combs. Publishes 1 picture book/year; 1 middle reader/year. 100% of books by first-time authors. "We create books for children whose parents are lesbian, gay, bisexual or transgender. WE ONLY want stories featuring children and their gay or lesbian parents."

Fiction Picture books, young readers, middle readers: contemporary.

How to Contact Fiction: Query. Responds to queries/mss in 3 months. Publishes book 2-3 years after acceptance. Will consider e-mail submissions, simultaneous submissions, previously published work.

Illustration Works with 2 illustrators/year. Uses color artwork only. Query ms/illustration packages. Contact: Bobbie Combs, publisher. Illustrations only: Send postcard sample with brochure, photocopies. Contact: Bobbie Combs, publisher. Responds only if interested. Samples filed.

Terms Pays authors royalty of 5-10% based on retail price. Offers advances (average amount: $250). Pays illustrators royalty of 5-10% based on retail price. Sends galleys to authors. Originals returned to artist at job's completion. Catalog available on website.

Ⓐ TYNDALE HOUSE PUBLISHERS, INC.

351 Executive Dr.P.O. Box 80, Wheaton IL 60189. (630)668-8300. Website: www.tyndale.com. **Manuscript Acquisitions:** Katara Washington Patton. **Art Acquisitions:** Talinda Iverson. Publishes approximately 15 Christian children's titles/year.

• Tyndale House no longer reviews unsolicited mss, only agented material.

Fiction Juvenile.

Nonfiction Bible, devotionals, Bible storybooks.

Illustration Uses full-color for book covers, b&w or color spot illustrations for some nonfiction. Illustrations only: Query with photocopies (color or b&w) of samples, résumé.

Photography Buys photos from freelancers. Works on assignment only.

Terms Pay rates for authors and illustrators vary.

Tips "All accepted manuscripts will appeal to Evangelical Christian children and parents."

UNLIMITED PUBLISHING LLC

P.O. Box 3007, Bloomington IN 47402. **Contact:** Acquisitions Manager (short nonfiction with a clear audience). "We prefer short nonfiction and fiction with a clear audience, and expect authors to be actively involved in publicity. A detailed marketing plan is required with all submissions. Moderate to good computer skills are necessary." Receives 1,000 queries/year; 500 manuscripts/year.

Fiction Submit proposal package, including: outline and 10-page excerpt in rich text format, author bio and detailed marketing plan.

Nonfiction Submit proposal package, including: outline and 10-page excerpt in rich text format, a standard 'save-as option with Microsoft Word', author bio and detailed marketing plan.

Tips "The growth of online bookselling allows authors and publishers to jointly cultivate a tightly targeted grassroots audience in specialty or niche markets before expanding to mainstream book industry channels based on proven public demand."

Ⓝ VIEWPOINT PRESS

PMB 400 785 Tucker Road #G Tehachapi, CA. 93561. Phone: (661)821-5110. Fax: (661)821-7515. E-mail: joie99@aol.com. We are not accepting manuscripts at this time. **Contact:** Dr. B.J. Mitchell. We have been in business for 25 years and have two children's books: *The Secret of Hilhouse* and *The Huckenpuck Papers*. Our website is viewpointpress.com.

VIKING CHILDREN'S BOOKS

Penguin Group Inc., 345 Hudson St., New York NY 10014-3657. (212)414-3600. Fax: (212)414-3399. Website: www.penguin.com. **Acquisitions:** Catherine Frank, executive editor (picture books, middle grade and young adult fiction, and nonfiction); Tracy Gates, associate editorial director (picture books, middle grade, and young adult fiction); Joy Peskin, executive editor (middle grade and young adult fiction); Kendra Levin, associate editor (picture books, middle grade and young adult fiction); Leila Sales, editorial assistant. **Art Acquisitions:** Denise Cronin, Viking Children's Books. Publishes hardcover originals. Publishes 55 books/year. Receives 7,500 queries/year. 25% of books from first-time authors; 33% from unagented writers. "Viking Children's Books is known for humorous, quirky picture books, in addition to more traditional fiction. We publish the highest quality fiction, nonfiction, and picture books for pre-schoolers through young adults." Publishes book 1-2 years after acceptance of artwork. Hesitantly accepts simultaneous submissions.

• Viking Children's Books is not accepting unsolicited submissions at this time.

Fiction All levels: adventure, animal, contemporary, fantasy, history, humor, multicultural, nature/environment, poetry, problem novels, romance, science fiction, sports, suspense/mystery. Recently published *Llama Llama Misses Mama*, by Anna Dewdney (ages 2 up, picture book); *Wintergirls*, by Laurie Halse Anderson (ages 12 and up); *Good Luck Bear*, by Greg Foley (ages 2 up); *Along for the Ride*, by Sarah Dessen (ages 12 up). **Nonfiction** All levels: biography, concept, history, multicultural, music/dance, nature/environment, science, and sports. Recently published *Harper Lee*, by Kerry Madden (ages 11 up, biography); *Knucklehead*, by Jon Scieszka (ages 7up, autobiography); *Marching for Freedom* by Elizabeth Partridge (ages 11 up, nonfiction).

Illustration Works with 30 illustrators/year. Responds to artist's queries/submissions only if interested. Samples returned with SASE only or samples filed. Originals returned at job's completion.

Terms Pays 2-10% royalty on retail price or flat fee. Advance negotiable.

WALKER & COMPANY

Books for Young Readers, 175 Fifth Ave., New York NY 10010. Website: www.bloomsburykids. com and www.bloomsburyteens.com. **Manuscript Acquisitions:** Emily Easton, publisher; Stacy Cantor, editor Mary Kate Castellani, associate editor. Publishes 10-15 picture books/year; 5-10 nonfiction books/year; 5-10 middle readers/year; 10-20 young adult titles/year. 5% of books by first-time authors; 75% of books from agented writers. Website:www.bloomsburykids.com and www.bloomsburyteens.com

Fiction Picture books: adventure, history, humor. Middle readers: coming-of-age, adventure, contemporary, history, humor, multicultural. Young adults: adventure, contemporary, romance, humor, historical fiction, suspense/mystery. Recently published *Even Monsters Need Haircuts*, by Matthew McElligott (ages 6-10, picture book); *The Summer of Moonlight Secrets*, by Danette Haworth (8-12, middle grade novel); *Rules of Attraction*, by Simone Elkeles (ages 14 and up).

Nonfiction Picture book, middle readers: biography, history. Recently published *Poop Happened: A History of the World from the Bottom Up*, by Sarah Albee, illustrated by Robert Leighton, (ages 8-12, middle grade nonfiction); *I, Matthew Henson*, by Carole Boston Weahterford, illustrated by Eric Velasquez (ages 7-12, picture book history); *101 Things to Do Before You're Old and Boring* , by Richard Horne (ages 12 and up). Multicultural needs include "contemporary, literary fiction and historical fiction written in an authentic voice. Also high interest nonfiction with trade appeal."

How to Contact Fiction/nonfiction: Submit outline/synopsis and sample chapters; complete ms for picture books. Send SASE for writer's guidelines.

Illustration Works with 20-25 illustrators/year. Editorial department reviews ms/illustration packages from artists. Query or submit ms with 4-8 samples. Illustrations only: Tearsheets. "Please do not send original artwork." Responds to art samples only if interested.

Terms Pays authors royalty of 5-10%; pays illustrators royalty or flat fee. Offers advance payment against royalties. Original artwork returned at job's completion. Sends galleys to authors. Ms guidelines for SASE.

Tips Writers: "Make sure you study our catalog before submitting. We are a small house with a tightly focused list. Illustrators: Have a well-rounded portfolio with different styles." Does not want to see folktales, ABC books, paperback series. "Walker and Company is committed to introducing talented new authors and illustrators to the children's book field."

WEIGL PUBLISHERS INC.

350 5th Ave., 59th floor, New York NY 10118-0069. (866)649-3445. Fax: (866)449-3445. E-mail: linda@weigl.com. Website: www.weigl.com. **Manuscript/Art Acquisitions:** Heather Hudak.

Publishes 25 young readers/year; 40 middle readers/year; 20 young adult titles/year. 15% of books by first-time authors. "Our mission is to provide innovative high-quality learning resources for schools and libraries worldwide at a competitive price."

Nonfiction Young readers: animal, biography, geography, history, multicultural, nature/environment, science. Middle readers: animal, biography, geography, history, multicultural, nature/environment, science, social issues, sports. Young adults: biography, careers, geography, history, multicultural, nature/environment, social issues. Average word length: young readers—100 words/page; middle readers—200 words/page; young adults—300 words/page. Recently published *Amazing Animals* (ages 9 and up, science series); *U.S. Sites and Symbols* (ages 8 and up, social studies series); *Science Q&A* (ages 9 and up, social studies series).

How to Contact Nonfiction: Query, by e-mail only. Publishes book 6-9 months after acceptance. Will consider e-mail submissions, simultaneous submissions.

Terms Work purchased outright from authors. Pays illustrators by the project. Pays photographers per photo. Originals returned to artist at job's completion. Book catalog available for 9½ × 11 SASE. Catalog available on website.

WHITECAP BOOKS

351 Lynn Ave., North Vancouver BC V7J 2C4 Canada. (604)980-9852. Fax: (604)980-8197. E-mail: whitecap@whitecap.ca. Website: www.whitecap.ca. **Manuscript Acquisitions:** Rights and Acquisitions. **Illustration Acquisitions:** Michelle Mayne, art director. Publishes 0-1 young readers/year; 0-1 middle readers/year; 3-4 young adult/year.

Fiction Whitecap Books is currently de-emphasizing the children's and YA adventure in series only. Recently published *Wild Horse Cree #2; Coyote Canyon*, by Sharon Siamon.

Nonfiction Young Children's and middle reader's non-fiction focusing mainly on nature, wildlife and animals. Recently published *Canadian Girls Who Rocked The World; Revised and Expanded Edition*, by Tanya Lloyd Kyi.

How to Contact Query to Rights and Acquisitions. Accepts unagented work and multiple submissions. Responds to queries/ms in 6 months. Publishes a book approximately 1 year after acceptance. Include SASE with sufficient return postage. Mark envelopes "submissions." Please send international postal vouchers with SASE if submission is form U.S.A. No e-mail submissions.

Illustration Works with 1-2 illustrators/year. Uses color artwork only. Reviews ms/illustration packages from artists. Query. Contact: Rights and Acquisitions. Illustrations only: Send postcard sample with tearsheets. Contact: Michelle Mayne, art director. Responds only if interested.

Photography Buys stock and assigns work. Model/property releases required; captions required. Only accepts digital photography. Submit stock photo list.

Terms Pays authors a negotiated royalty or purchases work outright. Offers advances. Pays illustrators and photographers negotiated amount. Originals returned to artist at job's completion. Manuscript guidelines available on website.

Tips "Check submission guidelines on our website before submitting. Don't send U.S. postage SASE to Canada. It can't be used in Canada and no reply will be sent."

WHITE MANE KIDS

Imprint of White Mane Publishing, P.O. Box 708, Shippensburg PA 17257. (717)532-2237. Fax: (717)532-6110. Website: www.whitemane.com. **Manuscript Acquisitions:** Send attention acquisitions dept.

Fiction Middle readers, young adults/teens: history. Recently published *Drumbeat: The Story of a Civil War Drummer Boy*, by Rober J. Trout; *The Witness Tree and the Shadow of the Noose: Mystery, Lies, and Spies in Manassas*, by K.E.M. Johnston

Nonfiction Middle readers, young adults: history. Recently published *Hey, History Isn't Boring Anymore! A Creative Approach to Teaching the Civil War*, by Kelly Ann Butterbaugh.

How to Contact Fiction/nonfiction: Query. Responds to queries in 1 month; mss in 3-4 months. Publishes book 12-18 months after acceptance. Will consider simultaneous submissions.

Illustration Works with 2-3 illustrators/year. Uses color artwork only. Artwork for book covers only. Reviews ms/illustration packages from artists. Query. Illustrations only: Query with samples. Responds only if interested. Samples not returned; samples filed.

Terms Pays authors royalties. Pays illustrators by the project. Sends galleys to authors. Originals returned to artist at job's completion. Book catalog available; ms guidelines available for SASE. All imprints included in a single catalog.

Tips "We are interested in historically accurate fiction for middle and young adult readers. We do *not* publish picture books. Our primary focus is the American Civil War and some America Revolution topics."

ALBERT WHITMAN & COMPANY

6340 Oakton St, Morton Grove, IL 60053-2723. (847)581-0033. Fax: (847)581-0039. Website: www. albertwhitman.com. **Manuscript Acquisitions:** Kathleen Tucker, editor-in-chief. Art Acquisitions: Carol Gildar. Publishes 30 books/year. 20% of books by first-time authors; 15% off books from agented authors.

Fiction Picture books, young readers, middle readers: adventure, concept (to help children deal with problems), fantasy, history, humor, multicultural, suspense. Middle readers: problem novels, suspense/mystery. "We are interested in contemporary multicultural stories-stories with holiday themes and exciting distinctive novels. We publish a wide variety of topics and are interested in stories that help children deal with their problems and concerns. Does not want to see, "religion-oriented, ABCs, pop-up, romance, counting." Recently published fiction: *Three Little Gators*, by Hellen Ketteman, illustrated by Will Terry; *Peace Week in Miss Fox's Class*, by Eileen Spinelli, Anne Kennedy (Illustrator); *The Bully-Blockers Club*, by Teresa Bateman, illustrated by Jackie Urbanovic; *The Truth about Truman School*, by Dori Hillestad Butler.

Nonfiction Picture books, young readers, middle readers: animal, arts/crafts, health, history, hobbies, multicultural, music/dance, nature/environment, science, sports, special needs. Does not want to see, "religion, any books that have to be written in, or fictionalized biographies."Recently published *Abe Lincoln Loved Animals*, by Ellen Jackson, illustrated by Doris Ettllinger; *An Apple for Harriet Tubman*, by Glennette Tilly Turner.

How to Contact Fiction/nonfiction: Submit query, outline, and sample chapter. For picture books send entire ms. Include cover letter. Responds to submissions in 4 months. Publishes a book 18 months after acceptance. Will consider simultaneous submissions "if notified."

Illustration "We are not accepting Illustration samples at this time. Submissions will not be returned."

Photography Publishes books illustrated with photos, but not stock photos-desires photos all taken for project. "Our books are for children and cover many topics; photos must be taken to match text. Books often show a child in a particular situation (e.g. kids being home-schooled, a sister whose brother is born prematurely)." Photographers should query with samples; send unsolicited photos by mail.

Terms Pays author's, illustrator's, and photographer's royalties. Book catalog for 8 × 10 SAE and 3 first-class stamps.

Tips "In both picture books and nonfiction, we are seeking stories showing life in other cultures and the variety of multicultural life in the U.S. We also want fiction and nonfiction about mentally or physically challenged children-some recent topics have been autism, stuttering, and diabetes.

Look up some of our books first to be sure your submission is appropriate for Albert Whitman & Co."

WILLIAMSON BOOKS

An imprint of Ideals Publications, 2636 Elm Hill Pike, Ste. 120, Nashville TN 37214. Website: www. idealsbooks.com. **Manuscript and Art Acquisitions:** Williamson Books Submission. Publishes 2-4 titles/year. 50% of books by first-time authors; 10% of books from agented authors. Publishes "very successful nonfiction series (Kids Can! Series) on subjects such as history, science, arts/crafts, geography, diversity, multiculturalism. Little Hands series for ages 2-6, Kaleidoscope Kids series (age 7 and up) and Quick Starts for Kids! series (ages 8 and up). "Our goal is to help every child fulfill his/her potential and experience personal growth."

Nonfiction Hands-on active learning books, animals, African-American, arts/crafts, Asian, biography, diversity, careers, geography, health, history, hobbies, how-to, math, multicultural, music/dance, nature/environment, Native American, science, writing and journaling. Does not want to see textbooks, picture books, fiction. "Looking for all things African American, Asian American, Hispanic, Latino, and Native American including crafts and traditions, as well as their history, biographies, and personal retrospectives of growing up in U.S. for grades pre K-8th. We are looking for books in which learning and doing are inseparable." Recently published *Keeping Our Earth Green; Leap Into Space; China! and Big Fun Craft Book.*

How to Contact Query with annotated TOC/synopsis and 1 sample chapter. Responds to queries/mss in 4 months. Publishes book "about 1 year" after acceptance. Writers may send a SASE for guidelines or reply to submission.

Illustration Works with at least 2 illustrators and 2 designers/year. "We're interested in expanding our illustrator and design freelancers." Uses primarily 2-color and 4-color artwork. Responds only if interested. Samples returned with SASE; samples filed.

Photography Buys photos from freelancers; uses archival art and photos.

Terms Pays authors advance against future royalties based on wholesale price or purchases outright. Pays illustrators by the project. Pays photographers per photo. Sends galleys to authors.

Tips "Please do not send any fiction or picture books of any kind—those should go to Ideals Children's Books. Look at our books to see what we do. We're interested in interactive learning books with a creative approach packed with interesting information, written for young readers ages 3-7 and 8-14. In nonfiction children's publishing, we are looking for authors with a depth of knowledge shared with children through a warm, embracing style. Our publishing philosophy is based on the idea that all children can succeed and have positive learning experiences. Children's lasting learning experiences involve their participation."

WINDRIVER PUBLISHING, INC.

72 N. WindRiver Rd., Silverton ID 83867-0446. (208)752-1836. Fax: (208)752-1876. E-mail: info@ windriverpublishing.com. **Contact:** E. Keith Howick, Jr., president; Gail Howick, vice president/editor-in-chief. "Authors who wish to submit book proposals for review must do so according to our Submissions Guidelines, which can be found on our website, along with an on-line submission form, which is our preferred submission method. We do not accept submissions of any kind by email." Publishes hardcover originals and reprints, trade paperback originals, and mass market originals. 1,000 queries received/year. 300 mss received/year.

Fiction Follow online instructions.

Nonfiction Follow online instructions for submitting proposal, including synopsis and 3 sample chapters. *Ms submissions by invitation only.*

Tips "We do not accept manuscripts containing graphic or gratuitous profanity, sex, or violence. See online instructions for details."

☐ WINDWARD PUBLISHING

An imprint of the Finney Company, 8075 215th Street West, Lakeville MN 55044. (952)469-6699. Fax: (952)469-1968. E-mail: feedback@finneyco.com. Website: www.finneyco.com. **Manuscript/ Art Acquisitions:** Alan E. Krysan. Publishes 2 picture books/year; 4-6 young readers, middle readers, young adult titles/year. 50% of books by first-time authors.

Fiction Young readers, middle readers, young adults: adventure, animal, nature/environment. Recently published *Storm Codes*, by Tracy Nelson Maurer (ages 6-12, picture book); *Wild Beach*, by Marion Coste (ages 4-8, picture book).

Nonfiction Young readers, middle readers, young adults: activity books, animal, careers, nature/ environment, science. Young adults: textbooks. Recently published *My Little Book of Manatees*, by Hope Irvin Marston (ages 4-8, introductions to the wonders of nature); *Space Station Science*, by Marianne Dyson (ages 8-13, science).

How to Contact Fiction: Query. Nonfiction: Submit outline/synopsis and 3 sample chapters. Responds to queries in 1 month; mss in 2 months. Publishes book 6-12 months after acceptance. Will consider simultaneous submissions and previously published work.

Illustration Reviews ms/illustration packages from artists. Send ms with dummy. Query with samples. Responds in 2 months. Samples returned with SASE; samples filed.

Photography Buys stock and assigns work. Photography needs depend on project-mostly ocean and beach subject matter. Uses color, 4 × 6, glossy prints. Submit cover letter, résumé, stock photo list.

Terms Author's payment negotiable by project. Offers advances (average amount: $500). Illustrators and photographers payment negotiable by project. Sends galleys to authors; dummies to illustrators. Originals returned to artist at job's completion. Book catalog available for 6 × 9 SAE and 3 first-class stamps; ms guidelines available for SASE on website, www.finneyco.com/authoring.html. Catalog mostly available on website.

PAULA WISEMAN BOOKS

Imprint of Simon & Schuster, 1230 Sixth Ave.New York NY 10020. (212)698-7000. Website: http:// kids.simonandschuster.com/. Publishes 15 picture books/year; 4 middle readers/year; 2 young adult titles/year. 10% of books by first-time authors.

Fiction Considers all categories. Average word length: picture books-500; others standard length. Recently published *Which Puppy?*, by Kate Feiffer, illustrated by Jules Feiffer.

Nonfiction Picture books: animal, biography, concept, history, nature/environment. Young readers: animal, biography, history, multicultural, nature/environment, sports. Average word length: picture books-500; others standard length.

How to Contact Do not submit original artwork. **Do not accept unsolicted or unagented manuscript submissions.**

Illustration Works with 15 illustrators/year. DO NOT ACCEPT UNSOLICITED OR UNAGENTED ILLUSTRATIONS SUBMISSIONS.

WM KIDS

Imprint of White Mane Publishing Co. Inc. P.O. Box 708, 73 W. Burd St. Shippensburg PA 17257. (717)532-2237. Fax: (717)532-6110. E-mail: marketing@whitemane.com. Website: www.whitemane. com. Acquisitions: Harold Collier, acquisitions editor. Imprints: White Mane Books, Burd Street Press, White Mane Kids, Ragged Edge Press. Publishes 7 middle readers/year. 50% of books are by first-time authors.

Fiction Middle readers, young adults: history (primarily American Civil War). Average word length: middle readers-30,000. Does not publish picture books. Recently published *The Witness Tree and* *the Shadow of the Noose: Mystery, Lies, and Spies in Manassas,* by K.E.M. Johnston and *Drumbeat: The Story of a Civil War Drummer Boy,* by Robert J. Trout (grades 5 and up).

Nonfiction Middle readers, young adults: history. Average word length: middle readers-30,000. Does not publish picture books. Recently published *Hey, History Isn't Boring Anymore! A Creative Approach to Teaching the Civil War,* by Kelly Ann Butterbaugh (young adult).

How to Contact Fiction: Query. Nonfiction: Submit outline/synopsis and 2-3 sample chapters. Responds to queries in 1 month; mss in 3 months. Publishes a book 18 months after acceptance. Will consider simultaneous submissions.

Illustration Works with 4 illustrators/year. Illustrations used for cover art only. Responds only if interested. Samples returned with SASE.

Photography Buys stock and assigns work. Submit cover letter and portfolio.

Terms Pays authors royalty of 7-10%. Pays illustrators and photographers by the project. Sends galleys for review. Originals returned to artist at job's completion. Book catalog and writer's guidelines available for SASE. All imprints included in a single catalog.

WORDSONG

815 Church St. Honesdale PA 18431. Website: www. wordsongpoetry.com. Estab. 1990. An imprint of Boyds Mills Press, Inc. 5% of books from agented writers. "We publish fresh voices in contemporary poetry."

Fiction Nonfiction All levels: All types of quality children's poetry.

How to Contact Fiction/ nonfiction: Submit complete ms or submit through agent. Label package "Manuscript Submission" and include SASE. "Please send a book-length collection of your own poems. Do not send an initial query." Responds in 3 months.

Illustration Works with 10 illustrators/year works with approx. 7 illustrators/year. Reviews ms/ illustration packages from artists. Submit complete ms with 1 or 2 pieces of art. Illustrations only: Query with samples best suited to the art (postcard, 8½ × 11, etc.). Label package "Art Sample Submission." Responds only if interested. Samples returned with SASE.

Photography Assigns work.

Terms Authors paid royalty or work purchased outright. Offers advances. Illustrators paid by the project or royalties; varies. Photographers paid by the project, per photo, or royalties; varies. Manuscripts/artist's guidelines available on website.

Tips "Collections of original poetry, not anthologies, are our biggest need at this time. Keep in mind that the strongest collections demonstrate a facility with multiple poetic forms and offer fresh images and insights. Check to see what's already on the market and on our website before submitting."

⬚ WORLD BOOK, INC.

233 N. Michigan Ave.Suite 2000, Chicago IL 60601. (312)729-5800. Fax: (312)729-5600. Website: www.worldbook.com. **Manuscript Acquisitions:** Paul A. Kobasa, Editor-in-Chief. **Art Acquisitions:** Sandra Dyrlund, art/design manager. World Book, Inc. (publisher of The World Book Encyclopedia), publishes reference sources and nonfiction series for children and young adults in the areas of science, mathematics, English-language skills, basic academic and social skills, social studies, history, and health and fitness. We publish print and non-print material appropriate for children ages 3-14. WB does not publish fiction, poetry, or wordless picture books."

Nonfiction Young readers: animal, arts/crafts, careers, concept, geography, health, reference. Middle readers: animal, arts/crafts, careers, geography, health, history, hobbies, how-to, nature/ environment, reference, science. Young adult: arts/crafts, careers, geography, health, history, hobbies, how-to, nature/environment, reference, science.

How to Contact Nonfiction: Submit outline/synopsis only; no mss. Responds to queries/mss in 2 months. Unsolicited mss will not be returned. Publishes a book 18 months after acceptance. Will consider simultaneous submissions.

Illustration Works with 10-30 illustrators/year. Illustrations only: Query with samples. Responds only if interested. Samples returned with SASE; samples filed "if extra copies and if interested."

Photography Buys stock and assigns work. Needs broad spectrum; editorial concept, specific natural, physical and social science spectrum. Model/property releases required; captions required. Uses color 8 × 10 glossy and matte prints, 35mm, 2¼ × 2¼, 4 × 5, 8 × 10 transparencies. Submit cover letter, résumé, promo piece (color and b&w).

Terms Payment negotiated on project-by-project basis. Sends galleys to authors. Book catalog available for 9 × 12 SASE. Manuscript and art guidelines for SASE.

N ZUMAYA PUBLICATIONS, LLC

3209 S. Interstate 35, #1086, Austin TX 78741. E-mail: acquisitions@zumayapublications.com. **Contact:** Elizabeth Burton, executive editor. Publishes trade paperback and electronic originals and reprints 1,000 queries received/year. 100 mss received/year.

Fiction "We are currently oversupplied with speculative fiction and are reviewing submissions in SF, fantasy and paranormal suspense by invitation only. We are much in need of GLBT and YA/middle grade, historical and western, New Age/inspirational (no overtly Christian materials, please), non-category romance, thrillers. As with nonfiction, we encourage people to review what we've already published so as to avoid sending us more of the same, at least, insofar as the plot is concerned. While we're always looking for good specific mysteries, we want original concepts rather than slightly altered versions of what we've already published." Electronic query only.

Nonfiction "The easiest way to figure out what I'm looking for is to look at what we've already done. Our main nonfiction interests are in collections of true ghost stories, ones that have been investigated or thoroughly documented, memoirs that address specific regions and eras and books on the craft of writing. That doesn't mean we won't consider something else." Electronic query only.

Tips "We're catering to readers who may have loved last year's best seller but not enough to want to read 10 more just like it. Have something different. If it does not fit standard pigeonholes, that's a plus. On the other hand, it has to have an audience. And if you're not prepared to work with us on promotion and marketing, it would be better to look elsewhere."

Canadian & International Book Publishers

While the United States is considered the largest market in children's publishing, the children's publishing world is by no means strictly dominated by the U.S. After all, the most prestigious children's book extravaganza in the world occurs each year in Bologna, Italy, at the Bologna Children's Book Fair and some of the world's most beloved characters were born in the United Kingdom (i.e., Winnie-the-Pooh and Mr. Potter).

In this section you'll find book publishers from English-speaking countries around the world from Canada, Australia, New Zealand and the United Kingdom. The listings in this section look just like the U.S. Book Publishers section; and the publishers listed are dedicated to the same goal—publishing great books for children.

Like always, be sure to study each listing and research each publisher carefully before submitting material. Determine whether a publisher is open to U.S. or international submissions, as many publishers accept submissions only from residents of their own country. Some publishers accept illustration samples from foreign artists, but do not accept manuscripts from foreign writers. Illustrators do have a slight edge in this category as many illustrators generate commissions from all around the globe. Visit publishers' websites to be certain they publish the sort of work you do. Visit online bookstores to see if publishers' books are available there. Write or e-mail to request catalogs and submission guidelines.

When mailing requests or submissions out of the United States, remember that U.S. postal stamps are useless on your SASE. Always include International Reply Coupons (IRCs) with your SAE. Each IRC is good for postage for one letter. So if you want the publisher to return your manuscript or send a catalog, be sure to enclose enough IRCs to pay the postage. For more help visit the United State Postal Service website at www.usps.com/global. Visit www.timeanddate.com/worldclock and American Computer Resources, Inc.'s International Calling Code Directory at www.the-acr.com/codes/cntrycd.htm before calling or faxing internationally to make sure you're calling at a reasonable time and using the correct numbers.

As in the rest of *Children's Writer's & Illustrator's Market*, the maple leaf (◻) symbol identifies Canadian markets. Look for International (◻) symbol throughout *Children's Writer's & Illustrator's Market* as well. Several of the Society of Children's Book Writers and Illustrator's (SCBWI) international conferences are listed in the Conferences & Workshops section along with other events in locations around the globe. Look for more information about SCBWI's international chapters on the organization's website, www.scbwi.org. You'll also find international listings in Magazines and Young Writer's & Illustrator's Markets. See Useful Online Resources on page 363 for sites that offer additional international information.

☒ ANNICK PRESS LTD.

15 Patricia Ave., Toronto ON M2M 1H9, Canada. **Creative Director:** Sheryl Shapiro. Publishes 5 picture books/year; 6 young readers/year; 8 middle readers/year; 9 young adult titles/year. 25% of books by first-time authors. "Annick Press maintains a commitment to high-quality books that entertain and challenge. Our publications share fantasy and stimulate judgment and abilities."

• Annick Press does not accept unsolicited manuscripts.

Fiction Recently published *The Apprentice's Masterpiece: A Story of Medieval Spain*, by Melanie Little, ages 12 and up; *Chicken, Pig, Cow series*, written and illustrated by Ruth Ohi, ages 2-5; *Single Voices series*, Melanie Little, Editor, ages 14 and up; *Crusades*, by Laura Scandiffio, illustrated by John Mantha, ages 9-11.

Nonfiction Recently published *Pharaohs and Foot Soldiers: One Hundred Ancient Egyptian Jobs you Might Have Desired or Dreaded*, by Kristin Butcher, illustrations by Martha Newbigging, ages 9-12; *The Bite of the Mango*, by Mariatu Kamara with Susan McClelland, ages 14 and up; *Adventures on the Ancient Silk Road*, by Priscilla Galloway with Dawn Hunter, ages 10 and up; *The Chinese Thought of it: Amazing Inventions and Innovations*, by Ting-xing Ye, ages 9-11.

Illustration Works with 20 illustrators/year. Illustrations only: Query with samples. Contact: Creative Director. Samples cannot be returned. Response sent only if SASE included and submission being kept on file.

Terms Pays authors royalty of 5-12% based on retail price. Offers advances (average amount: $3,000). Pays illustrators royalty of 5% minimum. Originals returned to artist at job's completion. Book catalog available on website.

⊕ BUSTER BOOKS

Imprint of Michael O'Mara Books, 16 Lion Yard, Tremadoc Rd., London SW4 7NQ United Kingdom. (44)(207)772-8643. Fax: (44)(207)819-5934. E-mail: enquiries@mombooks.com. Website: www.mombooks.com/busterbooks. "We are dedicated to providing irresistible and fun books for children of all ages. We typically publish black-and-white nonfiction for children aged 8-12 novelty titles-including doodle books."

Nonfiction Middle readers.

How to Contact Prefers synopsis and sample text over complete mss. Responds to queries/mss in 6 weeks. Will consider e-mail submissions.

Tips "We do not accept fiction submissions. Please do not send original artwork as we cannot guarantee its safety." Visit website before submitting.

ℕ ⊕ CHILD'S PLAY (INTERNATIONAL) LTD.

Child's Play International, Ashworth Rd., Bridgemead, Swindon, Wiltshire SN5 7YD United Kingdom. (44)(179)361-6286. Fax: (44)(179)351-2795. E-mail: office@childs-play.co. Website: www.childs-play.com. Estab. 1972. Specializes in nonfiction, fiction, educational material, multicultural material. **Manuscript Acquisitions:** Sue Baker, Neil Burden. **Art Acquisitions:** Annie Kubler, art director. Produces 30 picture books/year; 10 young readers/year; 2 middle readers/year. 20% of books by first-time authors. "A child's early years are more important than any other. This is when children learn most about the world around them and the language they need to survive and grow. Child's Play aims to create exactly the right material for this all-important time."

Fiction Picture books: adventure, animal, concept, contemporary, folktales, multicultural, nature/environment. Young readers: adventure, animal, anthology, concept, contemporary, folktales, humor, multicultural, nature/environment, poetry. Average word length: picture books-0-1,500; young readers-2,000. Recently published *The Wim Wom from the Mustard Mill*, by Polly Peters (ages 3-8, traditional tale); *Ten Little Ducks,* illustrated Airlie Anderson (ages 3-6 years, novelty); *Pick and Choose,* illustrated Anthony Lewis (ages 0-2 years, novelty board).

Nonfiction Picture books: activity books, animal, concept, multicultural, music/dance, nature/ environment, science. Young readers: activity books, animal, concept, multicultural, music/dance, nature/environment, science. Average word length: picture books-2,000; young readers-3,000. Recently published *Roly Poly Discovery, by Kees Moerbeek (ages 3 + years, novelty).*

How to Contact Accepts international submissions. Fiction/nonfiction: Query or submit complete ms. Responds to queries in 10 weeks; mss in 15 weeks. Publishes book 2 years after acceptance. Considers simultaneous submissions, electronic submissions.

Illustration Accepts material from international illustrators. Works with 10 illustrators/year. Uses color artwork only. Reviews ms/illustration packages. For ms/illustration packages: Query or submit ms/illustration packages to Sue Baker, editor. Reviews work for future assignments. If interested in illustrating future titles, query with samples, CD, website address. Submit samples to Annie Kubler, art director. Responds in 10 weeks. Samples not returned. Samples filed.

Terms Work purchased outright from authors (range: $500-15,000). Pays illustrators by the project (range: $500-15,000). Author sees galleys for review. Originals not returned. Catalog on website. Offers writer's, artist's guidelines for SASE.

Tips "Look at our website to see the kind of work we do before sending. Do not send cartoons. We do not publish novels. We do publish lots of books with pictures of babies/toddlers."

🌐 CHRISTIAN FOCUS PUBLICATIONS

Geanies House, Tain Ross-shire IV20 1TW, Scotland, UK. Estab. 1975. 44 (0) 1862 871 011. Fax: 44 (0) 1862 871 699. E-mail: info@christianfocus.com. Website: www.christianfocus.com. Specializes in Christian material, nonfiction, fiction, educational mat erial. **Manuscript Acquisitions:** Catherine Mackenzie. Publishes 4-6 picture books/year; 4-6 young readers/year; 10-15 middle readers/year; 4-6 for young adult books/year. 2% of books by first-time authors.

Fiction Picture books, young readers, adventure, history, religion. Middle readers: adventure, problem novels, religion. Young adult/teens: adventure, history, problem novels religion. Average word length: young readers-5,000; middle readers-max 10,000; young adult/teen-max 20,000. Recently published *Back Leg of a Goat,* by Penny Reeve, illustrated by Fred Apps (middle reader Christian/world issues); *Trees in the Pavement, by* Jennifer Grosser (teen fiction/Christian/Islamic and multicultural issues); *The Duke's Daughter*, by Lachlan Mackenzie; illustrated by Jeff Anderson (young reader folk tale/Christian).

Nonfiction All levels: activity books, biography, history, religion, science. Average word length: picture books-2-5,000; young readers-5,000; middle readers-5,000-10,000; young adult/ teens-10,000-20,000. Recently published *Moses the Child-Kept by God*, by Carine Mackenzie, illustrated by Graham Kennedy (young reader, bible story); *Hearts and Hands-History Lives vol. 4,* by Mindy Withrow, cover illustration by Jonathan Williams (teen, church history); *Little Hands Life of Jesus,* by Carine Mackenzie, illustrated by Rafaella Cosco (picture book, bible stories about Jesus).

How to Contact Fiction/nonfiction: Query or submit outline/synopsis submit outline/synopsis and 3 sample chapters. Responds to queries in 2 weeks/mss in 3 months. Publishes 1 year after acceptance. Will consider electronic submissions and previously published work.

Illustration Works on 15-20 potential projects. "Some artists are chosen to do more than one. Some projects just require a cover illustration, some require full color spreads, others black and white line art." **Contact:** Catherine Mackenzie, Children's Editor. Responds in two weeks only if interested. Samples are not returned.

Photography "We only purchase royalty free photos from particular photographic associations. However portfolios can be presented to our designer." **Contact:** Daniel van Straatten. Photographers should send cover letter, résumé, published samples client list portfolio.

Terms Authors: "We do not discuss financial details of this type in public. Contracts can vary depending on the needs of author/publisher. Illustrators/Photographers: "Each project varies-we determine our budget by determining possible sales-but each illustrator is paid a fee. Originals generally are not returned. We keep them on file so that we can rescan if necessary in the future but they may be sent back to the artist on the proviso that we will be able to obtain them again for the future reprints if necessary. For catalog visit our website at www.christianfocus.com." Writers and artists are available for SASE.

Tips "Be aware of the international market as regards writing style/topics as well as illustration styles. Our company sells rights to European as well as Asian countries. Fiction sales are not as good as they were. Christian fiction for youngsters is not a product that is performing well in comparison to nonfiction such as Christian Biography/bible stories/church history etc."

◼️ COTEAU BOOKS

(306)777-0170. Fax: (306)522-5152. E-mail: coteau@coteaubooks.com. **Contact:** Geoffrey Ursell, publisher. "Our mission is to publish the finest in Canadian fiction, nonfiction, poetry, drama, and children's literature, with an emphasis on Saskatchewan and prairie writers. De-emphasizing science fiction, picture books." Publishes trade paperback originals and reprints 200 queries received/year. 200 mss received/year.

Fiction *Canadian authors only*. No science fiction. No children's picture books. Submit bio, complete ms, SASE.

Nonfiction *Canadian authors only*. Submit bio, 3-4 sample chapters, SASE.

Tips "Look at past publications to get an idea of our editorial program. We do not publish romance, horror, or picture books but are interested in juvenile and teen fiction from Canadian authors. Submissions, even queries, must be made in hard copy only. We do not accept simultaneous/multiple submissions. Check our website for new submission timing guidelines."

◼️ COTEAU BOOKS LTD.

2517 Victoria Ave., Regina SK S4P 0T2 Canada. (306)777-0170. E-mail: coteau@coteaubooks.com. Website: www.coteaubooks.com. **Acquisitions:** Acquisition editor. Publishes 6 juvenile and/or young adult books/year; 14-16 books/year; 25% of books by first-time authors. "Coteau Books publishes the finest Canadian fiction, poetry, drama and children's literature, with an emphasis on western writers."

- Coteau Books publishes Canadian writers and illustrators only; mss from the U.S. are returned unopened.

Fiction Teen, young readers, middle readers, young adults: adventure, contemporary, fantasy, history, humor, multicultural, nature/environment, science fiction, suspense/mystery. "No didactic, message pieces, nothing religious, no horror. No picture books. Recently published *New: Run Like Jäger*, by Karen Bass (ages 15 and up); *Longhorns & Outlaws,* by Linda Aksomitis (ages 9 and up); *Graveyard of the Sea*, by Penny Draper (ages 9 and up).

Nonfiction Young readers, middle readers, young adult/teen: biography, history, multicultural, nature/environment, social issues.

How to Contact Accepts unsolicited mss— fiction accepted from Jan. 1 to April 30; Children's/Teen novels from May 1 to August 31, poetry from September 1 to December 31, Nonfiction accepted any time. Submit complete manuscript, or 3-4 sample chapters, author bio. Responds in 2-3 months to queries; 6 months to mss. No simultaneous submissions. Sometimes comments on rejected mss.

No e-mail submissions or queries. Include SASE. Responds to queries/mss in 4 months. Publishes a book 1-2 years after acceptance.

Illustration Works with 1-4 illustrators/year. Illustrations only: Submit nonreturnable samples. Responds only if interested. Samples returned with SASE; samples filed.

Photography "Very occasionally buys photos from freelancers." Buys stock and assigns work.

Terms Pays authors royalty based on retail price. Pays illustrators and photographers by the project. Sends galleys to authors; dummies to illustrators. Original artwork returned at job's completion. Book catalog free on request with 9 × 12 SASE.

N ⊕ A EMMA TREEHOUSE

Treehouse Children's Books, The Studio, Church Street, Nunney, Somerset BA11 4LW, United Kingdom. (44)(373)836-233. Fax: (44)(373)836-299. E-mail: sales@emmatreehouse.com. Website: www.emmatreehouse.com. Estab. 1992. Publishes mass market books, trade books. "We are an independent book packager/producer." **Manuscript Acquisitions:** David Bailey, director. **Art Acqusitions:** Richard Powell, creative director. Imprints: Treehouse Children's Books. Produces 100 young readers/year.

Fiction Picture books: adventure, animal, concept, folktales, humor.

Nonfiction Picture books: activity books, animal, concept.

How to Contact Only interested in agented material. Accepts international submissions. Fiction: Submit outline/synopsis. Nonfiction: Submit complete ms. Responds to queries in 3 weeks. No simultaneous, electronic, or previously published submissions.

Illustration Only interested in agented illustration submissions. Accepts material from international illustrators. Works with 10 illustrators/year. Uses color artwork only. Reviews ms/illustration packages. For ms/illustration packages: Send ms with dummy. Submit ms/illustration packages to Richard Powell, creative director. Reviews work for future assignments. If interested in illustrating future titles, arrange personal portfolio review. Submit samples to Richard Powell, creative director. Responds in 3 weeks. Samples returned with SASE. Samples not filed.

Terms Work purchased outright. Pays illustrators by the project. Illustrators see dummies for review. Catalog available for SASE. All imprints included in single catalog.

⊕ FABER AND FABER

Bloomsbury House, 74-77 Great Russell St., London WC2B 3DA, United Kingdom. 020 7927 3800. Fax: 020 7927 3801. E-mail: gachildren@faber.co.uk.

Fiction Recently published Grubtown Tales: The Wrong End of the Dog, by Philip Ardagh (ages 7-10); Holidays According to Humphrey, by Betty G. Birney (ages 7-9); The Chamber of Shadows, by Justin Richards (ages 10 +); New and Collected Poems for Children, by Carol Ann Duffy (ages 5-7)

How to Contact "Faber and Faber published a wide range of children's fiction and poetry titles. For more information and a full set of our titles, please see www.faber.co.uk/kids. *Faber and Faber does not currently accept any unsolicited submissions to the children's list.*"

⊠ FENN PUBLISHING CO.

34 Nixon Rd.Bolton ON L7E 1W2 Canada. (905)951-6600. Fax: (905)951-6601. E-mail: fennpubs@hbfenn.com. Website: www.hbfenn.com. Manuscript/Art Acquisitions: C. Jordan Fenn, publisher. Publishes 35 books/year. Publishes children's and young adult fiction.

Fiction Picture books: adventure, animal, sports. adult sports.

How to Contact Query or submit complete ms. Responds to queries/mss in 2 months.

Illustration Reviews ms/illustration packages from artists. Responds only if interested. Samples not returned or filed.

⊕ DAVID FICKLING BOOKS

31 Beaumont St.Oxford OX1 2NP United Kingdom. (018)65-339000. Fax: (018)65-339009. E-mail: tburgess@randomhouse.co.uk. Website: www.avidficklingbooks.co.uk/. Publishes 12 fiction titles/year.

Fiction Considers all categories. Recently published *Once Upon a Time in the North*, by Phillip Pullman; *The Curious Incident of the Dog in the Night-time*, by Mark Haddon; *The Boy in the Striped Pyjamas*, by John Boyne.

How to Contact Submit 3 sample chapters to David Fickling. Please send submission rather than query letter. Responds to mss in approximately three months.

Illustration Reviews ms/illustration packages from artists. Illustrations only: query with samples.

Photography Submit cover letter, résumé, promo pieces.

⊠ FITZHENRY & WHITESIDE LTD.

195 Allstate Pkwy. Markham ON L3R 4T8 Canada. (905)477-9700. Fax: (905)477-9179. E-mail: charkin@fitzhenry.ca. Website: www.fitzhenry.ca. Book publisher. **President:** Sharon Fitzhenry; Children's Publisher: Cathy Sandusky. Publishes 3 picture books/year; 4 middle novels/year; 3 young adult titles/year; 3 juvenile nonfiction titles/year. 10% of books by first-time authors. Publishes fiction and nonfiction-social studies, visual arts, biography, environment. Emphasis on Canadian authors and illustrators, subject or perspective.

How to Contact Submissions Editor: Christie Harkin. Fiction/nonfiction. Publishes a book 12-24 months after acceptance. See full submission guidelines on website www.fitzhenry.com.

Illustration Works with approximately 10 illustrators/year. Reviews ms/illustration packages from artists. Submit outline and sample illustration (copy). Illustrations only: Query with samples and promo sheet. Samples not returned unless requested.

Photography Buys photos from freelancers. Buys stock and assigns work. Captions required. Uses b&w 8 × 10 prints; 35mm and 4 × 5 transparencies, 300+ dpi digital images. Submit stock photo list and promo piece.

Terms Pays authors 8-10% royalty with escalations. Offers "respectable" advances for picture books, 50/50 split between author and illustrator. Pays illustrators by the project and royalty. Pays photographers per photo. Sends galleys to authors; dummies to illustrators.

Tips "We respond to quality."

⊕ FRANCES LINCOLN CHILDREN'S BOOKS

Frances Lincoln. 4 Torriano Mew, Torriano Ave., London NW5 2RZ United Kingdom. +00442072844009. E-mail: flcb@franceslincoln.com. Website: www.franceslincoln.com. Estab. 1977. Specializes in trade books, nonfiction, fiction, multicultural material. **Manuscript Acquisitions:** Emily Sharatt, editor assistant. **Art Acquisitions:** Jane Donald, designer. Publishes 84 picture books/year; 2 young readers/year; 11 middle readers/year; 2 young adult titles/readers; 6% of books by first-time authors. "Our company was founded by Frances Lincoln in 1977. We published our first books two years later, and we have been creating illustrated books of the highest quality ever since, with special emphasis on gardening, walking and the outdoors, art, architecture, design and landscape. In 1983 we started to publish illustrated books for children. Since then we have won many awards and prizes with both fiction and non-fiction children's books. "

Fiction Picture books, young readers, middle readers, young adults: adventure, animal, anthology, fantasy, folktales, health, history, humor, multicultural, nature/environment, special needs, sports. Average word length: picture books—1,000; young readers— 9,788; middle readers— 20,653; young adults— 35,407. Recently published *The Sniper*, by James Riordan (young adult/teen novel); *Amazons! Women Warriors of the World*, by Sally Pomme Clayton, illustrated by Sophie

Herxheimer (picture book); *Young Inferno,* by John Agard, illustrated by Satoshi Kitamura (graphic novel/picture book).

Nonfiction Picture books, young readers, middle readers, young adult: activity books, animal, biography, careers, cooking, graphic novels, history, multicultural, nature/environment, religion, social issues, special needs. Average word length: picture books—1,000; middle readers—29,768. Recently published *Tail-End Charlie,* by Mick Manning and Brita Granstroöm. (picture book); *Our World of Water*, by Beatrice Hollyer, with photographers by Oxfam (picture book); *Look! Drawing the Line in Art*, by Gillian Wolfe (picture book).

How to Contact Fiction/nonfiction: Submit query (by e-mail- letter queries are rarely responded to). Responds as soon as possible; mss in minimum 6 weeks. Publishes a book 18 months after acceptance. Will consider e-mail submissions, simultaneous submissions, and previously published work.

Illustration Works with approx 56 illustrators/year. Uses both color and b&w. Reviews ms/ illustration packages from artist. Sample illustrations. Contact: Jane Donald, designer. Illustrations only: Query with samples. Contact: Jane Donald, designer. Responds only if interested. Samples are returned with SASE. Samples are kept on file only if interested.

Photography Buys stock images and assign work. Contact: Jane Donald, designer. Uses children, multicultural photos. Submit cover letter, published samples, or portfolio.

Terms Pays authors royalty. Offers advances. Originals returned to artist at job's completion. Catalog available on website.

▨ GROUNDWOOD BOOKS

110 Spadina.Suite 801, Toronto ON M5V 2K4 Canada. (416)363-4343. Fax: (416)363-1017. Website: www.groundwoodbooks.com. **Manuscript Acquisitions:** Acquisitions Editor. **Art Acquisitions:** Art Director. Publishes 10 picture books/year; 3 young readers/year; 5 middle readers/year; 5 young adult titles/year, approximately 2 nonfiction titles/year. 10% of books by first-time authors; Nonfiction: Recently published *Hip Hop* (A Ground Group), by Dalton Higgins; Picture Books: Recently published *When Stella Was Very, Very Small,* by Marie-Louise Gay (ages 2-5); *Bella's Tree*, by Janet Russell, illustrated by Jirina Marton; *Alego*, by Ningeokuluk Teevee; *A Coyote Solstice Tale*, by Thomas King, illustrated by Gary Clement. Fiction: Recently published *Against The Odds*, by Marjolijn Hof; *Rex Zero, The Great Pretender*, by Tim Wynne-Jones; *Poster Boy*, by Dede Crane.

Fiction Recently published *The Shepherd's Granddaughter*, by Anne Laurel Carter (y/a); *The Saver*, by Edeet Ravel (y/a).

How to Contact Fiction: Submit synopsis and sample chapters. Responds to mss in 6-8 months. Will consider simultaneous submissions.

Illustration Works with 20 illustrators/year. Reviews ms/illustration packages from artists. Illustrations only: Send resume, promo sheet, slides, color or b&w copies, and tearsheets. Responds only if interested. Samples not returned.

Terms Offers advances. Pays illustrators by the project for cover art; otherwise royalty. Sends galleys to authors; dummies to illustrators. Originals returned to artist at job's completion. Backlist available on website.

Tips "Try to familiarize yourself with our list before submitting to judge whether or not your work is appropriate for Groundwood. Visit our website for guidelines."

⊕ ▢ ▥ HINKLER BOOKS

45-55 Fairchild St., Heatherton, Victoria Australia 3202. (61)(3)9552-1333. Fax: (61)(3)9552-2566. E-mail: tracey.ahern@hinkler.com.au. Website: www.hinklerbooks.com. **Acquisitions:** Tracey Ahern, publisher. "Hinkler Books publishes quality books affordable to the average family."

☑ Ⓐ KEY PORTER BOOKS

6 Adelaide St. E, Toronto ON M5C 1H6 Canada. (416)862-7777. Fax: (416)862-2304. E-mail: info@keyporter.com. Website: www.keyporter.com. Book publisher. Key Porter Books is the largest independent, 100% Canadian-owned trade publisher.

Fiction Picture books: biographies, memoirs. Middle readers, young adult: adventure, anthology, sports.

Nonfiction Picture books: animal, arts/crafts, cooking, geography, nature/environment, reference, science, photography. Middle readers: history and business. Recently published *Crusade*, by John Wilson; *Gordon Ramsay's Weekend Brunch*, by Gordon Ramsay; *Contact Charlie*, by Chris Wattie; *Stampede: The Rise of the West and Canada's New Power Elite*, by Gordon Pitts; *Hockey Night in Canada: By the Numbers*, by Scott Morrison; *Ted Reader's Napoleon's Everyday Gourmet Grilling*, by Ted Reader; *Global Warring*, by Cleo Paskal; *The Meaning of Puck*, by Bruce Dowbiggin; *The China Wall*, by Johnny Bower; *Canada*, by Mike Grandmaison.

How to Contact Only interested in agented material; no unsolicited mss. "Although Key Porter Books does not review unsolicited manuscript submissions, we do try and review queries and proposals." Responds to queries/proposals in 6 months.

Photography Buys photos from freelancers. Buys stock and assigns work. Captions required. Uses 35mm transparencies. Submit cover letter, résumé, duplicate slides, stock photo list.

Tips "Please note that all proposals and accompanying materials will be discarded unless sufficient postage has been provided for their return. Please do not send any original artwork or other irreplaceable materials. We do not accept responsibility for any materials you submit."

☑ KIDS CAN PRESS

29 Birch Ave., Toronto ON M4V 1E2, Canada.

- •Kids Can Press is currently accepting unsolicited manuscripts from Canadian adult authors only.

Fiction Fiction Picture books, young readers: concepts. We do not accept young adult fiction or fantasy novels for any age. Adventure, animal, contemporary, folktales, history, humor, multicultural, nature/environment, special needs, sports, suspense/mystery. Average word length: picture books 1,000-2,000; young readers 750-1,500; middle readers 10,000-15,000; young adults over 15,000. Recently published *Rosie & Buttercup*, by Chieri Ugaki, illustrated by Shephane Jorisch (picture book); *The Landing*, by John Ibbitson (novel); *Scaredy Squirrel*, by Melanie Watt, illustrated by Melanie Watt, (picture book).

Nonfiction Picture books: activity books, animal, arts/crafts, biography, careers, concept, health, history, hobbies, how-to, multicultural, nature/environment, science, social issues, special needs, sports. Young readers: activity books, animal, arts/crafts, biography, careers, concept, history, hobbies, how-to, multicultural. Middle readers: cooking, music/dance. Average word length: picture books 500-1,250; young readers 750-2,000; middle readers 5,000-15,000. Recently published *The Kids Book of Canadian Geography*, by Jane Drake and Ann Love, illustrated by Heather Collins, written and illustrated by Briony Penn (informational activity); *Science, Nature, Environment*; *Moving Day*, by Pamela Hickman, illustrated by Geraldo Valerio (animal/nature); *Everywear*, by Ellen Warwick, illustrated by Bernice Lum (craft book).

How to Contact Fiction/nonfiction: Submit outline/synopsis and 2-3 sample chapters. For picture books submit complete ms. Responds within 6 months only if interested. Publishes a book 18-24 months after acceptance.

Illustration Works with 40 illustrators/year. Reviews ms/illustration packages from artists. Send color copies of illustration portfolio, cover letter outlining other experience. Contact: Art Director. Illustrations only: Send tearsheets, color photocopies. Responds only if interested.

🌐 KOALA BOOKS

P.O. Box 626, Mascot NSW 1460 Australia. (61)02 9667-2997. Fax: (61)02 9667-2881. E-mail: admin@koalabooks.com.au. Website: www.koalabooks.com.au. **Manuscript Acquisitions:** Children's Editor. Art Acquisitions: Children's Designer, deb@koalabooks.com.au. KOALA Books is an independent wholly Australian-owned children's book publishing house. Our strength is providing quality books for children at competitive prices.

How to Contact Accepts material from residents of Australia only. Hard copy only. Picture books only: Submit complete ms, blurb, brief author biography, list of author's published works. Also SASE large enough for ms return. Responds to mss in 3 months.

Illustration Accepts material from residents of Australia only. Illustrations only: Send cover letter, brief bio, list of published works and samples (color photographs or photocopies) in A4 folder suitable for filing." Contact: Children's Designer. Responds only if interested. Samples not returned; samples filed.

Terms Pays authors royalty of 10% based on retail price or work purchased outright occasionally (may be split with illustrator).

Tips "Take a look at our website to get an idea of the kinds of books we publish. A few hours research in a quality children's bookshop would be helpful when choosing a publisher."

🌐 LITTLE TIGER PRESS

1 The Coda Centre, 189 Munster Rd., London En SW6 6AW, United Kingdom.

Fiction Picture books: animal, concept, contemporary, humor. Average word length: picture books-750 words or less. Recently published *Gruff the Grump*, by Steve Smallman and Cee Biscoe (ages 3-7, picture book); *One Special Day*, by M. Christina Butler and Tina Macnaughton (ages 3-7, touch-and-feel, picture book).

Illustration Digital submissions preferred please send in digital samples as pdf or jpeg attachments to artsubmissions@littletiger.co.uk. Files should be flattened and no bigger than1.0mb per attachment. Include name and contact details on any attachments. Printed submissions please send in printed color samples as A4 printouts. Do not send in original artwork as we cannot be held responsible for unsolicited original artwork being lost or damaged in the post. We aim to acknowledge unsolicited material and to return material if so requested within three months. Please include S.A.E. if material if so requested.

Tips "Every reasonable care is taken of the manuscripts and samples we receive, but we cannot accept responsibility for any loss or damage. Try to read or look at as many books on the Little Tiger Press list before sending in your material. Refer to our website www.littletigerpress.com for further details."

◩ LOBSTER PRESS

1620 Sherbrooke St. W., Suites C&D, Montreal QC H3H 1C9 Canada. (514)904-1100. Fax: (514)904-1101. E-mail: editoria@lobsterpress.com. Website: www.lobsterpress.com. **Editorial Director**: Meghan Nolan. Publishes picture books, young readers and YA fiction and nonfiction. "Driven by a desire to produce quality books that bring families together." 75 Lobster Press is currently accepting manuscripts and queries for everything except picture books. **Fiction** Young readers, middle readers, young adults: adventure, animal, contemporary, health, history, literary, multicultural, nature/environment, special needs, sports, suspense/mystery, science fiction, historical fiction, teen issues. Average word length: picture books-200-1,000. Average word length: middle, YA readers-40,000-70,000. Recently published *When I Visited the Farm*, written and illustrated by Crystal Beshara (picture book, 3-5); *Grim Hill; The Forgotten Secret* (ages 9 +); *If You Live Like Me*, by Lori Weber (novel, 13 +).

Nonfiction Young readers, middle readers and adults/teens: animal, biography, Canadian history/culture, careers, geography, hobbies, how-to, multicultural, nature/environment, references, science, self-help, social issues, sports, travel. Recently published *Our Powerful Planet: The Curious Kid's guide to Tornadoes, Earthquakes, and other Phenomena,* by Tim O'Shei (ages 8+); *Pier 21: Stories from Near & Far,* by Anne Renaud (ages 8+).

How to Contact "Please address all submissions to Editorial, Lobster Press and specify the genre of your work on the envelope; e-mailed or faxed submissions will not be considered. No editorial comment will be forthcoming unless Lobster Press feels that a manuscript is publishable."

Illustration Works with approx. 3 illustrators/year. Uses line drawings as well as digital and color artwork. Reviews ms/illustration packages from artists. Query with samples. Illustrations only: query with samples. Samples not returned; samples kept on file.

Terms Pays authors 5-10% royalty based on retail price. Original artwork returned to artist at job's completion. Writer's and artist's guidelines available on website.

🌐 MANTRA LINGUA

Global House, 303 Ballards Lane, London N12 8NP United Kingdom. (44)(208)445-5123. Website: www.mantralingua.com. **Manuscript Acquisitions:** Series Editor. Mantra Lingua "multicultural resources and innovative technologies to support teachers and children."

- Mantra Lingua publishes dual-language books in English and more that 42 languages. They also publish talking books and resources with their Talking Pen technology, which brings sound and interactivity to thier products. They will consider good contemporary stories, myths and folklore for picture books only.

Fiction Picture books, young readers, middle readers: folktales, multicultural stories, myths. Average word length: picture books—1,000-1,500; young readers—1,000-1,500. Recently published *Keeping Up With Cheetah,* by Lindsay Camp, illustrated by Jill Newton (ages 3-7); *Lion Fables,* by Heriette Barkow, illustrated by Jago Ormerod (ages 6-10).

How to Contact Fiction: Submit outline/synopsis (250 words); mail submissions. Include SASE if you'd like ms returned.

Illustration Uses 2D animations for CD-ROMs. Query with samples. Responds only if interested. Samples not returned; samples filed.

🎭 MOOSE ENTERPRISE BOOK & THEATRE PLAY PUBLISHING

Imprint of Moose Hide Books, 684 Walls Rd., Sault Ste. Marie ON P6A 5K6 Canada. E-mail: mooseenterprises@on.aibn.com. Website: www.moosehidebooks.com. **Manuscript Acquisitions:** Edmond Alcid. Publishes 2 middle readers/year; 2 young adult titles/year. 75% of books by first-time authors. Editorial philosophy: "To assist the new writers of moral standards."

- This publisher does not offer payment for stories published in its anthologies and/or book collections. Be sure to send a SASE for guidelines.

Fiction Middle readers, young adults: adventure, fantasy, humor, suspense/mystery, story poetry. Recently published *Realm of the Golden Feather,* by C.R. Ginter (ages 12 and up, fantasy); *Tell Me a Story,* short story collection by various authors (ages 9-11, humor/adventure); *Spirits of Lost Lake,* by James Walters (ages 12 and up, adventure); *Rusty Butt-Treasure of the Ocean Mist,* by R.E. Forester.

Nonfiction Middle readers, young adults: biography, history, multicultural.

How to Contact Fiction/nonfiction: Query. Responds to queries in 1 month; mss in 3 months. Publishes book 1 year after acceptance. Will consider simultaneous submissions.

Illustration Uses primarily b&w artwork for interiors, cover artwork in color. Illustrations only: Query with samples. Responds in 1 month, if interested. Samples returned with SASE; samples filed.

Terms Pays royalties. Originals returned to artist at job's completion. Manuscript and art guidelines available for SASE.

Tips "Do not copy trends, be yourself, give me something new, something different."

ORCA BOOK PUBLISHERS

1030 N. Park St., Victoria BC V8T 1C6, Canada. 1016 Balmoral St.Victoria BC V8T 1A8 Canada. (250)380-1229. Fax: (250)380-1892. Website: www.orcabook.com. **Acquisitions:** Christi Howes, children's book editor (young readers); Andrew Wooldridge, editor (Orca Soundings); Bob Tyrrell, editor (teen fiction); Sarah Harvey, editor (juvenile fiction); Melanie Jeffs, editor (Orca Currents). Publishes 7 picture books/year; 16 middle readers/year; 10 young adult titles/year. 25% of books by first-time authors.

• Orca only considers authors who are Canadian or who live in Canada.

Fiction Picture books: animals, contemporary, history, nature/environment. Middle readers: contemporary, history, fantasy, nature/environment, problem novels, graphic novels. Young adults: adventure, contemporary, hi-lo (Orca Soundings), history, multicultural, nature/environment, problem novels, suspense/mystery, graphic novels. Average word length: picture books—500-1,500; middle readers—20,000-35,000; young adult—25,000-45,000; Orca Soundings—13,000-15,000; Orca Currents—13,000-15,000. Published *Tall in the Saddle*, by Anne Carter, illustrated by David McPhail (ages 4-8, picture book); *Me and Mr. Mah*, by Andrea Spalding, illustrated by Janet Wilson (ages 5 and up, picture book); *Alone at Ninety Foot*, by Katherine Holubitsky (young adult).

How to Contact Fiction: Submit complete ms if picture book; submit outline/synopsis and 3 sample chapters. "All queries or unsolicited submissions should be accompanied by a SASE." Responds to queries in 2 months; mss in 3 months. Publishes a book 18-36 months after acceptance. Submission guidelines available online.

Illustration Works with 8-10 illustrators/year. Reviews ms/illustration packages from artists. Submit ms with 3-4 pieces of final art. "Reproductions only, no original art please." Illustrations only: Query with samples; provide résumé, slides. Responds in 2 months. Samples returned with SASE; samples filed.

Terms Pays authors royalty of 5% for picture books, 10% for novels, based on retail price. Offers advances (average amount: $2,000). Pays illustrators royalty of 5% minimum based on retail price and advance on royalty. Sends galleys to authors. Original artwork returned at job's completion if picture books. Book catalog available for SASE with $2 first-class postage. Manuscript guidelines available for SASE. Art guidelines not available.

Tips "We are not seeking seasonal stories, board books, or 'I Can Read' Books. Orca Sounding/ Currents lines offer high interest teen novels aimed at reluctant readers. The story should reflect the universal struggles young people face, but need not be limited to 'gritty' urban tales. Can include adventure, mystery/suspense, fantasy, etc. There's a definite need for humorous stories that appeal to boys and girls. Protagonists are between 14 and 17 years old."

PEMMICAN PUBLICATIONS, INC.

150 Henry Ave., Winnipeg MB R3B 0J7, Canada. (204)589-6346. Fax: (204)589-2063. E-mail: pemmican@pemmican.mb.ca. **Contact:** Randal McILroy, managing editor (Metis culture & heritage). "Pemmican Publications is a Metis publishing house, with a mandate to publish books by Metis authors and illustrators and with an emphasis on culturally relevant stories. We encourage writers to learn a little about Pemmican before sending samples. Pemmican publishes titles in the

following genres: Adult Fiction, which includes novels, story collections and anthologies; Non-Fiction, with an emphasis on social history and biography reflecting Metis experience; Children's and Young Adult titles; Aboriginal languages, including Michif and Cree." Publishes trade paperback originals and reprints 120 queries received/year. 120 mss received/year.

Fiction All manuscripts must be Metis culture and heritage related. Submit proposal package including outline and 3 sample chapters.

Nonfiction All mss must be Metis culture and heritage related. Submit proposal package including outline and 3 sample chapters.

Tips "Our mandate is to promote Metis authors, illustrators and stories. No agent is necessary."

⊕ PICCADILLY PRESS

5 Castle Rd., London NW1 8PR United Kingdom. (44)(207)267-4492. Fax: (44)(207)267-4493. E-mail: books@piccadillypress.co.uk Website: www.piccadillypress.co.uk.

Fiction Picture books: animal, contemporary, fantasy, nature/environment. Young adults: contemporary, humor, problem novels. Average word length: picture books-500-1,000; young adults-25,000-35,000. Recently published *Desperate Measures,* by Laura Summers (young adult); *The Worst of Me,* Kate le Vann (young adult); *Hattori Hachi: The Revenge of Praying Mantis,* by Jane Prowse (young adult); *Where's the Bus?,* by Eileen Browne and James Croft (picture book); Don't Kicke up a Fuss, Gus, by Adria Meserve (picture book).

Nonfiction Young adults: self help (humorous). Average word length: young adults-25,000-35,000. Recently published *Mates, Dates & Saving the Planet: A Girl's Guide To Going Green,* by Cathy Hopkins; *Totally Pants: A Brilliant Guide To Boys'Bits,* by Tricia Kreitman, Dr. Neil Simpson, Dr. Rosemary Jones.

How to Contact Fiction: Submit complete ms for picture books or submit outline/synopsis and 2 sample chapters for YA. Enclose a brief cover letter and SASE for reply. Nonfiction: Submit outline/synopsis and 2 sample chapters. Responds to mss in approximately 6 weeks.

Illustration Illustrations only: Query with samples (do not send originals).

Tips "Keep a copy of your manuscript on file."

⊕ PIPERS' ASH LTD.

Church Rd., Christian Malford, Chippenham Wiltshire SN15 4BW United Kingdom. (44) (124)972-0563. E-mail: pipersash@supamasu.com. Website: www.supamasu.com. **Manuscript Acquisitions:** Manuscript Evaluation Desk. Publishes 1 middle reader/year; 2 young adult titles/year. 90% of books by first-time authors. Editorial philosophy is "to discover new authors with talent and potential."

Fiction Young readers, middle readers: adventure. Young adults: problem novels. Average word length: young readers-10,000; middle readers-20,000; young adults-30,000. Visit website.

Nonfiction Young readers: history, multicultural, nature/environment. Middle readers: biography, history, multicultural, nature/environment, sports. Young adults: self help, social issues, special needs. Average word length: young readers-10,000; middle readers-20,000; young adults-30,000.

How to Contact Fiction/nonfiction: Query. Responds to queries in 1 week; mss in 3 months. Publishes book 2 months after acceptance. Will consider e-mail submissions, previously published work.

Terms Pays authors royalty of 10% based on wholesale price. Sends galleys to authors. Offers ms guidelines for SASE. "Include adequate postage for return of manuscript plus publisher's guidelines."

Tips "Visit our website-note categories open to writers and word link to pages of submission guidelines."

🌐 MATHEW PRICE LTD.

2 Greenhill Court, Sherborne, Dorset VI DT94EP, United Kingdom. E-mail: mathewp@mathewprice. com. Website: www.mathewprice.com. **Manuscript Acquisitions:** Mathew Price, chairman. Publishes 2-3 picture books/year; 2 young readers/year; novelty/year; 1-2 gift book/year. We accept submissions by e-mail only. Looking especially for stories for 2- to 4-year-olds and fiction for young adults, especially fantasy. "Mathew Price Ltd. works to bring to market talented authors and artists profitably by publishing books for children that lift the hearts of people young and old all over the world."

Fiction Will consider any category.

Illustration Accepts material from artists in other countries. Uses color artwork only. Reviews ms/illustration packages from artists sent by e-mail only. Illustrations only: send PDFs or JPEGs by e-mail.

Terms Originals returned to artist at job's completion. Book catalog available. All imprints included in a single catalog. Catalog available on website.

Tips "Study the market, keep a copy of all your work."

N 🌐 QED PUBLISHING

Quarto Publishing plc, 226 City Road, London EC1V 2TT United Kingdom. (44)(207)812-8600. Fax: (44)(207)253-4370. E-mail: zetad@quarto.com and AmandaA@quarto.com. Website: www. qed-publishing.co.uk. Estab. 2003. Specializes in trade books, educational material, multicultural material. **Manuscripts Acquisitions:** Amanda Askew, managing editor. **Art Acquisitions:** Zeta Davies, creative director. Produces 8 picture books/year; 20 nonfiction readers/year, 40 general reference book/year. Strives for "editorial excellence with ground-breaking design."

Fiction Average word length: picture books—500; young readers—3,000; middle readers—3,500. Recently published *The Tickety Tale Teller*, by Maureen Haselhurst, illustrated by Barbara Vagnozzi (ages 4 +); *The Thief of Bracken Farm*, by Emma Barnes, illustrated by Hannah Wood (ages 4 +); *The Big Fuzzy*, by Caroline Castle, illustrated by Daniel Howarth (ages 4 +).

Nonfiction Picture books: animal, arts/crafts, biography, geography, reference, science. Young readers: activity books, animal, arts/crafts, biography, geography, reference, science. Middle readers: activity books, animal, arts/crafts, biography, geography, science. Average word length: picture books—500; young readers—3,000; middle readers—3,500. Recently published *Exploring the Earth*, by Peter Grego (ages 7 and up); *The Ancient Egyptians*, by Fiona Macdonald (ages 7 +, science); *The Great Big Book of Pirated*, by John Malam (ages 7 +, history).

How to Contact Fiction/nonfiction: Query.

Illustration Accepts material from international illustrators. Works with 25 illustrators/year. For ms/illustration packages: Submit ms with 2 pieces of final art. Submit ms/illustration packages to Zeta Davies, creative director. Reviews work for future assignments. Submit samples to Amanda Askew, editor. Responds in 2 weeks. Samples filed.

Photography Buys stock images and assigns work. Submit photos to Zeta Davies, creative director. Uses step-by-step photos. For first contact, send CD of work or online URL.

Tips "Be persistent."

🌐 RANDOM HOUSE CHILDREN'S BOOKS

61-63 Uxbridge Rd., London W5 5SA England. (44)(208)579-2652. Fax: (44)(208)579-5479. E-mail: enquiries@randomhouse.co.uk. Website: www.kidsatrandomhouse.co.uk. Book publisher. **Manuscript Acquisitions:** Philippa Dickinson, managing director. Imprints: Doubleday, Corgi, Johnathan Cape, Hutchinson, Bodley Head, Red Fox, David Fickling Books, Tamarind Books. Publishes 120 picture books/year; 120 fiction titles/year.

Fiction Picture books: adventure, animal, anthology, contemporary, fantasy, folktales, humor, multicultural, nature/environment, poetry, suspense/mystery. Young readers: adventure, animal, anthology, contemporary, fantasy, folktales, humor, multicultural, nature/environment, poetry, sports, suspense/mystery. Middle readers: adventure, animal, anthology, contemporary, fantasy, folktales, humor, multicultural, nature/environment, problem novels, romance, sports, suspense/mystery. Young adults: adventure, contemporary, fantasy, humor, multicultural, nature/environment, problem novels, romance, science fiction, suspense/mystery. Average word length: picture books—800; young readers—1,500-6,000; middle readers—10,000-15,000; young adults—20,000-45,000.

How to Contact Only interested in agented material. No unsolicited mss or picture books.

Illustration Works with 50 illustrators/year. Reviews ms/illustration packages from artists. Query with samples. Contact: Margaret Hope. Samples are returned with SASE (IRC).

Photography Buys photos from freelancers. Contact: Margaret Hope. Photo captions required. Uses color or b&w prints. Submit cover letter, published samples.

Terms Pays authors royalty. Offers advances. Pays illustrators by the project or royalty. Pays photographers by the project or per photo.

Tips "Although Random House is a big publisher, each imprint only publishes a small number of books each year. Our lists for the next few years are already full. Any book we take on from a previously unpublished author has to be truly exceptional. Manuscripts should be sent to us via literary agents."

◪ RED DEER PRESS

195 Allstate Parkway, Markham ON L9P 1R4 Canada. (800)-387-9776/(905)477-9700. Fax: (800)260-9777/(905)477-2834. E-mail: rdp@reddeerpress.com. Website: www.reddeerpress.com. **Manuscript/Art Acquisitions:** Peter Carver, children's editor. Publishes 3 to 5 picture books/year; 4 young adult titles/year per season. Red Deer Press is known for their "high-quality international children's program that tackles risky and/or serious issues for kids."

• Red Deer only publishes books written and illustrated by Canadians.

Fiction Picture books, young readers: adventure, contemporary, fantasy, folktales, history, humor, multicultural, nature/environment, poetry. Middle readers, young adult/teens: adventure, contemporary, fantasy, folktales, hi-lo, history, humor, multicultural, nature/environment, problem novels, suspense/mystery. Recently published *Egghead*, by Caroline Pignat; *Dooley Takes the Fall*, by Norah McClintock; *The End of The World As We Know It*, by Lesley Choyce.

How to Contact Fiction/nonfiction: Query or submit outline/synopsis. Responds to queries in 2 months; mss in 8 months. Publishes a book 18 months after acceptance.

Illustration Works with 4-6 illustrators/year. Illustrations only: Query with samples. Responds only if interested. Samples not returned; samples filed for six months. Canadian illustrators only.

Photography Buys stock and assigns work. Model/property releases required. Submit cover letter, résumé and color promo piece.

Terms Pays authors royalty (negotiated). Advances (negotiated). Pays illustrators and photographers by the project or royalty (depends on the project). Sends galleys to authors. Originals returned to artist at job's completion. Guidelines not available on website.

Tips "Writers, illustrators, and photographers should familiarize themselves with Red Deer Press's children's publishing program, including the kinds of books we do and do not publish."

◪ RONSDALE PRESS

3350 W. 21st Ave., Vancouver BC V6S 1G7, Canada. (604)738-4688. Fax: (604)731-4548. E-mail: ronsdale@shaw.ca. Website: ronsdalepress.com. Estab. 1988. Book publisher. **Manuscript/Art**

Acquisitions: Veronica Hatch, children's editor. Publishes 3 children's books/year. 40% of titles by first-time authors. "Ronsdale Press is a Canadian literary publishing house that publishes 12 books each year, three of which are children's titles. Of particular interest are books involving children exploring and discovering new aspects of Canadian history."

Fiction Young adults: Canadian novels. Average word length: middle readers and young adults-50,000. Recently published *Red Goodwin*, by John Wilson (ages 10-14); *Tragic Links*, by Cathy Beveridge (ages 10-14); *Dark Times*, edited by Ann Walsh (anthology of short stories, ages 10 and up); *Submarine Outlaw*, by Phillip Roy; *The Way Lies North*, by Jean Rae Baxter (ages 10-14).

Nonfiction Middle readers, young adults: animal, biography, history, multicultural, social issues. Average word length: young readers-90; middle readers-90.

How to Contact Accepts material from residents of Canada only. Fiction/nonfiction: Submit complete ms. Responds to queries in 2 weeks; mss in 2 months. Publishes a book 1 year after acceptance. Will consider simultaneous submissions.

Illustration Works with 2 illustrators/year. Reviews ms/illustration packages from artists. Requires only cover art. Responds in 2 weeks. Samples returned with SASE. Originals returned to artist at job's completion.

Terms Pays authors royalty of 10% based on retail price. Pays illustrators by the project $400-800. Sends galleys to authors. Book catalog available for 8½ × 11 stet and $1 postage; ms and art guidelines available for SASE.

❦ SCHOLASTIC CANADA LTD.

604 King St. West, ON M5V 1E1 Canada. (416)915-3500. Fax: (416)849-7912. Website: www.scholastic.ca; for ms/artist guidelines: www.scholastic.ca/aboutscholastic/manuscripts.htm. **Acquisitions:** Editor, children's books. Publishes hardcover and trade paperback originals. Imprints: Scholastic Canada; North Winds Press; Les Editions Scholastic. Publishes 70 titles/year; imprint publishes 4 titles/year. 3% of books from first-time authors; 50% from unagented writers. Canadian authors, theme or setting required.

- At press time Scholastic Canada was not accepting unsolicited manuscripts. For up-to-date information on their current submission policy, call their publishing status line at (905)887-7323, ext. 4308 or view their submission guidelines on their website.

Fiction Picture books, young readers, young adult. Average word length: picture books-under 1,000; young readers-7,000-10,000; middle readers-15,000-30,000; young adult-25,000-40,000.

Nonfiction Animals, biography, history, hobbies, nature, recreation, science, sports. Reviews artwork/photos as part of ms package. Send photocopies.

How to Contact Query with synopsis, 3 sample chapters and SASE. Nonfiction: Query with outline, 1-2 sample chapters and SASE (IRC or Canadian stamps only). Responds in 3 months. Publishes book 1 year after acceptance.

Illustration Illustrations only: Query with samples; send résumé. Never send originals. Contact: Ms. Yuksel Hassan.

Terms Pays authors royalty of 5-10% based on retail price. Offers advances. Book catalog for 8½ × 11 SAE with $2.55 postage stamps (IRC or Canadian stamps only).

❦ SECOND STORY PRESS

20 Maud St., Suite 401, Toronto ON M5V 2M5 Canada. (416)537-7850. Fax: (416)537-0588. E-mail: info@secondstorypress.ca. Website: www.secondstorypress.ca.

Fiction Considers non-sexist, non-racist, and non-violent stories, as well as historical fiction, chapter books, picture books. Recently published *Lilly and the Paper Man*, by Rebecca Upjohn; *Mom and Mum Are Getting Married!*, by Ken Setterington.

Nonfiction Picture books: biography. Recently published *Hiding Edith: A True Story*, by Kathy Kacer (a new addition to our Holocaust remembrance series for young readers).

How to Contact Accepts appropriate material from residents of Canada only. Fiction and nonfiction: Submit complete ms or submit outline and sample chapters by postal mail only. No electronic submissions or queries.

THISTLEDOWN PRESS LTD.

633 Main St., Saskatoon SK S7H 0J8 Canada. (306)244-1722. Fax: (306)244-1762. E-mail: tdpress@ thistledown.sk.com. Website: www.thistledown.com. **Acquisitions:** Allan Forrie, publisher. Publishes numerous middle reader and young adult titles/year. "Thistledown originates books by Canadian authors only, although we have co-published titles by authors outside Canada. We do not publish children's picture books."

• Thistledown publishes books by Canadian authors only.

Fiction Middle readers, young adults: adventure, anthology, contemporary, fantasy, humor, poetry, romance, science fiction, suspense/mystery, short stories. Average word length: young adults-40,000. Recently published *Up All Night*, edited by R.P. MacIntyre (young adult, anthology); *Offside*, by Cathy Beveridge (young adult, novel); *Cheeseburger Subversive*, by Richard Scarsbrook; *The Alchemist's Daughter*, by Eileen Kernaghan.

How to Contact Submit outline/synopsis and sample chapters. **"We don not accept unsolicted full-length manuscripts. These will be returned."** Responds to queries in 4 months. Publishes a book about 1 year after acceptance. No simultaneous submissions. No e-mailed submissions.

Illustration Prefers agented illustrators but "not mandatory." Works with few illustrators. Illustrations only: Query with samples, promo sheet, slides, tearsheets. Responds only if interested. Samples returned with SASE; samples filed.

Terms Pays authors royalty of 10-12% based on net dollar sales. Pays illustrators and photographers by the project (range: $250-750). Sends galleys to authors. Original artwork returned at job's completion. Book catalog free on request. Manuscript guidelines for #10 envelope and IRC.

Tips "Send cover letter including publishing history and SASE."

TRADEWIND BOOKS

202-1807 Maritime Mews, Vancouver BC V6H 3W7, Canada. **Manuscript Acquisitions**: Michael Katz, publisher. **Art Acquisitions:** Carol Frank, art director. Senior Editor: R. David Stephens. Publishes 2-3 picture books; 3 young adult titles/year; 1 book of poetry; 1 chapter book. 15% of books by first-time authors.

Fiction Picture books: adventure, multicultural, folktales. Average word length: 900 words. Recently published City Kids, by X.J. Kennedy and illustrated by Phillpe Beha; *Roxy,* by PJ Reece; *Viva Zapata!,* by Emilie Smith and illustrated by Stefan Czernecki.

How to Contact Picture books: submit complete ms. YA novels by Canadian authors only. Chapter books by US authors considered. Will consider simultaneous submissions. Do not send query letter. Responds to mss in 12 weeks. Unsolicited submissions accepted only if authors have read a selection of books published by Tradewind Books. Submissions must include a reference to these books.

Illustration Works with 3-4 illustrators/year. Reviews ms/illustration packages from artists. Send illustrated ms as dummy. Illustrations only: Query with samples. Responds only if interested. Samples returned with SASE; samples filed.

Terms Royalties negotiable. Offers advances against royalties. Originals returned to artist at job's completion. Catalog available on website.

USBORNE PUBLISHING

83-85 Saffron Hill, London EC1N 8RT United Kingdom. Fax: (44)(20)743-1562. Website: www. usborne.com. **Manuscript Acquisitions:** Fiction Editorial Assistant. **Art Acquisitions:** Usborne Art Department. "Usborne Publishing is a multiple-award winning, world-wide children's publishing company specializing in superbly researched and produced information books with a unique appeal to young readers."

Fiction Young readers, middle readers: adventure, contemporary, fantasy, history, humor, multicultural, nature/environment, science fiction, suspense/mystery, strong concept-based or character-led series Average word length: young readers-5,000-10,000; middle readers-25,000-50,000. Recently published *Secret Mermaid series,* by Sue Mongredien (ages 7 and up); *School Friends,* by Ann Bryant (ages 9 and up).

How to Contact Refer to guidelines on website or request from above address. Fiction: Acquisitions: No unsolicited submissions accepted. Does not accept submissions for nonfiction or picture books.

Illustration Works with 100 illustrators per year. Illustrations only: Query with samples. Samples not returned; samples filed.

Photography Contact: Usborne Art Department. Submit samples.

Terms Pays authors royalty.

Tips "Do not send any original work and, sorry, but we cannot guarantee a reply."

WHITECAP BOOKS

351 Lynn Ave., North Vancouver BC V7J 2C4 Canada. (604)980-9852. Fax: (604)980-8197. E-mail: whitecap@whitecap.ca. Website: www.whitecap.ca. **Manuscript Acquisitions:** Rights and Acquisitions. **Illustration Acquisitions:** Michelle Mayne, art director. Publishes 0-1 young readers/year; 0-1 middle readers/year; 3-4 young adult/year.

Fiction Whitecap Books is currently de-emphasizing the children's and YA adventure in series only. Recently published *Wild Horse Cree #2; Coyote Canyon,* by Sharon Siamon.

Nonfiction Young Children's and middle reader's non-fiction focusing mainly on nature, wildlife and animals. Recently published *Canadian Girls Who Rocked The World; Revised and Expanded Edition,* by Tanya Lloyd Kyi.

How to Contact Query to Rights and Acquisitions. Accepts unagented work and multiple submissions. Responds to queries/ms in 6 months. Publishes a book approximately 1 year after acceptance. Include SASE with sufficient return postage. Mark envelopes "submissions." Please send international postal vouchers with SASE if submission is form U.S.A. No e-mail submissions.

Illustration Works with 1-2 illustrators/year. Uses color artwork only. Reviews ms/illustration packages from artists. Query. Contact: Rights and Acquisitions. Illustrations only: Send postcard sample with tearsheets. Contact: Michelle Mayne, art director. Responds only if interested.

Photography Buys stock and assigns work. Model/property releases required; captions required. Only accepts digital photography. Submit stock photo list.

Terms Pays authors a negotiated royalty or purchases work outright. Offers advances. Pays illustrators and photographers negotiated amount. Originals returned to artist at job's completion. Manuscript guidelines available on website.

Tips "Check submission guidelines on our website before submitting. Don't send U.S. postage SASE to Canada. It can't be used in Canada and no reply will be sent."

Magazines

Children's magazines are a great place for unpublished writers and illustrators to break into the market. Writers, illustrators and photographers alike may find it easier to get book assignments if they have tearsheets from magazines. Having magazine work under your belt shows you're professional and have experience working with editors and art directors and meeting deadlines.

But magazines aren't merely a breaking-in point. Writing, illustration and photo assignments for magazines let you see your work in print quickly, and the magazine market can offer steady work and regular paychecks (a number of them pay on acceptance). Book authors and illustrators may have to wait a year or two before receiving royalties from a project. The magazine market is also a good place to use research material that didn't make it into a book project you're working on. You may even work on a magazine idea that blossoms into a book project.

TARGETING YOUR SUBMISSIONS

It's important to know the topics typically covered by different children's magazines. To help you match your work with the right publications, we've included several indexes in the back of this book. The **Subject Index** lists both book and magazine publishers by the fiction and nonfiction subjects they're seeking.

If you're a writer, use the Subject Index in conjunction with the **Age-Level Index** to narrow your list of markets. Targeting the correct age group with your submission is an important consideration. Many rejection slips are sent because a writer has not targeted a manuscript to the correct age. Few magazines are aimed at children of all ages, so you must be certain your manuscript is written for the audience level of the particular magazine you're submitting to. Magazines for children (just as magazines for adults) may also target a specific gender.

If you're a poet, refer to the **Poetry Index** to find which magazines publish poems.

Each magazine has a different editorial philosophy. Language usage also varies between periodicals, as does the length of feature articles and the use of artwork and photographs. Reading magazines *before* submitting is the best way to determine if your material is appropriate. Also, because magazines targeted to specific age groups have a natural turnover in readership every few years, old topics (with a new slant) can be recycled.

If you're a photographer, the **Photography Index** lists children's magazines that use photos from freelancers. Using it in combination with the subject index can narrow your search. For instance, if you photograph sports, compare the Magazine list in the Photography

Index with the list under Sports in the Subject Index. Highlight the markets that appear on both lists, then read those listings to decide which magazines might be best for your work.

Since many kids' magazines sell subscriptions through direct mail or schools, you may not be able to find a particular publication at bookstores or newsstands. Check your local library, or send for copies of the magazines you're interested in. Most magazines in this section have sample copies available and will send them for a SASE or small fee.

Also, many magazines have submission guidelines and theme lists available for a SASE. Check magazines' websites, too. Many offer excerpts of articles, submission guidelines, and theme lists and will give you a feel for the editorial focus of the publication.

Watch for the Canadian (🍁) and International (🌐) symbols. These publications' needs and requirements may differ from their U.S. counterparts.

Magazines

ADVENTURES

WordAction Publications, 6401 The Paseo, Kansas City MO 64131. (816)333-7000. Fax: (816)333-4439. E-mail: dfillmore@nazarene.org. **Articles Editor:** Donna Filmore. Weekly magazine. "Adventures is a full-color story paper for first and second graders. It is designed to connect Sunday School learning with the daily living experiences of the early elementary child. The reading level should be beginning. The intent of Adventures is to provide a life-related paper enabling Christian values, encouraging good choices and providing reinforcement for biblical concepts taught in WordAction Sunday School curriculum." Entire publication aimed at juvenile market.
Fiction Picture-Oriented Material: contemporary, inspirational, religious. Young Readers: contemporary, inspirational, religious. Byline given.
How to Contact Fiction: Send complete ms. Responds to queries in 6 weeks; to mss in 6 weeks.
Terms Pays on acceptance. Buys all rights. Writer's guidelines free for SASE.
Tips "Send SASE for themes and guidelines or e-mail acallison@nazarene.org. Stories should realistically portray the life experiences of first- and second-grade children from a variety of ethnic and social backgrounds. We also need simple puzzles, easy recipes and easy-to-do craft ideas."

ADVOCATE, PKA'S PUBLICATION

PKA Publication, 1881 Little Westkill Rd., Prattsville NY 12468. (518)299-3103. **Publisher:** Patricia Keller. Bimonthly tabloid. Estab. 1987. Circ. 12,000. "Advocate advocates good writers and quality writings. We publish art, fiction, photos and poetry. Advocate 's submitters are talented people of all ages who do not earn their livings as writers. We wish to promote the arts and to give those we publish the opportunity to be published."

• Gaited Horse Association newsletter is included in this publication. Horse-oriented stories, poetry, art and photos are currently needed.

Fiction Middle readers, young adults/teens; adults: adventure, animal, contemporary, fantasy, folktales, health, humorous, nature/environment, problem-solving, romance, science fiction, sports, suspense/mystery. Looks for "well written, entertaining work, whether fiction or nonfiction." Buys approximately 42 mss/year. Prose pieces should not exceed 1,500 words. Byline given. Wants to see more humorous material, nature/environment and romantic comedy.
Nonfiction Middle readers, young adults/teens: animal, arts/crafts, biography, careers, concept, cooking, fashion, games/puzzles, geography, history, hobbies, how-to, humorous, interview/profile, nature/environment, problem-solving, science, social issues, sports, travel. Buys 10 mss/year. Prose pieces should not exceed 1,500 words. Byline given.
Poetry Reviews poetry any length.
How to Contact Fiction/nonfiction: send complete ms. Responds to queries in 6 weeks; mss in 2 months. Publishes ms 2-18 months after acceptance.

Illustration Uses b&w artwork only. Uses cartoons. Reviews ms/illustration packages from artists. Submit a photo print (b&w or color), an excellent copy of work (no larger than 8 × 10) or original. Prints in black and white but accepts color work that converts well to gray scale. Illustrations only: "Send previous unpublished art with SASE, please." Responds in 2 months. Samples returned with SASE; samples not filed. Credit line given.

Photos Buys photos from freelancers. Model/property releases required. Uses color and b&w prints (no slides). Send unsolicited photos by mail with SASE. Responds in 2 months. Wants nature, artistic and humorous photos.

Terms Pays on publication with contributor's copies. Acquires first rights for mss, artwork and photographs. Pays in copies. Sample copies for $ 5. For a yearly subscription, published 6 times per year $16.50. Writer's/illustrator/photo guidelines with sample copy.

Tips " Please, no simultaneous submissions, work that has appeared on the Internet, pornography, overt religiousity, anti-environmentalism or gratuitous violence. Artists and photographers should keep in mind that we are a b&w paper. Please do not send postcards. Use envelope with SASE."

AIM MAGAZINE

P.O. Box 390, Milton WA 98354-0390.

Fiction Young adults/teens: adventure, folktales, humorous, history, multicultural, "stories with social significance." Wants stories that teach children that people are more alike than they are different. Does not want to see religious fiction. Buys 20 mss/year. Average word length: 1,000-4,000. Byline given.

Nonfiction Young adults/teens: biography, interview/profile, multicultural, "stuff with social significance." Does not want to see religious nonfiction. Buys 20 mss/year. Average word length: 500-2,000. Byline given.

How to Contact Fiction: Send complete ms. Nonfiction: Query with published clips. Responds to queries/mss in 1 month. Will consider simultaneous submissions.

Illustration Buys 6 illustrations/issue. Preferred theme: Overcoming social injustices through nonviolent means. Reviews ms/illustration packages from artists. Query first. Illustrations only: Query with tearsheets. Responds to art samples in 1 month. Samples filed. Original artwork returned at job's completion "if desired." Credit line given.

Photos Wants "photos of activists who are trying to contribute to social improvement."

Terms Pays on acceptance. Buys first North American serial rights. Pays $15-25 for stories/articles. Pays in contributor copies if copies are requested. Pays $25 for b&w cover illustration. Photographers paid by the project. Sample copies for $5.

Tips "Write about what you know."

AMERICAN CAREERS

6701 W. 64th St., Overland Park KS 66202. (913)362-7788. Fax: (913)362-4864. Published 1 time/year. Circ. 400,000. Publishes career and education information for students in grades 6-12. Website: www.carcom.com. Jerry Kanabel, art director. **Contact:** Mary Pitchford, articles editor.

Nonfiction Buys 5 mss/year. Average word length: 300-800. Byline given.

How to Contact Query with résumé and published clips. Acknowledges queries within 30 days. Keeps queries on file up to 2 years. Accepts simultaneous submissions with notification.

Terms Pays on acceptance. Pays writers variable amount.

AMERICAN CHEERLEADER

American Cheerleader Media LLC,110 William St., 23rd Floor, New York NY 10038. (646)459-4800. Fax: (646)459-4900. E-mail: acmail@americancheerleader.com. Website: www.americancheerleader.

com. **Publisher:** Joanna Schwartz. **Editor:** Marisa Walker. Bimonthly magazine. Estab. 1995. Circ. 150,000. Special interest teen magazine for kids who cheer.

Nonfiction Young adults: biography, interview/profile (sports personalities), careers, fashion, beauty, health, how-to (cheering techniques, routines, pep songs, etc.), problem-solving, sports, cheerleading specific material. "We're looking for authors who know cheerleading." Buys 20 mss/ year. Average word length: 750-2,000. Byline given.

How to Contact Query with published clips. Responds to queries/mss in 3 months. Publishes ms 3 months after acceptance. Will consider electronic submission via disk or e-mail.

Illustration Buys 2 illustrations/issue; 12-20 illustrations/year. Works on assignment only. Reviews ms/illustration packages from artists. Illustrations only: Query with samples; arrange portfolio review. Responds only if interested. Samples filed. Originals not returned at job's completion. Credit line given.

Photos Buys photos from freelancers. Looking for cheerleading at different sports games, events, etc. Uses 35mm, 2¼ × 2¼ transparencies and 5 × 7 prints. Query with samples; provide résumé, business card, tearsheets to be kept on file. "After sending query, we'll set up an interview." Responds only if interested.

Terms Pays on publication. Buys all rights for mss, artwork and photographs. Pays $100-300 for stories. Pays illustrators $50-200 for b&w inside, $100-300 for color inside. Pays photographers by the project $300-750; per photo (range: $25-100). Sample copies for $4.

Tips "Authors: We invite proposals from freelance writers who are involved in or have been involved in cheerleading—i.e. coaches, sponsors or cheerleaders. Our writing style is upbeat, and 'sporty' to catch and hold the attention of our teen readers. Articles should be broken down into lots of sidebars, bulleted lists, etc. Photographers and illustrators must have teen magazine experience or high profile experience."

AMERICAN GIRL

8400 Fairway Place, Middleton WI 53562-0984. (608)836-4848. Website: www.americangirl.com. **Contact:** Editorial Dept. Assistant. Bimonthly magazine. Estab. 1992. Circ. 600,000. girls ages 8-12.

Fiction Not currently accepting fiction. **Nonfiction** How-to, interview/profile. Any articles aimed at girls ages 8-12. Buys 3-10 mss/year. Average word length: 600. Byline sometimes given. No historical profiles about obvious female heroines Annie Oakley, Amelia Earhart; no romance or dating.

How to Contact Fiction: Query with published clips. Nonfiction: Query. Responds to queries/mss in 3 months. Will consider simultaneous submissions.

Illustration Works on assignment only.

Terms Pays on acceptance. Buys first North American serial rights. Pays $500 minimum for stories; $300 minimum for articles. Sample copies for $4.95 and 9 ½ × 12 SASE with $1.98 in postage (send to Magazine Department Assistant). Writer's guidelines free for SASE.

Tips Keep (stories and articles) simple but interesting. Kids are discriminating readers, too. They won't read a boring or pretentious story. We're looking for short (maximum 175 words) how-to stories and short profiles of girls for 'Girls Express' section.

APPLESEEDS

Cobblestone Publishing, A Division of Carus Publishing, 30 Grove Street, Suite C,, Peterborough NH 03458.

- Requests for sample issues should be mailed to Cobblestone directly. See website for current theme list www.cobblestonepub.com/guidesAAP.html.

How to Contact Nonfiction: Query only. Send all queries to Susan Buckley. See website for submission guidelines and theme list. E-mail queries only. See website for editorial guidelines.
Illustration Contact Ann Dillon at Cobblestone. See website for illustration guidelines.
Tips "Submit queries specifically focused on the theme of an upcoming issue. We generally work 6 months ahead on themes. We look for unusual perspectives, original ideas, and excellent scholarship. We accept **no unsolicited manuscripts**. Writers should check our website at cobblestonepub.com/pages/writersAPPguides/html for current guidelines, topics, and query deadlines. We use very little fiction. Illustrators should not submit unsolicited art."

N ⊕ AQUILA

New Leaf Publishing, P.O. Box 2518, Eastbourne BN22 8AP United Kingdom. (44)(132)343-1313. Fax: (44)(132)373-1136. E-mail: info@aquila.co.uk. Website: www.aquila.co.uk. **Submissions Editor:** Jackie Berry and Anji Ansty-Holroyd. Monthly magazine. Estab. 1993. "Aquila is an educational magazine for readers ages 8-13 including factual articles (no pop/celebrity material), arts/crafts and puzzles." Entire publication aimed at juvenile market.
Fiction Young Readers: animal, contemporary, fantasy, folktales, health, history, humorous, multicultural, nature/environment, problem solving, religious, science fiction, sports, suspense/mystery. Middle Readers: animal, contemporary, fantasy, folktales, health, history, humorous, multicultural, nature/environment, problem solving, religious, romance, science fiction, sports, suspense/mystery. Buys 6-8 mss/year. Byline given.
Nonfiction Considers Young Readers: animal, arts/crafts, concept, cooking, games/puzzles, health, history, how-to, interview/profile, math, nature/environment, science, sports. Middle Readers: animal, arts/crafts, concept, cooking, games/puzzles, health, history, interview/profile, math, nature/environment, science, sports. Buys 48 mss/year. Average word length: 350-750.
How to Contact Fiction: Query with published clips. Nonfiction: Query with published clips. Responds to queries in 6-8 weeks. Publishes ms 1 year after acceptance. Considers electronic submissions via disk or e-mail, previously published work.
Illustration Color artwork only. Works on assignment only. For first contact, query with samples. Submit samples to Jackie Berry, Editor. Responds only if interested. Samples not returned. Samples filed.
Terms Buys exclusive magazine rights. Buys exclusive magazine rights rights for artwork. Pays 150-200 for stories; 50-100 for articles. Additional payment for ms/illustration packages. Additional payment for ms/photo packages. Pays illustrators $130-150 for color cover. Sample copies (5 sterling) this must be bankers cheque in sterling, not US dollars. Writer's guidelines free for SASE. Publishes work by children.
Tips "We only accept a high level of educational material for children ages 8-13 with a good standard of literacy and ability."

ASK

Carus Publishing, 70 E. Lake Street, Suite 300, Chicago IL 60601. (312) 701-1720. E-mail: ask@caruspub.com. Website: www.askmagkids.com. Editor: Liz Huyck. Art Director: Karen Kohn. Magazine published 9 times/year. Estab. 2002. Ask is a magazine of arts and sciences for curious kids who like to find out how the world works.
Nonfiction Young readers, middle readers: science, engineering, machines, archaeology, animals, nature/environment, history, history of science. Average word length: 150-1,600. Byline given
How to Contact *Ask* commissions most articles, but welcomes queries from authors on all nonfiction subjects. Particularly looking for odd, unusual, and interesting stories likely to interest science-oriented kids. Contact ask@caruspub.com to request a current issue theme list and calendar.

Writers interested in working for ask should send a resume and writing sample (including at least one page un-edited) for consideration.

Illustration Buys 10 illustrations/issue; 60 illustrations/year. Works on assignment only. For illustrations, send query with samples.

BABAGANEWZ

Jewish Family & Life, P.O. Box 9129, Newton, MA 02464. (888) 458-8535. Fax: (617) 965-7772. Website: www.babaganewz.com. **Articles Editor:** Mark Levine. **Managing Editor:** Jean Max. Monthly magazine. Estab. 2001. Circ. 40,000. "BabagaNewz helps middle school students explore Jewish values that are at the core of Jewish beliefs and practices."

Fiction Middle readers: religious, Jewish themes. Buys 1 ms/year. Average word length: 1,000-1,500. Byline given.

Nonfiction Middle readers: arts/crafts, concept, games/puzzles, geography, history, humorous, interview/profile, nature/environment, religion, science, social issues. Most articles are written by assignment. Average word length: 350-1,000. Byline given.

How to Contact Queries only for fiction; queries preferred for nonfiction. No unsolicited manuscripts.

Illustration Uses color artwork only. Works on assignment only. Illustrations only: Send postcard sample with promo sheet, resume, URL. Responds only if interested. Credit line given.

Photos Photos by assignment.

Terms Pays on acceptance. Usually buys all rights for mss. Original artwork returned at job's completion only if requested. Sample copies free for SAE 9 × 12 and 4 first-class stamps.

Tips "Most work is done on assignment. We are looking for freelance writers with experience writing non-fiction for 9- to 13-year-olds, especially on Jewish-related themes. No unsolicited manuscripts."

BABYBUG

Carus Publishing Company, 70 E. Lake St., Suite 300, Chicago IL 60601. Website: www.babybugmagkids.com. **Associate Editor:** Jenny Gillespie. **Art Director:** Suzanne Beck. Published 10 times/year (monthly except for combined May/June and July/August issues). Estab. 1994. "A listening and looking magazine for infants and toddlers ages 6 to 24 months, Babybug is 6 × 7, 24 pages long, printed in large type on high-quality cardboard stock with rounded corners and no staples."

Fiction Looking for very simple and concrete stories, 4-6 short sentences maximum.

Nonfiction Must use very basic words and concepts, 10 words maximum.

Poetry Maximum length 8 lines. Looking for rhythmic, rhyming poems.

How to Contact "Please do not query first." Send complete ms with SASE. "Submissions without SASE will be discarded." Responds in 6 months.

Illustration Uses color artwork only. Works on assignment only. Reviews ms/illustration packages from artists. "The manuscripts will be evaluated for quality of concept and text before the art is considered." Contact: Suzanne Beck. Illustrations only: Send tearsheets or photo prints/photocopies with SASE. "Submissions without SASE will be discarded." Responds in 3 months. Samples filed.

Terms Pays on publication for mss; after delivery of completed assignment for illustrators. Rights purchased vary. Original artwork returned at job's completion. Rates vary ($25 minimum for mss; $250 minimum for art). Sample copy for $5. Guidelines free for SASE or available on website, FAQ at www.cricketmag.com.

Tips "*Babybug* would like to reach as many children's authors and artists as possible for original contributions, but our standards are very high, and we will accept only top-quality material. Before attempting to write for *Babybug*, be sure to familiarize yourself with this age child."

BOYS' LIFE

Boy Scouts of America, 1325 W. Walnut Hill Lane, Irving TX 75015-2079. (972)580-2366. Fax: (972)580-2079. Website: www.boyslife.org. **Managing Editor:** Michael Goldman. **Senior Writer:** Aaron Derr. **Fiction Editor:** Paula Murphey. **Director of Design:** Scott Feaster. Monthly magazine. Estab. 1911. Circ. 1.1 million. Boys' Life is "a 4-color general interest magazine for boys 8 to 18 who are members of the Cub Scouts, Boy Scouts or Venturers."

Fiction Young readers, middle readers, young adults: adventure, animal, contemporary, history, humor, multicultural, nature/environment, problem-solving, sports, science fiction, spy/mystery. Does not want to see animals and adult reminiscence." Buys only 12-16 mss/year. Average word length: 1,000-1,500. Byline given.

Nonfiction Young readers, middle readers, young adult: animal, arts/crafts, biography, careers (middle readers and young adults only), cooking, health, history, hobbies, how-to, interview/profile, multicultural, nature/environment, problem-solving, science, sports. Matter is broad. We cover everything from professional sports to American history to how to pack a canoe. A look at a current list of the BSA's more than 100 merit badge pamphlets gives an idea of the wide range of subjects possible. Even better, look at a year's worth of recent issues. Column subjects are science, nature, earth, health, sports, space and aviation, cars, computers, entertainment, pets, history, music and others." Average word length: 500-1,500. Columns 300-750 words. Byline given.

How to Contact Fiction: Send complete ms with cover letter and SASE to fiction editor. Nonfiction: Major articles query senior editor. Columns query associate editor with SASE for response. Responds to queries/mss in 2 months.

Illustration Buys 10-12 illustrations/issue; 100-125 illustrations/year. Works on assignment only. Reviews ms/illustration packages from artists. "Query first." Illustrations only: Send tearsheets. Responds to art samples only if interested. Samples returned with SASE. Original artwork returned at job's completion. Credit line given.

Terms Pays on acceptance. Buys first rights. Pays $750 and up for fiction; $400-1,500 for major articles; $150-400 for columns; $250-300 for how-to features. Pays illustrators $1,500-3,000 for color cover; $100-1,500 color inside. Pays photographers by the project. Sample copies for $3.95 plus 9 × 12 SASE. Writer's/illustrator's/photo guidelines available for SASE.

Tips "We strongly urge you to study at least a year's issues to better understand the type of material published. Articles for *Boys' Life* must interest and entertain boys ages 8 to 18. Write for a boy you know who is 12. Our readers demand crisp, punchy writing in relatively short, straightforward sentences. The editors demand well-reported articles that demonstrate high standards of journalism. We follow *The New York Times* manual of style and usage. All submissions must be accompanied by SASE with adequate postage."

BOYS' QUEST

P.O. Box 227, Bluffton OH 45817-0227. (419)358-4610. Fax: (419)358-5027. Website: www. boysquest.com. **Articles Editor:** Marilyn Edwards. Bimonthly magazine. Estab. 1995. "Boys' Quest is a magazine created for boys from 5 to 14 years, with youngsters 8, 9 and 10 the specific target age. Our point of view is that every young boy deserves the right to be a young boy for a number of years before he becomes a young adult. As a result, Boys' Quest looks for articles, fiction, nonfiction, and poetry that deal with timeless topics, such as pets, nature, hobbies, science, games, sports, careers, simple cooking, and anything else likely to interest a young boy."

Fiction Picture-oriented material, young readers, middle readers: adventure, animal, history, humorous, multicultural, nature/environment, problem-solving, sports. Does not want to see violence, teenage themes. Buys 30 mss/year. Average word length: 200-500. Byline given.

Nonfiction Picture-oriented material, young readers, middle readers: animal, arts/crafts, cooking, games/puzzles, history, hobbies, how-to, humorous, math, problem-solving, sports. Prefer photo support with nonfiction. Buys 30 mss/year. Average word length: 200-500. Byline given.

Poetry Reviews poetry. Maximum length: 21 lines. Limit submissions to 6 poems.

How to Contact All writers should consult the theme list before sending in articles. To receive current theme list, send a SASE. Fiction/nonfiction: Query or send complete ms (preferred). Send SASE with correct postage. No faxed or e-mailed material. Responds to queries in 2 weeks; mss in 2 weeks (if rejected); 5 weeks (if scheduled). Publishes ms 3 months-3 years after acceptance. Will consider simultaneous submissions and previously published work.

Illustration Buys 10 illustrations/issue; 60-70 illustrations/year. Uses b&w artwork only. Works on assignment only. Reviews ms/illustration packages from artists. Illustrations only: Query with samples, tearsheets. Responds in 1 month only if interested and a SASE. Samples returned with SASE; samples filed. Credit line given.

Photos Photos used for support of nonfiction. "Excellent photographs included with a nonfiction story is considered very seriously." Model/property releases required. Uses b&w, 5 × 7 or 3 × 5 prints. Query with samples; send unsolicited photos by mail. Responds in 3 weeks.

Terms Pays on publication. Buys first North American serial rights for mss. Buys first rights for artwork. Pays 5/word for stories and articles. Additional payment for ms/illustration packages and for photos accompanying articles. Pays $150-200 for color cover; $25-35 for b&w inside. Pays photographers per photo (range: $5-10). Originals returned to artist at job's completion. Sample copies for $6 (there is a direct charge by the post office of $4.50 per issue for airmail to other countries); $8 for Canada, and $10.50 for all other countries. Writer's/illustrator's/photographer's guidelines and theme list are free for SASE.

Tips "First be familiar with our magazines. We are looking for lively writing, most of it from a young boy's point of view—with the boy or boys directly involved in an activity that is both wholesome and unusual. We need nonfiction with photos and fiction stories—around 500 words—puzzles, poems, cooking, carpentry projects, jokes and riddles. Nonfiction pieces that are accompanied by black and white photos are far more likely to be accepted than those that need illustrations. We will entertain simultaneous submissions as long as that fact is noted on the manuscript."

BREAD FOR GOD'S CHILDREN

Bread Ministries, Inc., P.O. Box 1017, Arcadia FL 34265-1017. (863)494-6214. Fax: (863)993-0154. E-mail: bread@breadministries.org. Website: www.breadministries.org. **Editor:** Judith M. Gibbs. Bimonthly magazine. Estab. 1972. Circ. 10,000 (U.S. and Canada). "Bread is designed as a teaching tool for Christian families." 85% of publication aimed at juvenile market.

Fiction Young readers, middle readers, young adult/teen: adventure, religious, problem-solving, sports. Looks for "teaching stories that portray Christian lifestyles without preaching." Buys approximately 10-15 mss/year. Average word length: 900-1,500 (for teens); 600-900 (for young children). Byline given.

Nonfiction All levels: how-to. "We do not want anything detrimental to solid family values. Most topics will fit if they are slanted to our basic needs." Buys 3-4 mss/year. Average word length: 500-800. Byline given.

How to Contact Fiction/nonfiction: Send complete ms. Responds to mss in 6 months "if considered for use." Will consider simultaneous submissions and previously published work.

Illustration "The only illustrations we purchase are those occasional good ones accompanying an accepted story."

Terms Pays on publication. Pays $30-50 for stories; $30 for articles. Sample copies free for 9 × 12 SAE and 5 first-class stamps (for 2 copies).

Tips "We want stories or articles that illustrate overcoming obstacles by faith and living solid, Christian lives. Know our publication and what we have used in the past. Know the readership and publisher's guidelines. Stories should teach the value of morality and honesty without preaching. Edit carefully for content and grammar."

BRILLIANT STAR

National Spiritual Assembly of the Bahá'ís of the U.S.1233 Central St., Evanston IL 60201. (847)853-2354. Fax: (847)425-7951. E-mail: brilliant@usbnc.org. Website: www.brilliantstarmagazine.org. **Associate Editor:** Susan Engle. **Art Director:** Amethel Parel-Sewell. Publishes 6 issues/year. Estab. 1969. Magazine is designed for children ages 8-12. Brilliant Star presents Bahá'í history and principles through fiction, nonfiction, activities, interviews, puzzles, cartoons, games, music, and art. Universal values of good character, such as kindness, courage, creativity, and helpfulness are incorporated into the magazine.

Fiction Middle readers: contemporary, fantasy, folktale, multicultural, nature/environment, problem-solving, religious. Average word length: 700-1,400. Byline given.

Nonfiction Middle readers: arts/crafts, games/puzzles, geography, how-to, humorous, multicultural, nature/environment, religion, social issues. Buys 6 mss/year. Average word length: 300-700. Byline given.

Poetry Only publish poetry written by children at the moment."

How to Contact Fiction: Send complete ms. Nonfiction: Query. Responds to queries/mss in 6 weeks. Publishes ms 6 months-1 year after acceptance. Will consider e-mail submissions.

Illustration Works on assignment only. Reviews ms/illustration packages from artists. Illustrations only: Query with samples. Contact: Aaron Kreader, graphic designer. Responds only if interested. Samples kept on file. Credit line given.

Photos Buys photos with accompanying ms only. Model/property release required; captions required. Responds only if interested.

Terms Pays 2 copies of issue. Buys first rights and reprint rights for mss. Buys first rights and reprint rights for artwork; first rights and reprint rights for photos. Sample copies for $3. Writer's/illustrator's/photo guidelines for SASE.

Tips "*Brilliant Star's* content is developed with a focus on children in their 'tween' years, ages 8-12. This is a period of intense emotional, physical, and psychological development. Familiarize yourself with the interests and challenges of children in this age range. Protagonists in our fiction are usually in the upper part of our age-range: 10-12 years old. They solve their problems without adult intervention. We appreciate seeing a sense of humor but not related to bodily functions or put-downs. Keep your language and concepts age-appropriate. Use short words, sentences, and paragraphs. Activities and games may be submitted in rough or final form. Send us a description of your activity along with short, simple instructions. We avoid long, complicated activities that require adult supervision. If you think they will be helpful, please try to provide step-by-step rough sketches of the instructions. You may also submit photographs to illustrate the activity."

CADET QUEST

Calvinist Cadet Corps, P.O. Box 7259, Grand Rapids MI 49510. (616)241-5616. E-mail: submissions@calvinistcadets.org. Website: www.calvinistcadets.org. **Editor:** G. Richard Broene. Magazine published 7 times/year. Circ. 7,500. "Our magazine is for members of the Calvinist Cadet Corps—boys aged 9-14. Our purpose is to show how God is at work in their lives and in the world around them. Our magazine offers nonfiction articles and fast-moving fiction—everything to appeal to the interests and concerns of boys and teach Christian values."

Fiction Middle readers, boys/early teens: adventure, humorous, multicultural, problem-solving, religious, sports. Buys 12 mss/year. Average word length: 900-1,500.

Nonfiction Middle readers, boys/early teens: arts/crafts, games/puzzles, hobbies, how-to, humorous, interview/profile, problem-solving, science, sports. Buys 6-12 mss/year. Average word length: 400-900.

How to Contact Fiction/nonfiction: Send complete ms by mail with SASE or by e-mail. Please note: e-mail submissions must have material in the body of the e-mail. Will not open attachments." Responds to mss in 2 months. Will consider simultaneous submissions.

Illustration Buys 2 illustration/issue; buys 12 illustrations/year. Works on assignment only. Reviews ms/illustration packages from artists. Responds in 5 weeks. Samples returned with SASE. Originals returned to artist at job's completion. Credit line given.

Photos Buys photos from freelancers. Wants nature photos and photos of boys.

Terms Pays on acceptance. Buys first North American serial rights; reprint rights. Pays 4-5 cent a word for stories/articles. Pays illustrators $200-300 for full page illustrations—inside or cover and $100 - $200 for smaller illustrations—inside. Sample copy free with 9 × 12 SAE and 3 first-class stamps.

Tips "Our publication is mostly open to fiction; look for new themes at our website. We use mostly fast-moving fiction from a Christian perspective and based on our themes for each issue. Articles on sports, outdoor activities, science, crafts, etc. should emphasize a Christian perspective. Best time to submit material is February-April. Themes available on our website February 1."

CALLIOPE

Exploring World History, 30 Grove St., Peterborough NH 03458. (603)924-7209. Fax: (603)924-7380. Website: www.cobblestonepub.com. **Editorial Director:** Lou Waryncia. **Co-editors:** Rosalie Baker and Charles Baker. **Art Director:** Ann Dillon. Magazine published 9 times/year. "Calliope covers world history (East/West), and lively, original approaches to the subject are the primary concerns of the editors in choosing material."

• For themes and queries deadlines, visit the Calliope web site at: www.cobblestonepub.com/ magazine/CAL.

Fiction Middle readers and young adults: adventure, folktales, plays, history, biographical fiction. Material must relate to forthcoming themes. Word length: up to 1,000.

Nonfiction Middle readers and young adults: arts/crafts, biography, cooking, games/puzzles, history. Material must relate to upcoming themes. Word length: 300-1,000.

How to Contact "A query must consist of the following to be considered (please use nonerasable paper): a brief cover letter stating subject and word length of the proposed article; a detailed one-page outline explaining the information to be presented in the article; an bibliography of materials the author intends to use in preparing the article; a self-addressed stamped envelope. Writers new to *Calliope* should send a writing sample with query. In all correspondence, please include your complete address as well as a telephone number where you can be reached. A writer may send as many queries for one issue as he or she wishes, but each query must have a separate cover letter, outline and bibliography as well as a SASE. Telephone and e-mail queries are not accepted. Handwritten queries will not be considered. Queries may be submitted at any time, but queries sent well in advance of deadline *may not be answered for several months*. Go-aheads requesting material proposed in queries are usually sent 10 months prior to publication date. Unused queries will be returned approximately three to four months prior to publication date."

Illustration Illustrations only: Send tearsheets, photocopies. Original work returned upon job's completion (upon written request).

Photos Buys photos from freelancers. Wants photos pertaining to any upcoming themes. Uses b&w/color prints, 35mm transparencies and 300 DPI digital images. Send unsolicited photos by mail (on speculation).

Terms Buys all rights for mss and artwork. Pays 20-25¢/word for stories/articles. Pays on an individual basis for poetry, activities, games/puzzles. "Covers are assigned and paid on an individual basis." Pays photographers per photo ($15-100 for b $25-100 for color). Sample copy for $5.95 and SAE with $2 postage. Writer's/illustrator's/photo guidelines for SASE.

CAREERS AND COLLEGES

A division of Alloy Education, an Alloy Media + Marketing Company, 10 Abeel Road, Cranbury NJ 08512. (609) 619- 8739. Website: www.careersandcolleges.com. **SVP/Managing Director:** Jayne Pennington. Editor: Don Rauf. Magazine published 3 times a year (2 issues direct-to-home in July and 1 to 10,000 high schools in December). Circulation: 760,000. Distributed to 760,000 homes of 15- to 17-year-olds and college-bound high school graduates, and 10,000 high schools. Careers and Colleges magazine provides juniors and seniors in high school with editorial, tips, trends, and Web sites to assist them in the transition to college, career, young adulthood, and independence.

Nonfiction Young adults/teens: careers, college, health, how-to, humorous, interview/profile, personal development, problem-solving, social issues, sports, travel. Buys 10-20 mss/year. Average word length: 1,000-1,500. Byline given.

How to Contact Nonfiction: Query. Responds to queries in 6 weeks. Will consider electronic submissions.

Illustration Buys 2 illustrations/issue; buys 8 illustrations/year. Works on assignment only. Reviews samples online. Query first. Credit line given.

Terms Pays on acceptance plus 45 days. Buys all rights. Pays $100-600 for assigned/unsolicited articles. Additional payment for ms/illustration packages "must be negotiated." Pays $300-1,000 for color illustration; $200-700 for b&w/color inside illustration. Pays photographers by the project. Sample copy $5. Contributor's Guidelines are available electronically.

Tips " Articles with great quotes, good reporting, good writing. Rich with examples and anecdotes. Must tie in with the objective to help teenaged readers plan for their futures. Current trends, policy changes and information regarding college admissions, financial aid, and career opportunities."

CARUS PUBLISHING COMPANY

P.O. Box 300, Peru IL 61354.

- See listings for *Babybug, Cicada, Click, Cricket, Ladybug, Muse, Spider* and *ASK*. Carus Publishing owns Cobblestone Publishing, publisher of *AppleSeeds, Calliope, Cobblestone, Dig, Faces* and *Odyssey*.

CATHOLIC FORESTER

Catholic Order of Foresters, P.O. Box 3012, 355 Shuman Blvd., Naperville IL 60566-7012. (630)983-4900. E-mail: magazine@CatholicForester.com. Website: www.catholicforester.com. **Articles Editor:** Patricia Baron. **Assistant V.P. Communication:** Mary Ann File. **Art Director:** Keith Halla. Quarterly magazine. Estab. 1883. Circ. 85,000. Targets members of the Catholic Order of Foresters. In addition to the organization's news, it offers general interest pieces on health, finance, family life. Also use inspirational and humorous fiction.

Fiction Buys 6-10 mss/year. Average word length: 500-1,500.

How to Contact Fiction: Submit complete ms. Responds in 4 months. Will consider previously published work.

Illustration Buys 2-4 illustrations/issue. Uses color artwork only. Works on assignment only.

Photos Buys photos with accompanying ms only.

Terms Pays on acceptance. Buys first North American serial rights, reprint rights, one-time rights. Sample copies for 9 × 12 SASE with 3 first-class stamps. Writer's guidelines free for SASE.

CELEBRATE

Word Action Publishing Co., Church of the Nazarene, 2923 Troost Ave, Kansas City MO 64109. (816)931-1900, ext. 8228. Fax: (816)412-8306. E-mail: dxb@nph.com. Website: www.wordaction. com. **Editor:** Abigail L. Takala. **Assistant Editor:** Danielle J. Broadbooks. Weekly publication. Estab. 2001. Circ. 30,000. "This weekly take-home paper connects Sunday School learning to life for preschoolers (age 3 and 4), kindergartners (age 5 and 6) and their families." 75% of publication aimed at juvenile market; 25% parents.

Nonfiction Picture-oriented material: arts/crafts, cooking, poems, action rhymes, piggyback songs (theme based). 50% of mss nonfiction. Byline given.

Poetry Reviews poetry. Maximum length: 4-8 lines. Unlimited submissions.

How to Contact Nonfiction: query. Responds to queries in 1 month. Responds to mss in 6 weeks. Publishes ms 1 year after acceptance. Will accept electronic submission via e-mail.

Terms Pays on acceptance. Buys all rights, multi-use rights. Pays $15 for activities, crafts, recipes, songs, rhymes, and poems. Compensation includes 2 contributor copies. Sample copy for SASE.

Tips "We are accepting submissions at this time."

🌐 CHALLENGE

Pearson Education Australia, 20 Thackray Rd., Port Melbourne VIC 3205 Australia. (61)03 9245 7111. Fax: (61)03 9245 7333. E-mail: magazines@pearson.com.au. Website: www.pearson.com.au/ schools. **Articles Editor:** Petra Poupa. **Fiction Editor:** Meredith Costain. Quarterly Magazine. Circ. 20,000. "Magazines are educational and fun. We publish mainly nonfiction articles in a variety of genres and text types. They must be appropriate, factually correct, and of high interest. We publish interviews, recounts, informational and argumentative articles."

- *Challenge* is a theme-based publication geared to ages 11-14. Check the website to see upcoming themes and deadlines.

Fiction Middle readers, young adults: adventure, animal, contemporary, fantasy, folktale, humorous, multicultural, problem-solving, science fiction, sports, suspense/mystery. Buys 12 mss/ year. Average word length: 400-1,000. Byline given.

Nonfiction Middle readers, young adults: animal, arts/crafts, biography, careers, cooking, fashion, geography, health, history, hobbies, how-to, humorous, interview/profile, math, multicultural, nature/environment, problem-solving, science, social issues, sports, travel (depends on theme of issue). Buys 100 ms/year. Average word length: 200-600. Byline given.

Poetry Reviews poetry.

How to Contact Fiction/nonfiction: Send complete ms. Responds to queries in 4-5 months; mss in 3 months. Publishes ms 3 months after acceptance. Will consider simultaneous submissions and electronic submissions via disk or e-mail.

Photos Looking for photos to suit various themes; photos needed depend on stories. Model/ property release required; captions required. Uses color, standard sized, prints, high resolution digital images and 35mm transparencies. Provide résumé, business card, promotional literature and tearsheets to be kept on file.

Terms Pays on publication. Buys first Australian serial rights. Pays $80-200 (Australian) for stories; $100-220 (Australian) for articles.

Tips "Check out our website for information about our publications." Also see listings for *Comet* and *Explore*.

☐ CHEMMATTERS

American Chemical Society, 1155 16th Street, NW, Washington DC 20036. (202)872-6164. Fax: (202)833-7732. E-mail: chemmatters@acs.org. Website: http://www.acs.org/chemmatters. **Editor:** Pat Pages. **Art Director:** Cornithia Harris. Quarterly magazine. Estab. 1983. Circ. 35,000.

• *ChemMatters* only accepts e-mail submissions.

How to Contact Query with published clips. E-mail or mail submissions will be considered. Responds to queries/mss in 2 weeks. Publishes ms 6 months after acceptance. Will consider simultaneous submissions, e-mail submissions.

Illustration Buys 3 illustrations/issue; 12 illustrations/year. Uses color artwork only. Works on assignment only. Reviews manuscript/illustration packages from artists. Query. Contact: Cornithia Harris, art director *ChemMatters*. Illustrations only: Query with promo sheet, resume. Responds in 2 weeks. Samples returned with self-addressed stamped envelope; samples not filed. Credit line given.

Photos Looking for photos of high school students engaged in science-related activities. Model/property release required; captions required. Uses color prints, but prefers high-resolution PDFs. Query with samples. Responds in 2 weeks.

Terms Pays on acceptance. Minimally buys first North American serial rights, but prefers to buy all rights, reprint rights, electronic rights for manuscripts. Buys all rights for artwork; non-exclusive first rights for photos. Pays $500-$1,000 for article. Additional payment for manuscript/illustration packages and for photos accompanying articles. Sample copies free for self-addressed stamped envelope 10 inches × 13 inches and 3 first-class stamps. Writer's guidelines free for self-addressed stamped envelope (available as e-mail attachment upon request).

Tips Be aware of the content covered in a standard high school chemistry textbook. Choose themes and topics that are timely, interesting, fun, *and* that relate to the content and concepts of the first-year chemistry course. Articles should describe real people involved with real science. Best articles feature young people making a difference or solving a problem.

CHILDREN'S BETTER HEALTH INSTITUTE

1100 Waterway Blvd.P.O. Box 567, Indianapolis IN 46206. See listings for Children's Digest, Children's Playmate, Humpty Dumpty's Magazine, Jack and Jill, Turtle and U*S* Kids.

CHILDREN'S DIGEST

Children's Better Health Institute, 1100 Waterway Blvd., P.O. Box 567, Indianapolis IN 46206. (317)634-1100. Fax: (317)684-8094. Website: www.childrensdigestmag.org. For children ages 10-12.

• See website for submission guidelines.

CICADA

Carus Publishing Company, 70 East Lake Street, Suite 300, Chicago IL 60601. E-mail: mail@cicadamag.com. Website: www.cricketmag.com. **Editor-in-Chief:** Marianne Carus. **Executive Editor:** Deborah Vetter. **Art Director**: John Sandford. Bimonthly magazine. Estab. 1998. Cicada publishes fiction and poetry with a genuine teen sensibility, aimed at the high school and college-age market. The editors are looking for stories and poems that are thought-provoking but entertaining.

Fiction Young adults: adventure, contemporary, fantasy, historical, humor/satire, multicultural, nature/environment, romance, science fiction, sports, suspense/mystery. Buys up to 42 mss/year. Average word length: about 5,000 words for short stories; up to 10,000 for novellas (one novella per issue).

Nonfiction Young adults: first-person, coming-of-age experiences that are relevant to teens and young adults (example: life in the Peace Corps). Buys up to 6 mss/year. Average word length: about 5,000 words. Byline given.

Poetry : Reviews serious, humorous, free verse, rhyming (if done well) poetry. Maximum length: up to 25 lines. Limit submissions to 5 poems.

How to Contact Fiction/nonfiction: send complete ms. Responds to mss in 3 months. Publishes ms 1-2 years after acceptance. Will consider simultaneous submissions if author lets us know. Important: See www.cricketmag.com. For updated submissions guidelines as editorial needs fluctuate.

Illustration Buys 20 illustrations/issue; 120 illustrations/year. Uses color artwork for cover; b&w for interior. Works on assignment only. Reviews ms/illustration packages from artists. To submit samples, e-mail a link to your online portfolio to: mail@cicadamag.com. You may also e-mail a sample up to a maximum attachment size of 50 KB. We will keep your samples on file and contact you if we find an assignment that suits your style. Credit line given.

Photos Wants documentary photos (clear shots that illustrate specific artifacts, persons, locations, phenomena, etc. cited in the text) and "art" shots of teens in photo montage/lighting effects etc.

Terms Pays on publication. Rates and contract rights vary.

Tips "Cicada is currently open to submissions from adult contributors who have previously published in the magazine. We are also open to general submissions from young people ages 14-23. See YA guidelines at www.cicadamag.com. In addition, The Slam, our online micro fiction and poetry forum, is open to young people ages 14-23. Check www.cricketmag.com for updates on our submissions policy."d\fi720\sl480\slmult1d

THE CLAREMONT REVIEW

4980 Wesley Road, Victoria BC V8Y 1Y9 Canada. (250)685-5221. Fax: (250)658-5387. E-mail: bashford@islandnet.com. Website: www.theClaremontReview.ca. Magazine 2 times/year. Estab. 1992. Circ. 500. "Publish quality fiction and poetry of emerging writers aged 13 to 19."

Fiction Young adults: multicultural, problem-solving, social issues, relationships. Average word length: 1,500-3,000.

Poetry Maximum length: 60 lines. No limit on submissions.

How to Contact Fiction: Send complete ms. Responds to queries in 2 weeks; mss in 2 months. Publishes ms 6 months after acceptance.

Terms Buys first North American rights for mss. Pays contributor's copies when published. Sample copies for $10. Writer's guidelines for SASE.

Tips "Looking for good, concrete narratives with credible dialogue and solid use of original detail. It must be unique, honest and have a glimpse of some truth. Send an error-free final draft with a short covering letter and bio. Read our magazine first to familiarize yourself with what we publish."

CLICK

30 Grove Street, Suite C, Peterborough, NH 03458. E-mail: click@caruspub.com. Website: www.cricketmag.com. **Editor:** Amy Tao. **Art Director:** Deb Porter. 9 issues/year. Estab. 1998. "Click is a science and exploration magazine for children ages 3 to 7. Designed and written with the idea that it's never too early to encourage achild's natural curiosity about the world, Click 's 40 full-color pages are filled with amazing photographs, beautiful illustrations, and stories and articles that are both entertaining and thought-provoking."

Nonfiction Young readers: animals, nature/environment, science. Average word length:100-900. Byline given.

How to Contact *Click* does not accept unsolicited manuscripts or queries. All articles are commissioned. To be considered for assignments, experienced science writers may send a resume and three published clips.

Illustration Buys 10 illustrations/issue; 100 illustrations/year. Works on assignment only. Query with samples. Responds only if interested. Credit line given.

COBBLESTONE

Discover American History, 30 Grove St., Suite C, Peterborough NH 03458. (603)924-7209. Fax: (603)924-7380. Website: www.cobblestonepub.com. **Editor:** Meg Chorlian. **Art Director:** Ann Dillon. **Editorial Director:** Lou Waryncia. Magazine published 9 times/year. Circ. 27,000. "Cobblestone is theme-related. Writers should request editorial guidelines which explain procedure and list upcoming themes. Queries must relate to an upcoming theme. It is recommended that writers become familiar with the magazine (sample copies available)."

• *Cobblestone* themes and deadline are available on website or with SASE.

Fiction Middle readers, young adults: folktales, history, multicultural.

Nonfiction Middle readers (school ages 9-14): arts/crafts, biography, geography, history (world and American), multicultural, social issues. All articles must relate to the issue's theme. Buys 120 mss/year. Average word length: 600-800. Byline given.

Poetry Up to 100 lines. "Clear, objective imagery. Serious and light verse considered." Pays on an individual basis. Must relate to theme.

How to Contact Fiction/nonfiction: Query. "A query must consist of all of the following to be considered: a brief cover letter stating the subject and word length of the proposed article, a detailed one-page outline explaining the information to be presented in the article, an extensive bibliography of materials the author intends to use in preparing the article, a SASE. Writers new to *Cobblestone* should send a writing sample with query. If you would like to know if your query has been received, please also include a stamped postcard that requests acknowledgment of receipt. In all correspondence, please include your complete address as well as a telephone number where you can be reached. A writer may send as many queries for one issue as he or she wishes, but each query must have a separate cover letter, outline, bibliography and SASE. Telephone queries are not accepted. Handwritten queries will not be considered. Queries may be submitted at any time, but queries sent well in advance of deadline *may not be answered for several months*. Go-aheads requesting material proposed in queries are usually sent five months prior to publication date. Unused queries will not be returned."

Illustration Buys 5 color illustrations/issue; 45 illustrations/year. Preferred theme or style: Material that is fun, clear and accurate but not too juvenile. Historically accurate sources are a must. Works on assignment only. Reviews ms/illustration packages from artists. Query. Illustrations only: Send photocopies, tearsheets, or other nonreturnable samples. "Illustrators should consult issues of *Cobblestone* to familiarize themselves with our needs." Responds to art samples in 1 month. Samples are not returned; samples filed. Original artwork returned at job's completion (upon written request). Credit line given.

Photos Photos must relate to upcoming themes. Send transparencies and/or color prints. Submit on speculation.

Terms Pays after publication. Buys all rights to articles and artwork. Pays 20-25¢/word for articles/stories. Pays on an individual basis for poetry, activities, games/puzzles. Pays photographers per photo ($50-100 for color). Sample copy $5.95 with 9 × 12 SAE and 4 first-class stamps; writer's/illustrator's/photo guidelines free with SAE and 1 first-class stamp.

Tips Writers: "Submit detailed queries which show attention to historical accuracy and which offer interesting and entertaining information. Study past issues to know what we look for. All feature articles, recipes, activities, fiction and supplemental nonfiction are freelance contributions."

Illustrators: "Submit color samples, not too juvenile. Study past issues to know what we look for. The illustration we use is generally for stories, recipes and activities."

CRICKET

Carus Publishing Company, 70 East Lake, Suite 300, Chicago, IL 60601. (312)701-1270. Website: www.cricketmag.com. **Editor-in-Chief:** Marianne Carus. **Executive Editor:** Lonnie Plecha. **Senior Art Director:** Karen Kohn. Publishes 9 issues/year. Estab. 1973. Circ. 55,000. Children's literary magazine for ages 9-14.

Fiction Middle readers, young adults/teens: contemporary, fantasy, folk and fairy tales, history, humorous, science fiction, suspense/mystery. Buys 70 mss/year. Maximum word length: 2,000. Byline given.

Nonfiction Middle readers, young adults/teens: adventure, architecture, archaeology, biography, foreign culture, games/puzzles, geography, natural history, science and technology, social science, sports, travel. Multicultural needs include articles on customs and cultures. Requests bibliography with submissions. Buys 30 mss/year. Average word length: 200-1,500. Byline given.

Poetry Reviews poems, 1-page maximum length. Limit submission to 5 poems or less.

How to Contact Send complete ms. Do not query first. Responds to mss in 4-6 months. Does not like but will consider simultaneous submissions. SASE required for response, IRC's for international submissions.

Illustration Buys 22 illustrations (7 separate commissions)/issue; 198 illustrations/year. Preferred theme for style: "stylized realism; strong people, especially kids; good action illustration; whimsical and humorous. All media, generally full color." Reviews ms/illustration packages from artists, "but reserves option to re-illustrate." Send complete ms with sample and query. Illustrations only: Provide link to web site or tearsheets and good quality photocopies to be kept on file. SASE required for response/return of samples.

Photos Purchases photos with accompanying ms only. Model/property releases required. Uses 300 DPI digital files, color glossy prints.

Terms Pays 30 days after publication. Rights purchased vary. Do not send original artwork. Pays up to 25¢/word for unsolicited articles; up to $3/line for poetry. Pays $750 for color cover; $150-250 for color inside. Writer's/illustrator's guidelines for SASE. Sample issue for $5, check made out to Cricket Magazine Group.

Tips Writers: "Read copies of back issues and current issues. Adhere to specified word limits. *Please* do not query." Would currently like to see more fantasy and science fiction." Illustrators: "Send only your best work and be able to reproduce that quality in assignments. Put name and address on *all* samples. Know a publication before you submit your style appropriate?"

DAVEY AND GOLIATH'S DEVOTIONS

Augsburg Fortress Publishers, P.O. Box 1209, Minneapolis MN 55440-1209. E-mail: cllsub@ augsburgfortress.org. Website: www.augsburgfortress.org. **Editor:** Becky Carlson. Quarterly magazine. Circ. approximately 40,000. This is a booklet of interactive conversations and activities related to weekly devotional material. Used primarily by Lutheran families with elementary school-aged children. "Davey and Goliath's devotions is a magazine with concrete ideas that families can use to build biblical literacy and share faith and serve others. It includes bible stories, family activities, crafts, games, and a section of puzzles, and mazes."

How to Contact Visit www.augsburgfortress.org/media/company/downloads/FamilyDevotional SampleBriefing.oc to view sample briefing. Follow instructions in briefing if interested in submitting a sample for the devotional. Published material is 100% assigned.

Terms Pays on acceptance of final ms assignment. Buys all rights. Pays $40/printed page on assignment. Free sample and information for prospective writers. Include 6 × 9 SAE and postage.

Tips "Pay attention to details in the sample devotional. Follow the process laid out in the information for prospective writers. Ability to interpret Bible texts appropriately for children is required. Content must be doable and fun for families on the go."

DIG

30 Grove St., Suite C, Peterb0rough NH 03450. (603)924-7209. Fax: (603)924-7380. **Editor:** Rosalie Baker. **Editorial Director:** Lou Waryncia. **Art Director:** Ann Dillon. Magazine published 9 times/year. Estab. 1999. Circ. 18,000. An archaeology magazine for kids ages 8-14. Publishes entertaining and educational stories about discoveries, artifacts, archaeologists.

• *Dig* was purchased by Cobblestone Publishing, a division of Carus Publishing.

Nonfiction Middle readers, young adults: biography, games/puzzles, history, science, archaeology. Buys 50 mss/year. Average word length: 400-800. Byline given.

How to Contact Fiction/nonfiction: Query. "A query must consist of all of the following to be considered: a brief cover letter stating the subject and word length of the proposed article, a detailed one-page outline explaining the information to be presented in the article, a bibliography of materials the author intends to use in preparing the article, and a SASE. Writers new to *Dig* should send a writing sample with query." Multiple queries accepted, may not be answered for many months. Go-aheads requesting material proposed in queries are usually sent 10 months prior to publication date. Unused queries will be returned approximately 3-4 months prior to publication date.

Illustration Buys 10-15 illustrations/issue; 60-75 illustrations/year. Prefers color artwork. Works on assignment only. Reviews ms/illustration packages from artists. Query. Illustrations only: Query with samples. Arrange portfolio review. Send tearsheets. Responds in 2 months only if interested. Samples not returned; samples filed. Credit line given.

Photos Uses anything related to archaeology, history, artifacts, and current archaeological events that relate to kids. Uses color prints and 35mm transparencies and 300 DPI digital images. Provide resume, promotional literature or tearsheets to be kept on file. Responds only if interested.

Terms Pays on publication. Buys all rights for mss. Buys first North American rights for photos. Original artwork returned at job's completion. Pays 20-25¢/word. Additional payment for ms/illustration packages and for photos accompanying articles. Pays per photo.

Tips "We are looking for writers who can communicate archaeological concepts in a conversational, interesting, informative and *accurate* style for kids. Writers should have some idea where photography can be located to support their articles."

DRAMATICS MAGAZINE

Educational Theatre Association, 2343 Auburn Ave., Cincinnati OH 45219. (513)421-3900. E-mail: dcorathers@edta.org. Website: www.edta.org. **Articles Editor:** Don Corathers. **Graphic Design:** Kay Walters. Published monthly September-May. Estab. 1929. Circ. 35,000. "Dramatics is for students (mainly high school age) and teachers of theater. Mix includes how-to (tech theater, acting, directing, etc.), informational, interview, photo feature, humorous, profile, technical. We want our student readers to grow as theater artists and become a more discerning and appreciative audience. Material is directed to both theater students and their teachers, with strong student slant."

Fiction Young adults: drama (one-act and full-length plays). Does not want to see plays that show no understanding of the conventions of the theater. No plays for children, no Christmas or didactic "message" plays. "We prefer unpublished scripts that have been produced at least once." Buys 5-9 plays/year. Emerging playwrights have better chances with résumé of credits.

Nonfiction Young adults: arts/crafts, careers, how-to, interview/profile, multicultural (all theater-related). "We try to portray the theater community in all its diversity." Does not want to see academic treatises. Buys 50 mss/year. Average word length: 750-3,000. Byline given.

How to Contact Send complete ms. Responds in 3 months (longer for plays). Published ms 3 months after acceptance. Will consider simultaneous submissions and previously published work occasionally.

Illustration Buys 0-2 illustrations/year. Works on assignment only. Arrange portfolio review; send résumé, promo sheets and tearsheets. Responds only if interested. Samples returned with SASE; sample not filed. Credit line given.

Photos Buys photos with accompanying ms only. Looking for "good-quality production or candid photography to accompany article. We very occasionally publish photo essays." Model/property release and captions required. Prefers hi-res jpg files. Will consider prints or transparencies. Query with résumé of credits. Responds only if interested.

Terms Pays on acceptance. Buys one-time print and short term Web rights. Buys one-time rights for artwork and photos. Original artwork returned at job's completion. Pays $100-500 for plays; $50-500 for articles; up to $100 for illustrations. Pays photographers by the project or per photo. Sometimes offers additional payment for ms/illustration packages and photos accompanying a ms. Sample copy available for 9 × 12 SAE with 4 ounces first-class postage. Writer's and photo guidelines available for SASE or via website.

Tips "Obtain our writer's guidelines and look at recent back issues. The best way to break in is to know our audience—drama students, teachers and others interested in theater—and write for them. Writers who have some practical experience in theater, especially in technical areas, have an advantage, but we'll work with anybody who has a good idea. Some freelancers have become regular contributors."

🌐 EXPLORE

Pearson Education Australia, 20 Thackray Rd., Port Melbourne VIC 3207 Australia. (61)03 3245 7111. Fax: (61)03 9245 7333. E-mail: magazines@pearson.com.au. Website: www.pearson.com.au/schools. Quarterly Magazine. Circ. 20,000. Pearson Education publishes "educational magazines that include a variety of nonfiction articles in a variety of genres and text types (interviews, diary, informational, recount, argumentative, etc.). They must be appropriate, factually correct and of high interest.

• *Explore* is a theme based publication. Check the website to see upcoming themes and deadlines.

Fiction Young readers, middle readers: adventure, animal, contemporary, fantasy, folktale, humorous, multicultural, nature/environment, problem-solving, suspense/mystery. Middle readers: science fiction, sports. Average word length: 400-1,000. Byline given.

Nonfiction Young readers, middle readers: animal, arts/crafts, biography, careers, cooking, health, history, hobbies, how-to, interview/profile, math, multicultural, nature/environment, problem-solving, science, social issues, sports, travel. Young readers: games/puzzles. Middle readers: concept, fashion, geography. Average word length: 200-600. Byline given.

Poetry Reviews poetry.

How to Contact Fiction/nonfiction: Send complete ms. Responds to queries in 1 month; mss in 3 months. Publishes ms 3 months after acceptance. Will consider simultaneous submissions and electronic submissions via disk or e-mail.

Photos Looking for photos to suit various themes; photos needed depend on stories. Model/property release required; captions required. Uses color, standard sized, prints, high resolution digital images and 35mm transparencies. Provide résumé, business card, promotional literature and tearsheets to be kept on file.

Terms Pays on publication. Buys first Australian rights. Pays $80-200 (Australian) for stories; $100-220 (Australian) for articles.

Tips "Check out our website for information about our publications." Also see listings for *Challenge* and *Comet*.

FACES

People, Places & Cultures, 30 Grove St., Peterborough NH 03458. (603)924-7209. Fax: (603)924-7380. E-mail: facesmag@yahoo.com. Website: www.cobblestonepub.com. **Editor:** Elizabeth Crooker Carpentiere. **Editorial Director:** Lou Warnycia. **Art Director:** Ann Dillon. Magazine published 9 times/year (September-May) with combined issues in May/June, July/August, and November/December. Circ. 15,000. Faces is a theme-related magazine; writers should send for theme list before submitting ideas/queries. Each month a different world culture is featured through the use of feature articles, activities and photographs and illustrations.

• See website for 2009-2010 theme list for *Faces*.

Fiction Middle readers, young adults/teens: adventure, folktales, history, multicultural, plays, religious, travel. Does not want to see material that does not relate to a specific upcoming theme. Buys 9 mss/year. Maximum word length: 800. Byline given.

Nonfiction Middle readers and young adults/teens: animal, anthropology, arts/crafts, biography, cooking, fashion, games/puzzles, geography, history, how-to, humorous, interview/profile, nature/environment, religious, social issues, sports, travel. Does not want to see material not related to a specific upcoming theme. Buys 63 mss/year. Average word length: 300-600. Byline given.

How to Contact Fiction/nonfiction: Query with published clips and 2-3 line biographical sketch. "Ideas should be submitted six to nine months prior to the publication date. Responses to ideas are usually sent approximately four months before the publication date." Guidelines on website.

Illustration Buys 3 illustrations/issue; buys 27 illustrations/year. Preferred theme or style: Material that is meticulously researched (most articles are written by professional anthropologists); simple, direct style preferred, but not too juvenile. Works on assignment only. Roughs required. Reviews ms/illustration packages from artists. Illustrations only: Send samples of b&w work. "Illustrators should consult issues of *Faces* to familiarize themselves with our needs." Responds to art samples only if interested. Samples returned with SASE. Original artwork returned at job's completion (upon written request). Credit line given.

Photos Wants photos relating to forthcoming themes.

Terms Pays on publication. Buys all rights for mss and artwork. Pays 20-25¢/word for articles/stories. Pays on an individual basis for poetry. Covers are assigned and paid on an individual basis. Pays illustrators $50-300 for color inside. Pays photographers per photo ($25-100 for color). Sample copy $6.95 with 712 × 1012 SAE and 5 first-class stamps. Writer's/illustrator's/photo guidelines via website or free with SAE and 1 first-class stamp.

Tips "Writers are encouraged to study past issues of the magazine to become familiar with our style and content. Writers with anthropological and/or travel experience are particularly encouraged; *Faces* is about world cultures. All feature articles, recipes and activities are freelance contributions." Illustrators: "Submit b&w samples, not too juvenile. Study past issues to know what we look for. The illustration we use is generally for retold legends, recipes and activities."

THE FRIEND MAGAZINE

The Church of Jesus Christ of Latter-day Saints, 50 E. North Temple St., Salt Lake City UT 84150-3226. (801)240-2210. E-mail: friend@ldschurch.org. Website: www.lds.org. **Editor:** Vivian Paulsen. **Art Director:** Mark Robison. Monthly magazine for 3-12 year olds. Estab. 1971. Circ. 275,000.

Nonfiction Publishes children's/true stories—adventure, ethnic, some historical, humor, mainstream, religious/inspirational, nature. Length: 1,000 words maximum. Also publishes family- and gospel-oriented puzzles, games and cartoons. Simple recipes and handicraft projects welcome.

Poetry Reviews poetry. Maximum length: 20 lines. "We are looking for easy-to-illustrate poems with catchy cadences. Poems should convey a sense of joy and reflect gospel teachings. Also brief poems that will appeal to preschoolers."

How to Contact Send complete ms. Responds to mss in 2 months.

Illustration Illustrations only: Query with samples; arrange personal interview to show portfolio; provide résumé and tearsheets for files.

Terms Pays on acceptance. Buys all rights for mss. Pays $100-150 (400 words and up) for stories; $30 for poems; $20 minimum for activities and games. Contributors are encouraged to send for sample copy for $1.50, 9 × 12 envelope and four 41-cent stamps. Free writer's guidelines.

Tips "*The Friend* is published by The Church of Jesus Christ of Latter-day Saints for boys and girls up to eleven years of age. All submissions are carefully read by the *Friend* staff, and those not accepted are returned within two months for SASE. Submit seasonal material at least one year in advance. Query letters and simultaneous submissions are not encouraged. Authors may request rights to have their work reprinted after their manuscript is published."

FUN FOR KIDZ

P.O. Box 227, Bluffton OH 45817-0227. (419)358-4610. Fax: (419)358-5027. Website: www.funforkidz.com. **Articles Editor:** Marilyn Edwards. Bimonthly magazine. Estab. 2002. "Fun for Kidz is a magazine created for boys and girls ages 5-14, with youngsters 8, 9, and 10 the specific target age. The magazine is designed as an activity publication to be enjoyed by both boys and girls on the alternative months of Hopscotch and Boys' Quest magazines."

• *Fun for Kidz* is theme-oriented. Send SASE for theme list and writer's guidelines.

Fiction Picture-oriented material, young readers, middle readers: adventure, animal, history, humorous, problem-solving, multicultural, nature/environment, sports. Average word length: 300-700.

Nonfiction Picture-oriented material, young readers, middle readers: animal, arts/crafts, cooking, games/puzzles, history, hobbies, how-to, humorous, problem-solving, sports, carpentry projects. Average word length: 300-700. Byline given.

Poetry Reviews poetry.

How to Contact Fiction/nonfiction: Send complete ms. Responds to queries in 2 weeks; mss in 5 weeks. Will consider simultaneous submissions. "Will not respond to faxed/e-mailed queries, mss, etc."

Illustration Works on assignment mostly. "We are anxious to find artists capable of illustrating stories and features. Our inside art is pen & ink." Query with samples. Samples kept on file.

Photos "We use a number of back & white photos inside the magazine; most support the articles used."

Terms Pays on publication. Buys first American serial rights. Buys first American serial rights and photos for artwork. Pays 5/word; $10/poem or puzzle; $35 for art (full page); $25 for art (partial page). Pays illustrators $5-10 for b&w photos. Sample copies available for $6 (there is a direct charge by the post office of $4.50 per issue for airmail to other countries); $8 for Canada, and $10.50 for all other countries.

Tips "Our point of view is that every child deserves the right to be a child for a number of years before he or she becomes a young adult. As a result, *Fun for Kidz* looks for activities that deal with timeless topics, such as pets, nature, hobbies, science, games, sports, careers, simple cooking, and anything else likely to interest a child."

GIRLS' LIFE

Monarch, 4529 Harford Rd., Baltimore MD 21214. (410)426-9600. Fax: (410)254-0991. E-mail: katiea@girlslife.com. Website: www.girlslife.com. **Contact:** Katie Abbondanza, associate editor. Bimonthly·magazine for girls, ages 9-15. Estab.1994. Circ. 400,000.

Fiction "We accept short fiction. They should be stand-alone stories and are generally 2,500-3,500 words."

Nonfiction "Features and articles should speak to young women ages 10-15 looking for new ideas about relationships, family, friends, school, etc. with fresh, savvy advice. Front-of-the -book columns and quizzes are a good place to start." Buys 40mss/year. Length: 700-2,000 words. Pays $350/regular column; $500/feature.

How to Contact Accepts queries by mail or e-mail. Query by with published clips. Submit complete mss on spec only. Responds in 3 month to queries.

Photos State availability with submission if applicable. Reviews contact sheets, negatives, transparencies. Negotiates payment individually. Captions, identification of subjects, model releases required.

Terms Pays on publication. Publishes ms an average of 3 months after acceptance Byline given. Buys all rights. Editorial lead time 4 months. Submit seasonal material 5 months in advance. Sample copy for $5 or online. Writer's guidelines online.

Tips "Send thought-out queries with published writing samples and detailed résumé. Have fresh ideas and a voice that speaks to our audience-not down to them. And check out a copy of the magazine or visit girlslife.com before submitting."

☙ GREEN TEACHER

Green Teacher, 95 Robert Street, Toronto ON M2S 2K5.(416)960-1244. Fax: (416)925-3474. E-mail: info@greenteacher.com. Website: www.greenteacher.com. **Article Editor/Photo Editor:** Gail Littlejohn and Tim Grant. Estab. 1991. Circ. 15,000. " Green Teacher is a magazine that helps youth educators enhance environmental and global education inside and outside of schools."

Nonfiction Considers all levels: multicultural, nature/environment. Buys 0 — volunteer mss/year. Average word length: 750-2,500.

How to Contact Nonfiction: Query. Responds to queries in 1 weeks; Publishes ms 8 months after acceptance. Considers electronic submissions via disk or e-mail.

Illustration Buys 3 illustrations/issue from freelancers; 10 illustrations/year from freelancers. Black & white artwork only. Works on assignment only. Reviews ms/illustration packages from artists. Query. **Contact:** Gail Littlejohn, Editor. Illustrations only: Query with samples; tearsheets. Contact: Gail Littlejohn, Editor. Responds only if interested. Samples not returned. Samples filed. Credit line given.

Photos Purchases photos both separately and with accompanying mss. "Activity photos, environmental photos." Uses b&w prints. Query with samples. Responds only of interested.

Terms Pays on acceptance.

GUIDE MAGAZINE

Review and Herald Publishing Association, 55 W. Oak Ridge Dr., Hagerstown MD 21740. (301)393-4037. Fax: (301)393-4055. E-mail: guide@rhpa.org. Website: www.guidemagazine.org. **Editor:** Randy Fishell. **Designer:** Brandon Reese. Weekly magazine. Estab. 1953. Circ. 27,000. "Ours is a weekly Christian journal written for middle readers and young teens (ages 10-14), presenting true stories relevant to the needs of today's young person, emphasizing positive aspects of Christian living."

Nonfiction Middle readers, young adults/teens: adventure, animal, character-building, contemporary, games/puzzles, humorous, multicultural, problem-solving, religious. "We need true, happenings, not merely true-to-life. Our stories and puzzles must have a spiritual emphasis." No violence. No articles. "We always need humor and adventure stories." Buys 150 mss/year. Average word length: 500-600 minimum, 1,200-1,300 maximum. Byline given.

How to Contact Nonfiction: Send complete ms. Responds in 6 weeks. Will consider simultaneous submissions. "We can pay half of the regular amount for reprints." Responds to queries/mss in 6 weeks. Credit line given. "We encourage e-mail submissions."

Terms Pays on acceptance. Buys first world serial rights; first rights; one-time rights; second serial (reprint rights); simultaneous rights. Pays 6-12¢/word for stories and articles. "Writer receives three complimentary copies of issue in which work appears." Sample copy free with 6 × 9 SAE and 2 first-class stamps. Writer's guidelines for SASE.

Tips "Children's magazines want mystery, action, discovery, suspense and humor—no matter what the topic. For us, truth is stronger than fiction."

HIGHLIGHTS FOR CHILDREN

803 Church St., Honesdale PA 18431. (570)253-1080. E-mail: eds@highlights-corp.com. Website: www.Highlights.com. **Contact:** Manuscript Coordinator. **Editor-in-Chief:** Christine French Clark. **Art Director:** Cindy Smith. Monthly magazine. Estab. 1946. Approx. 2 million. "Our motto is 'Fun With a Purpose.' We are looking for quality fiction and nonfiction that appeals to children, encourages them to read, and reinforces positive values. All art is done on assignment."

Fiction Picture-oriented material, young readers, middle readers: adventure, animal, contemporary, fantasy, folktales, history, humorous, multicultural, problem-solving, sports. Multicultural needs include first-person accounts of children from other cultures and first-person accounts of children from other countries. Does not want to see war, crime, violence. "We see too many stories with overt morals." Would like to see more contemporary, multicultural and world culture fiction, mystery stories, action/adventure stories, humorous stories, and fiction for younger readers. Buys 150 mss/year. Average word length: 500-800. Byline given.

Nonfiction Picture-oriented material, young readers, middle readers: animal, arts/crafts, biography, careers, games/puzzles, geography, health, history, hobbies, how-to, interview/profile, multicultural, nature/environment, problem-solving, science, sports. Multicultural needs include articles set in a country *about* the people of the country. Does not want to see trendy topics, fads, personalities who would not be good role models for children, guns, war, crime, violence. "We'd like to see more nonfiction for younger readers—maximum of 500 words. We still need older-reader material, too—500-800 words." Buys 200 mss/year. Maximum word length: 800. Byline given.

How to Contact Send complete ms. Responds to queries in 1 month; mss in 6 weeks.

Illustration Buys 25-30 illustrations/issue. Preferred theme or style: Realistic, some stylization. Works on assignment only. Reviews ms/illustration packages from artists. Illustrations only: photocopies, promo sheet, tearsheets, or slides. Résumé optional. Portfolio only if requested. Contact: Art Director. Responds to art samples in 2 months. Samples returned with SASE; samples filed. Credit line given.

Terms Pays on acceptance. Buys all rights for mss. Pays $50 and up for unsolicited articles. Pays illustrators $700 for color front cover; $25-200 for b&w inside, $100-500 for color inside. Sample copies $3.95 and send SASE with 4 first-class stamps. Writer's/illustrator's guidelines free with SASE and on website.

Tips "Know the magazine's style before submitting. Send for guidelines and sample issue if necessary." Writers: "At *Highlights* we're paying closer attention to acquiring more nonfiction for young readers than we have in the past. Illustrators: "Fresh, imaginative work encouraged. Flexibility in working relationships a plus. Illustrators presenting their work need not confine themselves to just children's illustrations as long as work can translate to our needs. We also use animal illustrations, real and imaginary. We need crafts, puzzles and any activity that will stimulate children mentally and creatively. We are always looking for imaginative cover subjects. Know our publication's standards and content by reading sample issues, not just the guidelines. Avoid tired themes, or put a fresh twist on an old theme so that its style is fun and lively. We'd like to see stories with subtle messages, but the fun of the story should come first. Write what inspires you, not what you think the market needs."

[N] HIGHLIGHTS HIGH FIVE

803 Church St., Honesdale PA 18431. Fax: (570)251-7847. Website: http://www.highlights.com/high-five-magazine-for-kids. **Contact:** Linda Rose, assistant editor; Christine French Clark, editor. "Highlights High Five was created to help you encourage your young child's development—and have fun together at the same time. Based on sound educational principles and widely accepted child-development theories, each monthly issue brings a 40-page, high-quality mix of read-aloud stories and age appropriate puzzles and activities that will help you set your child firmly on the path to becoming a lifelong learner." "Stories for younger readers (ages three to seven) should have 500 words or fewer and should not seem babyish to older readers." Guidelines available at website online.

Fiction "Puzzles that lend themselves to strong visuals are a big plus."

Tips "Writers may also find it helpful to search the magazine index or peruse the Fun Finder at www.HighlightsKids.com."

HOPSCOTCH

The Magazine for Girls P.O. Box 164, Bluffton OH 45817-0164. (419)358-4610. Fax: (419)358-5027. Website: hopscotchmagazine.com. **Editor:** Marilyn Edwards. Bimonthly magazine. Estab. 1989. Circ. 14,000. For girls from ages 5- 14, featuring traditional subjects—pets, games, hobbies, nature, science, sports, etc.—with an emphasis on articles that show girls actively involved in unusual and/or worthwhile activities."

Fiction Picture-oriented material, young readers, middle readers: adventure, animal, history, humorous, nature/environment, sports, suspense/mystery. Does not want to see stories dealing with dating, sex, fashion, hard rock music. Buys 30 mss/year. Average word length: 300-700. Byline given.

Nonfiction Picture-oriented material, young readers, middle readers: animal, arts/crafts, biography, cooking, games/puzzles, geography, hobbies, how-to, humorous, math, nature/environment, science. Does not want to see pieces dealing with dating, sex, fashion, hard rock music. "Need more nonfiction with quality photos about a *Hopscotch*-age girl involved in a worthwhile activity." Buys 46 mss/year. Average word length: 400-700. Byline given.

Poetry Reviews traditional, wholesome, humorous poems. Maximum word length: 300; maximum line length: 20. Will accept 6 submissions/author.

How to Contact All writers should consult the theme list before sending in articles. To receive a current theme list, send a SASE. Fiction: Send complete ms. Nonfiction: Query or send complete ms. Responds to queries in 2 weeks; mss in 5 weeks. Will consider simultaneous submissions.

Illustration Buys approximately 10 illustrations/issue; buys 60-70 articles/year. "Generally, the illustrations are assigned after we have purchased a piece (usually fiction). Occasionally, we will use a painting—in any given medium—for the cover, and these are usually seasonal." Uses b&w artwork only for inside; color for cover. Reviews ms/illustration packages from artists. Query first or send complete ms with final art. Illustrations only: Send résumé, portfolio, client list and tearsheets. Responds to art samples only if interested and SASE in 1 month. Samples returned with SASE. Credit line given.

Photos Purchases photos separately (cover only) and with accompanying ms only. Looking for photos to accompany article. Model/property releases required. Uses 5 × 7, b&w prints; 35mm transparencies. Black & white photos should go with ms. Should show girl or girls ages 6-12.

Terms For mss: pays on publication. For mss, artwork and photos, buys first North American serial rights; second serial (reprint rights). Original artwork returned at job's completion. Pays 5¢/word and $5-10/photo. "We always send a copy of the issue to the writer or illustrator." Text and art are treated separately. Pays $200 maximum for color cover; $25-35 for b&w inside. Sample copy for $6 (there is a direct charge by the post office of $4.50 per issue for airmail to other countries) and 8 × 12 SASE; $8 for Canada, and $10.50 for all other countries. Writer's/illustrator's/photo guidelines, theme list free for #10 SASE.

Tips "Remember we publish only six issues a year, which means our editorial needs are extremely limited. Please look at our guidelines and our magazine.. and remember, we use far more nonfiction than fiction. Guidelines and current theme list can be downloaded from our website. If decent photos accompany the piece, it stands an even better chance of being accepted. We believe it is the responsibility of the contributor to come up with photos. Please remember, our readers are 6-12 years—most are 8-10—and your text should reflect that. Many magazines try to entertain first and educate second. We try to do the reverse. Our magazine is more simplistic, like a book to be read from cover to cover. We are looking for wholesome, non-dated material."

⚡ HORSEPOWER

Horse Publications Group, P.O. Box 670, Aurora ON L4G 4J9, Canada. 800)505-7428. Fax: (905)841-1530. E-mail: info@horse-canada.com. Bimonthly 16-page magazine, bound into *Horse Canada*, a bimonthly family horse magazine. Estab. 1988. Circ. 17,000. "Horsepower offers how-to articles and stories relating to horse care for kids ages 6-16, with a focus on safety." Website: www.horse-canada.com. **Contact:** Susan Stafford.

• *Horsepower* no longer accepts fiction.

Nonfiction Middle readers, young adults: arts/crafts, biography, careers, fashion, games/puzzles, health, history, hobbies, how-to, humorous, interview/profile, problem-solving, travel. Buys 6-10 mss/year. Average word length: 500-1,200. Byline given.

How to Contact Fiction: query. Nonfiction: send complete ms. Responds to queries in 6 months; mss in 3 months. Publishes ms 6 months after acceptance. Will consider simultaneous submissions, electronic submission via disk or e-mail, previously published work.

Illustration Buys 3 illustrations/year. Reviews ms/illustration packages from artists. Contact: Editor. Query with samples. Responds only if interested. Samples returned with SASE; samples kept on file. Credit line given.

Photos Look for photos of kids and horses, instructional/educational, relating to riding or horse care. Uses color matte or glossy prints. Query with samples. Responds only if interested. Accepts TIFF or JPEG 300 dpi, disk or e-mail. Children on horseback must be wearing riding helmets or photos cannot be published.

Terms Pays on publication. Buys one-time rights for mss. Original artwork returned at job's completion if SASE provided. Pays $50-75 for stories. Additional payment for ms/illustration packages and for photos accompanying articles. Pays illustrators $25-50 for color inside. Pays photographers per photo (range: $15). Sample copies for $4.50. Writer's/illustrator's/photo guidelines for SASE.

Tips "Articles must be easy to understand, yet detailed and accurate. How-to or other educational features must be written by, or in conjunction with, a riding/teaching professional. Fiction is not encouraged, unless it is outstanding and teaches a moral or practical lesson. Note: preference will be given to Canadian writers and photographers due to Canadian content laws. Non-Canadian contributors accepted on a very limited basis."

HUMPTY DUMPTY'S MAGAZINE

Children's Better Health Institute, 1100 Waterway Blvd., Indianapolis IN 46206. (317)636-8881. Fax: (317)684-8094. Website: www.humptydumptymag.org. **Editor/Art Director:** Phyllis Lybarger. Magazine published 6 times/year. HDM is edited for children ages 4-6. It includes fiction (easy-to-reads; read alouds; rhyming stories; rebus stories), nonfiction articles (some with photo illustrations), poems, crafts, recipes, and puzzles. Content encourages development of better health habits.

- *Humpty Dumpty's* publishes material promoting health and fitness with emphasis on simple activities, poems and fiction.

Fiction Picture-oriented stories: adventure, animal, contemporary, fantasy, folktales, health, humorous, multicultural, nature/environment, problem-solving, science fiction, sports. Also, talking inanimate objects are very difficult to do well. Beginners (and maybe everyone) should avoid these." Buys 8-10 mss/year. Maximum word length: 300. Byline given.

Nonfiction Picture-oriented articles: animal, arts/crafts, concept, games/puzzles, health, how-to, humorous, nature/environment, no-cook recipes, science, social issues, sports. Buys 6-10 mss/year. Prefers very short nonfiction pieces—200 words maximum. Byline given. Send ms with SASE if you want ms returned.

How to Contact Send complete ms. Nonfiction: Send complete ms with bibliography if applicable. "No queries, please!" Responds to mss in 3 months. Send seasonal material at least 8 months in advance.

Illustration Buys 5-8 illustrations/issue; 30-48 illustrations/year. Preferred theme or style: Realistic or cartoon. Works on assignment only. Illustrations only. Query with slides, printed pieces or photocopies. Samples are not returned; samples filed. Responds to art samples only if interested. Credit line given.

Terms Writers: Pays on publication. Artists: Pays within 2 months. Buys all rights. "One-time book rights may be returned if author can provide name of interested book publisher and tentative date of publication." Pays up to 22¢/word for stories/articles; payment varies for poems and activities. 10 complimentary issues are provided to author with check. Pays $275 for color cover illustration; $35-90 per page b&w inside; $70-155 for color inside. Sample copies for $3.95. Writer's/illustrator's guidelines free with SASE.

IMAGINATION CAFÉ

Imagination Cafe, P.O. Box 1536, Valparaiso IN 46384.(219)510-4467. E-mail: editor@imagination-cafe.com. Website: www.imagination-cafe.com. **Articles Editor:** Rosanne Tolin. **Art Director:** Photo Editor. Estab. 2006. "Imagination Café is dedicated to empowering kids and tweens by encouraging curiosity in the world around them, as well as exploration of their talents and aspirations. Imagination Café's mission is to offer children tools to discover their passions by providing them with reliable information, resources and safe opportunities for self-expression. Imagination Café publishes general interest articles with an emphasis on career exploration for kids. There is also material on school, science, history, and sports. Plus, celebrity briefs, recipes, animals, and other general interest pieces." Publication is aimed at juvenile market.

Nonfiction Buys 72 mss/year. Average word length: 150-500. Byline given.

How to Contact Agented submissions only. Nonfiction: Query or query with published clips. Send complete ms. Responds to queries in 1 day to 2 weeks. Publishes ms 1 month after acceptance. Considers simultaneous submissions.

Terms Pays on acceptance. Buys electronic and non-exclusive print rights. Originals not returned. Pays 15-75 for stories. Additional payment for ms/illustration packages.

Tips "Imagination Café is not a beginner's market. Most of our contributors are published writers. Please study the web site before submitting, and make sure your writing is clearly directed to a kid audience, no adults. That means informative, interesting text written in a clear, concise, even clever manner that suitable for the online reader. Have fun with it and be sure include web-friendly, relevant links and sidebars."

JACK AND JILL

Children's Better Health Institute, 1100 Waterway Blvd., P.O. Box 567, Indianapolis IN 46202. (317)634-1100. Fax: (317)684-8094. Website: www.cbhi.org/magazines/jackandjill/index.shtml. **Editor:** Daniel Lee. **Art Director:** Jennifer Webber. Magazine for children ages 7-10, published 6 times/year. Estab. 1938. Circ. 360,000. "Write entertaining and imaginative stories for kids, not just about them. Writers should understand what is funny to kids, what's important to them, what excites them. Don't write from an adult 'kids are so cute' perspective. We're also looking for health and healthful lifestyle stories and articles, but don't be preachy."

Fiction Young readers and middle readers: adventure, contemporary, folktales, health, history, humorous, nature, sports. Buys 30-35 mss/year. Average word length: 700. Byline given.

Nonfiction Young readers, middle readers: animal, arts/crafts, cooking, games/puzzles, history, hobbies, how-to, humorous, interview/profile, nature, science, sports. Buys 8-10 mss/year. Average word length: 500. Byline given.

Poetry Reviews poetry.

How to Contact Fiction/nonfiction: Send complete ms. Queries not accepted. Responds to mss in 3 months. Guidelines by request with a #10 SASE.

Illustration Buys 15 illustrations/issue; 90 illustrations/year. Responds only if interested. Samples not returned; samples filed. Credit line given.

Terms Pays on publication; up to 17¢/word. Pays illustrators $275 for color cover; $35-90 for b&w, $70-155 for color inside. Pays photographers negotiated rate. Sample copies $1.25. Buys all rights to mss and one-time rights to photos.

Tips Publishes writing/art/photos by children.

KEYS FOR KIDS

CBH Ministries, Box 1001, Grand Rapids MI 49501-1001. (616)647-4971. Fax: (616)647-4950. E-mail: hazel@cbhministries.org. Website: www.cbhministries.org. **Fiction Editor:** Hazel Marett. Bimonthly devotional booklet. Estab. 1982. "This is a devotional booklet for children and is also widely used for family devotions."

Fiction Young readers, middle readers: religious. Buys 60 mss/year. Average word length: 400.

How to Contact Fiction: Send complete ms. Will consider simultaneous submissions,

Terms Pays on acceptance. Buys reprint rights or first rights for mss. Pays $25 for stories. Sample copies free for SAE 6 × 9 and 3 first-class stamps. Writer's guidelines for SASE.

Tips "Be sure to *follow* guidelines after studying sample copy of the publication."

THE KIDS HALL OF FAME NEWS

The Kids Hall of Fame, 3 Ibsen Court, Dix Hills NY 11746. (631)242-9105. Fax: (631)242-8101. E-mail: VictoriaNesnick@TheKidsHallofFame.com. Website: www.TheKidsHallofFame.com. **Publisher:** Dr. Victoria Nesnick. **Art/Photo Editor:** Amy Gilvary. Online publication. Estab. 1998. "We spotlight and archive extraordinary positive achievements of contemporary and historical kids internationally under age 20. These inspirational stories are intended to provide positive peer role models and empower others to say, 'If that kid can do it, so can I,' or 'I can do better.' Our magazine is the prelude to The Kids Hall of Fame set of books (one volume per age) and museum."

How to Contact Query with published clips or send complete mss with SASE for response. Go to website for sample stories and for The Kids Hall of Fame nomination form.

Tips "Nomination stories must be positive and inspirational, and whenever possible, address the 7 items listed in the 'Your Story and Photo' page of our website. Request writers' guidelines and list of suggested nominees. Day and evening telephone queries acceptable."

KIDZ CHAT

8805 Governor's Hill Drive, Suite 400, Cincinnati OH 45249. 513-931-4050. Fax: 1-877-867-5751. E-mail: mredford@standardpub.com. Standard Publishing. Website: www.standardpub.com. **Editor:** Marjorie Redford. Weekly magazine. Circ. 55,000. Website: www.standardpub.com.
- *Kidz Chat* has decided to reuse much of the material that was a part of the first publication cycle. They will not be sending out theme lists, sample copies or writers guidelines or accepting any unsolicited material because of this policy.

KID ZONE

WordAction Publishing Co.2923 Troost Ave., Kansas City MO 64109. (816)931-1900. Fax: (816)412-8306. E-mail: lslohberger@wordaction.com. **Editor:** Virginia L. Folsom. **Senior Editor:** Melissa Hammer. **Assistant Editor:** Laura Lohberger. Take-home paper. "Kid Zone is a leisure-reading piece for third- and fourth-graders. It is published weekly by WordAction Publishing. The major purpose of the magazine is to provide a leisure-reading piece which will build Christian behavior and values and provide reinforcement for Biblical concepts taught in the Sunday School curriculum. The focus of the reinforcement will be life-related, with some historical appreciation. Kid Zone's target audience is children ages eight to ten in grades three and four. The readability goal is third to fourth grade." Request guidelines and theme list by e-mail or send SASE.

LADYBUG

The Magazine for Young Children 70 E. Lake St., Suite 300, Chicago IL 60601. (312)701-1720. **Editor:** Alice Letvin. **Art Director:** Suzanne Beck. Monthly magazine. Estab. 1990. Circ. 130,000. Literary magazine for children 3-6, with stories, poems, activities, songs and picture stories.
Fiction Picture-oriented material: adventure, animal, fantasy, folktales, humorous, multicultural, nature/environment, problem-solving, science fiction, sports, suspense/mystery. "Open to any easy fiction stories." Buys 50 mss/year. Story length: limit 800 words. Byline given.
Nonfiction Picture-oriented material: activities, animal, arts/crafts, concept, cooking, humorous, math, nature/environment, problem-solving, science. Buys 35 mss/year. Story length: limit 800 words.
Poetry Reviews poems, 20-line maximum length; limit submissions to 5 poems. Uses lyrical, humorous, simple language, action rhymes.
How to Contact Fiction/nonfiction: Send complete ms. Queries not accepted. Responds to mss in 6 months. Publishes ms up to 3 years after acceptance. Will consider simultaneous submissions if informed. Submissions without SASE will be discarded.
Illustration Buys 12 illustrations/issue; 145 illustrations/year. Prefers "bright colors; all media, but use watercolor and acrylics most often; same size as magazine is preferred but not required." To be considered for future assignments: Submit promo sheet, slides, tearsheets, color and b&w photocopies. Responds to art samples in 3 months. Submissions without SASE will be discarded.
Terms Pays on publication for mss; after delivery of completed assignment for illustrators. Rights purchased vary. Original artwork returned at job's completion. Pays 25¢/word for prose; $3/line for poetry. Pays $750 for color (cover) illustration, $50-100 for b&w (inside) illustration, $250/page for color (inside). Sample copy for $5. Writer's/illustrator's guidelines free for SASE or available on website, FAQ at www.cricketmag.com.
Tips Writers: "Get to know several young children on an individual basis. Respect your audience. We want less cute, condescending or 'preachy-teachy' material. Less gratuitous anthropomorphism.

More rich, evocative language, sense of joy or wonder. Keep in mind that people come in all colors, sizes, physical conditions. Be inclusive in creating characters. Set your manuscript aside for at least a month, then reread critically." Illustrators: "Include examples, where possible, of children, animals, and—most important—action and narrative (i.e., several scenes from a story, showing continuity and an ability to maintain interest)." (See listings for *Babybug*, *Cicada*, *Cricket*, *Muse* and *Spider*.)

LEADING EDGE

4087 JKB, Provo UT 84602. E-mail: fiction@leadingedgemagazine.com; poetry@ leadingedgemagazine.com. Twice yearly magazine. "We strive to encourage developing and established talent and provide high quality speculative fiction to our readers." Does not accept mss with sex, excessive violence, or profanity. Website: www.leadingedgemagazine.com.

Fiction Young adults: fantasy, science fiction. Buys 16 mss/year. Average word length: up to 15,000. Byline given.

How to Contact Fiction: Send complete ms c/o Fiction Director. Responds to queries/mss in 4 months. Publishes ms 2-6 months after acceptance.

Illustration Buys 24 illustrations/issue; 48 illustrations/year. Uses b&w artwork only. Works on assignment only. Contact: Art Director. Illustrations only: Send postcard sample with portfolio, samples, URL. Responds only if interested. Samples filed. Credit line given.

Terms Pays on publication. Buys first North American serial rights for mss. Buys first North American serial rights for artwork. Original artwork returned at job's completion. Pays $0.01/word for stories. Pays illustrators $50 for color cover, $30 for b&w inside. Sample copies for $5.95. Writer's/illustrator's guidelines for SASE or visit the web site.

LISTEN

Drug-Free Possibilities for Teens, 55 West Oak Ridge Dr., Hagerstown MD 21740. (301)393-4019. Fax: (301)393-3294. E-mail: listen@healthconnection.org. **Editor:** Céleste Perrino-Walker. Monthly magazine, 9 issues. Estab. 1948. Circ. 12,000. "Listen offers positive alternatives to drug use for its teenage readers. Helps them have a happy and productive life by making the right choices."

Nonfiction How-to, health, humorous, life skills, problem-solving, social issues, drug facts, drug-free living. Wants to see more factual articles on drug abuse. Buys 50 mss/year. Average word length: 500. Byline given.

How to Contact Fiction/nonfiction: Query. Considers manuscripts once a year, in October. Will consider simultaneous submissions, e-mail and previously published work.

Illustration Buys 3-6 illustrations/issue; 50 illustrators/year. Reviews ms/illustration packages from artists. Manuscript/illustration packages and illustration only: Query. Contact: Bill Kirstein bkirstein@rhpa.org, designer. Responds only if interested. Originals returned at job's completion. Samples returned with SASE. Credit line given.

Photos Purchases photos from freelancers. Photos purchased with accompanying ms only. Uses color and b&w photos; digital, 35mm, transparencies or prints. Query with samples. Looks for "youth oriented—action (sports, outdoors), personality photos."

Terms Pays on acceptance. Buys exclusive magazine rights for mss. Buys one-time rights for artwork and photographs. Pays $80-200 for articles. Pays illustrators $500 for color cover; $75-225 for b&w inside; $135-450 for color inside. Pays photographers by the project (range: $125-500); pays per photo (range: $125-500). Additional payment forms/illustration packages and photos accompanying articles. Sample copy for $2 and 9 × 12 SASE and 2 first class stamps. Writer's guidelines free with SASE

Tips "*Listen* is a magazine for teenagers. It encourages development of good habits and high ideals of physical, social and mental health. It bases its editorial philosophy of primary drug prevention on total abstinence from tobacco, alcohol, and other drugs. Because it is used extensively in public high school classes, it does not accept articles and stories with overt religious emphasis. Four specific purposes guide the editors in selecting materials for *Listen*: (1) To portray a positive lifestyle and to foster skills and values that will help teenagers deal with contemporary problems, including smoking, drinking, and using drugs. This is *Listen*'s primary purpose. (2) To offer positive alternatives to a lifestyle of drug use of any kind. (3) To present scientifically accurate information about the nature and effects of tobacco, alcohol, and other drugs. (4) To report medical research, community programs, and educational efforts which are solving problems connected with smoking, alcohol, and other drugs. Articles should offer their readers activities that increase one's sense of self-worth through achievement and/or involvement in helping others. They are often categorized by three kinds of focus: (1) Hobbies. (2) Recreation. (3) Community Service."

LIVE WIRE

8805 Governor's Hill Drive, Suite 400, Cincinnati OH 45249. (513)931-4050. Fax: (877)867-5751. E-mail: mredford@standardpub.com. Standard Publishing. E-mail: Website: www.standardpub. com. **Editor:** Marjorie Redford. Published quarterly in weekly parts. Circ. 40,000.

- *Live Wire* has decided to reuse much of the material that was a part of the first publication cycle. They will not be sending out theme lists, sample copies, or writers guidelines or accepting any unsolicited material because of this policy.

MUSE

Carus Publishing, 70 E Lake St., Suite 300, Chicago IL 60601. (312)701-1720. Fax: (312)701-1728. E-mail: muse@caruspub.com. Website: www.cricketmag.com. **Editor:** Elizabeth Preston. **Art Director:** John Sandford. **Photo Editor:** Carol Parden. Estab. 1996. Circ. 40,000. "The goal of Muse is to give as many children as possible access to the most important ideas and concepts underlying the principal areas of human knowledge. Articles should meet the highest possible standards of clarity and transparency aided, wherever possible, by a tone of skepticism, humor, and irreverence."

Nonfiction Middle readers, young adult: animal, arts, history, math, nature/environment, problem-solving, science, social issues.

How to Contact *Muse* is not accepting unsolicited mss or queries. All articles are commissioned. To be considered for assignments, experienced science writers may send a résumé and 3 published clips.

Illustration Works on assignment only. Credit line given. Send prints or tearsheets, but please, no portfolios or original art, and above all, DO NOT SEND SAMPLES THAT NEED TO BE RETURNED.

Photos Needs vary. Query with samples to photo editor.

NATIONAL GEOGRAPHIC KIDS

National Geographic Society, 1145 17th St. NW, Washington DC 20036-4688. (202)857-7000. Fax: (202)775-6112. Website: www.nationalgeographic.com/ngkids. **Editor:** Melina Gerosa Bellows. **Art Director:** Jonathan Halling. **Photo Director:** Jay Sumner. Monthly magazine. Estab. 1975. Circ. 1.3 million.

NATURE FRIEND MAGAZINE

4253 Woodcock Lane, Dayton VA 22821 (540)867-0764. Fax: (540)867-9516. Website: www. naturefriendmagazine.com. **Articles Editor:** Kevin Shank. Monthly magazine. Estab. 1983. Circ. 10,000.

Fiction Picture-oriented material, conversational, no talking animal stories.

Nonfiction Picture-oriented material: animal, how-to, nature, photo-essays. No talking animal stories. No evolutionary material. Buys 50 mss/year. Average word length: 500. Byline given.

Photos Submit on CD with a color printout. Photo guidelines free with SASE.

Terms Pays on publication. Buy one-time rights. Pays $75 for front cover photo; $50 for back cover photo, $25 inside photo. Offers sample copy is and writer's/photographer's guidelines for $10. Pays .05¢ per edited word.

Tips Needs stories about unique animals or nature phenomena. "Please examine samples and writer's guide before submitting." The best way to learn what we use is to be a subscriber.

NEW MOON

The Magazine for Girls & Their Dreams New Moon Girl Media, LLC.2 W. First St.#101, Duluth MN 55802. (218)728-5507. Fax: (218)728-0314. E-mail: girl@newmoongirlmedia.com. Website: www. newmoongirls.com. **Managing Editor:** Heather Parfitt. Bimonthly magazine. Estab. 1992. Circ. 30,000. "New Moon Girls is for every girl who wants her voice heard and her dreams taken seriously. New Moon Girls portrays strong female role models of all ages, backgrounds and cultures now and in the past.": The Magazine for Girls & Their Dreams New Moon Girl Media, LLC.2 W. First St.#101, Duluth MN 55802. (218)728-5507. Fax: (218)728-0314. E-mail: girl@newmoongirlmedia.com. Website: www.newmoongirls.com. **Managing Editor:** Heather Parfitt. Bimonthly magazine. Estab. 1992. Circ. 30,000. "New Moon Girls is for every girl who wants her voice heard and her dreams taken seriously. New Moon Girls portrays strong female role models of all ages, backgrounds and cultures now and in the past."

Fiction Middle readers, young adults: adventure, contemporary, fantasy, folktales, history, humorous, multicultural, nature/environment, problem-solving, religious, science fiction, sports, suspense/mystery, travel. Buys 6 mss/year. Average word length: 1,200-1,600. Byline given.

Nonfiction Middle readers, young adults: animal, arts/crafts, biography, careers, cooking, games/puzzles, health, history, hobbies, humorous, interview/profile, math, multicultural, nature/environment, problem-solving, science, social issues, sports, travel, stories about real girls. Does not want to see how-to stories. Wants more stories about real girls doing real things written *by girls*. Buys 6-12 adult-written mss/year; 30 girl-written mss/year. Average word length: 600. Byline given.

How to Contact Fiction/Nonfiction: Does not return or acknowledge unsolicited mss. Send copies only. Responds only if interested. Will consider simultaneous and e-mail submissions.

Illustration Buys 6-12 illustrations/year from freelancers. *New Moon Girls* seeks 4-color cover illustrations. Reviews ms/illustrations packages from artists. Query. Submit ms with rough sketches. Illustration only: Query; send portfolio and tearsheets. Samples not returned; samples filed. Responds in 6 months only if interested. Credit line given.

Terms Pays on publication. Buys all rights for mss. Buys one-time rights, reprint rights, for artwork. Original artwork returned at job's completion. Pays 6-12 ¢/word for stories and articles. Pays in contributor's copies. Pays illustrators $400 for color cover; $50-300 for color inside. Sample copies for $7. Writer's/cover art guidelines for SASE or available on website.

Tips "Please refer to a copy of *New Moon Girls* to understand the style and philosophy of the magazine, or visit us online at www.NewMoonGirls.com. Writers and artists who understand our goals have the best chance of publication. We're looking for stories about real girls, women's careers, and historical profiles. We publish girl's and women's writing only." Publishes writing/art/photos by girls.

NICK JR. FAMILY MAGAZINE

Nickelodeon Magazine Group, 1515 Broadway, 37th Floor, New York NY 10036. (212)846-4985. Fax: (212)846-1690. Website: www.nickjr.com/magazine. **Deputy Editor:** Wendy Smolen. **Creative Director:** Don Morris. Published 9 times/year. Estab. 1999. Circ. 1,100,000. A magazine where kids play to learn and parents learn to play. 30% of publication aimed at juvenile market.

Fiction Picture-oriented material: adventure, animal, contemporary, humorous, multicultural, nature/environment, problem-solving, sports. Byline sometimes given.

Nonfiction Picture-oriented material: animal, arts/crafts, concept, cooking, games/puzzles, hobbies, how-to, humorous, math, multicultural, nature/environment, problem-solving, science, social issues, sports. Byline sometimes given.

How to Contact Fiction/nonfiction: Query or submit complete ms. Responds to queries/mss in 3-12 weeks.

Illustration Only interested in agented material. Works on assignment only. Reviews ms/illustration packages from artists. Query or send ms with dummy. Contact: Don Morris, creative director. Illustrations only: arrange portfolio review; send résumé, promo sheet and portfolio. Responds only if interested. Samples not returned; samples kept on file. Credit line sometimes given.

Tips "Writers should study the magazine before submitting stories. Read-Together Stories must include an interactive element that invited children to participate in telling the story: a repeating line, a fill-in-the-blank rhyme, or rebus pictures."

ODYSSEY

Adventures in Science, 30 Grove St., Suite C, Peterborough NH 03458. (603)924-7209. Fax: (603)924-7380. E-mail: odyssey@caruspub.com. Website: www.odysseymagazine.com. **Editor:** Elizabeth E. Lindstrom. **Executive Director:** Lou Waryncia. **Art Director:** Ann Dillon. Magazine published 9 times/year. Estab. 1979. Circ. 22,000. Magazine covers general science and technology for children ages 10-16. All material must relate to the theme of a specific upcoming issue in order to be considered.

• *Odyssey* themes can be found on website.

Fiction Middle readers and young adults/teens: science fiction, science, astronomy. Does not want to see anything not theme-related. Average word length: 900-1,200 words.

Nonfiction Middle readers and young adults/teens: interiors, activities. Don't send anything not theme-related. Average word length: 750-1,200, depending on section article is used in.

How to Contact Query by mail. "A query must consist of all of the following to be considered (please use nonerasable paper): a brief cover letter stating the subject and word length of the proposed article; a detailed one-page outline explaining the information to be presented in the article; an extensive bibliography of materials/interviews the author intends to use in preparing the article; a SASE. Writers new to *Odyssey* should send a writing sample with query. If you would like to know if your query has been received, please also include a stamped postcard that requests acknowledgment of receipt. In all correspondence, please include your complete address as well as a telephone number and e-mail address where you can be reached. A writer may send as many queries for one issue as he or she wishes, but each query must have a separate cover letter, outline, bibliography, and SASE. Telephone queries are not accepted. Handwritten queries will not be considered. Queries may be submitted at any time."

Illustration Buys 4 illustrations/issue; 36 illustrations/year. Works on assignment only. Reviews ms/illustration packages from artists. Query. Contact: Beth Lindstrom, editor. Illustration only: Query with samples. Send tearsheets, photocopies. Responds in 2 weeks. Samples returned with SASE; samples not filed. Original artwork returned upon job's completion (upon written request).

Photos Wants photos pertaining to any of our forthcoming themes. Uses color prints; 35mm transparencies, digital images. Photographers should send unsolicited photos by mail on speculation.

Terms Pays on publication. Buys all rights for mss and artwork. Pays 20-25¢/word for stories/articles. Covers are assigned and paid on an individual basis. Pays photographers per photo ($15-100 for b $25-100 for color). Sample copy for $4.95 and SASE with $2 postage. Writer's/illustrator's/photo guidelines for SASE.

ON COURSE

A Magazine for Teens, 1445 Boonville Ave., Springfield MO 65802-1894. (417)862-2781. Fax: (417)862-1693. E-mail: oncourse@ag.org. Website: www.oncourse.ag.org. **Editor:** Amber Weigand-Buckley. **Art Director:** Ryan Strong. Bi- annual magazine. Estab. 1991. Circ. 160,000. On Course is a magazine to empower students to grow in a real-life relationship with Christ.

• *On Course* no longer uses illustrations, only photos.

Fiction Young adults: Christian discipleship, contemporary, humorous, multicultural, problem-solving, sports. Average word length: 800. Byline given.

Nonfiction Young adults: careers, interview/profile, multicultural, religion, social issues, college life, Christian discipleship.

How to Contact Works on assignment basis only. Resumes and writing samples will be considered for inclusion in Writer's File to receive story assignments.

Photos Buys photos from freelancers. "Teen life, church life, college life; unposed; often used for illustrative purposes." Model/property releases required. Uses color glossy prints and 35mm or 2¼ × 2¼ transparencies. Query with samples; send business card, promotional literature, tearsheets or catalog. Responds only if interested.

Terms Pays on acceptance. Buys first or reprint rights for mss. Buys one-time rights for photographs. Pays $30 per assigned stories/articles. Pays illustrators and photographers "as negotiated." Sample copies free for 9 × 11 SA SE. Writer's guidelines for SASE.

N PASSPORT

2923 Troost Ave., Kansas City MO 64109. (816)931-1900. Fax: (816)412-8343. **Editor:** Ryan R. Pettit. Weekly take-home paper. "Passport looks for a casual, witty approach to Christian themes. We want hot topics relevant to preteens. We are not accepting stories."

POCKETS

Devotional Magazine for Children, 1908 Grand Ave., P.O. Box 340004, Nashville TN 37203-0004. (615)340-7333. Fax: (615)340-7267. E-mail: pockets@upperroom.org. Website: www.pockets.org. **Articles/Fiction Editor:** Lynn W. Gilliam. **Art Director:** Chris Schechner, 408 Inglewood Dr., Richardson TX 75080. Magazine published 11 times/year. Estab. 1981. "Pockets is a Christian devotional magazine for children ages 6-11. Stories should help children experience a Christian lifestyle that is not always a neatly wrapped moral package but is open to the continuing revelation of God's will."

Fiction Picture-oriented, young readers, middle readers: adventure, contemporary, occasional folktales, multicultural, nature/environment, problem-solving, religious. Does not accept violence or talking animal stories. Buys 25-30 mss/year. Average word length: 600-1,400. Byline given. *Pockets* also accepts short-short stories (no more than 600 words) for children 5-7. Buys 11 mss/year.

Nonfiction Picture-oriented, young readers, middle readers: cooking, games/puzzles. "*Pockets* seeks biographical sketches of persons, famous or unknown, whose lives reflect their Christian commitment, written in a way that appeals to children." Does not accept how-to articles. "Nonfiction reads like a story." Multicultural needs include: stories that feature children of various racial/ethnic groups and do so in a way that is true to those depicted. Buys 10 mss/year. Average word length: 400-1,000. Byline given.

How to Contact Fiction/nonfiction: Send complete ms. "We do not accept queries." Responds to mss in 6 weeks. Will consider simultaneous submissions.

Illustration Buys 25-35 illustrations/issue. Preferred theme or style: varied; both 4-color. Works on assignment only. Illustrations only: Send promo sheet, tearsheets.

RAINBOW RUMPUS

The Magazine for Kids with LGBT Parents, P.O. Box 6881, Minneapolis MN 55406. (612)721-6442. E-mail: fictionandpoetry@rainbowrumpus.org. Website: www.rainbowrumpus.org. **Article Editors:** Deb Carver, Al Onkka, Aja McCullough. **Fiction Editor:** Beth Wallace. **Art/photo Acquisitions:** Beth Wallace. Monthly online magazine. Estab. 2005. Circ. 250 visits/day. "Rainbow Rumpus is an online magazine for 4- to 18-year-olds who have lesbian, gay, bisexual or transgender (LGBT) parents. The magazine has three sections: one for children, one for grownups. We are looking for children's fiction, young adult fiction, and poetry. Rainbow Rumpus publishes and reviews work that is written from the point of view of youth who have LGBT parents or connections with the LGBT community, celebrates the diversity of LGBT-headed families, and is of high quality." 75% of publication aimed at young readers.

Fiction All levels: adventure, animal, contemporary, fantasy, folktales, history, humorous, multicultural, nature/environment, problem solving, science fiction, sports, suspense/mystery. Buys 24 mss/year. Average word length: 800-5,000. Byline given.

Nonfiction All levels: interview/profile, social issues. Average word length: 800-5,000. Byline given.

Poetry Maximum of 5 poems per submission.

How to Contact Send complete ms via email to fictionandpoetry@rainbowrumpus.org with the word "Submission" in the subject line. Responds to mss in 6 weeks. Considers electronic submission and previously published work.

Illustration Buys 1 illustration/issue. Uses both b&w and color artwork. Reviews ms/illustration packages from artists: Query. Illustrations only: query with samples. Contact: Beth Wallace, Editor in Chief. Samples not returned; samples filed depending on the level of interest. Credit line given.

Terms Pays on publication. Buys first rights for mss; may request print anthology and audio or recording rights. Buys first rights rights for artwork. Pays $75 per story. Pays illustrators $100 for $300 for color. Writer's guidelines available on website.

Tips If you wish to submit nonfiction, please query by e-mail to editorinchief@rainbowrumpus.org. Emerging writers encouraged to submit. You do not need to be a member of the LGBT community to participate.

RANGER RICK

National Wildlife Federation, 11100 Wildlife Center Dr., Reston VA 20190. (703)438-6000. Website: www.nwf.org/rangerrick. **Editor:** Mary Dalheim. **Design Director:** Donna Miller. Monthly magazine. Circ. 550,000. "NWF's mission is to inspire Americans to protect wildlife for our children's future."

• Ranger Rick does not accept submissions or queries.

Fiction Middle readers: animal (wildlife), fables, fantasy, humorous, multicultural, plays, science fiction. Average word length: 900. Byline given.

Nonfiction Middle readers: animal (wildlife), conservation, humorous, nature/environment, outdoor adventure, travel. Buys 15-20 mss/year. Average word length: 900. Byline given.

How to Contact No longer accepting unsolicited queries/mss.

Illustration Buys 5-7 illustrations/issue. Preferred theme: nature, wildlife. Works on assignment only. Illustrations only: Send résumé, tearsheets. Responds to art samples in 2 months.

Terms Pays on acceptance. Buys exclusive first-time worldwide rights and non-exclusive worldwide rights thereafter to reprint, transmit, and distribute the work in any form or medium. Original artwork returned at job's completion. Pays up to $700 for full-length of best quality. For illustrations, buys one-time rights. Pays $150-250 for b $250-1,200 for color (inside, per page) illustration. Sample copies for $2.15 plus a 9 × 12 SASE.

READ

Weekly Reader Publishing Group, 1 Reader's Digest Rd., Pleasantville NY 10570. Website: www. weeklyreader.com. READ no longer accepts unsolicited manuscripts. Those that are sent will not be read, responded to, or returned.

REUNIONS MAGAZINE

Reunions magazine, Inc., P.O. Box 11727, Milwaukee WI 53211. (414)263-4567. Fax: (414)263-6331. E-mail: editor@reunionsmag.com. Website: reunionsmag.com. Articles Editor: Edith Wagner. Art Director: Jennifer Rueth. Quarterly Monthly magazine. Estab. 1990. Circ. 20,000. "Reunions magazine is a reader driven how-to book for persons planning family, class, military and other reunions. Includes articles about the detao's pf reunion planning.

Nonfiction For parents of all ages of kids: cooking, games, genealogy/history. Must be about Reunions. Buys 85% mss/year. Average word length: 300-1,500. Byline given.

How to Contact Prefer e-mailed Microsoft Word attachments or responds to queries quickly instead if they're e-mailed; mss up to 1 year. Publishes ms can be up to a year for seasonal material after acceptance. Considers simultaneous submissions, electronic submissions via disk or e-mail, previously published work.

Illustration Uses material that illustrates copy. Samples returned with SASE. Credit line given.

Photos Buys photos including payments: no extra pay. Uses digital: 300 dpi or higher.

Terms Pays on publication. Buys first rights for mss. We don't buy any rights for artwork. Included in whatever we pay rights for photos. Sometimes pays for stories; Pays with contributor copies. "Almost all: we pay very few contributors" No additional payment for ms/illustration packages. Free for SASE. Sample copies for $3. Writer's guidelines free for SASE and available on our web site.

Tips "Do not waste your time sending anything other that material about reunions and reunion planning.

SCIENCE WEEKLY

P.O. Box 70638, Chevy Chase MD 20813. (301)680-8804. Fax: (301)680-9240. E-mail: scienceweekly@ erols.com. Website: www.scienceweekly.com. **Publisher:** Dr. Claude Mayberry, CAM Publishing Group, Inc. Magazine published 14 times/year. Estab. 1984. Circ. 200,000. Science Weekly uses freelance writers to develop and write an entire issue on a single science topic. Send résumé only, not submissions. Authors preferred within the greater D.C., Virginia, Maryland area. Science Weekly works on assignment only.

Nonfiction Young readers, middle readers, (K-6th grade): science/math education, education, problem-solving.

Terms Pays on publication. Prefers people with education, science and children's writing background. *Send resume only.* Samples copies free with SAE and 3 first-class stamps. Free samples on website www.scienceweekly.com

SHARING THE VICTORY

Fellowship of Christian Athletes, 8701 Leeds, Kansas City MO 64129. (816)921-0909. Fax: (816)921-8755. Website: www.sharingthevictory.com. **Articles/Photo Editor:** Jill Ewert. **Art Director:** Mat Casner. Magazine published 9 times a year. Estab. 1982. Circ. 80,000. Purpose is to serve as a ministry tool of the Fellowship of Christian Athletes (FCA) by aligning with its mission to present to athletes and coaches and all whom they influence, the challenge and adventure of receiving Jesus Christ as Savior and Lord.

Nonfiction Young adults/teens: religion, sports. Average word length: 700-1,200. Byline given. How to Contact/Writers Nonfiction: Query with published clips. Publishes ms 3 months after acceptance. Will consider electronic submissions via e-mail.

Photos Purchases photos separately. Looking for photos of sports action. Uses color prints and high resolution electronic files of 300 dpi or higher.

Terms Pays on publication. Buys first rights and second serial (reprint) rights. Pays $150-400 for assigned and unsolicited articles. Photographers paid per photo. Sample copies for 9 × 12 SASE and $1. Writer's/photo guidelines for SASE.

Tips "All stories must be tied to FCA ministry."

SHINE BRIGHTLY

GEMS Girls' Clubs, P.O. Box 7259, Grand Rapids MI 49510. (616)241-5616. Fax: (616)241-5558. E-mail: shinebrightly@gemsgc.org. Website: www.gemsgc.org. **Editor:** Jan Boone. **Senior Editor:** Sara Lynne Hilton. Monthly (with combined June/July/August summer issue) magazine. Circ.17000. "SHINE brightly is designed to help girls ages 9-14 see how God is at work in their lives and in the world around them."

Fiction Middle readers: adventure, animal, contemporary, health, history, humorous, multicultural, nature/environment, problem-solving, religious, sports. Does not want to see unrealistic stories and those with trite, easy endings. We are interested in manuscripts that show how girls can change the world. Buys 30 mss/year. Average word length: 400-900. Byline given.

Nonfiction Middle readers: animal, arts/crafts, careers, cooking, fashion, games/puzzles, health, hobbies, how-to, humorous, nature/environment, multicultural, problem-solving, religious, service projects, social issues, sports, travel, also movies, music and musicians, famous people, interacting with family and friends. We are currently looking for inspirational biographies, stories from Zambia, Africa, and articles about living a green lifestyle. Buys 9 mss/year. Average word length: 100- 800. Byline given.

How to Contact Annual theme update available online. Fiction/nonfiction: E-mail complete manuscript. Place manuscript within body of e-mail. No attachments. Send complete ms. Responds to mss in 3 months. Will consider simultaneous submissions. Guidelines on website.

Illustration Buys 3 illustrations/year. Prefers ms/illustration packages. Works on assignment only. Responds to submissions in 3 months. Samples returned with SASE. Credit line given.

Terms Pays on publication. Buys first North American serial rights, first rights, second serial (reprint rights) or simultaneous rights. Original artwork not returned at job's completion. Pays $35 for stories, assigned articles and unsolicited articles. Poetry is $5-15. Games and Puzzles are $5-10. "We send complimentary copies in addition to pay." Pays $25-50 for color inside illustration. Writer's guidelines online at www.gemsgc.org

Tips Writers: "Please check our website before submitting. We have a specific style and theme that deals with how girls can impact the world. The stories should be current, deal with pre-adolescent problems and joys, and help girls see God at work in their lives through humor as well as problem-solving."

⚡ SKIPPING STONES

A Multicultural Children's Magazine, P.O. Box 3939, Eugene OR 97403. (541)342-4956. E-mail: editor@skippingstones.org. Website: www.skippingstones.org. **Articles/Photo/Fiction Editor:** Arun N. Toke. Bimonthly magazine. Estab. 1988. Circ. 2,500. "Skipping Stones is an award-winning multicultural, nonprofit magazine designed to encourage cooperation, creativity and celebration of cultural and ecological richness. We encourage submissions by children of color, minorities and under-represented populations."

- Send SASE for *Skipping Stones* guidelines and theme list for detailed descriptions of the topics they want. *Skipping Stones*, now in it's 22nd year, has won EDPRESS, National Association for Multicultural Education (N.A.M.E.), Writer Magazine, Newsstand Resources and Parent's Choice Awards.

Fiction Middle readers, young adult/teens: contemporary, meaningful, humorous. All levels: folktales, multicultural, nature/environment. Multicultural needs include: bilingual or multilingual pieces; use of words from other languages; settings in other countries, cultures or multi-ethnic communities.

Nonfiction All levels: animal, biography, cooking, games/puzzles, history, humorous, interview/profile, multicultural, nature/environment, creative problem-solving, religion and cultural celebrations, sports, travel, social and international awareness. Does not want to see preaching, violence or abusive language; no poems by authors over 18 years old; no suspense or romance stories. Average word length: 1,000, max. Byline given.

How to Contact Fiction: Query/complete ms. Nonfiction: Send query. Responds to queries in 1 month; mss in 4 months. Will consider simultaneous submissions; reviews artwork for future assignments. Please include your name and address on each page.

Illustration Prefers illustrations by teenagers and young adults. Will consider all illustration packages. Manuscript/illustration packages: Query; submit complete ms with final art; submit tearsheets. Responds in 4 months. Credit line given.

Photos Black & white photos preferred, but color photos with good contrast are welcome. Needs: youth 7-17, international, nature, celebrations.

Terms Acquires first and non-exclusive reprint rights for mss and photographs. Pays in copies for authors, photographers and illustrators. Sample copy for $5 with SAE and 4 first-class stamps. Writer's/illustrator's guidelines for 4 × 9 SASE.

Tips "We want material meant for children and young adults/teenagers with multicultural or ecological awareness themes. Think, live and write as if you were a child, tween or teen." Wants "material that gives insight to cultural celebrations, lifestyle, customs and traditions, glimpse of daily life in other countries and cultures. Photos, songs, artwork are most welcome if they illustrate/highlight the points. Translations are invited if your submission is in a language other than English. Upcoming themes will include cultural celebrations, living abroad, challenging, hospitality customs of various cultures, cross-cultural understanding, African, Asian and Latin American cultures, humor, international understanding, turning points and magical moments in life, caring for the earth, spirituality, and Multicutural Awareness."

SPARKLE

GEMS Girls' Clubs, 1333 Alger SE, P,P. Box 7295, Grand Rapids MI 49510. (616)241-5616. Fax: (616)241-5558. E-mail: sparkle@gemsgc.org. Website: www.gemsgc.org. **Senior Editor:** Sara Lynn Hilton **Art Director/Photo Editor:** Sara DeRidder. Magazine published 6 times/year. Estab. 2002. Circ. 5,119. "Our mission is to prepare young girls to live out their faith and become world-changers-. We strive to help girls make a difference in the world. We look at the application of scripture to everyday life. We strive to delight the reader and cause the reader to evaluate her own life in light of the truth presented. Finally, we strive to teach practical life skills.

Magazines

Fiction Young readers: adventure, animal, contemporary, fantasy, folktale, health, history, humorous, multicultural, music and musicians, nature/environment, problem-solving, religious, recipes, service projects, sports, suspense/mystery, interacting with family and friends. We currently Looking for inspirational biographies, stories form Zambia, Africa, and ideas on how to live a green lifestyle. Buys 10 mss/year. Average word length: 100-400. Byline given.

Nonfiction Young readers: animal, arts/crafts, biography, careers, cooking, concept, games/puzzles, geography, health, history, hobbies, how-to, interview/profile, math, multicultural, nature/environment, problem-solving, quizzes, science, social issues, sports, travel, personal experience, inspirational, music/drama/art. Buys 15 mss/year. Average word length: 100-400. Byline given.

Poetry Looks for simple poems about God's creation or traditional Bible truths. Maximum length: 15 lines.

How to Contact Fiction/nonfiction: E-mail complete manuscript. Place Manuscript within body of e-mail. No attachments. Send complete ms. Responds to ms in 6 weeks. Publishes ms 6 months after acceptance. Will consider simultaneous submissions, and previously published work.

Illustration Buys 1-2 illustrations/issue; 8-10 illustrations/year. Uses color artwork only. Works on assignment only. Reviews ms/illustration packages from artists. Send ms with dummy. Contact: Sara DeRidder, graphic and web designer. Illustrations only: send promo sheet. Contact: Sara DeRidder. Responds in 3 weeks only if interested. Samples returned with SASE; samples filed. Credit line given.

Terms Pays on publication. Buys first North American serial rights, second serial (reprint rights) or simultaneous rights for mss, artwork and photos. Pays $20 minimum for stories and articles. Pays illustrators $50 for color cover; $25 for color inside. Original artwork not returned at job's completion. Sample copies for $1. Writer's/illustrator/photo guidelines free for SASE or available on Web site.Tips "Keep it simple. We are writing to 1st-3rd graders. It must be simple yet interesting. Manuscripts should build girls up in Christian character but not be preachy. They are just learning about God and how He wants them to live. Manuscripts should be delightful as well as educational and inspirational."

SPIDER

Carus Publishing Company,, 70 East Lake Street, Suite 300, Chicago IL 60601. (312)701-1720. Magazine published 9x/year, monthly except for combined May/June, July/August, and November/December issues. Circ. 50,000. Spider publishes high-quality literature for beginning readers, primarily ages 6-9. Sue Beck, senior art director. **Contact:** Editor-in-Chief: Alice Letvin; Margaret Mincks, associate editor.

Fiction Young readers: adventure, contemporary, fantasy, folktales, humor, science fiction. "Authentic stories from all cultures are welcome. No didactic, religious, or violent stories, or anything that talks down to children." Average word length: 300-1,000. Byline given.

Nonfiction Young readers: animal, arts/crafts, cooking, games/puzzles, geography, history, human interest, math, multicultural, nature/environment, problem-solving, science. "Well-researched articles on topics are welcome. Would like to see more games, puzzles, and activities, especially ones adaptable to *Spider*'s takeout pages. No encyclopedic or overtly educational articles." Average word length: 300-800. Byline given.

Poetry Serious, humorous. Maximum length: 20 lines.

How to Contact Fiction/nonfiction: Send complete ms with SASE. Do not query. Responds to mss in 6 months. Publishes ms 2-3 years after acceptance. Will consider simultaneous submissions and previously published work.

Illustration Buys 5-10 illustrations/issue; 45-90 illustrations/year. Uses color artwork only. "We prefer that you work on flexible or strippable stock, no larger than 20 × 22 (image area 19 × 21). This will allow us to put the art directly on the drum of our separator's laser scanner. Art on disk CMYK, 300 dpi. We use more realism than cartoon-style art." Works on assignment only. Reviews ms/illustration packages from artists. Illustrations only: Send promo sheet and tearsheets. Responds in 3 months. Samples returned with SASE; samples filed. Credit line given.

Photos Buys photos from freelancers. Buys photos with accompanying ms only. Model/property releases and captions required. Uses 35mm, 2¼ × 2¼ transparencies or digital files. Send unsolicited photos by mail; provide résumé and tearsheets. Responds in 3 months.

Terms Pays on publication. Rights purchased vary. Buys first and promotional rights for artwork; one-time rights for photographs. Original artwork returned at job's completion. Pays up to 25¢/word for previously unpublished stories/articles. Authors also receive 6 complimentary copies of the issue in which work appears. Additional payment for ms/illustration packages and for photos accompanying articles. Pays illustrators $750 for color cover; $200-300 for color inside. Pays photographers per photo (range: $25-75). Sample copies for $5. Writer's/illustrator's guidelines online at www.cricketmag.com or for SASE.

Tips Writers: "Read back issues before submitting."

TURTLE MAGAZINE

For Preschool Kids, 1100 Waterway Blvd., Indianapolis IN 46206-0567. (317)636-8881. Fax: (317)684-8094. Website: www.turtlemag.org. **Editor:** Terry Harshman. **Art Director:** Bart Rivers. Bimonthly magazine published 6 times/year. Circ. 300,000. Turtle uses read-aloud stories, especially suitable for bedtime or naptime reading, for children ages 2-5. Also uses poems, simple science experiments, easy recipes and health-related articles.

Fiction Picture-oriented material: health-related, medical, history, humorous, multicultural, nature/environment, problem-solving, sports, recipes, simple science experiments. Avoid stories in which the characters indulge in unhealthy activities. Buys 20 mss/year. Average word length: 150-300. Byline given. Currently accepting submissions for Rebus stories only.

Nonfiction Picture-oriented material: cooking, health, sports, simple science. "We use very simple experiments illustrating basic science concepts. These should be pretested. We also publish simple, healthful recipes." Buys 24 mss/year. Average word length: 100-300. Byline given.

Poetry "We're especially looking for short poems (4-8 lines) and slightly longer action rhymes to foster creative movement in preschoolers. We also use short verse on our inside front cover and back cover."

How to Contact Fiction/nonfiction: Send complete mss. Queries are not accepted. Responds to mss in 3 months.

Terms Pays on publication. Buys all rights for mss. Pays up to 22¢/word for stories and articles (depending upon length and quality) and 10 complimentary copies. Pays $25 minimum for poems. Sample copy $ 3.95. Writer's guidelines free with SASE and on website.

Tips "Our need for health-related material, especially features that encourage fitness, is ongoing. Health subjects must be age-appropriate. When writing about them, think creatively and lighten up! Always keep in mind that in order for a story or article to educate preschoolers, it first must be entertaining—warm and engaging, exciting, or genuinely funny. Here the trend is toward leaner, lighter writing. There will be a growing need for interactive activities. Writers might want to consider developing an activity to accompany their concise manuscripts."

U.S. KIDS

Children's Better Health Institute, 1100 Waterway Blvd., P.O. Box 567, Indianapolis IN 46202. (317)636-8881. Website: www.uskidsmag.org. **Editor:** Daniel Lee. **Art Director:** Greg Vanzo. Magazine for children ages 6-11, published 6 times a year. Estab. 1987. Circ. 230,000.

Fiction Young readers: adventure, animal, contemporary, health, history, humorous, multicultural, nature/environment, problem-solving, sports, suspense/mystery. Buys limited number of stories/year. Query first. Average word length: 500-800. Byline given.

Nonfiction Young readers: animal, arts/crafts, cooking, games/puzzles, health, history, hobbies, how-to, humorous, interview/profile, multicultural, nature/environment, science, social issues, sports, travel. Wants to see interviews with kids ages 5-10, who have done something unusual or different. Buys 30-40 mss/year. Average word length: 400. Byline given.

Poetry Maximum length: 8-24 lines.

How to Contact Fiction: Send complete ms. Responds to queries and mss in 3 months.

Illustration Buys 8 illustrations/issue; 70 illustrations/year. Color artwork only. Works on assignment only. Reviews ms/illustration packages from artists. Query. Illustrations only: Send resume and tearsheets. Responds only if interested. Samples returned with SASE; samples kept on file. Does not return originals. Credit line given.

Photos Purchases photography from freelancers. Looking for photos that pertain to children ages 5-10. Model/property release required. Uses color and b&w prints; 35mm, 2¼ × 2¼, 4 × 5 and 8 × 10 transparencies. Photographers should provide resume, business card, promotional literature or tearsheets to be kept on file. Responds only if interested.

Terms Pays on publication. Buys all rights for mss. Purchases all rights for artwork. Purchases one-time rights for photographs. Pays 17¢/word minimum. Additional payment for ms/illustration packages. Pays illustrators $155/page for color inside. Photographers paid by the project or per photo (negotiable). Sample copies for $3.95. Writer's/illustrator/photo guidelines for #10 SASE.

Tips "Write clearly and concisely without preaching or being obvious."

WHAT IF?

Canada's Creative Magazine for Teens, 19 Lynwood Place, Guelph ON N1G 2V9 Canada. (519)823-2941. Fax: (519)823-8081. E-mail: editor@whatifmagazine.com. Website: www.whatifmagazine.com. **Articles/Fiction Editor:** Mike Leslie. **Art Director:** Jean Leslie. Quarterly magazine. Estab. 2003. Circ. 5,000. "The goal of What If? is to help Canadian young adults get published for the first time in a quality literary setting."

Fiction Young adults: adventure, contemporary, fantasy, folktale, health, humorous, multicultural, nature/environment, problem-solving, science fiction, sports, suspense/mystery. Buys 48 mss/year. Average word length: 500-3,000. Byline given.

Nonfiction Young adults: Personal essays and opinion pieces to a maximum of 1,500 words. Byline given.

Poetry Reviews poetry: all styles. Maximum length: 20 lines. Limit submissions to 4 poems.

How to Contact Fiction/Nonfiction: Send complete ms. Responds to mss in 3 months. Publishes ms 4 months after acceptance. Will consider e-mail submissions, previously published work if the author owns all rights.

Illustration Uses approximately 150 illustrations/year. Reviews ms/illustration packages from young adult artists. Send ms with dummy. Query with samples. Contact: Jean Leslie, production manager. Responds in 2 months. Samples returned with SASE. Credit line given.

Terms Pays on publication. Acquires first rights for mss and artwork. Original artwork returned at job's completion. Pays 2 copies for stories; 2 copy for articles; 2 copies for illustration and 2 copies for poems. Sample copies for $10.00 Writer's/illustrator's guidelines for SASE or available by e-mail.

Tips "Read our magazine. The majority of the material we publish (90%) is by Canadian young adults. Another 10% is staff written. We are currently accepting material from Canadian teens only."

YES MAG

Canada's Science Magazine for Kids 501-3960 Quadra St., Victoria, BC, V8X 4A3 Canada. Fax: (250)477-5390. E-mail. website:www.yesmag.ca. **Publisher:** David Garrison. **Editor:** Shannon Hunt. **Art/Photo Director:** Sam Logan. Managing Editor: Jude Isabella. Bimonthly magazine. Estab. 1996. Circ. 22,000. "YES Mag is designed to make science accessible, interesting, exciting, and fun. Written for children ages 10 to 15, YES Mag covers a range of topics including science and technology news, environmental updates, do-at-home projects and articles about Canadian science and scientists."

Nonfiction Middle readers: all the sciences-math, engineering, biology, physics, chemistry, etc. Buys 30 mss/year. Average word length: 250- 800. Byline given.

How to Contact Nonfiction: Query with published clips. "We prefer e-mail queries." Responds to queries/mss in 6 weeks. Generally publishes ms 3 months after acceptance. **Emphasis on Canadian writers**.

Illustration Buys 2 illustrations/issue; 10 illustrations/year. Uses color artwork only. Works on assignment only. Reviews ms/illustration packages from artists. Query. Illustration only: Query with samples. Responds in 6 weeks. Samples filed. Credit line given.

Photos "Looking for science, technology, nature/environment photos based on current editorial needs." Photo captions required. Uses color prints. Provide resume, business card, promotional literature, tearsheets if possible. Will buy if photo is appropriate. Usually uses stock agencies.

Terms Pays on publication. Buys one-time rights for mss. Buys one-time rights for artwork/photos. Original artwork returned at job's completion. Pays $70-200 for stories and articles. Sample copies for $5. Writer's guidelines available on the website under "Contact" information.

Tips We do not publish fiction or science fiction or poetry. Visit our website for more information and sample articles. Articles relating to the physical sciences and mathematics are encouraged."

YOUNG RIDER

The Magazine for Horse and Pony Lovers, P.O. Box 8237, Lexington KY 40533. (859)260-9800. Fax: (859)260-9814. Website: www.youngrider.com. **Editor:** Lesley Ward. Bimonthly magazine. Estab. 1994. "Young Rider magazine teaches young people, in an easy-to-read and entertaining way, how to look after their horses properly, and how to improve their riding skills safely."

Fiction Young adults: adventure, animal, horses, horse celebrities, famous equestrians. Buys 10 mss/year. Average word length: 1,500 maximum. Byline given.

Nonfiction Young adults: animal, careers, health (horse), sports, riding. Buys 20-30 mss/year. Average word length: 1,000 maximum. Byline given.

How to Contact Fiction/nonfiction: Query with published clips. Responds to queries in 2 weeks. Publishes ms 6-12 months after acceptance. Will consider simultaneous submissions, electronic submissions via disk or modem, previously published work.

Illustration Buys 2 illustrations/issue; 10 illustrations/year. Works on assignment only. Reviews ms/illustration packages from artists. Query. Contact: Lesley Ward, editor. Illustrations only: Query with samples. Contact: Lesley Ward, editor. Responds in 2 weeks. Samples returned with SASE. Credit line given.

Photos Buys photos with accompanying ms only. **Uses high-res digital images only-in focus, good light**. Model/property release required; captions required. Query with samples. Responds in 2 weeks.

Terms Pays on publication. Buys first North American serial rights for mss, artwork, photos. Original artwork returned at job's completion. Pays $150 maximum for stories; $250 maximum for articles. Additional payment for ms/illustration packages and for photos accompanying articles. Pays $70-140 for color inside. Pays photographers per photo (range: $65-155). Sample copies for $3.50. Writer's/illustrator's/photo guidelines for SASE.

Tips "Fiction must be in third person. Read magazine before sending in a query. No 'true story from when I was a youngster.' No moralistic stories. Fiction must be up-to-date and humorous, teen-oriented. Need horsy interest or celebrity rider features. No practical or how-to articles-all done in-house."

Agents & Art Reps

T his section features listings of literary agents and art reps who either specialize in, or represent a good percentage of, children's writers and/or illustrators. While there are a number of children's publishers who are open to non-agented material, using the services of an agent or rep can be beneficial to a writer or artist. Agents and reps can get your work seen by editors and art directors more quickly. They are familiar with the market and have insights into which editors and art directors would be most interested in your work. Also, they negotiate contracts and will likely be able to get you a better deal than you could get on your own.

Agents and reps make their income by taking a percentage of what writers and illustrators receive from publishers. The standard percentage for agents is 10 to 15 percent; art reps generally take 25 to 30 percent. We have not included any agencies in this section that charge reading fees.

WHAT TO SEND

When putting together a package for an agent or rep, follow the guidelines given in their listings. Most agents open to submissions prefer initially to receive a query letter describing your work. For novels and longer works, some agents ask for an outline and a number of sample chapters, but you should send these only if you're asked to do so. Never fax or e-mail query letters or sample chapters to agents without their permission. Just as with publishers, agents receive a large volume of submissions. It may take them a long time to reply, so you may want to query several agents at one time. It's best, however, to have a complete manuscript considered by only one agent at a time. Always include a self-addressed, stamped envelope (SASE).

For initial contact with art reps, send a brief query letter and self-promo pieces, following the guidelines given in the listings. If you don't have a flier or brochure, send photocopies. Always include a SASE.

For those who both write and illustrate, some agents listed will consider the work of author/illustrators. Read through the listings for details.

As you consider approaching agents and reps with your work, keep in mind that they are very choosy about who they take on to represent. Your work must be high quality and presented professionally to make an impression on them. For more information on approaching agents and additional listings, see *Guide to Literary Agents* (Writer's Digest Books). For additional listings of art reps see *Artist's & Graphic Designer's Market* (Writer's Digest Books).

Information on agents and art reps listed in the previous edition but not included in this edition of *Children's Writer's & Illustrator's Market* may be found in the General Index.

An Organization for Agents

In some listings of agents you'll see references to AAR (The Association of Authors' Representatives). This organization requires its members to meet an established list of professional standards and code of ethics.

The objectives of AAR include keeping agents informed about conditions in publishing and related fields; encouraging cooperation among literary organizations; and assisting agents in representing their author-clients' interests. Officially, members are prohibited from directly or indirectly charging reading fees. They offer writers a list of member agents on their website. They also offer a list of recommended questions an author should ask an agent and other FAQs, all found on their website. They can be contacted at AAR, 676A 9th Ave. #312, New York NY 10036. (212)840-5777. E-mail: aarinc@mindspring.com. Website: www.aar-online.org.

AGENTS

ADAMS LITERARY

7845 Colony Rd., #215, Charlotte NC 28226. (704)542-1440. Fax: (704)542-1450. E-mail: info@adamsliterary.com. Website: www.adamsliterary.com. **Contact:** Tracey Adams, Josh Adams, Quinlan Lee. Member of AAR. Other memberships include SCBWI and WNBA.

Terms Agent receives 15% commission on domestic sales; 20% on foreign sales. Offers written contract.

How to Contact "Guidelines are posted (and frequently updated) on our website."

BOOKS & SUCH

52 Mission Circle, Suite 122, PMB 170, Santa Rosa CA 95409-5370. (707)538-4184. E-mail: etta@booksandsuch.biz. Website: www.booksandsuch.biz. **Contact:** Etta Willson. Estab. 1996. Member of SCWBI, WNBA, and associate member of CBA. Represents 25 clients. 5% of clients are new/unpublished writers. Places projects in the general and relgious market. Represents 70% juvenile books. Considers: nonfiction, fiction for middle grades, and picture books.

- Before becoming an agent with Books & Such, Etta Wilson was a packager and agent with March Media and an editor at Abingdon Press.

Recent Sales *The Sweetest Story Bible* (Zonderkidz); *Rumble, Zap, Pow* (Tyndale); *Police Officers on Patrol* (Viking).

Terms Agent receives 15% commission on domestic and foreign sales. Offers written contract.

Tips "The heart of my motivation is to help authors develop their writing talent for children and to be successful in having it published."

BOOKSTOP LITERARY AGENCY

67 Meadow View Rd., Orinda CA 94563. Website: www.bookstopliterary.com. Seeking both new and established writers and illustrators. Estab. 1983. 100% of material handled is books for children and young adults.

Terms Agent receives 15% commission on domestic sales. Offers written contract, binding for 1 year.

How to Contact Please send: cover letter, entire ms for picture books; and first 30 pages of novels, proposal and sample chapters ok for nonfiction. E-mail submissions: Paste cover letter and first

10 pages of manuscript into body of e-mail, send to info@bookstopliterary.com. Send sample illustrations only if you are an illustrator.

CURTIS BROWN, LTD.

Ten Astor Place., New York NY 10003. Seeking both new and established writers. Estab. 1914. Members of AAR and SCBWI. Signatory of WGA. **Staff includes:** Nathan Bransford, Ginger Clark, Elizabeth Harding, Ginger Knowlton, Mitchell Waters, and Anna J. Webman.

Terms Agent receives 15% commission on domestic sales; 20% on foreign sales. Offers written contract. 75 days notice must be given to terminate contract.

How to Contact Query with SASE. If a picture book, send only one picture book ms. Considers simultaneous queries, "but please tell us." Returns material only with SASE. Obtains clients through recommendations from others, queries/solicitations, conferences.

ANDREA BROWN LITERARY AGENCY, INC.

1076 Eagle Dr., Salinas CA 93905. (831)422-5925. Website: www.andreabrownlit.com. **President:** Andrea Brown. Estab. 1981. Member of SCBWI and WNBA. 20% of clients are new/previously unpublished writers. Specializes in "all kinds of children's books—illustrators and authors."

- Prior to opening her agency, Andrea Brown served as an editorial assistant at Random House and Dell Publishing and as an editor with Alfred A. Knopf.

Recent Sales *Thirteen Reasons Why,* by Jay Asher (Penguin); three book series, by Ellen Hopkins (S&S); *Downside Up,* by Neal Shusterman (Simon & Schuster).

Terms Agent receives 15% commission on domestic sales; 20% on foreign sales. Written contract.

How to Contact Query. Responds in 3 months to queries and mss. E-mail queries only.

Tips Query first. "Taking on very few picture books. Must be unique—no rhyme, no anthropomorphism. Do not call or fax queries or manuscripts. E-mail queries first. Check website for details."

⊞ LIZA DAWSON ASSOCIATES

350 7th Ave, Suite 2003, New York, NY 10001. E-mail: anna@olswanger.com. Website: www.olswanger.com. **Contact:** Anna Olswanger. Member of SCBWI, WNBA, Authors Guild. Represents 10 clients. 30% of clients are new/unpublished writers. 75% of material handled is books for young readers.

Terms Agent receives 15% commission on domestic sales; 20% commission on foreign sales. Offers written contract.

How to Contact Query with first 5 pages. Query by e-mail only. No phone calls. Considers simultaneous queries. Responds in 4 weeks to queries; 8 weeks to mss. Obtains most new clients through recommendations and queries.

DUNHAM LITERARY, INC.

156 Fifth Ave, Suite 625, New York NY 10010-7002. E-mail: dunhamlit@yahoo.com. **Contact:** Jennie Dunham. Seeking both new and established writers but prefers to work with established writers. Estab. 2000. Member of AAR, signatory of SCBWI. Represents 50 clients. 15% of clients are new/previously unpublished writers. 50% of material handled is books of young readers. Website: www.dunhamlit.com.

Recent Sales Sold 30 books for young readers in the last year. *Peter Pan,* by Robert Sabuda (Little Simon); *Flamingos On the Roof,* by Calef Brown (Houghton); *Adele and Simon In America,* by Barbara McClintock (Farrar, Straus & Giroux); *Caught Between the Pages,* by Marlene Carvell

(Dutton); *Waiting For Normal*, by Leslie Connor (HarperCollins), *The Gollywhopper Games*, by Jody Feldman (Greenwillow).

Terms Agent receives 15% commission on domestic sales; 20-25% on foreign sales. Offers written contract. 60 days notice must be given to terminate contract.

How to Contact Query with SASE. Consider simultaneous queries and submissions. Responds in 2 week s to queries; 2 months to mss. Returns material only with SASE. Obtains clients through recommendations from others.

⒩ DYSTEL & GODERICH LITERARY MANAGEMENT

1 Union Square West, Suite 904, New York NY 10003. (212)627-9100. Fax: (212)627-9313. E-mail: mbourret@dystel.com. Website: www.dystel.com. **Contact:** Michael Bourret and Jim McCarthy.

Represents Fiction, picture books, middle grade, and young adult novels.

Recent Sales Sold 20 books in the past year for young readers. The Slayer Journals, by Heather Brewer (Dutton); Shooting Kabul, by Naheed Hasnat (Simon & Schuster); Vampire Academy sequels, by Richelle Mead (Razorbill); Whisper, by Phoebe Kitanidis (Balzer & Bray). Other clients represented Sara Zarr, Lisa McMann, Suzanne Selfors, Nova Ren Suma, Emily Wing Smith, Dawn Metcalf, Dale Basye, Mindi Scott, Victoria Laurie, Cyn Balog, Michelle Rowen, Carrie Ryan, James Dashner, Jill Alexander, N.H. Senzai, Joe Fenton, Anne Rockwell, Dori Jones Yang, Jenna Helland, Pat Lowery Collins, Joelle Anthony, Jewell Parker Rhodes, Debbie Lytton, Antonio Pagliarulo.

Terms Agent receives 15% commission on domestic sales, 20% commission on foreign sales. Offers written contract.

How to Contact Query with SASE. Please include the first three chapters in the body of the e-mail. E-mail queries preferred; Michael Bourret only accepts email queries; will accept mail. Accepts simultaneous submissions. Responds within 8 weeks. Returns mss only with SASE. Obtains new clients by recommendations from others, queries/solicitations, and conferences.

▢ EDUCATIONAL DESIGN SERVICES LLC

5750 Bou Ave, Ste. 1508, N. Bethesda, MD 20852. E-mail: blinder@educationaldesignservices.com. Website: www.educationaldesignservices.com. **Contact:** B. Linder. Handles only certain types of work educational materials aimed at teacher development or the K-12 Market. Estab. 1981. 80% of clients are new/previously unpublished writers.

Recent Sales *How to Solve Word Problems in Mathematics*, by Wayne (McGraw-Hill*); Preparing for the 8th Grade Test in Social Studies*, by Farran-Paci (Amsco); *Minority Report*, by Gunn-Singh (Scarecrow Education); *No Parent Left Behind*, by Petrosino & Spiegel (Rowman & Littlefield); *Teaching Test-taking Skills* (R&L Education); *10 Languages You'll Need Most in the Classroom*, by Sundem, Krieger, Pickiewicz (Corwin Press); *Kids, Classrooms & Capital Hill*, by Flynn (R&L Education).

Terms Agent receives 15% commission on domestic sales; 25% on foreign sales. Offers written contract, binding until any party opts out. Terminate contract through certified letter.

How to Contact Query by e-mail or with SASE or send outline and 1 sample chapter. Considers simultaneous queries and submissions if so indicated. Responds in 6-8 weeks to queries/mss. Returns material only with SASE. Obtains clients through recommendations from others, queries/ solicitations, or through conferences.

ETHAN ELLENBERG LITERARY AGENCY

548 Broadway, #5-E, New York NY 10012. (212)431-4554. Fax: (212)941-4652. E-mail: agent@ethanellenberg.com. Website: EthanEllenberg.com. **Contact:** Ethan Ellenberg. Estab. 1983.

Represents 80 clients. 10% of clients are new/previously unpublished writers. "Children's books are an important area for us."

- Prior to opening his agency, Ethan Ellenberg was contracts manager of Berkley/Jove and associate contracts manager for Bantam. Represents 2002 Cladecott Medal winner Eric Rohmann, for *My Friend Rabbit*, adapted by Nelvana and running in an animated series fall 2007 on NBC and for his most recent titles *A Kitten Tale* (Knopf 2008); *Last Song* (Roaring Brook Press 2010). Other client's recent publications include Renee Watson's *A Place Where Hurricanes Happen* (Random House 2010); Bryan W. Fields' *Froonga Planet* (Henry Holt 2008); *Lunchbox And The Aliens* (Square Fish 2008); *Sharon Shinn's General Winston's Daughter* (Viking 2009); *Gateway* (Viking 2009); *Piper Banks' Geek High* (Nal 2007); *Geek Abroad* (Nal 2008); *Summer of The Geek* (Nal 2010); *Marthe Jocelyn's Would You* (Wendy Lamb/Random House 2008); and *Folly* (Wendy Lamb/Random House 2010).

Terms Agent receives 15% on domestic sales; 20% on foreign sales. Offers written contract, "flexible." Charges for "direct expenses only: photocopying for manuscript submissions, postage for submission and foreign rights sales."

How to Contact Picture books—send full ms with SASE. Illustrators: Send a representative portfolio with color copies and SASE. No original artwork. Young adults—send outline plus 3 sample chapters with SASE. Accepts queries by e-mail; does not accept attachments to e-mail queries or fax queries. Considers simultaneous queries and submissions. Responds in six weeks to snail mail queries; only responds to e-mail queries if interested. Returns materials only with SASE. "See website for detailed instructions, please follow them carefully." No phone calls.

Tips "We are actively taking new clients, both published and unpublished, in all areas of children's books. We're most interested in natural storytellers, people who let their imaginations soar. This includes all age groups and genres. If we love your work, we'll also give you sound editorial feedback and help you develop it so it can be successfully sold." For illustrators we must love you artwork and prefer author/illustrators. This continues to be a prime area of our interest and we look forward to your submission.

THE ELAINE P. ENGLISH LITERARY AGENCY

4710 41st St. NW, Suite D, Washington DC 20016. (202)362-5190. Fax: (202)362-5192. E-mail: elaine@elaineenglish.com; naomi@elaineenglish.com. **Contact:** Elaine English; Naomi Hackenberg.

Represents Actively seeking women's fiction, including single-title romances, and young adult fiction. Does not want to receive any science fiction, time travel, or picture books.

Recent Sales have been to Sourcebooks, Tor, Harlequin

Terms Agent receives 15% commission on domestic sales. Agent receives 20% commission on foreign sales. Offers written contract; 30-day notice must be given to terminate contract. Charges only for shipping expenses; generally taken from proceeds.

How to Contact Generally prefers e-queries sent to queries@elaineenglish.com or YA sent to naomi@elaineenglish.com. If requested, submit synopsis, first 3 chapters, SASE. Please check website for further details. Responds in 4-8 weeks to queries; 3 months to requested submissions Obtains most new clients through recommendations from others, conferences, submissions.

FLANNERY LITERARY

1140 Wickfield Ct., Naperville IL 60563. (630)428-2682. Fax: (630)428-2683. E-mail: FlanLit@aol.com. **Contact:** Jennifer Flannery.

Represents This agency specializes in children's and young adult fiction and nonfiction. It also accepts picture books.

Terms Agent receives 15% commission on domestic sales. Agent receives 20% commission on foreign sales. Offers written contract, binding for life of book in print; 1-month notice must be given to terminate contract.

How to Contact Query with SASE. No e-mail submissions or queries. Responds in 2 weeks to queries. Responds in 1 month to mss. Obtains most new clients through recommendations from others, submissions.

Tips "Write an engrossing, succinct query describing your work. We are always looking for a fresh new voice."

BARRY GOLDBLATT LITERARY LLC

320 Seventh Ave.#266, Brooklyn NY 11215. (718)832-8787. Fax: (718)832-5558. Website: www. bgliterary.com. Estab. 2000. Member of AAR, SCBWI. **Staff includes:** Barry Goldblatt, Beth Fleisher and Joe Monti. Represents 95% juvenile and young adult books. Considers graphic novels, fiction, nonfiction, middle grade, and young adult.

Recent Sales The Infernal Devices trilogy, by Cassandra Clare; *Clappy as a Ham*, by Michael Ian Black; *Pearl*, by Jo Knowles; *The Book of Blood and Shadows,* by Robin Wasserman; *Summerton,* by Karen Healey; *The Deviners,* by Libba Bray.

Terms Agent receives 15% commission on domestic sales; 20% on foreign and dramatic sales. Offers written contract. 60 days notice must be given to terminate contract.

How to Contact "Please see our website for specific submission guidelines and information on agents' particular tastes." Obtains clients through referrals, queries, and conferences.

Tips "We're a group of hands-on agents, with wide ranging interests. Get us hooked with a great query letter, then convince us with an unforgettable manuscript."

THE GREENHOUSE LITERARY AGENCY

11308 Lapham Drive, Oakton VA 22124. **Contact:** Sarah Davies. Young agency actively seeking clients. Seeking both new and established writers. Estab. 2008. Member of SCBWI. Represents 20 authors. 100% fiction for young readers. Staff includes Sarah Davies in USA and Julia Churchill in UK.

- Sarah Davies has had an editorial and management career in children's publishing spanning 25 years; for 5 years prior to launching the Greenhouse she was Publishing Director of Macmillan Children's Books in London, and publishing leading authors from both sides of the Atlantic.

Recent Sales *Princess for Hire*, by Lindsey Leavitt (Hyperion); *What Happened on Fox Street*, by Tricia Springstubb (Harpercollins); *The Replacement*, by Brenna Yovanoff (Razorbill); *Just Add Magic*, by Cindy Callaghan (Aladdin).

Terms Receives 15% commission on sales to both US and UK; 25% on foreign sales. Offers written contract.Sarah Davies attends Bologna Children's Bookfair in Bologna, Italy; SCBWI conferences; BookExpo America; and other conferences—see website for information.

How to Contact See website for full submission criteria. Email queries only; short letter containing a brief outline, biography and any writing 'credentials'. Up to the first five pages of text may be pasted into the email. All submissions are answered; usual response time 2-3 weeks; allow 6 weeks before chasing. If interested will ask to see full manuscript; allow 6-8 weeks for response on fulls. Obtains new authors through recommendations, queries/solicitations, conferences. Simultaneous submissions accepted but prioritizes exclusives.

Tips "It's very important to me to have a strong, long-term relationship with clients. Having been 25 years in the publishing industry, I know the business from the inside and have excellent contacts in both the US and UK. I work hard to find every client the very best publisher and deal for their writing. My editorial background means I can work creatively with authors where necessary; I aim to submit high-quality manuscripts to publishers while respecting the role of the editor who will have their own publishing vision. Before submitting, prospective authors should read up-to-date submissions guidelines on website and also look at the Greenhouse's 'Top 10 tips for authors of children's fiction', which can be found on www.greenhouseliterary.com.

BARBARA S. KOUTS, LITERARY AGENT

P.O. Box 560, Bellport NY 11713. (631)286-1278. **Contact:** Barbara Kouts. Currently accepting new clients. Estab. 1980. Member of AAR. Represent 50 clients. 10% of clients are new/previously unpublished writers. Specializes in children's books.

Recent Sales *Code Talker*, by Joseph Bruchac (Dial); *The Penderwicks*, by Jeanne Birdsall (Knopf); *Frogg y's Baby Sister*, by Jonathan London (Viking).

Terms Agent receives 10% commission on domestic sales; 20% on foreign sales. Charges for photocopying.

How to Contact Accepts queries by mail only. Responds in 1 week to queries; 6 weeks to mss.

Tips "Write, do not call. Be professional in your writing."

THE MCVEIGH AGENCY

345 West 21st St., New York NY 10011. (917)913-6388. Fax: (646)619-4944. E-mail: queries@themcveighagency.com. Website: www.themcveighagency.com. Contact: Mark McVeigh.

Recent Sales Sold 1 book last year. Also represents: Steve Björkman (Illustrator of over 80 children's books, including NY TIMES best seller Dirt On My Shirt); Terry Trueman (Printz-Honor Author; Labor Carrick Hill, Author of Dave the Potter (Little, Brown); Robyn Schneider, Author of Best-Seller Knightley Academy; Patrick Jones; Nicole Rubel; Don Tate; Stacia Deutsch and Rhody Cohon, NY Times Best-Selling Authors; James St.James, Author Freakshow, SLJ's Best of 2007; Chris Eboch (Author of over ten books, including the Haunted series for Simon and Schuster.) Verge Entertainment, Inc: Joseph Phillip Illidge, Shawn Martinbrough, Milo Stone Wilfred Santiago (Graphic novelist, author of 21: The Roberto Clemente story (Fantagraphics, 2010). Rebecca Van Slyke (Picture book author); BD Wong (actor, author); Linda Zinnen Author of The Truth About Rats, Rules and The Seventh Grade; The Dragons Of Spratt, Ohio (both HarperCollins), and Third (Dutton).

Terms Agent receives 15% on domestic sales, 15% on foreign sales. Offers written contract. 30 days notice must be given for termination of contract.

How to Contact E-mail query. Considers simultaneous queries, submissions. Responds 2 weeks after query; 4 weeks after ms. Returns mss only with SASE. Obtains new clients through recommendations from others, queries/solicitations, conferences.

Tips "I am a very hands-on, old-school agent who likes to edit manuscripts as much as I like to negotiate deals. My favorite agents were always what I called "honest sharks, 'out to get the best deal for their client, always looking ahead, but always conduced business in such a way that everyone came away as happy as possible. In short-they had integrity and determination to represent their clients to the best of their abilities, and that's what I aspire to."

ERIN MURPHY LITERARY AGENCY

2700 Woodlands Village, #300-458, Flagstaff AZ 86001-7127. (928)525-2056. E-mail: alwayserin@earthlink.com. Website: http://emliterary.com. **Contact**: Erin Murphy, President; Ammi-Joan Paquette, Associate Agent. Closed to unsolicited queries and submissions. Considers both new and established writers, by referral from industry professionals she knows or personal contact (such as conferences) only. Estab. 1999. Member of SCBWI. Represents 70 active clients. 25% of clients are new/previously unpublished writers. 100% of material handled is books of young readers.

- Prior to opening her agency, Erin Murphy was editor-in-chief at Northland Publishing/Rising Moon. (Agency is not currently accepting unsolicited queries or submissions.)

Terms Agent receives 15% commission on domestic sales; 25% on foreign sales. Offers written contract. 30 days notice must be given to terminate contract.

MUSE LITERARY MANAGEMENT

189 Waverly Place #4, New York NY 10014-3135. Seeking both new and established writers. Estab. 1998. Agency is member of Children's Literature Network. Represents 10 clients. 90% new writers. 60% books for young readers. **Contact:** Deborah Carter.

Recent Sales Sold 1 book for young readers in 2008. *The Adventures of Molly Whuppie and Other Appalachian Folktales*, by Anne Shelby (University of North Carolina Press). Winner of 2008 AESOP Accolade from American Folklore Society.

Terms Agent receives 15% commission on domestic sales; 20% on foreign sales. Offers written contract. Contract binding for 1 year. One day's notice must be given for termination of contract.

How to Contact Accepts queries by e-mail, mail. Considers simultaneous queries, submissions. Responds in 1-2 weeks to queries; 2-3 weeks to ms.

Tips "I give editorial feedback and work on revisions on spec. Agency agreement is offered when the writer and I feel the manuscript is ready for submission to publishers. Writers should also be open to doing revisions with editors who express serious interest in their work, prior to any offer of a publishing contract. All aspects of career strategy are discussed with writers, and all decisions are ultimately theirs. I make multiple and simultaneous submissions when looking for rights opportunities, and share all correspondence. All agreements are signed by the writers. Reimbursement for expenses is subject to client's approval, limited to photocopying (usually press clips) and postage. I always submit fresh manuscripts to publishers printed in my office with no charge to the writer."

JEAN V. NAGGAR LITERARY AGENCY, INC.

216 E. 75th Street, Suite 1E, New York NY 10021. Seeking both new and established writers. Estab. 1978. Member of AAR, SCBWI. Represents 150 clients. Large percentage of clients are new/previously unpublished writers. 25% material handled is books for young readers.

Recent Sales See website for information.

How to Contact Accepts queries by e-mail. Prefers to read materials exclusively. Responds in 2 weeks to queries; response time for ms depends on the agent queried. Obtains new clients through recommendations from others, queries/solicitations, conferences.

ALISON PICARD, LITERARY AGENT

P.O. Box 2000, Cotuit MA 02635. **Contact:** Alison Picard. Seeking both new and established writers. Estab. 1985. Represents 50 clients. 40% of clients are new/previously unpublished writers. 20% of material handled is books for young readers.

- Prior to opening her agency, Alison Picard was an assistant at a large New York agency before co-founding Kidde, Hoyt & Picard in 1982. She became an independent agent in 1985.

Recent Sales *Funerals and Fly Fishing*, by Mary Bartek (Henry Holt & Co.); *Playing Dad's Song*, by Dina Friedman (Farrar Straus & Giroux); *Escaping into the Night*, by Dina Friedman (Simon & Schuster); *Celebritrees* and *The Peace Bell*, by Margi Preus (Henry Holt & Co.)

Terms Receives 15% commission on domestic sales; 20-25% on foreign sales. Offers written contract, binding for 1 year. 1-week notice must be given to terminate contract.

How to Contact Query with SASE. Accepts queries by e-mail with no attachments. Considers simultaneous queries and submissions. Responds in 2 weeks to queries; 4 months to mss. Returns material only with SASE. Obtains clients through queries/solicitations.

Tips "We currently have a backlog of submissions."

PROSPECT AGENCY

551 Valley Road, PMB 377, Upper Montclair NJ 02043. (718)788-3217. Fax: (718)360-9582. E-mail: esk@prospectagency.com. Website: www.prospectagency.com. **Contact:** Emily Sylvan Kim, Becca Stumpf, Rachel Orr, Teresa Keitlinski. Seeking both new and established writers. Estab. 2005. Agent is member of AAR. Represents 55 clients and growing. 70% of clients are new/previously unpublished writers. 60% of material handled is books for young readers. Staff includes Emily Sylvan, Becca Stumpf, and Rachel Orr are agents. Emily handles Young Adult, tween and middle grade literary and commercial fiction, with a special interest in edgy books and books for boys. Becca Stumpf handals Young adult and middle grade literary and commercial fiction, with a special interest in fantasy and science fiction with cross-genre appeal. Rachel Orr handles picture books, beginning readers, chapter books, middle-grade/YA novels, children's non-fiction, and children's illustrators. Teresa Kietlinski hadles picte books authors and illustrators as well as MG and YA books. She also seeks children's picture book illustrators and graphic novels.

- For some of us, it's all we've ever known. Others have worked in various facets of publishing and law.

Recent Sales Sold 2 books for young readers in the last year. (Also represents adult fiction.) Recent sales include: *Ollie and Claire*, Philomel, *Vicious*, Bloomsbury, *Temptest Rising*, Walker Books, *Where do Diggers Sleep at Night*, Random House Children's, *A DJ Called Tomorrow*, Little,Brown, The *Princesses of Iowa*, Candlewick and others. .

Terms Agent receives 15% on domestic sales, 20% on foreign sales. Offers written contract.

How to Contact Send outline and 3 sample chapters. Accepts queries through website ONLY. Considers simultaneous queries submissions. However, we do not accept submissions to multiple Prospect agents (please submit to only one agent at Prospect Agency). Responds in 1 week to 3 months following an initial query. 1 week to two months after a mss has been requested. All submissions are electronic; manuscripts and queries that are not a good fit for our agency are rejected via e-mail. We obtain new clients through conferences, recommendations, queries, and some scouting.

WENDY SCHMALZ AGENCY

P.O. Box 831, Hudson NY 12534. (518)672-7697. E-mail: wendy@schmalzagency.com. Website: www.schmalzagency.com. **Contact:** Wendy Schmalz. Seeking both new and established writers. Estab. 2002. Member of AAR. Represents 35 clients. 10% of clients are new/previously unpublished writers. 70% of material handled is books for young readers.

- Prior to opening her agency, Wendy Schmalz was an agent for 23 years at Harold Ober Associates.

Recent Sales Sold 25 books for young readers in the last year.

Terms Agent receives 15% commission on domestic sales; 20% on foreign sales. Fees for photocopying and FedEx.

How to Contact Query with SASE. Accepts queries by e-mail. Responds in 4 weeks to queries; 4-6 weeks to mss. Returns material only with SASE. Obtains clients through recommendations from others.

N SUSAN SCHULMAN LITERARY AGENCY

454 W. 44th, New York NY 10036. (212)713-1633. Fax: (212)581-8830. E-mail: schulman@aol.com. Website: www.Schulmanagency.com. **Contact**: Susan Schulman. Seeking both new and established writers. Estab. 1980. Member of AAR, WGA, SCBWI, Dramatists Guild, New York Women in Film, League of New York Theater Professional Women, Women's Media Group; 15% of material handled is books for young readers. Staff includes Emily Uhry, YA; Linda Kiss, picture books.

Recent Sales Of total agency sales, approximately 20% is children's literature. Recent sales include: *Pirates of Crocodile Swamp*, by Jim Arnosky; *Spotting for Nelliel*, by Pamela Lowell (Marshall Cavendish); *I Get All Better*, by Vickie Cobb (4-book series with Lerner); film rights to *100 Girls to MTV*; film rights to *Social Climbers Guide to High School*, by Robyn Schneider to ABC Family.

Terms Agent receives 15% on domestic sales, 20% on foreign sales.

How to Contact Query with SASE. Accepts queries by e-mail but responds only to e-mail queries which interest agency. Considers simultaneous queries and submissions. Returns mss only with SASE. Obtains new clients through recommendations from others, queries/solicitations, conferences.

Tips Schulman describes her agency as "professional boutique, long-standing, eclectic."

S©OTT TREIMEL NY

0434 Lafayette St., New York, NY 10003. (212)505-8353. E-mail: stny@verizonnet. Website: scotttreimelnycom.

Recent Sales Recent Sales Sold 32 new titles in the last year. *Boy and Boy*, by Ame Dyckman (Knopf) (debut); *Dark Song*, by Gail Giles (Little, Brown); *Girl Parts*, by John M. Cusick (Candlewick) (debut); *How To Create Your Own Country*, by Rick Walton (Bloomsbury); *Weiner Wolf*, by Jeff Crosby (Hyperion); *Old Robert And The Troubadour Cats*, text by Barbara Joosse, illustrations for Jan Jutte (Philomel); *Sleeping Bootsie*, by Maribeth Boelts; *The P.S. Brothers*, by Maribeth Boelts (Harcourt); *Wink: The Ninja Who Wanted to Nap*, by J.C. Phillipps (Viking); *The First Five Fourths*, by Pat Hughes (Viking); *Aphrodite Figures It Out*, by Janice Repka (Dutton); *Haunted*, by Barbara Haworth-Attard (HarperCanada); *Ends*, by David Ward (Abrams); *Fire In The Sky*, by David Ward (Scholastic Canada); *The Blending Time*, by Michael Kinch (Flux)(debut); Audio sales to Listening Library, Brilliance, and Audible.

Terms Agent receives 15-20% commission on domestic sales; 25% on foreign sales. Offers verbal or written contract, binding on a "contract-by-contract basis." Submission accepted via website. Offers extensive editorial guidance. To ensure submissions are of the high quality for which we are known.

How to Contact Submissions accepted via website submission form.

Tips "We look for dedicated authors and illustrators able to sustain longtime careers in our increasingly competitive field. I want fresh, not derivative story concepts with overly-familiar characters. We look for gripping stories, characters, pacing, and themes. We remain mindful of an authentic (to the age) point-of-view, and look for original voices. We spend significant time hunting for the best new work, and do launch debut talent each year. It is best *not* to send manuscripts with lengthy submission histories already."

WRITERS HOUSE

21 W. 26th St., New York NY 10010. (212)685-2400. Fax: (212)685-1781. Website: www.writershouse. com. Estab. 1974. Member of AAR. Writers house represents all types of fiction and nonfiction, specializing in children's and young adult literature, form picture books to YA, authors and illustrators. Client include winners of the Caldecott, Newbery, and Printz Medals and Honors in addition to recipients of the National Book Award in young people's literature and numerous other prizes. Clients' books have appeared on the New York Times Children's picture book, chapter book, paperback, and series lists including the phenomenon, twilight. Information on submissions policies and specific agent guidelines can be found on our website. New clients are found through unsolicited submissions as well as other means.

Terms Agent receives 15% commission on domestic sales; 20% on foreign sales. Offers written contract.

Tips Follow submission guidelines and please do not simultaneously submit your work to more than one writers house agent.

ART REPS

ART FACTORY

925 Elm Grove Rd., Elm Grove WI 53122. (262)785-1940. Fax: (262)785-1611. E-mail: tstocki@ artfactoryltd.com. Website: www.artfactoryillustrators.com. **Contact:** Tom Stocki. Commercial illustration representative. Estab. 1978. Represents 9 illustrators including: Tom Buchs, Tom Nachreiner, Todd Dakins, Linda Godfrey, Larry Mikec, Bill Scott, Gary Shea, Terry Herman, Troy Allen. 10% of artwork handled is children's book illustration. Currently open to illustrators seeking representation. Open to both new and established illustrators.
Represents Illustration.
Terms Receives 25-30% commission. Offers written contract. Advertising costs are split: 75% paid by illustrators; 25% paid by rep. "We try to mail samples of all our illustrators at one time and we try to update our website; so we ask the illustrators to keep up with new samples." Advertises in *Picturebook*, *Workbook*. **How to Contact** For first contact, send query letter, tearsheets. Responds only if interested. Call to schedule an appointment. Portfolio should include tearsheets. Finds illustrators through queries/solicitations.
Tips "Have a unique style."

ASCIUTTO ART REPS.INC.

1712 E. Butler Circle, Chandler AZ 85225. (480)899-0600. Fax: (480)899-3636.Website: www. Aartreps.com E-mail: Aartreps@cox.net. **Contact:** Mary Anne Asciutto, art agent, Children's book illustration representative since 1980. Specializing in childrens illustrations for childrens educational text books, grades K thru 8, childrens trade books, childrens magazines, posters, packaging, etc.
Recent Sales *Bats, Sharks, Whales, Snakes, Penguins, Alligators and Crocodiles*, illustrated by Meryl Henderson for Boyds Mills Press.
Terms Agency receives 25% commission. Advertising and promotion costs are split: 75% paid by talent; 25% paid by representative. US citizens only.
How to Contact Send samples via email with a cover letter résumé. Submit sample portfolio for review with an SASE for it's return. Responds in 2 to 4 weeks. Portfolio should include at least 12 samples of original art, printed tearsheets, photocopies or color prints of most recent work.
Tips In obtaining representation, "be sure to connect with an agent who handles the kind of work, you (the artist) *want*."

CAROL BANCROFT & FRIENDS

P.O. Box 2030, Danbury, CT 06813 (203)730-8270 or (800)720-7020. Fax: (203)730-8275. E-mail: cbfriends@sbcglobal.net. Website: www.carolbancroft.com. **Owner:** Joy Elton Tricarico. **Founder:** Carol Bancroft. Estab. 1972. Illustration representative for all aspects of children's publishing and design. Text and trade; any children's related material. Member of, Society of Illustrators, Graphic Artists Guild, National Art Education Association, SCBWI. Represents 30+ illustrators. Specializes in illustration for children's publishing-text and trade; any children's-related material. Clients include, but not limited to, Scholastic, Houghton Mifflin, HarperCollins, Dutton, Harcourt, Marshall Cavendish, Mcgraw Hill, Hay House.
Represents Illustration for children of all ages including young adult.

Terms Rep receives 25% commission. Advertising costs are split: 75% paid by talent; 25% paid by representative. For promotional purposes, artists must provide "laser copies (not slides), tearsheets, promo pieces, good color photocopies, etc.; 6 pieces or more is best; narrative scenes and children interacting." Advertises in Picture Book, Directory of Illustration.

How to Contact Send either 2-3 samples with your address to the e-mail address above or mail 6-10 samples, along with a self Addressed, stamped envelope (SASE) to the above P.O. box."

PEMA BROWNE LTD.

11 Tena Place, Valley Cottage NY 10989. (845)268-0029. **Contact:** Pema Browne. Estab. 1966. Represents 2 illustrators. 10% of artwork handled is children's book illustration. Specializes in general commercial. Markets include: all publishing areas; children's picture books. Clients include HarperCollins, Holiday House, Bantam Doubleday Dell, Nelson/Word, Hyperion, Putnam. Client list available upon request.

Represents Fiction, nonfiction, picture books, middle grade, young adult, manuscript/illustration packages. Looking for "professional and unique" talent.

Recent Sales *The Daring Ms. Quimby*, by Suzanne Whitaker (Holiday House).

Terms Rep receives 30% illustration commission; 20% author commission. Exclusive area representation is required. For promotional purposes, talent must provide color mailers to distribute. Representative pays mailing costs on promotion mailings.

How to Contact For first contact, send query letter, direct mail flier/brochure and SASE. If interested will ask to mail appropriate materials for review. Portfolios should include tearsheets and transparencies or good color photocopies, plus SASE. Accepts queries by mail only. Obtains new talent through recommendations and interviews (portfolio review).

Tips "We are doing more publishing—all types—less advertising." Looks for "continuity of illustration and dedication to work."

CATUGEAU: ARTIST AGENT, LLC

3009 Margaret Jones Lane, Williamsburg VA 23185. (757)221-0666. Fax: (757)221-6669. E-mail: chris@catugeau.com. Website: www.CATugeau.com. **Owner/Agent:** Christina Tugeau. Children's publishing trade book, mass market, educational. Estab. 1994. Member of SPAR, SCBWI, Graphic Artists Guild. Represents about 38 illustrators. 95% of artwork handled is children's book illustration.

• Accepting limited new artists from North America only.

Represents Illustration ONLY (and book ideas from agency artists).

Terms Receives 25% commission. "Artists responsible for providing samples for portfolios, promotional books and mailings." Exclusive representation required in educational. Trade "house accounts" acceptable. Offers written contract. Advertises in *Picturebook* and directory of illustration.

How to Contact For first contact, e-mail samples and live website link, with note. No CDs. Responds ASAP. Finds illustrators through recommendations from others, conferences, personal search.

Tips "Do research, read articles on CAT website, study picture books at bookstores, promote yourself a bit to learn the industry. Be professional.. know what you do best, and be prepared to give rep what they need to present you! Do have e-mail and scanning capabilities, too."

CORNELL & MCCARTHY, LLC

2-D Cross Hwy., Westport CT 06880. (203)454-4210. Fax: (203)454-4258. E-mail: contact@cmartreps.com. Website: www.cmartreps.com. **Contact:** Merial Cornell. Children's book illustration representatives. Estab. 1989. Member of SCBWI and Graphic Artists Guild. Represents 30 illustrators. Specializes in children's books: trade, mass market, educational.

Represents Illustration.

Terms Agent receives 25% commission. Advertising costs are split: 75% paid by talent; 25% paid by representative. For promotional purposes, talent must provide 10-12 strong portfolio pieces relating to children's publishing.

How to Contact For first contact, send query letter, direct mail flier/brochure, tearsheets, photocopies and SASE or e-mail. Responds in 1 month. Obtains new talent through recommendations, solicitation, conferences.

Tips "Work hard on your portfolio."

CREATIVE FREELANCERS, INC.

P.O. Box 366, Tallevast FL 34270 (800)398-9544. Website: www.illustratorsonline.com. **Contact:** Marilyn Howard. Commercial illustration representative. Estab. 1988. Represents over 30 illustrators. "Our staff members have art direction, art buying or illustration backgrounds." Specializes in children's books, advertising, architectural, conceptual. Markets include: advertising agencies; corporations/client direct; design firms; editorial/magazines; paper products/greeting cards; publishing/books; sales/promotion firms.

Represents Illustration. Artists must have published work.

Terms Rep receives 30% commission. Exclusive area representation is preferred. Advertising costs are split: 75% paid by talent; 25% paid by representative. For promotional purposes, talent must provide scans of artwork. Advertises in *American Showcase, Workbook*.

How to Contact For first contact, send tearsheets, low res jpegs or "whatever best shows work." Responds back only if interested.

Tips Looks for experience, professionalism and consistency of style. Obtains new talent through "word of mouth and website."

DIMENSION

13420 Morgan Ave. S., Burnsville MN 55337. (952)201-3981. Fax: (952)895-9315. E-mail: jkoltes@dimensioncreative.com. Website: www.dimensioncreative.com. **Contact:** Joanne Koltes. Commercial illustration representative. Estab. 1982. Member of MN Book Builder. Represents 12 illustrators. 65% of artwork handled is children's book illustration. Staff includes Joanne Koltes.

Terms Advertises in *Picturebook* and *Minnesota Creative*.

How to Contact Contact with samples via e-mail. Responds only if interested.

DWYER & O'GRADY, INC.

P.O. Box 790, Cedar Key FL 32625-0790. (352)543-9307. Fax: (603)375-5373. Website: www. dwyerogrady.com. Contact: Jeffrey P. Dwyer. Agents for authors and illustrators of children's books. Estab. 1990. Member of Society of Illustrators, Author's Guild, SCBWI, Graphic Artist's Guild. Represents 12 illustrators and 20 writers. Staff includes Elizabeth O'Grady and Jeffrey Dwyer. Specializes in children's books (picture books, middle grade and young adult). Markets include: publishing/books, audio/film. Dwyer & O'Grady is not accepting new clients.

Recent Sales *The Rain School* (HoughtonMifflinHarcourt) and *From the Good Mountain* (Roaring Brook), by James Rumford; *Country Fair* (Putnam), by Richard Michelson with illustrations by Mary Azarian; *Lip Pike* (Sleeping Bear), by Richard Michelson; Christmas in the Time of Billy Lee (Hyperion) illustrated by Barry Moser, O Harry (Roaring Brook) by Maxine Kumin illustrated by Barry Moser, *The Shih Tzu's Haiku* (Candlewick) illustrated by Mary Azarian, and *Tea Cakes for Tosh* (Putnam) by Kelly Starling Lyons.

Terms Receives 15% commission domestic, 20% foreign. Additional fees are negotiable. Exclusive representation is required (world rights). Advertising costs are paid by representative.

How to Contact For first contact, send query letter by postal mail only.

🌐 THOROGOOD KIDS

+44(0) 20 8859 7507. Fax: +44(0) 20 8333 7677. E-mail: draw@goodillustration.com; doreen@thorogood.net. Represents 30 illustrators including: Bill Dare, Kanako and Yuzuru, Shaunna Peterson, Nicola Slater, Dan Hambe, David Bromley, Robin Heighway-Bury, Anja Boretzki, Olivier Latyk, Al Sacui, John Woodcock, Carol Morley, Leo Timmers, Christiane Engel, Anne Yvonne Gilbert, Philip Nicholson, Adria Fruitos, Ester Garcia Cortes, Lisa Zibamanzar, Alessandra Cimatoribus, Marta and Leonor, Iryna Bodnaruk. Staff includes Doreen Thorogood, Steve Thorogood, Tom Thorogood and Kate Webber. Open to illustrators seeking representation. Accepting both new and established illustrators. Guidelines not available. Website: www.goodillustration.coms.
Represents Accepts illustration, illustration/manuscript packages.
Recent Sales Anne Yvonn
How to Contact For first contact, send tearsheets, photocopies, SASE, direct mail flyer/brochure. After initial contact, we will contact the illustrator if we want to see the portfolio. Portfolio should include tearsheets, photocopies. Finds illustrators through queries/solicitations, conferences.
Tips "Be unique and research your market. Talent will win out!"

PAT HACKETT/ARTIST REP

7014 N. Mercer Way, Mercer Island WA 98040-2130. (206)447-1600. Website: www.pathackett.com. **Contact:** Pat Hackett. Commercial illustration representative. Estab. 1979. Member of Graphic Artists Guild. Represents 8 illustrators. 10% of artwork handled is children's book illustration. Currently open to illustrators seeking representation. Open to both new and established illustrators.
Represents Illustration. Looking for illustrators with unique, strong, salable style.
Terms Receives 25-33% commission. Advertising costs are split: 75% paid by illustrators; 25% paid by rep. Illustrator must provide portfolios (2-3) and promotional pieces. Advertises in *Picturebook*, *Workbook*.
How to Contact For first contact, send query letter, tearsheets, SASE, direct mail flier/brochure, or e-mail. Responds only if interested. Wait for response.
Tips "Send query plus 1-2 samples, either by regular mail or e-mail."

HANNAH REPRESENTS

1472 Dudley Avenue, Ventura, CA 93004. (818)378-1644. E-mail: hannahrepresents@yahoo.com. **Contact:** Hannah Robinson. Literary representative for illustrators. Estab. 1997. 100% of artwork handled is children's book illustration. Looking for established illustrators only.
Represents Manuscript/illustration packages.

LEVY CREATIVE MANAGEMENT

250 E. 54th St., Suite 15c, New York NY 10022. (212)687-6465. Fax: (212)661-4839. E-mail: info@levycreative.com. Website: www.levycreative.com. **Contact:** Sari Levy. Estab. 1998. Member of Society of Illustrators, Graphic Artists Guild, Art Directors Club. Represents 13 illustrators including: Kako, Orbit Berman, Michael Byers, Robin Eley, Brian Hubble, Rory Kurtz, Jorge Mascarenhas, Christopher Nelsen, Laura Osorno, Trip Park, Kyung Soon Park, Koren Shadmi, Jason Tharp, Andrea Wicklund. 30% of artwork handled is children's book illustration. Currently open to illustrators seeking representation. Open to both new and established illustrators. Submission guidelines available on website.
Represents Illustration, manuscript/illustration packages.
Terms Exclusive representation required. Offers written contract. Advertising costs are split: 75% paid by illustrators; 25% paid by rep. Advertises in *Picturebook*, *American Showcase*, *Workbook*, *Alternative Pick and others*.

How to Contact For first contact, send tearsheets, photocopies, SASE. "See website for submission guidelines." Responds only if interested. Portfolio should include professionally presented materials. Finds illustrators through recommendations from others, word of mouth, competitions.

MARLENA AGENCY, INC.

322 Ewing St., Princeton NJ 08540. (609)252-9405. Fax: (609)252-1949. E-mail: marlena@ marlenaagency.com. Website: www.marlenaagency.com. Commercial illustration representative. Estab. 1990. Member of Society of Illustrators. Represents over 30 international illustrators including: Gerard Dubois, Linda Helton, Paul Zwolak, Martin Jarrie, Serge Bloch, Hadley Hooper, Jean-François Martin Perre Mornet, Pep Montserrat, Tomasz Walenta, Istvan Orosz, Lorenzo Petrantoni, Scott Mckowen and Carmen Segovia. Staff includes Marlena Torzecka, Marie Joanne Wimmer, Anna Pluskota, Sophie Mialhe. Currently open to illustrators seeking representation. Open to both new and established illustrators. Submission guidelines available for #10 SASE.
Represents Illustration.
Recent Sales *Sees Behind Trees*, by Linda Helton (Harcourt); *Ms. Rubinstein's Beauty, by Pep Montserrat* (Sterling);ABC USA, by Martin Jarrie (Sterling); *My Cat*, by Linda Helton (Scholastic); *The McElderry Book of Greek Myths*, by Pep Monserrat (McElderly Books)
Terms Exclusive representation required. Offers written contract. Requires printed portfolios, digital files, direct mail piece (such as postcards) printed samples. Advertises in *Workbook*.
How to Contact For first contact, send tearsheets, photocopies, or e-mail low resolution samples only. Responds only if interested. Drop off or mail portfolio, photocopies. Portfolio should include tearsheets, photocopies. Finds illustrators through queries/solicitations, magazines and graphic design.
Tips "Be creative and persistent."

MB ARTISTS

(formerly HK Portfolio), 775 Sixth Ave., #6 , New York NY 10001. (212)689-7830. E-mail: mela@ mbartists.com. Website: www.mbartists.com. **Contact:** Mela Bolinao. Illustration representative. Estab. 1986. Member of SPAR, Society of Illustrators and Graphic Artists Guild. Represents over 60 illustrators. Specializes in illustration for juvenile markets. Markets include: advertising agencies; editorial/magazines; publishing/books, Tos, games boards, stationary, etc.
Represents Illustration.
Recent Sales *Bunion Burt*, illustrated by Jack E. Davis (Simon & Schuster); *Dear Tyrannosaurus Rex*, illustrated by John Manders (Random House); *The Adventures of Granny Clearwater*, illustrated by by Laura Huliska Beith (Henery Holtt); *Pre School Hooray*, illustrated by Hiroe Nakata (Scholastic); *Alred Sector, Book Collector*, illustrated by Macky Pamintuan (HarperCollins).
Terms Rep receives 25% commission. No geographic restrictions. Advertising costs are split: 75% paid by talent; 25% paid by representative. Advertises in *Picturebook*, *Directory of Illustration*, *Play* and *Workbook*.
How to Contact No geographic restrictions. For first contact, send query letter, direct mail flier/ brochure, website address, tearsheets, slides, photographs or color copies and SASE or send website link to mela@mbartists.com. Responds in 1 week. Portfolio should include at least 12 images appropriate for the juvenile market.

THE NEIS GROUP

14600 Sawyer Ranch Rd, Dripping Springs TX 78620. (616)450-1533. **Contact:** Judy Neis. Commercial illustration representative. Estab. 1982. Represents 45 illustrators including: Lyn Boyer, Pam Thomson, Dan Sharp, Terry Workman, Garry Colby, Clint Hansen, Julie Borden, Diana Magnuson, Jacqueline Rogers, Johnna Hogenkamp, Jack Pennington, Gary Ferster, Mark and Lee Fullerton,

James Palmer, Brandon Reese, Joel Spector, John White, Neverne Covington, Ruth Pettis, Laura Nikiel, Brandon Fall, Carol Newsom, Joel Aaron Carlson, Gary Freeman. 60% of artwork handled is children's book illustration. Currently open to illustrators seeking representation. Looking for established illustrators only. Website: www.neisgroup.com.

Represents Illustration, photography and calligraphy/manuscript packages.

Terms Receives 25% commission. "I prefer portfolios on disc, color printouts and e-mail capabilities whenever possible." Advertises in *Picturebook*, & *Creative Black Book*.

How to Contact For first contact, send bio, tearsheets, direct mail flier/brochure. Responds only if interested. After initial contact, drop off portfolio of nonreturnables. Portfolio should include tearsheets, photocopies. Obtains new talent through recommendations from others and queries/solicitations.

WANDA NOWAK/CREATIVE ILLUSTRATORS AGENCY

231 E. 76th St.5D, New York NY 10021. (212)535-0438. E-mail: wanda@wandanow.com. Website: www.wandanow.com. **Contact:** Wanda Nowak. Commercial illustration representative. Estab. 1996. Represents 20 illustrators including: Emilie Chollat, Thea Kliros, Frederique Bertrand, Ilja Bereznickas, Boris Kulikov, Yayo, Laurence Cleyet-Merle, E. Kerner, Ellen Usdin, Stephane Jorisch, Oliver Latyk, Benoit Laverdiere, Anne-Sophie Lanquetin, Andre Letria. 50% of artwork handled is children's book illustration. Staff includes Wanda Nowak. Open to both new and established illustrators.

Represents Illustration. Looking for "unique, individual style."

Terms Receives 30% commission. Exclusive representation required. Offers written contract. Advertising costs are split: 70% paid by illustrators; 30% paid by rep. Advertises in *Picturebook*, *Workbook*, *The Alternative Pick*.

How to Contact For first contact, send SASE. Responds only if interested. Drop off portfolio. Portfolio should include tearsheets. Finds illustrators through recommendations from others, sourcebooks like *CA*, *Picture Book* exhibitions.

Tips "Develop your own style. Send a little illustrated story, which will prove you can carry a character in different situations with facial expressions, etc."

RENAISSANCE HOUSE

465 Westview Ave., Englewood NJ 07631. (800)547-5113. Fax: (201)408-5011. E-mail: info@ renaissancehouse.net. Website: www.renaissancehouse.net. **Contact:** Raquel Benatar. Children's, educational, multicultural, and textbooks, advertising rep. Estab. 1991. Represents 80 illustrators. 95% of artwork handled is children's book illustration. Currently open to illustrators and photographers seeking representation. Open to both new and established illustrators.

Represents Illustration and photography.

Recent Sales Maribel Suarez (Little Brown, Hyperion); Gabriel Pacheco (MacMillan)Ana Lopez (Scholastic); Ruth Araceli (Houghton Mifflin); Vivi Escriva (Albert Whitman); Marie Jara (Sparknotes); Sheli Petersen (McGraw-Hill).

Terms Exclusive and non-exclusive representation. Illustrators must provide scans of illustrations. Advertises in own website and catalog of illustrators.

How to Contact For first contact send tearsheets. Responds in 2 weeks. Finds illustrators through recommendations from others, conferences, direct contact.

ⓝ SALZMAN INTERNATIONAL

1751 Charles Ave., Arcate CA 95521. Phone/fax: (707)822-5500. E-mail: rs@salzint.com. Website: www.salzint.com. Commercial illustration representative. Estab. 1982. Represents 20 illustrators.

20% of artwork is children's book illustration. Staff includes Richard Salzman. Open to illustrators seeking representation. Accepting both new and established illustrators.

Represents Accepts illustration.

Terms Receives 25% commission. Offers written contract. 100% of advertising costs paid by illustrator. Advertises in *Workbook*, ispot.com, altpick.com.

How to Contact For first contact, send link to website or printed samples. Portfolio should include tearsheets, photocopies; "best to post samples on website and send link." Finds illustrators through queries/solicitations.

S.I. INTERNATIONAL

43 E. 19th St., New York NY 10003. (212)254-4996. Fax: (212)995-0911. E-mail: information@ si-i.com. Website: www.si-i.com. Commercial illustration representative. Estab. 1983. Member of SPAR, Graphic Artists Guild. Represents 50 illustrators. Specializes in license characters, educational publishing and children's illustration, digital art and design, mass market paperbacks. Markets include design firms; publishing/books; sales/promotion firms; licensing firms; digital art and design firms.

Represents Illustration. Looking for artists "who have the ability to do children's illustration and to do license characters either digitally or reflectively."

Terms Rep receives 25-30% commission. Advertising costs are split: 70% paid by talent; 30% paid by representative. "Contact agency for details. Must have mailer." Advertises in *Picturebook*.

How to Contact For first contact, send query letter, tearsheets. Responds in 3 weeks. After initial contact, write for appointment to show portfolio of tearsheets, slides.

GWEN WALTERS ARTIST REPRESENTATIVE

1801 S. Flagler Dr., #1202, W. Palm Beach FL 33401. (561)805-7739. E-mail: artincgw@aol. com. Website: www.gwenwaltersartrep.com. **Contact:** Gwen Walters. Commercial illustration representative. Estab. 1976. Represents 18 illustrators. 90% of artwork handled is children's book illustration. Currently open to illustrators seeking representation. Looking for established illustrators only.

Represents Illustration.

Recent Sales Sells to "All major book publishers."

Terms Receives 30% commission. Artist needs to supply all promo material. Offers written contract. Advertising costs are split: 70% paid by illustrator; 30% paid by rep. Advertises in *Picturebook*, *RSVP*, *Directory of Illustration*.

How to Contact For first contact, send tearsheets. Responds only if interested. Finds illustrators through recommendations from others.

Tips "Go out and get some first-hand experience. Learn to tell yourself to understand the way the market works."

WENDYLYNN & CO.

504 Wilson Rd., Annapolis MD 21401. (401)224-2729. E-mail: wendy@wendylynn.com. Website: www.wendylynn.com. **Contact:** Wendy Mays. Children's illustration representative. Estab. 2002. Member of SCBWI. Represents 30 illustrators. 100% of artwork handled is children's illustration. Staff includes Wendy Mays, Janice Onken. Currently open to considering illustrators seeking representation. Open to both new and established illustrators. Not interested in cartoon style illustration. Submission guidelines available on website.

Represents Illustration.

Terms Receives 25% commission. Exclusive representation required. Offers written contract. Requires 20 images submitted on disk in high and low resolution versions. Requires participation in a children's illustrators website that cost the artist $200 annually. Pays 100% of all other promotion.

How to Contact For first contact, e-mail 4-5 jpg samples and link to website. Responds if interested. Portfolio should include a minimum of 20 strong images. Finds illustrators through recommendations from others and from portfolio reviews.

Tips "Work on making your characters consistent and vibrant, showing movement and emotion. Be able to scan your artwork and send digital files. Create an interesting and user-friendly website of your illustrations."

DEBORAH WOLFE LTD.

731 N. 24th St., Philadelphia PA 19130. (215)232-6666. Fax: (215)232-6585. E-mail: info@ illustrationOnline.com. Website: www.illustrationOnline.com. **Contact:** Deborah Wolfe. Commercial illustration representative. Estab. 1978. Member of Graphic Artist Guild. Represents 30 illustrators. Currently open to illustrators seeking representation.

Represents Illustration.

Terms Receives 25% commission. Exclusive representation required. Offers written contract. Advertising costs are split: 75% paid by illustrators; 25% paid by rep. Advertises in *Picturebook, Directory of Illustration, The Workbook.*

How to Contact Responds in 2 weeks. Portfolio should be sent as jpgs or you should direct us to your website. Finds illustrators through queries/solicitations.

Clubs & Organizations

Contacts made through organizations such as the ones listed in this section can be quite beneficial for children's writers and illustrators. Professional organizations provide numerous educational, business, and legal services in the form of newsletters, workshops, or seminars. Organizations can provide tips about how to be a more successful writer or artist, as well as what types of business cards to keep, health and life insurance coverage to carry, and competitions to consider.

An added benefit of belonging to an organization is the opportunity to network with those who have similar interests, creating a support system. As in any business, knowing the right people can often help your career, and important contacts can be made through your peers. Membership in a writer's or artist's organization also shows publishers you're serious about your craft. This provides no guarantee your work will be published, but it gives you an added dimension of credibility and professionalism.

Some of the organizations listed here welcome anyone with an interest, while others are only open to published writers and professional artists. Organizations such as the Society of Children's Book Writers and Illustrators (SCBWI, www.scbwi.org) have varying levels of membership. SCBWI offers associate membership to those with no publishing credits, and full membership to those who have had work for children published. International organizations such as SCBWI also have regional chapters throughout the U.S. and the world. Write or call for more information regarding any group that interests you, or check the websites of the many organizations that list them. Be sure to get information about local chapters, membership qualifications, and services offered.

ARIZONA AUTHORS ASSOCIATION

6145 West Echo Lane, Glendale AZ 85302. E-mail: info@azauthors.com. Website: www.azauthors. com. **President:** Toby Heathcotte. Purpose of organization: to offer professional, educational and social opportunities to writers and authors, and serve as a network. Members must be authors, writers working toward publication, agents, publishers, publicists, printers, illustrators, etc. Membership cost: $45/year writers; $30/year students; $60/year other professionals in publishing industry. Holds regular workshops and meetings. Publishes bimonthly newsletter and Arizona Literary Magazine. Sponsors Annual Literary Contest in poetry, essays, short stories, novels, and published books with cash prizes and awards bestowed at a public banquet. Winning entries are also published or advertised in the Arizona Literary Magazine. First and second place winners in poetry, essay and short story categories are entered in the Pushcart Prize. Winner is in published categories receive free listings by www.fivestarpublications.com. Send SASE or view website for guidelines.

▨ CANADIAN SOCIETY OF CHILDREN'S AUTHORS, ILLUSTRATORS AND PERFORMERS (CANSCAIP)

104-40 Orchard View Blvd., Toronto ON M4R 1B9 Canada. (416)515-1559. E-mail: office@canscaip. org. Website: www.canscaip.org. **Administrative Director:** Lena Coakley. Purpose of organization: development of Canadian children's culture and support for authors, illustrators and performers working in this field. Qualifications for membership: Members—professionals who have been published (not self-published) or have paid public performances/records/tapes to their credit. Friends—share interest in field of children's culture. Membership cost: $85 (Members dues), $45 (Friends dues). Sponsors workshops/conferences. Manuscript evaluation services publishes newsletter: includes profiles of members; news round-up of members' activities countrywide; market news; news on awards, grants, etc; columns related to professional concerns.

FLORIDA FREELANCE WRITERS ASSOCIATION

Writers-Editors Network, P.O. Box A, North Stratford NH 03590. (603)922-8338. E-mail: FFWA@ Writers-Editors.com. Web sites: www.ffwamembers.com and www.writers-editors.com. **Executive Director:** Dana K. Cassell. Purpose of organization: To provide a link between Florida writers and buyers of the written word; to help writers run more effective editorial businesses. Qualifications for membership: "None. We provide a variety of services and information, some for beginners and some for established pros." Membership cost: $90/year. Publishes a newsletter focusing on market news, business news, how-to tips for the serious writer. Annual Directory of Florida Markets included in FFWA newsletter section and electronic download. Publishes annual Guide to CNW/Florida Writers, which is distributed to editors around the country. Sponsors contest: annual deadline March 15. Guidelines on website. Categories: juvenile, adult nonfiction, adult fiction and poetry. Awards include cash for top prizes, certificate for others. Contest open to nonmembers.

GRAPHIC ARTISTS GUILD

32 Broadway, Suite 1114, New York NY 10004. (212)791-3400. Fax: (212) 791-0333. E-mail: admin@ gag.org. Website: www.gag.org. **Executive Director:** Patricia Mckiernan. Purpose of organization: "To promote and protect the economic interests of member artists. It is committed to improving conditions for all creators of graphic arts and raising standards for the entire industry." Qualification for full membership: 50% of income derived from the creation of artwork. Associate members include those in allied fields, students and retirees. Initiation fee: $30. Full memberships: $200; student membership: $75/year. Associate membership: $170/year. Publishes Graphic Artists Guild Handbook, Pricing and Ethical Guidelines (members receive a copy as part of their membership).

NATIONAL WRITERS ASSOCIATION

10940 S. Parker Rd., #508, Parker CO 80138. (303)841-0246. Fax: (303)841-2607. E-mail: natlwritersassn@hotmail.com. Website: www.nationalwriters.com. **Executive Director:** Sandy Whelchel. Purpose of organization: association for freelance writers. Qualifications for membership: associate membership—must be serious about writing; professional membership—must be published and paid writer (cite credentials). Membership cost: $65 associate; $85 professional; $35 student. Sponsors workshops/conferences: TV/screenwriting workshops, NWAF Annual Conferences, Literary Clearinghouse, editing and critiquing services, local chapters, National Writer's School. Open to non-members. Publishes industry news of interest to freelance writers; how-to articles; market information; member news and networking opportunities. Nonmember subscription: $20. Sponsors poetry contest; short story contest; article contest; novel contest. Awards cash for top 3 winners; books and/or certificates for other winners; honorable mention certificate places 5-10. Contests open to nonmembers.

NATIONAL WRITERS UNION

E-mail: nwu@nwu.org. Website: www.nwu.org. Students welcome. Purpose of organization: Advocacy for freelance writers. Qualifications for membership: "Membership in the NWU is open to all qualified writers, and no one shall be barred or in any manner prejudiced within the Union on account of race, age, sex, sexual orientation, disability, national origin, religion or ideology. You are eligible for membership if you have published a book, a play, three articles, five poems, one short story or an equivalent amount of newsletter, publicity, technical, commercial, government or institutional copy. You are also eligible for membership if you have written an equal amount of unpublished material and you are actively writing and attempting to publish your work" Membership cost: annual writing income less than $5000-$120/year; $5001-15,000-$195; $15,001-30,000-$265/year; $30,001-$45,000-$315 a year; $45,001- and up -$340/year. Holds workshops throughout the country. Members only section on web site offers rich resources for freelance writers. Skilled contract advice and grievance help for members.

🌐 PLAYMARKET

P.O. Box 9767, Te Aro We New Zealand. (64)4 382-8462. Fax: +64 4 382 8461. E-mail: info@playmarket.org.nz. **Director:** Murray Lynch. **Script Development**: Jean Betts. **Administrator:** Pania Stevenson. **Agency Coordinator:** Murray Lynch. Purpose of organization: funded by Creative New Zealand, Playmarket serves as New Zealand's script advisory service and playwrights' agency. Playmarket offers script assessment, development and agency services to help New Zealand playwrights secure professional production for their plays. Playmarket runs the NZ Young Playwrights Competition, The Aotearoa Playwrights Conference and the Adam Playreading Series and administers the annual Bruce Mason Playwrighting Award. The organization's magazine, Playmarket News, is published biannually. Inquiries e-mail info@playmarket.org.nz. Website: www.playmarket.org.nz.

SOCIETY OF CHILDREN'S BOOK WRITERS AND ILLUSTRATORS

8271 Beverly Blvd., Los Angeles CA 90048. (323)782-1010. Fax: (323)782-1892 E-mail: scbwi@scbwi.org. Website: www.scbwi.org. **President:** Stephen Mooser. **Executive Director:** Lin Oliver. Chairperson, Board of Advisors: Frank Sloan. Purpose of organization: to assist writers and illustrators working or interested in the field. Qualifications for membership: an interest in children's literature and illustration. Membership cost: $70/year. Plus one time $85 initiation fee. Different levels of membership include: P.A.L. membership—published by publisher listed in SCBWI Market Surveys; full membership—published authors/illustrators (includes self-published); associate membership—unpublished writers/illustrators. Holds 100 events (workshops/conferences) worldwide each year. National Conference open to nonmembers. Publishes bi-monthly magazine on writing and illustrating children's books. Sponsors annual awards and grants for writers and illustrators who are members.

SOCIETY OF ILLUSTRATORS

128 E. 63rd St., New York NY 10021-7303. (212)838-2560. Fax: (212)838-2561. E-mail: info@ societyillustrators.org. **Contact:** Anelle Miller, director. "Our mission is to promote the art and appreciation of illustration, its history and evolving nature through exhibitions, lectures and education." Cost of membership. Annual dues for nonresident Illustrator members (those living more than 125 air miles from SI's headquarters): $300. Dues for Resident Illustrator Members: $500 per year; Resident Associate Members: $500." Artist Members shall include those who make illustration their profession and earn at least 60% of their income from their illustration. Associate Members are those who earn their living in the arts or who have made a substantial contribution to the art of illustration. This includes art directors, art buyers, creative supervisors, instructors, publishers and like categories. The candidate must complete and sign the application form which requires a brief biography, a listing of schools attended, other training and a résumé of his or her professional career. Candidates for Illustrators membership, in addition to the above requirements, must submit examples of their work." Website: www.societyillustrators.org.

SOUTHWEST WRITERS

3721 Morris NE, Suite A, Albuquerque NM 87111. (505)265-9485. Fax: (505)265-9483. E-mail: swwriters@juno.com. Website: www.southwestwriters.org. Non-profit organization dedicated to helping members of all levels in their writing. Members enjoy perks such as networking with professional and aspiring writers; substantial discounts on mini-conferences, workshops, writing classes, and annual and quarterly SWW writing contest; monthly newsletter; two writing programs per month; critique groups, critique service (also for nonmembers); discounts at bookstores and other businesses; and website linking. Cost of membership: Individual, $60/year, $100/2 years; Two People, $50 each/year; Student, $40/year; Student under 18, $25/year; Outside U.S.$65/year; Lifetime, $750. See website for information.

TEXT AND ACADEMIC AUTHORS ASSOCIATION TAA

P.O. Box 56359, St. Petersburg FL 33732-6359. (727)563-0020. Fax: (727)563-0500. E-mail: TextandAcademicAuthors@taaonline.net. Website: www.taaonline.net. **President:** Paul Siegel until June 30, 2010. After that, President is Don Collins. Purpose of organization: the only nonprofit membership association dedicated solely to assisting textbook and academic authors. TAA's overall mission is to enhance the quality of textbooks and other academic materials, such as journal articles, monographs and scholarly books, in all fields and disciplines. Qualifications for membership: all authors and prospective authors are welcome. Membership cost: $30 first year; graduated levels for following years. Workshops/conferences: June each year. Newsletter focuses on all areas of interest to text book and academic authors.

WESTERN WRITERS OF AMERICA, INC.

1012 Mesa Vista Hall, MSCO6 3770, 1 University of New Mexico, Albuquerque NM 87131-0001. (505)277-5234. E-mail: wwa@unm.edu; rod@holmesco.com. Website: www.westernwriters.org. **Executive Director:** Paul Andrew Hutton. Open to students. Purpose of organization: to further all types of literature that pertains to the American West. Membership requirements: must be a published author of Western material. Membership cost: $75/year ($90 foreign). Different levels of membership include: Active and Associate-the two vary upon number of books or articles published. Holds annual conference. The 2008 conference held in Scottsdale, AZ; 2009 held in Midwest City, Oklahoma. Publishes bimonthly magazine focusing on western literature, market trends, book reviews, news of members, etc. Nonmembers may subscribe for $30 ($50 foreign). Sponsors youth writing contests. Spur awards given annually for a variety of types of writing. Awards include plaque, certificate, publicity. Contest and Spur Awards open to nonmembers.

WRITERS GUILD OF ALBERTA

11759 Groat Rd., Edmonton AB T5M 3K6 Canada. (780)422-8174. Fax: (780)422-2663. E-mail: mail@writersguild.ab.ca. Website: www.writersguild.ab.ca. Purpose of organization: to support, encourage and promote writers and writing, to safeguard the freedom to write and to read, and to advocate for the well-being of writers in Alberta. Membership cost: $60/year; $30 for seniors/students. Holds workshops/conferences. Publishes a newsletter focusing on markets, competitions, contemporary issues related to the literary arts (writing, publishing, censorship, royalties etc.). Sponsors annual Literary Awards in five categories (novel, nonfiction, children's literature, poetry, drama). Awards include $1,500, leather-bound book, promotion and publicity. Open to nonmembers.

Conferences & Workshops

Writers and illustrators eager to expand their knowledge of the children's publishing industry should consider attending one of the many conferences and workshops held each year. Whether you're a novice or seasoned professional, conferences and workshops are great places to pick up information on a variety of topics and network with experts in the publishing industry, as well as with your peers.

Listings in this section provide details about what conference and workshop courses are offered, where and when they are held, and the costs. Some of the national writing and art organizations also offer regional workshops throughout the year. Write, call or visit websites for information.

Writers can find listings of more than 1,000 conferences on the WritersMarket.com Paid Services site—www.writersmarket.com/paidservices.

Members of the Society of Children's Book Writers and Illustrators can find information on conferences in national and local SCBWI newsletters. Nonmembers may attend SCBWI events as well. SCBWI conferences are listed in the beginning of this section under a separate subheading. For information on SCBWI's annual national conferences, contact them at (323)782-1010 or check their website for a complete calendar of national and regional events (www.scbwi.org).

CONFERENCES & WORKSHOPS CALENDAR

January
Gotham Writers' Workshop (New York NY) 328
Indianapolis Youth Lit Conference (Indianapolis IN) 329
Publishinggame.com Workshop 332
San Diego State University Writers' Conference (San Diego CA) 333
SCBWI—Florida Regional Conference (Miami FL) 319
SCBWI—Ventura/Santa Barbara; Retreat for Children's Authors and Illustrators 325
Winter Poetry & Prose Getaway in Cape May (Cape May NJ) 336

February
Fishtrap, Inc. 328
Publishinggame.com Workshop 332
San Francisco Writers Conference (San Francisco CA) 334

Multiple or Seasonal Events

The conference listings below include information on multiple or year-round events or events that are seasonal (held in fall or spring, for example). Please read the listings for more information on the dates and locations of these events and check the conferences' websites.

SCBWI CONFERENCES

SCBWI; ANNUAL CONFERENCES ON WRITING AND ILLUSTRATING FOR CHILDREN

8271 Beverly Blvd.Los Angeles CA 90048. (323)782-1010. Fax: (323)782-1892. E-mail: scbwi@scbwi.org. Website: www.scbwi.org. **Conference Director:** Lin Oliver. Writer and illustrator workshops geared toward all levels. **Open to students.** Covers all aspects of children's book and magazine publishing—the novel, illustration techniques, marketing, etc. Annual conferences held in August in Los Angeles and in New York in February. Cost of conference (LA): approximately $390; includes all 4 days and one banquet meal. Write for more information or visit website.

SCBWI—ARIZONA; EVENTS

P.O. Box 26384, Scottsdale AZ 85255-0123. E-mail: RegionalAdvisor@scbwi-az.org. Website: www.scbwi-az.org. **Regional Advisor:** Michelle Parker-Rock. SCBWI Arizona will offer a variety of workshops, retreats, intensives, conferences, meetings and other craft and industry-related events throughout 2010-2011. Open to members and nonmembers, published and nonpublished. Registration to major events is usually limited. Pre-registration always required. Visit website, write or e-mail for more information.

🌐 SCBWI BOLOGNA BIENNIAL CONFERENCE

The SCBWI Showcase Booth at the Bologna Book Fair: The next SCBWI Showcase Booth will take place during the 2012 Bologna Book Fair. It will feature authors and illustrators from SCBWI regions, SCBWI PAL members, and special author and illustrator events. For more information email: Angela@SCBWIBologna.org or Kathleen@SCBWIBologna.org

SCBWI—CAROLINAS; ANNUAL FALL CONFERENCE

E-mail: scbwicarolinas@earthlink.net. **Regional Advisor:** Teresa Fannin. Inventing Story: Oh, The Places We'll Go. September 24-26, 2010 at the Marriott Executive Park, Charlotte, NC. Speakers include: Alvina Ling, senior editor, Little Brown Publishing; Liz Waniewski, editor, Dial Books for Young Readers; Alan Gratz, author, The Brooklyn Nine; Chris Richman, agent, Upstart Crow Literary Agency; Steve Watkins, 2009 SCBWI Golden Kite Winner, Down Sand Mountain, 2K09 debut Author Fran Slayton, When the Whistle Blows. Friday afternoon manuscript and portfolio critiques, workshops focusing on the art and craft of writing and illustrating for children visit www.scbwicarolinas.org for more information.

📓 SCBWI CAROLINAS— SPRING RETREAT, THE ELEMENTS OF STORY

April 16-18, 2010 Aqueduct Conference Center, Chapel Hill, NC. Speakers include Jennifer Rees, senior editor, Scholastic Books; Stacey Cantor, editor, Walker Books for Young Readers; Bruce Hale, author, The Chet Gecko series. Join us for a weekend of inspiring and informative talks on story in the peaceful seclusion of the center's woodland setting. For more information and registration visit our website at www.scbwicarolinas.org.

SCBWI—DAKOTAS; SPRING CONFERENCE

2521 S 40th St., Grand Forks, ND 58201. E-mail: cdrylander@yahoo.com. Website: www. scbwidakotas.org. **Regional Advisor:** Chris Rylander. This is a conference for writers and illustrators of all levels. Previous conferences have included speakers Tim Gilner, S.T. Underdahl, Roxane Salonen, and Marilyn Kratz. Annual event held every spring. Check website for details.

SCBWI—DAKOTAS; WRITERS CONFERENCE IN CHILDREN'S LITERATURE

Grand Forks ND 58201. (701)720-0464. E-mail: cdrylander@yahoo.com. Website: www.und.edu/ dept/english/ChildrensLit.html or www.scbwidakotas.org. **Regional Advisor:** Chris Rylander. Conference sessions geared toward all levels. "Although the conference attendees are mostly writers, we encourage & welcome illustrators of every level." Open to students. "Our conference offers 3-4 children's authors, editors, publishers, illustrators, or agents. Past conferences have included Kent Brown (publisher, Boyds Mills Press); Alexandra Penfold (Editor, Simon & Schuster); Jane Kurtz (author); Anastasia Suen (author); and Karen Ritz (illustrator). Conference held each fall. "Please call or e-mail to confirm dates. Writers and illustrators come from throughout the northern plains, including North Dakota, South Dakota, Montana, Minnesota, Iowa, and Canada." Writing facilities available: campus of University of North Dakota. Local art exhibits and/or concerts may coincide with conference. Cost of conference includes Friday evening reception and sessions, Saturday's sessions, and lunch. A manuscript may be submitted 1 month in advance for critique (extra charge). E-mail for more information.

SCBWI—DAKOTAS/UND WRITERS CONFERENCE IN CHILDREN'S LITERATURE

Department. of English, Merrifield Hall, Room 110, 276 Centennial Drive, Stop 7209, Univeristy of North Dakota, Grand Forks ND 58202. (701)777-3321 or (701)777-3984. E-mail: cdrylander@ yahoo.com. Website: www.und.edu or www.scbwidakotas.com. **Regional Advisor:** Chris Rylander. Conference for all levels. "Our conference offers 3-4 chlidren's authors, editors, publishers, illustrators or agents. Past conferences have included Elaine Marie Alphin (author), Jane Kurtz (author), Alexandra Penfold (editor), Kent Brown (publisher), and Karen Ritz (illustrator)." Annual conference held every fall. "Please call or e-mail to confirm dates." Cost of conference to be determined. Cost included Friday evening sessions, Saturday sessions, and Saturday lunch. "We welcome writers, illustrators, and others who are interested in children's literature."

◫ SCBWI—EASTERN CANADA; ANNUAL EVENTS

E-mail: araEast@scbwicanada.org; raEast@scbwicanada.org. Website: www.scbwicanada. org/east. **Regional Advisor:** Lizann Flatt. Writer and illustrator events geared toward all levels. Usually offers one event in spring and another in the fall. Check website Events pages for updated information.

SCBWI—FLORIDA; REGIONAL CONFERENCE

(305)382-2677. E-mail: lindabernfeld@gmail.com. Website: www.scbwiflorida.com. **Regional Advisor:** Linda Rodriguez Bernfeld. Annual conference held in January in Miami. 2011 conference will be held January 14-16, 2011. Past keynote speakers have included Linda Sue Park, Richard Peck, Bruce Coville, Bruce Hale, Arthur A. Levine, Judy Blume, Kate Dicamillo. 2011 Speakers include Cinda Williams Chima, Lauren Myracle, Sarah Davies, and Michael Bourret. Cost of conference: approximately $225. The 3-day conference will have workshops Friday afternoon and a field trip to Books and Books Friday evening. There will be a general session all day Saturday covering all aspects of writing for children. There will be hands on workshops Sunday morning led by industry leaders. For more information, contact e-mail Linda Rodriguez Bernfeld at lindabernfeld@gmail.com.

SCBWI—IDAHO; EDITOR DAY

Email: neysajensen@msn.com. **Regional Advisor:** Sydney Husseman; **Assistant Regional Advisor:** Neysa Jensen. One day workshop focuses on the craft of writing, as well as getting to know an editor. One-on-one critiques available for an additional fee. Event held in Boise, Idaho every fall.

ⓝ SCBWI—ILLINOIS; PRAIRIE WRITERS DAY

Chicago, IL Email: biermanlisa@hotmail.com. Website: www.scbwi-illinois.org/events. Regional Advisors: Lisa Bierman and Alice McGinty. All-day conference November 13, 2010, at the Wojcik Conference Center, Harper College, 1200 W. Algonquin Rd., Palatine, IL 60067. Full day of guest speakers, editors/agents TBD.Ms. critiques available as well as break-out sessions on career and craft. See website for complete description.

SCBWI—IOWA CONFERENCES

P.O. Box 1436, Bettendorf IA 52722-0024. E-mail: hecklit@aol.com. Writer and illustrator workshopsin all genres of children writing. The Iowa Region offers conferences of high quality events usually over a three-day period with registration options. Recent speakers included Allyn Johnston, Marla Frazee, Lisa Graff, Ammi-Joan Paquette and other well-known edtiors from the finest publisheing houses, Holds spring and fall events on a regional level, and network events across that state. Individual critiques and portfolio review offerings vary with the program and presenters. For more information e-mail or visit website. Website: www.scbwi-iowa.org/. **Contact:** Connie Heckert, regional advisor.

SCBWI—LOS ANGELES; EVENTS

P.O. Box 1728, Pacific Palisades CA 90272. (310) 573-7318. Website: www.scbwisocal.org. **Co-regional Advisors:** Claudia Harrington (claudiascbwi@verizon.net) and Edie Pagliasotti (ediescbwi@sbcglobal.net). SCBWI—Los Angeles hosts 6 major events each year: **Writer's Workshop** (winter)—half-day workshop featuring speaker demonstrating nuts and bolts techniques on the craft of writing for childrens; **Writer's Day** (spring)—a one-day conference featuring speakers, a professional forum, writing contests and awards; **Critiquenic** (summer)—a free informal critiquing session for writers and illustrators facilitated by published authors/illustrators, held after a picnic lunch; **Writers & Illustrator's Sunday Field Trip** (fall)—hands-on creative field trip for writers and illustrators; **Working Writer's Retreat** (fall)—a 3-day, 2-night retreat featuring an editor/agent, speakers, and intensive critiquing. **Illustrator's Day** (winter)—A one-day conference featuring speakers, juried art competition, contests, portfolio review/display. See calendar of events on website for more details and dates.

SCBWI—METRO NEW YORK; PROFESSIONAL SERIES

P.O. Box 1475, Cooper Station, New York NY 10276-1475. (212) 545-3719. E-mail: scbwi_metrony@yahoo.com. Website: http://metro.nyscbwi.org. **Regional Advisors:** Nancy Lewis and Seta Toroyan. Writer and illustrator workshops geared toward all levels. The Metro New York Professional Series generally meets the second Tuesday of each month, from September to June, 7:15-9:15 p.m. Check website to confirm location, dates, times and speakers. Cost of workshop: $15 for SCBWI members;

$20 for nonmembers. "We feature an informal evening with coffee, cookies, and top editors, art directors, agents, publicity and marketing people, librarians, reviewers and more."

SCBWI—MIDATLANTIC; ANNUAL FALL CONFERENCE

Mid-Atlantic SCBWI, P.O. Box 3215, Reston, VA 20195-1215. E-mail: midatlanticscbwi@tidalwave. net or teaganek@hotmail.com. Website: www.scbwi-midatlantic.org. **Conference Co-Chairs:** Sydney Dunlap and Erin Teagan. Regional Advisor: Ellen Braaf. Conference takes place Saturday, October 22, 2011 in Arlington, VA from 8 to 5. Keynote speaker TBA. For updates and details visit website. Registration limited to 200. Conference fills quickly. Cost: $115for SCBWI members; $145 for nonmembers. Includes continental breakfast. Lunch is on your own. (The food court at the Ballston Common Mall is two blocks away.)

SCBWI—MIDSOUTH FALL CONFERENCE

P.O. Box 396, Cordova TN 38088. E-mail: expressdog@bellsouth.net or cameron_s_e@yahoo. com. Website: www.scbwi-midsouth.org. **Conference Coordinators:** Genetta Adair and Sharon Cameron. Conference for writers and illustrators of all experience. In the past, workshops were offered on Plotting Your Novel, Understanding the Language of Editors, Landing an Agent, How to Prepare a Portfolio, Negotiating a Contract, The Basics for Beginners, and many others. Attendees are invited to bring a manuscript and/or art portfolio to share in the optional, no-charge critique group session. Illustrators are invited to bring color copies of their art (not originals) to be displayed in the illustrators' showcase. For an additional fee, attendees may schedule a 15-minute manuscript critique or portfolio critique by the editor, art director or other expert consultant. Annual conference held in September. Registration limited to 130 attendees. Cost to be determined. The 2010 Midsouth Fall Conference included Balzer & Bray editor Ruta Rimas; Nonfiction book pakager and editor Lionel Bender from London, England; Andrea Brown agent Kelly Sonnack; ICM agent Tina Wexler; Award-winning author Linda Sue Park and more.

SCBWI—MISSOURI; CHILDREN'S WRITER'S CONFERENCE

St. Charles County Community College, P.O. Box 76975, 103 CEAC, St. Peters MO 63376-0975. (636)922-8233, ext. 4108. Website: www.moscbwi.org. **Regional Advisor:** Stephanie Bearce. Writer and illustrator conference geared toward all levels. **Open to students.** Speakers include editors, writers, agents, and other professionals. Topics vary from year to year, but each conference offers sessions for both writers and illustrators as well as for newcomers and published writers. Previous topics included: "What Happens When Your Manuscript is Accepted" by Dawn Weinstock, editor; "Writing—Hobby or Vocation?" by Chris Kelleher; "Mother Time Gives Advice: Perspectives from a 25 Year Veteran" by Judith Mathews, editor; "Don't Be a Starving Writer" by Vicki Berger Erwin, author; and "Words & Pictures: History in the Making," by author-illustrator Cheryl Harness. Annual conference held in early November. For exact date, see SCBWI Website: www.scbwi.org or the events page of the Missouri SCBWI website. Registration limited to 75-90. Cost of conference includes one-day workshop (8 a.m. to 5 p.m.) plus lunch. Write for more information.

SCBWI—NEW ENGLAND; ANNUAL CONFERENCE

Nashua NH 03063.E-mail: northernnera@scbwi.org. Website: www.nescbwi.org. **Regional Advisor:** Janet Arden. Conference all levels of writers and illustrators. **Open to students.** "We offer many workshops at each conference, and often there is a multi-day format. Examples of subjects addressed: manuscript development, revision, marketing your work, productive school visits, picture book dummy formatting, adding texture to your illustrations, etc." Annual conference held May 14,15,16 at the Fitchburg Courtyard Marriott on Route 2 in Fitchburg MA. Registration limited to 450. Cost: TBD; includes pre-conference social, great keynote speaker, many workshop options, lunch, snacks, etc. "Keynote speaker for 2008 conference is Laurie Halse Anderson." Details (additional speakers, theme, number of workshop choices, etc.) will be posted to our website as they become available. Registration will not start until March 2008. Opportunities for one-on-one manuscript critiques and portfolio reviews will be available at the conference".

SCBWI—NEW JERSEY; ANNUAL SPRING CONFERENCE

SCBWI—NEW JERSEY; ANNUAL SPRING CONFERENCEE-mail: njscbwi@newjerseyscbwi.com. Website: www.newjerseyscbwi.com. Regional Advisor: Kathy Temean. This two day conference is always held the first weekend in June in Princeton, NJ. "How to" workshops, first page sessions, pitch sessions and interaction with the faculty of editors, agents, art director and authors are some of the highlights of the weekend. Writers and illustrators will find workshops to fit their level of expertise. Illustrators can attend a special session with an art director to discuss promotional materials. Published authors attending the conference are invited to do a book signing and sell their books on Saturday afternoon, Illustrators have the opportunity to display their artwork during this time. Attendees have the option to participate in group critiques, one-on-one critiques and portfolio reviews. Meals are included with the cost of admission. Continental breakfast and two lunches are included with the cost of admission. Illustrators' intensive and various writing intensives held before conference for additional cost. Conference is known for its high ratio of faculty to attendees.

SCBWI—NEW JERSEY; FIRST PAGE SESSIONS

E-mail: njscbwi@newjerseyscbwi.com. Website: www.newjerseyscbwi.com. Held 4 times a year in Princeton, NJ. Two editors/agents give their first impression of a first page and let participants know if they would read more. These sessions are held late afternoon during the week and are limited to 30 people. Attendees can choose to have dinner with the editors after the session. Please visit www.newjerseyscbwi.com for more information.

SCBWI—NEW JERSEY; MENTORING WORKSHOPS

E-mail: njscbwi@newjerseyscbwi.com. Website: www.newjerseyscbwi.com. **Regional Advisor:** Kathy Temean. These workshops have become very popular and fill quickly. Workshops provide an inspiring environment for writers to work on their manuscript and have personal contact with their mentor/editor. Each workshop consists of 14 writers and two editors or 28 people and 4 editors. Weekend workshops allow writers to spend 45 minutes, one-on-one, with their mentor to discuss their manuscript and career direction, first page critiques, pitch sessions and other fun writing activities. One day workshops consist of 20 minute one-on-one critiques and Q & A session, plus first page critiques. These workshops are held in the Winter, Spring and Fall each year Princeton, New Jersey. Please visit www.newjerseyscbwi.com for more information

SCBWI—NEW MEXICO; HANDSPRINGS: A CONFERENCE FOR CHILDREN'S WRITERS AND ILLUSTRATORS

P.O. Box 1084, Socorro NM. E-mail: handsprings@scbwi-nm.org. Website: www.scbwi-nm.org. **Registrar:** Lois Bradley. **Regional Advisor:** Chris Eboch. Conference for beginner and intermediate writers and illustrators. "The 2010 conference features four keynote speakers —editors, agents, art directors and/or illustrators and authors. 2010 speakers include Kendra Levin, Associate Editor, Viking Children's Books, Penguin Group (USA); Kate Sullivan, Assistant Editor, Little, Brown Young Readers; Jamie Weiss Chilton, Associate Agent Andrea Brown Literary Agency, Inc. Deborah Kapalan, Vice President, Executive Art Director, Penguin Young Readers Group Fiction, Puffin

Books. Speakers will lead 2 ½ hour intensive, craft-based workshops. Annual conference held in April or May. Registration limited to 100. "Offers intensive craft-based workshops and large-group presentations." Cost: $110-150 for basic Saturday registration dependent on registration; $40-50 for private critiques (lowest prices are for SCBWI members). "The Friday evening party included social time, a First Page critique panel with our visiting editors, mini book launches and an illustrators' portfolio display. Saturday features a full day of keynote speeches by visiting editors, agents and/ or art directors; breakout workshops on the craft and business of writing; and optional written critiques with the editors or written portfolio review by the art director."

SCBWI—NORCA (SAN FRANCISCO/SOUTH); GOLDEN GATE CONFERENCE AT ASILOMAR

Website: www.scbwisf.org. **Co-Regional Advisors:** Amy Laughlin and Kristin Howell. We welcome published and "not-yet-published" writers and illustrators. Lectures and workshops are geared toward professionals and those striving to become professional. Program topics cover aspects of writing or illustrating, and marketing, from picture books to young adult novels. Past speakers include editors, agents, art directors, Newbery Award-winning authors, and Caldecott Award-winning illustrators. Annual conference, generally held third or fourth weekend in February; Friday evening through Sunday lunch. Registration limited to approximately 140. Manuscript or portfolio review available. Most rooms shared with one other person. Additional charge for single when available. Desks available in most rooms. All rooms have private baths. Conference center is set in wooded campus on Asilomar Beach in Pacific Grove, California. Approximate cost: $465 for SCBWI members, $610 for nonmembers; includes shared room, 6 meals and all conference activities. Vegetarian meals available. Coming together for shared meals and activities builds a strong feeling of community among the speakers and conferees. Scholarships available to SCBWI members. Registration opens end of October/November.For more information, including exact costs and dates, visit our website.

SCBWI—NORTHERN OHIO; ANNUAL CONFERENCE

E-mail: vselvaggio@windstream.net. Website: www.nohscbwi.org. Regional Advisor: Victoria A. Selvaggio. Northern Ohio's conference is crafted for all levels of writers and illustrators of children's literature. The dates for our 2010 Conference are September 10th and 11th. Our annual event will be held at the Sheraton Cleveland Airport Hotel. Conference costs will be posted on our website with registration information. SCBWI members receive a discount. Additional fees apply for late registration, critiques, or portfolio reviews. Cost includes an optional Friday evening Opening Banquet form 6-10 p.m. with a keynote speaker; Saturday event from 8:30 a.m. to 5 p.m. which includes breakfast snack, full-day conference with headliner presentations, general sessions, breakout workshops, lunch, panel discussion, bookstore, and autograph session. The Illustrator Showcase is open to all attendees at no additional cost. Grand door prize drawn at the end of the day Saturday, is free admission to the following year's conference. Further information, including Headliner Speakers will be posted on our website. All questions can be directed to vselvaggio@windstream.net

SCBWI—OREGON CONFERENCES

E-mail: robink@scbwior.com. Website: www.scbwior.com. **Regional Advisor:** Robin Koontz. Writer and illustrator workshops and presentations geared toward all levels. "We invite editors, teachers, agents, attorneys, authors, illustrators and others in the business of writing and illustrating for children. They present lectures, workshops, and on-site critiques on a first-registered basis." Critique group network for local group meetings and regional retreats; see website for details.

Two main events per year: Writers and Illustrators Retreat: Retreat held near Portland Thursday-Sunday the 2nd weekend in October. Cost of retreat: $345 plus $35.00 critique fee includes double occupancy and all meals; Spring Conference: Held in the Portland area (2 day event the third Fri-Sat in May); cost for presentations and workshops: about $150 includes continental breakfast and lunch on Saturday, critique fee $35.00-attendees only; Friday intensive cost about $45 per a-la-carte-session with writer and illustrator tracks includes snacks and coffee. Registration limited to 300 for the conference and 55 for the retreat. SCBWI Oregon is a regional chapter of the SCBWI. SCBWI Members receive a discount for all events. Oregon and S. Washington members get preference.

SCBWI—ROCKY MOUNTAIN; EVENTS

E-mail: denise@rmcscbwi.org. or ttuell@yahoo.com. Website: www.rmcscbwi.org. Co-Regional Advisors: Denise Vega and Todd Tuell. SCBWI Rocky Mountain chapter (CO/WY) offers special events, schmoozes, meetings and conferences throughout the year. Major events: Summer Retreat (odd years in July), "Big Sur in the Rockies" (even years, spring), Fall Conference (yearly, Sept). More info on Web site.

SCBWI—SAN DIEGO; CHAPTER MEETINGS & WORKSHOPS

San Diego—SCBWI, San Diego CA. E-mail: ra-sd@sandiego-scbwi.org. Website: www.sandiego-scbwi.org. **Regional Advisor:** Janice M. Yuwiler. Writer and illustrator meetings and workshops geared toward all levels. Topics vary but emphasize writing and illustrating for children. Check website, e-mail or call (619)713-5462 for more information. "The San Diego chapter holds meetings the second Saturday of each month from September-May at the University of San Diego from 2-4 p.m.; cost $7 (members), $9 (nonmembers). Check web site for room, speaker and directions." 2011 meeting schedule: January 8, February 12, March 12, April 9, May 14, September 10, October 8, November 12, and December 10. December 2011 meeting: Published members share lessons learned and holiday book sale. 2011 conference to be held February 12, 2011, Writer's Retreat in May 2011—Check website for details. Season tickets include all regular chapter meetings during the season and newsletter issues for one calendar year as well as discounts on conferences/retreats. If interested in taking a class, Inside Children's Books through University of San Diego Continuing Education for 2 units college credit. Class in September 11, 2010 and ends May 14, 2011. See the website for conference/workshop dates, times and prices. Chapter also helps members find critique groups for on-going enhancement of skills.

SCBWI—SOUTHERN BREEZE; SPRINGMINGLE

P.O. Box 26282, Birmingham AL 35260. E-mail: JSKittinger@gmail.com. Website: www.southern-breeze.org. **Regional Advisors:** Jo Kittinger and Donna Bowman. Writer and illustrator conference geared toward intermediate, advanced and professional levels. Speakers typically include agents, editors, authors, art directors, illustrators. **Open to SCBWI members, non-members and college students.** Annual conference held in Atlanta, Georgia. Usually held in late February. Registration limited. Cost of conference: approximately $225; Typically includes Friday dinner, Saturday lunch and Saturday banquet. Manuscript critiques and portfolio reviews available for additional fee. Pre-registration is necessary. Send a SASE to Southern Breeze, P.O. Box 26282, Birmingham AL 35260 for more information or visit Website: www.southern-breeze.org.

SCBWI—SOUTHERN BREEZE; WRITING AND ILLUSTRATING FOR KIDS

P.O. Box 26282, Birmingham AL 35260. E-mail: sjkittinger@gmail.com. Writer and illustrator workshops geared toward all levels. Open to SCBWI members, non-members and college students. All sessions pertain specifically to the production and support of quality children's literature. This one-day conference offers about 30 workshops on craft and the business of writing. Picture books, chapter books, novels covered. Entry and professional level topics addressed by published writers and illustrators, editors and agents. Annual conference. Fall conference is held the third weekend in October in the Birmingham, AL metropolitan area. (Museums, shopping, zoo, gardens, universities and colleges are within a short driving distance.) All workshops are limited to 30 or fewer people. Pre-registration is necessary. Some workshops fill quickly. Cost of conference: approximately $110 for members, $135 for nonmembers, $120 for students; program includes keynote speaker, 4 workshops (selected from 30), lunch, and Friday night dessert party. Mss critiques and portfolio reviews are available for an additional fee; mss must be sent early. Registration is by mail ahead of time. Manuscript and portfolio reviews must be pre-paid and scheduled. Send a SASE to: Southern Breeze, P.O. Box 26282, Birmingham AL 35260 or visit website. Fall conference is always held in Birmingham, Alabama. Room block at a hotel near conference site (usually a school) is by individual reservation and offers a conference rate. Keynote for WIK10 was Darcy Pattison. Additional speakers include editors, agents, art directors, authors, and/or illustrators. WIK11 speakers to be announced. Website: www.southern-breeze.org. **Contact:** Jo Kittinger.

SCBWI—VENTURA/SANTA BARBARA; FALL CONFERENCE

E-mail: alexisinca@aol.com. Website: www.scbwisocal.org/calendar. Writers'conference geared toward all levels. Speakers include editors, authors, illustrators and agents. Fiction and nonfiction picture books, middle grade and YA novels, and magazine submissions addressed. Annual writing contest in all genres plus illustration display. Conference held October 29, 2011 at California Lutheran University in Thousand Oaks, California in cooperation with the CLU School of Education. For fees and other information e-mail or go to website.

SCBWI—VENTURA/SANTA BARBARA; RETREAT FOR CHILDREN'S AUTHORS AND ILLUSTRATORS

E-mail: alexisinca@aol.com. Website: www.scbwisocal.org. The Winter Retreat, held in Santa Barbara in January, focuses on craft or business issues. Go to website or e-mail for upcoming date, theme and fee.

SCBWI—WESTERN WASHINGTON STATE; RETREATS & CONFERENCE

SCBWI Western Washington; Conference and Retreat P.O. Box 156, Enumclaw WA 98022. Email: info@scbwi-washington.org. Website: www.scbwi-washington.org. **Co-Regional Advisors:** Joni Sensel and Laurie Thompson. "The Western Washington region of SCBWI hosts an annual conference each spring, as well as a weekend retreat in November. Please visit the website for complete details."

SCBWI—WISCONSIN; FALL RETREAT FOR WORKING WRITERS

3446 Hazelnut Lane, Milton WI 53563. E-mail: pjberes@centurytel.net. Website: www.scbwi-wi.com. **Regional Advisor:** Pam Beres. Writer and illustrator conference geared toward all levels. All our sessions pertain to children's writing/illustration. Faculty addresses writing/illustrating/publishing. Annual conference held October. Registration limited to 90. Conference center has retreat-style bedrooms with desks that can be used to draw/write. Cost of conference: $375 for SBCWI member; $450 for non-members; includes program, meals, lodging, ms critique. Write or go to our website for more information: www.scbwi-wi.com.

OTHER CONFERENCES

AMERICAN CHRISTIAN WRITERS CONFERENCE

P.O. Box 110390, Nashville TN 37222-0390. 1(800)21-WRITE or (615)834-0450. Fax: (615)834-7736. Website: www.ACWriters.com. **Director:** Reg Forder. Writer and illustrator workshops geared toward beginner, intermediate and advanced levels. Classes offered include: fiction, nonfiction, poetry, photography, music, etc. Workshops held in 3 dozen U.S. cities. Call or write for a complete schedule of conferences. 75 minutes. Maximum class size: 30 (approximate). Cost of conference: $150, 1-day session; $250, 2-day session (discount given if paid 30 days in advance) includes tuition only.

ANNUAL SPRING POETRY FESTIVAL

City College, 138th St. at Convent Ave., New York NY 10031. (212)650-6356. **Director, Poetry Outreach Center:** Pam Laskin. Writer workshops geared to all levels. **Open to students.** Annual poetry festival. Festival held May 16, 2008. Registration limited to 325. Cost of workshops and festival: free. Write for more information.

BIG SUR WRITING WORKSHOP

Henry Miller Library, Highway One, Big Sur CA 93920. Phone/fax: (831)667-2574. E-mail: magnus@ henrymiller.org. Website: www.henrymiller.org/CWW.html. **Contact:** Magnus Toren, executive director. Annual workshops are held in December and March focusing on children's and young adult writing. Workshop held in Big Sur Lodge in Pfeiffer State Park. Cost of workshop: $720; included meals, lodging, workshop, Saturday evening reception; $600 if lodging not needed. www. henrymiller.org.

CAPE COD WRITER'S CONFERENCE

Cape Cod Writer's Center, P.O. Box 408, Osterville MA 02655. (508)420-0200. Fax: (508)420-0212. E-mail: writers@capecodwriterscenter.org; www.capecodwriterscenter.org. Annual conference held third week in August in a rustic retreat center on Nantucket Sound, Cape Cod; 48th annual conference: August 15-20, 2010. This year we will offer numerous 5-day, 4-day, 3-day, 2-day, and 1-day courses in fiction, nonfiction, screenwriting, children and young adult, memoir, humor, travel writing, marketing, finding an agent, self-publishing, and more. Evening programs include keynote speakers, panels, poetry, and prose readings. Manuscript evaluations and mentoring with faculty, literary agents, publishers, and editors. No registration fee for Cape Cod Writers Center members. The Young Writers' Workshop for 12- to 17-year-olds on prose and poetry held concurrent with the conference. Pricing available on the web page by May 1.

CAT WRITERS' ASSOCIATION ANNUAL WRITERS CONFERENCE

66 Adams Street, Jamestown NY 14701. (716)484-6155. E-mail: dogwriter@windstream.net. The Cat Writers' Association holds an annual conference at varying locations around the US. The agenda for the conference is filled with seminars, editor appointments, an autograph party, networking breakfast, reception and annual awards banquet, as well as the annual meeting of the association. See website for details. Website: www.catwriters.org. **Contact:** Susan M. Ewing, president.

CHILDREN'S AUTHORS' BOOTCAMP

P.O. Box 231, Allenspark CO 80510. (303)747-1014. E-mail: CABootcamp@msn.com. Website: www.WeMakeWriters.com. **Contact:** Linda Arms White. Writer workshops geared toward beginner and intermediate levels. "Children's Authors' Bootcamp provides two full, information-packed days on the fundamentals of writing fiction for children. The workshop covers developing strong, unique characters; well-constructed plots; believable dialogue; seamless description and pacing; point of view; editing your own work; marketing your manuscripts to publishers, and more. Each day also includes in-class writing exercises and small group activities." Workshop held several times per year at various locations throughout the United States. Please check our website for upcoming dates and locations. Maximum size is 55; average workshop has 40-50 participants. Cost of workshop varies; see website for details. Cost includes tuition for both Saturday and Sunday (9:00 a.m. to 4:30 p.m.); morning and afternoon snacks; lunch; handout packet. "Check website for details."

CONFERENCE FOR WRITERS & ILLUSTRATORS OF CHILDREN'S BOOKS

Book Passage, 51 Tamal Vista Blvd., Corte Madera CA 94925. (415)927-0960, ext. 239. Fax: (415)927-3069. E-mail: kathryn@bookpassage.com. Website: www.bookpassage.com. **Conference Coordinator:** Kathryn Petrocelli. Writer and illustrator conference geared toward beginner and intermediate levels. Sessions cover such topics as the nuts and bolts of writing and illustrating, publisher's spotlight, market trends, developing characters/finding voice in your writing, and the author/agent relationship. Four-day conference held each summer. Includes opening night dinner, 3 lunches and a closing reception.

THE DIY BOOK FESTIVAL

7095 Hollywood Blvd., Suite 864, Los Angeles CA 90028-0893. (323)665-8080. Fax: (323)372-3883. E-mail: diyconvention@aol.com. Website: www.iyconvention.com. **Managing Director:** Bruce Haring. Writer and illustrator workshops geared toward beginner and intermediate levels. **Open to students.** Festival focus on getting your book into print, book marketing and promotion. Annual workshop. Workshop held February-October, various cities. Cost of workshop: $50; includes admission to event, entry to prize competition, lunch for some events. Check out our website for current dates and locations.

DUKE UNIVERSITY YOUTH PROGRAMS: CREATIVE WRITERS' WORKSHOP

Campus Box 90700, Room 201, The Bishop's House, Durham NC 27708. **Contact:** Duke Youth Programs. Writer workshops geared toward intermediate to advanced levels. **Open to students.** The Creative Writers' Workshop provides an intensive creative writing experience for advanced high school age writers who want to improve their skills in a community of writers. "The interactive format gives participants the opportunity to share their work in small groups, one-on-one with instructors, and receive feedback in a supportive environment. The review and critique process helps writers sharpen critical thinking skills and learn how to revise their work." Annual workshop. Every summer there is one 2-week residential session. Costs for 2010—$1,740 for residential campers; $1,120 for extended day campers/ day camper $865. Visit website for more information.

EAST OF EDEN WRITERS CONFERENCE

California Writers Club, P.O. Box 3254, Santa Clara, CA 95055. (408)247-1286. Fax: (408)927-5224. E-mail: eastofeden@southbaywriters.com. Website: www.southbaywriters.com. Writer workshops geared toward beginner, intermediate and advanced levels. Open discounts for students. Bi-annual conference. Next held September 5-7, 2008, in Salinas, CA (at the National Steinbeck Center and the Salinas Community Center.) Registration is limited to 400. Cost of conference: around $300, depending on options chosen; See website for fees. Registration includes all events and all meals, lodging is available at reduced rate from five of several hotels in the neighborhood includes Friday night dinner and program; Saturday breakfast, lunch, and full day of workshops and panels; "Night

Owl" sessions; Saturday dinner program and Sunday brunch at John Steinbeck's family home are available for a small additional fee. "This conference, run presented by the nonprofit California Writers Club, will include many 48 top-notch workshops following five tracks seminars on the art craft and business of writing. Critique opportunities, writing contests, Ask-An-Agent, and reading programs are available. See our website (above) for the details. We'll have panels where writers can meet literary agents and editors and an Ask-A-Pro program, where writers can sign up to speak individually with faculty members of their choice."

FESTIVAL OF FAITH AND WRITING

Department of English, Calvin College 1795 Knollcrest Circle SE, Grand Rapids MI 49546. (616)526-6770. E-mail: ffw@calvin.edu. Website: www.calvin.edu/festival. E-mail all inquiries about attendance (for registration brochures, program information, etc.). Geared toward all levels of readers and writers. Open to students. The Festival of Faith and Writing has talks, panel discussions, and workshops by nearly 100 individuals, many of whom compose, write, illustrate, and publish children's books and books for young adults. Each break-out will have a session on children's books/young adult books. Conference held in April of the even years. Registration limited to approximately 1,900 people.

FISHTRAP, INC.

400 Grant Street, P.O. Box 38, Enterprise OR 97828-0038. (541)426-3623. E-mail: director@fishtrap.org. Website: www.fishtrap.org. **Director:** Rick Bombaci. Writer workshops geared toward beginner, intermediate, advanced and professional levels. Open to students, scholarships available. A series of eight writing workshops and a writers' gathering is held each July; a winter gathering concerning writing and issues of public concern is held each February. During the school year Fishtrap brings writers into local schools and offers workshops for teachers and writers of children's and young adult books. A **Children's Lit Writing Workshop is held each fall.** Other programs include writing and K-12 teaching residencies, writers' retreats, and lectures. College credit available for many workshops. See website for full program descriptions and to get on the e-mail and mail lists.

FLORIDA CHRISTIAN WRITERS CONFERENCE

Lake Yale Conference center, Leesburg FL. E-mail: billiewilson@cfl.rr.com. Website: www.flwriters.org. **Conference Director:** Billie Wilson. Writer workshops geared toward all levels. **Open to students.** "We offer 72 one-hour workshops and 9 six-hour classes. Approximately 15 of these are for the children's genre." Annual workshop held in March. "We have 30 publishers and publications represented by editors teaching workshops and reading manuscripts from the conferees. The conference is limited to 250 people. Advanced or professional workshops are by invitation only via submitted application. Cost of conference: $465; includes tuition and ms critiques and editor review of your ms plus personal appointments with editors. Write or e-mail for more information.

GOTHAM WRITERS' WORKSHOP

(877)974-8377. Fax: (212)307-6325. **Director, Student Affairs:** Dana Miller. Creative writing workshops taught by professional writers are geared toward beginner, intermediate and advanced levels. **Open to students.** "Workshops cover the fundamentals of plot, structure, voice, description, characterization, and dialogue appropriate to all forms of fiction and nonfiction for pre-schoolers through young adults. Students can work on picture books or begin middle-readers or young adult novels." Annual workshops held 4 times/year (10-week and 1-day workshops). Workshops held January, April, July, September/October. Registration limited to 14 students/in-person (NYC) class; 18 students/online class; 40 students for in-person (NYC) one-day workshops are held 4 times per year. Cost of workshop: $420 for 10-week workshops; $150 for 1-day workshops; 10-week NYC classes meet once a week for 3 hours; 10-week online classes include 10 week-long, asynchronous "meetings"; 1-day workshops are 7 hours and are held 8 times/year. E-mail for more information.

HIGHLIGHTS FOUNDATION WRITERS WORKSHOP AT CHAUTAUQUA

814 Court St., Honesdale PA 18431. (570)253-1192. Fax: (570)253-0179. E-mail: contact@ highlightsfoundation.org. To view faculty and other details please got to Website. The intensive, week-long conference at Chautauqua is designed for individuals at all levels of experience, from beginning to published, who are interested in writing and illustrating for children. The conference includes seminars, small-group workshops, and one-on-one sessions with some of the most accomplished and prominent authors, illustrators, editors, critics, and publishers in the world of children's literature. Classes include: Writing Poetry, Book Promotion, Characterization, Developing a Plot, How to Promote Your Book, and many many more. Annual. Workshop held: July 17-24, 2010, at Chautauqua Institution, Chautauqua, NY. Registration limited to 100. Tuition, meals, conference supplies. Cost does not include housing. Call for availability and pricing. Scholarships are available for first-time attendees. Call for more information or visit the website. In addition to the flagship Writers Workshop at Chautauqua, the Highlights Foundation holds various thematic Founders Workshops throughout the year. Website: http://www.highlightsfoundation.org/pages/current/chautauqua_top.html. **Contact:** Kent L. Brown, Jr., executive director. July 17-24, 2010

INDIANAPOLIS YOUTH LITERATURE CONFERENCE

Chaired by Dr. Marilyn Irwin, School of Library and Information Science, Indiana University, Purdue University, Indianapolis. Phone 317-278-2375 Annual conference held the last Saturday of January each year featuring top writers in the field of children's literature. Registration limited to 300. Cost of conference:$75. Three plenary addresses, 2 workshops, book signing, reception and conference bookstore. The conference is geared toward three groups: teachers, librarians and writers/illustrators. Co-sponsors include the Indianapolis Marion County Public Library, Indiana State Library, and Kids Ink Children's Bookstore.

INTERNATIONAL WOMEN'S WRITING GUILD "REMEMBER THE MAGIC" ANNUAL SUMMER CONFERENCE

P.O. Box 810, Gracie Station, New York NY 10028. (212)737-7536. Fax: (212)737-9469. E-mail: iwwg@iwwg.org. Writer and illustrator workshops geared toward all levels. Offers over 50 different workshops—some are for children's book writers and illustrators. Also sponsors other events throughout the U.S. Annual workshops. "Remember the Magic" workshops held every summer for a week. Length of each session: 90 minutes; sessions take place for an entire week. Registration limited to 500. Cost of workshop: $1,399 (includes complete program, room and board). Write for more information. "This workshop takes place at Brown University in Providence, RI." Website: www.iwwg.org. **Contact:** Hannelore Hahn, executive director.

IOWA SUMMER WRITING FESTIVAL

C215 Seashore Hall, Iowa City IA 52242. (319)335-4160. Fax: (319)335-4743. E-mail: iswfestival@ uiowa.edu. Website: www.uiowa.edu/ ~ iswfest. **Director:** Amy Margolis. Writer workshops geared toward beginner, intermediate and advanced levels. Open to writers age 21 and over. "We offer writing workshops across the genres, including workshops for children's writers in picture books, structuring writing for children, the young adult novel, and nonfiction." Annual workshop held June and July. Registration limited to 12/workshop. Workshops meet in university classrooms.

Cost of workshop: $560/week-long session; $280/weekend. Housing is separate and varies by facility. Write or call for more information.

LAJOLLA WRITERS CONFERENCE

P.O. Box 178122, San Diego CA 92177. (858)467-1978. Website: www.lajollawritersconference.com. Contact: Jared Kuritz, director. Established 2001. Annual. 2010 Conference held November 5-7 at the Paradise Point Resort & Spa (San Diego). Conference duration: 3 days. Maximum attendance limited to 200. The La Jolla Writers Conference welcomes writers of all levels of experience. This three-day event, now in its 9th year, always boasts exciting, interactive workshops, lectures, and presentations by an outstanding and freely accessible faculty comprised of best-selling authors, editors from major publishing houses, and literary agents, all of whom value meeting and working with a diverse group of creative people passionate about writing. The LJWC uniquely covers the art, craft, and business of writing for both fiction and non-fiction with a 5 to 1 student to faculty ratio. Costs $295 Early, $385 Regular, $435 after August 1. Conference registration includes access to more than 75 classes, three keynote addresses, two meals, appetizer reception, and faculty author signing. Additional Information: Private Read & Critiques for an additional fee of $50 each.

THE MANUSCRIPT WORKSHOP IN VERMONT

P.O. Box 529, Londonderry VT 05148. (802)824-3968 or (212)877-4457. E-mail: aplbrk2@earthlink. net. Website: www.barbaraseuling.com. **Director:** Barbara Seuling. Writer workshop for all levels. Annual workshop estab. 1992. Generally held mid to late July and August and sometimes early September. The time is divided among instructive hands-on sessions in the mornings, writing time in the afternoons, and critiquing in the evenings. A guest speaker from the world of children's books may be a guest at the workshops. Registration is limited to 8 in the regular workshop, 6 in the advanced workshop (revising your novel; developing your story; mystery writing). Cost of workshop: $750 per person; applicants are responsible for their accommodations and meals at the inn.

MONTROSE CHRISTIAN WRITER'S CONFERENCE

5 Locust St., Montrose PA 18801-1112. (570)278-1001. Fax: (570)278-3061. E-mail: mbc@ montrosebible.org. Writer workshops geared toward beginner, intermediate and advanced levels. Annual workshop held in July. Cost of workshop: $160 tuition (2010 rate). Brochure available in April. Website: www.montrosebible.org. **Contact:** Jim Fahringer, executive director; Donna Kosik, secretary-registrar.

MOUNT HERMON CHRISTIAN WRITERS CONFERENCE

Mount Hermon Christian Conference Center, Mount Hermon CA 95041-0413. (831)335-4466. Fax: (831)335-9413. E-mail: rachel.williams@mounthermon.org. Website: www.mounthermon.org/ writers. **Writers Conferences Director:** Rachel A. Williams; **Conference Host:** David Talbott. Writer workshops geared toward all levels. **Open to students over 16 years** with special teen track. All genre of writing. 12 Major Morning Sessions including mentoring tracks and all-day career track; 70 optional afternoon workshops include every genre of writing. Held annually over Palm Sunday weekend: April 15-19, 2011. Length of each session: 5-day residential conference held annually. Registration limited 45/class, but most are 20-30. Conference center with hotel-style accommodations. Cost of workshop: $700-1500 variable; includes tuition, web binder, free critiques refreshment breaks, full room and board for 13 meals and 4 night. Conference information posted annually on website by December 1. Write or e-mail for more information or call toll-free to 1-888-MH-CAMPS.

NORTH CAROLINA WRITERS' NETWORK FALL CONFERENCE

P.O. Box 954, Carrboro NC 27510-0954. (919)967.9540. Fax: (919)929.0535. E-mail: mail@ncwriters. org. Website: www.ncwriters.org. Writing workshops and services geared toward beginning, intermediate and advanced or published levels. **Open to students.** We offer workshops, keynote, presentations and critique sessions in a variety of genres: fiction, poetry, creative nonfiction, children, youth, etc. Past youth and children writing faculty include Louise Hawes, Jackie Ogburn, Clay Carmichael, Carole Boston Weatherford, Susie Wilde, Stephanie Greene, Joy Neaves, and Frances O'Roark Dowell. Annual Conference to be held next at the Marriott Winston-Salem Twin City Quarter. Date: Usually the second weekend of November. Cost of conference usually $250/ members, $350/nonmembers, including all workshops, panels, roundtables, social activities and four meals. Extra costs for accommodations, master classes and critique sessions.

OHIO KENTUCKY INDIANA CHILDREN'S LITERATURE CONFERENCE

Northern Kentucky University, 405 Steely Library, Highland Heights, KY 41099. (859)572-6620. Fax: (859)572-5390. E-mail: smithjen@nku.edu. Website:http://oki.nku.edu. **Staff Development Coordinator:** Jennifer Smith. Writer and illustrator conference geared toward all levels. **Open to University.** Annual conference. Emphasizes multicultural literature for children and young adults. Conference held annually in November. Contact Jennifer Smith for more information. Registration limited to 250. Cost of conference: $75; includes registration/attendance at all workshop sessions, Tri-state Authors and Illustrators of Childrens Books Directory, continental breakfast, lunch, author/illustrator signings. Manuscript critiques are available for an additional cost. E-mail or call for more information.

OKLAHOMA WRITERS' FEDERATION, INC. ANNUAL CONFERENCE

3925 S. Boulevard St., Edmond, OK 73013. (405)348-3325. E-mail: Marcia@marciapreston.com. **Contact: 2009 President: Marcia Preston** (please see website for most current info): www.owfi. org. Writer workshops geared toward all levels. **Open to students.** "Forty seminars, with 30 speakers consisting of editors, literary agents and many best-selling authors. Topics range widely to include craft, marketing, and all genres of writing." Annual conference. Held first weekend in May each year. Writing facilities available: book room, autograph party, two lunch workshops. Cost of conference: $150 before March 15; $175 after March 15; $70 for single days; $25 for lunch workshops. Full tuition includes 2-day conference (all events except lunch workshops) and 2 dinners plus one 10-minute appointment with an attending editor or agent of your choice (must be reserved in advance). "If writers would like to participate in the annual writing contest, they must become members of OWFI. You don't have to be a member to attend the conference." See website for more information.

THE PACIFIC COAST CHILDREN'S WRITERS WORKSHOP

P.O. Box 244, Aptos CA 95001. This ninth annual seminar serves intermediate through professional levels; beginners may attend with modified participation. Intensive focus on craft as a marketing tool. Open to students ages 15 and up, with independent and intergenerational programs. "All enrollees must demonstrate competence in story-crafting or come prepared to learn from highly skilled writers. Focus sessions and team-taught master classes(manuscript critique clinics) explore topics such as 'A Novelist's Toolkit: Architecture, Archetypes, and Arcs.' Presenters have included esteemed NY editors and agents, plus literary master Marion Dane Bauer.Several enrollees have landed contracts as a direct result of our event." Upcoming seminars: August 20-22, 2010 and August 19-21, 2011; in-depth craft session Sunday afternoon. Registration limited to 35; continuous close contact with all faculty. Pajaro Dunes' private beachfront facility offers free use of business center with DSL Internet access in enrollees' condos. Cost of workshop: $339-629; includes basic program, most meals, and up to 3 faculty critiques (written and/or in person). Limited work scholarships. "Our e-application includes essay questions about each writer's manuscript. For the most critique options, submit sample chapters and synopsis with e-application by mid-April. Open until filled. Content: Literary, character-driven novels with protagonists ages 11 and older. Collegial format; 90 percent hands-on, with dialogues between seasoned faculty and savvy, congenial peers. Faculty critiques openings, as well as optional later chapters and synopses. Our pre-workshop prep (e.g., peer anthology) maximizes learning and networking. Details: visit our website and email us via the contact form." Website: www.childrenswritersworkshop.com.

PACIFIC NORTHWEST CHILDREN'S BOOK CONFERENCE

Portland State University, Continuing Education, Graduate School of Education, P.O. Box 751, Portland OR 97207. (503)725-9786 or (800)547-8887, ext. 9786. Fax: (503)725-5595. E-mail:katagiri@pdx.edu. Website: www.ceed.pdx.edu/children/. Focus on the craft of writing and illustrating for children while working with an outstanding faculty of acclaimed editors, authors, and illustrators. Daily afternoon faculty-led writing and illustration workshops. Acquire specific information on how to become a professional in the field of children's literature. Annual workshop for all levels. 11th annual conference held July 19-23 2010 on the campus of Reed College, Portland, Oregon. Cost depends on options selected, including: noncredit or 3 graduate credits or graduate credits; individual ms/portfolio reviews and room and board at Reed campus. E-mail katagiri@pdx.edu for more information. Linda Zuckerman, editor, coordinates conference and brings together knowledgeable and engaging presenters every year.

PACIFIC NORTHWEST WRITER ASSN. SUMMER WRITER'S CONFERENCE

PMB 2717, 1420 NW Gilman Blvd, Suite 2, Issaquah, WA 98027. (425) 673-BOOK (2665). E-mail: staff@pnwa.org. Website: www.pnwa.org. Writer conference geared toward beginner, intermediate, advanced and professional levels. Meet agents and editors. Learn craft from renowned authors. Uncover new marketing secrets. PNWA's 55th Anniversary Conference was held July 22-25, 2010 at the Seattle Airport Hilton, Seattle, WA 98188. Annual conference held every July.

PIMA WRITERS' WORKSHOP

Pima College, 2202 W. Anklam Rd., Tucson AZ 85709-0170. (520)206-6084. Fax: (520)206-6020. E-mail: mfiles@pima.edu. **Director:** Meg Files. Writer conference geared toward beginner, intermediate and advanced levels. **Open to students.** The conference features presentations and writing exercises on writing and publishing stories for children and young adults, among other genres. Annual conference. Workshop held in May. Cost of workshop: $85; includes tuition, manuscript consultation. Write for more information.

PUBLISHINGGAME.COM WORKSHOP

Newton MA 02459. (617)630-0945. E-mail: Alyza@publishinggame.com. Website: www.publishinggame.com. **Coordinator:** Alyza Harris. Fern Reiss, author of the popular "Publishing Game" book series and CEO of Expertizing.com, will teach this one-day workshop. Writer workshops geared toward beginner, intermediate and advanced levels. Sessions will include: Find A Literary Agent, Self-Publish Your Children's Book, Book Promotion For Children's Books. September—New York; October—Boston; November—New York; December—Philadelphia; January—Washington, DC; February—New York; March—New York; April—New York; May—Boston; June—Los Angeles, CA; July—San Francisco; August—Boston. Please see http://www.publishinggame.com for current schedule. Registration limited to 18. Fills quickly! Cost of workshop: $195; included information-packed course binder and light refreshments. E-mail for more information. Workshop now available as a 5-CD audio workshop. For information on getting more media attention for your children's book, see Fern Reiss' complementary Expertizing workshop at www.expertizing.om.

ROBERT QUACKENBUSH'S CHILDREN'S BOOK WRITING AND ILLUSTRATING WORKSHOP

Studio address: 223 East 79th St, .New York, NY 10075. Mailing address: 460 East 79th St., New York, NY 10075. (212)744-3822. Fax: (212)861-2761. E-mail: Rqstudios@aol.com. Website: www.rquackenbush.com. **Contact:** Robert Quackenbush. A four-day extensive workshop on writing and illustrating books for young readers held annually the second week in July at author/artist Robert Quackenbush's Manhattan studio for beginning and advance writers and illustrators. The focus of this workshop is on creating manuscripts and/or illustrated book dummies from start to finish for picture books and beginning reader chapter books ready to submit to publishers. Also covered is writing fiction and nonfiction for middle grades and young adults, if that is the attendee's interest. In addition, attention is given to review of illustrator's portfolios and new trends in illustration, including animation for films, are explored. During the four days, the workshop meets from 9 a.m-4 p.m. including one hour for lunch. Registration is limited to 10. Some writing and/or art supplies are available at the studio and there is an art store nearby, if needed. There are also electrical outlets for attendee's laptop computers. Cost of workshop is $750. A $100 non-refundable deposit is required to enroll; balance is due three weeks prior the workshop. Attendees are responsible for arranging for their own hotel and meals. On request, suggestions are given for economical places to stay and eat. Recommended by Foder's Great American Learning Vacations, which says, "This unique workshop, held annually since 1982, provides the opportunity to work with Robert Quackenbush, a prolific author and illustrator of children's books with more than 200 fiction and nonfiction books for young readers to his credit, including mysteries, biographies and songbooks. The workshop attracts both professional and beginning writers and artists of different ages from all over the world." Brochure available. Also inquire about fall, winter and spring workshops that meet once a week for ten weeks each that are offered to artists and writers in the New York area.

◼ SAGE HILL WRITING EXPERIENCE

Writing Children's & Young Adult Fiction Workshop, Box 1731, Saskatoon SK S7K 3S1 Canada. Phone: (306) 652-7395. Fax: (306)244-0255. E-mail: sage.hill@sasktel.net. Website: www.sagehillwriting.ca. **Executive Director:** Paula Jane Remlinger. Writer conference geared toward intermediate level. This program occurs every 3 years. Most recently in summer 2009. The Sage Hill Conference is annual. Conference held in July. Registration limited to 6 participants for this program, and to 37 for full program. Cost of conference approximately $1195; includes instruction, meals, accommodation. Require ms samples prior to registration. Write or visit the website for more information and workshop dates. Summer 2009 facilitator: Arthur Slade. Program dates: July 20-31, 2009.

SAN DIEGO STATE UNIVERSITY WRITERS' CONFERENCE

The College of Extended Studies, San Diego CA 92182-1920. (619)594-2517. Fax: (619)594-8566. E-mail: extended.std@sdsu.edu. Website: www.ces.sdsu.edu/writers **Conference Facilitator:** Rose Brown. Writer workshops geared toward beginner, intermediate and advanced levels. Emphasizes nonfiction, fiction, screenwriting, advanced novel writing; includes sessions specific to writing and illustrating for children. Workshops offered by children's editors, agents and writers. Annual workshops. Workshops held January 29-31, 2010. Registration limited. Cost of workshops: approximately $350. Call for more information or visit website.

SAN FRANCISCO WRITERS CONFERENCE

1029 Jones St., San Francisco CA 94109 (415)673-0939. Web site: www.sfwriters.org. This conference has a children's book track featuring agents, editors and authors who specialize in children's writing and illustrating. Held President's day weekend each year in San Francisco, SFWC also features a writing contest with a children's writing category and tracks on craft, marketing and the business of publishing.

◼ SASKATCHEWAN FESTIVAL OF WORDS AND WORKSHOPS

217 Main Street, Moose Jaw SK S6J 0W1 Canada. E-mail: word.festival@sasktel.net. Writer workshops geared toward beginner and intermediate levels. **Open to students.** Readings that include a wide spectrum of genres—fiction, creative non-fiction, poetry, songwriting, screenwriting, playwriting, dramatic reading with actors, graphic novels, Great Big Book Club Discussion with author, children's writing, panels, independent film screening, panels, slam poetry, interviews and performances. Annual festival. Workshop held third weekend in July. Cost of workshop varies from $10 for a single reading to $160 for a full pass (as of 2010). Trivia Night Fun ticket is extra. Visit website for more information. Website: www.festivalofwords.com. **Contact:** Donna Lee Howes.

SOUTH COAST WRITERS CONFERENCE

P.O. Box 590, 29392 Ellensburg Ave., Gold Beach OR 97444. (541)247-2741. E-mail: scwc@socc. edu. **Coordinator:** Karim Shumaker. Writer workshops geared toward beginner, intermediate levels. **Open to students.** Include fiction, nonfiction, nuts and bolts, poetry, feature writing, children's writing, publishing. Annual workshop. Workshop held Friday and Saturday of President's Day weekend in February. Registration limited to 25-30 students/workshop. Cost of workshop: $60 before January 31, $70 after; includes Friday night author's reading and book signing, Saturday conference, 4 workshop sessions, Saturday evening writers' circle (networking and critique). Write or email for more information. "We also have four six-hour workshops Friday for more intensive writing exercises. The cost is an additional $55."

SOUTHEASTERN WRITERS ASSOCIATION—29TH ANNUAL WRITERS WORKSHOP

161 Woodstone, Athens GA 30605. E-mail: purple@southeasternwriters.com. **Open to all writers**. Contests with cash prizes. Instruction offered for novel and short fiction, nonfiction, writing for children, humor, inspirational writing, and poetry. Manuscript deadline April 1st, includes evaluation conference(s) with instructor(s). Agent in residence. Annual 4-day workshop held in June. Cost of workshop: $395 for four days or $150-350 daily tuition. Accommodations: Offers overnight accommodations on workshop site. Visit website for more information and cost of overnight accommodations. E-mail or send SASE for brochure. Website: www.southeasternwriters. com. **Contact:** Amy Munnell & Sheila Hudson, presidents.

SOUTHWEST WRITERS CONFERENCES

3721 Morris NE, Suite A, Albuquerque NM 87111. (505)265-9485. Fax: (505)265-9483. E-mail: swwriters@juno.com. Website: www.southwestwriters.org. **Open to adults and students.** Writer workshops geared toward all genres at all levels of writing. Various aspects of writing covered, including children's. Mini-conference, periodic workshops, and writing classes. Examples from mini-conferences: Novel Conference for all Genres with JET literary agent Lis Trupin-Pulli; William Morrow editor Gabe Robinson; Avon Books executive editor Carrie Feron; speakers Jo-Anne Power, Michael McGarrity, Walter Jon Williams, Jane Lindshold, Sandra K. Toro et al. SWW Memoir Conference with Jeff Herman literary agent Deborah Herman; author Lisa Dale Norton; Outskirts Press VP Brent Sampson; KOAT-TV reporter Mitch Blacher; Sun Managing Editor Tim McKee; author Dina Wolff; UNM Press Editor-in-Chief Clark Whitehorn and UNM Press Director Luther Wilson. Prices vary, but usually $79-$179. Also offers annual and quarterly contests, two monthly programs, writing classes, periodic workshops, monthly newsletter, critique service, e-lerts, website linking and various discount perks. See website for information.

SPLIT ROCK ARTS PROGRAM

Split Rock Arts Program, University of Minnesota, 360 Coffey Hall, 1420 Eckles Ave., St. Paul MN 55108-6084. (612)625-8100. Fax: (612)624-5359. E-mail: splitrockarts@umn.edu. Website: www.cce.umn.edu/Split-Rock-Arts-Program. Summer workshops and seasonal retreats, including autobiography, poetry, fiction, creative nonfiction, memoir, screenwriting, writing for children; book arts, calligraphy, picture books illustration, and a variety of visual forms, are taught by renowned writers and illustrators.. Held on the Twin Cities campus and at the University's Cloquet Forestry Center in northern Minnesota. Past and current faculty includes Marcia Brown, Marion Dane Bauer, Candace Fleming, Jan Spivey Gilchrist, David Haynes, Gerald McDermott, Daniel Powers, Ilse Plume, Eric Rohmann, Lauren Stringer, Jane Resh Thomas, Carole Boston Weatherford and others. Three-day season retreats are offered in March, April, and October; summer workshops and retreats begin every Sunday in June and July. Registration limited to 17 per workshop/retreat. Graduate/undergraduate credit, scholarships and on-campus accommodations available. Cost of workshop: $370-555. Registration is ongoing.

✂ SURREY INTERNATIONAL WRITERS CONFERENCE

SIWC c/o SD 36, Unit 400, 9260-140 Street, Surrey, BC, Canada, V3V 5Z4. (604)589-2221. Fax: (604)588-9286. E-mail:contest@siwc.ca. Website: www.siwc.ca. Coordinator: Kathy Chung. Writer and illustrator workshops geared toward beginners, intermediate and advanced levels. More than 70 workshops, panels, on all topics and genres. Blue Pencil and Agent/Editor Pitch sessions included. Annual Conference held every October. Different conference price packages available. Check our website for more information, or email conference coordinator Kathy Chung at kathychung@siwc. ca.

⊕ SYDNEY CHILDREN'S WRITERS AND ILLUSTRATORS NETWORK

The Hughenden Boutique Hotel, 14 Queen St., Woollahra NS 2025Australia . (61) 2 9363 4863. Fax: (61) 2 9362 0398. Website: www.sgervay.com.au. **Contact:** Susanne Gervay. Writer and illustrator network geared toward professionals. Topics emphasized include networking, information and expertise about Australian children's publishing industry. Network held the first Wednesday of every month, except for January, commencing at 10:30 a.m. Registration limited to 30. Writing facilities available: internet and conference facilities. Payment of personal beverages and lunch. As a prerequisite must be published in a commercial or have a book contract. E-mail for more information. "This is a professional meeting which aims at an interchange of ideas and information between professional children's authors and illustrators. Editors and other invited guests speak from time to time."

UMKC/WRITERS PLACE WRITERS WORKSHOPS

5300 Rockhill Rd., Kansas City MO 64110-2450. (816)235-2736. Fax: (816)235-5279. E-mail: seatons@umkc.edu. Website: www.newletters.org/writingConferences.asp. **Contact:** Kathi Wittfeld. Mark Twain Workshop will be Monday, June 7 -25, 2010 in 104 Cockefair Hall and New Letters Weekend Writing Conference will be held on Friday, Saturday and Sunday, June 25-27, 2010 at Diastole. New Letters Writer's Conference and Mark Twain Writer's Workshop is geared toward intermediate, advanced and professional levels. Workshops open to students and community. Annual workshops. Workshops held in Summer. Cost of workshop varies. Write for more information.

WINTER POETRY & PROSE GETAWAY IN CAPE MAY

18 N. Richards Ave., Ventnor NJ 08406. (888)887-2105. E-mail: info@wintergetaway.com. Website: www.wintergetaway.com. Annual conferences. Estab. 1994. Join Peter E. Murphy & friends for the 18th Annual Winter Poetry & Prose getaway on the oceanfront in historic Cape May, NJ January 14-17, 2011. This is not your typical writers' conference. Energize you writing with challenging and supportive workshops that focus on starting new material. Advance your craft with feedback from our award-winning faculty including Pultizer Prize & National book award winners. Thousands of people have enjoyed the getaway over the past 17 years, developing their craft as writers and making lifelong friends. The focus isn't on our award-winning faculty, it's on helping you improve and advance your skills. This intensive three-day conference features a variety of poetry and prose workshops, each with 10 or fewer participants. Our writing for the children's market workshop explores different genres of juvenile literature and focuses on creating character, plot, setting, and dialogue. Writing exercises and prompts provide springboards for discussion and feedback. Previous faculty has included Pamela Curtis Swallow, Carol Plum-Ucci, and Joyce McDonald. Workshops also available in poetry, memoir, creative non-fiction, novel, short story, song writing & more. Visit the website or call for current fee information: www.wintergetaway.com, 1-888-887-2105.

WRITE-BY-THE-LAKE WRITER'S WORKSHOP & RETREAT

21 N. Park St., 7th Floor,, Madison WI 53715. **Coordinator:** Christine DeSmet. Writer workshops geared toward beginner, intermediate, and advanced levels. **Open to students** (1-3 graduate credits available in English). "One week-long session is devoted to writing for children." Annual workshop. Workshop held June 14-18, 2010. Registration limited to 15. Writing facilities available: computer labs. Cost of workshop: $335 before May 17; $365 after May 17. Cost includes instruction, welcome luncheon, and pastry/coffee each day. E-mail for more information. "Brochure goes online every January for the following June."

⚃ WRITE! CANADA

P.O. Box 1243, Trenton, ON, Canada. E-mail: info@thewordguild.com. Website: www.writecanada.org. Estab. 1984. Annual conference for writers who are Christian. Hosted by The WordGuild, www.thewordguild.com an association of Canadian writers and editors who are Christian. The Word Guild seeks to connect, develop, and promote its members. Keynote speaker, continuing classes, workshops, panels, editor appointments, reading times, critiques, and more. For all levels of writers from beginner to professional. Held in mid-June. Check web site for details.

WRITE ON THE SOUND WRITERS CONFERENCE

700 Main St., Edmonds WA 98020-3032. (425)771-0228. Fax: (425)771-0253. E-mail: wots@ci.edmonds.wa.us. Website: www.ci.edmonds.wa.us/ArtsCommission/wots.stm. **Conference Organizer:** Kris Gillespie. Writer workshops geared toward beginner, intermediate, advanced and professional levels with some sessions on writing for children. Annual conference held in Edmonds,

on Puget Sound, on the first weekend in October with 2.5 days of workshops. Registration limited to 200. Cost of conference: approximately $119 for early registration, $139 for late registration; includes two days of workshops plus one ticket to keynote lecture. Brochures are mailed in August. Attendees must pre-register. Write, e-mail or call for brochure. Writing contest and manuscript critique appointments for conference participants.

⬛ THE WRITERS RETREATS' NETWORK

E-mail: info@writersretreat.com. Website: www.writersretreat.com. Contact: Micheline Cote. This is the only organization featuring a network of worldwide residential retreats opened year-round with on-site mentoring. The retreats cater to writers of all genres and offer on-site support such as mentoring, workshops, editing, and lodging; some of them offer scholarships. Residency rates vary between $200 and $1,000 per week depending on the location. To start and operate a retreat in your area, contact The Writers' Retreat; We're here to help.

WRITE-TO-PUBLISH CONFERENCE

9118 W. Elmwood Dr.#1G, Niles IL 60714-5820. (847)296-3964. Fax: (847)296-0754. E-mail: lin@ writetopublish.com. Website: www.writetopublish.com. **Director:** Lin Johnson. Writer workshops geared toward all levels. **Open to students.** Conference is focused for the Christian market and includes classes on writing for children. Annual conference held in June 8-11, 2011. Cost of conference approximately: $475; includes conference and banquet. For information e-mail brochure@writetopublish.com. Conference takes place at Wheaton College in the Chicago area.

Contests, Awards & Grants

Publication is not the only way to get your work recognized. Contests and awards can also be great ways to gain recognition in the industry. Grants, offered by organizations like SCBWI, offer monetary recognition to writers, giving them more financial freedom as they work on projects.

When considering contests or applying for grants, be sure to study guidelines and requirements. Regard entry deadlines as gospel and follow the rules to the letter.

Note that some contests require nominations. For published authors and illustrators, competitions provide an excellent way to promote your work. Your publisher may not be aware of local competitions such as state-sponsored awards—if your book is eligible, have the appropriate person at your publishing company nominate or enter your work for consideration.

To select potential contests and grants, read through the listings that interest you, then send for more information about the types of written or illustrated material considered and other important details. A number of contests offer information through Web sites given in their listings.

If you are interested in knowing who has received certain awards in the past, check your local library or bookstores or consult *Children's Books: Awards & Honors*, compiled and edited by the Children's Book Council (www.cbcbooks.org). Many bookstores have special sections for books that are Caldecott and Newbery Medal winners. Visit the American Library Association website, www.ala.org, for information on the Caldecott, Newbery, Coretta Scott King and Printz Awards. Visit www.hbook.com for information on The Boston Globe-Horn Book Award. Visit www.scbwi.org/awards.htm for information on The Golden Kite Award.

⊕ ACADEMY OF CHILDREN'S WRITERS' WRITING FOR CHILDREN COMPETITION

Academy of Children's Writers, P.O. Box 95, Huntington Cambridgeshire PE28 5RL England. 01487 832752. Fax: 01487 832752. E-mail: enquiries@childrens-writers.co.uk **Contact:** Roger Dewar, contest director. Annual contest for the best unpublished short story writer for children. **Deadline:** March 31.Visit website for guidelines: www.childrens-writers.co.uk. **Charges $10 (US) Bill;** Prize: 1st Prize: $4,000; 2nd Prize: $600; 3rd Prize: $400. Judged by a panel appointed by the Academy of Children's Writers. Open to any writer.

🍁 ALCUIN CITATION AWARD

The Alcuin Society, P.O. Box 3216, Vancouver BC V6B 3X8 Canada. (604)732-5403. E-mail: awards@alcuinsociety.com. Website: www.alcuinsociety.com /awards. Annual award. Estab. 1981. Purpose of contest: Alcuin Citations are awarded annually for excellence in Canadian book design. Previously published submissions from the year prior to the Award's Call for Entries (i.e. 2005 awards went to books published in 2004). Submissions made by the publisher, author or designer. Deadline for entries: mid-March. Entry fee is $25/book for Society members; $30/book for non-members; include cheque and entry form with book; downloadable entry form available at web site. Awards certificate. Winning books are exhibited nationally, and internationally at the Frankfurt and Leipzig Book Fairs, and are Canada's entries in the international competition in Leipzig, "Book Design from all over the World" in the following Spring. Judging by professionals and those experienced in the field of book design. Requirements for entrants: Winners are selected from books designed and published in Canada. Awards are presented annually at an appropriate ceremonies held in each year.

AMERICA & ME ESSAY CONTEST

Farm Bureau Insurance, P.O. Box 30400, 7373 W. Saginaw, Lansing MI 48909-7900. (517)323-7000. Fax: (517)323-6615. E-mail: lfedewa@fbinsmi.com. Website: www.farmbureauinsurance-mi.com. **Contest Coordinator:** Lisa Fedewa. Annual contest. **Open to students only.** Estab. 1968. Purpose of the contest: to give Michigan 8th graders the opportunity to express their thoughts/feelings on America and their roles in America. Unpublished submissions only. Deadline for entries: mid-November. SASE for contest rules and entry forms. "We have a school mailing list. Any school located in Michigan is eligible to participate." Entries not returned. No entry fee. Cash awards savings bonds and plaques for state top ten ($1,000), certificates and plaques for top 3 winners from each school. Each school may submit up to 10 essays for judging. Judging by home office employee volunteers. Requirements for entrants: participants must work through their schools or our agents' sponsoring schools. No individual submissions will be accepted. Top ten essays and excerpts from other essays are published in booklet form following the contest. State capitol/ schools receive copies."

AMERICAN ASSOCIATION OF UNIVERSITY WOMEN, NORTH CAROLINA DIVISION, AWARD IN JUVENILE LITERATURE

4610 Mail Service Center, Raleigh NC 27699-4610. **Contact:** Mr. Michael Hill. Annual award. Purpose of award: to recognize the year's best work of juvenile literature by a North Carolina resident. Book must be published during the year ending June 30. Submissions made by author, author's agent or publisher. Deadline for entries: July 15. SASE for contest rules. Awards a cup to the winner and winner's name inscribed on a plaque displayed within the North Carolina Office of Archives and History. Judging by Board of Award selected by sponsoring organization. Requirements for entrants: Author must have maintained either legal residence or actual physical residence, or a combination of both, in the state of North Carolina for three years immediately preceding the close of the contest period. Only published work (books) eligible.

AMERICAS AWARD

CLASP Committee on Teaching and Outreach, c/o Center for Latin American and Caribbean Studies, P.O. Box 413, Milwaukee WI 53201. (414)229-5986. Fax: (414)229-2879. E-mail: jkline@uwm.edu. Website: http://www4.uwm.edu/clacs/aa/index.cfm. **Coordinator:** Julie Kline. Annual award. Estab. 1993. Purpose of contest: Up to two awards are given each spring in recognition of U.S. published works (from the previous year) of fiction, poetry, folklore or selected nonfiction (from picture books to works for young adults) in English or Spanish which authentically and engagingly relate to Latin America, the Caribbean, or to Latinos in the United States. By combining both and linking the "Americas," the intent is to reach beyond geographic borders, as well as multicultural-international boundaries, focusing instead upon cultural heritages within the hemisphere. Previously published submissions only. Submissions open to anyone with an interest in the theme of the award. Deadline for entries: January 15. Visit website or send SASE for contest rules and any committee changes. Awards $500 cash prize, plaque and a formal presentation at the Library of Congress, Washington DC. Judging by a review committee consisting of individuals in teaching, library work, outreach and children's literature specialists.

🌐 HANS CHRISTIAN ANDERSEN AWARD

IBBY International Board on Books for Young People, Nonnenweg 12, Postfach CH-4003 Basel Switzerland. (004161)272 29 17. Fax: (004161)272 27 57. E-mail: ibby@ibby.org. Website: www.ibby.org. **Director:** Liz Page. Award offered every two years. Purpose of award: A Hans Christian Andersen Medal shall be awarded every two years by the International Board on Books for Young People (IBBY) to an author and to an illustrator, living at the time of the nomination, who by the outstanding value of their work are judged to have made a lasting contribution to literature for children and young people. The complete works of the author and of the illustrator will be taken into consideration in awarding the medal, which will be accompanied by a diploma. Candidates are nominated by National Sections of IBBY in good standing. The Hans Christian Andersen Award, is the highest international recognition given to an author and an illustrator of children's books. The Author's Award has been given since 1956, the Illustrator's Award since 1966. Her Majesty Queen Margrethe II of Denmark is the Patron of the Hans Christian Andersen Awards. The Hans Christian Andersen Jury judges the books submitted for medals according to literary and artistic criteria. The awards are presented at the biennial congresses of IBBY.

▤ ATLANTIC WRITING COMPETITION

Writer's Federation of Nova Scotia, 1113 Marginal Rd., Halifax NS B3H 4P7 Canada. (902)423-8116. Fax: (902)422-0881. E-mail: talk@writers.ns.ca. Website: www.writers.ns.ca/awc.html. Annual contest. Purpose is to encourage emerging writers in Atlantic Canada to explore their talents by sending unpublished work to any of five categories: novel, short story, poetry, writing for younger children, writing for juvenile/young adult. Unpublished submissions only. Only open to residents of Atlantic Canada who are unpublished in category they enter. Visit website for more information.

AUSTIN PUBLIC LIBRARY FRIENDS FOUNDATION AWARDS FOR BEST CHILDREN'S BOOK ($500) AND BEST YOUNG ADULT BOOK ($500)

Dallas TX 75225. Website: www.smu.edu/english/creativewriting/The_Texas_Institute_of_Letters.htm. Offered annually for work published January 1-December 31 of previous year to recognize the best book for children and young people. Writer must have been born in Texas or have lived in the state for at least 2 consecutive years at one time, or the subject matter must be associated with the state. See website for information on eligibility, deadlines, and the judges names and addresses to whom the books should be sent. Prize: $500 for each award winner. **Contact:** Darwin Payne.

☒ MARILYN BAILLIE PICTURE BOOK AWARD

40 Orchard View Blvd., Suite 101, Toronto ON M4R 1B9 Canada. (416)975-0010. Fax: (416)975-8970. E-mail: meghan@bookcentre.ca. Website: www.bookcentre.ca. "To be eligible, the book must be an original work in English, aimed at children ages 3-8, written and illustrated by Canadians and first published in Canada. Eligible genres include fiction, nonfiction and poetry. Books must be published between Jan. 1 and Dec. 31 of the previous calendar year." "Honours excellence in the illustrated picture book format." **Charges Deadline: mid-December.** Prize: $20,000.

☒ ☒ THE GEOFFREY BILSON AWARD FOR HISTORICAL FICTION FOR YOUNG PEOPLE

The Canadian Children's Book Centre, 40 Orchard View Blvd., Suite 101, Toronto ON M4R 1B9 Canada. (416)975-0010. Fax: (416)975-8970. Website: www.bookcentre.ca. Created in Geoffrey Bilson's memory in 1988. Awarded annually to reward excellence in the writing of an outstanding work of historical fiction for young readers, by a Canadian author, published in the previous calendar year. Open to Canadian citizens and residents of Canada for at least 2 years. Deadline: Mid- December. Prize: $5,000. Please visit website for submissions guidelines and eligibility criteria, as well as specific submission deadline.

THE IRMA S. AND JAMES H. BLACK BOOK AWARD

Bank Street College of Education, New York NY 10025-1898. (212)875-4458. Fax: (212)875-4558. E-mail: kfreda@bankstreet.edu. Website: http://www.bankstreet.edu/childrenslibrary/irmasimontonblackhome.html. **Contact:** Kristin Freda. Annual award. Estab. 1972. Purpose of award: "The award is given each spring for a book for young children, published in the previous year, for excellence of both text and illustrations." Entries must have been published during the previous calendar year (between January '08 and December '08 for 2009 award). Deadline for entries: mid-December. "Publishers submit books to us by sending them here to me at the Bank Street Library. Authors may ask their publishers to submit their books. Out of these, three to five books are chosen by a committee of older children and children's literature professionals. These books are then presented to children in selected first, second, and third grade classes here and at a number of other cooperating schools. These children are the final judges who pick the actual award winner. A scroll (one each for the author and illustrator, if they're different) with the recipient's name and a gold seal designed by Maurice Sendak are awarded in May."

WALDO M. AND GRACE C. BONDERMAN BIENNIAL NATIONAL YOUTH THEATRE PLAYWRITING COMPETITION AND DEVELOPMENT WORKSHOP AND SYMPOSIUM

Bonderman Youth Theatre Playwriting Workshop, Indiana Repertory Theatre, 140 West Washington St., Indianapolis, IN 46204. E-mail: bonderma@iupui.edu. Website: www.Irtlive.com. **Artistic Director**: Dorothy Webb. Open to professional and non-professional American playwrights. Next deadline, (Tentative) August 16, 2010. Established 1985. Entries not returned. No entry fee. Judging by professional theatre directors, teachers, and artists. Requirements for entrants: Contest opens only to American playwrights with plays not previously produced professionally and not currently in development with a theatre.

ANN CONNOR BRIMER AWARD

Nova Scotia Library Association, P.O. Box 36036, Halifax NS B3J 3S9 Canada. (902)490-5991. Fax: (902)490-5889. Website: http://nsla.ns.ca/aboutnsla/brimeraward.html. **Award Director:** Heather MacKenzie. Annual award. Estab. 1991. Purpose of the contest: to recognize excellence in writing. Given to an author of a children's book who resides in Atlantic Canada. Previously published submissions only. Submissions made by the author's agent or nominated by a person or group of people. Must be published in previous year. Deadline for entries: October 15. SASE for contest rules and entry forms. No entry fee. Awards $1,000 and framed certificate. Judging by a selection committee. Requirements for entrants: Book must be intended for use up to age 15; in print and readily available; fiction or nonfiction except textbooks.

BUCKEYE CHILDREN'S BOOK AWARD

Website: www.bcbookaward.info. **President:** Christine Watters. Correspondence should be sent to Christine Watters via the website. **Open to Ohio students.** Award offered every year. Estab. 1981. Purpose of the award: The Buckeye Childeren's Book Award Program was designed to encourage children to read literature critically, to promote teacher and librarian involvement in children's literature programs, and to commend authors of such literature, as well as to promote the use of libraries. Nominees are submitted by students between January 1 and March 15. Votes are cast between September 1 and November 10. Winning titles are posted on the website on December 1.

CALLIOPE FICTION CONTEST

Writers' Specialized Interest Group (SIG) of American Mensa, Ltd.2506 SE Bitterbrush Dr., Madras, OR 97741. E-mail: cynthia@theriver.com. Website: www.calliopewriters.org. **Fiction Editor:** Sandy Raschke. **Open to students.** Annual contest. Estab. 1991. Purpose of contest: "To promote good writing and opportunities for getting published. To give our member/subscribers and others an entertaining and fun exercise in writing." Unpublished submissions only (all genres, no violence, profanity or extreme horror). Submissions made by author. Deadline for entries: Changes annually. Entry fee is $5 for nonsubscribers; subscribers get first entry fee. Awards small amount of cash (up to $75 for 1st place, to $10 for 3rd), certificates, full or mini-subscriptions to Calliope and various premiums and books, depending on donations. All winners are published in subsequent issues of Calliope. Judging by fiction editor, with concurrence of other editors, if needed. Requirements for entrants: winners must retain sufficient rights to have their stories published in the January/February issue, or their entries will be disqualified; one-time rights. Open to all writers. No special considerations—other than following the guidelines. Contest theme, due dates and sometimes entry fees change annually. Always send SASE for complete rules; available after March 15 each year. Sample copies with prior winners are available for $3.

CANADA COUNCIL GOVERNOR GENERAL'S LITERARY AWARDS

350 Albert St., Ottawa ON K1P 5V8 Canada. (613)566-4410, ext. 5573. Fax: (613)566-4410. E-mail: diane.miljours@canadacouncil.ca. **Program Officer, Writing and Publishing Section:** Diane Miljours. Annual award. Estab. 1937. Purpose of award: given to the best English-language and the best French-language work in each of the seven categories of Fiction, Literary Non-fiction, Poetry, Drama, Children's Literature (text), Children's Literature (illustration) and Translation. Books must be first-edition trade books that have been written, translated or illustrated by Canadian citizens or permanent residents of Canada. In the case of Translation, the original work written in English or French, must also be a Canadian-authored title. English titles must be published between September 1, 2009 and September 30, 2010. Books must be submitted by publishers. Deadlines depend on the book's publication date. For books published in English: March 15, June 1 and August 7. For books published in french: March 15 and July 15. The awards ceremony is scheduled mid-November. Amount of award: $25,000 to winning authors; $1,000 to non-winning finalists.

SANDRA CARON YOUNG ADULT POETRY PRIZE

National League of American Pen Women, Nob Hill, San Francisco Branch, 1544 Sweetwood Dr., Broadmoor Vlg.Colma CA 94015-2029. E-mail: pennobhill@aol.com. Website: www. soulmakingcontest.us. **Contact:** Eileen Malone. **Open to students.** Three poems/entry; one poem/page; one-page poems only from poets in grades 9-12 or equivalent. Annually. Deadline: November 30. Guidelines for SASE. Charges $5/entry (make checks payable to NLAPW, Nob Hill Branch). Prize: 1st Place: $100; 2nd Place: $50; 3rd Place: $25. Open to any writer in grade 9-12.

CHILDREN'S AFRICANA BOOK AWARD

c/o Rutgers University, 132 George St., New Brunswick NJ 08901. (732)932-8173. Fax: (732)932-3394. Website: www.africanstudies.org. Administered by Africa Access, P.O. Box 8028, Silver Spring MD 20910. (301)585-9136. E-mail: africaaccess@aol.com. Website: www.africaaccessreview. org. **Chairperson**: Brenda Randolph. Annually. Estab. 1991. Purpose of contest: "The Children's Africana Book Awards are presented annually to the authors and illustrators of the best books on Africa for children and young people published or republished in the U.S. The awards were created by the Outreach Council of the African Studies Association (ASA) to dispel stereotypes and encourage the publication and use of accurate, balanced children's materials about Africa. The awards are presented in 2 categories: Young Children and Older Readers. Since 1991, books have been recognized." Entries must have been published in the calendar year previous to the award. No entry fee. Awards plaque, announcement each spring, reviews published at Africa Access Review website and in Sankofa: Journal of African Children's & Young Adult Literature. Judging by Outreach Council of ASA and children's literature scholars. "Work submitted for awards must be suitable for children ages 4-18; a significant portion of books' content must be about Africa; must by copyrighted in the calendar year prior to award year; must be published or republished in the US."

CHILDREN'S BOOK GUILD AWARD FOR NONFICTION

E-mail: theguild@childrensbookguild.org. Annual award. Estab. 1977. Purpose of award: "to honor an author or illustrator whose total work has contributed significantly to the quality of nonfiction for children." Award includes a cash prize and an engraved crystal paperweight. Judging by a jury of Children's Book Guild specialists, authors, and illustrators. "One doesn't enter. One is selected. Our jury annually selects one author for the award." Website: www.childrensbookguild. org. **Contact:** President changes yearly.

COLORADO BOOK AWARDS

(303)894-7951, ext. 21. Fax: (303)864-9361. E-mail: long@coloradohumanities.org. **Contact:** Margaret Coval, exec. dir., or Jennifer Long, Prog. Adjudicator. Offered annually for work published by December of previous year. "The purpose is to champion all Colorado authors, editors, illustrators, and photographers, and in particular, to honor the award winners raising the profiles of both their work and Colorado as a state whose people promote and support reading, writing, and literacy through books. The categories are generally: children's literature, young adult and juvenile literature, fiction, genre fiction (romance, mystery/thriller, science fiction/fantasy, historical), biography, history, anthology, poetry, pictorial, graphic novel/comic, creative nonfiction, and general nonfiction, as well as other categories as determined each year. Open to authors who reside or have resided in Colorado." Deadline: January 15, 2010. **Charges $50 fee.**

CRICKET LEAGUE

Cricket League, P.O. Box 300, Peru IL 61354. E-mail: mail@cricketmagkids.com. Website: www.cricketmagkids.com/contests. Open to all ages. Nine contests per year. Estab. 1973. "The purpose of Cricket League contests is to encourage creativity and give young people an opportunity to express themselves in writing, drawing, painting or photography. There is a contest in each issue. Possible categories include story, poetry, art, or photography. Each contest relates to a specific theme described on each Cricket issue's Cricket League page and on the website. Signature verifying originality, age and address of entrant and permission to publish required. Entries which do not relate to the current month's theme cannot be considered." Unpublished submissions only. Deadline for entries: the 25th of the month. Cricket League rules, contest theme, and submission deadline information can be found in the current issue of Cricket and via website. " We prefer that children who enter the contests subscribe to the magazine or that they read Cricket in their school or library." No entry fee. Awards certificate suitable for framing and children's books or art/writing supplies. Judging by Cricket editors. Obtains right to print prizewinning entries in magazine and/or on the website. Refer to contest rules in current Cricket issue. Winning entries are published on the Cricket League pages in a subsequent Cricket magazine. Current theme, rules, and prizewinning entries also posted on the website.

DOROTHY CANFIELD FISHER CHILDREN'S BOOK AWARD

Vermont Department of Libraries, Northeast Regional Library, 109 State St., Montpelier VT 05609. (802)828-6954. E-mail: grace.greene@state.vt.us. Website: www.dcfaward.org. **Chair:** Mary Linney. Annual award. Estab. 1957. Purpose of the award: to encourage Vermont children to become enthusiastic and discriminating readers by providing them with books of good quality by living American or Canadian authors published in the current year. Deadline for entries: December of year book was published. E-mail for entry rules. No entry fee. Awards a scroll presented to the winning author at an award ceremony. Judging is by the children grades 4-8. They vote for their favorite book. Requirements for entrants: "Titles must be original work, published in the United States, and be appropriate to children in grades 4 through 8. The book must be copyrighted in the current year. It must be written by an American author living in the U.S. or Canada, or a Canadian author living in Canada or the U.S."

⊠ ⊠ THE NORMA FLECK AWARD FOR CANADIAN CHILDREN'S NONFICTION

The Canadian Children's Book Centre, 40 Orchard View Blvd., Suite 101, Toronto ON M4R 1B9 Canada. (416)975-0010. Fax: (416)975-8970. E-mail: info@bookcentre.ca. Website: www.bookcentre.ca. **Contact:** Naseem Hrab, librarian. The Norma Fleck Award was established by the

Fleck Family Foundation in May 1999 to honour the life of Norma Marie Fleck, and to recognize exceptional Canadian non-fiction books for young people. Publishers are welcome to nominate books using the online form. Offered annually for books published between January 1 and December 31 of the previous calendar year. Open to Canadian citizens or landed immigrants. The jury will always include at least 3 of the following: a teacher, a librarian, a bookseller, and a reviewer. A juror will have a deep understanding of, and some involvement with, Canadian children's books. The Canadian Children's Book Centre will select the jury members. **Deadline: Mid-December (annually).** Prize: $10,000 goes to the author (unless 40% or more of the text area is composed of original illustrations, in which case the award will be divided equally between the author and the artist).

DON FREEMAN MEMORIAL GRANT-IN-AID

Society of Children's Book Writers and Illustrators, 8271 Beverly Blvd., Los Angeles CA 90048. (323)782-1010 Fax: (323) 782-1892 E-mail: scbwi@scbwi.org. Website: www.scbwi.org. Estab. 1974. Purpose of award: to "enable picture book artists to further their understanding, training and work in the picture book genre." Applications and prepared materials are available in October and must be postmarked between February 1 and March 1. Grant awarded and announced in August. SASE for award rules and entry forms. SASE for return of entries. No entry fee. Annually awards one grant of $1,500 and one runner-up grant of $500. "The grant-in-aid is available to both full and associate members of the SCBWI who, as artists, seriously intend to make picture books their chief contribution to the field of children's literature."

GOLDEN KITE AWARDS

Society of Children's Book Writers and Illustrators, 8271 Beverly Blvd., Los Angeles CA 90048. (323)782-1010. E-mail: scbwi@scbwi.org. Website: www.scbwi.org. **Contact:** SCBWI Golden Kite Coordinator. Annual award. Estab. 1973. "The works chosen will be those that the judges feel exhibit excellence in writing, and in the case of the picture-illustrated books—in illustration, and genuinely appeal to the interests and concerns of children. For the fiction and nonfiction awards, original works and single-author collections of stories or poems of which at least half are new and never before published in book form are eligible—anthologies and translations are not. For the picture-illustration awards, the art or photographs must be original works (the texts—which may be fiction or nonfiction—may be original, public domain or previously published). Deadline for entries: December 15. SASE for award rules. No entry fee. Awards, in addition to statuettes and plaques, the four winners receive $2,500 cash award plus trip to LA SCBWI Conference. The panel of judges will consist of professional authors, illustrators, editors or agents." Requirements for entrants: "must be a member of SCBWI and books must be published in that year." Winning books will be displayed at national conference in August. Books to be entered, as well as further inquiries, should be submitted to: The Society of Children's Book Writers and Illustrators, above address.

⊠ ⊠ GOVERNOR GENERAL'S LITERARY AWARDS

Canada Council for the Arts, 350 Albert St., P.O. Box 1047, Ottawa ON K1P 5V8 Canada. (613)566-4414, ext. 5573. Fax: (613)566-4410. Website: www.canadacouncil.ca/prizes/ggla. Submissions in English must be published between September 1, 2009 and September 30, 2010; submissions in French between July 1, 2009 and June 30, 2010. Publishers submit titles for consideration. Deadlines depend on the book's publication date. For books published in English: March 15, June 1 and August 7. For books published in French: March 15 and July 15. Prize: Each laureate receives $25,000; non-winning finalists receive $1,000.

HRC SHOWCASE THEATRE

P.O. Box 940, Hudson NY 12534. (518)851-7244. E-mail: jangrice2002@yahoo.com. Annual contest. HRCs Showcase Theatre is a not-for-profit professional theater company dedicated to the advancement of performing in the Hudson River Valley area through reading of plays and providing opportunities for new and established playwrights. Unpublished submissions only. Submissions made by author and by the author's agent. Deadlines for entries: May 15th. SASE for contest rules and entry forms. Entry fee is $5. Awards $500 cash plus concert reading by professional actors for winning play and $100 for each of the four other plays that will be given a staged reading. Judging by panel selected by Board of Directors. Requirements for entrants: Entrants must live in the northeastern U.S.

IRA CHILDREN'S AND YOUNG ADULT'S BOOK AWARD

(302)731-1600. Fax: (302)731-1057. E-mail: exec@reading.org. Annual award. Awards are given for an author's first or second published book for fiction and nonfiction in three categories: primary (ages preschool-8), intermediate (ages 9-13), and young adult (ages 14-17). This award is intended for newly published authors who show unusual promise in the children's book field. Deadline for entries: October 15, 2010. Awards $1000. For guidelines write or e-mail. Website: www.reading.org.

KENTUCKY BLUEGRASS AWARD

Lincoln County High School Media Center, 60 Educat, 521 Lancaster Ave., Stanford KY 40484. (606)365-9111. Fax: (606)365-1750. E-mail: kay.hensley@lincoln.kyschools.us. **Award Director:** Kay Renee Hensley. Submit entries to: Kay Renee Hensley. Annual award. Estab. 1983. Purpose of award: to promote readership among young children and young adolescents. Also to recognize exceptional creative efforts of authors and illustrators. Previously published submissions only. Submissions made by author, made by author's agent, nominated by teachers or librarians. Must be published no more than 3 years prior to the award year. Deadline for entries: March 15. Contest rules and entry forms are available from the website. No entry fee. Awards a framed certificate and invitation to be recognized at the annual luncheon of the Kentucky Bluegrass Award. Judging by children who participate through their schools or libraries. "Books are reviewed by a panel of teachers and librarians before they are placed on a Master List for the year. These books must have been published within a three year period prior to the review. Winners are chosen from this list of preselected books. Books are divided into four divisions, K-2, 3-5, 6-8, 9-12 grades. Winners are chosen by children who either read the books or have the books read to them. Children from the entire state of Kentucky are involved in the selection of the annual winners for each of the divisions." Website: www.kyreading.org.

CORETTA SCOTT KING BOOK AWARDS

Coretta Scott King Book Awards Committee, Ethnic and Multicultural Information Exchange Round Table, American Library Association, 50 E. Huron St., Chicago IL 60611. (800)545-2433 ext: 4297. Fax: (312)280-3256. E-mail: olos@ala.org. Website: www.ala.org/csk. "The Coretta Scott King Book Awards is an annual award celebrating African American experience. A new talent award may also be selected. An awards jury of Children's Librarians judge the books form the previous year, and select the winners in January at the ALA Midwinter meeting. A copy of an entry must be sent to each juror by December 1 of the juried year. A copy of the jury list and directions for submitting titles can be found on website. Call or e-mail ALA Office for Literacy and Outreach Services for jury list. Awards breakfast held on Tuesday morning during ALA. Annual Conference in June. See schedule at website.

ⓝ ⓥ THE VICKY METCALF AWARD FOR CHILDREN'S LITERATURE

The Writers' Trust of Canada, 90 Richmond St. E., Suite 200, Toronto ON M5C 1P1 Canada. (416)504-8222. Fax: (416)504-9090. E-mail: info@writerstrust.com. Website: www.writerstrust.com. **Contact:** James Davies. The Vicky Metcalf Award is presented each fall to a Canadian writer for a body of work in children's literature at The Writers' Trust Awards event in Toronto. Prize: $20,000. Open to Canadian residents only.

MILKWEED PRIZE FOR CHILDREN'S LITERATURE

Milkweed Editions, 1011 Washington Ave. S., Suite 300, Minneapolis MN 55415-1246. (612)332-3192. Fax: (612)215-2550. E-mail: editor@milkweed.org. Website: www.milkweed.org. **Award Director:** Daniel Slager, Publisher. Annual award. Estab. 1993. Purpose of the award: to recognize an outstanding literary novel for readers ages 8-13 and encourage writers to turn their attention to readers in this age group. Unpublished submissions only "in book form." Please send SASE or visit website for award guidelines. The prize is awarded to the best work for children ages 8-13 that Milkweed agrees to publish in a calendar year. The Prize consists of a $10,000 advance against royalties agreed to at the time of acceptance. Submissions must follow our usual children's guidelines.

NATIONAL CHILDREN'S THEATRE FESTIVAL

Actors' Playhouse at the Miracle Theatre, 280 Miracle Mile, Coral Gables FL 33134. (305)444-9293, ext. 615. Fax: (305)444-4181. E-mail: maulding@actorsplayhouse.org. Website: www.actorsplayhouse.org. **Director:** Earl Maulding. **Open to students.** Annual contest. Estab. 1994. Purpose of contest: to bring together the excitement of the theater arts and the magic of young audiences through the creation of new musical works and to create a venue for playwrights/composers to showcase their artistic products. Submissions must be unpublished. Submissions are made by author or author's agent. Deadline for entries: April 1 annually. Visit website or send SASE for contest rules and entry forms. Entry fee is $10. Awards: first prize of $500, full production, and transportation to Festival weekend based on availability. Final judges are of national reputation. Past judges include Joseph Robinette, Moses Goldberg and Luis Santeiro.

NATIONAL PEACE ESSAY CONTEST

1200 17th St. NW, Washington DC 20036. (202)457-1700. Fax: (202)429.6063. E-mail: essaycontest@usip.org. **Open to high school students.** Annual contest. Estab. 1987. "The contest gives students the opportunity to do valuable research, writing and thinking on a topic of importance to international peace and conflict resolution. Teaching guides are available for teachers who allow the contest to be used as a classroom assignment." Deadline for entries is February 1, 2011. "Interested students, teachers and others may visit the website to download or request contest materials. Please do not include SASE." Guidelines and rules on website. No entry fee. State Level Awards are $1,000 college scholarships. National winners are selected from among the 1st place state winners. National winners receive scholarships in the following amounts: first place $10,000; second $5,000; third $2,500. National amount includes State Award. First place state winners invited to an expenses-paid awards program in Washington, DC in June. Judging is conducted by education professionals from across the country and by the Board of Directors of the United States Institute of Peace. "All submissions become property of the U.S. Institute of Peace to use at its discretion and without royalty or any limitation. Students grades 9-12 in the U.S., its territories and overseas schools may submit essays for review by completing the application process. U.S. citizenship required for students attending overseas schools. National winning essays will be published by the U.S. Institute of Peace." Website: www.usip.org/NPEC.

NEW ENGLAND BOOK AWARDS

New England Independent Booksellers Association, 297 Broadway, #212, Arlington MA 02474. (781)316-8894. Fax: (781)316-2605. E-mail: nan@neba.org. Website: www.newenglandbooks.org/ Default.aspx?pageId=234046. **Assistant Executive Director:** Nan Sorensen. Annual award. Estab. 1990. Purpose of award: "to promote New England authors who have produced a body of work that stands as a significant contribution to New England's culture." Previously published submissions only. Submissions made by New England booksellers; publishers. "Award is given to a specific title, fiction, nonfiction, children's. The titles must be either about New England, set in New England or by an author residing in the New England. The titles must be hardcover, paperback original or reissue that was published between September 1 and August 31. Entries must be still in print and available. No entry fee. Judging by NEIBA membership. Requirements for entrants: Author/ illustrator must live in New England. Submit written nominations only; actual books should not be sent. Member bookstores receive materials to display winners' books. Submission deadline: July 2.

NEW VOICES AWARD

Lee & Low Books, 95 Madison Ave., New York NY 10016. (212)779-4400. Fax: (212)532-6035. E-mail: general@leeandlow.com. Website: www.leeandlow.com. **Editor-in-chief:** Louise May. **Open to students.** Annual award. Estab. 2000. Purpose of contest: To encourage writers of color to enter the world of children's books. Lee & Low Books is one of the few minority-owned publishing companies in the country. We have published more than 85 first-time writers and illustrators. Winning titles include The Blue Roses, winner of a Patterson Prize for Books for Young People, Janna and the Kings, an IRA Children's Book Award Notable, and Sixteen Years in Sixteen Seconds, selected for the Texas Bluebonnet Award Masterlist. Submissions made by author. Deadline for entries: September 30. SASE for contest rules or visit website. No entry fee. Awards New Voices Award—$1,000 prize and standard publication contract (regardless of whether or not writer has an agent) along with an advance against royalties; New Voices Honor Award—$500 prize. Judging by Lee & Low editors. Restrictions of media for illustrators: The author must be a writer of color who is a resident of the U.S. and who has not previously published a children's picture book. For additional information, send SASE or visit Lee & Low's website.

NORTH AMERICAN INTERNATIONAL AUTO SHOW HIGH SCHOOL POSTER CONTEST

Detroit Auto Dealers Association, 1900 W. Big Beaver Rd., Troy MI 48084-3531. (248)643-0250. Fax: (248)283-5148. E-mail: sherp@dada.org. Website: www.naias.com. **Contact:** Sandy Herp. **Open to students.** Annual contest. Submissions made by the author and illustrator. Contact: Detroit Auto Dealers Association, DADA. for contest rules and entry forms or retrieve rules from website. No entry fee. Awards in the High School Poster Contest are as follows: Chairman's Award—$1,000; Designer's Best of Show (Digital and Traditional)—$500; Best Theme—$250; Best Use of Color—$250; Most Creative—$250. A winner will be chosen in each category from grades 10, 11 and 12. Prizes: 1st place in 10, 11, 12—$500; 2nd place—$250; 3rd place—$100. The winners of the Designer's Best of Show Digital and Traditional will each receive $500. The winner of the Chairman's Award will receive $1,000. Entries will be judged by an independent panel of recognized representatives of the art community. Entrants must be Michigan high school students enrolled in grades 10-12. Winning posters may be displayed at the NAIAS 2009 and reproduced in the official NAIAS program, which is available to the public, international media, corporate executives and automotive suppliers. Winning posters may also be displayed on the official NAIAS website at the sole discretion of the NAIAS.

ORBIS PICTUS AWARD FOR OUTSTANDING NONFICTION FOR CHILDREN

The National Council of Teachers of English, 1111 W. Kenyon Rd., Urbana IL 61801-1096. (217)328-3870. Fax: (217)328-0977. E-mail: dzagorski@ncte.org. Website: www.ncte.org/awards/ orbispictus. **Chair, NCTE Committee on the Orbis Pictus Award for Outstanding Nonfiction for Children:** Kim Ford, Memphis TN. Annual award. Estab. 1989. Purpose of award: To promote and recognize excellence in the writing of nonfiction for children. Previously published submissions only. Submissions made by author, author's agent, by a person or group of people. Must be published January 1-December 31 of contest year. Deadline for entries: November 30. Call for award information. No entry fee. Awards a plaque given at the NCTE Elementary Section Luncheon at the NCTE Annual Convention in November. Judging by a committee. "The name Orbis Pictus commemorates the work of Johannes Amos Comenius, 'Orbis Pictus—The World in Pictures' (1657), considered to be the first book actually planned for children."

HELEN KEATING OTT AWARD FOR OUTSTANDING CONTRIBUTION TO CHILDREN'S LITERATURE

Church and Synagogue Library Association, 2920 SW Dolph Ct Ste 3A, Portland OR 97219. (503)244-6919. Fax: (503)977-3734. E-mail: csla@worldaccessnet.com. Website: www.cslainfo. org. **Chair of Committee:** Jeri Baker. Annual award. Estab. 1980. "This award is given to a person or organization that has made a significant contribution to promoting high moral and ethical values through children's literature." Deadline for entries: April 1. "Recipient is honored in July during the conference." Awards certificate of recognition , the awards banquet, and one nights stay in the hotel. "A nomination for an Award may be made by anyone. An application form is available by contacting Judy Janzen, Administrator of CSLA via e-mail at csla@worldaccessnet.com or by calling 1-800-LIB-CSLA. Elements of creativity and innovation will be given high priority by the judges."

PATERSON PRIZE FOR BOOKS FOR YOUNG PEOPLE

Poetry Center at Passaic County Community College, One College Blvd., Paterson NJ 07505-1179. (973)684-6555. Fax: (973)523-6085. E-mail: mgillan@pccc.edu. Website: www.pccc.edu/poetry. **Executive Director:** Maria Mazziotti Gillan. Estab. 1996. Part of the Poetry Center's mission is "to recognize excellence in books for young people." Published submissions only. Submissions made by author, author's agent or publisher. Must be published between January 1-December 31 of year previous to award year. Deadline for entries: March 15. SASE for contest rules and entry forms or visit website. Awards $500 for the author in either of 3 categories: PreK-Grade 3; Grades 4-6, Grades 7-12. Judging by a professional writer selected by the Poetry Center. Contest is open to any writer/illustrator.

PENNSYLVANIA YOUNG READERS' CHOICE AWARDS PROGRAM

Pennsylvania School Librarians Association, 148 S. Bethlehem Pike, Ambler PA 19002-5822. (215)643-5048. Fax: (215)646-7250. E-mail: bellavance@verizon.net. Website: www.psla.org. **Coordinator:** Jean B. Bellavance. Annual award. Estab. 1991. Submissions nominated by a person or group. Must be published within 5 years of the award for example, books published in 2005 to present are eligible for the 2009-2010 award. Deadline for entries: September 1. SASE for contest rules and entry forms. No entry fee. Framed certificate to winning authors. Judging by children of Pennsylvania (they vote). Requirements for entrants: currently living in North America. Reader's Choice Award is to promote reading of quality books by young people in the Commonwealth of Pennsylvania, to promote teacher and librarian involvement in children's literature, and to honor authors whose work has been recognized by the children of Pennsylvania. Four awards are given, one for each of the following grade level divisions: K-3, 3-6, 6-8, YA. View information at the Pennsylvania School Librarians website.

PNWA ANNUAL LITERARY CONTEST

Pacific Northwest Writers Association, PMB 2717-1420 NW Gilman Blvd, Ste 2, Issaquah, WA 98027. (425)673-2665. E-mail: staff@pnwa.org. Website: www.pnwa.org. **Open to students.** Annual contest. Purpose of contest: "Valuable tool for writers as contest submissions are critiqued (2 critiques)." Unpublished submissions only. Submissions made by author. Deadline for entries: February 19, 2010. Entry fee is $35/entry for members, $50/entry for nonmembers. Awards $600-1st; $300-2nd; $150-3rd. Awards in all 12 categories.

EDGAR ALLAN POE AWARD

Mystery Writers of America, Inc.1140 Broadway, Suite 1507, New York NY 10001. (212)888-8171. Fax: (212)888-8107. E-mail: mwa@mysterywriters.org. Website: www.mysterywriters.org. **Administrative Manager:** Margery Flax. Annual award. Estab. 1945. Purpose of the award: to honor authors of distinguished works in the mystery field. Previously published submissions only. Submissions made by the author, author's agent; "normally by the publisher." Work must be published/produced the year of the contest. Deadline for entries: Must be received by November 30. Submission information can be found at: www.mysterywriters.org. No entry fee. Awards ceramic bust of "Edgar" for winner; scrolls for all nominees. Judging by professional members of Mystery Writers of America (writers). Nominee press release sent in mid January. Winner announced at the Edgar[[PIRg]] Banquet, held in late April/early May.

QUILL AND SCROLL INTERNATIONAL WRITING/PHOTO CONTEST

Quill and Scroll, School of Journalism and Mass Communication, University of Iowa, Iowa City IA 52242-2004. (319)335-3457. Fax: (319)335-3989. E-mail: quill-scroll@uiowa.edu. Website: www. uiowa.edu/~quill-sc. **Contest Director:** Vanessa Shelton. **Open to students.** Annual contest. Previously published submissions only. Submissions made by the author or school newspaper adviser. Must be published within the last year. Deadline for entries: February 5. SASE for contest rules and entry forms or visit website for more information and forms. Entry fee is $2/entry. Awards engraved plaque to junior high and high school level sweepstakes winners. Judging by various judges. Quill and Scroll acquires the right to publish submitted material in its magazine or website if it is chosen as a winning entry. Requirements for entrants: must be students in grades 9-12 for high school division; grades 6-8 for junior high school division. Entry form available on website.

TOMAS RIVERA MEXICAN AMERICAN CHILDREN'S BOOK AWARD

Texas State University-San Marcos, EDU, 601 University Dr., San Marcos TX 78666-4613. (512)245-3839. Fax: (512)245-7911. E-mail: jb23@txstate.edu. Website: www.education.txstate.edu. **Award Director:** Dr. Jennifer Battle. Competition open to adults. Annual contest. Estab. 1995. Purpose of award: "To encourage authors, illustrators and publishers to produce books that authentically reflect the lives of Mexican Americans appropriate for children and young adults in the United States." Unpublished mss not accepted. Submissions made by "any interested individual or publishing company." Must be published during the two years prior to the year of consideration for the appropriate category "Works for Younger Children" or " Works for Older Children". Deadline for entries: November 1 of publication year. Contact Dr. Jennifer Battle for information and send copy of book. No entry fee. Awards $3,000 per book. Judging of nominations by a regional committee, national committee judges finalists. Annual ceremony honoring the book and author/illustrator is held during Hispanic Heritage Month at Texas State University-San Marcos in collaboration with the Texas Book Festival.

✿ ROCKY MOUNTAIN BOOK AWARD: ALBERTA CHILDREN'S CHOICE BOOK AWARD

Rocky Mountain Book Award Committee, Box 42, Lethbridge AB T1J 3Y3 Canada. (403)381-0855. E-mail: rockymountainbookaward@shaw.ca. Website: http://rmba.lethsd.ab.ca. **Contest Director:** Michelle Dimnik. Submit entries to: Richard Chase, board member. Open to students. Annual contest. Estab. 2001. Purpose of contest: "Reading motivation for students, promotion of Canadian authors, illustrators and publishers." Previously unpublished submissions only. Submissions made by author's agent or nominated by a person or group. Must be published between 2008-2010. Deadline for entries: January 17, 2010. SASE for contest rules and entry forms. No entry fee. Awards: Gold medal and author tour of selected Alberta schools. Judging by students. Requirements for entrants: Canadian authors and illustrators only.

✿ SASKATCHEWAN BOOK AWARDS: CHILDREN'S LITERATURE

Saskatchewan Book Awards, 205B-2314 11th Avenue, Regina SK S4P 0K1 Canada. (306)569-1585. Fax: (306)569-4187. E-mail: director@bookawards.sk.ca. Website: www.bookawards.sk.ca. **Award Director:** Jacki Lay. Open to Saskatchewan authors only. Annual award. Estab. 1995. Purpose of contest: to celebrate Saskatchewan books and authors and to promote their work. Previously published submissions only. Submissions made by author, author's agent or publisher by September 15. SASE for contest rules and entry forms. Entry fee is $25 (Canadian). Awards $2,000 (Canadian). Judging by three children's literature authors outside of Saskatchewan. Requirements for entrants: Must be Saskatchewan resident; book must have ISBN number; book must have been published within the last year. Award-winning book will appear on TV talk shows and be pictured on bookmarks distributed to libraries, schools and bookstores in Saskatchewan.

SCBWI MAGAZINE MERIT AWARDS

Society of Children's Book Writers and Illustrators, 8271 Beverly Blvd., Los Angeles CA 90048. Fax: (323)782-1010. E-mail: scbwi@scbwi.org. Website: www.scbwi.org. **Award Coordinator:** Stephanie Gordon. Annual award. Estab. 1988. Purpose of the award: "to recognize outstanding original magazine work for young people published during that year and having been written or illustrated by members of SCBWI." Previously published submissions only. Entries must be submitted between January 1 and December 15 of the year of publication. For rules and procedures see website. No entry fee. Must be a SCBWI member. Awards plaques and honor certificates for each of 4 categories (fiction, nonfiction, illustration, poetry). Judging by a magazine editor and two "full" SCBWI members. "All magazine work for young people by an SCBWI member—writer, artist or photographer—is eligible during the year of original publication. In the case of co-authored work, both authors must be SCBWI members. Members must submit their own work." Requirements for entrants: 4 copies each of the published work and proof of publication (may be contents page) showing the name of the magazine and the date of issue. The SCBWI is a professional organization of writers and illustrators and others interested in children's literature. Membership is open to the general public at large.

SCBWI WORK-IN-PROGRESS GRANTS

Society of Children's Book Writers and Illustrators, 8271 Beverly Blvd., Los Angeles CA 90048. (323)782-1010. Fax: (323)782-1892. E-mail: scbwi@scbwi.org. Website: www.scbwi.org. Annual award. "The SCBWI Work-in-Progress Grants have been established to assist children's book writers in the completion of a specific project." Four categories: (1) General Work-in-Progress Grant. (2) Grant for a Contemporary Novel for Young People. (3) Nonfiction Research Grant. (4) Grant for a Work Whose Author Has Never Had a Book Published. Requests for applications may be made beginning October 1. Completed applications accepted February 1-April 1 of each year. SASE for applications for grants. In any year, an applicant may apply for any of the grants except the one awarded for a work whose author has never had a book published. (The recipient of this grant will be chosen from entries in all categories.) Five grants of $1,500 will be awarded annually. Runner-up grants of $500 (one in each category) will also be awarded. "The grants are available to both full and associate members of the SCBWI. They are not available for projects on which there are already contracts." Previous recipients not eligible to apply.

SHUBERT FENDRICH MEMORIAL PLAYWRITING CONTEST

Pioneer Drama Service, Inc., P.O. Box 4267, Englewood CO 80155-4267. Fax: (303)779-4315. E-mail: submissions@pioneerdrama.com. Website: www.pioneerdrama.com. **Director:** Lori Conary. Annual contest. Estab. 1990. Purpose of the contest: "To encourage the development of quality theatrical material for educational and family theater." Previously unpublished submissions only. Open to all writers not currently published by Pioneer Drama Service. Deadline for entries: December 31. SASE for contest rules and guidelines. No entry fee. Cover letter, SASE for return of ms, and proof of production or staged reading must accompany all submissions. Awards $1,000 royalty advance and publication. Upon receipt of signed contracts, plays will be published and made available in our next catalog. Judging by editors. All rights acquired with acceptance of contract for publication. Restrictions for entrants: Any writers currently published by Pioneer Drama Service are not eligible.

SKIPPING STONES BOOK AWARDS

Skipping Stones, P.O. Box 3939, Eugene OR 97403-0939. (541)342-4956. E-mail: editor@ skippingstones.org. Website: www.skippingstones.org. Open to published books, publications/ magazines, educational videos, and DVDs. Annual awards since 1994. Purpose of contest: To recognize exceptional, literary and artistic contributions to juvenile/children's literature, as well as teaching resources and educational audio/video resources in the areas of multicultural awareness, nature and ecology, social issues, peace and nonviolence. Submissions made by the author or publishers and/or producers. Deadline for entries: February 1. Send request for contest rules and entry forms or visit website. Entry fee is $50; 50% discount for small nonprofit publishers. Each year, an honor roll of about 20 to 25 books and A/V with teaching resources are selected by a multicultural selection committee of editors, students, parents, teachers and librarians. Winners receive gold honor award seals, attractive honor certificates and publicity via multiple outlets. Many educational publications announce the winners of our book awards. The reviews of winning books and educational videos/DVDs are published in the May-August issue of Skipping Stones, now in its 22nd year.

SKIPPING STONES YOUTH HONOR AWARDS

P.O. Box 3939, Eugene OR 97403-0939. (541)342-4956. E-mail: editor@SkippingStones.org. **Open to students.** Annual awards. Purpose of contest: "to recognize youth, 7 to 17, for their contributions to multicultural awareness, nature and ecology, social issues, peace and nonviolence. Also to promote creativity, self-esteem and writing skills and to recognize important work being done by youth organizations." Submissions made by the author. Deadline for entries: June 25. SASE for contest rules. Entries must include certificate of originality by a parent and/or teacher and a cover letter that included cultural background information on the author. Submissions can either be mailed or e-mailed. Entry fee is $3. Everyone who enters the contest receives the September-October issue featuring Youth Awards. Judging by Skipping Stones ' staff. "Up to ten awards are given in three categories: (1) Compositions—(essays, poems, short stories, songs, travelogues, etc.) should be typed (double-spaced) or neatly handwritten. Fiction or nonfiction should be limited to 1,000 words; poems to 30 lines. Non-English writings are also welcome. (2) Artwork—(drawings, cartoons, paintings or photo essays with captions) should have the artist's name, age and address on the back of each page. Send the originals with SASE. Black & white photos are especially welcome. Limit: 8 pieces. (3) Youth Organizations—Tell us how your club or group works to: (a) preserve the nature and ecology in your area, (b) enhance the quality of life for low-income, minority or disabled or (c) improve racial or cultural harmony in your school or community. Use the same format as for compositions." The winners are published in the September-October issue of Skipping Stones. Now in its 2 1st year, Skipping Stones is a winner of N.A.M.E.EDPRESS, Newsstand Resources and Parent's Choice Awards. Website: www.SkippingStones.org.

KAY SNOW WRITERS' CONTEST

9045 SW Barbur Blvd. #5A, Portland OR 97219-4027. (503)452-1592. Fax: (503)452-0372. E-mail: wilwrite@teleport.com. Annual contest. **Open to students.** Purpose of contest: "to encourage beginning and established writers to continue the craft." Unpublished, original submissions only. Submissions made by the author. Deadline for entries: April 23rd. SASE for contest rules and entry forms. Entry fee is $10, Williamette Writers' members; $15, nonmembers; free for student writers grades 1-12. Awards cash prize of $300 per category (fiction, nonfiction, juvenile, poetry, script writing), $50 for students in three divisions: 1-5, 6-8, 9-12. Judges are anonymous. Website: www.willamettewriters.com. **Contact:** Lizzy Shannon, contest director.

SOUTHWEST WRITERS ANNUAL CONTEST

SouthWest Writers, 3721 Morris NE, Suite A, Albuquerque NM 87111. (505)265-9485. Fax: (505)265-9483. E-mail: swwriters@juno.com. Website: www.southwestwriters.org. Submit entries to: Contest Chair. **Open to adults and students.** Annual contest. Estab. 1982. Purpose of contest: to encourage writers of all genres. Also offers mini-conferences, critique service (for $60/year, offers 2 monthly programs, monthly newsletter, annual writing and quarterly writing contests, other workshops, various discount perks, website linking, e-mail addresses, classes and critique service (open to nonmembers). See website for more information or call or write.

▨ SYDNEY TAYLOR BOOK AWARD

Association of Jewish Libraries, P.O. Box 1118, Teaneck, NJ 07666. (212)725-5359. E-mail: chair@sydneytaylorbookaward.org. Website: www.sydneytaylorbookaward.org. **Contact:** Barbara Bietz, chair. Offered annually for work published during the current year. "Given to distinguished contributions to Jewish literature for children. One award for younder readers, one for older readers, and one for teens." Publishers submit books. Deadline: December 31, but we cannot guarantee that books received after December 1 will be considered. Guidelines on website. Awards certificate, cash award, and gold or silver seals for cover of winning book.

SYDNEY TAYLOR MANUSCRIPT COMPETITION

Association of Jewish Libraries, 204 Park St., Montclair NJ 07042. E-mail: stmacajl@aol.com. Website: www.jewishlibraries.org. **Coordinator:** Aileen Grossberg. **Open to students** and to any unpublished writer of fiction. Annual contest. Estab. 1985. Purpose of the contest: "This competition is for unpublished writers of fiction. Material should be for readers ages 8-11, with universal appeal that will serve to deepen the understanding of Judaism for all children, revealing positive aspects of Jewish life." Unpublished submissions only. Deadline for entries: December 15. Download rules and forms from website. No entry fee. Awards $1,000. Award winner will be notified in April, and the award will be presented at the convention in June. Judging by qualified judges from within the Association of Jewish Libraries. Requirements for entrants: must be an unpublished fiction writer; also, books must range from 64-200 pages in length. "AJL assumes no responsibility for publication, but hopes this cash incentive will serve to encourage new writers of children's stories with Jewish themes for all children."

THEMATIC ANTHOLOGIES!

Creative With Words Publications, Carmel CA 93922. Fax: (831)655-8627. E-mail: geltrich@mbay.net. Website: members.tripod.com/CreativeWithWords. **Contest Director:** Brigitta Geltrich. **Open to all ages:** pre-school, school, and adult. Eight times a year. Estab. 1975. Purpose: to further creative writing in children and offer all ages an opportunity to be published. Unpublished submissions only. Can submit year round on any theme (theme list available upon request and SASE). Deadlines for entries: year round. SASE for guidelines and submittal forms. SASE for return of entries "if not accepted." No entry fee. All selected poems are published in an anthology. Judging by selected guest editors and educators. Anthologies open to all ages. Writer should request guidelines. Include SASE with all correspondence. Age of child and home address must be stated and ms must be verified of its authenticity. Each story or poem must have a title. Creative with Words Publications (CWW) publishes the top 50-100 mss submitted to any theme. CWW also publishes two anthologies "The Eclectics" for adult poets and writers only. Focus of all anthologies is on Nature, Seasons, Animals, School/Education, and on Folklore.

◼ THE TORONTO BOOK AWARDS

City of Toronto, 100 Queen St. W, 2nd Floor, West Tower, Toronto ON M5H 2N2 Canada. (416)392-4674. E-mail: bkurmey@toronto.ca. **Submit entries to:** Bev Kurmey, Protocol Officer. Annual award. Estab. 1974. Recognizes books of literary or artistic merit that are evocative of Toronto. Submissions made by author, author's agent or nominated by a person or group. Must be published the calendar year prior to the award year. Deadline for entries: last week day of March annually. Awards $15,000 in prize money. Judging by committee.

VEGETARIAN ESSAY CONTEST

The Vegetarian Resource Group, P.O. Box 1463, Baltimore MD 21203. (410)366-VEGE. Fax: (410)366-8804. E-mail: vrg@vrg.org. Website: www.vrg.org. Annual contest. **Open to students.** Estab. 1985. Purpose of contest: to promote vegetarianism in young people. Unpublished submissions only. Deadline for entries: May 1 of each year. SASE for contest rules and entry forms. No entry fee. Awards $50 savings bond. Judging by awards committee. Acquires right for The Vegetarian Resource Group to reprint essays. Requirements for entrants: age 18 and under. Winning works may be published in Vegetarian Journal, instructional materials for students. Submit 2-3 page essay on any aspect of vegetarianism, which is the abstinence of meat, fish and fowl. Entrants can base paper on interviewing, research or personal opinion. Need not be vegetarian to enter.

VFW VOICE OF DEMOCRACY

Veterans of Foreign Wars of the U.S.406 W. 34th St., Kansas City MO 64111. (816)968-1117. Fax: (816)968-1149. Website: www.vfw.org. **Open to high school students.** Annual contest. Estab. 1960. Purpose of contest: to give high school students the opportunity to voice their opinions about their responsibility to our country and to convey those opinions via the broadcast media to all of America. Deadline for entries: November 1. No entry fee. Winners receive awards ranging from $1,000-30,000. Requirements for entrants: "Ninth-twelfth grade students in public, parochial, private and home schools are eligible to compete. Former first place state winners are not eligible to compete again. Contact your participating high school teacher, counselor, our website www.vfw.org or your local VFW Post to enter."

WESTERN HERITAGE AWARDS

National Cowboy & Western Heritage Museum, 1700 NE 63rd St., Oklahoma City, OK 73111-7997. (405)478-2250. Fax: (405)478-4714. E-mail: ssimpson@nationalcowboymuseum.org. Website: www.nationalcowboymuseum.org. **Western Heritage Award:** Shayla Simpson. Annual award. Estab. 1961. Purpose of award: The WHA are presented annually to encourage the accurate and artistic telling of great stories of the West through 16 categories of western literature, television, film and music; including fiction, nonfiction, children's books and poetry. Previously published submissions only; must be published the calendar year before the awards are presented. Deadline for literary entries: November 30. Deadline for film, music and television entries: December 31. Entries not returned. Entry fee is $50/entry. Awards a Wrangler bronze sculpture designed by famed western artist, John Free. Judging by a panel of judges selected each year with distinction in various fields of western art and heritage. Requirements for entrants: The material must pertain to the development or preservation of the West, either from a historical or contemporary viewpoint. Literary entries must have been published between December 1 and November 30 of calendar year. Film, music or television entries must have been released or aired between January 1 and December 31 of calendar year of entry. Works recognized during special awards ceremonies held annually at the museum. There is an autograph party preceding the awards. Awards ceremonies are sometimes broadcast.

JACKIE WHITE MEMORIAL NATIONAL CHILDREN'S PLAY WRITING CONTEST

1800 Nelwood, Columbia MO 65202-1447. (573)874-5628. E-mail: bybetsy@yahoo.com. Send scripts to 309 Parkade Blvd., Columbia MO 65202. Annual contest. Estab. 1988. Purpose of contest: "To encourage writing of family-friendly scripts." Previously unpublished submissions only. Submissions made by author. Deadline for entries: June 1, 2011. SASE for contest rules and entry forms. Entry fee is $25. Awards $500 with production possible. Judging by current and past board members of CEC and by non-board members who direct plays at CEC. Play may be performed during the following season. We reserve the right to award 1st place and prize monies without a production. All submissions will be read by at least three readers. Author will receive a written evaluation of the script. Website: www.cectheatre.org. **Contact:** Betsy Phillips, contest director.

⧉ RITA WILLIAMS YOUNG ADULT PROSE PRIZE

National League of American Pen Women, Nob Hill, San Francisco Branch, 1544 Sweetwood Dr., Broadmoor Vlg.CA 94015-2029. E-mail: pennobhill@aol.com. Website: www.soulmakingcontest.us. **Contact:** Eileen Malone. **Open to students.** Up to 3,000 words in story, essay, journal entry, creative nonfiction, or memoir by writers in grades 9-12. Annual prize. Deadline: November 30. Guidelines for SASE or at www.soulmakingcontest.us. Charges $5/entry (make checks payable to NLAPW, Nob Hill Branch) International entrants please send Travelers Check drawn on a USA Bank. Prize: 1st Place: $100; 2nd Place: $50; 3rd Place: $25. Open to any writer in grade 9-12. or equivalent.

PAUL A. WITTY OUTSTANDING LITERATURE AWARD

International Reading Association, Special Interest Group, Reading for Gifted and Creative Learning, School of Education, P.O. Box 10034, Lamar University, Beaumont, TX 77710. (409)286-5941. Fax: (409)880-8384. Website: http://www.reading.org/General/AdvocacyandOutreach/SIGS/ReadingGiftedSIG.aspx. **Award Director:** Dorothy Sisk. **Open to students.** Annual award. Estab. 1979. Categories of entries: poetry/prose at elementary, junior high and senior high levels. Unpublished submissions only. Deadline for entries: February 1. SASE for award rules and entry forms. SASE for return of entries. No entry fee. Awards $25 and plaque, also certificates of merit. Judging by 2 committees for screening and awarding. "The elementary students' entries must be legible and may not exceed 1,000 words. Secondary students' prose entries should be typed and may exceed 1,000 words if necessary. At both elementary and secondary levels, if poetry is entered, a set of five poems must be submitted. All entries and requests for applications must include a self-addressed, stamped envelope."

PAUL A. WITTY SHORT STORY AWARD

P.O. Box 8139, 800 Barksdale Rd., Newark DE 19714-8139. (302)731-1600. E-mail: exec@reading.org. "The entry must be an original short story appearing in a young children's periodical for the first time. The short story should serve as a literary standard that encourages young readers to read periodicals." Deadline for entries: The entry must have been published for the first time in the eligibility year; the short story must be submitted during the calendar year of publication. Anyone wishing to nominate a short story should send it to the designated Paul A. Witty Short Award Subcommittee Chair by November 1. Award is $1,000 and recognition at the annual IRA Convention. Website: www.reading.org.

JOHN WOOD COMMUNITY COLLEGE CREATIVE WRITING CONTEST

Business Office—Writing Contest, John Wood Community College, 1301 S. 48th Street, Quincy IL 62305. (217)641-4940. Fax: (217)641-4900. E-mail: KLangston@jwcc.edu. Website: www.jwcc.edu/communityed. **Contact:** Kelli Langston, community education specialist. The college sponsors a writing contest for poetry, fiction and nonfiction. Entries for the contest are accepted January-March of each year. Please see the JWCC website for more details or e-mail. KLangston@jwcc.edu for more information. In addition, the college sponsors a student art show in February. A recycled art contest in April. A photography show in May and an annual art competition for adults only in November.

☒ ALICE WOOD MEMORIAL OHIOANA AWARD FOR CHILDREN'S LITERATURE

Ohioana Library Association, 274 E. First Ave., Suite 300, Columbus OH 43201. (614)466-3831. Fax: (614)728-6974. E-mail: ohioana@sloma.state.oh.us or Ohioana@Ohioana.org. Website: www.ohioana.org. **Contact:** Linda R. Hengst. Offered to an author whose body of work has made, and continues to make, a significant contribution to literature for children or young adults and through their work as a writer, teacher, administrator, and community member, interest in children's literature has been encouraged and children have become involved with reading. Nomination forms for SASE. Recipient must have been born in Ohio or lived in Ohio at least 5 years. Deadline: December 31. Awards $1,000 cash prize.

WRITERS-EDITORS NETWORK ANNUAL INTERNATIONAL WRITING COMPETITION

(formerly Florida State Writing Competition), CNW/FFWA, P.O. Box A, North Stratford NH 03590. (603)922-8338. Fax: (603)922-8339. E-mail: contest@writers-editors.com. Website: www. writers-editors.com. **Executive Director:** Dana K. Cassell. Annual contest. Estab. 1984. Categories include children's literature (length appropriate to age category). Entry fee is $5 (members), $10 (nonmembers) or $10-20 for entries longer than 3,000 words. Awards $100 first prize, $75 second prize, $50 third prize, certificates for honorable mentions. Judging by librarians, editors and published authors. Judging criteria: interest and readability within age group, writing style and mechanics, originality, salability. Deadline: March 15. For copy of official entry form, send #10 SASE or visit website. List of winners on website.

WRITING CONFERENCE WRITING CONTESTS

The Writing Conference, Inc., P.O. Box 664, Ottawa KS 66067. Phone/fax: (785)242-1995. E-mail: jbushman@writingconference.com. Website: www.writingconference.com. **Contest Director:** John H. Bushman. **Open to students.** Annual contest. Estab. 1988. Purpose of contest: to further writing by students with awards for narration, exposition and poetry at the elementary, middle school and high school levels. Unpublished submissions only. Submissions made by the author or teacher. Deadline for entries: January 8. Consult website for guidelines and entry form. No entry fee. Awards plaque and publication of winning entry in The Writers' Slate online, April issue. Judging by a panel of teachers. Requirements for entrants: must be enrolled in school—K-12th grade- - or home schooled.

❖ YOUNG ADULT CANADIAN BOOK AWARD

Canadian Library Association/ Association canndienne des bibliothèques, 328 Frank St., Ottawa ON K2P 0X8 Canada. (613)232-9625. Fax: (613)563-9895. Website: www.cla.ca. **Contact:** Committee Chair. Annual award. Estab. 1981. This award recognizes an author of an outstanding English language Canadian book which appeals to young adults between the ages of 13 and 18. To be eligible for consideration, the following must apply; it must be a work of fiction (novel, collection of short stories, or graphic novel), the title must be a Canadian publication in either hardcover or paperback, and the author must be a Canadian citizen or landed immigrant. The award is given annually, when merited, at the Canadian Library Association's annual conference. The winner will receive a leather-bound book with the title, author and award seal embossed on the cover in gold. Established in 1980 by the Young Adult Caucus of the Saskatchewan Library Association, the Young Adult Canadian Book Award is administered by the Young Adult Services Interest Group of the Canadian Library Association. Nominations should be sent by December 31, annually.

THE YOUTH HONOR AWARD PROGRAM

Skipping Stones, P.O. Box 3939, Eugene OR 97403. (514)342-4956. E-mail: editor@skippingstones. org. Website: www.skippingstones.org. **Director of Public Editor:** Arun N. Toke. **Open to students.** Annual contest. Estab. 1994. Purpose of contest: "To recognize creative and artistic works by young people that promote multicultural awareness and nature appreciation." Unpublished submissions only. Submissions made by author. Deadline for entries: June 25. SASE for contest rules and entry forms also available on our website. Entry fee is $3; low-income entrants, free. "Ten winners will be published in our fall issue. Winners will also receive an Honor Award Certificate, a subscription to Skipping Stones and five nature and/or multicultural books." Requirements for entrants: Original writing (essays, interviews, poems, plays, short stories, etc.) and art (photos, paintings, cartoons, etc.) are accepted from youth ages 7 to 17. Non-English and bilingual writings are welcome. Also, you must include a certificate of originality signed by a parent or teacher. "Include a cover letter telling about yourself and your submissions, your age, and contact information. Every student who enters will receive a copy of Skipping Stones featuring the ten winning entries."

THE ANNA ZORNIO MEMORIAL CHILDREN'S THEATRE PLAYWRITING AWARD

University of New Hampshire, Department of Theatre and Dance, Paul Creative Arts Center, 30 Academic Way. Durham NH 03824-3538. (603)862-3038. Fax: (603)862-0298. E-mail: mike.wood@ unh.edu. Website: www.unh.edu/theatre-dance/zornio.html. **Contact:** Michael Wood. Contest every 4 years; next contest is November 2012 for 2013-2014 season. Estab. 1979. Purpose of the award: "to honor the late Anna Zornio, an alumna of The University of New Hampshire, for dedication to and inspiration of playwriting for young people, K-12th grade. Open to playwrights who are residents of the U.S. and Canada. Plays or musicals should run about 45 minutes." Unpublished submissions only. Submissions made by the author. Deadline for entries: March 2, 2012. No entry fee. Awards $500 plus guaranteed production. Judging by faculty committee. Acquires rights to campus production. For entry form and more information visit website.

Helpful Books & Publications

The editors of *Children's Writer's & Illustrator's Market* suggest the following books and periodicals to keep you informed on writing and illustrating techniques, trends in the field, business issues, industry news and changes, and additional markets.

BOOKS

An Author's Guide to Children's Book Promotion, Ninth edition, by Susan Salzman Raab, 345 Millwood Rd., Chappaqua NY 10514. (914)241-2117. E-mail: info@raabassociates.com. Website: www.raabassociates.com/authors.htm.

The Business of Writing for Children, by Aaron Shepard, Shepard Publications. Available on www.amazon.com.

Children's Writer Guide, (annual), The Institute of Children's Literature, 93 Long Ridge Rd., West Redding CT 06896-0811. (800)443-6078. Website: www.writersbookstore.com.

The Children's Writer's Reference, by Berthe Amoss and Eric Suben, Writer's Digest Books, 4700 E. Galbraith Rd., Cincinnati OH 45236. (800)448-0915. Website: www.writersdigest. com.

Children's Writer's Word Book, Second edition, by Alijandra Mogilner & Tayopa Mogilner, Writer's Digest Books, 4700 E. Galbraith Rd., Cincinnati OH 45236. (800)448-0915. Website: www.writersdigest.com.

The Complete Idiot's Guide(r) to Publishing Children's Books, Second Edition, by Harold D. Underdown, Alpha Books, 201 W. 103rd St., Indianapolis IN 46290. Website: www.un derdown.org/cig.htm.

Creating Characters Kids Will Love, by Elaine Marie Alphin, Writer's Digest Books, 4700 E. Galbraith Rd., Cincinnati OH 45236. (800)448-0915. Website: www.writersdigest.com.

Formatting & Submitting Your Manuscript, Second Edition, by Cynthia Laufenberg and the editors of Writer's Market, Writer's Digest Books, 4700 E. Galbraith Rd., Cincinnati OH 45236. (800)448-0915. Website: www.writersdigest.com.

Guide to Literary Agents, edited by Chuck Sambuchino, Writer's Digest Books, 4700 E. Galbraith Rd., Cincinnati OH 45236. (800)448-0915. Website: www.writersdigest.com.

How to Write a Children's Book and Get It Published, Third Edition, by Barbara Seuling, John Wiley & Sons, 111 River St., Hoboken NJ 07030. (201)748-6000. Website: www.wiley.com.

How to Write and Illustrate Children's Books and Get Them Published, edited by Treld Pelkey Bicknell and Felicity Trottman, Writer's Digest Books, 4700 E. Galbraith Rd., Cincinnati OH 45236. (800)448-0915. Website: www.writersdigest.com.

How to Write Attention-Grabbing Query & Cover Letters, by John Wood, Writer's Digest Books, 4700 E. Galbraith Rd., Cincinnati OH 45236. (800)448-0915. Website: www.writers digest.com.

Illustrating Children's Books: Creating Pictures for Publication, by Martin Salisbury, Barron's Educational Series, 250 Wireless Blvd., Hauppauge NY 11788. (800)645-3476. Website: www.barronseduc.com.

It's a Bunny-Eat-Bunny World: A Writer's Guide to Surviving and Thriving in Today's Competitive Children's Book Market, by Olga Litowinsky, Walker & Company, 104 Fifth Ave., New York NY 10011. (212)727-8300. Website: www.walkerbooks.com.

Page After Page: discover the confidence & passion you need to start writing & keep writing (no matter what), by Heather Sellers, Writer's Digest Books, 4700 E. Galbraith Rd., Cincinnati OH 45236. (800)448-0915. Website: www.writersdigest.com.

Picture Writing: A New Approach to Writing for Kids and Teens, by Anastasia Suen, Writer's Digest Books, 4700 E. Galbraith Rd., Cincinnati OH 45236. (800)448-0915. Website: www.writersdigest.com.

Story Sparkers: A Creativity Guide for Children's Writers, by Marcia Thornton Jones and Debbie Dadey, Writer's Digest Books, 4700 E. Galbraith Rd., Cincinnati OH 45236. (800)448-0915. Website: www.writersdigest.com.

Take Joy: A Writer's Guide to Loving the Craft, by Jane Yolen, Writer's Digest Books, 4700 E. Galbraith Rd., Cincinnati OH 45236. (800)448-0915. Website: www.writersdigest.com.

A Teen's Guide to Getting Published; Publishing for Profit, Recognition and Academic Success, Second edition, by Jessica Dunn & Danielle Dunn, Prufrock Press, P.O. Box 8813, Waco TX 76714-8813. (800)998-2208. Website: www.prufrock.com.

The Writer's Guide to Crafting Stories for Children, by Nancy Lamb, Writer's Digest Books, 4700 E. Galbraith Rd., Cincinnati OH 45236. (800)448-0915. Website: www.writersdigest.com.

Writing and Illustrating Children's Books for Publication: Two Perspectives, Revised Edition, by Berthe Amoss and Eric Suben, Writer's Digest Books, 4700 E. Galbraith Rd., Cincinnati OH 45236. (800)448-0915. Website: www.writersdigest.com.

Writing & Selling the YA Novel, by K.L. Going, Writer's Digest Books, 4700 E. Galbraith Rd., Cincinnati OH 45236. (800)448-0915. Website: www.writersdigest.com.

Writing for Young Adults, by Sherry Garland, Writer's Digest Books, 4700 E. Galbraith Rd., Cincinnati OH 45236. (800)448-0915. Website: www.writersdigest.com.

Writing With Pictures: How to Write and Illustrate Children's Books, by Uri Shulevitz, Watson-Guptill Publications, 770 Broadway, New York NY 10003. (800)278-8477. Website: www.watsonguptill.com/products.html.

You Can Write Children's Books, by Tracey E. Dils, Writer's Digest Books, 4700 E. Galbraith Rd., Cincinnati OH 45236. (800)448-0915. Website: www.writersdigest.com.

You Can Write Children's Books Workbook, by Tracey E. Dils, Writer's Digest Books, 4700 E. Galbraith Rd., Cincinnati OH 45236. (800)448-0915. Website: www.writersdigest.com.

PUBLICATIONS

Book Links: Connecting Books, Libraries and Classrooms, editor Laura Tillotson, American Library Association, 50 E. Huron St., Chicago IL 60611. (800)545-2433. Website: www.ala.org/BookLinks. *Magazine published 6 times a year (September-July) for the purpose of connecting books, libraries and classrooms. Features articles on specific topics followed by bibliographies recommending books for further information. Subscription: $39.95/year.*

Children's Book Insider, editor Laura Backes, 901 Columbia Rd., Ft. Collins CO 80525-1838. (970)495-0056 or (800)807-1916. E-mail: mail@write4kids.com. Website: www.write4kids.com. *Monthly newsletter covering markets, techniques and trends in children's publishing. Subscription: $29.95/year; electronic version $26.95/year.*

Children's Writer, editor Susan Tierney, The Institute of Children's Literature, 93 Long Ridge Rd., West Redding CT 06896-0811. (800)443-6078. Website: www.childrenswriter.com. *Monthly newsletter of writing and publishing trends in the children's field. Subscription: $24/year; special introductory rate: $19.*

The Five Owls, editor Dr. Mark West, P.O. Box 235, Marathon TX 79842. (432)386-4257. Website: www.fiveowls.com. *Quarterly online newsletter for readers personally and professionally involved in children's literature. Subscription: $35/year.*

The Horn Book Magazine, editor-in-chief Roger Sutton, The Horn Book Inc., 56 Roland St., Suite 200, Boston MA 02129. (800)325-1170. E-mail: info@hbook.com or cgross@hbook.com. Website: www.hbook.com. *Bimonthly guide to the children's book world including views on the industry and reviews of the latest books. Subscription: $34.95/year for new subscriptions; $49/year for renewals.*

The Lion and the Unicorn: A Critical Journal of Children's Literature, editors George Bodmer, Lisa Paul and Sandra Beckett, The Johns Hopkins University Press, P.O. Box 19966, Baltimore MD 21211-0966. (800)548-1784 or (410)516-6987 (outside the U.S. and Canada). E-mail: jrlncirc@press.jhu.edu. Website: www.press.jhu.edu/journals/lion_and_the_unicorn/. *Magazine published 3 times a year serving as a forum for discussion of children's literature featuring interviews with authors, editors and experts in the field. Subscription: $33/year.*

Once Upon a Time, editor Audrey Baird, 553 Winston Court, St. Paul MN 55118. (651)457-6223. E-mail: audreyouat@comcast.net. Website: www.onceuponatimemag.com. *Quarterly support magazine for children's writers and illustrators and those interested in children's literature. Subscription: $27/year.*

Publishers Weekly, editor-in-chief Sara Nelson, Reed Business Information, a division of Reed Elsevier Inc., 360 Park Ave. S., New York NY 10010. (800)278-2991. Website: www.publishersweekly.com. *Weekly trade publication covering all aspects of the publishing* *industry; includes coverage of the children's field and spring and fall issues devoted solely to children's books. Subscription: $239.99/year. Available on newsstands for $8/issue. (Special issues are higher in price.)*

Society of Children's Book Writers and Illustrators Bulletin, editors Stephen Mooser and Lin Oliver, SCBWI, 8271 Beverly Blvd., Los Angeles CA 90048. (323)782-1010. E-mail: bulletin@scbwi.org. Website: www.scbwi.org/pubs.htm. *Bimonthly newsletter of SCBWI covering news of interest to members. Subscription with $60/year membership.*

Useful Online Resources

The editors of *Children's Writer's & Illustrator's Market* suggest the following Web sites to keep you informed on writing and illustrating techniques, trends in the field, business issues, industry news and changes, and additional markets.

Amazon.com: www.amazon.com
Calling itself "A bookstore too big for the physical world," Amazon.com has more than 3 million books available on their website at discounted prices, plus a personal notification service of new releases, reader reviews, bestseller and suggested book information.

America Writes for Kids: http://usawrites4kids.drury.edu
Lists book authors by state along with interviews, profiles and writing tips.

Artlex Art Dictionary: www.artlex.com
Art dictionary with more than 3,200 terms

Association for Library Service to Children: www.ala.org
This site provides links to information about Newbery, Caldecott, Coretta Scott King, Michael L. Printz and Theodor Seuss Geisel Awards as well as a host of other awards for notable children's books.

Association of Authors' Representatives: www.aar-online.org
The website of the AAR offers a list of agent members, links, and frequently asked questions including useful advice for authors seeking representation.

Association of Illustrators: www.theaoi.com
This U.K.-based organization has been working since 1973 to promote illustration, illustrators' rights and standards. The website has discussion boards, artists' directories, events, links to agents and much more.

Authors and Illustrators for Children Webring: www.geocities.com/heartland/shores/2084/
Here you'll find a list of links of sites of interest to children's writers and illustrators or created by them.

The Authors Guild Online: www.authorsguild.org
The website of The Authors Guild offers articles and columns dealing with contract issues, copyright, electronic rights and other legal issues of concern to writers.

Barnes & Noble Online: www.barnesandnoble.com
The world's largest bookstore chain's website contains 600,000 in-stock titles at discount prices as well as personalized recommendations, online events with authors and book forum access for members.

The Book Report Network: includes www.bookreporter.com; www.readinggroupguides.com; www.authorsontheweb.com; www.teenreads.com and www.kidsreads.com.
All the sites feature giveaways, book reviews, author and editor interviews, and recommended reads. A great way to stay connected.

Bookwire: www.bookwire.com
A gateway to finding information about publishers, booksellers, libraries, authors, reviews and awards. Also offers frequently asked publishing questions and answers, a calendar of events, a mailing list and other helpful resources.

Canadian Children's Book Centre: www.bookcentre.ca
The site for the CCBC includes profiles of illustrators and authors, information on recent books, a calendar of upcoming events, information on CCBC publications, and tips from Canadian children's authors.

Canadian Society of Children's Authors, Illustrators and Performers: www.canscaip.org
This organization promotes all aspects of children's writing, illustration and performance.

The Children's Book Council: www.cbcbooks.org
This site includes a complete list of CBC members with addresses, names and descriptions of what each publishes, and links to publishers' Web sites. Also offers previews of upcoming titles from members; articles from *CBC Features*, the Council's newsletter; and their catalog.

Children's Literature: www.childrenslit.com
Offers book reviews, lists of conferences, searchable database, links to over 1,000 author/ illustrator Web sites and much more.

Children's Literature Web Guide: www.ucalgary.ca/ ~ dkbrown
This site includes stories, poetry, resource lists, lists of conferences, links to book reviews, lists of awards (international), and information on books from classic to contemporary.

Children's Writer's & Illustrator's Market Web Page: www.cwim.com
Visit the new web page for market updates and sign up for a free e-newsletter.

Children's Writing Supersite: www.write4kids.com
This site (formerly Children's Writers Resource Center) includes highlights from the newsletter *Children's Book Insider*; definitions of publishing terms; answers to frequently asked questions; information on trends; information on small presses; a research center for Web information; and a catalog of material available from *CBI*.

The Colossal Directory of Children's Publishers Online: www.signaleader.com/
This site features links to Web sites of children's publishers and magazines and includes information on which publishers offer submission guidelines online.

Cynthia Leitich Smith's website: www.cynthialeitichsmith.com
In addition to information about her books and appearances and a blog, Cynthia Leitich Smith has assembled a site chock full of great useful and inspiring information including

interviews with writers and illustrators, favorite reads, awards, bibliographies, and tons of helpful links, many to help writers explore diversity.

Database of Award-Winning Children's Literature: www.dawcl.com

A compilation of over 4,000 records of award-winning books throughout the U.S., Canada, Australia, New Zealand and the U.K. You can search by age level, format, genre, setting, historical period, ethnicity or nationality of the protagonist, gender of protagonist, publication year, award name, or even by keyword. Begin here to compile your reading list of award-winners.

The Drawing Board: http://thedrawingboardforillustrators.blogspot.com

This site for illustrators features articles, interviews, links and resources for illustrators from all fields.

Editor & Publisher: www.editorandpublisher.com

The Internet source for *Editor & Publisher*, this site provides up-to-date industry news, with other opportunities such as a research area and bookstore, a calendar of events and classifieds.

International Board on Books for Young People: www.ibby.org

Founded in Switzerland in 1953, IBBY is a nonprofit that seeks to encourage the creation and distribution of quality children's literature. They cooperate with children's organizations and children's book institutions around the world.

International Reading Association: www.reading.org

This website includes articles; book lists; event, conference and convention information; and an online bookstore.

Kid Magazine Writers: www.kidmagwriters.com

Writer Jan Fields created this site to offer support and information to the often-neglected children's magazine writer. The website features editor interviews, articles on technique, special reports, an A to Z magazine market guide, and archives of monthly features.

National Association for the Education of Young Children: www.naeyc.org

This organization is comprised of over 100,000 early childhood educators and others interested in the development and education of young children. Their website makes a great introduction and research resource for authors and illustrators of picture books.

National Writers Union: www.nwu.org

The union for freelance writers in U.S. Markets. The NWU offers contract advice, grievance assistance, health and liability insurance and much more.

Once Upon a Time: www.onceuponatimemag.com

This companion site to *Once Upon A Time* magazine offers excerpts from recent articles, notes for prospective contributors, and information about *OUAT*'s 11 regular columnists.

Picturebook: www.picture-book.com

This site brought to you by *Picturebook* sourcebook offers tons of links for illustrators, portfolio searching, and news, and offers a listserv, bulletin board and chatroom.

Planet Esme: A Wonderful World of Children's Literature: www.planetesme.com

This site run by author Esme Raji Codell, offers extensive lists of children's book recommendations, including the latest titles of note for various age groups, a great list of

Resources

links, and more. Be sure to click on "join the club" to receive Codell's delightful e-mail newsletter.

Publishers' Catalogues Home Page: www.lights.ca/publisher

A mammoth link collection of more than 6,000 publishers around the world arranged geographically. This site is one of the most comprehensive directories of publishers on the Internet.

The Purple Crayon: www.underdown.org

Editor Harold Underdown's site includes articles on trends, business, and cover letters and queries as well as interviews with editors and answers to frequently asked questions. He also includes links to a number of other sites helpful to writers and excerpts from his book *The Complete Idiot's Guide to Publishing Children's Books*.

Slantville: www.slantville.com

An online artists community, this site includes a yellow pages for artists, frequently asked questions and a library offering information on a number of issues of interest to illustrators. This is a great site to visit to view artists' portfolios.

Smartwriters.com: www.smartwriters.com

Writer, novelist, photographer, graphic designer, and co-founder of 2-Tier Software, Inc., Roxyanne Young, runs this online magazine, which is absolutely stuffed with resources for children's writers, teachers and young writers. It's also got contests, interviews, free books, advice and well—you just have to go there.

Society of Children's Book Writers and Illustrators: www.scbwi.org

This site includes information on awards and grants available to SCBWI members, a calendar of events listed by date and region, a list of publications available to members, and a site map for easy navigation. Follow the Regional Chapters link to find the SCBWI chapter in your area.

The Society of Illustrators: www.societyillustrators.org

Since 1901, this organization has been working to promote the interest of professional illustrators. Information on exhibitions, career advice, and many other links provided.

U.K. Children's Books: www.ukchildrensbooks.co.uk

Filled with links to author sites, illustrator sites, publishers, booksellers, and organizations—not to mention help with website design and other technicalities—visit this site no matter which side of the Atlantic you rest your head.

United States Board on Books for Young People: www.usbby.org

Serves as the U.S. national section of the International Board on Books for Young People.

United States Postal Service: www.usps.com

Offers domestic and International postage rate calculator, stamp ordering, zip code look up, express mail tracking and more.

Verla Kay's website: www.verlakay.com

Author Verla Kay's website features writer's tips, articles, a schedules of online workshops (with transcripts of past workshops), a good news board and helpful links.

Writersdigest.com: www.writersdigest.com

Brought to you by *Writer's Digest* magazine, this site features articles, resources, links, writing prompts, a bookstore, and more.

Writersmarket.com: www.writersmarket.com

This gateway to the *Writer's Market* online edition offers market news, FAQs, tips, featured markets and web resources, a free newsletter, and more.

Writing-world.com: www.writing-world.com/children/

Site features reams of advice, links and offers a free bi-weekly newsletter.

Glossary

AAR. Association of Authors' Representatives.

ABA. American Booksellers Association.

ABC. Association of Booksellers for Children.

Advance. A sum of money a publisher pays a writer or illustrator prior to the publication of a book. It is usually paid in installments, such as one half on signing the contract, one half on delivery of a complete and satisfactory manuscript. The advance is paid against the royalty money that will be earned by the book.

ALA. American Library Association.

All rights. The rights contracted to a publisher permitting the use of material anywhere and in any form, including movie and book club sales, without additional payment to the creator.

Anthology. A collection of selected writings by various authors or gatherings of works by one author.

Anthropomorphization. The act of attributing human form and personality to things not human (such as animals).

ASAP. As soon as possible.

Assignment. An editor or art director asks a writer, illustrator or photographer to produce a specific piece for an agreed-upon fee.

B&W. Black and white.

Backlist. A publisher's list of books not published during the current season but still in print.

BEA. BookExpo America.

Biennially. Occurring once every 2 years.

Bimonthly. Occurring once every 2 months.

Biweekly. Occurring once every 2 weeks.

Book packager. A company that draws all elements of a book together, from the initial concept to writing and marketing strategies, then sells the book package to a book publisher and/or movie producer. Also known as book producer or book developer.

Book proposal. Package submitted to a publisher for consideration usually consisting of a synopsis, outline and sample chapters. (See Before Your First Sale, page 7.)

Business-size envelope. Also known as a #10 envelope. The standard size used in sending business correspondence.

Camera-ready. Refers to art that is completely prepared for copy camera platemaking.

Caption. A description of the subject matter of an illustration or photograph; photo captions include persons' names where appropriate. Also called cutline.

CBC. Children's Book Council.

Clean-copy. A manuscript free of errors and needing no editing; it is ready for typesetting.

Clips. Samples, usually from newspapers or magazines, of a writer's published work.

Concept books. Books that deal with ideas, concepts and large-scale problems, promoting an understanding of what's happening in a child's world. Most prevalent are alphabet and counting books, but also includes books dealing with specific concerns facing young people (such as divorce, birth of a sibling, friendship or moving).

Contract. A written agreement stating the rights to be purchased by an editor, art director or producer and the amount of payment the writer, illustrator or photographer will receive for that sale. (See Running Your Business, page 13.)

Contributor's copies. The magazine issues sent to an author, illustrator or photographer in which her work appears.

Co-op publisher. A publisher that shares production costs with an author, but, unlike subsidy publishers, handles all marketing and distribution. An author receives a high percentage of royalties until her initial investment is recouped, then standard royalties. (*Children's Writer's & Illustrator's Market* does not include co-op publishers.)

Copy. The actual written material of a manuscript.

Copyediting. Editing a manuscript for grammar usage, spelling, punctuation and general style.

Copyright. A means to legally protect an author's/illustrator's/photographer's work. This can be shown by writing ÞCR, the creator's name, and year of work's creation. (See Running Your Business, page 13.)

Cover letter. A brief letter, accompanying a complete manuscript, especially useful if responding to an editor's request for a manuscript. May also accompany a book proposal. (See Before Your First Sale, page 7.)

Cutline. See caption.

Division. An unincorporated branch of a company.

Dummy. A loose mock-up of a book showing placement of text and artwork.

Electronic submission. A submission of material by modem or on computer disk.

Final draft. The last version of a polished manuscript ready for submission to an editor.

First North American serial rights. The right to publish material in a periodical for the first time, in the United States or Canada. (See Running Your Business, page 13.)

F&Gs. Folded and gathered sheets. An early, not-yet-bound copy of a picture book.

Flat fee. A one-time payment.

Galleys. The first typeset version of a manuscript that has not yet been divided into pages.

Genre. A formulaic type of fiction, such as horror, mystery, romance, science fiction or western.

Glossy. A photograph with a shiny surface as opposed to one with a non-shiny matte finish.

Gouache. Opaque watercolor with an appreciable film thickness and an actual paint layer.

Halftone. Reproduction of a continuous tone illustration with the image formed by dots produced by a camera lens screen.

Hard copy. The printed copy of a computer's output.

Hardware. All the mechanically-integrated components of a computer that are not software—circuit boards, transistors and the machines that are the actual computer.

Hi-Lo. High interest, low reading level.

Home page. The first page of a website.

IBBY. International Board on Books for Young People.

Imprint. Name applied to a publisher's specific line of books.

Internet. A worldwide network of computers that offers access to a wide variety of electronic resources.

IRA. International Reading Association.

IRC. International Reply Coupon. Sold at the post office to enclose with text or artwork sent to a recipient outside your own country to cover postage costs when replying or returning work.

Keyline. Identification of the positions of illustrations and copy for the printer.

Layout. Arrangement of illustrations, photographs, text and headlines for printed material.

Line drawing. Illustration done with pencil or ink using no wash or other shading.

Mass market books. Paperback books directed toward an extremely large audience sold in supermarkets, drugstores, airports, newsstands, online retailers, and bookstores.

Mechanicals. Paste-up or preparation of work for printing.

Middle grade or mid-grade. See middle reader.

Middle reader. The general classification of books written for readers approximately ages 9-11. Often called middle grade or mid-grade.

Ms (mss). Manuscript(s).

Multiple submissions. See simultaneous submissions.

NCTE. National Council of Teachers of English.

One-time rights. Permission to publish a story in periodical or book form one time only. (See Running Your Business, page 13.)

Outline. A summary of a book's contents; often in the form of chapter headings with a descriptive sentence or two under each heading to show the scope of the book.

Package sale. The sale of a manuscript and illustrations/photos as a "package" paid for with one check.

Payment on acceptance. The writer, artist or photographer is paid for her work at the time the editor or art director decides to buy it.

Payment on publication. The writer, artist or photographer is paid for her work when it is published.

Picture book. A type of book aimed at preschoolers to 8-year-olds that tells a story using a combination of text and artwork, or artwork only.

Print. An impression pulled from an original plate, stone, block, screen or negative; also a positive made from a photographic negative.

Proofreading. Reading text to correct typographical errors.

Query. A letter to an editor or agent designed to capture interest in an article or book you have written or propose to write. (See Before Your First Sale, page 7.)

Reading fee. Money charged by some agents and publishers to read a submitted manuscript. (*Children's Writer's & Illustrator's Market* does not include agencies that charge reading fees.)

Reprint rights. Permission to print an already published work whose first rights have been sold to another magazine or book publisher. (See Running Your Business, page 13.)

Response time. The average length of time it takes an editor or art director to accept or reject a query or submission and inform the creator of the decision.

Rights. The bundle of permissions offered to an editor or art director in exchange for printing a manuscript, artwork or photographs. (See Running Your Business, page 13.)

Rough draft. A manuscript that has not been checked for errors in grammar, punctuation, spelling or content.

Roughs. Preliminary sketches or drawings.

Royalty. An agreed percentage paid by a publisher to a writer, illustrator or photographer for each copy of her work sold.

SAE. Self-addressed envelope.

SASE. Self-addressed, stamped envelope.

SCBWI. The Society of Children's Book Writers and Illustrators. (See listing in Clubs & Organizations section.)

Second serial rights. Permission for the reprinting of a work in another periodical after its first publication in book or magazine form. (See Running Your Business, page 13.)

Semiannual. Occurring every 6 months or twice a year.

Semimonthly. Occurring twice a month.

Semiweekly. Occurring twice a week.

Serial rights. The rights given by an author to a publisher to print a piece in one or more periodicals. (See Running Your Business, page 13.)

Simultaneous submissions. Queries or proposals sent to several publishers at the same time. Also called multiple submissions. (See Before Your First Sale, page 7.)

Slant. The approach to a story or piece of artwork that will appeal to readers of a particular publication.

Slush pile. Editors' term for their collections of unsolicited manuscripts.

Software. Programs and related documentation for use with a computer.

Solicited manuscript. Material that an editor has asked for or agreed to consider before being sent by a writer.

SPAR. Society of Photographers and Artists Representatives.

Speculation (spec). Creating a piece with no assurance from an editor or art director that it will be purchased or any reimbursements for material or labor paid.

Subsidiary rights. All rights other than book publishing rights included in a book contract, such as paperback, book club and movie rights. (See Running Your Business, page 13.)

Subsidy publisher. A book publisher that charges the author for the cost of typesetting, printing and promoting a book. Also called a vanity publisher. (*Children's Writer's & Illustrator's Market* does not include subsidy publishers.)

Synopsis. A brief summary of a story or novel. Usually a page to a page and a half, single-spaced, if part of a book proposal.

Tabloid. Publication printed on an ordinary newspaper page turned sideways and folded in half.

Tearsheet. Page from a magazine or newspaper containing your printed art, story, article, poem or photo.

Thumbnail. A rough layout in miniature.

Trade books. Books sold in bookstores and through online retailers, aimed at a smaller audience than mass market books, and printed in smaller quantities by publishers.

Transparencies. Positive color slides; not color prints.

Unsolicited manuscript. Material sent without an editor's, art director's or agent's request.

Vanity publisher. See subsidy publisher.

Work-for-hire. An arrangement between a writer, illustrator or photographer and a company under which the company retains complete control of the work's copyright. (See Running Your Business, page 13.)

YA. See young adult.

Young adult. The general classification of books written for readers approximately ages 12-18. Often referred to as YA.

Young reader. The general classification of books written for readers approximately ages 5-8.

Names Index

This index lists the editors, art directors, agents and art reps listed in *Children's Writer's & Illustrator's Market*, along with the publisher, publication or company for which they work. Names were culled from Book Publishers, Canadian & International Books Publishers, Magazines, and Agents & Art Reps.

Age-Level Index

This index lists book and magazine publishers by the age-groups for which they publish. Use it to locate appropriate markets for your work, then carefully read the listings and follow the guidelines of each publisher. Use this index in conjunction with the Subject Index to further narrow your list of markets. **Picture Books and Picture-Oriented Material** are for preschoolers to 8-year-olds; **Young Readers** are for 5- to 8-year-olds; **Middle Readers** are for 9- to 11-year-olds; and **Young Adults** are for ages 12 and up.

BOOK PUBLISHERS

Picture Books

Young Readers

Middle Readers

Young Adults/Teens

Subject Index

This index lists book and magazine publishers by the fiction and nonfiction subject areas in which they publish. Use it to locate appropriate markets for your work, then carefully read the listings and follow the guidelines of each publisher. Use this index in conjunction with Age-Level Index to further narrow your list of markets.

BOOK PUBLISHERS - FICTION

Adventure

Animal

Anthology

Board Books

Concept

Contemporary

Fantasy

Folktales

Health

Humor

Multicultural

Nature/Environment

Poetry

Problem Novels

Religion

Science Fiction

BOOK PUBLISHERS - NONFICTION

Activity Books

Animal

Arts/Crafts

Biography

Careers

Hobbies

How-to

Multicultural

Self Help

Social Issues

Textbooks

MAGAZINES - FICTION

Adventure

Religious

Romance

Science Fiction

Suspense/Mystery

Social Issues

Sports

Travel

Photography Index

This index lists markets that buy photos from freelancers and is divided into **Book Publishers** and **Magazines**. Its important to carefully read the listings and follow the guidelines of each publisher to which you submit.

MAGAZINES

General Index

General Index